Masculinities and Queer Perspectives in Transitional Justice

This book addresses the theory and practice of transitional justice through the lens of masculinities and queer perspectives.

What and where are the intersections between masculinities and queer theories and frameworks for better understanding lived experiences of violence, justice, and transitions? How can masculinities and queer perspectives enhance and "complexify" our understandings of the intersections between gender, sexualities, armed conflict and (post-)conflict transitions? Incorporating masculinities and queer perspectives in transitional justice in tandem, and alongside one another, this book contributes empirically, conceptually, and methodologically to an exploration of gender in processes of dealing with violent pasts. More specifically, and by taking on the task of combining, bringing into conversation, and utilizing both masculinities and queer perspectives, the book aims to facilitate and contribute toward more inclusive, holistic, and intersectional approaches of gender in dealing with the past.

This book will appeal to scholars and students working in the areas of transitional justice, peace and conflict research, international relations, gender studies, and socio-legal studies.

Philipp Schulz is Postdoctoral Researcher at the Institute for Intercultural and International Studies (InIIS) at the University of Bremen, Germany.

Brandon Hamber is John Hume and Thomas P. O'Neill Chair in Peace based at the International Conflict Research Institute (INCORE) at Ulster University, United Kingdom.

Heleen Touquet is a visiting professor at the University of Antwerp, Belgium.

Part of the Transitional Justice series
Series editor Kieran McEvoy
Queen's University Belfast, UK

A GlassHouse book

For more information about this series, please visit: www.routledge.com/Transitional-Justice/book-series/TRANJ

Masculinities and Queer Perspectives in Transitional Justice

Edited by Philipp Schulz, Brandon Hamber, and Heleen Touquet

Routledge
Taylor & Francis Group
a GlassHouse Book

First published 2025
by Routledge
4 Park Square, Milton Park, Abingdon, Oxon OX14 4RN

and by Routledge
605 Third Avenue, New York, NY 10158

Routledge is an imprint of the Taylor & Francis Group, an informa business

A GlassHouse book

The Open Access version of this book has been funded by the University of Bremen, Ulster University and the German Research Foundation.

British Library Cataloguing-in-Publication Data
A catalogue record for this book is available from the British Library

Library of Congress Cataloging-in-Publication Data
Names: Schulz, Philipp, editor. | Hamber, Brandon, editor. | Touquet, Heleen, editor.
Title: Masculinities and queer perspectives in transitional justice / edited by Philipp Schulz, Brandon Hamber, and Heleen Touquet.
Description: Abingdon, Oxon [UK] ; New York , NY : Routledge, 2025. | Series: Transitional justice | Includes bibliographical references and index.
Identifiers: LCCN 2024027711 (print) | LCCN 2024027712 (ebook) | ISBN 9781032857176 (hardback) | ISBN 9781032857213 (paperback) | ISBN 9781003519522 (ebook)
Subjects: LCSH: Transitional justice. | Homosexuality—Law and legislation. | Gay people—Legal status, laws, etc. | Masculinity. | Men—Psychology.
Classification: LCC K5250 .M38 2025 (print) | LCC K5250 (ebook) | DDC 342.08/7—dc23/eng/20240621
LC record available at https://lccn.loc.gov/2024027711
LC ebook record available at https://lccn.loc.gov/2024027712

ISBN: 9781032857176 (hbk)
ISBN: 9781032857213 (pbk)
ISBN: 9781003519522 (ebk)

DOI: 10.4324/9781003519522

Typeset in Sabon
by Apex CoVantage, LLC

Contents

About the Contributors viii
List of Abbreviations xi
Acknowledgments xv

SECTION 1
Seeking Intersections Between Masculinities and Queer Perspectives in Transitional Justice 1

1 Introduction: Masculinities and Queer Perspectives in Transitional Justice 3
PHILIPP SCHULZ, BRANDON HAMBER, HELEEN TOUQUET, AND GIULIA MESSMER

2 Transitional Justice and Masculinities: A Critical Mapping of the Field 29
BRANDON HAMBER, PHILIPP SCHULZ, HELEEN TOUQUET, AND GIULIA MESSMER

3 Queering Transitional Justice: Reviewing the Field of Transitional Justice and Looking Toward Queer Possibilities 51
KATHERINE FOBEAR

SECTION 2
Theories, Processes, and Practices – Toward Inclusive Gender in TJ 67

4 "Queering" Transitional Justice From African Decolonial Perspectives? 69
KATHARINA HOFFMANN AND THOKOZANI MBWANA

5 Linking a Queer Legal Theoretical Perspective and Transitional Justice: Challenges and Possibilities 93
E. İREM AKI

6 The Heterosexual System Denuded: Ecuador's Truth Commission 113
PASCHA BUENO-HANSEN

7 Peacebuilding and Transitional Justice in Colombia: Institutionalized and Challenged Meanings of Gender 136
ANIKA OETTLER

SECTION 3
Gendering Justice and Transitions Across Contexts 159

8 Justice and Forced Marriage and Pregnancy in Wartime: A Gender-Inclusive Approach 161
CAMILE OLIVEIRA AND ERIN BAINES

9 Delineating Perpetratorhood: On Race, Masculinities, and Fighting Impunity for Sexual Violence in DRC 181
CHLOÉ LEWIS AND SUSANNE ALLDÉN

10 Croatian Veteran Masculinities and Exclusive Narratives: Points of Identification With the "Myth of the Homeland War" in the 2010s 208
CATHERINE BAKER AND HELEEN TOUQUET

11 Possibilities and Improbabilities: Reflections on "Queering" Transitional Justice in Colombia and Lebanon/Syria 228
HENRI MYRTTINEN, LAURA CAMILA BARRIOS SABOGAL, AND CHARBEL MAYDAA

SECTION 4
Beyond Violation-Centric Views 249

12 Queering Transitional Justice From Below: Some Inputs From Queer Masculinities 251
JOSÉ FERNANDO SERRANO-AMAYA

13 **Reclaiming the Post-War Self: Masculinities, Political Prisoners, and Transitional Justice in El Salvador** 278
URSULA MOSQUEIRA

14 **Mind and Body: Civilian Enactment of Masculinity in the North of Ireland and the Occupied Palestinian Territories** 300
SEAMUS CAMPBELL

15 **Civilian and Caring Masculinities and the Questions of Justice in Kashmir** 325
AMYA AGARWAL

16 **Queering Post-War Transitions: Exploring Queer Potentials of the "Butterfly for Democracy" Movement in Sri Lanka** 344
THIYAGARAJA WARADAS

17 **Concluding Thoughts and Calls to Action** 368
HELEEN TOUQUET, PHILIPP SCHULZ, PASCHA BUENO-HANSEN, JOSÉ FERNANDO SERRANO-AMAYA, BRANDON HAMBER, AND KATHERINE FOBEAR

Index *374*

About the Contributors

Amya Agarwal is a lecturer in international relations at the University of Sheffield. Her research explores the gender dimension of armed conflict in South Asia, paying close attention to masculinities, motherhood, and art. She is the author of *Contesting Masculinities and Women's Agency in Kashmir*.

E. İrem Akı works as a research assistant at Ankara University, Faculty of Law, Department of Philosophy and Sociology of Law. She was a post-doctoral fellow at Marburg University, Centre for Conflict Studies. Her research interests include transitional justice and feminist and queer theory.

Susanne Alldén is a senior lecturer and researcher at Linnaeus University, Sweden. Her work highlights the causes and consequences of armed conflicts, with a special focus on women's rights and situation during and after armed conflicts. Her research focuses on sexual violence during armed conflict and on women, peace, and security, in particular in DR Congo.

Erin Baines is an associate professor at the School of Public Policy and Global Affairs at the University of British Columbia. She is the author of *Buried in the Heart* (2017) and the co-principal investigator of an SSHRC partnership grant, the Transformative Memory International Network.

Catherine Baker is a reader in twentieth-century history in the School of Humanities, University of Hull. Her work uses feminist and queer lenses to understand the everyday politics of militarism, conflict, and security, especially through popular culture.

Pascha Bueno-Hansen is an associate professor of women and gender studies and political science and international relations at the University of Delaware, USA. Her current book project is titled *Dissident Genders and Sexualities in the Andes*.

Seamus Campbell was a doctoral student and, subsequently, a postdoctoral research associate at the Transitional Justice Institute, Ulster University. His work explores civilian masculinities during violent and protracted conflict.

Katherine Fobear is an associate professor in the Department of Women's, Gender, and Sexuality Studies at California State University, Fresno. Her work focuses on the intersections of gender identity and sexuality in migration, refugee rights, and transitional justice.

Brandon Hamber is the John Hume and Thomas P. O'Neill chair in peace at Ulster University at the International Conflict Research Institute (INCORE). He is a member of the Transitional Justice Institute and a visiting professor at the Geneva Academy.

Katharina Hoffmann holds a PhD in history and worked as a historian for projects on remembering the atrocities of national socialism and as a lecturer in gender studies. Her main research areas are memory cultures, gender and "transitional justice," migration, and diversity.

Chloé Lewis is a Research Fellow at the Minerva Global Security Programme, Blavatnik School of Government, University of Oxford and a Senior Research Associate with the Global Security Programme, Pembroke College, University of Oxford. She was previously a post-doctoral research associate at the School of Politics and International Relations at Queen Mary, University of London and a member of the UKRI GCRF Gender, Justice and Security Hub. Her independent and collaborative research sits at the intersection of scholarship, policy, and practice relating to gender and armed conflict.

Charbel Maydaa is the founder and former director of MOSAIC, a holistic program committed to the improvement of the health and wellness of LGBTIQ persons in the MENA region, and is the co-chair and West Asian representative of ILGA ASIA. Since 2004, they have been promoting LGBTIQ rights.

Thokozani Mbwana (he/they) is a human rights researcher, poet, and PhD candidate in African studies at the University of Cape Town. Thokozani's work centers queer narratives in transitional justice issues, freedom of expression, and association rights, as well as creative expression practices.

Giulia Messmer holds an MSSc in peace and conflict studies from Uppsala University and currently works as a media strategy officer at Sea-Watch e.V., as well as a project manager for the Safe Passage Foundation in Berlin.

Ursula Mosqueira is a research associate at the Catholic University of Chile Law School. Her applied work and research explore human rights issues affecting vulnerable communities in various contexts, such as political violence survivors in post-authoritarian Chile and El Salvador.

Henri Myrttinen is a visiting researcher with the Institute for Intercultural and International Studies at Universität Bremen. He has collaborated with MOSAIC MENA on research on diverse SOGIESC refugees in Lebanon and Turkey. He holds a PhD from the University of KwaZulu-Natal, South Africa.

Anika Oettler is a professor of sociology at Philipps Universität Marburg. She has published on transitional justice, collective memory, gender, and social inequality. She is a member of the network "Postcolonial Hierarchies in Peace and Conflict," funded by the German BMBF.

Camile Oliveira is a policy professional with a background in research and advocacy in various subject areas, including the women, peace, and security (WPS) agenda, children born of war, and wartime sexual violence. She holds an MPhil in multidisciplinary gender studies from the University of Cambridge.

Laura Camila Barrios Sabogal is a doctoral researcher at the Peace Research Institute Frankfurt (PRIF). Her research focuses on gender, DDR, and peacebuilding in Colombia. Previously, she was the director of the master's program in conflict, memory, and peace at Universidad del Rosario (Bogota).

Philipp Schulz is a post-doctoral researcher at the Institute for Intercultural and International Studies (InIIS) at the University of Bremen. His work engages with the gender dynamics of armed conflict, political violence, and post-conflict transitions.

José Fernando Serrano-Amaya is an assistant professor in the Department of Languages and Culture, Universidad de los Andes (Colombia). His research and teaching interests include gender, sexualities, and peacebuilding. He is the author of *Homophobic Violence in Armed Conflict and Political Transition.*

Heleen Touquet is a visiting professor at the Department of Politics at the University of Antwerp. Their research interests and work center on issues related to gender, conflict, political violence, and masculinities.

Thiyagaraja Waradas is a Sri Lankan Tamil queer activist. He works as a lecturer at the Department of Social and Policy Sciences at the University of Bath and was previously a senior lecturer at the Department of International Relations of the University of Colombo.

Abbreviations

ACHPR	African Commission on Human and Peoples' Rights
AFSPA	The Armed Forces Special Powers Act
AI	Acuerdo Final para la Terminación del Conflicto y la Construccion de una Paz Estable y Duradera, 24 August 2016 (Final Agreement to End the Armed Conflict and Build a Stable and Lasting Peace)
AII	Acuerdo Final para la Terminación del Conflicto y la Construccion de una Paz Estable y Duradera, 24 November 2016 (Final Agreement to End the Armed Conflict and Build a Stable and Lasting Peace)
APDP	Association of Parents of Disappeared Persons
AU	African Union
AVC	Alfaro Vive, ¡Carajo!
B4D	Butterflies for Democracy
BiH	Bosnia-Herzegovina
BJP	Bhartiya Janata Party
CAIN	Conflict Archive on the Internet
CDHES	Comision de Derechos Humanos de El Salvador (Human Rights Commission of El Salvador)
CEPDIPO	Centro de Pensamiento y Diálogo Político
CEV	truth commission
CIASE	Corporación de Investigación y Acción Social y Económica
CLS	critical legal studies
CMO	Cour Militaire Opérationelle
CNMH	Centro National de Memoria Histórica (National Center for Historical Memory)
CNR	*Consejo Nacional de Reincorporación*
COJ	companions on a journey
CONPES	Consejo Nacional de Política Económina y Social
CONPES 3931	Política Nacional para la Reincorporación Social y Económica D Exintegrantes De Las FARC-EP (The National

	Policy for the Social And Economical Reintegration of Former Members of the FARC-EP)
COPPES	Committee of Former Political Prisoners of El Salvador
CRSV	conflict-related sexual violence
CSIVI	Comisión de Seguimiento, Impulso y Verificación a la Implementación (Implementation, Follow-Up, Promotion, and Verification Committee)
CSMM	critical scholarship on men and masculinities
DIGNAS	Mujeres por la Dignidad y la Vida (Women for Dignity and Life)
DRC	Democratic Republic of Congo
ECCC	Extraordinary Chambers in the Courts of Cambodia
ECHR	European Court of Human Rights
ELN	Ejército de Liberasión Nacional
EU	European Union
FARC	Fuerzas Armadas Revolucionarias de Colombia – Ejército del Pueblo (Revolutionary Armed Forces of Colombia – People's Army)
FARC-EP	Revolutionary Armed Forces of Colombia – People's Army
FARDC	Forces Armées de la République Démocratique du Congo (The Armed Forces of the Democratic Republic of the Congo)
FCO	Foreign, Commonwealth Office
GMH	Historical Memory Group
GoSL	Government of Sri Lanka
GUSCO	Gulu Support the Children Organization
HDZ	Croatian Democratic Union
HIV	human immunodeficiency virus
HNS	Croatian Football Association
HOS	Croatian Defence Forces
HRW	Human Rights Watch
HVIDRA	Association of Croatian Homeland War Military Invalids
HVO	Croat Defence Council
ICC	International Criminal Court
ICRC	International Committee of the Red Cross
ICTR	International Criminal Tribunal for Rwanda
ICTY	International Criminal Tribunal for the former Yugoslavia
IDHUCA	*El Instituto de Derechos Humanos de la Universidad Centroamericana*
INREDH	*Fundación Regional de Asesoría de Derechos Humanos*
J&K	Jammu and Kashmir
JEP	Special Jurisdiction for Peace
JKCCS	Jammu and Kashmir Coalition of Civil Society
JNA	Yugoslav People's Army

JRP	Justice and Reconciliation Project
JVP	Peoples' Liberation Front
KGK	Kolinda Grabar-Kitarović
LGBTQI+	***lesbian, gay, bisexual, trans, queer, inter***
LLRC	Lessons Learnt and Reconciliation Commission
LRA	Lord's Resistance Army
LTTE	Liberation Tigers of Tamil Eelam
M-19	Movimento 19 de Abril
MAQL	*Movimiento Armado Quintín Lame*
NATO	North Atlantic Treaty Organization
NDH	Independent State of Croatia
NGO	non-governmental organization
OML	Organización de Mujeres Lesbianas de Ecuador (Ecuadorian Organization of Lesbian Women)
OMP	Office on Missing Persons
ONU	Organización de las Naciones Unidas (The United Nations)
OSF	Open Society Foundations
OSISA	Open Society Initiatives for Southern Africa
PTA	Prevention of Terrorism Act
QQIAAAP2+	queer, questioning, intersex, asexual, ally, androgynous, pansexual, two-spirit
RTI	Right to Information Act
RUF	Revolutionary United Front
SEA	sexual exploitation and abuse
SGBV	sexual and gender-based violence
SHRC	State Human Rights Commission
SIT	special investigation team
SMUG	Sexual Minorities Uganda
SOGIESC	sexual orientation, gender identity, gender expression, and sex characteristics
SVAM	sexual violence against men
TERF	trans-exclusionary radical feminist(s)
TJ	transitional justice
TJFB	transitional justice from below
TNA	Tamil National Alliance
UBPD	Unit to Search for the Disappeared
UCA	Universidad Centroamericana "José Simeón Cañas" (Jesuit University of El Salvador)
UN	United Nations
UNDP	United Nations Development Programme
UNGA	United Nations General Assembly
UNHCR	United Nations High Commissioner for Refugees
UNJHRO	United Nations Joint Human Rights Office
UNJHRO	United Nations Joint Human Rights Office

UNSCR	United Nations Security Council Resolution
UP	Union Patriótica
WAN	Women's Advocacy Network
WEF	World Economic Forum
YP +10	Yogyakarta Principles plus 10

Acknowledgments

This edited volume was a long time in the making. It would not have been possible without the patience, dedication, commitment, curiosity, and insights of the authors and contributors to this volume. Since 2020, the editors and contributors have worked closely with one another, over various rounds of drafts and feedback and a collaborative author workshop, and we are thankful for this slowed-down and collective process of knowledge production and the insights it has garnered.

We also collectively acknowledge, and are thankful for, the commitment and interest invested into this process and this scholarship by the various groups of interlocutors, collaborators, research partners across various contexts which informed the work across these chapters, shaping our understanding of the gender dynamics of transitional justice processes.

The edited volume was initially commissioned by Mina Rauschenbach, Stephan Parmentier, and Jeremy Sarkin for the Intersentia Series on Transitional Justice. We are immensely grateful for their support and encouragement throughout this period, and for their dedication to this project. This book would not have been what it is without their involvement in it.

At Routledge, we are thankful to Kieran McEvoy and our editors, Colin Perrin and Naomi Round Cahalin, for so enthusiastically welcoming us and the project and for offering a home for this volume in the transitional justice series. Thank you also to Giulia Messmer for supporting the process and dedicated editorial assistance.

The process of writing and editing this volume, and its open-access publication in particular, has benefited from generous support and funding from various sources and institutions: the German Research Council (DF), project nr. 426849903; Ulster University; and the Staats- und Universitätsbibliothek Bremen.

Section 1

Seeking Intersections Between Masculinities and Queer Perspectives in Transitional Justice

Chapter 1

Introduction

Masculinities and Queer Perspectives in Transitional Justice

Philipp Schulz, Brandon Hamber, Heleen Touquet, and Giulia Messmer

Introduction

At the 75th UN General Assembly, the United Nations Special Rapporteur on the promotion of truth, justice, reparation, and guarantees of non-recurrence, Fabián Salvioli, presented his report on gender perspectives in transitional justice (Salvioli, 2020). The report signals a significant change in the sphere of policy, as it explicitly highlights and emphasizes the experiences of people with diverse sexual orientations, gender identities and expressions and sex characteristics (SOGIESC), as well as men in processes of transitional justice. While the report draws attention to some of the issues that this present book engages with, it nevertheless also falls into some of the traps and shortcomings of emerging debates about broadening the scope and advancing more inclusive conceptions of peacebuilding and transitional justice – something that this volume seeks to engage with and remedy.

For example, Salvioli importantly acknowledges that the mandates of truth commissions have largely privileged men's experiences and that "adding gender perspectives can solve this problem" (2020: 3). This is somewhat contradictory: the report, on the one hand, says that male experiences have been privileged, while also saying that they have been ignored. In fact, we contend that both are true: transitional justice has traditionally been a field where male values have dominated under the veil of "neutrality," but this has also meant that men's experiences are not analyzed or seen as *gendered*, thus missing how they are connected to patriarchy, power differentials in society, and gender inequality. In essence, the failure to perceive these connections blinds us to the very systems that contribute and sustain conflict.

Salvioli then goes on to demonstrate how the experiences of men and SOGIESC should be incorporated:

> [A]ddressing and preventing gender-based abuses requires that due consideration be given to the complexity and intersectionality of the experiences not only of women, but also of men in the face of gender-based violence and of lesbian, gay, bisexual and transgender persons.
>
> (2020: 4)

DOI: 10.4324/9781003519522-2

> It is also evident that men have been forgotten and rendered invisible in the face of sexual and gender-based violence, especially in the case of lesbian, gay, bisexual and transgender persons. There is also a general lack of focus on sexual orientation and gender identity in the vast majority of truth-seeking processes.
>
> (2020: 5)

These paragraphs suggest what we in this volume refer to as a "violation-centric" logic: where the focus rests on violence against males and persons with diverse SOGIESC rather than on a broader understanding of the role of masculinities and queer bodies and perspectives in post-conflict contexts. We observe a similar pattern in the scholarly literature on gender and transitional justice: careful consideration for the roles of masculinities and for men's experiences as *gendered* (Hamber 2016) as well as for the lived realities of SOGIESC remains marginalized in scholarly debates about gendering TJ (Fobear 2014; Bueno-Hansen 2018). As previously argued by feminist anthropologist Kimberly Theidon, "from gender hearings to gender units and gender-sensitive truth commissions, 'adding gender' is policy-speak for 'adding women'" (2009: 4). Without a doubt, sustained attention to gender justice for women and girls is much needed and warranted, given the pervasive marginalization of women and female experiences in conflict and transitional settings (Ní Aoláin 2012; Enloe 2004; Moser and Clark 2001). Although scholars have paid more attention to masculinities and queer bodies in the context of transitional justice and queer issues in recent years (Gopalan 2023; Ritholtz et al. 2023), their work has similarly been dominated by a focus on violations in narrowly defined terms. As a result, more holistic and structural analyses of how masculinities and queer bodies, theories, and identities underpin, influence, shape, and condition processes of transitional justice remain largely under-developed (Fobear 2014; Bueno-Hansen 2018; Hamber 2016).

As editors of this volume, all three of us have worked individually and collectively on various dimensions related to armed conflict, political violence, as well as post-conflict and transitional justice processes, specifically with a focus on masculinities (Hamber 2016; Schulz 2020; Touquet et al. 2021). We first came together as a group in 2016, at a workshop at Ulster University in Belfast on *Masculinities, Violence, and (Post-)conflict*, organized by Philipp Schulz and Seamus Campbell, together with some of the authors represented in this volume (Heleen Touquet, Seamus Campbell, Henri Myrttinen, Chloé Lewis). In many ways, this event marked the beginning of our collective work on and engagement with questions related to masculinities in post-conflict and transitional spaces, even though we have all worked on this individually before. Brandon Hamber has written widely on masculinities perspectives in transitional justice, which in many ways has shaped the foundations of this sub-field of scholarly engagement. Building on this, Philipp Schulz, in 2020, published an article that called for more inclusive gender in transitional justice. Amongst others, this article argued for the importance of not only focusing on masculinities in TJ, which remain under-explored, but also placing that engagement in conversation with growing attention to queer perspectives in the field, highlighting the necessity of holistic and relational approaches to gender. Yet despite these calls, the article attests that careful consideration for the roles of masculinities and for the experiences of persons with diverse sexual orientations, gender identities and expressions, and sex characteristics (SOGIESC) remains strikingly absent – requiring further engagement and research and, in many ways, constituting the point of departure for this volume.

This previous and persisting inattentiveness to masculinities and queer curiosities and perspectives in transitional justice, then, forms the overarching gap in scholarship and policymaking which this book seeks to address. By incorporating masculinities and queer perspectives in transitional justice in tandem and alongside one another, this book contributes empirically, conceptually, and methodologically to an exploration of gender in processes of dealing with violent pasts. Specifically, by taking on the task of combining, bringing into conversation, and utilizing both masculinities and queer perspectives, this volume aims to facilitate and contribute toward more inclusive, holistic, and intersectional approaches of gender in dealing with the past (Ní Aoláin and Rooney 2007).

We specifically consider the gendered workings and power relations of socially constructed idea(l)s of masculinities and heterosexuality and examine how these shape the lived realities in times of conflict and its wake. We believe that the intersections between gender, sexualities, vulnerabilities, and power, specifically, lie at the core of post-conflict processes of dealing with the past but have, for the most part, remained underexplored. Our aim is thereby also to explicitly challenge dominant institutionalized, (neo)liberal, and patriarchal transitional justice toolkit approaches. These approaches, we maintain, are often caught up in the dominant heteronormative frames of transitional justice (Bueno-Hansen 2018) but are often ineffective in dealing with a wider and more inclusive range of gendered experiences, vulnerabilities, harms, and quests for redress (Schulz 2019) – hence requiring a broader understanding of and approach to justice in transition (Sharp 2014). This volume seeks to contribute to such broadened understandings of TJ, by identifying and exploring intersections between masculinities, queer perspectives, sexualities, and gender in a widened manner.

We emphasize that gendered violations and vulnerabilities ought to be taken fully into account by mechanisms and processes designed to deliver justice, facilitate transitions, and build peace. The chapters in this volume contribute toward developing thicker pathways of facilitating justice in transition, moving beyond narrow institutional understandings of what justice can look and feel like and how to facilitate it, and moving beyond binary understandings of gender. Grounded in the empirical, many of the chapters in this volume emphasize the myriad ways in which gender shapes and underpins how individuals and communities impacted by violence understand and make sense of violence, harm, justice, and repair, and how they remake worlds in the aftermath of violence, encompassing the complexities of how communities "read, endure, work through, break apart under, transcend" violence and social suffering (Das et al. 2001: 3; see Krystalli and Schulz 2022).

Importantly, we situate this book in the tradition of critical feminist inquiries regarding the roles of gender in social, cultural, and political structuring (Sjoberg 2016). Specifically, the chapters in this volume follow a deep-seated feminist commitment and curiosity to critically interrogate, undo, and move beyond patriarchal and heteronormative frames (Enloe 2004; Weber 2016) which continue to dominate social and political life across time and space (Cockburn 2010). Rather than simply making men and people with diverse SOGIESC visible in transitional settings, the authors in this volume systematically analyze structural issues regarding the (lack of) inclusion of masculinities and queer perspectives on the topic of justice in transition (Fineman and Zinsstag 2013; O'Rourke 2013; Buckley-Zistel and Stanley 2012). Crucially, we wish to emphasize that we do *not* position our consideration for men and masculinities and for persons with diverse SOGIESC in contrast to, or in competition with, a focus on women and girls. Instead, our approaches are underpinned by and geared toward intersectional and relational understandings of gender, recognizing the relationalities between all gender identities (Connell 2005), which cannot be decoupled from patriarchal gender hierarchies and structures more broadly (Enloe 2004; Sjoberg 2016). This relational approach "draws attention to the wider web of social entanglements through which power circulates and is contested" (Aijazi and Baines 2017: 468) in transitional settings.

The topics we explore and the questions raised and answered in this volume include, but are not limited to:

- What and where are the intersections between masculinities and queer theories and frameworks for better understanding lived experiences of violence, justice, and transitions?
- How can masculinities and queer perspectives enhance and "complexify" our understandings of the intersections between gender, sexualities, armed conflict, and (post-)conflict transitions?
- What are the lived realities of men and boys, as well as of persons with diverse SOGIESC, in post-conflict and transitional spaces, and how can (or cannot) diverse transitional justice mechanisms and attempts to remake a world in the wake of violence engage with and respond to these experiences?
- How do identities defined by gender, sexuality, class, race, ethnicity, socio-political status, or (dis)ability intersect, and how do these intersections shape individuals' and communities' post-war and transitional experiences?

- And what are the potential challenges associated with bringing attention to men's and SOGIESC experiences in transitional settings?

In engaging with these and related questions and issues, the chapters in this volume offer several contributions – in empirical, conceptual, and methodological terms – to the study of transitional justice through a gender lens. Taken together, by employing masculinities and queer perspectives to processes of dealing with violent pasts, the chapters all contribute toward a more holistic, inclusive, nuanced, and relational understanding of how gender shapes and operates within and across post-conflict and transitional contexts. This is important, we argue, to better understand the diversities and complexities of gendered experiences in times of violence, conflict, transition, and peace and of gendered harms, violations, and vulnerabilities that ought to be taken into account by mechanisms and processes designed to deliver justice, facilitate transitions, and build peace.

Transitional Justice and Gender: Situating This Volume

We understand *transitional justice* (TJ) broadly as "the set of measures implemented . . . to deal with the legacies of human rights abuses" (de Greiff 2012: 34) in the wake of armed conflict, political violence, or authoritarian regimes, seeking to aid societies transitioning from violence and conflict toward more just and peaceful futures. Since the end of the Cold War, the study and implementation of TJ expanded significantly (Hansen 2016) and, in many ways, experienced its own transition (McEvoy 2007), emerging from its exceptionalist origins toward becoming a standardized, institutionalized, and globalized practice (Teitel 2015). Initially, TJ was focused primarily on criminal accountability processes for serious human rights violations (Sooka 2006) and truth-seeking processes (Hayner 2011) in situations where new liberal democracies were established (Hansen 2016). However, TJ, over time, developed to include a whole variety of processes, measures, and instruments – including, for instance, criminal trials, truth-seeking processes, memorialization initiatives, reparations, vetting and lustration, or traditional justice, among others. Furthermore, TJ is now applied to a wide range of violence-affected settings, that is, "where either the transition in question concerns 'something else', such as peaceful transformation, or where no transition has occurred" (Hansen 2016: 15).

As Brandon Hamber noted elsewhere, "the field of TJ and peacebuilding itself is fraught with false distinctions and categorisations" (Hamber 2016: 14) (e.g., "post-conflict" or "transition") that often manifest in misleading dichotomies, such as "war vs. peace," "justice vs. impunity," "global vs. local," or "(male) perpetrators vs. (female) victims." Although we remain increasingly uncomfortable with trying to categorize different contexts in these terms – as "post-conflict," "post-agreement," or "society in transition" – what they ought to reflect is an assumption about a certain type of society in which armed conflict and/or political violence has taken place. While all these contexts differ significantly, the cases and contexts captured by these terms and included in this volume have "seen not only the loss of life and a range of other human rights violations (for example, torture, rape) but also the destruction of infrastructure and livelihoods," as well as social and inter-community relationships (Hamber 2016: 14). Importantly, throughout this volume, we not only understood violence not in a narrower sense as implying physical violence only (as inscribed into militarized masculinities) but also take into account structural forms of violence in transitional settings (Sharp 2014), many of which are heavily gendered (O'Rourke 2013). These violences often manifest in continuities spanning "war," "peace," and beyond (Cockburn 2010; Martin de Almagro and Schulz 2022) but which, for the most part, have remained marginalized in TJ research.

Likewise, the contexts covered in this volume are generally categorized by violent political conflict subsiding, at least to some degree, followed by some sort of peace process. This can include high-level political agreements, constitutional changes, the implementation of justice strategies (e.g., trials), and other mechanisms of dealing with the past (e.g., truth commissions, reparations), as well as peacebuilding and TJ strategies, from rebuilding infrastructure to people-to-people reconciliation work, such as dialogue, inter-group contact, or memorialization efforts, with varying degrees of success (and failure). Yet despite these broad characterizations, in reality, these processes are seldom linear, and reconstruction involves many processes that are not always captured by phrases such as *peacebuilding* or *TJ* (Hamber 2009) – a point that several of the chapters included in this volume aptly illustrate and emphasize (see Campbell or Agarwal, this volume).

In line with these developments, we approach TJ in a thickened and broadened conceptualization (McEvoy 2007). In addition to various institutionalized mechanisms and processes, as noted earlier, this also includes a variety of non-institutionalized measures and "everyday" practices of how individuals and communities reconstruct their lives and rebuild societies in the wake of conflict (Das et al. 2001; Kent 2014). In light of this, Riaño-Alcalá and Baines's understanding applies to many of the chapters' engagement with TJ, referring to

> the many individual and collective ways in which people pursue mundane activities and practices to restore the basic fabrics of meaningful social relations, negotiations or re-creative protective mechanisms and provide some sense of continuity in their lives and sense of self in relation to others in the aftermath of violence and conflict.
>
> (2012: 386)

As part of this general expansion process of transitional justice, critical voices and perspectives in the field (Palmer et al. 2012; Sharp 2019; Kurze and

Lamont 2021) have critically scrutinized, questioned, and developed the study and practice of TJ. This includes, among others, a localization of TJ (Shaw and Waldorf 2010; MacDonald 2013) which pays increasing attention to local lived realities and specific processes and conceptions of justice, redress, and harm (Kent 2018; Baines 2007); as well as attention to (post) colonial dynamics (Bueno-Hansen 2015; Moyo 2019; Rolston and Ní Aoláin 2018) or to socio-economic aspects (Lai 2020; Roht-Arriaza and Mariezcurrena 2006) of justice in transition. At the same time, feminist and queer perspectives and inquiries form an integral component of this growing critical engagement with and scrutinizing of transitional justice processes (Ní Aoláin 2012; Scanlon and Muddell 2009) – as explored in the following section.

Gendering Transitional Justice

Critical feminist interventions in particular have paid substantial attention to the gender dynamics of political transitions (O'Rourke 2013; Fineman and Zinsstag 2013) – the body of scholarship in which we situate this volume. The last two decades of transitional justice developments thereby radically altered an engagement with gender (Buckley-Zistel and Stanley 2012), including gendered rights, experiences, harms, vulnerabilities, and forms of violence, but also gendered patterns of participation and inclusion/exclusion in TJ processes (see de Almagro and Schulz 2020; Franke 2006). Especially, women's movements around the world have led important efforts to ensure that gender justice is put at the center of political, legal, and humanitarian agenda of transitional justice (Bell and O'Rourke 2007: 24), that sexual violence is considered a war crime (Schulz and Kreft 2022), and that TJ also addresses social, economic, and cultural rights, as well as collective rights to socio-economic development (Roht-Arriaza and Mariezcurrena 2006).

While much – although definitely not all – of the work on gender in transitional justice takes place in the academy (Weber 2021), there certainly are also important legal, normative, and political developments that have addressed gender and TJ. Much of this policy engagement is taking place within the realms of the United Nations Security Council (UNSC) and its mandate to maintain international peace and security, and specifically under the umbrella of the UN women, peace, and security (WPS) framework (Martin de Almagro 2017). Similarly, the resolution of the UN's Human Rights Council that established the mandate of the Special Rapporteur on truth, reparation, and guarantees of non-recurrence – through which much of the UN's engagement with transitional justice unfolds – specifically refers to *gender* (see O'Rourke 2017). In 2020, the Special Rapporteur, Fabián Salvioli, issued a report on gender perspectives in transitional justice, quoted in the opening paragraph of this chapter, which "considers the multiple aspects of adopting a gender perspective in the conceptualization, design and implementation of national transitional justice strategies and mechanisms" (2020: 1).

Despite these developments, critical voices nevertheless remark that a "feminist presence in transitional justice is complex, multilayered and still in the process of engagement" (Ní Aolaín 2012: 205). Fifteen years since Bell and O'Rourke's (2007) call for feminist TJ theorizing, there continues to be a "capture problem with gendered harms" (Ní Aoláin 2012: 20), while "gender parity remains elusive in transitional justice implementation" (Ní Aolaín 2019: 1). As such, numerous gender blind spots persist (Bueno-Hansen 2018; Moyo 2019; Gopalan 2023), various gendered experiences in post-conflict and transitional spaces remain unaccounted for (Schulz 2019), and existing TJ processes have largely fallen short in advancing transformations for women (Boesten and Wilding 2015).

In light of such critiques, feminist analytical lenses underscore the importance of breaking out of binary and dichotomous framings between (gendered) public and private spheres and forms of violence; simplified distinctions between pre-war, war, and post-war violence; or neat differentiation between physical and structural forms of violence and inequalities (Enloe 2004; True 2012). Instead, a more nuanced understanding is needed that points toward the continuities and fluidities between these different notions of gender and justice respectively (Ní Aoláin 2012) – a call we follow throughout this volume.

At the same time, and as noted earlier, the thriving discussion about gender and TJ largely continues to be one about whether or not, and how, transitional justice processes (can) do "gender justice" for female victims and survivors of violence (Boesten and Wilding 2015; Scanlon and Muddell 2009). The understanding of "gender" that underpins such analyses, however, is effectively an exclusive one, often read synonymous with "women and girls" (Theidon 2009; Dolan 2015). According to dominant understandings, conflict-related experiences and harms are only regarded as "gendered" when they represent or reinforce "the unequal position of women in society" (Pillay 2007: 317). Similar to much of the literature on gender in the context of armed conflict, political violence, and peacebuilding more broadly (Carpenter 2006; Duriesmith 2016; Duncanson 2009), throughout scholarship on transitional justice, employing a "gender perspective" has long meant, and continues to translate into, highlighting the roles, needs, rights, and vulnerabilities of women and girls (Theidon 2009). Despite the ongoing importance of this attention, the persistent equation of "gender" with "women and girls" nevertheless implies the risk of ignoring a whole variety of other gender-based experiences, identities, and different forms of gendered violence. This includes, in particular, masculinities and men's experiences as *gendered* (Hamber 2016), as well as queer people with diverse SOGIESC (Fobear 2014), all of which remain largely omitted from most gendered TJ analyses. These exclusions, then, result in incomplete and essentialist pictures of the gendered workings and dynamics of post-conflict and transitional justice processes – the gap that this volume engages with, with a view toward identifying intersections and fostering more holistic and inclusive conceptions and analyses of gender and TJ.

Conceptual Framings: Masculinities and Queer Perspectives in TJ

Against the backdrop of these looming gaps, critical researchers have increasingly called for attention to masculinities and SOGIESC questions in peacebuilding and TJ scholarship, respectively (see Hamber 2016; Fobear 2014; Bueno-Hansen 2018; Schulz 2019; Ritholz et al. 2023). Analyses focusing on masculinities and diverse sexual orientations and gender identities, however, only really appeared in the TJ literature in the last decade (Hamber 2016; McQuaid 2020; Fobear 2014; Fobear and Baines 2020). Likewise, the few existing studies that do engage with men and masculinities or with SOGIESC experiences exist primarily in silos and are often characterized by a unitary focus on *either* masculinities *or* on queer issues. What is more, and as attested earlier, the existing engagement is largely defined by violation-centric views, focusing on violences by or against men and against persons with SOGIESC alike but not yet examining the wider and more structural dimensions of masculinities and queer issues in transitional settings. By focusing on masculinities and queer perspectives in combination and relation, this volume aims to bring these critical interventions together, moving beyond unitary, potentially exclusionary, and violence-centric perspectives. In order to do that, the chapters in this volume all apply gendered lenses to the study of violence, conflict, and TJ, focusing "on gender as a particular kind of power relation, or to trace out the ways in which gender is central to understanding international processes" (Steans 1998: 5).

In addition to masculinities and queer perspectives as guiding concepts – which we shed conceptual light on in the following sections, as well as throughout the different chapters (see, in particular, Chapters 2 and 3) – there are other key conceptual framings that move across this volume, including, notably, the concepts of heteronormativity and intersectionality, which we briefly seek to define and conceptualize here.

Heteronormativity, as a concept grown out of queer theories and curiosities – and as such further clarified in their respective applications of the concept by, amongst others, Katherine Fobear, Pascha Bueno-Hansen, or Katharina Hoffmann and Thokozani Mbwana – conceptualizes heterosexuality, that is, the romantic and/or sexual attraction and interactions between people of the opposite sex and gender, as the preferred, normalized, and accept mode of sexual orientation (Ward and Schneider 2009). As such, heteronormativity assumes a binaric gender model and idealizes same-sexual relations and encounters, prizing them as superior to other sexual orientations and relations. Heteronormativity thereby creates, upholds, and privileges patriarchy and is founded upon homo-, bi-, and transphobia (Weber 2016). The way in which these dynamics play out in the context of transitional justice, and in post-conflict and transitioning settings, is that heteronormative and heterosexual ideas, expectations, and assumptions are being privileged and centralized in the design, conceptualization, and implementation of these processes, referring to and designed for male and female protagonists and thereby marginalizing queer experiences, bodies, perspectives, and actors.

Intersectionality, as a concept emerging out of Black feminist thinking (Crenshaw 1989; Collins 1990), offers a conceptual and analytical frame to think about and refer to the different intersections of people's various identities – including, but not limited to, gender, sex, race, caste, class, ethnicity, (dis)ability, weight, and many others – and how these combine to form different layers of privilege or discrimination (Simien 2007). As defined by Kimberly Crenshaw, "intersectionality is a metaphor for understanding the ways that multiple forms of inequality or disadvantage sometimes compound themselves and create obstacles that often are not understood among conventional ways of thinking" (1989: 149). In thinking about and employing the concept of intersectionality, of which there has been an increase in recent years (Sarkin and Morais 2022), it is fundamentally important to not lose sight of the origins of this work and its thinking around it (Henry 2017), as we emphasize again in the following chapter. Crenshaw specifically employed the term "intersectionality" to refer to the different layers of discriminations caused and enforced by racism and sexism, as experienced by Black women in the context of navigating law(s). In the context of this work in the volume, then, and without neglecting the origins of this concept, *intersectionality* refers to the intersecting layers of experiences and levels of violence and discrimination of people in conflict-affected and transitional contexts.

Masculinities Perspectives in Transitional Justice

Building on this, then, applying a masculinities perspective specifically refers "to analytical approaches that attend to constructions of masculinities as they relate to conflict and peacebuilding" (Wright 2020: 652) as well as TJ. As we discuss in greater detail in Chapter 2, *masculinities* can be understood as the multiple ways of "doing male" (Connell 2005), referring to socially constructed gender norms that include "anything which is associated with being a man in any given culture" (Wright 2014: 4). In speaking of masculinities perspectives, in the plural, we emphasize the multiplicities and variations of ways of "doing male," as well as of approaches to and perspectives on masculinities, across time and space – a point we develop more fully in the following chapter.

Despite resounding calls for more attention to and engagement with men and masculinities in relation to violence, war, and conflict (Duriesmith 2016; Myrttinen et al. 2017; Dery 2020; see Hamber et al. this volume), masculinities perspectives, specifically in TJ scholarship, for the most part, find themselves in an embryonic state (Hamber 2016). If and when masculinities in TJ contexts are analyzed, the focus is either on violent and militarized masculinities (Duncanson 2009) or is concerned with questions of how to transform them post-conflict (Theidon 2009). Alternatively, existing research is characterized by a persistent focus on masculine vulnerabilities (Dolan 2015), specifically on sexual violence against men and their justice needs (Schulz 2020; Touquet et al. 2021). What remains under-explored, however, are the manifold and structurally embedded ways in which masculinities operate as structural vectors of power, affecting various categories of people with all gender identities in conflict-affected settings, including civilian and non-militant men who are neither combatants nor victims of sexual abuse, which, in turn, impacts on women and those with diverse SOGIESC (also see Hamber et al., this volume).

Several chapters included in this volume begin to address and remedy these gaps. For instance, the chapters by Amya Agarwal, Seamus Campbell, and Ursula Mosqueira all focus on the experiences of civilian, non-combatant men and masculinities in post-war and transitional settings. Moving beyond a focus on men as either violent combatants or passive victims of (sexual) violence, these investigations instead provide a more detailed picture of how a diverse group of men experience violence, conflict, and transition, as well as how they are impacted by and engage with TJ processes, and how they enact processes of social repair, micro-level peacebuilding, and justice-making on their own terms (also see Oliveira and Baines, this volume). Taken together, these chapters demonstrate the various ways in which men – including civilians, former political prisoners, fathers of children born in war, or civil society activists and peacebuilding practitioners – navigate complex processes of justice, transitions, and social repair, and how these processes are structured and shaped by gender and masculinities.

Other chapters in this volume also specifically focus on structural aspects of masculinities, considering how multiple and intersecting "masculine cultures operate within a variety of hierarchies and social spaces" (Hamber 2016: 30) during periods of transition. For instance, Catherine Baker investigates the salient power of militarized masculinities in post-war Croatia and how these get reproduced through popular culture and media, posing complex challenges for post-war peacebuilding and transitional justice efforts that seek to undo these violent masculinities constructions. Similarly, Chloé Lewis and Susanne Alldèn deconstruct racialized and gendered constructions of masculine perpetratorhood of sexual violence in the eastern Democratic of the Congo (DRC). Focused on northern Uganda, Camile Oliveira and Erin Baines likewise utilize masculinities perspectives to investigate men's experiences of forced marriage, considering how men were subjected to the institutionalization of forced marriage and pregnancy contingent on gender expectations and roles, and how these experiences continue to shape their post-conflict lived realities. In combination, these differing approaches and perspectives advance our understanding of the multiple ways in which masculinities constructions operate in and shape transitional justice processes, and how different categories of men participate in and are impacted by processes of dealing with the past.

Queer Perspectives in Transitional Justice

Despite the importance of engaging with men and masculinities, however, such a focus also bears the risk of reinforcing binary constructions of gender, which remain remarkably consistent throughout research on armed conflict and peacebuilding in general (Hagen 2016; Sjoberg 2016), and on TJ specifically (Bueno-Hansen 2018). As such, careful attention is required to ensure that centering men and masculinities does not further ignore or marginalize queer experiences and perspectives. As demonstrated by Katherine Fobear's chapter in this volume, the question of "what it would mean to better incorporate and engage with queer bodies and theory in transitional justice" (39) remains continuously under-explored. McQuaid similarly argues that "on the subject of the particular justice needs and harms experienced by sexual minorities, much current transitional justice scholarship remains silent" (2017: 1). Thanks to critical interventions from scholars and activists alike, there has recently been some movement in the field in this regard (Fobear 2014; Bueno-Hansen 2018).

By incorporating queer perspectives, alongside masculinities, in this volume, we specifically seek to move beyond binary understandings of gender and instead pay attention to gender identities and experiences across and outside the gender spectrum. This includes, in particular, attention to the lived realities of people with diverse SOGIESC and how these are omitted from the heteronormative frames that operate within and alongside conventional TJ processes – a point made by Pascha Bueno-Hansen in this volume. In this vein, we understand "'queering' as disrupting heteronormative frameworks based on strict binary and dichotomous conceptions of sex and gender" (Schulz and Touquet 2020: 1171). *Queer approaches* and *perspectives* thus refer to investigating "the 'who' and 'how' that cannot or will not be made to signify monolithically in relation to gender, sex, and/or sexuality" (Weber 2016: 597). A queer analysis thereby uncovers a wider spectrum of factors along the intersections between sexualities and gender that do not neatly fit into binary categorizations (Cooper-Cunningham 2021). In this reading, *queering* should not be (mis)understood in narrow terms as referring only to attention for persons with diverse SOGIESC and LGBTQI+ individuals – although this attention, of course, forms an important part of this investigation – but rather should also be interpreted more broadly as referring to the open mesh of possibilities, lapses, and dissonances where gender and sexualities intersect as analytical categories beyond monolithic heteronormativity (Sedgwick 1993; Ahmed 2006).

As Katherine Fobear helpfully clarifies in her chapter,

> [q]ueering or to queer refers to two actions. The first is to bring to the forefront voices, issues, and experiences of non-heterosexual and/or non-cisgendered individuals and communities in literature and practice. The second is to challenge social constructions of gender and sexuality that are in turn used to support institutions of gendered and sexualized normative power and discourse.
>
> (39–40)

In employing queer perspectives, the chapters in this volume use varying terminologies to label and describe these identities and experiences, including "sexual and gender minorities" (e.g., Katherine Fobear), "lesbian, gay, bisexual, transgender, queer, and intersex+" (LGBTQI+) individuals (e.g., Anika Oettler), or most commonly, "persons with diverse sexual orientations, gender identities and expressions and sex characteristics" (SOGIESC) (e.g., İrem Akı, Thiyagaraja Waradas, Pascha Bueno-Hansen). We, as editors, have made the purposeful editorial choice to allow authors a certain degree of freedom and flexibility to work with terms and concepts that best work for them and the contexts in which they work. While we acknowledge and agree that not having one unitary set of terms may, at first sight, be confusing, we are mindful of wanting to give authors and their research participants space to recognize and represent the diversity of perspectives, approaches, and preferences across different spaces, including among different groups of interlocutors and cultural contexts.

At the same time, following Daigle and Myrttinen (2018), we, as editors (like several of the authors), have a preference for the SOGIESC term and concept: even though the LGBTQI(+) acronym prevails throughout much of the academic and policy discourses around gender and sexuality, the acronym is not necessarily used universally. This can make for a Western-centric representation of gender and sexuality that "is limited in its capacity to represent sexual and gender minorities across the globe" (Hagen 2016: 315). At the same time, LGBTQI(+) is an aggregate category that implies the risk of universalizing, mashing together and glossing over diverse, possibly intersectional, experiences within and between different groups included under this umbrella acronym (Daigle and Myrttinen 2018: 18; see İrem Akı, this volume). In contrast, the alternative reference to diverse SOGIESC does "not indicate any particular group, as all human beings have sexual orientations and gender identities" (Daigle and Myrttinen 2018: 18). Following this line of reasoning, the SOGIESC[1] terminology is employed most commonly and

1 Following the Yogyakarta Principles, "*sexual orientation* [emphasis added] is understood to refer to each person's capacity for profound emotional, affectional and sexual attraction to, and intimate and sexual relations with, individuals of a different gender or the same gender or more than one gender. Gender identity is understood to refer to each person's deeply felt internal and individual experience of gender, which may or may not correspond with the sex assigned at birth, including the personal sense of the body (which may involve, if freely chosen, modification of bodily appearance or function by medical, surgical or other means) and other expressions of gender, including dress, speech and mannerisms" (Yogyakarta Principles 2007: 6 footnote 1 and 2). *Gender expression* is "each person's presentation of the person's gender through physical appearance, including dress, hairstyles, accessories, cosmetics – and mannerisms, speech, behavioural patterns, names and personal references" and "may or may not conform to a person's gender identity" (Yogyakarta Principles plus 10 2017: 6). *Sex characteristics* is "each person's physical features relating to sex, including genitalia and other sexual and reproductive anatomy, chromosomes, hormones, and secondary physical features emerging from puberty" (Yogyakarta Principles plus 10 2017: 6). Also see Aki, this volume, for definitional clarification.

consistently throughout the volume "in an attempt to express the variation that exists between individuals, as well as to avoid privileging 'normative' (i.e. heteronormative) identities and groups" (Daigle and Myrttinen 2018: 18).

As demonstrated by Katherine Fobear's chapter in this volume, attention to queer bodies and theories in peacebuilding and transitional justice remains significantly underexplored. The limited existing research has primarily examined homophobic and anti-queer violence directed against persons with diverse SOGIESC and LGBTQI communities (Oettler 2019), often with a focus on sexual violence (Myrttinen et al. 2017). Making visible these violations, harms, and vulnerabilities, which, for the most part, have remained marginalized, is of inherent normative, political, and scholarly relevance (see Myrttinen et al., this volume). Yet what is furthermore needed are critical interrogations of how larger and intersecting systems of heteronormativity and heterosexuality, homophobia, transphobia, and patriarchy underpin and shape peacebuilding and TJ processes (Bueno-Hansen 2018; Hagen 2016; Ritholtz et al. 2023), and how these frames result in binary understandings of gender and justice, respectively (Moyo 2019). The chapters included in this volume again begin to address these gaps.

For instance, Pascha Bueno-Hansen's contribution offers a structural investigation of how heteronormativity and patriarchy underpin processes of dealing with the past, and how this reinforces binary understandings of gender, at the expense of recognition for people across and outside the gender spectrum. As İrem Akı illustrates in her contribution, these heterosexual categorizations are particularly pronounced in legal processes and entities, calling for queer legal theory perspectives to counter these heteronormative binaries. Queer mobilization can also contribute to the process of undoing this heterosexual matrix that underpins state violence, as Thiyagaraja Waradas shows in this volume. Drawing on autoethnographic insights from Sri Lanka, Thiyagaraja explores how a queer grassroots movement, the Butterflies for Democracy (B4D), contributes toward queer emancipation and democratization and influences the country's ongoing post-war transition period.

Several authors and chapters also specifically emphasize the need for queer, intersectional, and decolonial approaches (see Katharina Hoffmann and Thokozani Mbwana; Pascha Bueno-Hansen) that expose "how institutionalized categories and identities are used to regulate and socialize" (Fobear, this volume: 42) and that would contribute toward circumventing the neoliberal and heteronormative foundations of TJ. The chapters included in this volume again take up this task, among others critically interrogating the heteronormative systems that shape conflict and transitions and asking what TJ processes can do about these systems (Pascha Bueno-Hansen, this volume), and exploring the intersections between de- and anticolonial African thought with queer theory (Katharina Hoffmann and Thokozani Mbwana, this volume).

Taken together, and by utilizing masculinities and queer perspectives in the field of transitional justice, the chapters in this volume thus contribute toward a more nuanced and holistic engagement with gender in the context of dealing with violent pasts, facilitating justice, building peace, and remaking worlds in the wake of violence. These interventions allow us to move beyond binary framings of gender and elucidate the intertwined and complex intersections between gender, sexualities, vulnerabilities, power, agency, and justice that lie at the heart of these processes and of how people experience, make sense of, and enact transitions in the wake of violence.

Organization of the Book

The intention of the book is to identify and push forward intersections and integrations of masculinities and queer perspectives in the study and practice of transitional justice through an analytical conversation. To this end, it is structured across four separate sections, each defined by a combined thematic focus and followed by a conclusion. The specific geopolitical contexts covered in this volume are diverse and varied, including the former Yugoslavia, Syria, Northern Ireland, Palestine, Syria/Lebanon, Kashmir, Sri Lanka, Uganda, the Democratic Republic of Congo (DRC), Colombia, El Salvador, and Ecuador. Despite this geographical diversity, there is a particular focus on Latin America across the chapters, with reflections from Colombia, El Salvador, and Ecuador. This relative concentration on Latin America aligns with the multiple processes of dealing with the past in the region that "have expanded their purview to include human rights investigations of violence against sexual and gender minorities" (Schulz 2019: 10). In particular, Colombia serves as a contemporary example of the precedent-setting work for the inclusion of persons with diverse SOGIESC and their experiences in peacebuilding and TJ processes (Bueno-Hansen 2018: 5; Oettler 2019).

Section 1: Seeking Intersections between Masculinities and Queer Perspectives in Transitional Justice

Section 1 lays the conceptual and theoretical groundwork for the volume and the individual chapters to follow. This section offers an overview of how scholarship on masculinities and queer perspectives in TJ has developed in recent years, as exercises of mapping the field(s), seeking intersections between these two approaches.

To this end, Chapter 2, by Brandon Hamber, Philipp Schulz, Heleen Touquet, and Giulia Messmer, offers an overview of the state of research on masculinities in TJ, providing a framework for understanding key concepts around masculinities, including hegemonic masculinity and militarized masculinity. The chapter argues that the existing scholarship is dominated by a violation-centric lens, a focus on either violence committed by militarized men or violence against men. The chapter calls for a broader remit, including the experiences of civilian men impacted by conflict or insecurity, and the different manifestations and expressions of non-heteronormative and subordinate expressions of masculinities. This call for a broader and wider engagement with masculinities in post-conflict and transitional settings in many ways sets the frame for many of the following chapters and arguments across the separate sections.

Katherine Fobear then shifts the attention to queer possibilities and theories in the field, study, and practice of transitional justice, offering a concise overview of recent developments in terms of queering TJ. Fobear immerses the reader in her reflections about the current state of research on queer perspectives in TJ, emphasizing the violent structural elements of heteronormative matrices besides direct physical violence against persons with different SOGIESC. She specifically explores issues only marginally touched upon in research on gender and TJ, namely, violence against displaced LGBTQ persons and their (non-)incorporation into TJ processes.

Taken together, the two chapters open the conversation by laying the conceptual groundwork of seeking and identifying intersections between masculinities and queer perspectives in TJ. At the same time, this section critically reviews the literature in order to identify possibilities, challenges, gaps, and critical questions. The subsequent chapters in this book will tackle these issues and form the overarching framework of a broader research agenda of taking masculinities and queer perspectives in TJ into account.

Section 2: Theories, Processes, and Practices – toward Inclusive Gender in TJ

Section 2 moves closer toward advancing inclusive conceptions of gender in transitional justice. The chapters included in this section engage with a range of TJ-related and TJ-relevant theories, processes, and practices, and primarily apply queer perspectives to these, in order to facilitate more inclusive discussions about gender and TJ. The focus of these chapters is both theoretical and empirical, reflecting on broader possibilities of queering transitional justice from both decolonial and legal theoretical perspectives and reflecting on empirical examples from Ecuador and Colombia of how, in practice, to move toward more inclusive conceptions of gender in implementing broader peacebuilding and transitional processes in general, or truth commissions in particular.

Specifically, Chapter 4, by Katharina Hoffmann and Thokozani Mbwana, on "queering transitional justice from African decolonial perspectives" combines queer perspectives with de- and anticolonial approaches in the field of transitional justice. As Hoffmann and Mbwana note, an engagement with gender in TJ often ignores the polysemy of sex/gender and justice in different geopolitical and cultural regions. De- and anticolonial perspectives thereby help us move toward broader understandings of justice and gender, respectively, serving as an essential tool to critique dominant TJ concepts and practices. More precisely, the chapter argues that de- and anticolonial lenses are important avenues to discuss and reimagine ways of restructuring the social fabric by dismantling gendered orders based on continuities or new forms of domination, oppression, and subjection. Hoffmann and Mbwana argue that decolonial analytical tools are urgently needed to deconstruct the production of sexual minorities from local standpoints and address the past and present harms and oppressions of people who are categorized as deviant in post-conflict settings. This opens up various avenues of future research and programming.

Following a similar objective of contributing toward more inclusive ideas of gender, İrem Akı, in Chapter 5, specifically focuses on linking queer legal theory to transitional justice processes, highlighting both challenges and possibilities. Introducing a broader overview of the field of queer legal theory and showing how these theoretical perspectives and approaches imply numerous synergies and areas of further engagement with transitional justice, this investigation opens up avenues for (re)constructing legal systems – so central to TJ – in ways that are inclusive to persons with diverse SOGIESC. Put differently, her chapter centers on how to deconstruct heteronormative frameworks in TJ in order to rebuild these systems to include and protect persons of all genders and sexual orientations. Connecting to Katherine Fobear's chapter, Akı asks: What does queer (legal) theory bring to the field of transitional justice? The chapter thereby emphasizes the importance of legal recognition of the victimhood of persons with different SOGIESC.

Furthering a critical engagement with heteronormativity as a guiding principle of most transitional justice processes globally, Pascha Bueno-Hansen's chapter analyzes the approach to gender taken by the Ecuadorian Truth Commission. She thereby examines the truth commission's impact, based on notes from activist meetings and movement-based communications focusing specifically on sexual and gender-based violence. She highlights the heterosexual matrix that is the fundament of the nation-state and which causes discriminatory violence and state repression both in armed conflict and in peacetime. She explicitly questions the politics of knowledge production in the field of TJ, where she finds that misogyny, sexism, and lesbophobia are the primary vectors of oppression that function to suppress the recognition of feminist contributions by passively distancing from and/or actively rejecting radical critiques. This chapter therefore builds and further advances calls made in previous chapters and illuminates through its empirical richness how a feminist-informed approach can tackle heteronormativity and thereby push for more inclusive notions of gender and justice.

Chapter 7, by Annika Oettler, takes on a macro-level perspective to offer an inclusive and critical gender analysis of the Colombian peace agreement. Oettler's chapter provides a cohesive genealogy of the incorporation and the constant development of the definition of *gender* into the country's peace process over the years, bringing the roles of feminist, queer, and decolonial activists to the forefront. While demonstrating the gender-inclusive approach taken to the 2016 peace referendum and the subsequent agreement, Oettler also shows that gender sensitivity was highly controversial, with immediate implications for the overall peacebuilding and transitional justice process. As Oettler shows, the politicization of sexuality and gender becomes central in understanding conflicts over the prospects of peace between and within secular and religious discursive fields.

Section 3: Gendering Justice and Transitions Across Contexts

Building on these broader conceptual and macro-level observations and dynamics, Section 3, on "gendering justice and transitions across contexts," then moves toward the empirics and specificities of particular cases. To this end, the chapters included in this section reflect on a range of cases, contexts, and examples, employing masculinities and queer perspectives to better understand the dynamics, complexities, and lived realities of gendering justice and transition processes across the globe. Chapters 8–11 offer different micro-level case study analyses and thereby contribute empirical insights into how, precisely, a focus on masculinities and/or queer questions can illuminate new questions and possibilities of gendering transitional justice.

Chapter 8, by Camille Oliveira and Erin Baines, asks how forced marriage and pregnancy in war affect boys and men. While recent years have witnessed growing attention to forced marriage and pregnancy in war from the viewpoint of women and children, the perspectives of fathers and masculinities have remained mostly absent. Analyzing interviews with former male LRA combatants in Uganda, the authors advocate for holistic gendered perspectives on sexual and gender-based crimes in TJ to include boys, men, as well as children born out of and into these violent contexts. The authors move beyond perpetrator and victim binaries in order to reveal a complex mosaic of responsibility, harm, affectedness, agency, subjectivity and objectivity, parenthood, and care – viewed through an inclusive approach to gender.

Chapter 9, by Chloé Lewis and Susanne Alldén, deconstructs the racialized and gendered assumptions behind the notion of masculine "perpetratorhood" of sexual violence in armed conflict, through the case study of the Democratic Republic of the Congo (DRC) and against the backdrop of a critical masculinities perspective. The important but seldom-considered questions of who is persecuted and for what kinds of sexual crimes are taken as a baseline to explore the complex realities of sexual crimes and masculinities constructions in conflict-affected areas. This is also used to critique the pertinent presumptions in the current (inter)national fight against impunity. The authors dispute the use of the number of trials as a measure of the success of transitional justice policy and practice. In this way, they enhance our understanding of what needs to be considered and challenged in the fight for justice, and how this is linked to and shaped by constructions of masculinities.

In a similar vein, Catherine Baker, in Chapter 10, analyzes the construction of veteran masculinities in Croatia vis-á-vis the Homeland War narrative idealizing the War of Independence between 1991 and 1995. Baker analyzes how these militarized versions of masculinity travel through different spheres of civilian life until today, for example, in youth or music culture, constituting the hegemonic gender construct. As Baker argues, this enduring influence is an important tool to gauge the state of transitional justice, as veteran masculinities are intimately connected to the Homeland War narrative. Veteran masculinities are important to consider in the context of transitional justice not only because they influence the ways in which it is socially acceptable to relate to the wartime past among the generation(s) that fought but also because of their effect on the young, for whom they represent masculinities of their parents, and specifically their fathers' generation. This makes "the challenges of dislodging militarised masculinities from their hegemonic place in post-conflict societies" (142) not only visible but also constitutive in assessing the current state of transitional justice in Croatian society.

In Chapter 11, Henri Myrttinen, Laura Camila Barrios Sabogal, and Charbel Maydaa engage with SOGIESC-inclusive transitional justice in Colombia and in Lebanon/Syria, utilizing queer perspectives. The chapter explores what is possible in terms of queering transitional justice through the case of Colombia, where SOGIESC perspectives have been included to some extent, but also reflects upon the impossibilities and improbabilities of gender-inclusive and queer TJ in Lebanon and Syria. Critically reflecting on these cross-national patterns, the authors argue that the narrow mandates of TJ processes as focused on direct physical violence committed only by particular actors during a limited period of time fail to address the continuums of gendered violence against persons with diverse SOGIESC, let alone other gendered wrongs of conflict and oppression. In the absence of state-level transitional justice processes that take into account diverse SOGIESC experiences, the chapter ends with a call to widen the frame and focus more on localized, community- and civil society–based efforts to provide truth-seeking and social norm change opportunities. This call for a broader approach to justice and a move to the micro-level within the absence of processes and gender inclusivity at the macro-level thereby mirrors similar arguments and findings across other settings as made throughout this volume.

Section 4: Beyond Violation-Centric Views

One of the central themes and arguments of this book is the need to move beyond a violation-centric view that perpetuates a focus on either the violences perpetrated by mostly men or on various forms of physical (and mostly sexual) violence perpetrated against men and persons with diverse SOGIESC. As various chapters highlight, such a view often dominates emerging debates about masculinities and queer perspectives in TJ but narrows the potential frame of analyses and investigations, by over-emphasizing certain experiences and positionalities and shrinking the space for alternative narratives, lived realities, and structural and cultural understandings of violence (see Hamber et al., this volume; Fobear, this volume). This section tackles this over-emphasis by moving into the spotlight a range of experiences, beyond a focus on violence, through attention to masculinities and queer perspectives.

Directing our attention specifically to Colombia – a precedent-setting case for queering peacebuilding and transitional justice – José Fernando Serrano-Amaya takes a close and critical look at transitional justice from below. Critically combining both masculinities and queer perspectives, Chapter 12 asks to what extent bottom-up processes take subordinate masculinities perspectives into account and why the dichotomies between armed conflict and peace, chaos and normality do not fit the lived experiences of persons with different SOGIESC. Based on these observations, Serrano-Amaya advances an argument regarding the importance of queering transitional justice from below as an attempt to unsettle the illusion of transition from chaos to order and the return to "normality" after the conflict has ended. Importantly, the queer men whose stories and experiences lie at the heart of this chapter are not merely objects of study but, rather, agents of change themselves who actively transform TJ processes from below – thereby breaking out of the dominant violation-centric foci.

The three chapters that follow then direct our attention specifically toward the gendered experiences, positionalities, and viewpoints of a diverse group of men and masculinities in post-conflict and transitional settings – similarly moving beyond a focus on violence by or against men. Ursula Mosqueira, in Chapter 13, traces the fluid constructions of masculinities among former political prisoners in El Salvador. The author breaks apart binary constructions of vulnerability and agency. Advocating for the necessity of thick descriptions and holistic approaches to gendered experiences, the chapter challenges the often limited scope of victimhood, which gives rise to an artificially created hierarchy of acknowledgment and deservingness between survivors. Analyzing the effects of intersecting systems of power on survivors' masculinities, Mosqueira demonstrates how vulnerability and agency are two sides of the same coin. Bringing the gendered lived realities of male political prisoners to the forefront, Mosqueira unpacks the differential ways in which this often-marginalized group of men engages with their wartime experiences, thereby exercising agency and striving for post-war justice.

In Chapter 14, Seamus Campbell similarly focuses on the lived realities of non-armed men in conflict-affected and transitional spaces, focused on the North of Ireland and the Occupied Palestinian Territories. Drawing on rich empirical data, the chapter provides a textured and nuanced analysis of civilian masculinities and the continuum of men's experiences within conflict-affected and transitional settings. More specifically, it draws attention to the ways in which everyday experiences, such as engaging in a popular sport (in this case, boxing) or utilizing one's knowledge whilst crossing a security checkpoint, may enable individuals to cope with experiences of violence and insecurity in a manner compatible with their gender identities. Whilst such micro-level dynamics may be outside the purview of formal peacebuilding or transitional justice processes, they can nevertheless provide further nuance and insight on how masculinities operate within conflicted societies, as Campbell argues.

In Chapter 15, Amya Agarwal explores the role of civilian masculinities around questions of justice, care, and processes of social repair in the ongoing Kashmir conflict in India. Like in other contexts globally, Kashmir also entails a web of entangled masculinities, including competitive militarized masculinities of the state armed forces and militant groups, conflict-affected civilian masculinities, demobilized masculinities and other non-militarized forms of masculinity. In this context, studying the roles and identities of civilian men enables us to arrive at a more meaningful understanding of informal mechanisms of social repair, justice, and agency. Agarwal studies the particular case study of a prominent male human rights activist who enacts a caring notion of masculinity which, in turn, underpins his efforts of facilitating social repair, thereby moving beyond institutionalized and state-centric avenues of enacting transitions and achieving post-conflict justice.

Similarly focusing on the micro-level, this time specifically grounded in Sri Lanka, Chapter 16, by Thiyagaraja Waradas, paints an in-depth picture of queering post-war democratization processes. Thiyagaraja's chapter introduces the Sri Lankan "Butterflies for Democracy" (B4D) movement as an exemplary case of micro-level queer engagements in post-war settings, thereby unpacking the intersections between queer emancipation and democratization in a post-war and transitional context and on the grassroots level. The B4D movement specifically emerged in response to the so-called "butterfly speech" by President Sirisena, a state-sponsored homophobic hate speech, whereby "butterfly" was used as a derogatory slur for *queer*. However, thanks to advocacy by the B4D movement, the term is being turned into a symbol of unity, courage, and solidarity – demonstrating the agency of persons with diverse SOGIESC in transitional settings. This approach moves beyond a violation-centric lens that reduces experiences and lived realities to a focus on violence and suffering only. By focusing on this grassroots movement and its contribution to democratization and transitional justice processes, this chapter also moves beyond institutionalized and technocratic approaches to transitional justice.

To round off the volume, Chapter 17 offers concluding reflections, implications, and ways forward for integrating masculinities and queer perspectives. While the previous chapters have all offered in-depth and micro-level analyses of specific cases and contexts, this chapter zooms out again and reflects on the various theoretical, conceptual, methodological, empirical, and analytical implications of the work offered throughout this book. While the introductory section began with identifying intersections between masculinities and queer perspectives in TJ, which the subsequent chapters then engaged with, the concluding chapter seeks to move forward the process of then specifically integrating these different approaches toward a more integrated framework of analysis. This, the conclusion argues, is the task of academics and practitioners alike as they apply new critical lenses to gender. Formulated as a call to action directed at scholars and practitioners alike, the concluding chapter sets the agenda and illustrates ways forward for effectively facilitating a relational and inclusive engagement with gender in the context of transitional justice, drawing on and taking inspiration from feminist, queer, and masculinities perspectives alike and in combination.

References

Ahmed, S. (2006). *Queer Phenomenology: Orientations, Objects, Others*. Durham, NC: Duke University Press.

Aijazi, O. and E. Baines (2017). Relationality, Culpability and Consent in Wartime: Men's Experiences of Forced Marriage. *International Journal of Transitional Justice* 11(3): 463–483.

Alcalá, P. R. and E. Baines (2012). Editorial Note. *International Journal of Transitional Justice* 6(3): 385–393.

Baines, E. K. (2007). The Haunting of Alice: Local Approaches to Justice and Reconciliation in Northern Uganda. *The International Journal of Transitional Justice* 1(1): 91–114.

Bell, C. and C. O'Rourke (2007). Does Feminism Need a Theory of Transitional Justice? An Introductory Essay. *International Journal of Transitional Justice* 1(1): 23–44.

Boesten, J. and P. Wilding (2015). Transformative Gender Justice: Setting an Agenda. *Women's Studies International Forum* 51: 75–80.

Buckley-Zistel, S. and R. Stanley (2012). *Gender in Transitional Justice*. New York: Springer.

Bueno-Hansen, P. (2015). *Feminist and Human Rights Struggles in Peru: Decolonizing Transitional Justice*. Urbana, IL: Illinois University Press.

Bueno-Hansen, P. (2018). The Emerging LGBTI Rights Challenge to Transitional Justice in Latin America. *International Journal of Transitional Justice* 12(1): 126–145.

Carpenter, C. (2006). Recognizing Gender-Based Violence Against Civilian Men and Boys in Conflict Situations. *Security Dialogue* 37(1): 83–103.

Cockburn, C. (2010). Gender Relations as Causal in Militarization and War. *International Feminist Journal of Politics* 12(2): 139–157.

Collins, P. H. (1990). *Black Feminist Thought: Knowledge, Consciousness and the Politics of Empowerment*. New York: Routledge.

Connell, R. (2005). *Masculinities*. Berkeley: University of California Press.

Cooper-Cunningham, D. (2021). *The International Politics of Sex: Visual Activism in Response to Russian State Homophpia*. PhD dissertation, Copenhagen: University of Copenhagen.

Crenshaw, K. (1989). Demarginalizing the Intersection of Race and Sex: A Black Feminist Critique of Antidiscrimination Doctrine, Feminist Theory and Antiracist Politics. *University of Chicago Legal Forum* (1): 8.

Daigle, M. and H. Myrttinen (2018). Bringing Diverse Sexual Orientation and Gender Identity (SOGI) into Peacebuilding Policy and Practice. *Gender & Development* 26(1): 103–120.

Das, V., A. Kleinman, M. Lock, M. Ramphele and P. Reynolds (2001). *Remaking a World: Violence, Social Suffering and Recovery*. Berkeley: University of California Press.

de Greiff, P. (2012). Theorizing Transitional Justice. *Nomos* 51: 31–77.

Dery, I. (2020). Negotiating Positionality, Reflexivity and Power Relations in Research on Men and Masculinities in Ghana. *Gender, Place & Culture* 27(12): 1766–1784.

Dolan, C. (2015). Letting Go of the Gender Binary: Charting New Pathways for Humanitarian Interventions on Gender-Based Violence. *International Review of the Red Cross* 96(894): 485–501.

Duncanson, C. (2009). Forces for Good? Narratives of Military Masculinity in Peacekeeping Operations. *International Feminist Journal of Politics* 11(1): 63–80.

Duriesmith, D. (2016). *Masculinity and New War: The Gendered Dynamics of Contemporary Armed Conflict*. New York: Routledge.

Enloe, C. (2004). *The Curious Feminist: Searching for Women in a New Age of Empire*. Berkeley: University of California Press.

Fineman, A. and E. Zinsstag (2013). *Feminist Perspectives on Transitional Justice. From International and Criminal to Alternative Forms of Justice*. Cambridge: Intersentia Press.

Fobear, K. (2014). Queering Truth Commissions. *Journal of Human Rights Practice* 6(1): 51–68.

Fobear, K. and E. Baines (2020). Pushing the Conversation Forward: The Intersections of Sexuality and Gender Identity in Transitional Justice. *The International Journal of Human Rights* 24(4): 307–312.

Franke, K. M. (2006). Gendered Subject of Transitional Justice. *Columbia Journal of Gender and Law* 15(3): 813–828.

Gopalan, P. (2023). Breaking Binaries and Honing-in on Harms: Inclusive Approaches Towards Sexual and Gender-Based Crimes. In: Sendze, Takeh B. K., Adeboyejo, A., Morrison, H. and Ugwu, S. (eds.): *Contemporary International Criminal Law Issues: Contributions in Pursuit of Accountability for Africa and in the World*. New York: Asser Press, Springer.

Hagen, J. (2016). Queering Women, Peace and Security. *International Affairs* 92(2): 313–332.

Hamber, B. (2009). *Transforming Societies after Political Violence: Truth, Reconciliation, and Mental Health*. New York: Springer.

Hamber, B. (2016). There Is a Crack in Everything: Problematising Masculinities, Peacebuilding and Transitional Justice. *Human Rights Review* 17(1): 9–34.

Hansen, T. (2016). The Time and Space of Transitional Justice. *Transitional Justice Institute Research Paper* 16(11). Available at: https://ssrn.com/abstract=2801546. Accessed on: 21 April 2022.

Hayner, P. B. (2011). *Unspeakable Truths: Confronting State Terror and Atrocity*. New York: Routledge.

Henry, M. (2017). Problematizing Military Masculinity, Intersectionality and Male Vulnerability in Feminist Critical Military Studies. *Critical Military Studies* 3(2): 182–199.

Kent, L. (2014). Narratives of Suffering and Endurance: Coercive Sexual Relationships, Truth Commissions and Possibilities for Gender Justice in Timor-Leste. *International Journal of Transitional Justice* 8(2): 289–313.

Kent, L. (2018). *The Dynamics of Transitional Justice: International Models and Local Realities in East Timor*. London: Routledge.

Krystalli, R. and P. Schulz (2022). Taking Love and Care Seriously: An Emergent Research Agenda for Remaking Worlds in the Wake of Violence. *International Studies Review* 24(1): 1–25.

Kurze, A. and C. K. Lamont (2021). Breaking the Transitional Justice Machine: Exploring Spatiality, Space Travel, and Inbetween Spaces in Research Practice. *Political Anthropological Research on International Social Sciences (PARISS)* 2(1): 155–178.

Lai, D. (2020). What Has Justice Got to Do with It? Gender and the Political Economy of Post-War Bosnia and Herzegovina. *Review of International Political Economy* 27 (6): 1257–1279.

MacDonald, A. (2013). Local Understandings and Experiences of Transitional Justice: A Review of the Evidence. Justice and Security Research Programme, International Development Department, London School of Economics and Political Science, London, UK.

Martin de Almagro, M. (2017). Transitional Justice and Women, Peace and Security: A Critical Reading of the EU Framework. *LSE Women, Peace and Security Working Paper Series (5/2017)*. London: Centre for Women Peace and Security, London School of Economics and Political Science.

Martin de Almagro, M. and P. Schulz (2022). Gender and Transitional Justice. In: *Oxford Research Encyclopedia of International Studies*. Oxford: Oxford University Press.

McEvoy, K. (2007). Beyond Legalism: Towards a Thicker Understanding of Transitional Justice. *Journal of Law and Society* 34(4): 411–440.

McQuaid, K. (2020). 'There Is Violence Across, in All Arenas': Listening to Stories of Violence Amongst Sexual Minority Refugees in Uganda. *The International Journal of Human Rights* 24(4): 313–334.

Moser, C. and F. Clark (2001). *Victims, Perpetrators or Actors?: Gender, Armed Conflict and Political Violence*. London: Zed Books.

Moyo, K. (2019). *Postcolonial Transitional Justice. Zimbabwe and Beyond*. London: Routledge.

Myrttinen, H., L. Khattab and C. Maydaa (2017). 'Trust No One, Beware of Everyone': Vulnerabilities of LGBTI Refugees in Lebanon. In: Freedman, J., Kıvılcım, Z. and Baklacıoğlu, N. Ö. (eds.): *A Gendered Approach to the Syrian Refugee Crisis*. London: Routledge: 61–76.

Ní Aoláin, F. (2012). Advancing Feminist Positioning in the Field of Transitional Justice. *International Journal of Transitional Justice* 6(2): 205–228.

Ní Aoláin, F. (2019). Transformative Gender Justice? In: Gready, P. and Robins, S. (eds.): *From Transitional to Transformative Justice*. Cambridge: Cambridge University Press: 150–171.

Ní Aoláin, F. and E. Rooney (2007). Underenforcement and Intersectionality: Gendered Aspects of Transition for Women. *International Journal of Transitional Justice* 1: 388–354.

Oettler, A. (2019). The Struggle for Gendered Peace and LGBT Rights in Colombia. *Violence, Security, and Peace Working Papers* 2. London: LSE-GIGA-CCDP. Available at: https://www.lse.ac.uk/lacc/publications/PDFs/VSP2-Oettler-Gendered-Peace-LGBT-Rights-Colombia-web.pdf. Accessed on: 12 January 2022.

O'Rourke, C. (2013). *Gender Politics in Transitional Justice*. London: Routledge.

O'Rourke, C. (2017). Transitional Justice and Gender. In: Lawther, C., Moffett, L. and Jacobs, D. (eds.): *Research Handbook on Transitional Justice*. Cheltenham: Edward Elgar Publishing.

Palmer, N., P. Clark and D. Granville (2012). *Critical Perspectives in Transitional Justice*. Cambridge: Intersentia.

Pillay, N. (2007). Editorial Note. Special Issue: Gender and Transitional Justice. *International Journal of Transitional Justice* 1(3): 315–317.

Ritholtz, S., J. F. Serrano-Amaya, J. J. Hagen and M. Judge (2023). Under Construction: Toward a Theory and Praxis of Queer Peacebuilding. *Revista De Estudios Sociales* 83: 3–22.

Roht-Arriaza, N. and J. Mariezcurrena (2006). *Transitional Justice in the Twenty-First Century: Beyond Truth Versus Justice*. Cambridge: Cambridge University Press.
Rolston, B. and F. Ní Aoláin (2018). Colonialism, Redress and Transitional Justice: Ireland and Beyond. *State Crime Journal* 7(2): 329–348.
Salvioli, F. (2020). *The Gender Perspective in Transitional Justice Processes: Note by the Secretary General*, A/75/174. Available at: https://digitallibrary.un.org/record/3883379. Accessed on: 22 November 2022.
Sarkin, J. J. and T. Morais (2022). The Importance of Adopting an Intersectionality Approach to Refugee Status Determination Procedures: Lessons from Greece, Israel and Uganda. *International Journal of Migration, Health and Social Care* 18(3): 193–206.
Scanlon, H. and K. Muddell (2009). Gender and Transitional Justice in Africa. Progress and Prospects. *African Journal on Conflict Resolution* 9(2): 9–28.
Schulz, P. (2019). Towards Inclusive Gender in Transitional Justice: Gaps, Blind-Spots and Opportunities. *Journal of Intervention and Statebuilding* 14(5): 691–710.
Schulz, P. (2020). *Male Survivors of Wartime Sexual Violence: Perspectives from Northern Uganda*. Berkeley, CA: University of California Press.
Schulz, P. and A. K. Kreft (2022). Accountability for Conflict-Related Sexual Violence. *Oxford Research Encyclopedia of International Studies*: 1–25.
Schulz, P. and H. Touquet (2020). Queering Explanatory Frameworks for Wartime Sexual Violence Against Men. *International Affairs* 96(5): 1169–1187.
Sedgwick, E. (1993). *Tendencies*. Durham, NC: Duke University Press.
Sharp, D. (2014). Emancipating Transitional Justice from the Bonds of the Paradigmatic Transition. *International Journal of Transitional Justice* 9(1): 150–169.
Sharp, D. (2019). What Would Satisfy Us? Taking Stock of Critical Approaches to Transitional Justice. *International Journal of Transitional Justice* 13(3): 570–589.
Shaw, R. and L. Waldorf (2010). *Localizing Transitional Justice: Interventions and Priorities after Mass Violence*. Redwood City: Stanford University Press.
Simien, E. M. (2007). Doing Intersectionality Research: From Conceptual Issues to Practical Examples. *Politics & Gender* 3(2): 264–271.
Sjoberg, L. (2016). *Women as Wartime Rapists: Beyond Sensation and Stereotyping*. New York: New York University Press.
Sooka, Y. (2006). Dealing with the Past and Transitional Justice: Building Peace Through Accountability. *International Review of the Red Cross* 88(862): 311–325.
Steans, J. (1998). *Gender and International Relations: An Introduction*. New Brunswick, NJ: Rutgers University Press.
Teitel, R. (2015). *Globalizing Transitional Justice*. Oxford: Oxford University Press.
Theidon, K. (2009). Reconstructing Masculinities: The Disarmament, Demobilization, and Reintegration of Former Combatants in Colombia. *Human Rights Quarterly* 31(1): 1–34.
Touquet, H., C. Chynoweth, S. Martin, C. Reis, H. Myrttinen, P. Schulz, L. Turner and D. Duriesmith (2021). From 'It Rarely Happens' to 'It's Worse for Men': Dispelling Misconceptions about Sexual Violence Against Men and Boys in Conflict and Displacement. *Journal of Humanitarian Affairs* 2(3): 25–34.
True, J. (2012). *The Political Economy of Violence Against Women*. Oxford: Oxford University Press.
Ward, J. and B. Schneider (2009). The Reaches of Heteronormativity: An Introduction. *Gender & Society* 23(4): 433–439.
Weber, C. (2016). *Queer International Relations*. Oxford: Oxford University Press.
Weber, S. (2021). Gender and Transitional Justice. In: Yusuf, H. and van der Merwe, H. (eds.): *Transitional Justice: Theories, Mechanisms and Debates*. Oxford: Oxford University Press: 207–229.
Wright, H. (2014). *Masculinities, Conflict and Peacebuilding: Perspectives on Men Through a Gender Lens*. London: Saferworld.

Wright, H. (2020). 'Masculinities Perspectives': Advancing a Radical Women, Peace and Security Agenda? *International Feminist Journal of Politics* 22(5): 652–674.

Yogyakarta Principles (2007). *Principles on the Application of International Human Rights Law in Relation to Sexual Orientation and Gender Identity*. Geneva: International Commission of Jurists.

Yogyakarta Principles plus 10 (2017). *The Yogyakarta Principles Plus 10 Additional Principles and State Obligations on the Application of International Human Rights Law in Relation to Sexual Orientation, Gender Identity, Gender Expression and Sex Characteristics to Complement the Yogyakarta P*. Geneva: International Commission of Jurists.

Chapter 2

Transitional Justice and Masculinities

A Critical Mapping of the Field

Brandon Hamber, Philipp Schulz, Heleen Touquet, and Giulia Messmer

Introduction

The Russian invasion of Ukraine in February 2022 and the heavily gendered rhetoric around it illustrate the close connections between warfare, militarization, and violent masculinities (Enloe 2004; Gaufman 2022; Cockburn 2010; Maringira 2021). Like almost all wars, the Russian war against Ukraine is heavily underpinned by (militarized) masculinities, contributing to the onset, dynamic, mobilization, and perception of violence and hostilities (Bias 2022; Gaufman 2022). As Wojnicka, Mellström, and de Boise argue, in the context of Ukraine, "masculinity is mobilized as a rhetorical figure and symbolic resource in the brutal reality for all these young men and women that have to go into a war declared by older men" (2022: 83).

This assessment is reflective of a more broadly growing engagement in political, societal, and academic discourses with the gendered nature of warfare and the roles played by masculinities within this (Duriesmith 2016; Moser and Clark 2001; Sharoni et al. 2016). Over the past two decades, the scholarly literature has begun to pay critical attention to masculinities and their relations to and positioning in the global gender order (Connell and Messerschmidt 2005; Ratele 2008; Christensen and Kyed 2022; Vigoya 2001). In recent years, the discussion has also extended more specifically to masculinities and political violence, and a "fairly substantial amount of literature has been generated . . . regarding the forms of masculinity that emerge in times of armed conflict and war" in particular (Haynes et al. 2011: 104; see Duriesmith 2016; Duncanson 2013; Myrttinen et al. 2024).

The literature on post-conflict transitional justice, however, has not mirrored this process. Whilst transitional justice (TJ) is dominated by masculine values and actors and structured around the masculine nature of (semi-)legal processes, these aspects have, by and large, not been critically unpacked in the TJ literature (O'Rourke 2017; Cahn and Ní Aoláin 2010; Martin de Almagro and Schulz 2022). What remains under-developed is careful consideration of men's and boys' experiences as gendered, and conflict, peace, and transition and their relationships to certain types of masculinities, and

DOI: 10.4324/9781003519522-3

how they shape which groups of men have their experiences and views incorporated into TJ processes. As Cahn and Ní Aoláin (2010) point out, it is often an elite male post-conflict fraternity that continues to dominate the TJ landscape as societies are reconfigured, noting: "men who were in power are losing power, other men (domestic and international) are taking their place" (110). For instance, most signatories of peace agreements are men who negotiate with other men on how to disarm, demobilize, and transition mostly male combatants and soldiers, and who reproduce gendered narratives about masculine heroism and feminized enemies. The engagement of TJ processes with different catalogues of crimes and human rights violations is similarly gendered: torture, for example, is seen as a masculine crime, and SGBV as a feminine crime (see earlier text). Similar dynamics apply to the ways in which transitional justice reparations, such as reparation programs, are designed and implemented and are often addressed and tailored toward men as breadwinners and women as reproducing mothers and housewives. As such, analyses of TJ processes continue to "present a unique and under-analyzed site of examination for masculinities" (Cahn and Ní Aoláin 2010: 105; Schulz 2019a). Scholars such as Hamber (2007, 2016) and Cahn and Ní Aoláin (2010) have called out these absences, and a number of others have argued in favor of including masculinities perspectives in different dimensions of post-conflict justice processes (Ashe 2019; Hamber et al. 2023; Schulz 2019b; Theidon 2009).

Masculinity lenses offer important avenues for better understanding the diversity of gendered dynamics in processes of transition and seeking post-conflict justice. Interrogating armed conflicts through a masculinities perspective and paying attention to men's gendered lived realities must, however, not be misappropriated toward diverting attention away from women's experiences and femininities, or from queer perspectives. Indeed, feminist scholars have noted that attention to men and masculinities might deflect from women's experiences and potentially take away funding for gendered work with/for women. Dowd, however, rightfully argues that masculinities and feminist theory should and can inform each other

> what masculinities has to offer feminist theory, in general, is the enrichment, contextualization and refinement of theory. . . . What feminism has to offer masculinities theory is a set of tools to address much more strongly inequality, subordination and how to shift from power-over to power-with.
>
> (231)

Crucially, then, analyses of masculinities cannot be decoupled from examinations of femininities and non-binary gender identities as well as heteronormative and patriarchal gender hierarchies more broadly (Sjoberg 2016). Instead, studies of men's roles and experiences in (post-)conflict contexts must maintain a holistic, relational, and intersectional focus to ultimately understand and address the complexities of gender and violence in transition.

This chapter maps the emerging scholarship on masculinities and TJ and situates it within the broader framework of masculinities studies, linking it with the related concepts of hegemonic masculinities and militarized masculinity. Based on this, the chapter further outlines the importance of widening the scope of research beyond a violation-centric focus.

Conceptualizing Masculinities

We start by presenting the core concepts within masculinities studies that are most relevant for transitional justice: hegemonic masculinities and militarized masculinity. We note that these theoretical concepts have been developed by scholars from the Global North, largely based on observations of White middle-class men in the UK, US, Europe, and Australia (Connell 2014; Chakraborty 2017; Demetriou 2001; Barker 2005). Additionally, they originate out of non-conflict settings and, at times, do not travel well to contexts of violence, development, conflict, and transition (Barker and Ricardo 2005; Dery et al. 2022; Hollander 2014; Dolan 2002).

What are *masculinities*, then? At its core, *masculinities* are socially constructed gender norms that refer to "anything which is associated with being a man in any given culture" (Wright 2014: 4). According to Connell, *masculinities* are "simultaneously a place in gender relations, the practices through which men and women engage that place in gender, and the effects of these practices on bodily experience, personality and culture" (Connell 2009: 71). *Masculinities*, for this chapter, are therefore broadly understood as the multiple ways of "doing male" (Connell 2000; Hamber 2016; Vigoya 2001).

Most theorists working on this subject argue that it is more accurate to talk of masculinities (in plural) than of a singular *masculinity* (Connell 2005; Beasley 2008; Morrell 2001; Vigoya 2001). Further, as Wright notes (2014: 4), "interpretations of what is considered to be masculine, and what constitutes being a man, vary across time and space, as well as between and within cultures." Taking these pluralities into account, R. W. Connell's foundational work provides particularly useful frameworks for understanding the multiplicities and variations of masculinities, as well as for conceptualizing the inherent power relations within and between masculinities and gender hierarchies more broadly. Importantly, social constructions of masculinities in different places also always intersect with other social categories, such as class, race, age, cultural background, sexual orientation, or (dis)ability – necessitating intersectional and relational analyses (Henry 2017; Connell 2014). In using the term and concept of *intersectionality* (Crenshaw 1989; Collins and Bilge 2020) here, we echo Henry (2017), who critically questions how the concept of intersectionality is often misappropriated in many studies on (militarized) masculinities, which often neglect to pay attention to the origins of intersectional perspectives (marginalized Black women) (Collins 2019; Crenshaw 1989). In addition to these variations and the spatial, temporal, and cultural contingencies, significant power differences between and within gender constructions exist (Connell 2005), and not all forms of masculinities are valued equally (Dowd 2010). Within these multiple versions of manhood, some interpretations of being a man "are prized as being more valuable to aspire to than others" (Wright 2014: 4).

Hegemonic Masculinity

The conception of manhood that is prized as more valuable than others (Wright 2014) and that appears culturally dominant is labeled as *hegemonic masculinity* (Connell 2005; Cheng 1999), in relation to which various subordinate and subversive notions of masculinities exist, in a Gramscian way of hegemony and power. Consent and support for the gender order are thus (re)produced through hegemonic masculinity and not always with violence. *Hegemonic masculinity* can thereby be understood as

> [t]he pattern of practice (i.e., things done, not just a set of role expectations or an identity) that allowed men's dominance over women to continue. Hegemonic masculinity was distinguished from other masculinities, especially subordinated masculinities. Hegemonic masculinity was not assumed to be normal in the statistical sense; only a minority of men might enact it. . . . It embodied the currently most honored way of being a man, it required all other men to position themselves in relation to it, and it ideologically legitimated the global subordination of women to men.
>
> (Connell and Messerschmidt 2005: 832)

Masculinities are therefore relational and concern "power and relations of inequality *between* men and women on the one hand, and *among* men on the other hand" (Christofidou 2021: 83) – as well as in relation to non-binary gender identities. In many ways, masculinities in general, and hegemonic masculinity in particular, are defined in opposition to anything that would be associated with femininities and with anything that is not heteronormative. As such, misogyny and homophobia are central elements of (hegemonic) masculinities (Belkin 2002; Slootmaeckers 2019). Hegemonic masculinity is also framing, constraining, contested, and legitimating at the same time. Although most men aspire to a certain type of hegemonic masculinity in any given context and (almost) all men benefit from patriarchy, albeit to differing extents, they generally would not embody all that hegemonic masculinity implies (Connell and Messerschmidt 2005; Cheng 1999). As such, hegemonic masculinity is a political mechanism "referring to cultural/moral leadership to ensure popular or mass consent to particular forms of rule" (Beasley 2008: 88). Such masculinities are not maintained by naked force (although they could be) but rather through complicity and range of institutions, cultural practices, sanction, and persuasion (Connell and Messerschmidt 2005; Messerschmidt 2018).

While the concept of hegemonic masculinity has "influenced gender studies across many academic fields" (Connell and Messerschmidt 2005: 829), various scholars have articulated a number of challenges with the concept and especially its applicability (Myrttinen et al. 2016; Demetriou 2001; Hamber 2016). These tend to concern how the term is interpreted and used in different contexts in a globalized world (Beasley 2008). In other words, masculinity in itself is also at the risk of being essentialized rather than understood as nuanced, contextual, and relational. Moreover, hegemonic masculinity is often viewed, portrayed, and (mis)understood as a static and essentialized idea, rather than a relational, constantly evolving, and potentially shifting concept that is embedded in multiple power relations (Yang 2020). Two debates regarding the concept are particularly relevant to this chapter. First, as Beasley (2008) points out, there is a need to distinguish between dominant masculinities that carry and exercise power of a certain type and ideas of hegemonic masculinity. To this end, Beasley argues that in modern societies, those who may wield significant economic and institutional power (managers, financiers, celebrities, and politicians, for example) – and may exhibit specific stereotypical masculine personality traits, such as competitiveness, assertiveness, or greed – may represent a dominant type of masculinity, but not necessarily a hegemonic one. As such, *hegemonic* must be clearly distinguished from *dominance*, as hegemonic masculinities are not necessarily the most powerful or most widespread in any given social environment (Beasley 2008: 88).

Messerschmidt (2018) similarly acknowledges the importance of not slipping between hegemonic and dominant masculinities, reiterating that what makes masculinities hegemonic rather than dominant is their role in legitimatizing particularly "unequal relationship between men and women, masculinity and femininity, and among masculinities" (Messerschmidt 2018: 75). This debate is important to this chapter. We argue that dominant and hegemonic masculinities are key in transitional settings and, in times of conflict, in fact align more closely than at other times. In other words, the relationship between dominant and hegemonic masculinities in times of crises, as the Ukraine example at the start of this chapter highlights, can be accentuated and increase legitimating processes that reinforce hegemonic masculinity.

Secondly, it is also important not to conflate hegemonic masculinity with narrow understandings of the concept, whereby *hegemonic* is only understood through the lens of violent, militarized masculinity (Myrttinen et al. 2016; on militarized masculinities, see following text). Such false equations of hegemonic with militarized masculinities often present the relationship between violence and masculinities as natural and inevitable (Maringira 2021; Wright 2014) and, at the same time, can lead to violence being seen as the true marker of manliness (Hearn 1998; Higate 2001). Such conceptualizations, however, miss that the term *hegemonic* applies to the political mechanism of patriarchal legitimation that ensures consent to particular gendered rules (Cheng 1999), rather than a description of socially dominant and powerful types of men and specific personality traits (Beasley 2008) or behaviors.

Thus, hegemonic masculinities and militarized masculinities are not to be conflated and, instead, operate at different conceptual and analytical levels. *Hegemonic masculinity* is an abstract concept describing how certain masculinities are hegemonic in relation to others. *Militarized masculinity* is less abstract, referring to a specific construction and enactment of masculinity in military and/or militarized contexts. Militarized masculinities can be thought of as one legitimizing component of hegemonic masculinities, often its fiercest enforcer (Dietrich Ortega 2012).

Militarized Masculinities

Tapscott (2020), drawing on Enloe (2004), conceptualizes militarized masculinities as the processes of socialization that are enacted and performed (Tapscott 2020) primarily within a setting of militarization, the military, and armed conflict (Higate 2003; Parashar 2018). Enloe (2000) sees this as a "step-by-step process" (3) in which persons (and things) come to be controlled by the military and dependent on militaristic ideas. DiGiovanni (2017) further sees *militarized masculinity* as the gender formations "imposed through intersecting institutions (education, religion, government, military, media) in order to shape men into useful and disciplined members of a hierarchical and heteronormative state" (64).

Thus, although the military can be the primary vehicle for representing and producing masculinity (Enloe 2000) and the military can be a defining framework for hegemonic masculinity (Chowdry 2013), the way masculinities are militarized encompasses processes beyond military institutions (Duriesmith and Ismael 2019; Parashar 2018). This includes, for instance, cultural process, such as film, sports, and popular culture (Christensen and Kyed 2022; see Baker, this volume), but also education, religion, or the government (DiGiovanni 2017). Enloe (2000) reminds us that the list of what can be militarized is endless, including, among others, "toys, jobs, the profession of psychology, fashion, faith, voting, local economies, condoms, and movies stars" (4–5). That said, militarized masculinities are at their most dangerous, at least physically, when produced and enacted through the military or other structures that have the capacity to produce large-scale violence. As Duncanson (2013) notes, "the most visible manifestation of the problem of militarized masculinities is the harm done to civilian populations by the soldiers charged with protecting them" (19).

Nonetheless, masculinities in the military (or military masculinity) should not be conflated with militarized masculinities (the process of socialization that militarizes masculinities). Increasingly, militarized masculinities can be enacted in other spaces beyond formal military settings, such as private security agents, local leaders who can enact violence themselves, or the use of informal armed groups or supporters, paramilitaries and guerilla groups, and increasingly, organized and armed crime syndicates. In other words, the processes that enact, create, reinforce, and shape militarized masculinities vary within different militarized and cultural contexts. Furthermore, the gendering of militarization, as Enloe (2000) reminds us, is not only the product of men but also linked to a diversity of femininities (e.g., military wives, sex workers, nurses, women in the defense and fashion industry) and entangled with patriarchy. Sex/gender binaries have also been challenged, noting that (militarized) masculinities can be performed by, for instance, people with female bodies or trans men, noting the importance of "dislocating masculinity from the male body" (Christofidou 2021: 84).

That said, while processes of socialization and the sites and ways militarization takes place are certainly diverse, in their final elaborations, they generally entail the dichotomization between a peaceful feminized society and the masculine sphere of the military (Enloe 2000). Militarized masculinities generally emphasize the expectations of the protective role of men and are assumed to be performed most obviously within the context of the militarized "warrior" or combatant. But equally, militarized masculinities are not only associated with such actions but can instead also prize virtues such as sacrifice, compassion, cooperation, discipline, and service in the modern military (Tapscott 2020; Titunik 2008).

Militarized masculinities are, therefore, multiple and operate in different ways and in a multitude of spaces. They are not necessarily tied to specific roles (e.g., soldiers as peacekeepers compared to direct combat troops) or the actions associated with men and women in the military (or those with a range of gendered identities for that matter) and the roles they fulfil, but rather the types of gendered relations militarism often legitimizes and the processes of socialization accompanying this. As such, militarized masculinity is not a monolithic construct, and different manifestations persist across time and space. There is, as such, a dynamic composition of militarized masculinities which can manifest in multiple and contradictory forms comprising different characteristics. Still, the most prevalent type of militarized masculinity is a violent and aggressive warrior type relying on hypermasculinity[1] (Tapscott 2020; Kieran 2021).[2] Alternatives can be found in the "peacekeeper masculinity" model (Duncanson 2013), or the "compassionate soldier winning hearts and minds" (Hamber

1 Hypermasculinity can simply be thought of as the exaggerated forms of masculinity often associated with "typical" male behavior. This generally involves "structures against femininity and homosexuality" being intensified (Harris 2000: 793) and traits such "status, self-reliance, aggressive activities, dominance over others, and devaluation of emotion and cooperation."

2 Certainly, much more can be said and discussed about militarized masculinities, but a fuller and more exhaustive engagement would go beyond the scope of this chapter. For further discussion, see, among others: Duncanson (2009), Enloe (2000), Tapscott (2020).

2016), though these can be harmful in other ways. These constructions "disrupt elements of the traditional linkages between militarism and masculinity" (Duncanson 2009: 63) while, at the same time, nevertheless relying on constructions of a feminized and racialized "other" (Khalid 2011).

Masculinities and Transitional Justice

As we indicated in our introduction to this chapter, there has been a slowly growing engagement with masculinities and its core theoretical tenets in the transitional justice literature. These analyses of direct physical violence and related gendered harms provide a potential framework for unpacking the relationship between gender, violence, masculinity, and sexual politics. In this section, we give an overview of what has been accomplished here, before highlighting in the next section what has been missing. We specifically note that the focus so far has been either on violent and militarized masculinities, seeking to deconstruct and analyze the violations perpetrated by men, or on men as victims, and specifically incidences of sexual violence (Theidon 2009; Schulz 2020a).[3]

Violence Perpetrated by Men

TJ scholarship and practice have centered on militarized masculinities and the diverse forms of violence perpetrated by men in conflict-affected and transitional spaces. This focus on militarized masculinities is reflective of dominant research on men and masculinities in the context of war, insecurities, and beyond more broadly, which primarily examines the linkages between certain forms of masculinities and the various forms of violence associated with them (Myrttinen et al. 2016; Hearn 1998; Higate 2003; Henry 2017).

It is now well-established that violent and militarized masculinities play a crucial role in creating and maintaining certain types of violence (Cockburn 2010) and that, in situations of conflict, hypermasculinity can become dominant (Cahn and Ní Aoláin 2010; Higate 2001). The cultural and political economy of militarized masculinities has been identified as key to violence during times of political strife and its wake (Theidon 2007; Hutchings 2008). Over the last two decades, a substantial body of literature has emerged that shows how violent and militarized masculinities are causally linked to war and militarization in general (Hutchings 2008; Cockburn 2010; Duncanson 2013). More specifically, such masculinities are also directly associated with diverse forms of sexual and gender-based violence, including war rape (Alison 2007; Eriksson-Baaz and Stern 2013), intimate partner violence (Kelly et al. 2018; Ní Aoláin and McWilliams 2014), and a wide range of other violations in conflict

3 O'Rourke (2017) also notes that the emphasis on civil and political rights rather than an engaging more deeply with socio-economic and cultural rights reveals a gendered bias.

settings (e.g., torture, criminalization of sexual practices, homophobic assault, forced medical treatment and sterilizations, among others) often committed against women, but also men and persons with diverse SOGIESC.

Against this background, one specific concern of the existing literature on masculinities and TJ has centered on questions of how to disarm and transform violent and/or militarized masculinities in post-conflict and transitional periods (Cahn and Ní Aoláin 2010), for instance, through disarmament, demobilization, and reintegration (DDR) programming (Theidon 2009; see Baker this volume). As Cahn and Ní Aoláin (2010: 118) argue, one of the central quandaries for peacebuilding and TJ processes "is how to undo the [violent] masculinities learned during wartime." This focus is underpinned by the argument that facilitating transitions from conflict to peace requires that militarized masculinities enacted by (former) combatants are successfully transformed (Theidon 2009). For instance, Baker's examination in this volume illustrates the importance of engaging with militarized masculinities, showing how, when these masculinities remain unaddressed, they manifest and become reproduced over time and pose complex challenges for processes of dealing with the past. Research in Colombia by Kimberly Theidon (2009) similarly centralizes the importance of sustainably mobilizing former combatants to respond to the security challenges posed by them and the perceived loss of masculine privilege that often attends to such processes. Theidon argues that "transforming the hegemonic, militarized masculinities that characterize former combatants can help further the goals of both DDR and transitional justice processes . . . to contribute to building peace on both the battlefield and the home front" (2009: 34).

Despite emphasizing its importance, research also acknowledges the complexities and difficulties of these transformation processes, due to how masculinities constructions are socially embedded within patriarchal and nationalistic societal structures (Yuval-Davis 1997; Slootmaeckers 2019). It is often asserted that demobilization can often lead to a sense of "emasculation" and a resulting desire in some men to reassert their lost power and manhood through violence (Gear 2010). Enforced dependence and destitution (often the consequences of war) are also said to be experienced as particularly emasculating ways by some men (Sankey 2014; Dolan 2002). Poverty and rising expectations have "proved a tragic mixture of fostering violent masculinities" after conflicts (Morrell 2001: 19). In a situation where men are deprived of their masculine roles, they often use their physical strength, the one male attribute not affected by their social deprivation, to control their environment (Hollander 2014).[4] Many of these dynamics

4 Space does not permit a full discussion of the issue of intersectionality present in this type of debate, as it does risk linking socio-economic marginalization with violent masculinities. See Christofidou (2021) for more on this debate.

unfold particularly pronounced in relation to the linkages between militarized masculinities and sexual violence, embedded within sustained attention on the topic in recent years.[5] In this vein, it is argued that the impact of conflict and insecurity on men's compromised masculinities may often lead to heightened sexual violence as a particular means to reassert power and regain a sense of manhood.

The issue of how different forms of violence mutate and change from a period of intense civil conflict into the so-called peacebuilding context is a further area of significant discussion in the literature. It has been argued that the time horizons in the fields of TJ and peace studies are often too limited in scope and time, often embodied in such terms as "post-conflict" or "post-agreement" (Hamber and Palmary 2021). As such, concepts like "post-conflict" can fail to capture how the impact of mass atrocity can continue to destabilize society long after formal agreements or direct hostilities have ended (not to mention often returning at different moments in time). Several studies have focused on how violence continues (and changes) post-agreement or ceasefire and during times of political transition (Gregg 2014; Ní Aoláin and McWilliams 2014). In societies emerging from political conflict (such as South Africa and Northern Ireland), violence is often described as profoundly gendered and linked to masculinities that remain pervasive in the post-agreement period (Hamber and Murray 2022). Violence during political conflict has frequently been linked to violence against women in the home, with increased levels of domestic violence during periods of peace following a violent political conflict (Ní Aoláin and McWilliams 2014).

As such, the prevalence of certain types of violent masculinities "poses complex issues for undoing violence" (Cahn and Ní Aoláin 2010: 105), and an awareness of their impact is necessary for a successful transition to sustained peace (Theidon 2009). To this end, much work remains to be done in dealing with hypermasculinity in times of war and peace, and ongoing attention is required to the continued exploration of the ability for violent and militarized masculinities to linger and transform long after the formal political conflict is over. Research on how the changing nature of violence and militarized masculinities impact on people with diverse SOGIESC, and the tendency to consider political violence within beyond a heteronormative framework, is particularly underexplored and thus has room for growth (see Serrano-Amaya's chapter on queer masculinities in Colombia).

Violations Against Men

Putting the spotlight solely on militarized masculinities and how to disarm them, however, tends to (re)produce essentialist ideas as universal aggressors

5 For a critique of the hyper-visibility of and attention to sexual violence over other forms of gender-based violence and discrimination, see Eriksson-Baaz and Stern (2013).

and women as universal victims during armed conflicts (see Carpenter 2006), resulting in all-too-prevalent dichotomous categorizations of "all the men are in the militias, all the women are victims" (Enloe 2000: 99; see Schulz 2020a). This obscures the agency of women and girls in violence-affected settings (Parashar 2009), as well as masculine vulnerabilities (Carpenter 2006). To obtain a holistic and inclusive understanding of the workings of gender in conflict-affected and transitional societies, therefore, "the scope of studying masculinities in these situations must be broadened to go beyond merely examining the violences of men" (Myrttinen et al. 2016: 1). As such, we cannot ignore men's experiences of victimization (Carpenter 2006; Dolan 2015), which has become intertwined with understandings of masculinities in conflict settings (Schulz 2020a). One particularly relevant entry point for analyzing male vulnerabilities in (post-)conflict and transitional settings comes through an engagement with conflict-related SGBV against men and boys (Touquet et al. 2021).

Although consistently under-researched, a growing body of scholarship has begun to examine the dynamics surrounding these crimes (Dolan 2015; Touquet 2021; Sivakumaran 2007) and to explore male survivors' gendered harms (Schulz 2018), which are immediately underpinned by masculinities. It is now well established that there is a conceptual disjuncture between masculinities and vulnerabilities which prevents men from being vulnerable (Sivakumaran 2007). This, in turn, makes some men specifically vulnerable to violence, and in particular sexual violence, because it powerfully demonstrates men's vulnerability and thus their dependencies, weaknesses, and subordination (Sjoberg 2016; Dolan 2015). At the same time, masculinities also immediately shape the impact of these crimes on male survivors' masculinities, leading to what, in most of the literature, is termed as "emasculation" through "feminization" – the perceived loss of, or displacement from, survivors' masculine identities (Schulz 2018).

Despite this growing engagement with sexual violence against men (SVAM), however, several gaps persist, and especially "tailored intervention to address male-centered sexual harms remains elusive and marginalized" throughout scholarship and praxis (Ní Aoláin et al. 2015: 109). This holds true specifically for an engagement with SVAM in the context of TJ. As previously noted by Schulz, "whereas recent years have witnessed increasing consideration for redressing CRSV against women and girls, specific attention to justice for male-directed sexual violence remains remarkably absent" (2020a: 131). Despite increasing efforts in scholarship and at the policy level "to ensure that transitional justice processes address the full spectrum of gender-based and sexual violence," including the holistic "needs and opportunities of women, men, girls and boys" (UN 2014: 2), male survivors' justice concerns remain remarkably absent, both from the scholarly literature and from post-conflict programming globally. Except for a handful of cases involving SVAM in the international criminal justice arena – most notably at the International Criminal Tribunal for the former Yugoslavia (ICTY) – TJ instruments have thus far almost entirely turned a blind eye to the experiences of sexually violated men in conflict zones (Buckley-Zistel and Stanley 2012). These gaps are mirrored by broader, overall shortcomings and inadequacies of achieving prosecutions for all victims of SGBV, regardless of their genders, and across international courts and tribunals, including specifically at the ICC (Mibenge 2013). As such, "there is persistent impunity and a vacuum of justice and accountability for sexual violence crimes in most conflict-affected settings globally" (Schulz and Kreft 2022: 1).

At times, when crimes perpetrated specifically against men, including SVAM, have been addressed or included by TJ mechanisms, for instance, in the international criminal arena, these instances were often categorized and subsequently prosecuted as forms of torture, but not as sexual violence (Leiby 2009). This differentiation itself is also inherently gendered and heavily shaped by masculinities constructions, whereby torture is considered as "masculine," and sexual violence a "feminine" crime/violation. Therefore, integrating the viewpoints and experiences of male sexual violence survivors into debates about dealing with the past, and working toward accountability for male sexual harms (Schulz 2020b), can thus bring attention to masculine vulnerabilities in transitional settings and thereby facilitate a more inclusive conception of gender in TJ processes (Schulz 2019a).

More recently, however, there has been some attention to the intersections between SVAM and TJ, including analyses of how male survivors conceptualize and enact justice in post-conflict settings (Schulz 2020b; Clark 2019). Research on northern Uganda has highlighted male survivors' gender-specific justice needs and conceptions (Schulz 2020a, 2019b), but also how numerous gendered, cultural, and socio-political barriers often uphold a vacuum of justice and persistent impunity for most male survivors of sexual violence globally (Schulz 2020b). This work shows male survivors' justice priorities (in northern Uganda) primarily center on justice as recognition, acknowledgment, and reparations – implying the potential to respond to the misrecognition of male survivors' experiences and to remedy their sexual and gendered harms in a gender-sensitive capacity, while also moving beyond a persistent focus on criminal accountability in response to CRSV against women and girls alike.

In addition, emergent research has also begun to pay attention to how male survivors in post-conflict settings exercise different forms of agency, by way of coming to terms with their gendered harms. Heleen Touquet and Philipp Schulz, for instance, drawing on research in the former Yugoslavia and Uganda, show how survivors actively "respond to their vulnerabilities, thereby refuting stereotypical portrayals of the ever-vulnerable and passive victim" (2021: 214). These forms of agency include processes of navigating silence and disclosure (Touquet 2021) or joining and actively engaging in the context of survivors' groups, which constitute a form of justice-making on the micro-level for some male survivors (Schulz 2019a). Paying attention to male survivors' lived realities and their justice-related concerns, needs, and priorities is thereby important to address some of the persisting gendered gaps and blind spots inherent to most TJ processes globally.

Moving Beyond a Violation-Centric Lens

As can be seen from the preceding debates, there are important research gaps and areas in terms of focusing on the violence that flows from militarized masculinities, as well as violations against men, that require further development. However, focusing solely on these agendas also involves risks. We argue that the current work on masculinities in the TJ field should also engage with masculinities beyond male combatants or male victims, so as not to miss the structural dimensions of masculinities in transitional societies. Civilian men who are not involved in direct violence are nevertheless heavily impacted by it. These men and the ideas about masculinity they espouse simultaneously shape the effects of conflicts and transition and are part of structures of masculine power that maintain gender inequality. Similarly, non-heterosexual masculinities are still largely rendered invisible by heteronormative frames of conflict and TJ (see Serrano-Amaya, this volume).

A practical consequence of centering the conversation on violations by and against men has been the development of programs intended to make men behave less violently (Duriesmith and Holmes 2019). Whilst these programs are well-intended and respond to specific needs in communities, the analysis they put forward is often decontextualized from broader structural issues, such as the complex factors that give rise to violent masculinities in the first place (Duriesmith 2019; Flood 2018). The risk is that such work non-intentionally reinforces patriarchal norms (Myrttinen and Schulz 2022: 10). Additionally, these efforts at transforming masculinities can be compounded by heteronormative and neocolonial assumptions and expectations of "new" and, ultimately, "better" masculinities (Mertens and Myrttinen 2019). As Myrttinen and Schulz note, these messages and this explicit or implicit reassertion of heterosexual male agency "is sometimes a deliberate strategy, entry point, or message" and is "often what may make these interventions appealing to men who feel that their masculine self has been undermined" (2022: 10). Christifidou (2021) refers to this as changes in "micro-practices and notions of masculinity" that often lead to superficial change that does not change "gender regimes" (90).

Yet another potential danger with violation- and male-centric views in TJ, and specifically with attempts of seeking to remedy male sexual violence survivors' harms, is that it carries the risk of being closely interwoven with yearnings for a patriarchal golden age (El-Bushra et al. 2014), implying unintended drawbacks for gender justice more broadly (Myrttinen and Schulz 2022). Drawing on empirical research in Israel and Palestine, Meghan MacKenzie and Alana Foster argue that for men who feel their masculine identities has been impacted, the struggle for peace and security can become "a struggle to 'return' men to a supremacy status in the home and in the nation," creating a type of "masculinity nostalgia . . . that included men as heads of household, economic breadwinners, primary decision-makers and sovereigns of the family" (2017: 14–15). This mirrors similar dynamics across the globe, such as in South Africa, where post-apartheid advances for women and growing equality at social, political, and economic levels, even if not wholly realized, have led to men seeking to reassert and maintain their masculinized dominance in and outside the home (Hamber 2010). A quest for justice in transition can frequently take on a similar character, with justice often distorted into men's rights issues rather than of universal gender justice. Transition and social change can lead to a resurgence of "visions of the patriarch" (Sideris 2005) that offer the prospect of maintaining control over women and society while abandoning social justice. Therefore, quests for stability, security, and justice inevitably remain fraught if "dependent on, or intertwined with, a commitment to restoring oppressive gender norms" (MacKenzie and Foster 2017: 15) – and instead require broader transformative and transformational gender justice efforts (Ní Aoláin 2012).

To move beyond these limiting violation-centric foci, and to fully understand and highlight the fluid, tense, and ever-changing nature of masculinities in societies going through transitions, in-depth examinations and observations of the complex diversity of masculinities in peacebuilding and transitional justice processes at various residual levels, including the everyday, are needed. In doing this, the task at hand, as Kimberly Theidon (2009) reminds us, becomes one to open the space for alternative masculinities. The point of departure should be "to look into the cracks," as Hamber (2016) puts it, that are continually emerging between masculinities, rather than narrow the discussion from the start by over-analyzing violent masculinities and their ramifications or only focusing on the vulnerabilities of sexually violated men.

In part, then, this process of "looking into the cracks" involves an examination of civilian masculinities, given that civilian men arguably constitute the majority of men in conflict-affected settings (Wright 2014; and Campbell in this volume). In recent years, there has been some attention to the experiences of non-combatant and non-victimized men in contexts affected by conflict and insecurity (Hollander 2014; Dolan 2002; Carpenter 2006). Based on empirical research in the eastern territories of the Democratic Republic of the Congo (DRC), Hollander argues that civilian men renegotiated their masculinities in a context of economic insecurity in two distinct ways: either by taking on a "victimized" identity or by re-negotiating their masculinities and accepting "a lower status within the family and society" (2014: 417), that is, enacting what Hollander terms "effaced" masculinities.

Another area of engagement with civilian masculinities that has recently gained some traction is in the context of forced migration (Alsopp 2017). Indeed, in situations of refuge and displacement, civilian able-bodied teenage and adult men are frequently the first to leave their point of origin, because they risk being forcefully conscripted into armed forces, because of gendered expectations, according to which males must be(come) breadwinners (Krystalli et al. 2018), and because men are often seen as having the best chance of survival when fleeing. At the same time, shaped by stereotypical masculinities constructions, displaced and fleeing civilian men often face specific threats and circumstances that can, and often do, render them vulnerable (Turner 2021) to various forms of violence, abuse, exploitation, and harm. Simultaneously, then, host communities and countries often see these very men as an enemy, or as a threat toward their security and well-being (Alsopp 2017) – unearthing multiple complexities and realities all at once. However, because TJ has not yet fully engaged with forced displacement and migration (see Fobear, this volume), this emerging engagement with refugees' masculinities has not yet travelled into the field and practice of TJ. Against this background, and seeking to remedy these gaps, various chapters in this volume further advance an understanding of how masculinities operate in post-conflict and transitional sites in several ways and beyond a violation-centric view.

However, paying attention to the masculinities and gendered experiences of non-combatant, non-victimized, and civilian men must not result in false dichotomies of militarized versus civilian masculinities. Rather than being always neatly separated spheres, empirical realities in times of violence, conflict, and its wake often paint a more ambiguous and complex picture, showing how so-called civilian men may often take on, perform, or embody traits of militarized masculinities as well, or how the status of civilian vis-à-vis soldier/warrior is often much more fluid (Bulmer and Eichler 2017; Higate 2001). Amya Agarwal's examination in this volume of how masculinities operate in Kashmir, and how men frequently shift between civilian and semi-militaristic roles and identities, poignantly illustrates this fluidity of civilian and militarized masculinities.

At the same time, caution is required that attention to civilian masculinities does not lead to such identities being romanticized, as associated with either vulnerability or neutrality in conflict situations. Civilian men can often be responsible for perpetuating violence, including SGBV, against women, other men, and persons with diverse SOGIESC alike – both in times of conflict and in its wake (Myrttinen et al. 2016). Civilian men also make up the bulk of those who maintain gendered militarized violence and contribute to the militarization of masculinities, such as politicians and those who control the economic levers of warfare (e.g., investors in the arms industry) or, at a different level, the civilian fathers (and mothers, of course) who encourage their sons to join the military or their daughters to enact traditional femininities. From a research perspective, to understand masculinities, we thus need to understand and appreciate the diversity of men's experiences at different levels and as shaped by different masculinities constructs and idea(l)s.

Conclusion

A holistic and nuanced engagement with masculinities in transitional justice – that moves beyond a focus on physical violence and that considers the diverse gendered lived experiences of a holistic group of men and masculinities in post-conflict settings – is needed. This includes paying attention to, for instance, the experiences of civilian men impacted by conflict or insecurity and the different manifestations, expressions, and lived realities of non-heteronormative and other marginalized expressions of masculinities.

One way in which such an engagement with masculinities in TJ can be fostered, without necessarily falling back into binary and violation-centric foci, comes through a more structurally embedded power analysis in relation to masculinities (Connell 2005). This moves us away from thinking about masculinity merely as a set of violent and visibly oppressive practices but rather as an embedded social construct linked to the relationship between gender, race, ethnicity, and class that can adapt and change over time and space (Wright 2014; Messerschmidt 2018). These intersections frequently have specific manifestations in times of war, for example, feeding ethnic or nationalistic hierarchies at the core of conflict, class, and its role in controlling the political economy of warfare and peace, among others.

Therefore, a relational analysis of TJ and masculinity is vital (Ní Aoláin and Rooney 2007). Such an analysis must recognize that all masculinities influence one another (Morrell 2001) and operate in complex interrelated ways. To draw on Beasley's (2008) work, this type of analysis should always be concerned with hegemony as a political mechanism that can produce solidarity between different masculinities in a hierarchical order. This way of thinking is vital if we are to consider masculinity more seriously within societies in transition, characterized by the ending of armed conflict and the emergence of new forms of power.

By looking for the less-visible manifestation of (violent) masculinities, we can see how politics can also replicate (constantly changing) masculinities. Masculinity then provides a framework for thinking about how the guerilla-turned-peacemaker can still be perceived as the rational and decisive "big man" who brings the revolutionaries with him into a peace process and end hostilities but, at the same time, institutes a new government that is male-centric and masculinized, that continues to control resources and people through new, less (or differently) physically violent means. Militarized masculine figures and actions are often lauded during times of conflict and in peace processes, reinforcing male dominance even in peacetime politics (Ashe 2015), often reinforcing heteronormative understandings of peace. Masculinities are therefore profoundly entangled with the political systems (Enloe 2000; Zalewski 1995), and we need to carefully consider how masculinities are interconnected with post-conflict social, political, and economic outcomes. This requires intellectual and activist deconstruction of how the manifestations of masculinity that drive conflict are interlinked with many factors from private capital, post-conflict economics, and the availability of weapons that all exist within a web of interrelated local and global social relations – feeding into larger efforts of undoing capitalism, militarism, and patriarchy (Enloe 2017).

Earlier, we raised the issue of not conflating dominant, hegemonic, and militarized masculinities (Beasley 2008). Despite this importance, however, we would contend that, in conflict settings, dominant masculinities can become deeply entwined with reproducing militarized masculinities and thus legitimating specific hegemonic masculinities. War and conflict can alter the relationships between dominant (and even subordinate) masculinities and hegemonic masculinity, creating what could be considered a hypermasculine alignment between different expressions of masculinity. This entails a blurring between ordinary citizens and their gendered lives, dominant masculinities, militarized masculinities, political rhetoric and action, and ultimately, hegemonic masculinity that continue to legitimate and sustain unequal gendered relationships. This happens in the rhetoric of the tough-talking president (who himself may never have seen combat), the arms dealers and financiers of war who are lauded rather than shunned for their role in violence, the warmongering rhetoric of ordinary citizens on social media, the social media influencer spouting hate, the actor who aligns himself with a military cause, the narrative of the next blockbuster that portrays certain groups as enemies, the TV show about the stoic fortitude of military wives, the analysis and glorification of war in the media, and the public shaming of conscientious objectors or peaceniks.

In a similar way, although even less researched, different masculinities can operate within the very structures said to be essential to bringing and building peace in societies transitioning out of violence. We need to understand how structures such as truth commissions, government inquiries and committees, funding agencies, demobilization processes, transnational corporations, development processes, strategic plans, international monetary bodies, educational institutions, and the media, among many others, reinforce and are reproduced by different forms of masculinities and power, and perhaps most importantly can reinforce hegemonic masculinities (Enloe 2000).

The question is therefore not just how to prevent violent masculinities manifesting through the actions of individuals or groups of men (and some women) directly associated with combatants but also how to halt pervasive militarized masculinities that marginalize different parts of populations and shape the TJ landscape, not only through the naked exercise of power, but also through the hidden masculine cultures operating within a variety of hierarchies and social spaces in transitional political settings (Hamber 2016). Cynthia Enloe (2019) notes how masculinity has significant currency in organizations, and we should analyze the implications carefully. The questions we should investigate include, among others: "[W]hich sorts of masculinities appear to be dominant in each? When? Why? With what consequences? Where are diverse women in the operations of each?[6] When? Why? With what results?" (112).

6 True to the analysis raised earlier about "looking for the cracks," we might add, "Where are diverse men in the operations of each?"

References

Alison, M. (2007). Wartime Sexual Violence: Women's Human Rights and Questions of Masculinity. *Review of International Studies* 33(1): 75–99.

Alsopp, J. (2017). Agent, Victim, Soldier, Son. Intersecting Masculinities in the European 'Refugee Crisis'. In: Freedman, J., Kivilcim, Z. and Baklacioglu, N. Ö. (eds.): *A Gendered Approach to the Syrian Refugee Crisis*. London: Routledge.

Ashe, F. (2015). Gendering Demilitarisation and Justice in Northern Ireland. *The British Journal of Politics & International Relations* 17(4): 665–680.

Ashe, F. (2019). Sexuality and Gender Identity in Transitional Societies: Peacebuilding and Counterhegemonic Politics. *International Journal of Transitional Justice* 13(3): 435–457.

Barker, G. (2005). *Dying to Be Men. Youth, Masculinity and Social Exclusion*. London: Routledge.

Barker, G. and C. Ricardo (2005). Young Men and the Construction of Masculinity in Sub-Saharan Africa: Implications for HIV/Aids, Conflict, and Violence. *Social Development Paper No. 84*. Washington, DC: World Bank.

Beasley, C. (2008). Rethinking Hegemonic Masculinity in a Globalizing World. *Men and Masculinities* 11(1): 88.

Belkin, A. (2002). *Bring Me Men: Military Masculinity and the Benign Façade of American Empire*. London: Hurst Publishers.

Bias, L. (2022). Hello. My Name Is Vladimir (He/Him). *The Security Times*, February. Available at: https://www.the-security-times.com/hello-my-name-is-vladimir-he-him/. Accessed on: 16 March 2023.

Buckley-Zistel, S. and R. Stanley (2012). *Gender in Transitional Justice*. New York: Springer.

Bulmer, S. and M. Eichler (2017). Unmaking Militarized Masculinity: Veterans and the Project of Military-to-Civilian Transition. *Critical Military Studies* 3(2): 161–181.

Cahn, N. and F. D. Ní Aoláin (2010). Gender, Masculinities and Transition in Conflicted Societies. *New England Law Review* 44(1): 101–123.

Carpenter, R. C. (2006). Recognizing Gender-Based Violence Against Civilian Men and Boys in Conflict Situations. *Security Dialogue* 37(1): 83–103.

Chakraborty, C. (2017). *Mapping South Asian Masculinities Men and Political Crises*. London: Routledge.

Cheng, C. (1999). Marginalized Masculinities and Hegemonic Masculinity: An Introduction. *The Journal of Men's Studies* 7(3): 295–231.

Chowdry, P. (2013). Militarized Masculinities: Shaped and Reshaped in Colonial South-East Punjab. *Modern Asian Studies* 47(3): 713–750.

Christensen, A.-D. and M. Kyed (2022). From Military to Militarizing Masculinities. *NORMA* 17(1): 1–4.

Christofidou, A. (2021). Men and Masculinities: A Continuing Debate on Change. *NORMA: International Journal of Masculinity Studies* 16(2): 90.

Clark, J. N. (2019). The Vulnerability of the Penis: Sexual Violence Against Men in Conflict and Security Frames. *Men and Masculinities* 22(5): 778–800.

Cockburn, C. (2010). Gender Relations as Causal in Militarization and War. *International Feminist Journal of Politics* 12(2): 139–157.

Collins, P. H. (2019). *Intersectionality as Critical Social Theory*. Durham: Duke University Press.

Collins, P. H. and S. Bilge (2020). *Intersectionality*. Cambridge: Cambridge Polity Press.

Connell, R. (2000). Arms and the Man: Using the New Research on Masculinity to Understand Violence and Promote Peace in the Contemporary World. In: Breines, I., Connell, R. and Eide, I. (eds.): *Male Roles, Masculinities and Violence: A Culture of Peace Perspective*. Paris: UNESCO Publishing: 21–33.

Connell, R. (2005). *Masculinities*. Berkeley: University of California Press.
Connell, R. (2009). *Gender*. Cambridge: Polity.
Connell, R. (2014). Margin Becoming Centre: For a World-Centred Rethinking of Masculinities. *NORMA: International Journal for Masculinity Studies* 9(4): 217–231.
Connell, R. and J. Messerschmidt (2005). Hegemonic Masculinity: Rethinking the Concept. *Gender & Society* 19(6): 829–859.
Crenshaw, K. (1989). Demarginalizing the Intersection of Race and Sex: A Black Feminist Critique of Antidiscrimination Doctrine, Feminist Theory and Antiracist Politics. *University of Chicago Legal Forum*: 139–168.
Demetriou, D. (2001). Connell's Concept of Hegemonic Masculinity: A Critique. *Theory and Society* 30(3): 337–361.
Dery, I., C. Baataar and A. R. Khan (2022). Everyday Peacebuilding Among Ghanaian Men: Ambiguities, Resistances, and Possibilities. *Journal of the British Academy* 19: 35–53.
Dietrich Ortega, L. M. (2012). Looking Beyond Violent Militarized Masculinities. *International Feminist Journal of Politics* 14(4): 489–507.
DiGiovanni, L. (2017). Militarized Masculinity: Boys' Socialization and the Postwar Graphic Novel of Carlos Giménez. In: Ryan, L. and Corbalan, A. (eds.): *The Dynamics of Masculinity in Contemporary Spanish Culture*. New York: Routledge: 63–79.
Dolan, C. (2002). Collapsing Masculinities and Weak States: A Case Study of Northern Uganda. In: Cleaver, F. (ed.): *Masculinity Matters: Men, Masculinities and Gender Relations in Development*. London: Zed Books: 57–83.
Dolan, C. (2015). Letting Go of the Gender Binary: Charting New Pathways for Humanitarian Interventions on Gender-Based Violence. *International Review of the Red Cross* 96(894): 485–501.
Dowd, N. E. (2010). *The Man Question: Male Subordination and Privilege*. New York: New York University Press.
Duncanson, C. (2009). Forces for Good? Narratives of Military Masculinity in Peacekeeping Operations. *International Feminist Journal of Politics* 11(1): 63–80.
Duncanson, C. (2013). *Forces for Good? Military Masculinities and Peacebuilding in Afghanistan and Iraq*. New York: Palgrave Macmillan.
Duriesmith, D. (2016). *Masculinity and New War: The Gendered Dynamics of Contemporary Armed Conflict*. New York: Routledge.
Duriesmith, D. (2019). Engaging or Changing Men? Understandings of Masculinity and Change in the New 'Men, Peace and Security' Agenda. *Peacebuilding*: 1–14.
Duriesmith, D. and G. Holmes (2019). The Masculine Logic of DDR and SSR in the Rwanda Defence Force. *Security Dialogue* 50(4): 361–379.
Duriesmith, D. and N. Ismail (2019). Militarized Masculinities Beyond Methodological Nationalism: Charting the Multiple Masculinities of an Indonesian Jihadi. *International Theory* 11(2): 139–159.
El-Bushra, J., H. Myrttinen and J. Naujoks (2014). *Renegotiating the 'Ideal' Society – Gender Relations in the Wake of Conflict and Displacement in Uganda*. London: International Alert.
Enloe, C. (2000). *Maneuvers – The International Politics of Militarizing Women's Lives*. Berkeley: University of California Press.
Enloe, C. (2004). *The Curious Feminist: Searching for Women in a New Age of Empire*. Berkeley: University of California Press.
Enloe, C. (2017). *The Big Push: Exposing and Challenging the Persistence of Patriarchy*. Berkeley: University of California Press.
Enloe, C. (2019). Hypermasculinity and #MeToo: Backlash and Hurdles in Feminist Movements. An Interview with Cynthia Enloe. *Journal of International Affairs* 72(2): 119–124.

Eriksson Baaz, M. and M. Stern (2013). *Sexual Violence as a Weapon of War? Perceptions, Prescriptions, Problems in the Congo and Beyond*. London: Zed Books.
Flood, M. (2018). *Engaging Men and Boys in Violence Prevention*. New York: Palgrave.
Gaufman, L. (2022). Damsels in Distress: Fragile Masculinity in Digital War. *Media, War and Conflict*: 1–20.
Gear, S. (2010). Imprisoning Men in Violence: Masculinity and Sexual Abuse: A View from South African Prisons. *South African Crime Quarterly* 33: 25–32.
Gregg, M. R. (2014). *An Incomplete Transition? Explaining the Ongoing Prevalence of Violence Against Women in Post-Apartheid South Africa*. MA thesis, Simon Fraser University, Burnaby, B.C. Canada.
Hamber, B. (2007). Masculinity and Transitional Justice: An Exploratory Essay. *The International Journal of Transitional Justice* 1: 375–390.
Hamber, B. (2010). Masculinity and Transition: Crisis or Confusion in South Africa? *Journal of Peacebuilding and Development* 5(3): 75–88.
Hamber, B. (2016). There Is a Crack in Everything: Problematising Masculinities, Peacebuilding and Transitional Justice. *Human Rights Review* 17(1): 9–34.
Hamber, B. and C. Murray (2022). *Voices from the Margins: Young Men and Post-Conflict Masculinities in Northern Ireland*. Geneva: Interpeace.
Hamber, B. and I. Palmary (2021). A Dance of Shadows and Fires: Conceptual and Practical Challenges of Intergenerational Healing after Mass Atrocity. *Genocide Studies and Prevention: An International Journal* 15(3): 100–120.
Hamber, B., P. Schulz and G. Messmer (2023). Transitional Justice and Masculinities. In: Lawther, C. and Moffet, L. (eds.): *Research Handbook on Transitional Justice* (2nd ed.). Cheltenham: Edward Elgar Publishing.
Harris, A. P. (2000). Gender, Violence, Race, and Criminal Justice. *Stanford Law Review* 52 (777): 778–806.
Haynes, D. F., F. D. Ni Aolain and N. Cahn (2011). Masculinities and Child Soldiers in Post-Conflict Societies. *Minnesota Legal Studies Research Paper* 10(57): 104.
Hearn, J. (1998). *The Violences of Men: How Men Talk About and How Agencies Respond to Men's Violence to Women*. London: Sage.
Henry, M. (2017). Problematizing Military Masculinity, Intersectionality and Male Vulnerability in Feminist Critical Military Studies. *Critical Military Studies* 3(2): 182–199.
Higate, P. (2001). Theorizing Continuity: From Military to Civilian Life. *Armed Forces & Society* 27(3): 443–460.
Higate, P. (2003). *Military Masculinities: Identity and the State*. Westport, CT: Praeger.
Hollander, T. (2014). Men, Masculinities, and the Demise of a State: Examining Masculinities in the Context of Economic, Political, and Social Crisis in a Small Town in the Democratic Republic of the Congo. *Men and Masculinities* 17(4): 417–439.
Hutchings, K. (2008). Making Sense of Masculinity and War. *Men and Masculinities* 10(4): 389–404.
Kelly, J. T. D., E. Colantuoni, C. Robinson, et al. (2018). From the Battlefield to the Bedroom: A Multilevel Analysis of the Links Between Political Conflict and Intimate Partner Violence in Liberia. *BMJ Global Health*: 1–11.
Khalid, M. (2011). Gender, Orientalism and Representations of the 'Other' in the War on Terror. *Global Change, Peace and Security* 23(1): 15–29.
Kieran, D. (2021). 'It Changed Me as a Man:' Reframing Military Masculinity in the Army's 'Shoulder to Shoulder' Suicide Prevention Campaign. *Journal of War & Culture Studies* 14(3): 306–323.
Krystalli, R., A. Hawkins and K. Wilson (2018). 'I Followed the Flood': A Gender Analysis of the Moral and Financial Economies of Forced Migration. *Disasters* 42(1): 17–39.
Leiby, M. (2009). Digging in the Archives: The Promise and Perils of Primary Documents. *Politics Society* 37: 75–99.

MacKenzie, M. and A. Foster (2017). Masculinity Nostalgia: How War and Occupation Inspire a Yearning for Gender Order. *Security Dialogue* 48(3): 206–223.
Maringira, Godfrey (2021). Soldiers, Masculinities and Violence. *Current Anthropology* 62(23): 103–111.
Martin de Almagro, M. and P. Schulz (2022). Gender and Transitional Justice. *Oxford Research Encyclopedia of International Studies*: 1–27.
Mertens, C. and H. Myrttinen (2019). 'A Real Woman Waits' – Heteronormative Respectability, Neo-Liberal Betterment and Echoes of Coloniality in SGBV Programming in Eastern DR Congo. *Journal of Intervention and Statebuilding* 13(4): 418–439.
Messerschmidt, J. W. (2018). *Hegemonic Masculinity: Formulation, Reformulation, and Amplification*. Lanham, MD: Rowman & Littlefield.
Mibenge, C. S. (2013). *Sex and International Tribunals: The Erasure of Gender from the War Narrative*. Philadelphia: University of Pennsylvania Press.
Morrell, R. (2001). The Times of Change: Men and Masculinity in South Africa. In: Morrell, R. (ed.): *Changing Men in Southern Africa*. London: Zed Books.
Myrttinen, H., L. Khattab and J. Naujoks (2016). Re-thinking Hegemonic Masculinities in Conflict-Affected Contexts. *Critical Military Studies* 3(2): 103–119.
Myrttinen, H., C. Lewis, H. Touquet, P. Schulz, F. Yousaf and E. Laruni (2024). *The Routledge Handbook of Masculinities in Conflict and Peacebuilding*. London: Routledge.
Myrttinen, H. and P. Schulz (2022). Broadening the Scope But Reasserting Male Privilege? Potential Patriarchal Pitfalls of Inclusive Approaches to Gender-Based Violence. *International Feminist Journal of Politics*: 1–25.
Ní Aoláin, F. (2012). Advancing Feminist Positioning in the Field of Transitional Justice. *International Journal of Transitional Justice* 6(2): 205–228.
Ní Aoláin, F. and M. McWilliams (2014). 'There Is a War Going on You Know' – Addressing the Complexity of Violence Against Women in Conflicted and Post Conflict Societies. *Transitional Justice Institute Research Paper* 14(1): 1–25.
Ní Aoláin, F., C. O'Rourke and A. Swaine (2015). Transforming Reparations for Conflict-Related Sexual Violence: Principles and Practice. *Harvard Human Rights Journal* 28: 97–146.
Ní Aoláin, F. and E. Rooney (2007). Underenforcement and Intersectionality: Gendered Aspects of Transition for Women. *International Journal of Transitional Justice* 1: 388–354.
O'Rourke, C. (2017). Transitional Justice and Gender. In: Lawther, C., Moffett, L. and Jacobs, D. (eds.): *Research Handbook on Transitional Justice*. Cheltenham: Edward Elgar Publishing.
Parashar, S. (2009). Feminist International Relations and Women Militants: Case Studies from Sri Lanka and Kashmir. *Cambridge Review of International Affairs* 22(2): 235–256.
Parashar, S. (2018). Competing Masculinities, Militarization and the Conflict in Kashmir. *International Feminist Journal of Politics* 20(4): 663–665.
Ratele, K. (2008). Analysing Males in Africa: Certain Useful Elements in Considering Ruling Masculinities. *African and Asian Studies* 7(4): 515–536.
Sankey, D. (2014). Towards Recognition of Subsistence Harms: Reassessing Approaches to Socioeconomic Forms of Violence in Transitional Justice. *International Journal of Transitional Justice* 8(1): 121–140.
Schulz, P. (2018). Displacement from Gendered Personhood: Sexual Violence and Masculinities in Northern Uganda. *International Affairs* 94(5): 1101–1119.
Schulz, P. (2019a). Towards Inclusive Gender in Transitional Justice: Gaps, Blind-Spots and Opportunities. *Journal of Intervention and Statebuilding* 14(5): 691–710.
Schulz, P. (2019b). To Me, Justice Means to Be in a Group': Survivors' Groups as a Pathway to Justice in Northern Uganda. *Journal of Human Rights Practice* 11(1): 171–189.

Schulz, P. (2020a). *Male Survivors of Wartime Sexual Violence: Perspectives from Northern Uganda*. Berkeley, CA: University of California Press.
Schulz, P. (2020b). Examining Male Wartime Rape Survivors' Perspectives on Justice in Northern Uganda. *Social & Legal Studies* 29(1): 19–40.
Schulz, P. and A. K. Kreft (2022). Accountability for Conflict-Related Sexual Violence. *Oxford Research Encyclopedia of International Studies*: 1–25.
Sharoni, S., J. Welland, L. Steiner and J. Pedersen (2016). *Handbook on Gender and War*. Cheltenham: Edward Elgar Publishing.
Sideris, T. (2005). 'You Have to Change and You Don't Know How!': Contesting What It Means to Be a Man in a Rural Area of South Africa. In: Reid, G. and Walker, L. (eds.): *Men Behaving Differently: South African Men Since 1994*. Cape Town: Double Storey Books.
Sivakumaran, S. (2007). Sexual Violence Against Men in Armed Conflict. *European Journal of International Law* 18(2): 253–276.
Sjoberg, L. (2016). *Women as Wartime Rapists: Beyond Sensation and Stereotyping*. New York: New York University Press.
Slootmaeckers, K. (2019). Nationalism as Competing Masculinities: Homophobia as a Technology of Othering for Hetero- and Homonationalism. *Theory and Society* 48(2): 239–265.
Tapscott, R. (2020). Militarized Masculinity and the Paradox of Restraint: Mechanisms of Social Control Under Modern Authoritarianism. *International Affairs* 96(6): 1565–1584.
Theidon, K. (2007). Transitional Subjects: The Disarmament, Demobilization and Reintegration of Former Combatants in Colombia. *International Journal of Transitional Justice* 1(1): 66–90.
Theidon, K. (2009). Reconstructing Masculinities: The Disarmament, Demobilization, and Reintegration of Former Combatants in Colombia. *Human Rights Quarterly* 31(1): 1–34.
Titunik, R. (2008). The Myth of the Macho Military. *Polity* 40(2): 1–18.
Touquet, H. (2021). Silent or Inaudible? Male Survivor Stories in Bosnia-Herzegovina. *Social Politics*: 1–18.
Touquet, H., C. Chynoweth, S. Martin, C. Reis, H. Myrttinen, P. Schulz, L. Turner and D. Duriesmith (2021). From 'It Rarely Happens' to 'It's Worse for Men': Dispelling Misconceptions About Sexual Violence Against Men and Boys in Conflict and Displacement. *Journal of Humanitarian Affairs* 2(3): 25–34.
Touquet, H. and P. Schulz (2021). Navigating Vulnerabilities and Masculinities: How Gendered Contexts Shape the Agency of Male Sexual Violence Survivors. *Security Dialogue* 52(3): 213–230.
Turner, L. (2021). The Politics of Labeling Refugee Men as 'Vulnerable'. *Social Politics* 28(1): 1–23.
United Nations (UN) (2014). *Analytical Study Focusing on Gender-Based and Sexual Violence in Relation to Transitional Justice*. New York: Office of the United Nations High Commissioner for Human Rights.
Vigoya, M. V. (2001). Contemporary Latin American Perspectives on Masculinity. *Men and Masculinities* 3(3): 237–260.
Wojnicka, K., U. Mellström and S. de Boise (2022). On War, Hegemony and (Political) Masculinities. *NORMA* 17(2): 83–87.
Wright, H. (2014). *Masculinities, Conflict and Peacebuilding: Perspectives on Men Through a Gender Lens*. London: Saferworld.
Yang, Y. (2020). What's Hegemonic About Hegemonic Masculinity? Legitimation and Beyond. *Sociological Theory* 38(4): 318–333.
Yuval-Davis, N. (1997). *Gender and Nation*. London: SAGE.
Zalewski, M. (1995). Well, What Is the Feminist Perspective on Bosnia? *International Affairs* 71(2): 339–356.

Chapter 3

Queering Transitional Justice

Reviewing the Field of Transitional Justice and Looking Toward Queer Possibilities

Katherine Fobear

Introduction

"What would the incorporation of sexual and gender minority experiences in transitional justice mechanisms mean for sexual and gender minorities?" (Fobear 2014). This was the question I originally asked ten years ago when I wrote my exploratory article "Queering Truth Commissions" (2014). The world was witnessing a profound public consciousness of queer persecution with the passing of Uganda's infamous "Kill the Gays" bill, also known as the Anti-Homosexuality Act (2014), which broadened the criminalization of same-sex sexual acts, increasing the maximum punishment from imprisonment to the death penalty. In addition, Ugandan citizens living abroad could be extradited and tried in court for engaging in same-sex sexual activities or "aggravated homosexuality." The Anti-Homosexuality Act would eventually be annulled by the Ugandan Constitutional Courts, which stripped away the death penalty but maintained imprisonment and the criminalization of same-sex sexual acts.

Reaction in the Western world was a mixture of outrage and calls for international sanctions. Western donors suspended or redirected more than $200 million in aid to Uganda as a result. As horrific as the Anti-Homosexuality Act was, and the subsequent explosive rise of anti-queer violence in Uganda continues to be, what struck me most was the ahistorical framing of persecution against sexual and gender minorities in Western media and human rights rhetoric. Uganda is a country that has endured colonization, two decades of civil strife, a 30-year military dictatorship under President Yoweri Museveni, and more than two decades of civil war involving the Lord's Resistance Army and the Ugandan government. The violence and oppression faced by sexual and gender minorities in Uganda were intimately intertwined with the political, economic, and social oppression brought on by the country's civil unrest. It struck me as odd that these connections were not being addressed – especially since there was already international attention on social unrest and civil conflict in Uganda, in particular by the United Nations Human Rights Commission and the International Center for Transitional Justice.

DOI: 10.4324/9781003519522-4

Why were these connections not being made? Why were lesbian, gay, bisexual, transgender, and queer (LGBTQ)[1] rights treated as a separate issue from other human rights issues brought on by decades of conflict and unrest? It made me question how sexual and gender minorities were being silenced in other institutions and fields, especially in transitional justice.

While, through the decades, the field of transitional justice has grown substantially, research and engagement with sexual and gender minorities remain slow and limited. The question I asked six years ago regarding what it would mean to better incorporate and engage with queer bodies and theory in transitional justice is still very relevant today. However, it would be misleading to claim that there has not been some movement within the field of transitional justice to queer it.[2]

This chapter engages with the current state of transitional justice literature regarding sexual and gender minorities. The first section discusses the critical turn in transitional justice to interrogate underlying assumptions about reconciliation and peace. Feminist engagement with transitional justice pushes the field not only to recognize gender-based violence against women but also to address how gender norms and hierarchies are reproduced in post-conflict realities. From there, I turn to queering transitional justice. This involves the purposeful inclusion of sexual and gender minorities in transitional justice processes as well as a critical examination of homophobia, heteronormativity, and patriarchy in conflict and post-conflict. Although limited in application across states, efforts by some in recent decades to address sexual

1 For the purpose of trying to use as much inclusionary language in this chapter as possible, I use a variety of terminology to address sexual and gender minorities. *Lesbian*, *gay*, *bisexual*, and *transgender* are Western sexual and gender identity terms. While these terms have been adopted by many communities around the world, it is important to recognize that even in the adoption of these terms, there is difference in meaning by culture and location. I use *LGBTQ* as an umbrella term, much as I use *sexual and gender minorities* to address a wide variety of sexual orientation, gender identity, gender expression, and sex characteristics. The term "sexual and gender minorities" comes with its own challenges and critiques as being potentially marginalizing to non-Western sexualities and genders, as well as minoritizing large groups of people who may not identify politically or socially as a minority or a marginalized population. Language continues to evolve around sexuality and gender, and it is important to recognize not only the fluidity of it but also the potential political impact it may have.

2 For the purpose of this discussion, I use *queer* in two different ways. The first is as an umbrella term to describe a variety of sexual and gender expressions and actions outside of what would be considered in the West to be heterosexuality and/or cisgendered, recognizing fully that even as an umbrella term, *queer* is limited in the context of the vast variety of sexualities and gender expressions around the world. Second, I use *queer* as a verb. *Queering*, or *to queer*, refers to two actions. The first is to bring to the forefront voices, issues, and experiences of non-heterosexual and/or non-cisgendered individuals and communities in literature and practice. The second is to challenge social constructions of gender and sexuality that are, in turn, used to support institutions of gendered and sexualized normative power and discourse.

and gender minorities in transitional justice processes do show a growing trend for greater inclusion. However, as progressive as this may be, inclusion does not automatically mean acceptance or full recognition of citizenship. States' accountability to address systemic violence against sexual and gender minorities and uphold legislation is limited. The final section of this chapter is more exploratory and open-ended, focusing on the importance of a more concerted effort in transitional justice to engage sexual and gender minority refugees and displaced peoples. If the goal of transitional justice is to redress past violence fully, forced displacement and the voices of those displaced must be taken into account. This is especially true for sexual and gender minorities, as many are forced to relocate out of fear. Including displaced LGBTQ persons in transitional justice will allow for a greater understanding of the full scope of harms against sexual and gender minorities and create spaces for cross-border civic engagement and repair.

Critical Turns in Transitional Justice

In recent years in particular, there has been a "critical turn" in transitional justice literature, aiming to re-evaluate the field's underlying assumptions and moving toward greater inclusion of different forms of violations and harms, as well as justice mechanisms and processes (Sharp 2019). Part of this effort is motivated by the need to decenter Western frameworks in order to decolonize transitional justice and support non-Western and/or Indigenous actors, voices, cultures, and practices (Park 2020). These processes involve supporting Indigenous or traditional practices of social repair (Matsunaga 2016), the use of storytelling and memory (Anderson 2019; Baines and Stewart 2011), and the establishment of tribal or community courts to deliver justice (Izquierdo and Viaene 2018). At the same time, many of these concerns and moves towards a more critical engagement are raised in feminist scholarship around transitional justice. Feminist scholars' engagement has greatly contributed to widening the scope of harms to include gender-based violence – most notably, wartime rape and conflict-related sexual and gender-based violence (Ketelaars 2018: 409). Echoing critiques of transitional justice's failure to address systemic oppression and cast a critical eye on power relations in both conflict and post-conflict societies, feminists contest the limited scope of transitional justice in addressing gendered violence and the harmful power structures and societal norms that contribute to gender oppression (also see introduction to this volume).

As much as transitional justice, in all its manifestations, can never be apolitical, it is also never gender-neutral or sexuality-neutral. Instead, gender and sexual norms and constructions of power are inherent in the entire field. Nadine Naber and Ziena Zaatari (2014) write that in the chaos, immediacy, and conflicting needs of post-conflict communities, groups, identities, and experiences can be pitted against one another in a constructed competition for recognition and priority. This is very much the case when addressing sexual and gender minorities, as inclusion remains slow in most transitional justice literature and practice. Much of this is due to the general reluctance of states to address violence against sexual and gender minorities (Lemay Langlois 2018: 118). Recognizing anti-queer violence would also mean recognizing subject-hood, citizenship, and legal rights for sexual and gender minorities that may run counter to cultural norms and beliefs about sexuality and gender. Despite promising international resolutions such as the United Nations *Joint Statement on Ending Violence and Discrimination against* LGBTI People (2015), which called for ending violence and discrimination against sexual and gender minorities, there remains limited political and economic pressure for states to address anti-queer persecution. Even with this slow and limited pace, progress has been made in recent decades in addressing LGBTQ populations and anti-queer violence in transitional justice. In the next section, I explore what it means to queer transitional justice. Queering transitional justice includes not only addressing violence against sexual and gender minorities but also addressing larger systemic forms of homophobic and heteronormative oppression. From there, I review recent efforts by states to address anti-queer persecution in their transitional justice processes and explore both the gains in bringing queer voices to the forefront and limitations in holding states accountable for LGBTQ human rights.

Queering Transitional Justice: Connecting Homophobia, Heteronormativity, and Patriarchy

Within the past decade, there has been slow but growing recognition of sexual and gender minorities within the field of transitional justice. Same-sex sexualities, queer relations, and gender-nonconforming, fluid, or non-binary subjectivities exist in every culture around the world. Western conceptualizations of sexuality and gender expression as binary, a primary identity, and a political identity are historically relatively new. However, queerness around sexuality and gender expression is not.

Homophobia is not inherent in any society; it is a historical construction brought on by colonialism and imperialism that, through the years, has grown as a political tool and means of oppression. This historical construction is evidenced by the majority of current laws criminalizing same-sex sexualities, which have their roots in former European colonial laws forced upon colonized states (Rao 2014). This is certainly the case in Uganda, as reflected upon in this chapter's introduction. The purpose of these laws was to control the sexual and gender agency of colonized peoples and create a sexual and gendered hierarchy with colonizers at the top. These laws remained even when formerly colonized states gained independence. Through the decades, these laws have increasingly been enforced as a means to control and terrorize vulnerable populations.

this effort has been brought on by international and local LGBTQ activists demanding representation and participation in transitional justice processes (also see Bueno-Hansen, this volume). Pascha Bueno-Hansen's review of Latin American truth commissions shows a moderate effort by states to "extinguish roots of impunity surrounding violence against gender and sexual minorities while advocating for the realization of LGBTI people's full citizenship" (2018: 127). Much of this effort is directed toward including targeted acts of violence against sexual and gender minorities in states' truth commissions' final reports as part of their collective findings regarding terror, persecution, and violence by state, military, and local actors.

An example of including sexual and gender minority voices can be seen in the Paraguayan Truth and Justice Commission's (2004–2008) final report, which included two cases under the dictatorship of Alfredo Stroessner (1954–1989) that involved police persecution, raids, and torture of sexual and gender minorities. These two cases were considered representative of the everyday terror that LGBTQ individuals faced under Stroessner's dictatorship, in which sexual minorities were targeted under the guise of defending social morality (Bueno-Hansen 2018). Likewise, the Ecuadorian Truth Commission (2008–2009) included acts of violence against the LGBTQ community in their final report (see Bueno-Hansen, this volume), as did the Brazilian Truth Commission (2012–2014) investigation of human rights violations that occurred in the years 1946 to 1988.

These efforts to include past instances of persecution and their effects on the everyday existence of sexual and gender minorities are an important step toward greater visibility and recognition of citizenship for queer individuals in post-conflict societies. The challenge remains to make the important linkage between past harms and present realities. Looking at the status of LGBTQ individuals in Paraguay, Ecuador, and Brazil, it is clear that despite efforts toward greater inclusion in the transitional justice processes, violence against sexual and gender minorities remains at epidemic proportions (Amnesty International 2020a, 2020b; Lopez 2020). What happened in Paraguay, Ecuador, and Brazil is representative of other cases where violence against queer individuals increases during times of peace. An example can be seen in South Africa, known for being the first to address violence against sexual and gender minorities in its truth commission and the first country to include protection of sexual minorities in its Constitution. Violence against sexual and gender minorities, especially against Black queer women and transgender individuals, remains at epidemic proportions, with a recent study reporting that 41% of LGBTQ South Africans know someone who was murdered because of their sexual orientation and/or gender identity (Love Not Hate Campaign 2016). Facing this reality, we must critically look at transitional justice from a queer perspective. What are the challenges in transitional justice that must be addressed in order to not only address past anti-queer violence but also work collectively with state and local actors to support LGBTQ communities in the present? How do we go beyond LGBTQ persons surviving during conflict to thriving post-conflict?

One step has already been addressed, which is the greater inclusion of local queer communities and LGBTQ activists in transitional justice processes. This comes with its own challenges. In the case of Colombia (also see Oettler, this volume), LGBTQ activists collected more than 50 years of documented violence against sexual and gender minorities by state, paramilitary, and guerilla groups, drug cartels, and local communities (Lemay Langlois 2018). Despite the efforts by local LGBTQ organizations, it was difficult to distinguish and separate acts of violence from one another in the face of ongoing structural violence against LGBTQ individuals in broader society (Maier 2020). LGBTQ activists advocated for an inclusive gender perspective that recognized the differential impacts the conflict had on women and sexual and gender minorities. As incredibly progressive as this action might have been, it was unfortunately omitted in the finalized peace agreement, as it was criticized by opponents as advancing gay rights, which they perceived to have nothing to do with the armed conflict (Lemay Langlois 2018: 118; see Oettler, this volume).

Despite this setback, LGBTQ activists continued to be involved with transitional justice processes, such as with the Colombian Victims' Unit, which included an LGBTQ category in its victim registry. This has come with its own setbacks. Reporting problems have emerged, as there is limited training for state functionaries on sexuality and gender. It is difficult to reach out to and inform disenfranchised LGBTQ communities about these services, and there is fear of prejudice and discrimination when self-identifying (Pascha Bueno-Hansen 2018). While overall murder rates have fallen to the lowest level in four decades since the signing of the peace agreement, there has been no such drop in the number of LGBTQ people murdered (Reuters 2020). Particularly vulnerable are Indigenous and/or Black sexual and gender minorities, as well as those living in poverty and those living in more rural parts of the country. As the chapters by Oettler and Serrano-Amya in this volume also demonstrate, Colombia's case shows that the gender and sexual hierarchies and societal prejudices against sexual and gender minorities remain despite greater inclusion of LGBTQ voices in transitional justice processes. Inclusion alone does not guarantee a shifting of a country's attitudes toward sexual and gender minorities.

Even when there are actions and legal provisions to address LGBTQ inequality in peace agreements, traditional sexual and gender norms and the institutions that support them may restrain progress toward enacting these provisions to the fullest degree. An example can be seen in Northern Ireland, where a concerted effort to address LGBTQ rights in the peace agreements led to the creation of the Northern Ireland Act and the Equality Commission. The Northern Ireland Act provided employment protections for sexual and gender minorities, while the Equality Commission was charged with protecting the employment rights and access to services for minorities, including LGBTQ individuals. The Northern Ireland Human Rights Commission was also in charge of overseeing discrimination and the protection of human rights in justice matters. Several legislative acts have also come about since the signing of the Good Friday Agreement, such as the Civil Partnership Act (2004) and the Equality Act (2006), ensuring legally recognized same-sex unions and civil rights protections. Despite the progress that has been made, many of the institutional bodies created and much of the legislation passed to protect LGBTQ individuals remain unused, and inequality remains high for sexual and gender minorities. Moral conservatism, religion, and ethnonationalism continue to hold significant power in Northern Ireland, further bolstered by exemptions and other protective measures to ensure that any progressive LGBTQ legislation passed has little authority and accountability (Schulz 2017; Hayes and Nagle 2019). Incorporating LGBTQ language into peace agreements, creating institutions to protect against discrimination, and even enacting legislation can bear little fruit without direct accountability. The exemptions for religious organizations in Northern Ireland to discriminate publicly against LGBTQ individuals work to further erode the meaningfulness of past efforts for equal protection and recognition. These actions lead to LGBTQ rights being recognized in name only and progressive legislation not being used effectively.

What happened in Northern Ireland points to the need for state accountability to enact legislation and hold institutions accountable. But where does this accountability come from if states are unwilling or have little incentive? International pressure on Bosnia and Herzegovina to address rising violence against minorities after signing the Dayton Agreement in 1995 led to the creation of hate crime legislation (Sarajevski Otvoreni Centar 2017). Sexual and gender minorities were included in its language, but there has been very little action from the government and police to address homophobic hate crimes. What little pressure there is comes from international organizations (Schulz 2017). This creates a narrative of LGBTQ rights as foreign, based on pressure from outside international bodies. State actors are unaccountable for LGBTQ rights, leaving an already-marginalized and vulnerable community susceptible to more violence.

These cases show the pressing need to critically analyze transitional justice processes and how successfully queer issues and rights are being addressed both within transitional justice processes and after they are completed. While progress has been made in including sexual and gender minority voices in transitional justice as well as incorporating language addressing discrimination and violence against LGBTQ individuals in peace agreements and subsequent legislation, inclusion does not automatically mean acceptance or full recognition of citizenship. It is therefore crucial to critically interrogate how successfully sexual and gender minorities are being included in transitional justice processes and how their rights are being addressed in post-conflict societies. With every new inclusion of LGBTQ voices in transitional justice, progress is made. However, inclusion alone cannot be the final step.

In the next section, I turn my attention to what I frame as pushing the conversation forward in queering transitional justice. Pushing the conversation forward is about returning to assumptions and blind spots within transitional justice, especially as they relate to sexual and gender minorities. I focus on greater inclusion of and engagement with LGBTQ refugees and displaced populations. The aim is to open up a space for dialogue and further research.

Moving Outside of National Boundaries: Actively Engaging LGBTQ Refugees and Displaced Populations

One of the major challenges in gaining greater inclusion and engagement of LGBTQ populations involves access to these communities. The everyday persecution that many queer individuals face means they may have to hide or relocate to avoid violence. This is especially true during periods of conflict and social unrest, as sexual and gender minorities are increasingly targeted by states and local actors. It creates a constant fear that fractures relationships and makes it difficult to create collective spaces and a sense of community (also see Myrttinen et al., this volume). Every interaction could lead to exposure and the potential for violence. Those who can be public about their sexual orientation and gender identity have their own set of privileges and circumstances that provide them resources or space to be open with outsiders. What, then, about the experiences of those not afforded these circumstances: those who had to flee for their own safety, or those living in the diaspora? How can their experiences and voices be better accounted for in transitional justice? What would bringing in queer displaced voices do for addressing anti-queer and gender-based violence in transitional justice processes?

Transitional justice holds an uneven track record in addressing internally and cross-border displaced persons. The field has mostly focused on internal institutions within national borders. The majority of transitional justice processes in post-conflict states have either ignored or purposely excluded forcibly displaced persons (Rimmer 2010). Likewise, displaced populations, forced migration, and the field of refugee protection have evolved into a mostly humanitarian enterprise (Hovil 2013). This depoliticizing of forced migration has disconnected internally and cross-border displaced people from the wider political context and violence that led to their exile, which in turn has meant limited access to or involvement in transitional justice processes happening in their countries of origin (Hovil 2013). However, not incorporating voices of refugees and displaced peoples is a missed opportunity for social repair and reconciliation.

Yet internally and cross-border displaced peoples are important witnesses to the violations that occur during conflict, as they experience persecution that forces them to flee. Including and engaging refugees and displaced persons in transitional justice and peace processes is incredibly important for sexual and gender minorities. Many of those claiming asylum on the basis of sexual orientation and gender identity identify political, social, and economic persecution brought on by conflict, social instability, and oppressive regimes. Forcing people to flee – and, in the process, become economically and socially vulnerable, losing all their social connections and safety nets – is another effect of persecution. This violence is rarely addressed in transitional justice. Including queer diasporas and internally displaced in transitional justice processes will better address not only violence within the national borders of a country but also the violence that sexual and gender minorities experience across borders. As Katie McQuaid's work on forcibly displaced sexual and gender minorities living in refugee camps in Western Uganda shows, persecution may increase once sexual and gender minorities cross borders (2020). Sexual and gender minority refugees become hyper-visual and vulnerable to social exclusion, predatory intentions, and anti-queer violence. LGBTQ asylum-seekers have reported being beaten, raped, robbed, and exploited in their host countries. While transitional justice processes have traditionally been nationally bound, addressing violence across borders may lead to greater accountability for international actors and neighboring states in peacebuilding and regional stability. At the very least, it would fully encapsulate the persecution that sexual and gender minorities face and extend the discussion of gender-based violence beyond what happens within the confines of national borders. The violence LGBTQ refugees experience abroad should be accounted for in transitional justice processes, as it is connected to the original violence and persecution that causes them to flee.

A number of factors can prevent inclusive engagement of LGBTQ refugees and internally displaced communities in transitional justice processes. Some of them are logistical and are the same problems facing the inclusion of any refugees and internally displaced populations in state peacebuilding and transitional justice efforts. Forced migration is chaotic, with limited international and national support systems assisting displaced people to resettle in new places or return to their countries of origin. Trying to connect with such a distressed population is always going to be challenging. There is the added concern for sexual and gender minorities' safety, especially in regards to their identities being publicly revealed in transitional justice processes. Disclosure always holds the potential for violence and social rejection for LGBTQ populations. Some who claim and are granted asylum based on sexual and gender identity (regardless of where they ultimately settle) may not wish for their identities to be revealed to their communities or families living in their countries of origin. This comes out of fear of rejection from their families or a fear of their families or loved ones being targeted because of them. There is also concern about revealing their sexual orientation or gender identity to those living around them in their host countries.

These are serious concerns, and any effort to engage with sexual and gender minority refugees and internally displaced communities must have participants' safety and well-being at the forefront. Working with local LGBTQ activists as well as LGBTQ networks abroad can help address these concerns and build community trust. Local LGBTQ community members and activists can be important gateways to connect with LGBTQ refugees and internally displaced peoples. In their role as advocates and community support, many have assisted or provided guidance to those needing to flee. Many of these organizations might maintain contact with those who left. Every LGBTQ person represents a chain of relationships with other queer individuals that cross state borders. Connecting with LGBTQ activists, having them guide facilitation and engagement, allows for greater engagement of queer communities abroad.

A great example can be seen in Sexual Minorities Uganda (SMUG), based in Kampala, which has a worldwide network of queer Ugandans living abroad supporting its efforts. Many of those participating in SMUG's activities online and abroad connected with the organization prior to migrating or after being resettled. Connecting with LGBTQ refugee organizations abroad can also be useful for engaging and connecting with sexual and gender minority refugees. An example is the African Centre for Refugees in Ontario, Canada, started by Christopher Nkambwe, a transgender refugee from Uganda. The goal of the organization is to assist and connect LGBTQ asylum seekers coming from African states. There are also organizations like the LGBT Refugee Project in the UK, the Refugee Law Project in Uganda, and Rainbow Refugee in Canada which work to assist those seeking asylum on the basis of sexual orientation and gender identity. Connecting with these organizations may also lead to greater inclusion of LGBTQ refugees and internally displaced persons, as they can serve as intermediaries and provide additional support to vulnerable participants.

Working with local LGBTQ rights organizations and international LGBTQ refugee organizations is the first step for greater inclusion of displaced and refugee sexual and gender minorities. More research on displaced queer populations and transitional justice is also needed. What would transitional justice look like across borders? How would queering transitional justice need to take into account migration and settlement? How would transitional justice address internal displacement due to anti-queer violence and persecution? These questions are all much-needed areas of investigation and ones that will push the mission to queer transitional justice further. Concerted efforts to incorporate forcibly displaced LGBTQ populations into the discussion will not only provide a deeper understanding of anti-queer violence and how it has affected a wide and diverse population but also amplify the voices of LGBTQ participants in the transitional justice process.

Final Thoughts: The Possibilities of Queering Transitional Justice

What is the future of queering transitional justice? Will there be continued engagement with queer theory and queer lives? What is the ultimate goal of transitional justice in societies that are misogynistic, racist, heteronormative, and transphobic? Could participating in transitional justice mechanisms lead to further vulnerability and revictimization for LGBTQ people? These are the questions that remain. While there has been progress in the field, a general reluctance to fully engage with queering remains. Progress has come at the expense of critically interrogating the complexities and intersectionalities of gender and sexuality beyond identity politics. Transitional justice is not alone in this, as the majority of human rights rhetoric is framed around liberal identity categories. It should be seen as neither a surprise nor an excuse to throw in the towel. Queering is needed more than ever to understand at a deeper level the systems of power and control that drive conflict and frame repair. It is this process of queering transitional justice, pushing it beyond identity categories to address systemic oppression, that will allow the field to return to its own assumptions and work toward a more transformative future.

While the future remains open with regards to queering transitional justice, as more and more local sexual and gender minorities take on leadership, representation of marginalized queer voices will continue to grow. Not only will there be more representation of queer voices in transitional justice, but hopefully, this will also lead to further centering of non-Western, Indigenous, and/or refugee LGBTQ voices in LGBTQ rights globally. This is important more than ever as globalization and capitalism have led to a global apartheid which further disenfranchises non-Western and Indigenous LGBTQ communities and creates barriers for them to fully participate on the international stage. Western LGBTQ politics continues to frame sexual and gender minority rights around the world, creating a colonial narrative of Western exceptionalism and an othering of queer lives outside of the West. Not only does this contribute to the further erasure of non-Western, Indigenous, and/or refugee LGBTQ voices, but it also robs us all of the important analysis and insights these populations have to contribute in targeting anti-queer violence. Centering marginalized queer voices in transitional justice contributes to larger queer decolonizing goals that, in turn, will benefit LGBTQ rights globally. Queering transitional justice is not just about transitional justice or just about sexual and gender minorities but instead a movement to dismantle hegemonic sexual and gender norms and hierarchies that impact us all.

References

Amnesty International (2020a). *Paraguay 2020*. Available at: https://www.amnesty.org/en/location/americas/southamerica/paraguay/report-paraguay/. Accessed on: 29 November 2021.

Amnesty International (2020b). *Brazil 2020*. Available at: https://www.amnesty.org/en/countries/americas/brazil/report-brazil/. Accessed on: 29 November 2021.

Anderson, M. E. (2019). Community-Based Transitional Justice Via the Creation and Consumption of Digitalized Storytelling Archives: A Case Study of Belfast's Prisons Memory Archive. *International Journal of Transitional Justice* 13(1): 30–49.

Baines, E. and B. Stewart (2011). 'I Cannot Accept What I Have Not Done': Storytelling, Gender and Transitional Justice. *Journal of Human Rights Practice* 3(3): 245–263.

Bueno-Hansen, P. (2018). The Emerging LGBTI Rights Challenge to Transitional Justice in Latin America. *International Journal of Transitional Justice* 12(1): 126–145.

Fobear, K. (2014). Queering Truth Commissions. *Journal of Human Rights Practice* 6(1): 51–68.

Hayes, B. C. and J. Nagle (2019). Ethnonationalism and Attitudes Towards Same-Sex Marriage and Abortion in Northern Ireland. *International Political Science Review* 40(4): 455–469.

Hovil, L. (2013). *The Nexus between Displacement and Transitional Justice: A Gender-Justice Dimension*. ICTJ & the Brookings-LSE Project on Internal Displacement. Available at: https://www.ictj.org/sites/default/files/ICTJ-Research-Brief-Displacement-Gender-Hovil.pdf. Accessed on: 3 December 2021.

Izquierdo, B. and L. Viaene (2018). Decolonizing Transitional Justice from Indigenous Territories. *Peace in Progress 34*. Available at: https://www.ohchr.org/Documents/Issues/IPeoples/SR/IPAndJustice/22-LViaene.pdf. Accessed on: 29 November 2021.

Johnston, L. and R. Longhurst (2009). *Space, Place and Sex: Geographies of Sexualities*. Lanham, MD: Rowman and Littlefield.

Ketelaars, E. (2018). Gendering Tunisia's Transition: Transformative Gender Justice Outcomes in Times of Transitional Justice Turmoil? *International Journal of Transitional Justice* 12(3): 407–426.

Lemay Langlois, L. (2018). Gender Perspective in UN Framework for Peace Processes and Transitional Justice: The Need for a Clearer and More Inclusive Notion of Gender. *International Journal of Transitional Justice* 12(1): 146–167.

Lopez, O. (2020). *Ecuador's LGBT+ Community Seen Suffering Deadliest Year in a Decade*. New York: Reuters. Available at: https://www.reuters.com/article/us-ecuador-lgbt-murder/ecuadors-lgbt-community-seen-suffering-deadliest-year-in-a-decade-idUSKBN1ZK2I8. Accessed on: 29 November 2021.

Love Not Hate Campaign (2016). *Hate Crimes Against Lesbian, Gay, Bisexual and Transgender (LGBT) People in South Africa*. Available at: https://out.org.za/wp-content/uploads/2020/10/Hate-Crimes-Against-LGBT-People-in-South-Africa-21-November-2016-Web.pdf. Accessed on: 29 November 2021.

Maier, N. (2020). Queering Colombia's Peace Process: A Case Study of LGBTI Inclusion. *The International Journal of Human Rights* 24(4): 377–392.

Matsunaga, J. (2016). Two Faces of Transitional Justice: Theorizing the Incommensurability of Transitional Justice and Decolonization in Canada. *Decolonization: Indigeneity, Education & Society* 5(1): 24–44.

McQuaid, K. (2020). 'There Is Violence Across, in All Arenas': Listening to Stories of Violence Amongst Sexual Minority Refugees in Uganda. *The International Journal of Human Rights* 24(4): 313–334.

Myrttinen, H., A. Gibbs, L. Washington, Y. Sikweyiya and R. Jewkes (2020). Constructing, Reproducing and Challenging Masculinities in a Participatory Intervention in Urban Informal Settlements in South Africa. *Culture, Health & Sexuality* 22(5): 535–550.

Naber, N. and Z. Zaatari (2014). Reframing the War on Terror: Feminist and Lesbian, Gay, Bisexual, Transgender, and Queer (LGBTQ) Activism in the Context of the 2006 Israeli Invasion of Lebanon. *Cultural Dynamics* 26(1): 91–111.

Nagel, J. (2000). Ethnicity and Sexuality. *Annual Review of Sociology* 26(1): 107–133.

Park, A. S. (2020). Settler Colonialism, Decolonization and Radicalizing Transitional Justice. *International Journal of Transitional Justice* 14(2): 260–279.

Payne, W. J. (2016). Death-Squads Contemplating Queers as Citizens: What Colombian Paramilitaries Are Saying. *Gender, Place & Culture* 23(3): 328–344.

Rao, R. (2014). The Locations of Homophobia. *London Review of International Law* 2(2): 169–199.

Reuters (2020). *More Than 60 LGBT, Intersex People Killed in Colombia in First Eight Months of 2020*. New York: Reuters. Available at: https://www.reuters.com/article/us-colombia-lgbt/more-than-60-lgbt-intersex-people-killed-in-colombia-in-first-eight-months-of-2020-idUSKBN26634G. Accessed on: 29 November 2021.

Rimmer, S. H. (2010). Reconceiving Refugees and Internally Displaced Persons (IDPs) as Transitional Justice Actors. *Contemporary Readings in Law and Social Justice* 2(2): 163–180.

Sarajevski Otvoreni Centar (2017). *Pink Report 2017: Hate Crime and Incitement to Hatred*. Available at: https://soc.ba/en/hate-crime-and-incitement-to-hatred/. Accessed on: 29 November 2021.

Schulz, W. (2017). *Queering Peace Deals and Sustainable Peace*. Master Thesis. Leiden, NL: University of Leiden.

Serrano-Amaya, J. F. (2017). *Homophobic Violence in Armed Conflict and Political Transition*. Cham, Switzerland: Palgrave Macmillan.

Sharp, D. N. (2019). What Would Satisfy Us? Taking Stock of Critical Approaches to Transitional Justice. *International Journal of Transitional Justice* 13(3): 570–589.

United Nations (2015). *Ending Violence And Discrimination Against Lesbian, Gay, Bisexual, Transgender and Intersex People*. New York. Available at: https://www.ohchr.org/Documents/Issues/Discrimination/Joint_LGBTI_Statement_ENG.PDF. Accessed on: 29 November 2021.

Section 2

Theories, Processes, and Practices – Toward Inclusive Gender in TJ

Chapter 4

"Queering" Transitional Justice From African Decolonial Perspectives?

Katharina Hoffmann and Thokozani Mbwana

Introduction

The importance of gender perspectives in transitional justice theories, policies, and practices has gained momentum within the last years (Martin de Almagro and Schulz 2022). In recent years, there has also been a slow but emerging turn to move toward the recognition of multiple aspects of the nexus between gender, sex, and desire beyond an equation of "gender" with "women and girls" across the field of TJ (O'Rourke 2017; United Nations 2020a; Oosterveld 2018; Margalit 2018). Gender issues and a variety of collective identity constructions and ascriptions have also been included in *Transitional Justice Policy* of the African Union (AU) and further intergovernmental African agreements and policies concerning peace and security programs and strategies (AU 2019; Merwe and Masiko 2020; Hendricks 2017). Yet sexualized violence against men and the particular problems and the marginalization and oppression of *queer* people have not been addressed in these efforts. This omission is worrying, given that the African Commission on Human and Peoples' Rights (ACHPR), with the adoption of *Principles and Guidelines on the Implementation of Economic, Social and Cultural Rights in the African Charter* in 2011, referred to "sex, gender, sexual orientation" as ground of discrimination. This instrument also specifically considered "lesbian, gay, bisexual, transgendered and intersex people" as "[v]ulnerable and disadvantaged groups . . . who have faced and/or continue to face significant impediments to their enjoyment of economic, social and cultural rights" (ACHPR 2011: 8).

However, internationally circulating narratives of progress on gender-sensitive TJ approaches with references to human rights and the *rule of law as the principle of governance* (United Nations 2020b) often ignore the polysemy of sex/gender and justice in different geopolitical and cultural settings. In contrast to dominant understandings, critical scholars and activists in different world regions insist on a broader understanding of concepts of justice beyond (neo)liberal framings and universalism (Gathii 2020; Johnson and Hamandishe Karekwaivanane 2018). This also concerns times of

DOI: 10.4324/9781003519522-6

transition, where globalized TJ concepts have been harshly criticized for reproducing colonial power structures and aiming at implementations of representative democracies in line with neoliberal ideas and capitalist economic orders (Madlingozi 2010; Sott 2017; Gready and Robins 2019; Kurze and Lamont 2021; Moyo 2019).

In response to these critiques, critical approaches intend to move toward forms of transformative justice which meet specific ideas and needs in particular post-conflict settings and address structural inequities on all – social, political, and economic – levels. In this vein, processes of justice look at regional and local perspectives, experiences, ideas, and normative frameworks. The focus of these approaches often rests on the active inclusion of grassroots and subalterns for initiating processes of radical change (see, for example, Gready and Robins 2019; Rooney and Ní Aoláin 2018; Okello et al. 2012; Shaw et al. 2010). This is especially true for justice concepts and processes that not only take into account the multi-dimensional aspects of gender/sex/desire in and after recent conflicts, mass atrocities, or dictatorships but which have also considered colonial repercussions and recent entanglements with global power regimes (Rolston and Ní Aoláin 2018).

Against this background, it is important to acknowledge and incorporate post- and decolonial thinking[1] as an essential tool to criticize current dominant TJ concepts and practices as well as to ensure that we create alternatives that take into account the socio-political statuses of post-conflict states. More specifically, post- and decolonial lenses are important avenues to discuss and reimagine ways of restructuring the social fabric by dismantling gendered orders based on continuities or new forms of domination, oppression, and subjection. Decolonial analytical tools and already-available decolonial knowledge are urgently needed to deconstruct the production of sexual minorities from local standpoints and address the past and present harms and oppressions of people who are categorized as deviant or are abjected. This implies the necessity to do research and develop programs toward gender justice in cooperations with decolonial scholars, activists, and grassroots actors within, from, and for the particular contexts. Currently, post- and decolonial approaches in TJ discourses and practices are limited but have entered the academic discourse since a couple of years (see, for example, Bueno-Hansen 2015; Moyo 2019; Rolston and Ní Aoláin 2018; Maddison and Shepherd 2013). It is indeed questionable if TJ, with

1 We refer to both post- and decolonial approaches which have been developed in and between different geopolitical regions. Both overlap (see, for example, Bhambra 2014) and have travelled further. The plethora of theories offers a toolkit for the analyses of the aftermath of colonialism and its continuities and new forms of domination. We primarily use the term "decolonial" to make reading easier.

its normative assumptions for political change without the democratization of socio-economic orders (Franzki and Olarte 2014; Merwe and Brinton Lykes 2020), can be re-evaluated and give space for post- and decolonial concepts of justice from local perspectives. Nevertheless, we think it is crucial to discuss such perspectives in relation to restructuring gendered orders in accordance with multiple constructions of the nexus of gender/sex/desire. Instead of completely rejecting globalized TJ approaches, we think Spivak's idea of *affirmative sabotage* – using "the master's tools to dismantle the master's house" – (Davis et al. 2019; Dhawan 2014: 71) can contribute to the critical TJ discourse. "[T]ransitional contexts create," as Khanyisela Moyo argues from a postcolonial legal perspective, "opportunities for postcolonial agency which is made possible by both the ambivalence of the master's discourse and the Other's resistance to hegemony" (Moyo 2019: 188–189). Crucial for counter-discourses are intersectional and intercultural methodologies for not only addressing times of conflict and war but also continuing structural oppressions and injustices beyond the "Western bias in international law" that promotes "civil and political rights" (Moyo 2019: 3). This demands decentering gender-sensitive TJ concepts biased by liberal understandings of gender justice and its inclusion of *queers*. Decolonial shifts are necessary to initiate broader processes of justice based on investigations of the particular past and present of local and regional contexts.

In the following, we discuss the limitations and challenges of terms signifying (non)heteronormative people and delineate the critiques of dominant Western perspectives on the nexus gender/sex/desire in TJ processes in African contexts. We, the authors of the chapter, are activist-scholars situated in different academic, disciplinary, civil, and geopolitical contexts. From our perspective, discussions and critical approaches in TJ must be based on reflections on one's situatedness and, thus, limited perspectives in knowledge production. This contributes to fruitful cooperations between the possible linkages as well as differences of outsider and insider positions aiming at concepts of justice appropriate to the respective societies. The current debate among scholars and activists shows that US American and European concepts are not appropriate to capture complex realities of gendered orders outside their region. Typical for such concepts are not only blind spots but also perpetuating US–European domination. In order to comprehend the complexities in African contexts, it is crucial to be aware of the colonial imposition of gender regimes and their aftermath. With putting "queering" in quotation marks, we indicate the necessity to scrutinize in which ways (components of) *queer* theory, as other critical theories, developed in Western contexts, contribute, and miss decolonized epistemologies. In doing so, we keep in mind "the potential of theorising to do violence" (Biruk 2020: 493). Furthermore, it is important to be aware of the ambivalences of homophobia in Africa: international campaigns have been intertwined with processes of othering, and at the same time, violence and discrimination against *queers* are a serious problem in African countries. These analytical deliberations lead to decolonial perspectives on gender justice. Finally, we scrutinize in which ways justice from bottom-up processes meets decolonial perspectives. Bottom-up processes are often seen as a crucial approach for developing alternative TJ instruments, by acknowledging local perspectives and including grassroots people (Schulz 2019).

Limitations and Challenges of Circulating Terms for People Outside Heteronormativity

Queer has been used as an umbrella term for non-heteronormative sexualities and genders in Western political movements and theory but has also travelled to other world regions. Once a word for derogatory ascription, then converted to a positive meaning used by social movements of people who were unintelligible and objected within dominant sexual and gender regimes, *queer* has increasingly gained influence in African activism, politics, and academia (Ngidi et al. 2020). Vasu Reddy, Surya Monro, and Zethu Matebeni see *queer* as a signifier for "non-heterosexual and non-gender binaried people, including those who identify as lesbian, gay bisexual, transgender (LGBT)" (Reddy et al. 2018: 1). In other words, they are aware of identity constructions that have travelled from Western contexts to African ones, but do not exclusively link the term to identity constructions. Activists inside, but also outside, Africa have also appropriated (or rejected) acronyms of LGBT/Q/I/A+ to raise awareness of the precarious living conditions in gender regimes which ostracize, stigmatize, and criminalize people who do not follow the prescribed gender/sex normative (Rao 2020). However, it is questionable that one term allows to catch all forms of complexity in different contexts. This also concerns the term *people with diverse sexual orientation, gender identities, and sex expressions* (SOGIESC), which originated from international human rights discourses (George et al. 2021: 5; Daigle and Myrttinen 2018) and which is the terminology adopted by most authors in this volume (see "Introduction"). All terms which are in use have "a history, reflecting power relations and attempts to navigate contested spaces, and each compromises by emphasising some attributes over (or to the exclusion of) others" (George et al. 2021: 4).

In order to recognize diversities between groups and the multiple local/Indigenous concepts intertwined with gender/sex/desire, scholars and activists have preferred local significations or self-descriptions of same-gender/sex relationships (Matebeni and Msibi 2015; Matebeni et al. 2018; Nyeck 2020). Local or Indigenous references have been helpful to emphasize the diversity of understandings of the nexus between gender/sex/desire beyond identity regimes and politics. However, Rahul Rao (2020) points to the limitation of such strategies by discussing the understandings of and politics aligned with *kuchus* (Swahili word for *same*) for people outside the heterosexual box in Uganda. He concludes:

> The inadequacies of both queer and *kuchu* as comprehensive placeholders for gender and sexual non-normativity point to the limits of language and signification itself, suggesting that we ought to be more interested in the work that such placeholders do than in conjuring unimpeachable signs for them.
>
> (Rao 2020: 28)

Moreover, as Zethu Matebeni, Surya Monro, Vasu Reddy argue, "local terms . . . can be both stigmatising and/or empowering" (Matebeni et al. 2018: 81). To put it differently, we should scrutinize in which contexts and by whom the terms are used and understood. Having said that, it is also important to underline, with Manuela L. Picq (2019: 169), that

> [g]lobal sexual rights frameworks did not introduce referents to recognize alternative sexualities; Indigenous languages already had them, as their terminologies indicate. Indigenous sexualities both predate and defy contemporary LGBTI and queer frameworks. It is not the idioms that are untranslatable but the cultural and political fabric they represent.

Nevertheless, Desiree Lewis reminds us that "language use, terminology and theory have become irrevocably creolised." She demands to acknowledge hybridizations and "develop 'new' contestatory modes and theories" (Lewis 2004: 31).

In academic as well as in political discourses, it has been ignored that the term *queer* signifies not only different gender and sexual identities as political identities claiming recognition, decriminalization, and civil rights. The term also stands for a radical critique of identity politics, based on clear-cut gender/sex identities, and a strong challenge to gender essentialism (Rao 2020: 26–30; Matebeni et al. 2018; Msibi 2011). Since the 1990s, *queer theory*, coined by the Italian American feminist theorist Teresa de Lauretis, has contributed to critical epistemologies to deconstruct sex/gender normativities within regimes of power and subjection (also see Akı, this volume). Zethu Matebeni and Jabu Pereira (2014: 9) refer to the critical stance of *queer* with reference to Judith Butler's reflection in her essay "Critically Queer." Here she argues that the meaning of *queer* is contested and will

> never [be] fully owned, but always and only redeployed, twisted, queered from a prior usage and in the direction of urgent and expanding political purposes, and perhaps also yielded in favor of terms that do that political work more effectively.
>
> (Butler 1993: 9)

Kirk Fiereck, Neville Hoad, and Danai S. Mupotsa refer in their epistemological deliberations on "queerness from/within Africa" to Western theorizing. However, they stress "queer theory's Euro-American silent ethnocentrisms" and "secret normativities" like "an unmarked (secret) normative assemblage of personhood." From their perspective, *queer* can be understood as a process, as "queering-to-come" (Fiereck et al. 2020: 365, 364, 368, 363). Here it is urgent

> to understand where specific idioms and forms of cultural particularity – such as the antinormativity debates, customary forms, traditionalisms, and tribalisms – overlap and, most critically, where precisely they diverge.
> (Fiereck et al. 2020: 368)

In short, our understanding of "queering" refers to analyzing and coping with the entanglements of gender/sex/desire, power, domination, subjectivation, and marginalization in particular contexts. In this vein, we think that it is crucial that researchers and practitioners reflect on the colonial legacies of imposed gender regimes in societies, their own situatedness, and the limitations of concepts used. This is a basic prerequisite for the perception of different relationship structures and community formations. Moreover, it allows to capture the simultaneity of recognition and objection of globally circulating identity concepts by various actors in certain settings.

Sex(uality) and Gender in African Contexts

Reflections on the terms used in TJ gender-sensitive discourses with its current inclusion or demands for addressing *queer* people bring to light the bias of signifying terms not only for the latter but also for the basic ones used. If we respect the agency of those people who are addressed during transition periods, we have to ask for knowledge about colonial repercussions and, for instance, the effects of structural adjustments within particular contexts, instead of using prefabricated programs for revising gender regimes.

Having this in mind, it is crucial to take notice that the term *sexuality* and its intertwinement with *gender* have been problematized as Western constructions imposed on colonized people and still affecting contemporary postcolonial gender regimes in Africa. African feminist scholars and activists remind us of the close ties between sexuality and gender regimes in time and place, the various structures of power, dominance, and subjectivation in (previously) colonizing and (previously) colonized societies. At the same time, precolonial ways of intimate and social relationship have continued to shape modes of life. Consequently, there is no universal meaning of gender and sex; instead, we should avoid essentialism and develop methodologies that acknowledge multiple forms of sex/gender constellations despite the imposition of racist Western heterosexual gender regimes in the colonies (Tamale

2011, 2020; Hendriks and Spronk 2020; Gething 2015; Ekine and Abbas 2013; Feminist Africa 2005, 2006; Signe 2004). This includes the recognition of local and localized forms of (tacit) knowledge and speaking about meanings and interpretations of intimacy, eroticism, and desire within the respective gender regimes. In deference to Western contexts with an emphasis of speaking out and problematizing silence, "in many African cultures silence can be as powerful and as empowering as speech" (Tamale 2011: 13). Like Desiree Lewis (2004), Sylvia Tamale urges us to develop "home-grown theories of African sexuality" (Tamale 2011: 25). Yet she reminds us with reference to Bibi Bakare-Yusuf: "For millennia, Africa has been part of Europe, as Europe has been part of Africa, and out of this relation, a whole series of borrowed traditions from both sides has been and continues to be brewed and fermented" (quoted from Tamale 2011: 25). In many postcolonial African states, "the general social and legal structure . . . is based on a Western model" (Tamale 1999: 30). This includes continuations of imposed gendered divisions of labor as well as heterosexual orders. Recently, Tamale has re-emphasized in her theoretical deliberations on "decolonization and Afro-feminism" that the colonial "dual sex/gender system took over African Indigenous arrangements and understandings which were more pluralistic, elastic and accommodating" (Tamale 2020: 100). Referring to María Lugones's concept of the *coloniality of gender*, which stresses the interconnection of domination, racialization, and the governance of bodies and subjectivities, Tamale requests a decolonial shift in opposition to concepts of gender, neglecting, or even erasing, the particular historical contexts of gender regimes and their repercussions. This implies a critical view on the modernization of concepts in line with neoliberal politics.

The increasing advocacy for LGBT/Q/I/+ rights as human rights on a global scale has become a powerful tool for activists in Africa to get recognition and support. In this frame, NGOs have become an important vehicle for the diverse African (trans)national *queer* movements. Yet external funding, the NGO-ization of social and political activism, requires particular patterns of action, evaluation, and accountability compatible with the human rights regime and neoliberal forms of life (Currier and Cruz 2014; Bennett and Reddy 2015; Biruk 2020). The current globally propagated rights-based approaches go along with identity politics, which mold new identities. For example, Serena Owusua Dankwa (2021) encountered in her research on same-sex relations of working-class women in Ghana the request of an NGO leader for clear-cut lesbian identities. She writes: "He appealed to me to raise their consciousness by 'educating' them about 'who they are' – conveying, thereby, that the fullest and most liberating expression of loving a woman as a woman was to develop a sexual identity" (Dankwa 2021: 14). In contrast, she contacted many women who "were either unfamiliar or uncomfortable with terms like 'queer', 'lesbian', and 'bisexual' or simply did not provide the space for a 'coming out' narrative" (Dankwa 2021: 15).

This observation meets Tamale's statement that "Indigenous conceptualizations of same-sex erotics generally had no desire to pin them down or to burden them with identities; they kept its content in flux and left it elusive" Tamale 2020: 104). She stresses "'secrecy' in African sexualities" in opposition to "Western norms around the need for legitimate 'sex' to be public (i.e., out)." In other words, "inconspicuous sexual and gendered variance" have been possible "modes of being" (Tamale 2020: 105).

Thus, political activism in line with international advocacy for *queer* identities marginalizes same-sex intimacies outside the Western concept(s) of non-heteronormativity. As Henriette Gunkel (2010: 134) points out, the "metropolitan model . . . of a public lesbian identity has a restrictive effect on the forms of same-sex intimacy such as 'mummy-baby' relationships[2] but also women marriages.'" From her point of view, "the constitution and the interpretation of rights in post-apartheid South Africa is not a product of a wider deconstruction of the sexuality apparatus and its sex/gender regime, the major technologies of power that underwrote colonialism and apartheid" (Gunkel 2010: 135).

Binary understandings of gender and sexuality, which are also part of the human rights discourse, support and stabilize essentialist identities and subjectivities. In doing so, the past and present of fluid gender constructions and relations, even within heterosexual regimes, are overlooked or reinterpreted in dominant conceptions of gender and sex. For example, existing male homoerotic practices in Congolese cities, which do not question heterosexual family constellations, show the difficulties of clear-cut terms and identities (Hendriks 2018). Such a coexistence of same-sex relationships within heterosexual gender regimes questions the terms *heteronormativity* and *homonormativity*. Consequently, research, politics, and advocacy have to be aware about the "limited assumptions about sexuality and sexual practices, and that points to possibilities for alliances, sociality, and kinship, also within queer communities" (Gunkel 2013: 76). In this vein, one has to be aware of, for example, local living arrangements and "the various forms of temporary and patchwork household arrangements," which remain invisible "when applying a heterosexual nuclear family lens only" (Mertens and Myrttinen 2019: 9). Furthermore, a large amount of representations of sexual minorities in conflict zones categorize people according to "the assumptions of 'belonging' from the perspective of the center" (Moore and Barner 2017: 34) and thus empower particular speech acts and silence others. This goes along with representations of helpless victims which erase other axes of oppression and privilege or the messiness of living conditions in conflict zones.

2 Following Gunkel (2010), the term refers to a cultural form of female same-sex intimate relationship.

In short, scholars and practitioners should be aware of current distorted interpretations of realities. Yet Rachel Spronk and Thomas Hendriks underline that "a more radical unthinking of sexuality seems necessary." We should "open up conditions of possibility for *thinking sex otherwise*, triggered by and dedicated to the many ways people on the African continent themselves live, feel, and think about sex" (Hendriks and Spronk 2020: 5, emphasis in the original) However, the *coloniality of power* still marginalizes the production and circulation of knowledge on gender, sexuality, and justice from the *Global South* and promotes in particular findings that are intelligible for *Western eyes* within neoliberal frames of knowledge production (Mohanty 1988; Brown and Browne 2016).

In contrast to such knowledge production, conceptualizing gender justice demands the inclusion of decolonial epistemologies and alliances with different actors aiming at processes of justice to overcome oppression and marginalization in line with the paradigm of responsibility for the other. In this frame, particular policies dedicated to the vulnerability of *queer* people remain shortsighted, because they do not only separate groups of people but also neglect the linkages to other issues of justice and the possible alliances between groups of people.

Difficult Terrains: *African Homophobia*

Anti-homosexual laws and public discourses of homosexuality as *un-African* in many, but not all, African countries make it extremely difficult to dismantle nationalistic heterosexual social orders and initiate processes of gender-just social orders. In other words, the imposed heterosexual gender regimes with anti-homosexual penal codes during colonialism still show "the effects of colonization in modern subjectivities and modern forms of life" (Maldonado-Torres 2007: 261–262) Yet the legacies of colonialism, the current anti-homosexual biased variations of the *coloniality of gender*, differ in and between Africa regions, not at least because of the difference of European colonial governance and their gender regimes on local societies with a variety of social, political, economic, and cultural structures.

The recent waves of homophobia have been caused by external as well as internal factors. It is well-known that they stem from the politics of conservative, in particular US–American factions within Christian churches and/or from the transnational politics of fundamentalist Islamic groups (Tabengwa and Waites 2019; see for Uganda in detail Rao 2020; Tamale 2020: 181–186). On a global scale, not only "religious groups act as the guardians of morality to stop people living their sexualities" but also activists for sexual rights as civil and human rights (Seckinelgin 2012: 552). It should be mentioned that although the penal codes were usually not abolished in postcolonial African countries, the persecution of same-sex relations was not always the rule. Yet anti-homosexual political campaigns have become a serious issue with the increase of HIV/AIDS in a number of African countries since the 1990s. At the same time, African governments (e.g., South Africa, Lesotho, Mozambique, Seychelles) have decriminalized same-sex relations, or in other countries, existing laws are still not applied. In other words, the living conditions of *queer* people in Africa differ considerably (Tabengwa and Waites 2019; Mendos 2019: 87–99).

The public outcries and rallies of Western countries about homophobia in African countries usually revive the old colonial narrative that represents the Global North as the civilized world region which has saved, in this case, *queer* people from the dark, unenlightened continent. This – what is also described by the notion of *homonationalism*, introduced by Jasbir Puar (Rao 2020: 11–12) – calls for an implementation of rights for *queer* people but separates such rights further from issues of justice. Concerning international strategies to change political regimes in the *Global South*, *homocapitalism*, "an ideology forged in interaction between elite LGBT activists and technocrats in international financial institutions (IFIs) such as the World Bank and the International Monetary Fund (IMF)," has gained importance (Rao 2020: 25). Rao emphasizes that "homocapitalism offers a powerful and arguably more sophisticated alternative to homonationalism's heavy-handed tropes of civilisation and barbarism that tend to arouse anti-imperialist resistance" (Rao 2020: 151). *Homocapitalism* calls upon *queer* subjectivities within the frame of consumption and human capital. Although sharing key points with *homonationalism*, *homocapitalism* seems to be a more effective strategy with its promise of "a rosy future redolent with growth and productivity should a state embrace LGBT rights" (Rao 2020: 12).

However, the homophobic attitudes and politics in African countries cannot be reduced to the effects of global guardians and powers. Even some sections of African feminist theory and women's movements support anti-homosexual attitudes and politics (Graneß et al. 2019: 163). The labelling of homosexuality as *un-African* is helpful to keep conservative African politicians in power based on patriarchal gender orders and distracting main factions of the population from urgent issues (Msibi 2011). Recently, a study about violence against *queer* people in Namibia and South Africa shows that "[s]pace in Southern African countries is continuously constructed as heterosexual, putting queer individuals at risk of violence" (Ngidi et al. 2020: 18). This suggests that even with decriminalizing policies, as in the case of South Africa, societies remain at odds with accepting and living with gender- and sexually diverse populations. Yet it is important to note in which ways violence intersects with other axes of oppression. The study highlights that "[p]oor, black, township/rural dwellers, who are gender non-conforming and female-identifying, are perceived as at greatest risk of queerphobic violence" (Ngidi et al. 2020: 28). This highlights the continued difficulty *queer* individuals face in navigating both "liberal" and conservative societies as well as the implications of the nuanced experiences through identity, race, and physical presentation that impact which *queer* individuals could potentially engage in TJ processes in safer ways and which queer individuals cannot, that is, cisgender–homosexual individuals versus transgender individuals.

Gender Justice

The rich literature on transformative gender justice shows that "the task of transforming gender orders is not starting terra nullis, but has had decades – nay, centuries – of practice," as Fionnuala Ní Aoláin (2019: 164) states. Yet although "the polysemy of both the notion of 'gender' and of 'justice'" (Buckley-Zistel and Zolkos 2012: 5) has been acknowledged, in-depth research on local and regional sex/gender knowledge as well as visions of transformative gender justice are not prevalent. Moreover, concepts of gender justice often operate within gender binaries despite their requests for radical transformations (El Awady 2015; Goetz 2007; Bueno-Hansen in this volume). Nevertheless, there is a growing awareness that gendered justice necessitates to deconstruct hegemonic gender/sex regimes within long-term processes of justice (Shackel and Fiske 2019).

However, established perspectives on gender in transitional justice research and politics hinder an interrogation into substantial differences of local concepts beyond the recognition of the vernacularization of human rights frames with their specification of women's and LGBTQ rights (Levitt and Merry 2017). The new regional instrument of the AU, the *AU Transitional Policy*, addresses questions of gender but remains silent on radical forms of transformative (gender) justice. In this frame, *gender justice* refers in particular "to transform[ing] fundamental gender biases in transitional societies that hinder women from claiming and enjoying their socio-economic and political rights" (AU 2019: 3, 11).

Decolonial thinking requires not only a revision of gender concepts and the dismantling of the coloniality of gender but also a general revision of justice concepts. This includes critiques of rights-based approaches and the *rule of the law* as guiding principle. Desiree Lewis (2008: 77) is concerned about "the growth of moderate rights-based discourses" in different regions of the world. She states for South Africa:

> Where the language of gender transformation was formerly marked by a climate in which the class, regional and racial political interests of particular women drove them to struggle for distinct agendas for social transformation, our current rights-based discourse assumes that melioristic and state-engineered transformation can grant rights and entitlements in terms of generalised notions of what "women" of South Africa need and want. These abrupt changes in the first decade of democracy have gone hand in glove with a veering away from the notion of "justice", towards a veneration of "rights". "Rights" have levelling and universalised legal meaning. "Justice",

> on the other hand, is far broader, and implies a holistic understanding of ways in which certain groups and institutions can prevent others from realising their different liberties. Speaking for 'rights' can occur within the framework of formal procedures that ensure the nominal access of all to certain platforms or resources, without comprehensively considering whether all relationships and structures in society actually guarantee this access.
>
> (Lewis 2008: 82–83)

In a similar vein, Sylvia Tamale argues that

> [i]nstead of waving the Bill of Rights or CEAW for ordinary wananchi [folk] when discussing justice for women, couching the values in Indigenous terms that emphasise, for example, the fact that when you humiliate and diminish a woman (or a man for that matter), you are also diminished as part of the greater whole.
>
> (Tamale 2020: 230)

She underscores the necessity to focus on "the structural foundations of gender injustice . . . to address institutionalized forms of oppression such as sexism and racism" (Tamale 2020: 219, 220) and, what we suggest to include and emphasize, the structural dimensions that produce sexual minorities as deviant or abjected people. In doing so, it is important to be aware of the linkages between identity politics of single groups and the "coloniality of power," as they address aspects of justice within a given, reformed, or desired system in the interest of dominant global powers. Thus, broader alliances are needed to think and act beyond liberal notions of social equality (Tamale 2020: 206–207). In this vein, "The African LGBTI Manifesto" from 2010 demands "a re-imagination of our lives outside neo-colonial categories of identity and power" and situates the struggle for queer people within a broader frame. "As Africans," it reads "we stand for the celebration of our complexities and we are committed to ways of being which allow for self-determination at all levels of our sexual, social, political and economic lives." (Consequently, the demands for justice are not limited to *queer* people, but the "need for total liberation" requires economic, environmental, racial and ethnic, and erotic justice (Queer African Manifesto 2010)). As Varyanne Sika and Awino Okech put it: "The queering of societies is an attempt not only to liberate those who declare to be queer but also to transform all African struggles, to invest all African struggles against oppression with the fullest and truest revolutionary potential of the queer" (Sika and Okech 2019: 16). Thus, Jane Bennett and Vasu Reddy underline that "the struggle for lgbti justice" cannot be separated from decolonial and anti-neoliberal struggles it is deeply intertwined with (Bennett and Reddy 2015: 20).

As a matter of principle, it should also be recalled that the epistemological decolonization of justice shifts "from the paradigm of equality to the paradigm of responsibility for the other" (Graness 2015: 134). The latter paradigm is rooted in the ethical concept *Ubuntu*, to which African philosophers refer in their concepts of justice (Graness 2015). *Ubuntu* is an important reference point for the Ugandan scholar and feminist Sylvia Tamale. She understands *Ubuntu* as "the closest equivalent to the notion of 'human rights' in many African societies" (Tamale 2020: 221). In contrast to human rights with their basis on liberal philosophical ideas of personhood, Tamale highlights the common maxim expressed in the worldview of many Africans as *I am because you are*. In other words, an individual is seen "as an inherently-communal being, embedded in social relationships" (Tamale 2020: 224). For Tamale, *Ubuntu* is a useful tool, with its "moral and ethical foundation" of respecting each other, for achieving gender justice, "albeit after a careful interrogation and historicization of the concept itself" (Tamale 2020: 227, 229). Thus, *Ubuntu* encompasses understandings beyond its use during the transition in South Africa, stressing forgiveness and human dignity and neglecting the continuity of privileges and power relations (for a discussion of various perspectives on *Ubuntu*, see Moyo 2021).

Legal rights approaches, the rule of law to guarantee just gendered orders, do not meet the necessities of transforming justice in decolonial ways. Consequently, rights for *queer* people in frames of *homocapitalism* promote models of queer subjectivity as beneficiaries of economic growth and limit the potential for initiating transformative changes in times of transition. Fundamental shifts are needed that meet concepts of justice which understand personhood within the frame of inextricable links between the individual and others. Yet transforming gender orders remains a difficult endeavor, in particular in societies without regime changes, with political elites responsible for mass atrocities and promoting homophobia – such as in Uganda. In such environments, it is challenging to create safe spaces for activists and encourage public discussions about a broad understanding of gender justice. In particular, in such settings, even the recognition of sexualized violence against men and boys can lead to social stigmatizations of survivors, who fear to be criminalized as homosexuals (Schulz 2020; Edström et al. 2016). Moreover, disregarding the respective local situation can seriously endanger *queer* people and neglect forms of queerness outside the defined box (Seckinelgin 2012). In other words, it is crucial to be aware of the diverse challenges, but also possibilities for queer people within existing gender orders, based on different understandings of the terms and links between gender/sexuality/desire.

Toward a Justice From Bottom-Up Processes

The potentials and limitations of bottom-up processes have been a central point in TJ discourses (Martin 2016). Yet the perspectives on such processes have been linked to different approaches. In critical TJ approaches, the "local" is understood as a standpoint, as "the shifted centre from which the rest of the world is viewed" (Shaw and Waldorf 2010: 6, 26). Simultaneously, local justice notions – referring to "traditional, informal, or otherwise non-Western modalities of justice" (Sharp 2017: 144) – have gained importance in dominant approaches in order to gain acceptance for transitional justice programs by local communities (Sharp 2017: 142, 143). Regardless of different objectives, the preference for the local and the prioritization of bottom-up processes need to be analyzed with regard to the influence on transition processes by external guardians and global powers.

Nevertheless, the centrality of *the local* in critical approaches can be linked to decolonial perspectives. For example, Tamale's request for bottom-up approaches meets holistic approaches of transitional justice that include various instruments. The AU's TJ policy names "[t]raditional justice and complementary justice mechanisms" with their objectives toward restorative justice as "local processes, including rituals" for conflict resolution "in accordance with established community-based norms and practices" (AU 2019: 4). As particular examples for traditional justice instruments, "customary courts and community-based dialogue" are mentioned (AU 2019: 4).

Yet bottom-up approaches are not, per se, a useful tool to achieve justice from decolonial theory and practice. When Tamale regards "informal or community-based initiatives as part of Africa's decolonisation of the justice system" (Tamale 2020: 154), she does not refer to the fixed customary laws originally established during colonialism; she refers to "the practice of living customary law" (Tamale 2020: 151) and other forms of community justice. Furthermore, she highlights hybrid forms of gender justice in South Africa where the Constitutional Court has acknowledged the fairness of proceedings by "living customary law"(Tamale 2020: 153). From her perspective, community justice offers great potential to address gender issues in dealing with atrocities and violence (Tamale 2020: 153–161).

However, the processes of decolonizing community justice differ from understandings of community justice as bridging "local perceptions of social order and human rights ideas" (Corradi 2010: 94). In other words, decolonizing processes do not start from already-fixed concepts of ideas and concepts which have to be adjusted. Against the background of the limited success of Western-based systems of formal justice, the revival or reinvention of local, informal systems of justice has been linked to the efforts of global powers to broaden ways of implementing transitions in societies, which are compatible with neoliberal objectives (Allen and MacDonald 2013). In this vein, foreign donors support local systems of justice as well as instruments of (inter)national criminal justice (Clark 2015; Branch 2014; for the recent EU funding for the *Justice and Accountability Reform*, see European Union's diplomatic service 2017).

Research findings show that Western donors interlinked with national and local power constellations often hinder steps toward decolonized community justice. For example, in Uganda, international NGOs contributed to "an idealised and dehistoricised vision of traditional leadership as the solution to the situation in the north" (Dolan 2009: 233; Branch 2014). Sophie Komujuni (2019) shows in her research how customary authority in the Acholi region was reproduced by donors. Acholi customary chiefs, whose power had been questioned by women and younger generations during and shortly after the war (Lonergan 2012), became key players in the TJ programs but have lost power after the withdrawal of NGOs in the region and the regained strength of the state in northern Uganda. These local leaders were important for both donors' and the Ugandan state in order to get local legitimacy. They were trained and empowered in line with the donors' concepts of a gendered order that, in turn, were adjusted to the local patriarchal order. The Ugandan Women's Coalition for Peace was very critical about local justice during the peace negotiations concerning the conflict in northern Uganda. They emphasized that such a local instrument addresses only a limited cultural community. Moreover, they "were also concerned that many African traditional reconciliation processes use women's bodies in resolving conflict, for example by marrying off girls to compensate for losses on the side of opponents" (Nabukeera-Musoke 2009: 126). Additionally, they stressed that such local instruments were not experienced in resolving issues of sexualized violence (Nabukeera-Musoke 2009: 126; for insufficient instruments in general, see Kiss et al. 2020).

The critique of currently promoted so-called traditional instruments of dealing with the aftermath of conflict is not sufficient with focusing in particular on the usually applied gender perspectives, focusing on women and girls. Nevertheless, research on women and girls has already disclosed some limitations and recommended the inclusion of multiple experiences of women and youth in the processes of planning and conducting traditional justice (Justice and Reconciliation Project 2012). Yet currently there are no empirical studies toward the inclusion or exclusion of *queer* people in community-based justice. Nevertheless, Kirk Fiereck et al. (2020: 367) state: "What is 'queer' emerges within the vernacular of . . . rituals and traditions." This can be noted in cases of "disarticulat[ing] customary practice from customary authority and inflected community normativities" (*ibid.*).

Pursuing justice for *queers* may be very challenging in post-conflict societies with anti-homosexual laws or widely supported attitudes against non-heteronormative people. The difficulties of breaking the taboo of sexualized violence against men and boys show the rigidity of heteronormative gender regimes. If local systems of justice like in northern Uganda "are equally ill-equipped to remedy gendered harms, including sexual violence against men" (Schulz 2018: 542), how can one expect that harms of non-heteronormative people will be addressed? In such contexts, "informal, 'everyday,' and survivor-driven approaches of remaking a world in the aftermath of violence, suffering, and harm" gain importance, as Schulz (2020: 166) shows in his study on male survivors of sexualized violence.

Working with local communities has become a mantra for NGOs in the framework of TJ as well as in transnational *queer* activism (Farmer 2020). Yet the inclusion of grassroots and subalterns in processes of transitional justice has often failed or has been limited to some representatives (see, for the discussion on the failure of including non-elite women, Fiske 2019: 31). Although critical researchers and practitioners reflect on their situatedness and privileges as outsider researcher/practitioner or outsider–insider researcher/practitioner or hierarchies of power during the research process/working in communities, further epistemological tools are often not included. Initiating local or localized processes of decolonial justice requires for all involved to create practices of learning and unlearning, as well as delinking gender and sex from modes of coloniality. If we take the involvement in processes of justice of grassroots people seriously, those who are already situated in powerful, privileged positions have to unlearn their privileges of speaking, being heard, and listening shaped by epistemic frames that consolidate their social position. This also includes being silent in such situations when one's own privilege might be threatened. Following such an approach might allow subalterns to be heard. Yet for developing processes of transformative gender justice, it also demands steps to unlearn oppression (Dhawan 2007; Brunner 2017). Last but not the least, "new criteria and new forms of judgement" are needed for "[c]hallenging universal blueprints of implementing justice" (Dhawan 2012: 277–278). In this vein, instead of fulfilling the criteria of NGOs, programs towards transformative local gender justice have to be evaluated within the frame of decolonization by local communities. However, as "non-Western measures" are currently marginalized, further research as well as activism is urgent to support counter-discourses (Moyo 2019: 195).

It is important to note that the consideration of TJ processes and mechanisms by donors and global powers as tools for justice on the African continent is rooted in colonialism and neo-colonialism (Chelin and van der Merwe 2018). Conflicts on the African continent have linkages to colonial legacies. These legacies impact socio-political dynamics and cultures throughout the life span of conflicts. This, coupled with the West's influence and their financial and political interest in conflicts on the African continent, disrupts decolonial attempts at TJ processes (Novic 2021). TJ processes and mechanisms (nationally and internationally) that do not recognize the impact and implications of neo-colonialism and, in turn, the implications of global powers determining a Western-lens usage of language around gender and sexuality, as well as concepts of justice in conflict, fail to decolonize TJ in the ways that African states need to engage in (An-Na'im 2013). The top-down approach to TJ is rooted in Western conceptions of "modernization" as well as a dismissal of African and Indigenous ideologies around justice (An-Na'im 2013: 198). However, this is not to say that the bottom-up approach only consists of its merits. In engaging with bottom-up approaches, regardless of their necessity, we need to also unpack and decolonize the amalgamation of long-held colonial ideologies of gender as well as African patriarchy.

In that sense, decolonizing TJ requires working from the back to the front regarding the inclusion of *queer* identities. Socio-economic and political spheres pre-, during, and post-conflict make it difficult for *queer* individuals to engage safely in TJ processes (Fobear and Baines 2020). *Queer* identities, specifically on the African continent, experience societal and cultural erasure and silencing in their everyday lives due to anti-LGBTIQ+ laws and constitutions. This leads to exclusion from any recourse during TJ processes due to their pre-existing socio-economic, political, and legal ostracization.

Gender binarism in donors' and global powers' involvement in post-conflict countries also contributes to which individuals can hypothetically gain access to TJ processes (women and girls) and which ones cannot (*queer* individuals, men and boys). However, even recourse within and outside of gender binarism is difficult to attain due to the exclusion of women and *queer* individuals from the developing and planning of TJ processes and mechanisms (Matandela 2020).

The Western ideologies of capitalism and individualism continue to impact how justice is perceived and engaged with on the African continent. The decolonization of justice and, in turn, TJ in Africa needs to take an Indigenous approach that includes African duty-bearers unlearning harmful gender ideologies and separating African patriarchy from state, as well as the West discarding their concept of African struggles and White saviorism.

Concluding Remarks

Our understanding of "queering" transitional justice in this chapter challenges perceptions of the nexus of gender/sexuality/desire on different levels within the TJ field (also see Fobear, this volume). As we have tried to show, dominant gender-sensitive approaches have to be questioned with regard to their adequacy in African post-conflict societies. Neglecting the polyphony of voices on justice and leaving little or no room for (developing) radical local solutions follow the tracks of (epistemic) violence already used during colonial times. By doing so, the empowerment of people to restructure their society is limited within the frame of (neo)liberal ideas. The veneration of rights to transform gender orders will hardly introduce radical changes for those who struggle to make their living. Within the frame of (neo)liberal politics and economies, the recognition of *queer* subjectivity is intertwined with offers of integration into capitalist modes of production and consumption. By such approaches, alliances between different groups of people fighting for transformative justice can be seriously hampered. Alliances between different oppressed and marginalized groups are an efficient tool to overcome injustices in particular post-conflict settings. This requires linking decolonial politics and epistemologies on gender/sexuality/desire. Thus, "queering" TJ means more than implementing rights for LGBT/Q/I/+ people. Its particular meaning has to be discussed, developed, and constantly revised on grassroots level in cooperation with experts who are committed to deconstruct the *coloniality of gender* and *power*. In other words, instead of assuming that one already knows in which ways gender and sex have been intertwined with other forms of (post)colonial forms of domination and applying prefabricated concepts for the revision of gender regimes, dialogues between all involved should take place without neglecting existing power relations as well as the variety of understandings, forms of deviations, and resistance in the respective constellations.

We focused on current applied local justice instruments to shed light on their limitations and potentials for radical changes. Such instruments are usually supported by international NGOs, similar to other instruments of TJ. In line with decolonial scholars and activists, we stress that the problem is not so much that, for example, traditional instruments have been reinvented, as they have already been regulated and ossified by colonial powers. It is much more significant to note and acknowledge decolonial perspectives. In this vein, dialogues with locals have to find out and create practices of local justice which support addressing the harms of people regardless of their ascribed gender and sexuality. Such dialogues need to be accompanied by unlearning processes of all involved.

In short, epistemological shifts are crucial for TJ approaches, also for critical ones. More attention is needed to (secret) normativities and theorizing as well as developing and applying instruments that require radical positionings. In other words, reflections on one's own embeddedness in certain frames of privileged knowledge production and, in particular, on the limitations of gender-sensitive concepts and programs embedded in US–European episteme should be obligatory. Such gender programs tend to overlook fluid gender constructions and relations within and outside respective gender orders. Concerning the people who are assigned as *queers* to the list of vulnerable victims and addressing them primarily through special policies miss chances for transformative justice. It is urgent for researchers as well as for practitioners to include hitherto marginalized theorizing, based on knowledge of the nexus of gender/sexuality/desire within African contexts. This also means that justice processes understood as queering-to-come can only be initiated and implemented in alliance with grassroots actors as well as critical scholars within, from, and for African contexts.

References

ACHPR (2011). *Principles and Guidelines on the Implementation of Economic, Social and Cultural Rights in the African Charter*. Available at: https://www.achpr.org/legalinstruments/detail?id=30. Accessed on: 20 February 2022.

Allen, T. and A. MacDonald (2013). *Post-Conflict Traditional Justice: A Critical Overview. Justice and Security Research Programme*, Paper 3. London School of Economics and Political Science. Available at: http://eprints.lse.ac.uk/56357. Accessed on: 27 February 2022.

An-Na'im, A. A. (2013). Editorial Note: From the Neocolonial 'Transitional' to Indigenous Formations of Justice. *International Journal of Transitional Justice* 7(2): 197–204.

AU (2019). *Transitional Justice Policy*. Available at: https://au.int/en/documents/20190425/transitional-justice-policy. Accessed on: 20 February 2022.

Bennett, J. and V. Reddy (2015). 'African Positionings': South African Relationships with Continental Questions of LGBTI Justice and Rights. *Agenda* 29(1): 10–23.

Bhambra, G. K. (2014). Postcolonial and Decolonial Dialogues. *Postcolonial Studies* 17(2): 115–121.

Biruk, C. (2020). 'Fake Gays' in Queer Africa: NGOs, Metrics, and Modes of (Queer) Theory. *GLQ: A Journal of Lesbian and Gay Studies* 26(3): 477–502.

Branch, A. (2014). The Violence of Peace: Ethnojustice in Northern Uganda. *Development and Change* 45(3): 608–630.

Brown, G. and K. Browne (eds.) (2016). *The Routledge Research Companion to Geographies of Sex and Sexualities*. London and New York: Routledge.

Brunner, C. (2017). Vom Sprechen und Schweigen und (Zu)hören in der Kolonialität des Wissens – Paradoxe Überlegungen zur Analyse, Kritik und Entgegnung (nicht nur) epistemischer Gewalt. In: Niederle, H. (ed.): *Sprache und Macht. Dokumentation des Symposiums*. Wien: Löcker: 30–71.

Buckley-Zistel, S. and M. Zolkos (2012). Introduction: Gender in Transitional Justice. In: Buckley-Zistel, S. and Stanley, R. (eds.): *Gender in Transitional Justice*. Basingstoke and New York: Palgrave Macmillan: 1–33.

Bueno-Hansen, P. (2015). *Feminist and Human Rights Struggles in Peru: Decolonizing Transitional Justice*. Urbana; Chicago; Springfield: University of Illinois Press.

Butler, J. (1993). Critically Queer. *GLQ: A Journal of Lesbian and Gay Studies* 1(1): 17–32.

Chelin, R. and H. van der Merwe (2018). *Policy Brief: Transitional Justice and Colonialism*. CSVR: 1–8. Available at: http://csvr.org.za. Accessed on: 22 July 2024.

Clark, P. (2015). 'All these Outsiders Shouted Louder Than Us': Civil Society Engagement with Transitional Justice in Uganda. *Working Paper SiT/WP/03/15*. Available at: http://securityintransition.org/wp-content/uploads/2015/11/CS-and-TJ-working-paper_Uganda.pdf. Accessed on: 27 February 2022.

Corradi, G. (2010). Human Rights Promotion in Post Conflict Sierra Leone: Coming to Grips with Plurality in Customary Justice. *Journal of Legal Pluralism and Unofficial Law* 42(60): 73–103.

Currier, A. and J. Cruz (2014). Civil Society and Sexual Struggles in Africa. In: Obadare, E. (ed.): *The Handbook of Civil Society in Africa*. New York: Springer: 337–360.

Daigle, M. and H. Myrttinen (2018). Bringing Diverse Sexual Orientation and Gender Identity (SOGI) into Peacebuilding Policy and Practice. *Gender & Development* 26(1): 103–120.

Dankwa, S. (2021). *Knowing Women: Same-Sex Intimacy, Gender and Identity in Postcolonial Ghana*. Cambridge: Cambridge University Press.

Davis, A. and G. C. Spivak in conversation with N. Dhawan (2019). Planetary Utopias. *Radical Philosophy* 2(5): 67–77.

Dhawan, N. (2007). *Impossible Speech. On the Politics of Silence and Violence*. Sankt Augustin: Academia.

Dhawan, N. (2012). Transitions to Justice. In: Buckley-Zistel, S. and Stanley, R. (eds.): *Gender in Transitional Justice*. New York: Palgrave MacMillan: 264–283.

Dhawan, N. (2014). Affirmative Sabotage of the Master's Tools: The Paradox of Postcolonial Enlightenment. In: Dhawan, N. (ed.): *Decolonizing Enlightenment:*

Transnational Justice, Human Rights and Democracy in a Postcolonial World. Opladen, Berlin and Toronto: Barbara Budrich: 19–78.

Dolan, Ch. (2009). *Social Torture. The Case of Northern Uganda, 1986–2006*. New York and Oxford: Berghahn Books.

Edström, J., Dolan, C. and Shahrokh, T. with O. David (2016). *Therapeutic Activism: Men of Hope Refugee Association Uganda Breaking the Silence over Male Rape in Conflict-related Sexual Violence*. IDS Evidence Report 182. Brighton: IDS.

Ekine, S. and H. Abbas (2013). *Queer African Reader*. Dakar: Pambazuka Press.

El Awady, M. (2015). *Does Gender Justice Matter?* New York: United Nations. Accessed on: 20 February 2022. Available at: http://unescwa.org.

Farmer, M. (2020). *Transnational LGBT Activism and UK-Based NGOs. Colonialism and Power*. Cham: Springer International Publishing.

Feminist Africa (2005). *Sexual Cultures*. Issue 5. Available at: http://www.agi.ac.za/agi/feminist-africa/05. Accessed on: 20 February 2022.

Feminist Africa (2006). *Subaltern Sexualities*. Issue 6. Available at: http://www.agi.ac.za/agi/feminist-africa/06. Accessed on: 20 February 2022.

Fiereck, K., N. Hoad and D. Mupotsa (2020). A Queering-to-Come. *GLQ: A Journal of Lesbian and Gay Studies* 26(3): 363–376.

Fiske, L. (2019). The Rise (and Fall?) of Transitional Gender Justice: A Survey of the Field. In: Shackel, R. & Fiske, L. (eds.): *Rethinking Transitional Gender Justice. Transformative Approaches in Post-Conflict Settings*. Cham: Springer International Publishing. Imprint: Palgrave Macmillan: 17–36.

Fobear, K. and E. Baines (2020). Pushing the Conversation Forward: The Intersections of Sexuality and Gender Identity in Transitional Justice. *The International Journal of Human Rights* 24(4): 307–312.

Franzki, H. and M. Olarte (2014). Understanding the Political Economy of Transitional Justice. A Critical Theory Perspective. In: Buckley-Zistel, S., Koloma Beck, T., Braun, C. and Mieth, F. (eds.): *Transitional Justice Theories*. Oxon: Routledge: 201–221.

Gathii, J. (2020). *The Promise of International Law: A Third World View*. Grotius Lecture Presented at the 2020 Virtual Annual Meeting of the American Society of International Law. Available at: https://ssrn.com/abstract=3635509. Accessed on: 20 February 2022.

George, R., J. Rivett, F. Samuels and E. Dwyer (2021). *Intersecting Exclusions. Displacement and Gender-Based Violence Among People with Diverse Sexualities and Gender Identities in Kenya. Literature Review*. London: ODI. Available at: https://odi.org/en/publications/intersecting-exclusions-displacement-and-gender-based-violence-among-people-with-diverse-sexualities-and-gender-identities-in-kenya/. Accessed on: 20 February 2022.

Gething, L. (2015). 'Non-Normative' Sexual and Gender Diversities in Africa. *Agenda* 29(1): 1–2.

Goetz, A. M. (2007). Gender Justice, Citizenship and Entitlements – Core Concepts, Central Debates and New Directions for Research. In: Mukhopadhyay, M. and Singh, N. (eds.): *Gender Justice, Citizenship and Development*. New Delhi: Zubaan Publications: 15–57.

Graneß, A., M. Kopf and M. Kraus (2019). *Feministische Theorien aus Afrika, Asien und Lateinamerika*. Wien: Facultas Verlag.

Graness, A. (2015). Is the Debate on 'Gobal Justice' a Global One? Some Considerations in View of Modern Philosophy in Africa. *Journal of Global Ethics* 11(1): 126–140.

Gready, P. and S. Robins (eds.) (2019). *From Transitional to Transformative Justice*. Cambridge: Cambridge University Press.

Gunkel, H. (2010). *The Cultural Politics of Female Sexuality in South Africa*. New York and London: Routledge and Taylor & Francis Group.

Gunkel, H. (2013). Some Reflections on Postcolonial Homophobia, Local Interventions, and LGBTI Solidarity Online: The Politics of Global Petitions. *African Studies Review* 56(2): 67–81.

Hendricks, Ch. (2017). Progress and Challenges in Implementing the Women, Peace and Security Agenda in the African Union's Peace and Security Architecture. *Africa Development* XLII(3): 73–98.

Hendriks, Th. (2018). "Erotiques Cannibales": A Queer Ontological Take on Desire from Urban Congo. *Sexualities* 21(5–6): 853–867.

Hendriks, T. and R. Spronk (2020). Introduction: Reading 'Sexualities' from 'Africa'. In: Spronk, R. and Hendriks, T. (eds.): *Readings in Sexualities from Africa*. Bloomington: Indiana University Press: 1–17.

Johnson, J. and G. Hamandishe Karekwaivanane (2018). *Pursuing Justice in Africa: Competing Imaginaries and Contested Practices*. Athens, OH: Ohio University Press.

Justice and Reconciliation Project (2012). *Gender and Generation in Acholi Traditional Justice Mechanisms*. JRP Field Note XVII. Available at: Gender-and-Generations-in-Acholi-Traditional-Mechanisms-Web.pdf. Accessed on: 20 February 2022.

Kiss, L., M. Quinlan-Davidson, L. Pasquero, P. Ollé Tejero, C. Hogg, J. Theis, A. Park, C. Zimmerman and M. Hossain (2020). Male and LGBT Survivors of Sexual Violence in Conflict Situations: A Realist Review of Health Interventions in Low-and Middle-Income Countries. *Conflict and Health* 14(11). Available at: https://doi.org/10.1186/s13031-020-0254-5. Accessed on: 12 December 2021.

Komujuni, S. (2019). *To Be a Chief and to Remain a Chief: The Production of Customary Authority in Post-post Conflict Northern Uganda*. PhD, Ghent University. Available at: https://biblio.ugent.be/publication/8612807. Accessed on: 27 February 2022.

Kurze, A. and C. Lamont (2021). Breaking the Transitional Justice Machine: Exploring Spatiality, Space Travel, and Inbetween Spaces in Research Practice. *Political Anthropological Research on International Social Sciences* 2(1): 155–178.

Levitt, P. and S. Engle Merry (2017). The Vernacularization of Women's Human Rights. In: Vinjamuri, L., Snyder, J. and Hopgood, S. (eds.): *Human Rights Futures*. Cambridge: Cambridge University Press: 213–236.

Lewis, D. (2004). African Gender Research and Postcoloniality: Legacies and Challenge. In: Arnfred, S. (ed.): *African Gender Scholarship: Concepts, Methodologies and Paradigms*. Dakar: CODESRIA: 27–41.

Lewis, D. (2008). Discursive Challenges for African Feminisms. *Quest: An African Journal of Philosophy* 20: 77–96.

Lonergan, K. (2012). *Gender and Generation in Acholi Traditional Justice Mechanisms*. Justice and Reconciliation Project Field Note VXII. Available at: http://justiceandreconciliation.com/wp-content/uploads/2012/11/Gender-and-Generations-in-Acholi-Traditional-Mechanisms-Web.pdf. Accessed on: 21 February 2022.

Maddison, S. and L. Shepherd (2013). Peacebuilding and the Postcolonial Politics of Transitional Justice. *Peacebuilding* 2(3): 253–269.

Madlingozi, T. (2010). On Transitional Justice Entrepreneurs and the Production of Victims. *Journal of Human Rights Practice* 2(2): 208–228.

Maldonado-Torres, N. (2007). On the Coloniality of Being. *Cultural Studies* 21(2–3): 240–270.

Margalit, A. (2018). Still a Blind Spot: The Protection of LGBT Persons During Armed Conflict and Other Situations of Violence. *International Review of the Red Cross* 100(907/908/909). Available at: https://international-review.icrc.org/reviews/irrc-no100-150-years-humanitarian-reflection. Accessed on: 20 February 2022.

Martin, L. (2016). Practicing Normality: An Examination of Unrecognizable Transitional Justice Mechanisms in Post-Conflict Sierra Leone. *Journal of Intervention and Statebuilding* 10(3): 400–418.

Martin de Almagro, M. and P. Schulz (2022). Gender and Transitional Justice. In: *Oxford Research Encyclopedia of International Studies*. Available at: https://oxfordre.com/internationalstudies/display/10.1093/acrefore/9780190846626.001.0001/acrefore-9780190846626-e-669. Accessed on: 22 July 2024.

Matandela, M. (2020). *Addressing Gender Justice and Colonialism Through Transitional Justice in Africa*. Available at: https://www.csvr.org.za/addressing-gender-justice-and-colonialism-through-transitional-justice-in-africa/. Accessed on: 28 October 2022.

Matebeni, Z., S. Monro and V. Reddy (eds.) (2018). *Queer in Africa: LGBTQ Identities, Citizenship, and Activism*. London and New York: Routledge.

Matebeni, Z. and T. Msibi (2015). Vocabularies of the Non-normative. *Agenda* 29(1): 3–9.

Matebeni, Z. and J. Pereira (2014). Preface. In: Matebeni, Z. (ed.): *Reclaiming Afrikan. Queer Perspectives on Sexual and Gender Identities*. Athlone: Modjaij Books: 7–9.

Mendos, L. R. (2019). *State-Sponsored Homophobia*. Geneva: International Lesbian, Gay, Bisexual, Trans and Intersex Association. Available at: https://apo.org.au/organisation/226656. Accessed on: 20 February 2022.

Mertens, C. and H. Myrttinen (2019). 'A Real Woman Waits' – Heteronormative Respectability, Neo-Liberal Betterment and Echoes of Coloniality in SGBV Programming in Eastern DR Congo. *Journal of Intervention and Statebuilding* 13(4): 418–439.

Merwe, H. van der and M. Brinton Lykes (2020). Racism and Transitional Justice. *International Journal of Transitional Justice* 14(3): 415–422.

Merwe, H. van der and N. Masiko (2020). Policy Brief: Addressing Diversity and Inclusion Through Transitional Justice. *Centre for the Study of Violence and Reconciliation*. Available at: https://www.africaportal.org/publications/addressing-diversity-and-inclusion-through-transitional-justice. Accessed on: 20 February 2022.

Mohanty, C. (1988). Under Western Eyes: Feminist Scholarship and Colonial Discourses. *Boundary* 2(12/13): 333–358.

Moore, M. and J. Barner (2017). Sexual Minorities in Conflict Zones: A Review of the Literature. *Aggression and Violent Behaviour* 35: 33–37.

Moyo, K. (2019). *Postcolonial Transitional Justice Zimbabwe and Beyond*. Oxon and New York: Routledge.

Moyo, O. (2021). *Africanity and Ubuntu as Decolonizing Discourse*. Cham: Springer International Publishing.

Msibi, T. (2011). The Lies We Have Been Told: On (Homo) Sexuality. *Africa Today* 58(1): 54–77.

Nabukeera-Musoke, H. (2009). Transitional Justice and Gender in Uganda: Making Peace, Failing Women During the Peace Negotiation Process. *African Journal on Conflict Resolution* 9(2): 121–129.

Ngidi, N., M. Ramphalile, Z. Essack and H. van Rooyen (2020). Exploring Queerphobic Geographies in Southern Africa. *Agenda* 34(2): 18–31.

Ní Aoláin, F. (2019). Transformative Gender Justice? In: Gready, P. and Robins, S. (eds.): *From Transitional to Transformative Justice*. Cambridge: Cambridge University Press: 150–171.

Novic, E. (2021). Transitional Justice to Address Colonial Legacies: Decolonising Transitional Justice First? *Society for Cultural Anthropology*. Available at: https://culanth.org/fieldsights/transitional-justice-to-address-colonial-legacies-decolonizing-transitional-justice-first. Accessed on: 12 November 2022.

Nyeck, S. (ed.) (2020). *Routledge Handbook of Queer African Studies*. London and New York: Routledge and Taylor, Francis Group.

Okello, M., C. Dolan, U. Whande, N. Mncwabe and S. Oola (eds.) (2012). *Where Law Meets Reality. Forging African Transitional Justice*. Cape Town: Pambazuka Press.

Oosterveld, V. (2018). The ICC Policy Paper on Sexual and Gender-Based Crimes: A Crucial Step for International Criminal Law. *William & Mary Journal of Race, Gender and Social Justice* 24(3): 443–457.

O'Rourke, C. (2017). Transitional Justice and Gender. In: Lawther, C., Moffett, L., Jacobs, D. and Elgar, E. (eds.): *Research Handbook on Transitional Justice*. Cheltenham, Northhamton: Edward Elgar Publishing: 117–141.

Picq, M. (2019). Decolonizing Indigenous Sexualities: Between Erasure and Resurgence. In: Bosia, M., McEvoy, S. and Rahman, M. (eds.): *The Oxford Handbook of Global LGBT and Sexual Diversity Politics*. Oxford: Oxford University Press.

Queer African Manifesto/Declaration from April 18, 2010, Nairobi, Kenya. In: Tamale, S. (ed.) (2011). *African Sexualities: A Reader*. Cape Town: Pambazuka Press: 182.

Rao, R. (2020). *Out of Time. The Queer Politics of Postcoloniality*. New York: Oxford University Press. Kindle-Version.

Reddy, V., S. Monro and Z. Matebeni (2018). Introduction. In Matebeni, Z., S. Monro and V. *Reddy Queer in Africa. LGBTQI Identities, Citizenship, and Activism*. London: Routledge: 1–16, https://www.taylorfrancis.com/books/oa-edit/10.4324/9781315406749/queer-africa-zethu-matebeni-surya-monro-vasu-reddy. Accessed on: 22 July 2024.

Rolston, B. and F. Ní Aoláin (2018). Colonialism, Redress and Transitional Justice: Ireland and Beyond. *State Crime Journal* 7(2): 329–348.

Rooney, E. and F. Ní Aoláin (2018). Transitional Justice from the Margins: Intersections of Identities, Power and Human Rights. *International Journal of Transitional Justice* 12(1): 1–8.

Schulz, P. (2018). 'Luk pe Coo', or Compensation as Dowry? Gendered Reflections on Reparations for Conflict-Related Sexual Violence Against Men. *International Journal of Transitional Justice* 12(3): 537–548.

Schulz, P. (2019). Towards Inclusive Gender in Transitional Justice: Gaps, Blind-Spots and Opportunities. *Journal of Intervention and Statebuilding* 14(5): 691–710.

Schulz, P. (2020). *Male Survivors of Wartime Sexual Violence. Perspectives from Northern Uganda*. Oakland: University of California Press.

Seckinelgin, H. (2012). Global Civil Society as Shepherd: Global Sexualities and the Limits of Solidarity from a Distance. *Critical Social Policy* 32(4): 536–555.

Shackel, R. and L. Fiske (eds.) (2019). *Rethinking Transitional Gender Justice. Transformative Approaches in Post-Conflict Settings*. Cham: Springer International Publishing. Imprint: Palgrave Macmillan.

Sharp, D. (2017). Transitional Justice and 'Local' Justice. In: Lawther, C., Moffett, L., Jacobs, D. and Elgar, E. (eds.): *Research Handbook on Transitional Justice*. Cheltenham, Northhamton: Edward Elgar Publishing: 142–158.

Shaw, R. and L. Waldorf (2010). Introduction: Localizing Transitional Justice. In: Shaw, R. and Waldorf, L., with Hazan, P. (eds.): *Localizing Transitional Justice. Interventions and Priorities after Mass Violence*. Standford: Standford University Press: 3–26.

Shaw, R. and L. Waldorf, with P. Hazan (eds.) (2010). *Localizing Transitional Justice. Interventions and Priorities after Mass Violence*. Standford: Standford University Press.

Signe, A. (ed.) (2004). *Re-thinking Sexualities in Africa*. Uppsala: Nordic Africa Institute.

Sika, V. and A. Okech (2019). African Sexual Politics: A Pan-African Lesbian Perspective. In: Corrêa, S. and Parker, R. (eds.): *Sex Politics: Trends & Tensions in the 21st Century – Contextual Undercurrents* (vol. 2). Rio de Janeiro: Sexuality Policy Watch.

Sott, S. (2017). *Desartikulation Statt Transitional Justice? Subalterne Perspektiven in der kolumbianischen Vergangenheitsbewältigung*. Bielefeld: Transcript.

Tabengwa, M. and M. Waites (2019). Africa and the Contestation of Sexual and Gender Diversity: Imperial and Contemporary Regulation. In: Bosia, M., McEvoy, S. and Rahman, M. (eds.): *The Oxford Handbook of Global LGBT and Sexual Diversity Politics*. New York: Oxford University Press. Available at: http://doi.org/10.1093/oxfordhb/9780190673741.013.35. Accessed on: 20 February 2021.

Tamale, S. (1999). *When Hens Begin to Crow. Gender and Parliamentary Politics in Uganda*. Kampala: Fountain Publishers.
Tamale, S. (2011). Researching and Theorizing Sexualities in Africa. In: Tamale, S. (ed.): *African Sexualities: A Reader*. Cape Town: Pambazuka Press: 11–36.
Tamale, S. (2020). *Decolonization and Afro-Feminism*. Ottawa: Daraja Press.
United Nations (2020a). *Gender Perspective in Transitional Justice Processes*, A/75/174 2020. Available at: https://www.ohchr.org/EN/Issues/TruthJusticeReparation/Pages/CallGender.aspx. Accessed on: 20 February 2022.
United Nations (2020b). *What Is the Rule of Law*. Available at: https://www.un.org/ruleoflaw/what-is-the-rule-of-law. Accessed on: 29 December 2020.

Chapter 5

Linking a Queer Legal Theoretical Perspective and Transitional Justice

Challenges and Possibilities

E. İrem Akı

Introduction

Legal mechanisms and the law in general carry tremendous power in the context of transitional justice, as many and important mechanisms of transitional justice are based on legal texts, such as statutes, court verdicts, decrees, regulations, and mandates. To illustrate the point further: truth commissions are most generally established by mandates, that is, *general legal rules*. Even more so, criminal trials during post-conflict periods are based on legal rules too. Who will be held accountable, the definitions of crime, which people give testimonies – all these aspects, and more, will be formulized by legal texts. Moreover, not only in the transition period but also in post-violence settings, the way we accommodate the demands for justice of persons with diverse *sexual orientations* and *gender identities*, *gender expressions*, and *sex characteristics* (SOGIESC)[1] is crucially related to legal texts, as these regulate gender, gender relations, gender binaries, sexual categories, and desires in post-conflict societies.

Thus, the importance of legal rules in the transitional justice context necessitates not only queer theory but a queer *legal* theory as well. Echoing Fobear's argument about the need for queer legal theory, in this chapter I specifically explore ways to integrate queer legal perspectives into the theory and practice of transitional justice. More explicitly, in order to include persons with diverse SOGIESC in transitional and post-conflict settings, we should reflect on how a queer perspective should be translated into *legal knowledge*, *form*, and *language*. In reflecting on this translation, we realize that there

1 Let me explain briefly my preference about terminology: instead of *LGBTI* or other variations, such as *LGBTIQ+*, I prefer to use the terms *sexual orientation*, *gender identity*, *gender expression*, and *sex characteristic*. On this matter, I follow Megan Daigle and Henri Myrittinen's arguments (Daigle and Myrttinen 2018). Firstly, the acronym *LGBTI* is not used universally but mostly in the West. Secondly, the acronym *LGBTI* does not express all the categories that lie outside of the heteronormative system. Thirdly, while all persons have sexual orientation and gender identity, the term *LGBTI* refers to specific groups.

DOI: 10.4324/9781003519522-7

are also challenges that need to be overcome. Firstly, there is the challenge of relating queer, which is essentially against norms and categorizing, to the legal system, which is, by and large, based on the gender binary and built on norms and categories such as male/female.[2] A second challenge has to do with queer's characteristic of essentially challenging established norms. The argument is that the more persons with diverse SOGIESC become part of the legal system, or the more they get recognized by it (and by international law), the less they remain queer and the less *queer* maintains its radical potential to challenge established norms (Kapur 2017).

I think that these challenges are inextricable. Yet I argue that mutable sexual categories could be constructed within the legal system. I maintain that the use of terms such as *SOGIESC* in place of rigid innate sexual categories can make legal texts more inclusive, as it is the case with the Yogyakarta Principles (2006). As a result, a legal system which is not dependent on the male/female and/or the hetero/homosexual binary becomes possible. From another point of view, to thus deconstruct these two binaries, which are, more often than not, taken for granted in most legal systems, is to, in a way, constitute a queer undertaking in itself. As for the second challenge, I argue that the admission of persons with diverse SOGIESC by a legal system is something already assisting in deconstructing the heterosexual matrix and gender binary (also see Bueno-Hansen, this volume). In that sense, their admittance can make the system more radical.

Keeping in mind these challenges, in this chapter I am engaging with the following question: What does queer (legal) theory bring to the field of transitional justice? To answer this question, I start with the presentation of some core arguments introduced by queer theory. Then, I explore possible ways of how queer theory and thinking can inform and enrich transitional justice. I argue that a queer lens that pays attention to intersectional dynamics and victim(hood) recognition can facilitate the inclusion of people with diverse SOGIESC as legal subjects in transitional contexts.

I then turn to the examination of queer legal theoretical perspectives. I contend that, in exposing the heterosexual fabric of the legal system, queer legal theory assists in the deconstruction of the heterosexual/homosexual and gender binaries in legal texts in the transitional context. The deconstruction of the binaries necessitates the recognition and protection of people with diverse SOGIESC as legal subjects. What is crucial for the transitional justice field is to explicitly recognize in legal texts, such as statutes of post-conflict criminal tribunals and mandates of truth commissions, that SOGIESC constitutes one of the grounds for persecution and violence (in addition to gender, race, ethnicity). Therefore, legal texts of transitional justice mechanisms

2 Other categories that a legal system can create can be "civil servant," "student," "unemployed," "married," etc.

(judicial or non-judicial) can address violence and discrimination based on SOGIESC and recognize the experiences of persons with diverse SOGIESC. The recognition and the protection of diverse SOGIESC is an important step to dismantle patriarchy and heterosexism and prevent violations against people with diverse SOGIESC in transitional and post-conflict settings. Although there is generally a gap between legal texts and their implementation, law as a social discourse can, without a doubt, reinforce mindsets and ways of thinking and practices. That is why it is enormously vital that diverse experiences and identities are recognized in and through legal texts.

Lastly, I look at how queer legal theory and transitional justice can converge through legal texts. I argue that one of the most important texts in transitional justice field, the Rome Statute – and even though it does not explicitly mention categories such as sexual orientation and gender identity – through a queer interpretative perspective, can facilitate the protection of the rights of people with diverse SOGIESC.

Queer Theory

Expounding the main arguments of queer theory will help us explore the possibilities and potential of a queer legal theoretical perspective in the transitional justice field, but also move beyond the tendency to wrongly treat the *LGBTI*[3] acronym as a synonym of *queer* (Kapur 2017; Cossman 2019) and to add the category of LGBTI to the category of women in the legal texts of transitional and post-conflict settings.

Queer is an umbrella term used to denote people who lie outside of heterosexual norms as well as for people who challenge the idea of the LGBTI mainstream (Jagose 1996; Barker and Scheele 2016). The term *queer* is used as a verb to indicate the act of challenging heteronormativity and gender binaries, as a noun for non-heterosexual or non-gender binary, but also as a shorthand for LGBTI (Monro 2020). Essentially, queer theory questions the relationship between sex, gender, and sexual desire. For queer theory, sex, gender, and sexual desire are contextual, that is, they have been understood and practiced in various and different ways in different cultures across time. Likewise, there is no true or wrong account of heterosexuality or homosexuality, as sexuality is not natural but rather discursively constructed (Sullivan 2003; Cossman 2019; Jagose 1996).

Many societies are constructed upon a duality, more often than not, in the form of heterosexuality/homosexuality and male/female. This holds true

3 *LGBT* refers to *lesbian*, *gay*, *bisexual*, and *trans*. In Latin American context, *I* (*intersex*) is included as well. In the US context, *Q* (*queer*) is included (Bueno-Hansen 2018). In this text, I will use the term *SOGIESC*. But sometimes, if context necessitates, I will choose to use the term *LGBTI*.

even in societies where homosexual marriage is legal or where the rights of transsexuals are not severely violated. This happens because, as long as those who are not heterosexual – that is, people with diverse SOGIESC – are conceptualized and held under control as sexual minorities, they do not present any danger to the heterosexual society and they can thus be accepted. Therefore, in such a society, there is a clear distinction between homosexuality and heterosexuality. Yet no matter how widespread, this duality is not natural. Queer theory and queer activists call this duality into question because, for them, "these dichotomies were themselves part of the problem. The homo/hetero distinction normalized heterosexuality and reinforced the very static and essentialist conceptions of sex, sexuality, gender, and desire" (Cossman 2019: 26). As a result, queer theory and activists' aims are not just to claim for themselves certain rights (for instance, right to marriage) that have already been recognized to heterosexuals (Craig 2010) or to add the "category 'transgender' to the mix" (Romero 2009: 190); rather, their aim is to expose and deconstruct discourses based on heteronormativity and the gender binary. As such, queer theory carries the potential to make us think about our bodies in ways different from existing social and legal norms, which draw on the male/female and heterosexual/homosexual binary. As Judith Butler (1990) attests, the reason behind the creation of these two sex categories of female and male and the coercion of individuals and bodies into one or the other is the formation of a society that is grounded on reproductive and heterosexual hegemonies.

In turn, heterosexual hegemony is based on certain norms. Butler (1990) refers to these norms as the "heterosexual matrix." The heterosexual matrix assumes that "there must be a stable sex expressed through a stable gender (masculine expresses male, feminine expresses female) that is oppositionally and hierarchically defined through the compulsory practice of heterosexuality" (Butler 1990: 194; also see Bueno-Hansen, this volume). As per these social constructions, the only acceptable, legitimate, and natural way of sexual desire or relationship is the heterosexual one, between man and woman. Thus, from a queer perspective, it is necessary to see and reveal how heterosexuality imposes itself on society and the rules regulating society, including legal norms and the legal system. Moreover, a legal system itself functions as a foundational pillar of the heteronormative matrix. Heterosexuality is realized with the assistance of legal norms. Since legal systems are predisposed toward heteronormativity, such norms are likely to be maintained in the mechanisms (judicial or non-judicial) we see in transitional justice. In this respect, queer legal theory primarily functions to expose the heteronormative character of the legal system.

The first thing, then, that queer theory–informed transitional justice scholarship can do is to acknowledge and promote awareness of the existence of genders beyond the binary and desires beyond heterosexuality, as well as of the plurality and intersectionality of diverse SOGIESC. Awareness of the plurality of diverse SOGIESC will make visible the violations based on them and pave the way for recognition of people with diverse SOGIESC as legal subjects in the transitional justice context.

The Legal Recognition of People with Diverse SOGIESC in the Transitional Justice Context

In respect to the potential that queer theory holds for the field of transitional justice, the question regarding the legal recognition of persons with diverse SOGIESC as victims and subjects of transitional justice is crucial. As victimhood touches upon almost all (judicial and non-judicial) mechanisms of transitional justice, to ascribe victimhood to persons with diverse SOGIESC and to recognize them as legal subjects is to extend the scope of transitional justice beyond the gender binary.

More specifically, who can be considered as victim is one of the most important and challenging issues in the theory and practice of transitional justice. The recognition of people as victims also includes the recognition of their sufferings, experiences, and the violence they have experienced (De Greiff 2006; Halderman 2008). Ascribing victimhood is thereby strongly linked to the act of legal recognition (Garcia-Godos 2017). Recognition of victimhood, then, may gain victims the right to speak in truth commissions, to participate as victims or witnesses in criminal trials, and to be beneficiary of reparation programs, for instance. In other words, recognized victims can actively participate in and potentially benefit from transitional justice processes, whether these are judicial or non-judicial.

As we know from feminist transitional justice scholarship, there are many categories of victims. Feminist scholarship has criticized the "hegemonic model of victimhood" and "the typical victim" of the non-White, poor, uneducated civilian woman and/or mother (Girelli 2017: 18). In such a conventional narrative, women are seen as typical victims and automatically fall within the same category as children, naturally and inevitably condemned to protection, devoid of agency. Men, on the other hand, are mostly seen as perpetrators. This narrative, in many ways, has obscured the empirical reality of men as victims (Dolan 2018; Touquet and Schulz 2020; Schulz 2021) and women as perpetrators (Sjoberg 2016), alongside the conventional categories of female victimhood and men's perpetration of violence (Girelli 2017).

Even if the hegemonic model of victimhood is criticized, this criticism is still based on the male/female binary, which thus strengthens patriarchy and heteronormativity. To avoid such a conclusion, transitional justice scholars must "sharpen their analytical lenses, to grow sensitized to the discursive production of sexual identities, and to be mindful of the insidious force of heteronormativity as fundamental organizing principle throughout the social order" (Gamson and Moon 2004: 48). In the practice and study of transitional justice, in place of dual representations of sexuality and gender, a queer awareness must be cultivated, and people with diverse SOGIESC should be recognized as legal subjects of transitional and post-conflict settings.

As unpacked earlier, a queer analysis brings forth and highlights the intersection of diverse identities (Gamson and Moon 2004). Therefore, a queer perspective enables us to recognize multilayered victimhood through an intersectional[4] analysis. More clearly, a queer and intersectional perspective can make visible identities that are usually excluded from transitional justice. In the following example, an intersectional approach focuses on the intersection of gender and sexual orientation: a report by Colombia's National Centre for Historical Memory on the experience of armed conflict by persons with diverse SOGIESC included the statement of a lesbian woman that she was sexually assaulted by an armed person in order to persuade her that she should love men (Maier 2019). If we analyze this case solely through a male/female distinction and a gender lens, we would miss the sexual violence against a lesbian woman who was raped specifically for being lesbian. We would, instead, only see the rape of a woman, but we would miss that the violence was based on sexual orientation. In extension, we would also miss the long catalogue of violations perpetrated against people with diverse SOGIESC by all sides of the conflict, paramilitary, police/army, and FARC (Espitia 2016).

Another example comes from Canada. In the pre-colonial period, there were fluid gender identities as Indigenous communities assumed that there existed more than two genders. In colonial times, though, heteronormativity and the gender binary became the established norm. Residential schools were one of the institutions through which the assimilation and the eventual extermination of the Indigenous population took place. Within a century, about 150,000 Indigenous children were assimilated in these schools (Robinson 2020). If we reflect on the violence experienced by these children only through the male/female lens, we will miss the violence perpetrated against various gender identities beyond the binary.

Considering the sexual desire of perpetrators is another good illustration of how queer lens can enrich transitional justice research. While the literature categorizes sexual violence against men as strategic within the heteronormative framework and the gender binary analysis, Schulz and Touquet (2020) use a queer framework based on empirical research to assert the connection of sexual violence against men with the sexual desire of perpetrators. In effect, an analysis which is based solely on the gender binary and heteronormativity

4 The American legal scholar Kimberlé Crenshaw coined the term. Crenshaw argued that a view in which race and gender are handled separately and domination is understood in a uniaxial framework renders the experiences of Black women invisible and conceals the specific discrimination they face as a result of the intersection of two different forms of domination. She uses the metaphor of intersection in traffic to explain how different lines of domination intersect, overlap, or intertwine (Crenshaw 1989).

will affect how one describes sexual violence against men. Such an analysis describes male violence solely as torture and not as sexual violence[5] (Moore and Barner 2017). In essence, behind such an analysis lies the assumption that a male cannot be a victim of sexual assault (Sivakumaran 2007; Charman 2018). This is a problematic approach because, in such an analysis, sexual violence is understood in a reductionist and essentialist way, solely in terms of penetration, and exclusively against girls and women (Schulz 2021).

In contrast to the preceding approach, a queer analysis that takes notice of intersectional dynamics discloses the experiences and voices of identities that are usually masked by other identities. That is, violence against transgenders, non-binaries, gays, or lesbians is habitually understood as violence against women or men. To address one type of violence and exclude the others is to conceal the fact that violence originates in various social, religious, economic, political, and national contexts (Fobear 2014; Daigle and Myrttinen 2018).[6]

Also, failing to recognize the experiences of diverse SOGIESC as victims perpetuates violence, exclusion, and trauma in post-conflict settings. In that sense, the recognition and the protection of people with diverse SOGIESC "is one step towards dismantling hegemonic norms of patriarchy, racial hierarchy, inequality, sexism, and heterosexism, whether brought on by colonization, state insecurity, or civil conflict" (Fobear 2014: 53).

This shift in victim perspective will also have important consequences for understanding the causes of violence against those who are perceived as victims. In other words, accepting people with diverse SOGIESC as victims in the field of transitional justice is important in terms of revealing the reasons of violence against them. In relation to gender, something similar happened in international criminal law. While the Nuremberg and Tokyo courts ignored the issue of violence and rape against women, the ICTY and ICTR have been an important shift in international law toward the recognition of violence and rape against women and the underlying causes of such crimes (Girelli 2017).

Queer Legal Theory

Transitional justice is a past-, present-, and future-oriented field. As a past-oriented field, it focuses on wrongdoings and human rights violations during conflict. Its focus on the present is related to the new political regime and

5 I should emphasize the difficulty of defining conflict-related sexual violence. My point here is to show the implications of an analysis which is based on gender binary and heteronormativity. For an analysis and overview about sexual violence, see Schulz (2021).

6 As feminist transitional justice scholars have demonstrated, violence is not limited to periods of armed conflict but exists before and after. Thus, it is necessary to take account of the "continuum of violence," that is, to holistically recognize all forms of violence and domination during and after the conflict (Sigsworth and Valji 2012).

institutions. As for the future, transitional justice mechanisms aim to prevent future violations, injustices, and crimes (Buckley-Zistel and Stanley 2012).

The definition of crimes and violence, the building of institutions in post-conflict settings, and the prevention of future violations and discrimination are primarily formalized through legal texts. What is more, the law as a social discourse has the power to shape sexuality and desires not only in transitional contexts but also in general. It is because of the centrality of the legal field, as text and everyday practice, that it is essential that we integrate queer legal perspectives into the theory and practice of transitional justice and reflect on the challenges that we will confront.

Before dwelling on queer legal perspectives, let me briefly present three main perspectives/schools in legal theory. We can generally differentiate between descriptive, normative, and critical perspectives to law. In defining law, the descriptive perspective does not treat questions of moral obligation (the law that ought to be), justice, and morality. Normative perspectives, though, in defining law, treat the concept of justice by arguing that law has to be compatible with justice. These two perspectives form the classic natural law–positive law debate (Murphy and Coleman 1990).

The third perspective deviates from the other two in that it brings a critique of the legal system as a whole and of the liberal character of legal systems. In that sense, critical legal studies and feminist legal theory stand very close to each other, as both theories express a total critique of the legal system. For instance, critical legal studies (CLS) raise the issue of the relation between law and politics. According to CLS, law is a mask that provides legitimacy to existing social structures and protects the rights of men and White people (Hasnas 1995).

But unlike CLS's focus on the political biases of the legal system, feminist legal scholars have instead emphasized its patriarchal fabric. Even if the origins of feminist legal theory are very diverse, most feminist legal scholars, especially in the 1970s and 1980s, focused on the issue of patriarchy.[7] They have argued that society, and necessarily the legal order, is patriarchal. Feminist legal theory has attempted to analyze the contribution of law to building, reinforcing, and maintaining patriarchy and looks at ways in which patriarchy can be undermined and ultimately eliminated. Another issue that feminist legal theory has explored is that of the mystification of the objectivity of law, which is also a point CLS has been emphasizing. According to both perspectives, the objectivity of law or of legal systems is a myth. Legal systems consist of norms. For instance, the main tenet of the liberal rule of law is that everybody is equal in front of the law. Yet feminist legal scholars have emphasized that, in legal systems, it is maleness that forms the norm of what is considered human (Freeman 1994). In short, CLS argues that the

7 This is especially the argument of the radical feminists (see MacKinnon 1983).

human being in front of the rule of law is predominately White and middle class, whilst feminist legal scholars underline the maleness of the law and the patriarchal character of the legal system.

In the 1990s, feminist scholarship tackled several philosophical and socio-political questions both in theory and in practice, seeking to answer questions about identity and difference (Lacey 2007). The sex/gender distinction and the gender binary have also been criticized by some feminist scholars (Butler 1990; Alsop et al. 2002). In addition to these critiques, feminist legal scholars in the 1990s questioned the role that powerful social discourse such as law played in the constitution of gendered identities. Feminist legal scholars specifically expounded that subjects do not arrive in legal texts already constituted as women or men, as lesbian/gay or heterosexual, emphasizing that the law in itself as a social discourse plays an active and dynamic role in the shaping of gendered and sexualized subjects (Lacey 2007).

Another significant issue feminist legal scholars have touched upon is the intersection of gender with several other attributes, such as race, culture, class, and sexual orientation (Barnett 1998; Lacey 2007). Barnett (1998), for instance, has argued that the concept of gender has been criticized for portraying women in an essentialist way in legal theory, uniformly as heterosexual, White, and middle-class. Feminist scholars have adopted the view that people are oppressed not solely or primarily on the basis of their gender but also on the basis of race, gender identity, sexual orientation, and other categories. There are many forms of inequality which could be explored through the prism of intersectionality (Crenshaw 1989; Harris 1990; Alsop et al. 2002).

Drawing on this theoretical background, queer legal theory, like feminist legal theory, belongs to this third, critical perspective to law. Both approaches – queer legal theory and feminist legal theory – are subversive because they criticize traditional and hegemonic understandings of sex and gender (Fineman 2009).[8]

In very general terms, queer legal theory[9] can be delineated as an "application of Queer theory to law and legal discourse" (McGill and Salyzyn 2014: 11).

8 In as much as there are scholars (Valdes 1995) who call for cooperation between queer and feminist legal theory, there are also scholars calling for a break between queer theory and feminism (Halley 2009).

9 Several scholars differentiate between queer legal theory and LGBTI legal studies. For example, Cossman (2019) presents four categories: (1) *queer* as a synonym/umbrella term for *LGBTI*; (2) *queer* as sexual minorities and non-normative sexual identities; (3) *queer* as referent to queer theory; and (4) no-name queer. I think numbers 1 and 2 could be classified under the title *LGBTI* studies, and 3 and 4 under queer legal theory. Libby Adler (2018) makes distinction between "LGBT equal rights discourse" and queer. Damian A. González Salzberg (2020) makes distinction between queer legal theory and "the doctrinal legal study of human rights of LGBT individuals." In this chapter, I focus on the deconstruction of the gender binary and the heterosexual matrix, and for this reason I draw on queer legal theory rather than LGBTI studies.

In that respect, a queer legal theory exposes that the law is a tool of heteronormative society and that sexuality is constructed socially, while it also shows the possibility of analyzing concepts beyond the male/female binary (Stychin 2004; González-Salzberg 2020). Indeed, through queer theory, we learn how sexuality is socially constructed and relative, that is, changing across time and space. Queer legal theory makes us think of the role of law as a social discourse used to create and maintain a heterosexual matrix, and to shape and name gendered and sexual legal subjects. In this regard, how legal texts and court decisions define, classify, or name cases or facts impacts the lives of legal subjects who have to live under the legal system. As Finley (1989: 888) states:

> Law can pronounce definitely what something is or is not and how a situation or event is to be understood. The concepts, categories, and terms that law uses, and the reasoning structure by which it expresses itself, organizes its practices, and constructs its meanings, has a particularly potent ability to shape popular and authoritative understandings of situations. Legal language does more than express thoughts. It reinforces certain world views and understandings of events. . . . Through its definitions and the way it talks about events, law has the power to silence alternative meanings – to suppress other stories.

Suppressed stories are, among other things, the experiences of those who are left out of the heterosexist legal system. To be able to listen to the stories of people with diverse SOGIESC in the transitional justice field, a queer legal perspective seems indispensable. A queer legal perspective facilitates the deconstruction of the heterosexist foundations of the legal system. As such, queer legal theory informs legal theory to recognize people with diverse SOGIESC as subjects or legal categories of transitional justice mechanisms. Besides, queer legal theory–informed transitional justice study and research will take into account that legal texts in the transitional justice field must include SOGIESC, next to race, gender, and ethnicity, as one of the grounds of human rights violations.

However, to argue for the deconstruction of the heterosexist foundations of the legal system through a queer legal perspective is to bring forth challenges that must be addressed. The first challenge originates from the law's essential dependence on norms and categories, on setting norms and categories. This dependence challenges the call for a queer lens in the legal mechanisms of transitional justice, because an essential attribute of queer or queerness is being against norms and categories. A second and related challenge arises with the incorporation of diverse SOGIESC into the legal system. The more they become part of and get recognized by the legal system (and by international law as well) as legal subjects, the less they retain their queerness (Kapur 2017).

Let me firstly deal with the second challenge. Indeed, the more persons with diverse SOGIESC become part of the legal system or the more they are recognized by the legal system (especially in the domain of family law), the more they become regulated by and fall under the control of state authorities and rules. However, I think that their recognition by a legal system is something already contributing to the deconstructing of the heterosexual matrix and gender binary, which continue to be foundational attributes of state authority and rules. Thus, this incorporation and subjection to state rules is a price worth paying as it holds significant prospects for a more inclusive transitional field and legal system.

As for the first challenge, I argue that mutable sexual categories could be constructed within a legal system in place of the existing rigid innate sexual categories. From a queer-informed legal theory point of view, a legal system that is not contained in the gender binary but recognizes and respects diverse SOGIESC is possible. More clearly, from a queer legal perspective, we should be prepared to see these binary categories deconstructed, because, although as a social discourse law may be repressive in its relationship to diverse SOGIESC, law is also a locus of struggle. In that sense, law can also be dynamic, unstable, and unpredictable (Stychin 2004) and, thus, function as a tool to change the heteronormative fabric of society.

This also holds true for the judicial mechanisms of transitional justice and how SOGIESC is handled therein, as exemplified in the case of the Rome Statute. In the following section, I explicate how queer legal perspectives could be reified through legal texts and/or interpretation of them and argue, through a queer-informed legal interpretation of the Rome Statute, that persecution based on SOGIESC can be addressed under international criminal law.

Queer Perspectives in Judicial Mechanisms of Transitional Justice

Created in 1998, the Rome Statute provided for the establishment of the International Criminal Court (ICC), which is one of the most important legal institutions and judicial mechanisms of transitional justice. The Rome Statute is also the first international law text that employed and defined the term *gender*. Yet in defining the term, the text reflects a heterosexist framework based on the gender binary. However, I will argue that from a queer point of view, we can expand the range of the Statute so that persecution based on SOGIESC can be addressed under it. In enumerating crimes against humanity Article 7(1)(h) includes

> Persecution against any identifiable group or collectivity on political, racial, national, ethnic, cultural, religious, gender as defined in paragraph 3, or other grounds that are universally recognized as impermissible under international law, in connection with any act referred to in this paragraph or any crime within the jurisdiction of the Court.
>
> (Rome Statute 2011: 3)

The first argument in favor of including SOGIESC under the protection of the Statue is, as Andrew Sumner Hagopian (2016) has argued, that persons with diverse SOGIESC could be considered persecuted on *political grounds*, as stated in the Article above. *Political grounds* here mostly refer to political activism. In that sense, people who take part in activism for individuals with diverse SOGIESC could be considered in the context of Article 7(1)(h) as being part of a political group. In many societies, publicly living as an LGBTI person is unmistakably seen as a political statement in itself, indicating the adherence to certain political positions or groups (Hagopian 2016). Accordingly, even the act of living openly as LGBTI can be, in itself, considered political action and, as such, be considered as falling under the protection of the Rome Statute.

Secondly, the incorporation of diverse SOGIESC into the provisions of the Rome Statute can be discussed from the viewpoint of gender. Article 7(1)(h) recognizes gender as one of the grounds for which people are persecuted. The Statue defines *gender* in Article 7(3):

> "[G]ender" refers to the two sexes, male and female, within the context of society. The term "gender" does not indicate any meaning different from the above.
>
> (Rome Statute 2011: 4)

This definition of *gender* was the result of many discussions and came as a compromise between countries that wanted to retain the term "gender" and those opposing its usage.[10] The opposition argued that the term *gender* should not be stated in an international criminal law text because its meaning is not clear. However, there was another reason certain countries were against it. They feared that the use of the term *gender* might lead to rights based on sexual orientation and the recognition of violence against sexual orientation (Oosterveld 2014). Those opposed would only accept a definition that mentioned men, women, and children, and explicitly of two sexes – male and female – because for them the term

> "gender" would expand from male and female to either include five "genders" (adding gay, lesbian, and transgendered) and/or include hermaphrodites, female hermaphrodites, and male pseudo hermaphrodites. They were convinced that if "male and female," the number "two," and the word "sex" were used, biology would be the foremost factor in the definition.
>
> (Oosterveld 2005: 72)

10 See Oosterveld (2014) for the battleground on the meaning of "gender" during the Rome Diplomatic Conference.

Conversely, the main concern of the countries supporting the term was that any definition accepted in the text would reflect that to be male and female is socially constructed. In the end, the definition was the result of compromise. On the one hand, Article 7(3) clearly states that there are two sexes, male and female, and thus satisfied those who opposed the use of the term *gender*. On the other hand, the Article includes the phrase "within the context of the society" (Rome Statute 2011: 4) and satisfied the supporters of gender (Oosterveld 2005) because it was thus accepted that gender is socially constructed and cannot be reduced to biological sex.

The definition did not *completely* satisfy both parties and left unanswered the question of whether sexual orientation should be evaluated within the context of gender, as defined in the Statute, and, thus, whether human rights violations based on sexual orientation will be protected under the Rome Statute (Oosterveld 2014; Hagopian 2016; Scheinert 2015). As a consequence, scholars hold different opinions regarding the question of whether SOGIESC can be read into the scope of Article 7(3). Rana Lehr-Lehnardt (2002) and Stephanie Farrior (2003) argue that sexual orientation cannot be considered under the Rome Statute, as the definition of *gender* therein "means male and female, not homosexual" (Lehr-Lehnnardt 2002: 340). In a similar vein, Michael Bohlander (2014) argues that the intention of the countries opposing the inclusion of the term *gender* was obvious, thus leaving no room for judges to interpret whether sexual orientation can or cannot be considered under Article 7(3).

However, other scholars do not share these conclusions. They argue that no consensus emerged whether the definition of *gender* explicitly excludes the term *sexual orientation*. The term *gender* is open to interpretation and covers *sexual orientation* (Copelon 2000; Oosterveld 2014; Scheinert 2015). Another reason to pursue the argument that Article 7(3) covers sexual orientation is that *gender* and *sexual orientation* are inseparably related to each other. According to Oosterveld (2005), Hagopian (2016), and Scheinert (2015), violence based on sexual orientation is linked to the societal expectations regarding what it means to be male or female. More specifically, violence against a gay man due to his sexual orientation is actually perpetrated because he is not obeying the societal expectation regarding manhood, that is, that a man can only be emotionally or sexually related to the opposite sex, to a woman. The same logic is behind violence against transgendered identities (Oosterveld 2005). Trans women, for instance, face violence specifically because they act against societal roles and expectations about what it means to be male or female.

The crucial point here is that even if we interpret Articles 7(1)(h) and 7(3) in favor of SOGIESC, this interpretation does not explicitly address diverse SOGIESC as one of the grounds of violence and persecution (Hagopian 2016). However, being aware of the Statute's missing the exact ground of persecution is, in itself, built upon a queer-informed legal perspective. It is worth noting that the ICC Office of the Prosecutor in the Policy Paper interpreted the term *gender* in line with Article 21(3)[11] and held an intersectional perspective. According to the Policy Paper (Office of the Prosecutor 2014: 16), the office will:

> [u]nderstand the intersection of factors such as gender, age, race, disability, religion or belief, political or other opinion, national, ethnic, or social origin, birth, sex, sexual orientation, and other status or identities which may give rise to multiple forms of discrimination and social inequalities.

It is important that the paper indicates the intersection between gender and sexual orientation and identity and other reasons. Although not legally bounding, the Policy Paper may have important potential regarding the protection of sexual orientation under the Rome Statute (see also Oosterveld 2014).

Lastly, the inclusion of diverse SOGIESC can also be discussed in the context of the phrase "other grounds that are universally recognized as impermissible under international law" (Rome Statute 2011: 3), as stated in Article 7(1)(h) of the Statue. Oosterveld (2005) and Scheinert (2015) argue that "other grounds" (Rome Statute 2011: 3) may include diverse SOGIESC, as many UN documents[12] protect diverse SOGIESC and many ECtHR verdicts[13] are in favor of diverse SOGIESC. Based on these data, we can argue that diverse SOGIESC is, indeed, protected and recognized within the scope of international and regional law and thus falls within the provisions of Article 7(1). However, this is not a unanimous understanding. For Hagopian (2016) and Bohlander (2014), considering that there are countries among the signatory states that criminalize diverse SOGIESC, it is difficult to say that the standard of "universally recognized as impermissible under international law" (Rome Statute 2011: 3) has been fulfilled.

Yet the debates on the inclusion/exclusion of sexual orientation and the consequent statement of the Office of the Prosecutor point to what seems to be a current tendency in international law toward the discussion, if not recognition, of sexual orientation as one of the reasons that should be addressed when persecution and human rights violations are investigated. This is even more evident in the Yogyakarta Principles. Although it is not directly connected to transitional justice research and practice and not legally bounding, I consider the Yogyakarta Principles as a very good example of a queer-informed (legal) text.

11 Article 21(3): "The application and interpretation of law pursuant to this article must be consistent with internationally recognized human rights and be without any adverse distinction founded on grounds such as gender as defined in Article 7, paragraph 3, age, race, colour, language, religion or belief, political or other opinion, national, ethnic or social origin, wealth, birth or other status" (Rome Statute 2011: 13).

12 See UN resolutions and soft law instruments about SOGIESC (Hagopian 2016).

13 See ECtHR's decisions (Dunne 2020; González-Salzberg 2020).

The horrifying human rights abuses committed around the world against persons on the basis of SOGIESC were the reason the Yogyakarta Principles (Yogyakarta Principles on the Application of International Human Rights Law in Relation to Sexual Orientation and Gender Identity) had to be developed. In 2006, in Yogyakarta, Indonesia, a group of international human rights experts met to outline a set of international principles regarding SOGIESC. They prepared a universal guide that presents legal standards by which all states should abide. It should be noted that the principles of Yogyakarta do not introduce a new set of rights. They instead remind states of their responsibilities in the context of international human rights and state that violations of human rights, such as right to life, education, health, on the basis of SOGIESC, cannot be accepted. In addition, the Principles stipulate that states should recognize the gender identity of individuals and that they cannot force upon them any surgery or medical treatment. In 2017, "Yogyakarta plus 10"[14] was adopted as a supplement to the Yogyakarta Principles.[15]

The Yogyakarta Principles are structured around the terms SOGIESC. SOGIESC was chosen over other terms, such as "homosexual," "lesbian," "gay," "bi-sexual," "intersex," etc., so that they "better reflect the universal reach and application of human rights law" (O'Flaherty 2015: 284). In other words, the Principles

> do not suggest specific standards for particular groups. . . . By expressing the rights in this way, the drafters have also sought to avoid the necessity of requiring individuals to absolutely *categorise themselves by identity labels* that may not be appropriate for all cultural contexts. The notions of sexual orientation and gender identity are fluid. Requiring a person to subscribe to a particular identity group would only perpetuate the oppression that the rights are seeking to combat. None of the rights in the Principles can be considered particular or unique to one group, but rather are enjoyed by all.
>
> (An Activist's Guide to The Yogyakarta Principles 2010: 23)[16]

14 Yogyakarta Plus 10's full title is "Additional Principles and State Obligations on the Application of International Human Rights Law in Relation to Sexual Orientation, Gender Identity, Gender Expression and Sex Characteristics to Complement the Yogyakarta Principles" (Yogyakarta Principles plus 10 2017).

15 The reason for the preparation of the principles is stated as follows: "The YP plus 10 was adopted on 10 November 2017 to supplement the Yogyakarta Principles. The YP plus 10 document emerged from the intersection of the developments in international human rights law with the emerging understanding of violations suffered by persons on grounds of sexual orientation and gender identity and the recognition of the distinct and intersectional grounds of gender expression and sex characteristics" (Yogyakarta Principles plus 10 2017).

16 Emphasis mine.

I consider the Yogyakarta Principles as a good example of a queer-informed (legal) text. I think that their adoption of SOGIESC over terms such as "homosexual," "lesbian," "gay," "bi-sexual," "intersex," and "trans" shows us a possible path through which queer-informed legal texts can be constructed. In that respect, the Yogyakarta Principles can function as a guide for prospective legal texts to be used in the transitional justice context.

Conclusion

In this chapter, I have argued that to include people with diverse SOGIESC in the field and practice of transitional justice, not only a queer perspective, but also specifically a queer *legal* perspective, is needed. One of the foremost reasons for this is the fact that transitional justice processes are typically, although certainly not exclusively, based on legal, or at least semi-legal, texts and statutes. This chapter is essentially an attempt to demonstrate what a queer legal theory brings to the field of transitional justice.

Firstly, the chapter has argued that queer legal theory exposes and deconstructs the heterosexist fabric of the legal system and legal texts. I have elaborated on the integration of queer legal theory in transitional justice through the recognition of victims as legal subjects, as victimhood relates to almost all mechanisms (judicial and non-judicial) of transitional justice. Who will be recognized as victim is often decided through legal texts. A queer legal perspective is thus enabling a holistic and intersectional understanding of the process of legal recognition of victimhood. In this way, hitherto invisible subjects of transitional justice become visible and form a part of the transitional justice process. Notwithstanding the gap between legal texts and their implementation, the recognition and protection of people with diverse SOGIESC is vital to preclude discrimination and violations against them and to break down heterosexism in transitional and post-conflict settings. Unquestionably, the power of the law has an important impact on the transitional justice field. As legal texts do not just classify or categorize people, they also form and reinforce understandings of situations, ways of thinking, mindsets, and practices. It is because of this that the acknowledgment of diverse experiences and identities through legal texts is crucial. Secondly, I have shown in the example of the Rome Statute that a queer legal perspective enables a reading which expands the scope of legal texts in a queer direction and can thus address the violations of human rights of persons with diverse SOGIESC extending their legal protection.

Finally, I have argued that queer legal theory prompts a discussion on how a queer perspective can be translated into *legal knowledge*, *form*, and *language*, while at the same time addressing the challenges inherent in this process of translation. Besides, these are the challenges we should overcome to bring a queer perspective to the transitional and post-conflict settings while including persons with diverse SOGIESC. The first challenge stems from the law's reliance on classifications and norms, *queer* being essentially against them. I have argued that, although legal rules are based on categories and norms, the plurality of SOGIESC can also be formalized through legal rules, as the Yogyakarta Principles have shown. To accomplish that, the Yogyakarta Principles employ the terms "sexual orientation," "gender identity," "gender expression," and "sex characteristic." The use of these terms instead of adding LGBTI categories or identities to legal texts demonstrates a queer perspective. I thus argue that mutable sexual and gender categories could become visible in a legal system in place of the existing rigid innate categories. In this regard, the important point is how legal systems regulate sexual and gender identities. For instance, the legal system in a post-conflict society that does not force sex-reassignment surgery upon trans individuals and recognizes non-binary genders or a third gender category holds the potential to recognize mutable sexual and gender categories.

The second challenge has to do with the fear that the recognition and incorporation of diverse SOGIESC into the legal system (national or international) might entail the loss of their essential character of being against rigid categorizations and norms. In that respect, I have argued that the acknowledgment of SOGIESC by a legal system is already contributing to the deconstructing of the heterosexual matrix and gender binary, which continue to be foundational components of state authority and rules. In that sense, subjection to state rules is a price worth paying as it holds important prospects for a more inclusive transitional justice field and legal system.

Acknowledgments

I would like to thank the editors of this book, especially Philipp Schulz and Heleen Touquet, as well as the anonymous reviewer, for their comments on an earlier draft of this chapter. I would also like to thank Susanne Buckley-Zistel and my colleagues at the Centre for Conflict Studies at Marburg University. This research has been supported by the Alexander von Humboldt Foundation Philipp Schwartz Initiative.

References

An Activist's Guide to the Yogyakarta Principles (2010). *An Activist's Guide to the Yogyakarta Principles on the Application of International Human Rights Law in Relation to Sexual Orientation and Gender Identity*. Available at: https://outright-international.org/sites/default/files/Activists_Guide_Yogyakarta_Principles.pdf. Accessed on: 9 January 2022.

Adler, L. (2018). *Gay Priori A Queer Critical Legal Studies Approach to Law Reform*. Durham: Duke University Press.

Alsop, R., A. Fitzsimons and K. Lennon (2002). *Theorizing Gender*. Malden: Blackwell.

Barker, M.-J. and J. Scheele (2016). *Queer a Graphic History*. London: Icon Books.

Barnett, H. (1998). *Introduction to Feminist Jurisprudence*. London and Sydney: Cavendish Publishing.

Bohlander, M. (2014). Criminalising LGBT Persons Under National Criminal Law and Article 7(1)(h) and (3) of the ICC Statute. *Global Policy* 5(4): 401–414.

Buckley-Zistel, S. and R. Stanley (2012). Introduction. In: Buckley-Zistel, S. and Stanley, R. (eds.): *Gender in Transitional Justice*. Basingstoke: Palgrave MacMillan: 1–33.

Bueno-Hansen, P. (2018). The Emerging LGBTI Rights Challenge to Transitional Justice in Latin America. *International Journal of Transitional Justice* 12(1): 126–145.

Butler, J. (1990). *Gender Trouble: Feminism and the Subversion of Identity, Gender Trouble: Feminism and the Subversion of Identity*. New York: Routledge.

Charman, T. (2018). Sexual Violence or Torture?: The Framing of Sexual Violence Against Men in Armed Conflict in Amnesty International and Human Rights Watch Reports. In: Zalewski, M., Drumond, P., Prugl, E. and Stern, M. (eds.): *Sexual Violence Against Men in Global Politics*. New York: Routledge: 198–210.

Copelon, R. (2000). Gender Crimes as War Crimes: Integrating Crimes Against Women into International Law. *McGill Law Journal* 46: 217–240.

Cossman, B. (2019). Queering Queer Legal Studies: An Unreconstructed Ode to Eve Sedwick (and Others). *Critical Analysis of Law* 6(1): 23–38.

Craig, E. (2010). Converging Feminist and Queer Legal Theories: Family Feuds and Family Ties. *Windsor Yearbook of Access to Justice* 28(1): 209–210.

Crenshaw, K. (1989). Demarginalizing the Intersection of Race and Sex: A Black Feminist Critique of Antidiscrimination Doctrine, Feminist Theory and Antiracist Politics. *The University of Chicago Legal Forum* 1: 139–167.

Daigle, M. and H. Myrttinen (2018). Bringing Diverse Sexual Orientation and Gender Identity (SOGI) into Peacebuilding Policy and Practice. *Gender and Development* 26(2): 103–120.

De Greiff, P. (2006). *The Handbook of Reparations*. Oxford: Oxford University Press.

Dolan, C. (2018). Victims Who Are Men. In: Ni Aolain, F., Cahn, N., Haynes, D. and Valji, N. (eds.): *The Oxford Handbook of Gender and Conflict*. Oxford: Oxford University Press: 86–104.

Dunne, P. (2020). Transgender Rights in Europe: EU and Council of Europe Movements Towards Gender Identity Equality. In: Ashford, C. and Maine, A. (eds.): *Research Handbook on Gender, Sexuality and the Law*. Cheltenham: Edward Elgar Publishing: 134–147.

Espitia, M. (2016). *LGBT in Colombia: A War Within, CUNY Academic Works*. Available at: https://academicworks.cuny.edu/gj_etds/150/. Accessed on: 4 January 2022.

Farrior, S. (2003). The Rights of Women in International Human Rights Law Textbooks: Segregation, Integration, or Omission? *Columbia Journal of Gender and the Law* 12(3): 587–599.

Fineman, M. (2009). Introduction: Feminist and Queer Legal Theory. In: Fineman, M., Sackson, J. and Romero, A. (eds.): *Feminist and Queer Legal Theory Intimate Encounters, Uncomfortable Conversations*. Farnham: Ashgate: 1–6.

Finley, L. (1989). Breaking Women's Silence in Law: The Dilemma of the Gendered Nature of Legal Reasoning. *Notre Dame Law Review* 64: 886–910.

Fobear, K. (2014). Queering Truth Commissions. *Journal of Human Rights Practice* 6(1): 51–68.

Freeman, M. (1994). *Lloyds Introduction To Jurisprudence*. London: Sweet & Maxwell.

Gamson, J. and D. Moon (2004). The Sociology of Sexualities: Queer and Beyond. *Annual Review of Sociology* 30: 47–64.

Garcia-Godos, J. (2017). Reparations. In: Simić, O. (ed.): *An Introduction to Transitional Justice*. New York: Routledge: 177–200.

Girelli, G. (2017). *Understanding Transitional Justice, Understanding Transitional Justice*. London: Palgrave MacMillan.

González-Salzberg, D. (2020). *Sexuality & Transsexuality Under the European Convention on Human Rights a Queer Reading of Human Rights Law*. Oxford: Hart Publishing.

Hagopian, A. (2016). Persecution and Protection of Sexual and Gender Minorities Under Article 7(1)(h) of the Rome Statute. *Soas Law Journal* 3(1): 55–69.

Halderman, F. (2008). Another Kind of Justice: Transitional Justice as Recognition. *Cornell International Law Journal* 41(3): 675–737.

Halley, J. (2009). Queer Theory by Men. In: Fineman, M., Jackson, J. and Romero, A. (eds.): *Feminist and Queer Legal Theory: Intimate Encounters, Uncomfortable Conversations*. Farnham: Ashgate: 9–28.

Harris, A. (1990). Race and Essentialism in Feminist Legal Theory. *Stanford Law Review* 42(3): 581–616.

Hasnas, J. (1995). Back to the Future: From Critical Legal Studies Forward to Legal Realism, or How Not to Miss the Point of the Indeterminacy Argument. *Duke Law Journal* 45(1): 84–132.

Jagose, A. (1996). *Queer Theory an Introduction*. New York: New York University Press.

Kapur, R. (2017). The (Im)possibility of Queering International Human Rights Law. In: Otto, D. (ed.): *Queering International Law: Possibilities, Alliances, Complicities, Risks*. London: Routledge Taylor & Francis Ltd.: 131–147.

Lacey, N. (2007). The Constitution of Identity: Gender, Feminist Legal Theory, and the Law and Society Movement. In: Sarat, A. (ed.): *The Blackwell Companion to Law and Society*.Oxford: Blackwell: 471–486.

Lehr-Lehnardt, R. (2002). One Small Step for Women: Female-Friendly Provisions in the Rome Statute of the International Criminal Court. *Brigham Young University Journal of Public Law* 16(2): 317–354.

MacKinnon, C. (1983). Feminism, Marxism, Method, and the State: Toward Feminist Jurisprudence. *Signs* 8(4): 635–658.

Maier, N. (2019). Queering Colombia's Peace Process: A Case Study of LGBTI Inclusion. *International Journal of Human Rights* 24(4): 1–16.

McGill, J. and A. Salyzyn (2014). Queer Insights on Women in the Legal Profession. *Legal Ethics* 17(2): 231–260.

Monro, S. (2020). Sexual and Gender Diversities: Implications for LGBTQ Studies. *Journal of Homosexuality* 67(3): 315–324.

Moore, M. and J. Barner (2017). Sexual Minorities in Conflict Zones: A Review of the Literature. *Aggression and Violent Behavior* 35: 33–37.

Murphy, J. and J. Coleman (1990). *Philosophy of Law: An Introduction to Jurisprudence, Dimensions of Philosophy Series*. London: Westviev Press.

Office of the Prosecutor (2014). *Policy Paper on Sexual and Gender-Based Crimes*. Available at: https://www.icc-cpi.int/iccdocs/otp/otp-policy-paper-on-sexual-and-gender-based-crimes--june-2014.pdf. Accessed on: 4 January 2022.

O'Flaherty, M. (2015). The Yogyakarta Principles at Ten. *Nordic Journal of Human Rights* 33(4): 280–298.

Oosterveld, V. (2005). The Definition of 'Gender' in the Rome Statute of the International Criminal Court: A Step Forward or Back for International Criminal Justice? *Harvard Human Rights Journal* 18(1): 55–84.

Oosterveld, V. (2014). Constructive Ambiguity and the Meaning of 'Gender' for the International Criminal Court. *International Feminist Journal of Politics* 16(4): 563–580.

Robinson, M. (2020). Two-Spirit Identity in a Time of Gender Fluidity. *Journal of Homosexuality* 67(12): 1675–1690.

Romero, A. (2009). Methodological Descriptions: 'Feminist' and 'Queer' Legal Theories. In: Fineman, M., Jackson, J. and Romero, A. (eds.): *Feminist and Queer Legal*

Theory: Intimate Encounters, Uncomfortable Conversations. Farnham: Ashgate: 179–198.

Rome Statute (2011). *Rome Statute of the International Criminal Court*. The Hague: International Crimina Court.

Scheinert, J. (2015). Is Criminalization Criminal?: Antisodomy Laws and the Crime Against Humanity of Persecution. *Law & Sexuality* 24: 99–144.

Schulz, P. (2021). *Male Survivors of Wartime Sexual Violence*. Oakland: University of California Press.

Schulz, P. and H. Touquet (2020). Queering Explanatory Frameworks for Wartime Sexual Violence Against Men. *International Affairs* 5(1): 1169–1187.

Sigsworth, R. and N. Valji (2012). Continuities of Violence Against Women and the Limitations of Transitional Justice: The Case of South Africa. In: Buckley-Zistel, S. and Stanley, R. (eds.): *Gender in Transitional Justice*.Basingstoke: Palgrave Macmillan: 115–135.

Sivakumaran, S. (2007). Sexual Violance Aganist Men in Armed Conflict. *The European Journal of International Law* 18(2): 253–276.

Sjoberg, L. (2016). *Women as Wartime Rapists: Beyond Sensation and Stereotyping*. New York: New York Univeristy Press.

Stychin, C. (2004). *Law's Desire Sexuality and the Limits of Justice*. New York: Routledge.

Sullivan, N. (2003). *A Critical Introduction to Queer Theory*. Edinburgh: Edinburgh University Press.

Touquet, H. and P. Schulz (2020). Navigating Vulnerabilities and Masculinities: How Gendered Contexts Shape the Agency of Male Sexual Violence Survivors. *Security Dialogue* 52(3): 1–18.

Valdes, F. (1995). Queers, Sissies, Dykes and Tomboys: Deconstructing the Conflation of 'Sex,' 'Gender,' and 'Sexual Orientation' in Euro-American Law and Society. *California Law Review* 83(1): 1–377.

Yogyakarta Principles (2006). *The Yogyakarta Principles on the Application of International Human Rights Law in Relation to Sexual Orientation and Gender Identity*. Available at: https://yogyakartaprinciples.org. Accessed on: 4 January 2022.

Yogyakarta Principles plus 10 (2017). *The Yogyakarta Principles Plus 10 Additional Principles and State Obligations on the Application of International Human Rights Law in Relation to Sexual Orientation, Gender Identity, Gender Expression and Sex Characteristics to Complement the Yogyakarta P*. Available at: http://yogyakartaprinciples.org/principles-en/yp10/. Accessed on: 4 January 2022.

Chapter 6

The Heterosexual System Denuded

Ecuador's Truth Commission

Pascha Bueno-Hansen

Introduction

The Ecuadorian Truth Commission final report chapter on sexual violence and patterns of human rights violations (2010: 251–252) notes that:

> Authoritarian regimes tend to exacerbate the social hierarchization of men and women and, as a corollary, the primacy of masculinity over femininity that is sustained through a heterosexual system. The creation of a 'national identity' has been harnessed to the construction of masculine and feminine identities that reproduce this ideology as part of its political organization and sexual division. These identities are an exacerbation of the gender system and its most recalcitrant manifestations.[1]

While feminist interventions in transitional justice practice and theory have made important strides over the last decades in recognizing harms against women and advocating for a gender (qua women) analysis, the heterosexual system endures as the default reference. The Ecuadorian Truth Commission final report refers to the heterosexual system as the traditional sex and gender social norms that reinforce a binary understanding of male and female, masculine and feminine, and assumes opposite sex coupling as the only acceptable sexual orientation and behavior. Paired seamlessly with the divide between the public and private spheres, this heterosexual system upholds patriarchal social control and obligates individuals to conform to rigid identities and roles. This chapter analyzes how the 2010 Ecuadorian Truth Commission's final report came to contain a gender approach that interrogates the heterosexual foundations of the nation-state. The aim here is to make visible the value of feminist movement–informed contributions to transitional justice processes and knowledge production, despite the significant conceptual, procedural, and structural constraints of its mechanisms. Most significantly, the

1 All translations from Spanish to English are by the author.

DOI: 10.4324/9781003519522-8

Ecuadorian final report evidences the way a feminist movement–informed gender approach frames the impact of sexual and gender-based violence against women, men, and people of non-conforming genders and sexualities in relation to each other, all mutually reinforcing manifestations of a heterosexual system of domination that goes hand in hand with authoritarianism. By understanding the varied violent manifestations of the heterosexual system as all coming from the same root, then the field and practice of transitional justice can expand its epistemic parameters to identify and address the systemic dynamics undergirding these harms.

While the last two decades have witnessed the mainstreaming of a gender analysis with a focus on sexual violence against women, the field of TJ has slowly begun to include knowledge produced about the role of masculinities and the impact of armed conflict, authoritarian regimes, and political repression against men (Theidon 2009; Hamber 2007, 2015; Green 2012) and people of non-normative genders and sexualities (Fobear 2014; Bueno-Hansen 2018; Ashe 2019; Schulz 2020; Fobear and Baines 2020). Following the path of gender mainstreaming, this process of inclusion has been piecemeal and "add-on" (Bueno-Hansen 2015, 2018), thereby leaving largely intact the default heterosexual system. The focus of the Ecuadorian Truth Commission, mandated by Rafael Correa in 2007, was to investigate political repression and violence committed under the León Febres Cordero administration between 1984 and 1988. Although the Ecuadorian Truth Commission did not include attention to gender in the mandate, one feminist staff person advocated for the inclusion of a gender approach; the Commission hired a gender consultant, and the final report contributes to the recognition of sexual and gender-based violence as a human rights violation against women, men, and the LGBTI population. While this contribution is noteworthy in terms of providing a contextual analysis of the political violence and repression under investigation, the Commission did not provide sufficient evidence to support any advances in justice and reparations for these harms. Nevertheless, the contributions of a feminist movement–informed gender analysis hold valuable lessons worth examination because it underscores the varied yet interlocking brutal expressions of the heterosexual system, as evidenced on the bodies of women, men, and people of non-normative genders and sexualities. Most importantly, this conceptual frame offers an alternative to the piecemeal and "add-on" inclusion. While gender disaggregation is needed to understand how the particular patterns of harm manifest, it can lead to the assumption that the victimhood, as experienced by women, men, and people of non-normative genders, is disconnected rather than relational. In practical terms, the formulation of the truth commission mandate, the selection of commissioners and staff, the research design and implementation, and the training processes would all benefit from incorporating this conceptual frame from the inception of the transitional justice mechanism.

The Ecuadorian Truth Commission final report demonstrates a feminist movement–informed gender approach that applied a holistic understanding of the logics and workings of the heterosexual system to examine sexual and gender-based violence against women, men, and the LGBTI population. For example, in relation to the violence experienced by the LGBTI population, the final report (Comisión de la Verdad 2010: 293) states:

> This gender-based violence is based in structurally asymmetrical power relations. Within the dominant discourse, these groups are considered a "threat" to social order because they do not obey heterosexual and patriarchal social norms. Because these groups question the social and traditional gender roles, they suffer daily moral condemnation, violence and social exclusion.

This approach to documenting and analyzing sexual and gender-based violence against people of all genders and sexualities is grounded in the doggedly committed work of two commission staff whose efforts draw from a feminist activist genealogy of praxis. My long-term personal and political commitments to feminist and lesbian activism and the networks I have become a part of over the years provide a unique vantage point to the discussion of gender and transitional justice.

Bringing light to this little-known case is especially relevant in that it predates the 2020 assertion by the UN Special Rapporteur on the promotion of truth, justice, reparation, and guarantees of non-recurrence, Fabián Salvioli:

> A gender perspective requires the complex experiences of sexual and gender-based violence, not only of women, but also of men and of lesbian, gay, bisexual and transgender persons, be consciously and duly recognized and captured by any transitional justice measures that have been designed and implemented, taking into account the criterion of intersectionality. Otherwise, the processes of truth-seeking, justice, comprehensive reparation, guarantees of non-repetition and memorialization would be incomplete.
>
> (UN 2020: 4)

At the time of the Ecuadorian Truth Commission, 2008–2011, truth commissions did not evidence this more capacious understanding of gender and sexuality. Indeed, only the more recent truth commissions of Timor-Leste and Colombia are currently recognized for setting a global precedent in this area (UN 2020: 6).

This analysis proceeds with a reflection on the politics of knowledge production and an explanation of the methodology of this study to show how a largely ignored feminist movement praxis contributes to queer, masculinities, and gender interventions in transitional justice. Such a reflection is necessary to situate the qualitative difference between a technocratic gender mainstreaming approach that adds women on the margins – and now, more recently, men and LGBTI people – and the feminist movement–informed gender approach evidenced in the Ecuadorian Truth Commission. This reflection underscores the significance of expanding the epistemic parameters of the field and practice of transitional justice. Then, returning to the case at hand, the next section sketches the contemporary and historic national and regional context to the Ecuadorian Truth Commission and explains when and why the feminist movement–informed gender approach was added to the Commission's work, how and why a gender consultant came on board, and the internal Commission dynamics surrounding her work. This context situates a close reading of the final report chapter "Sexual Violence and Gender Analysis" and exposes the common structural, procedural, and conceptual obstacles to a feminist movement–informed gender analysis. To understand how the Commission was able to forward its innovative feminist movement–informed gender approach, the following section explores the hidden genealogies of collective knowledge production rooted in the feminist and women's movements through the lives of the two key feminist protagonists on the Commission staff. Lastly, this chapter closes with a reflection on those human rights violations against people of non-normative genders and sexualities that fall outside the mandate and the national record.

The Politics of Knowledge Production and Methodological Considerations

While a global lineage of feminist activists and advocates of various genders and sexualities has examined the heterosexual system over the last decades, this genealogy has largely run parallel to queer, masculinities, and gender interventions in the TJ field. Generalized academic policing regarding knowledge production denies the legitimacy of collective analysis developed by advocates, organizers, activists, and others involved in movement struggles. The knock-on impact of this academic policing is an erasure of this knowledge, producing a generalized ignorance in academic circles and a knee-jerk repulsion and resistance most typically evidenced in the form of discomfort, silence, and looking way. Misogyny and cis-hetero-sexism are the primary vectors of oppression that function to suppress the recognition of these feminist contributions[2] by passively distancing from and/or actively rejecting radical critiques. These dynamics fragment the study of gender-based harms against women, men, and LGBTI populations, thereby curtailing a holistic understanding of the logics and workings of the heterosexual system and its imposition of cis- and heteronormativity as mechanisms of social control and

2 See Rothschild (2005) for a global look at how women's organizing, especially around sexual rights, is discredited, baited, and undermined.

political repression. Against these poor odds, this chapter uplifts the feminist movement–informed gender approach in forwarding a holistic understanding of sexual and gender-based violence as evidenced in the Ecuadorian Truth Commission's final report.

This analysis aligns with a genealogy of feminist activists that anchor their work in a broad-ranging understanding of gender and sexual rights, as expressed in 1996 by Rachel Rosenbloom in *Unspoken Rules: Sexual Orientation and Women's Human Rights* (xxv), published by the International Gay and Lesbian Human Rights Commission:

> The reports contained here present stark evidence of the need for a broad sexual rights movement that addresses the human rights of all women – including lesbians, bisexual women and transgendered women and other sexual minorities. Unless human rights organizations and women's organizations recognize these issues as their own, they will continue to be complicit in the silence that enables human rights violations against lesbians and other sexual minorities to occur.

The Ecuadorian Truth Commission exemplifies how this hidden genealogy of feminist resistance offers an important contribution to the growing field of queer, masculinities, and gender interventions in TJ. While this chapter places emphasis on this hidden genealogy of feminist resistance, it roundly condemns all transphobia. The broader research project in which this analysis is embedded aims to recognize important continuities of activist praxis between feminist movements of the 1980s and 1990s and current Latin American trans and travesti movement informed analytics.[3] Overall, this chapter calls readers to acknowledge that we can hold more than one truth at a time, humans are messy contradictions, and movements are neither monolithic nor homogenous.

The findings presented herein are part of an ongoing research project into the modes of resistance of people of non-normative genders and sexualities to political repression, internal armed conflict, and authoritarianism in Peru, Ecuador, and Colombia. Research includes attending activist-based gatherings, reviewing movement-based newspapers, magazines, reports, and communications, and extended interviews with veteran activists that are typically distrustful and reticent to concede their time. Why should they grant

3 See Berkins, L. (2006). Travestis: una identidad política. *Hemispheric Institute*. Available at https://hemisphericinstitute.org/en/emisferica-42/4-2-review-essays/lohana-berkins.html; Rizki, C. (2019). Latin/x American Trans Studies: Toward a Travesti-Trans Analytic. *Transgender Studies Quarterly* 6(2): 145–155; DiPietro, P. J. (2016). Of Huachafería, Así, and M'e Mati: Decolonizing Transing Methodologies. *Transgender Studies Quarterly* 1–2: 65–73; and DiPietro, P. J. (2016). Decolonizing Travesti Space in Buenos Aires: Race, Sexuality, and Sideways Relationality. *Gender, Place, and Culture* 23(5): 677–693.

academics access to their knowledge, given the data-extractivist approach of many researchers, the absence of personal and political commitments to movement struggles manifested by a lack of follow-up regarding the produces derived from the interview, and a general disregard for activist knowledge production that manifests in less-than-responsible citational practices?[4] A feminist methodological commitment to recognize social actors as knowledge producers is fundamental to building trust and respect, as well as decolonizing knowledge production.

In 2018, I conducted several weeks of preliminary qualitative research in Quito, including ten interviews and the collection of a large body of primary materials. My decades of work with feminist and lesbian organizations and activist groups in Peru and my contacts in Colombia and Ecuador, and transnationally, evidenced my personal and political convictions and facilitated the possibility of an extended interview with the Ecuadorian Truth Commission gender consultant, Tatiana Cordero, in Bogotá in 2019. Soon after the interview, I received the sad news that Tatiana Cordero passed away from cancer, and I dedicate this chapter in honor of her inspirational and courageous life. Given the pandemic-related limitations to conducting fieldwork as of 2020, I conducted desk research in the form of virtual interviews, ongoing email communications, and collection of primary materials. Most significantly, in 2021, I interviewed the member of the Commission's research team who advocated for contracting a gender consultant, Natalia Marcos. These are precarious and fragile herstories of struggle that could easily go undocumented. To contextualize the findings from this research, the next section explains the relevant national and regional history and a snapshot of the inner workings of the Ecuadorian Truth Commission.

National and Regional Context

The national legacy of impunity, which led to the need for a truth commission investigation, has its roots in the national security apparatus of the state established in the 1960s in the context of the Cold War. This national security apparatus dovetailed with Operation Condor in the 1970s (GlobalSecurity.org n.d.; Tremlett 2020). In 1976, a triumvirate of armed forces staged a coup and approved the law of national security, which provided the juridical framework for containing and repressing political opposition and protest. In the 1980s, the national police, armed forces, justice officers, and political authorities exercised political repression under the León Febres Cordero administration in alignment with the logic of national security. These forces, along with clandestine units, committed torture, illegal detention, forced disappearance, sexual violence, violations of the fundamental right to life, and extrajudicial

4 See the recommendations for researchers' section in Bueno-Hansen (2021).

executions to combat the internal enemy. Those that participated in subversive movements, such as Alvaro Vive ¡Carajo! and Montoneras Patria Libre (Peñafiel and Fernando 2015: 7–8), were understood to constitute a major threat, as well as any groups that opposed political control and the implementation of the Ecuadorian neoliberal project (Beristain 2014; Donoso 2018: 91).

The conformation of the Ecuadorian Commission responded to the confluence of Correa's political vision and ongoing demands for justice from victims of the political violence and repression under the Febres Cordero administration. Civil society demands by family members of those executed, tortured, or disappeared under the democratic regime of León Febres Cordero (1984–1988) and survivors of this political repression coincided with Rafael Correa's drive to hold the former president accountable for human rights violations that occurred under his administration (Comisión de la Verdad 2010). Correa's newly elected administration initially championed a democratizing agenda focused on inclusion and development and challenged the primacy of national security and neoliberalism, with a focus on the excesses of the Social Christian party exemplified by Febres Cordero's political repression and the imposition of a neoliberal model. The political goal of the Truth Commission was to morally condemn his administration and make an evidence-based claim that it was not a democratic regime, rather an authoritarian one that sought to implement a neoliberal model through an anti-terrorist program that would remove any popular resistance. Correa's citizen revolution and Truth Commission hoped to put an end to state violence and repression and the "long night of neoliberalism" (Solís Chiriboga 2018: 189).

Correa's initial nine-month presidential Truth Commission mandate in 2007 required a very focused and limited research design for the investigation that was to take place in 2008. Because the investigation yielded a significant quantity of inculpatory materials that incriminated the Febres Cordero administration and many testimonies of human rights violations that came after 1988, the Correa administration granted multiple extensions and expanded the investigation from 1984 to 2008. The Commission collected 800 testimonies and over 300,000 declassified documents from the National Police, Ministry of Defense, and National Security Council and completed the final report "Sin Verdad no Hay Justicia" in June of 2010.[5] One of the most significant conclusions of the final report is that the generalized and systematic patterns of violations of human rights under the Febres Cordero administration constitute crimes against humanity.

The Commission continued its work until November of 2011. According to Christian Bahamonde, the executive secretary of the Commission, during the period after the completion of the final report, the Commission staff was able

5 See Krupa (2013: 176–177) for a detailed breakdown of the Commission's research design, methodology, and data analysis.

to "defend, position and disseminate" the final report and its recommendations. The Truth Commission had prepared 119 legal cases[6] and passed them to the National Attorney General's Office. In March of 2012, the National Attorney General's Office established the Truth Commission and Human Rights Direction to prosecute the grave violations of human rights and crimes against humanity. Lastly, the Commission drafted and advocated for the Law for Reparation of Victims and Prosecution that came into effect in 2013.

There are several reasons that the Ecuadorian Commission has a low profile in the TJ field. First, the Commission's initial mandate was to investigate human rights violations related to political repression that occurred 25 years earlier during the administration of Febres Cordero (1984–1988). Unlike other cases in which the international community is made aware of current or recent atrocities committed during an internal armed conflict or an authoritarian regime, the Ecuadorian Commission did not kick the TJ field into a high gear of global attentiveness. Second, Ecuador holds the reputation as an "island of peace" according to former president Osvaldo Hurtado (Krupa 2013: 170). And last, while the Truth Commission received intense advocacy from the victims of political violence, there was no broad-based civil society engagement. For all these reasons, it failed to garner international media attention or activate human rights and donor networks.

Adding a Gender Approach

The Truth Commission of Ecuador (2008–2011) offers an overlooked example of an investigation that took an innovative, albeit belated, approach to investigate the gendered impact of political repression on women, men, and people of non-normative genders and sexualities. This conceptual innovation consistently hit up against and challenged the constricting procedural and structural parameters of the investigation already underway. I became aware of this case by coincidence when I participated in an event in Bogotá with Carlos Martín Beristain in 2017. As an international consultant for the Ecuadorian Truth Commission, he shared his reflections regarding the gender approach forwarded in that investigation as we rode together one early morning with our hosts to participate in the event. He mentioned a 2001 Amnesty International report, "Crimes of Hate Conspiracies of Silence Torture and Ill-Treatment Based on Sexual Identity," as an important source of information that brought the issue to the fore in the Commission.

The extensions on the initial nine-month mandate opened the possibility to expand the narrow focus of the investigation. Natalia Marcos, an Argentinian feminist sociologist and naturalized Ecuadorian with an impressive trajectory of leftist and feminist personal and political commitments

6 The Truth Commission includes cases 118A and 118B, which total 119 cases.

evidenced in both activism and academia, was one of the few women on the Commission's research team. She noted both the lack of a gender approach and growing evidence in the testimonies of systematic and generalized sexual violence during the administration of Febres Cordero that comprised a pattern of human rights violations. In an interview with Marcos, she explained that these concerns drove her to go before the Commissioners and argue for

> a research area that attended to human rights violations against women. Then, the inclusion of the LGBT population came a bit later when we found evidence in our bibliographical research, specifically the [aforementioned] AI report, violence against this population in Guayaquil during Febres Cordero administration in which Jaime Nebot, of the same Social Christian political party as Febres Cordero, who was the governor of Guayaquil exercised political repression against the LGBT population.

Marcos convinced the Commissioners of the need to contract a gender consultant, and that was how Tatiana Cordero ended up taking on the task.

Cordero's personal, ethical, and political commitments with women's rights and the human rights, feminist, and LGBT movements, her extensive contacts and networks, and her academic trajectory made her an incredible asset for the Commission. Moreover, Cordero worked on sexual violence in the Taller Comunicación Mujer/Women's Communication Workshop for many years, and she brought that accumulated experience and knowledge to the work of the Commission. While the gender consultant was contracted to include gender qua women in the investigation and final report, the previously mentioned Amnesty International report brought the issue of violence against the LGBTI population to global awareness, and given Cordero's own personal and political commitments, she extended the consultancy to investigate gender-based violence against people of all genders and sexualities. This is a powerful conceptual intervention, given the structural limitations circumscribing her work.

While political repression and human rights violations against gender and sexual minorities between 1984 and 2008 were mentioned in the final report of the Ecuadorian Truth Commission as contextual elements, they were not contemplated within the design of the Ecuadorian Truth Commission's investigation from its inception. Cordero and Marcos conducted supplementary research and prepared a chapter, "Sexual Violence and the Gender Perspective: Patterns of human rights violations in Ecuador," in the final report that included attention to sexual and gender-based violence against the LGBTI population, as well as cis and heterosexual women and men. Their analysis emerges from the rich trajectory of feminist organizing against the manifestations of heterosexual system in Ecuador and offers glimpses into the regional feminist genealogies of resistance that will be the focus of a subsequent section, titled "The Hidden Genealogy of Collective Activist Knowledge Production."

The research regarding sexual violence against all people during the period of political repression did not come out of a demand from movements, and the findings were not returned to movements, Tatiana Cordero explains. According to the final report (Comisión de la Verdad 2010: 259), the concentrated efforts of survivors and the families of those that endured the human rights violations did not create alliances with the feminist movement. Nevertheless, Tatiana Cordero found support and compatibility with Natalia Marcos, who was centrally involved in developing the gender-focused research design to investigate the human rights violations committed by state agents between 1979 and 2006 (Universidad de las Artes 2018). Cordero and Marcos conducted supplementary research to fill the gap of information regarding sexual violence in an institutional context of confusion, disorder, and constant rushing. Cordero reflects that the negotiation process regarding what would be included in the report was extremely difficult, and Marcos was key in advocating as Commission staff.

According to Christian Bahamond, when the Commission contracted Cordero as the expert to work on the issue of sexual violence, the issue of gender came into focus. Cordero and Marcos reviewed the cases the Commission had gathered and conducted focus groups as well as in-depth interviews with activist leaders (Comisión de la Verdad 2010: 292). According to Cordero and Marcos, the complementary research included an analysis of 79 existing testimonies by victims of sexual violence, three focus groups, and various in-depth interviews with a few men and women victims and families of victims of violence during the 1984–1988 period. One focus group was conducted with trans women and a few gay men in Guayaquil. Another focus group was conducted in Quito with women sex workers. The third focus group was conducted with women armed actors from the subversive groups. In addition, the research team conducted semi-structured interviews with representatives, such as Sandra Alvarez, from human rights organizations, the women's movement, LGBTI organizations, and sex worker collectives (Comisión de la Verdad 2010: 255). These sources brought to light violence by police, including extortion, torture, and arbitrary and indefinite detention.

The research findings of the gender consultancy were considered largely outside of the scope of the Commission's investigation, the preparation of the legal cases, and the content of the final report and were included as an "add-on." Bahamonde asserts that this supplemental research Cordero and Marcos conducted "fell outside of the logic of the Commission's investigation, so for [them] it ended up distracting from the type of cases the Commission was investigating." As Sebastian Yerovi Proaño (2015: 64) asserts, the Truth Commission depended on the juridical norms, conceptual foundations, and legitimacy in international human rights law. Bahamonde confirms that the focus of the Commission was juridical: the priority was to prepare legal cases. Since international human rights law does not offer a strong framework for the recognition of human rights violations against the LGBTI population, these violations fell outside of the Truth Commission research design.[7]

In an interview with Bahamonde, he remembered that the research Cordero coordinated, including violence against the trans population in Guayaquil, based on the findings of the 2001 Amnesty International report, "did not fit in the logic of the Commission." Although the gender consultant conducted significant supplementary research, the Commission decided to reduce the focus on those issues because, according to Bahamonde, "they took [them] away from the context of the rest of the issues." Bahamonde offers the following example. Cordero's research rendered, for example, 1,000 claims of sex workers against the police for arbitrary detentions, "and that was outside of the scope of the Commission's investigation, and it completely distracted [them]," Bahamonde reflected. Yet Bahamonde was sensitive to this issue, and he asserted, "Nevertheless, we didn't want to leave it out and we kept the issue in the report and focused one recommendation on the issue of violence against the LGBTI population." This dynamic of belatedly including a gender approach through an add-on effort is consistent with other cases, such as the Peruvian Truth and Reconciliation Commission final report (Bueno-Hansen 2015).

In the interviews with Cordero and Marcos, they both commented on the political and epistemic battles they waged from inside the Commission to address the methodological gaps that only now are gaining international attention at the level of the UN, as evidenced by the Special Rapporteur on the promotion of truth, justice, reparation, and guarantees of non-recurrence report titled "*Gender perspective in transitional justice processes*." As Marcos reflects, "We were the difficult ones and gained many enemies." Cordero and Marcos held a common personal and political commitment to challenge the default nature of the heterosexual system, which manifests in ignoring gender difference and then belatedly adding on gender qua women without questioning any of the research design's methodological limitations or the transitional justice mandate's conceptual gaps. This shared commitment centrally informs the analysis put forth in the final report chapter "Sexual Violence and Gender Perspective."

"Sexual Violence and Gender Perspective" Chapter

The Commission's belated inclusion of a gender approach was largely due to Marcos's intensive advocacy that expanded the openness and sensibility of a few people on the Commission staff, including Beristain and Bahamonde, and convinced the Commissioners that had less awareness of the issue. The add-on quality of the gender approach is consistent with the

7 Note the absence of engagement with sexual orientation and gender identity and expression rights and the Yogyakarta Principles (2006) (https://yogyakartaprinciples.org/).

global trend of truth commissions, yet Cordero and Marcos did not limit their investigation and analysis to women. Despite the severe limitations due to the lack of inclusion of a gender approach in the initial methodological design and the lack of conditions necessary to manage the risk of revictimization in the investigation of sexual violence, according to Tatiana Cordero, the chapter "Sexual Violence and Gender Analysis: Patterns of human rights violations in Ecuador" presents an integrated picture of how sexual violence impacted women, men, and the LGBTI population. The report (Comisión de la Verdad 2010: 310) concludes that sexual violence during the 1984–1998 period was perpetrated as a form of torture within the context of national security of the Christian Social administration of Febres Cordero against those considered subversives. During the 1989–2007 period, sexual violence was perpetrated as part of local security policies, such as that of Guayaquil, and quotidian political repression by state agents at the municipal level (Comisión de la Verdad 2010: 308).

Turning to an analysis of the content of the final report chapter "Sexual Violence and Gender Analysis," it is worth mentioning that the first paragraph contains reference to human rights violations of LGBTI people. "These violations are motivated by [rejection of] sexual difference and marginalization against lesbians, gays, bisexuals, and transgender, travesti and intersex people" (Comisión de la Verdad 2010: 251). The inclusion of this issue from the beginning of the chapter is anchored in what the authors assert to be an optic that analyzes the underlying gender logics and "heterosexual regulation" (ibid.). This optic is rooted in the feminist trajectory of resistance to the heterosexual system, with the broad understanding that such a system of oppression harms all people, even while it simultaneously privileges cis and hetero men. Marcos, reflecting on the work she and Cordero accomplished, asserts:

> The fact that we were able to not only conduct our supplementary investigation but also write a chapter that reflected our findings with no censorship, all our ideas were intact, that was a victory. Given the broader and ongoing theoretical and political disputes within the Commission, our work manifested our stance anchored in a feminist commitment to truth, reparation, and justice for the victims that were made invisible.

In terms of the feminist analysis, besides inclusion of sexual and gender-based violence against women and the LGBTI population, the chapter includes analysis of violations against men. Sexual and gender-based violence against women and men took place primarily during the 1984–1988 period against those suspected of being subversives and their families. Sexual violence was a torture tool with widespread use against women. Although it was not practiced in a widespread manner against detained men, the threat of penetration was a constant menace and troubled their claim to virility and heterosexuality (Comisión de la Verdad 2010: 256). As Cordero explains, in the dominant sociocultural gender logic, the act of penetration converts the penetrated man into a homosexual, thereby denying him claim to masculinity and its corresponding privileges.[8]

Men who took part in the uprising against Febres Cordero in 1987 on the Taura air force base in Guayaquil were the target of human rights violations, including sexual violence, by state agents. This attention to male victimhood in the late 2000s sets an important methodological standard given that "tailored intervention to address male-centered sexual harms remains elusive and marginalized" (Ni Aolain et al. 2015: 109). Lastly, police and state agents violated the rights of the LGBTI population on a permanent basis. While these violations did not correspond to a national policy, they were part of, or extensions of, the local security practices, especially in Guayaquil (Comisión de la Verdad 2010: 252).

It is not a coincidence that Guayaquil figures prominently as a place of rampant political repression, because it has been and continues to be a stronghold of the Social Christian party, that of Febres Cordero, that prioritizes national security (Comisión de la Verdad 2010: 304). As mentioned by Marcos, under the mayor Jaime Nebot of the Social Christian Party, the *More Security* campaign implemented a social cleansing project against all the populations considered undesirable. The Commission investigated the municipality of Guayaquil's *More Security* plan implemented in 2000 that subjected LGBT individuals and groups to detentions, torture, and cruel treatment by state agents (Comisión de la Verdad 2010: 298). Amnesty International (2001) relates this ill-treatment, particularly the targeting of transgender sex workers, to social extermination campaigns. In addition, political repression on the part of police has taken, and continues to take, the form of denial of free movement in public spaces. Cordero states that the trans population was the most impacted by the political repression and social cleansing campaigns by policy or state agents.

As Natalia Marcos explains in her interview, the social extermination campaign against transgender women in Guayaquil was part of the "More Security" program:

> These forms of punishment and harassment and the harms against human dignity have a patriarchal, sexist, misogynist, macho, and homo-lesbo-trans-phobic connotation that is fundamental to the politics of repression at the national level. The goal of this type of authoritarian society is submission and obedience. Gender hierarchies and differentiated and absolutely binary positions impose a moral sexual order that articulates with the dominant economic and political regime of the 1980's and 1990's in Latin America.

8 See Leiby (2009), Touquet (2018), and Schulz and Touquet (2020) for a more nuanced analysis of male victimhood. For supportive approaches to addressing male victimhood, see https://blogs.lse.ac.uk/gender/2018/11/21/sexual-violence-against-men-enabling-disclosure-in-the-face-of-denial/.

This framing of the analysis emphasizes the structural and systemic role of heterosexuality as the foundational logic of the nation-state that naturalizes and justifies sexual and gender-based violence and excuses the perpetrators. The heterosexual foundational logic of the nation-state permeates all institutions, programs, and policies, including TJ mechanisms and their products. The silences, gaps, and overlooked harms are evidence of the epistemological violence that undergirds the justification of human rights violations and their elision from the hegemonic narrative of national truth.

From the totality of victims of sexual violence, 73.3% were male and 26.7% were female, yet women were only 16.5% of the total victims of registered human rights violations, so they are disproportionately overrepresented as victims of sexual violence (Comisión de la Verdad 2010: 268). The most common sexual violence perpetrated by state agents was forced nudity, and that was committed against men and women evenly. Electric shock to the genitals and/or breasts was the second most common type of sexual violence, and that was committed more to men than women. The third most common type of sexual violence was beatings to the genitals and/or breasts that was perpetrated more to men than women. Rape comprised a smaller amount of the sexual violence and was perpetrated more against women.

The threat of rape against men was intimately tied to the threat of breaking their manhood and turning them into "*un maricón*," a gay man. One testimony demonstrates how these threats were also racialized. "Initially, the typical torture to make us declare that we were terrorists of the AVC included the threat of bringing a big black man to make me into '*un maricón*'" (Comisión de la Verdad 2010: 272). Given the hyper sexualization of Black men and the stereotypical assumption of a large phallus, this threat served to increase fear and shame. The issue of male victims of sexual violence is shrouded with silence and denial. When men do speak of these abuses, they typically remove those parts from their public testimony (Comisión de la Verdad 2010: 287), thereby indicating a sub-registry of sexual violence against men which is compounded by the lack of a methodological design that adequately attends to these particularly delicate aspects of documenting these human rights violations.[9] State agents perpetrated sexual violence against the LGBTI population, although there is scarce documentation of these harms. Various testimonies include information regarding sexual violence and rape perpetrated against travestis and trans women during detention and imprisonment by other inmates and guards (Comisión de la Verdad 2010: 306–307).

The logic that justifies sexual violence perpetrated against the LGBTI population conceives of this grouping as "a 'threat' to social order by the

9 See Leiby (2009) for a deep exploration of sexual violence against men and the sub-registry of sexual violence.

fact that they do not adhere to the heterosexual and patriarchal norms of society" (Comisión de la Verdad 2010: 293). In addition, dominant discourses about the pathological, abnormal, delinquent, and degenerate nature of this population further support the stripping of their humanity and human rights. Testimonies attest to police use of "public scandal" and "offense against public morals" as justifications for violent and discriminatory conduct even after the decriminalization of homosexuality (Comisión de la Verdad 2010: 295). The final report chapter highlights the systematic and structural nature of this discrimination as it is buttressed by mass media perpetuation of stereotypes and the church's role in propagating harmful myths. The human rights violations by state agents, such as arbitrary detentions, are intimately linked to the quotidian violence marked by "social condemnation and cultural prejudice," as well as overarching impunity (Comisión de la Verdad 2010: 296).

The final report chapter conclusion reiterates the nature of sexual violence against women, men, and the LGBTI population. State agents tortured women as punishment for "breaking the hegemonic gender order" (Comisión de la Verdad 2010: 309). Men were tortured for undermining the social order, and the most powerful tool to dominate them was rape or the threat of rape. The social understanding of this act converts the male victim into a homosexual and carries with it the ripping away of their masculine privilege. Sexual violence and gender discrimination against the LGBTI population by state agents were used to impose the heterosexual norm and evidence the lack of recognition of LGBTI people as subjects of the law (Comisión de la Verdad 2010: 311). Therefore, the feminist movement–informed gender approach reveals how gender-based and sexual violences in Ecuador against women, men, and LGBTI populations are interlocking phenomenon rooted in the violent enforcement of the heterosexual system. This analysis draws from a feminist activist genealogy of praxis that is largely ignored in the literature on gender and transitional justice.

The Hidden Genealogy of Collective Activist Knowledge Production

In my extended interview with the Ecuadorian Truth Commission gender consultant, feminist, and lesbian activist Tatiana Cordero, we took the work of Adrienne Rich, *Compulsory Heterosexuality and the Lesbian Existence* (1980), and her critique of compulsory heterosexuality as a common point of reference to understand heterosexuality as a political institution that orders and manages populations, conferring power and privilege to men over women. As the third paragraph of the chapter "Sexual Violence and a Gender Approach" contained the analysis of the heterosexual system, translated in the opening epigraph, and I had learned from Ecuadorian contacts and friends of Cordero's foundational role in the feminist movement, I knew that Rich's work would be a common reference point. Rich cites a 1976 feminist internationalist grassroots event, the Brussels Tribunal on Crimes against Women, as naming one of the crimes against women to be compulsory heterosexuality. While the heterosexual system benefits men who embody the ideal type in the pyramid of human worth, this system also measures out punishments to all those that do not conform, be it cisgender and heterosexual women and men or people of non-normative genders and sexualities. Two of the Brussels tribunal testimonies attest to persecution of lesbians: in Norway, through conversion therapy, including repeated rape over a period of six months, and in Mozambique, through rehabilitation camps (Rich 1980: 653). These punishments are largely about disciplining those that do not conform and who use violence as a pedagogical tool for communicating sex and gender norms and the consequences for betraying hegemonic sociocultural and/or political forces (Bueno-Hansen 2018).

In addition to contributing to the foundation analysis of compulsory heterosexuality, Adrienne Rich (1980) also asserts lesbian existence as a claim against the pathologizing of lesbians. "Lesbian existence suggests both the fact of the historical presence of lesbians and our continuing creation of the meaning of that existence" (Rich 1980: 648). Sara Ahmed (2017) picks up on this thread when she writes of lesbian feminism as a willfulness archive: "A willfulness archive would derive as much from our struggle to write ourselves into existence as from who appears in what we write" (Ahmed 2017: 230). On this note, this contribution to the TJ field is about writing ourselves and our legacies into existence with the "insistence that crafting a life is political work" (Ahmed 2017: 227). The contributions of Tatiana Cordero and Natalia Marcos, the Commission research team member with whom Cordero worked the closest, exemplify what is possible when this hidden feminist legacy takes shape in a Truth Commission investigation.

A brief look at the feminist movement trajectory traced through the life of Tatiana Cordero illuminates how the chapter that forwards a feminist movement analysis of sexual violence came to pass. Tatiana Cordero participated for decades in the feminist movement, most significantly in the Women's Communication Workshop/Taller de Comunicación Mujer, since 1997. She participated in creating the first national tribunal for women's economic, social, and cultural rights in Ecuador in 2005. The group that organized the tribunal made the strategic decision to prioritize sexual violence against women, and other forms of violence, as well as abortion and discrimination against lesbians, following the decades-long tradition of feminist grassroots tribunals, like the 1976 Brussels tribunal. This was particularly significant because, in 1997, the part of Article 516 of the Ecuadorian criminal code that criminalized homosexuality between men was found unconstitutional by the

Constitutional Court,[10] whilst female homosexuality was not acknowledged as existing and therefore was not legible under the law.[11]

While many feminist organizations found inroads into the state in the late 1980s and 1990s with the increase in non-governmental organizations (Alvarez 1999), Taller Comunicación Mujer and several other groups embraced an autonomous position that took on the issues put aside by the more mainstream groups, such as abortion and lesbianism. The members of Taller Comunicación Mujer, according to Tatiana Cordero, declared their organization to be an independent lesbian political collective. In the 2000s, lesbian groups started to become stronger in Ecuador, according to Tatiana Cordero and Sandra Alvarez, one of the founders of the Ecuadorian Organization of Lesbian Women/Organización de Mujeres Lesbianas de Ecuador (OML), the first lesbian collective. This movement trajectory evidences a commitment to questioning heteropatriarchy, especially in relation to bodily autonomy and reproductive and sexual rights. This is further evidenced in the joint advocacy of feminist and LGBTI organizations during the 1998 National Constituent Assembly and resulting Constitution that included the recognition of sexual orientation within equality law. In addition, the 1998 National Human Rights Plan included Article 26, that the government will "protect against persecution and harassment by agents and mechanisms of the security state against people due to their sexual orientation" (Comisión de la Verdad 2010: 295). Therefore, the gender analysis Cordero brought with her into the Truth Commission as a gender consultant carried with it a legacy of taking gender and sexuality seriously, and this includes masculine vulnerabilities and victimhood, as well as "the gendered positioning of the men in the sociopolitical context" (Touquet and Schulz 2020: 6).

In the period of the Correa administration, the constituent assembly and the new constitution of 2008 was when broader coalitions across differences really began to consolidate. The role of young women was fundamental in this shift according to Tatiana Cordero, since their understanding of their political subjectivity is defined by multiple identities and causes. Furthermore, the timing of the gender consultancy overlaps with hard-won gains in the legal recognition and protection of gender identity in the 2008 Constitution. Various gains in this area, including the two mentioned next, set the national political climate in a way that supports the exposure of human rights violations against the LGBTI population.

10 Constitutional Court Resolution 106, published in the Official Supplemental Registry 203 on 27 November 1997.

11 See Aguiar Roman (2018) for a detailed analysis of the legal history of homosexuality in Ecuador.

Article 11 number 2 prohibits discrimination against people due to their gender identity. This article "explicitly recognizes that women, men and trans people have the same rights" (Almeida and Vásquez 2010: 27). Moreover, Article 89 establishes the state obligation to sanction discriminatory acts against transgender people.

During the 1980s and 1990s in Ecuador, gay, travesti, and transexual people suffered extreme persecution and violent repression at the hands of the police, including extortion, arbitrary and indefinite detention, torture, and extrajudicial execution.[12] The Ecuadorian penal code condemned homosexuals to prison sentences of four to eight years. This population comprised another inextricably linked yet completely implicit threat to national security, an internal enemy, due to the undermining of the heterosexual system.[13] When Ecuador decriminalized homosexuality in 1997 due to intensive political organizing led by *la Asociación Gay Transgénero Coccinelle* along with other LGBTI, women's, and human rights groups, the police repression reduced slightly. This victory overlaps with the Ecuadorian political referendum that replaced President Abdalá Bucaram and resulted in the 1998 Constitutional Assembly. In this period, social movements, and in this case feminist and gay and trans movements, gained ground because of the lack of credibility of the state, according to Cordero. Nevertheless, neo-Nazi groups began social cleansing practices, otherwise understood as social extermination, against this population in the late 1990s and 2000s, including ongoing harassment, death threats, and assassinations.[14] As there were no accessible state entities to file a claim, these human rights violations were never investigated or sanctioned.

According to *Fundación Regional de Asesoría de Derechos Humanos* (INREDH)[15] executive director Luis Ángel Saavedra, the struggles, and victories, of *Coccinelle* were quickly forgotten in the 2000s, as was the pending debt of justice for the human rights violations against gender and sexual minorities in the 1980s and 1990s. When the truth commission began its investigation in the late 2000s, the organized political LGBTI groups had other political priorities and little historical memory. In an interview with Saavedra, he reflected that no one "assumed the re-vindication of those

12 See Pelayo (2021). Also, for a regional understanding of the term *travesti*, please see DiPietro (2016a and 2016b).

13 For a very interesting analysis of the LGBTI internal enemy discourse in Colombia, see Esguerra Muelle, C. (2017). Cómo hacer necropolíticas en casa: Ideología de género y acuerdos de paz en Colombia. *Sexualidad, Salud y Sociedad – Revista Latinoamericana* 27: 172–198.

14 For example, https://juventudrevolucionaria.wordpress.com/author/juventudrevolucionaria/page/57/.

15 https://www.inredh.org/.

killed." Ana Almeida and Elizabeth Vásquez reinforce this analysis of a generational and class divide in *Cuerpos Distintos* (2010: 32):

> After the decriminalization [of homosexuality] the gay groups lost interest in the defense of basic rights while trans people were still deeply impacted by labor and housing discrimination, as well as constant violent infringements upon their physical liberty and the right to move through public spaces.

While trans people continue fighting for basic rights, such as access to housing, medical attention, education, and labor without discrimination, the dominant LGBTI movement demands did not take up these issues.

During the Truth Commission investigation, which researched human rights violations between 1984 and 2008, none of the gay, lesbian, trans, and/or bisexual collectives or groups presented a formal claim of human rights violations. Only two people of non-normative genders and/or sexualities gathered the courage to offer their testimonies to the truth commission regarding their experiences with political repression, but there was no support or mobilization from civil society to accompany these individuals and their cases, according to Luis Angel Saavedra of INREDH. In a similar vein, veteran lesbian activist Sandra Alvarez asserts that there were several people that went to offer their testimonies to the Commission, but they were poorly received by the frontline public servants who replicate the discrimination and exclusion inherent within the heterosexual system. While Cordero and Marcos may have had the interests of LGBTI people in mind, the frontline public servants were not trained or prepared to attend to the LGBTI population as victims of political repression. Furthermore, there remain to this day harms that have yet to be acknowledged and investigated, which comprise pending debts.

Pending Debts

The Ecuadorian quest for truth, justice, and reconciliation requires much more research. During the period of the Truth Commission investigation, civil society–based groups, including the previously mentioned Taller Comunicación Mujer, exposed evidence of clandestine dehomosexualization clinics and related kidnapping and torture of LGBTI people. This issue was brought to attention in April 2005 when the Taller Comunicación Mujer organized a national tribunal for women's economic, social, and cultural rights in Guayaquil. According to Cordero, this is the first time the issue is documented in the national press in Ecuador. In addition, before the Commission started its investigation, a claim against the state had been filed regarding the kidnapping and torture of LGBT people in dehomosexualization clinics, according to Cordero. Nevertheless, this kidnapping, forced detention, and torture of LGBTI people fell outside the parameters of investigation due to the heteronormative logic underlying the Commission mandate and the fact that there is no evidence of programs or policies that stipulate the regulation of homosexuality through clinical therapies in the Ecuadorian health system. The clandestine nature of the human rights violations, compounded by the default heterosexual system foundational to the Truth Commission, sealed the resulting exclusion of these violations from the national record.

Nevertheless, the feminist movement–informed gender approach to sexual and gender-based violence implemented in the "Sexual Violence and Gender Perspective" chapter of the Ecuadorian Truth Commission final report (Comisión de la Verdad 2010) offers an important intervention in the field and practice of TJ. The TJ field has yet to comprehend how this hidden legacy of feminist activist–based praxis holds the key to integrating the analysis of sexual and gender-based violence against people of all genders and sexualities. In the 2020 report *The Gender Perspective in Transitional Justice Processes* (United Nations 2020: 5), Fabián Salvioli, the UN Special Rapporteur on the promotion of truth, justice, reparation, and guarantees of non-recurrence, writes regarding Truth Commission mandates:

> The mandate should comprehensively address the impact of gender, including sexual and other gender-based violence suffered by all persons, and consider the dimension of sexual orientation and gender identity. It is key to take into account, in all cases, an intersectional perspective that identifies how certain social markers of difference operate in a non-binary vision of gender.

This assertion faces a strong backlash, and the conservative political and religious commitment to the continuity of the heterosexual system should not be underestimated. As evidenced in Ecuador, these conservative commitments span the contemporary political administrations even though they represent varied positions on the political spectrum (Viteri 2020).

In conclusion, the Ecuadorian final report frames the impact of sexual and gender-based violence against women, men, and people of non-conforming genders and sexualities in relation to each other. This conceptual framing offers an alternative to the piecemeal and "add-on" inclusion of women, men, and people of non-normative genders and sexualities as discrete and distinct victims of gender and sexual violence. This chapter renders the significance of a feminist movement–informed gender approach in that it reveals the varied and interlocking violent manifestations of the heterosexual system as all coming from the same root. The field and practice of transitional justice benefit from this contribution by increasing the conceptual capacity to identify and address the systemic dynamics undergirding these harms. Moreover, in practical terms, incorporating this conceptual framing from the inception of the transitional justice mechanism would imply explicit inclusion in the Truth Commission mandate, the selection of commissioners and staff, the research design and implementation, and the training processes. There is much work to be done in this area, which will take courage as it challenges the heteropatriarchal underpinnings of the nation-state and demands an expansion of the epistemic parameters of transitional justice. In addition, there are many pending debts to those marginalized populations that must take the form of both recognizing the harms sustained and honoring their trajectories of collective knowledge production based in legacies of resistance praxis.

References

Aguiar Roman, J. (2018). Historia Legal de la Homosexualidad en el Ecuador. *Novedades Jurídicas: Ética y Deontología Jurídica* 146: 50–61.

Ahmed, S. (2017). *Living a Feminist Life*. Durham, NC: Duke University Press.

Almeida, A. and E. Vásquez (2010). *Cuerpos Distintos: Ocho años de Activismo Transfeminista en Ecuador*. Quito, Ecuador: Manthra Editores.

Alvarez, S. (1999). Advocating Feminism: The Latin American Feminist NGO 'Boom'. *International Feminist Journal of Politics* 1(2): 181–209.

Amnesty International (2001). *Crimes of Hate Conspiracies of Silence Torture and Ill-Treatment Based on Sexual Identity*, ACT 40/016/2001. Available at: https://www.amnesty.org/en/documents/act40/016/2001/en/. Accessed on: 22. November 2021.

Ashe, F. (2019). Sexuality and Gender Identity in Transitional Societies, Peacebuilding and Counterhegemonic Politics. *International Journal of Transitional Justice* 13: 435–457.

Beristain, C. (2014). Espejo de la Verdad. In: Égüez, P. (eds.): *Grito de la Memoria*. Quito: Fiscalía Genera del Estado: 103–115.

Berkins, Lohana (2006). *"Travestis: una identidad política " Hemispheric Institute*. Available at: https://hemisphericinstitute.org/en/emisferica-42/4-2-review-essays/lohana-berkins.html.

Bueno-Hansen, P. (2015). *Feminist and Human Rights Struggles in Peru: Decolonizing Transitional Justice*. Urbana, IL: Illinois University Press.

Bueno-Hansen, P. (2018). The Emerging LGBTI Rights Challenge to Transitional Justice in Latin America. *International Journal of Transitional Justice* 12(1): 126–145.

Bueno-Hansen, P. (2021). *The LGBTI Movement's Spiral Trajectory: From Peace Processes to Legal and Juridical Gains and Back Again*. New York: Astraea Foundation.

Comisión de la Verdad (2010). *Informe: sin verdad no hay justicia. Tomo 1: Violaciones de derechos humanos. Autoedición*. Available at: http://repositorio.dpe.gob.ec/handle/39000/2582. Accessed on: 11 January 2022.

DiPietro, Pedro Javier (2016a). Decolonizing Travesti Space in Buenos Aires: Race, Sexuality, and SidewaysRelationality. *Gender, Place, and Culture* 23(5): 677–693.

DiPietro, Pedro Javier (2016b). Of Huachafería, Así, and M'e Mati: Decolonizing Transing Methodologies. *Transgender Studies Quarterly* 1–2: 65–73.

Donoso, G. (2018). Psychosocial Implications of Political Trauma and Social Recognition I. In: Adlam, J., Kluttig, T. and Lee, B. X. (eds.): *Violent States and Creative States*. London: Jessica Kingsely Publisher: 87–100.

Esguerra Muelle, C. (2017). Cómo hacer necropolíticas en casa: Ideología de género y acuerdos de paz en Colombia. *Sexualidad, Salud y Sociedad – Revista Latinoamericana* 27: 172–198.

Fobear, K. (2014). Queering Truth Commissions. *Journal of Human Rights Practice* 6(1): 51–68.

Fobear, K. and E. Baines (2020). Pushing the Conversation Forward: The Intersections of Sexuality and Gender Identity in Transitional Justice. *The International Journal of Human Rights* 24(4): 307–312.

GlobalSecurity.org (n.d.). *Operation Condor/Operación Cóndor.* Global Security. Available at: https://www.globalsecurity.org/military/world/war/operation-condor.htm. Accessed on: 11 January 2022.
Green, J. (2012). 'Who Is the Macho Who Wants to Kill Me?' Male Homosexuality, Revolutionary Masculinity, and the Brazilian Armed Struggle of the 1960s and 1970s. *Hispanic American Historical Review* 92(3): 437–469.
Hamber, B. (2007). Masculinity and Transitional Justice: An Exploratory Essay. *International Journal of Transitional Justice* 1(3): 375–390.
Hamber, B. (2015). There Is a Crack in Everything: Problematising Masculinities, Peacebuilding and Transitional Justice. *Human Rights Review* 17(1): 9–34.
Krupa, C. (2013). Neoliberal Reckoning: Ecuador's Truth Commission and the Mythopoetics of Political Violence. In: Goodale, M. and Postero, N. (eds.): *Neoliberalism, Interrupted: Social Change and Contested Governance in Contemporary Latin America.* Stanford: Stanford University Press: 169–194.
Leiby, M. (2009). Digging in the Archives: The Promise and Perils of Primary Documents. *Politics and Society* 37(1): 75–99.
Ni Aolain, F., C. O'Rourke and A. Swaine (2015). Transforming Reparations for Conflict-Related Sexual Violence: Principles and Practice. *Harvard Human Rights Journal* 28: 97–146.
Pelayo, P. (2021). *Los fantasmas se cabrearon: crónicas de la despenalicación de la homosexualidad en el Ecuador.* Quito: Severo Editorial and USFQ Press.
Peñafiel, V. and D. Fernando (2015). *El Terrorismo de Estado en Ecuador: Autoritarismo, Seguridad y Derechos Humanos (1984–1988).* Master Thesis, Facultad Latinoamericana de Ciencias Sociales. Quito: FLASCO.
Rich, A. (1980). Compulsory Heterosexuality and Lesbian Existence. *Signs: Journal of Women in Culture and Society* 5(4): 631–660.
Rizki, C. (2019). Latin/x American Trans Studies: Toward a Travesti-Trans Analytic. *Transgender Studies Quarterly* 6(2): 145–155.
Rosenbloom, R. (1996). *Unspoken Rules: Sexual Orientation and Women's Human Rights.* New York: Cassell Wellington House, The International Gay and Lesbian Human Rights Commission.
Rothschild, C. (2005). *Written Out: How Sexuality Is Used to Attack Women's Organizing.* New York, NY: International Gay and Lesbian Human Rights Commission & Center for Women's Global Leadership.
Schulz, P. (2020). Towards Inclusive Gender in Transitional Justice: Gaps, Blind-Spots and Opportunities. *Journal of Intervention and Statebuilding* 14(5): 691–710.
Schulz, P. and H. Touquet (2020). Queering Explanatory Frameworks for Wartime Sexual Violence Against Men. *International Affairs* 96(5): 1169–1187.
Solís Chiriboga, M. (2018). Reparación a víctimas de violación de derechos humanos y crímenes de lesa humanidad en Ecuador. *Íconos: Revista de Ciencias Sociales* 62: 183–201.
Theidon, K. (2009). Reconstructing Masculinities: The Disarmament, Demobilization, and Reintegration of Former Combatants in Colombia. *Human Rights Quarterly* 31(1): 1–34.
Touquet, H. (2018). *Sexual Violence Against Men: Enabling Disclosure in the Face of Denial.* The London School of Economics. Available at: https://blogs.lse.ac.uk/gender/2018/11/21/sexual-violence-against-men-enabling-disclosure-in-the-face-of-denial/. Accessed on: 22 November 2021.
Touquet, H. and P. Schulz (2020). Navigating Vulnerabilities and Masculinities: How Gendered Contexts Shape the Agency of Male Sexual Violence Survivors. *Security Dialogue* 52(3): 1–18.

Tremlett, G. (2020). *Operation Condor: The Cold War Conspiracy that Terrorised South America*. London: The Guardian. Available at: https://www.theguardian.com/news/2020/sep/03/operation-condor-the-illegal-state-network-that-terrorised-south-america. Accessed on: 2 November 2021.

United Nations, General Assembly (2020). *The Gender Perspective in Transitional Justice Processes: Note by the Secretary General*, A/75/174. Available at: https://digitallibrary.un.org/record/3883379. Accessed on: 22 November 2022.

Universidad de las Artes (2018). *Natalia Carolina Marcos, investigadora y docente de la UArtes*. Universidad de las Artes. Available at: http://www.uartes.edu.ec/Natalia-Carolina-Marcos-investigadora-y-docente-de-la-UArtes.php. Accessed on: 23 July 2020.

Viteri, M. (2020). *Políticas Antigénero en America Latina: Ecuador*. Rio de Janeiro, Brazil: Observatorio de Sexualidad y Política (SPW).

Yerovi Proaño, S. (2015). Derechos humanos en las comisiones de verdad de Ecuador y Perú. *URVIO Revista Latinoamericana de Estudios de Seguridad* 16: 53–68.

Chapter 7

Peacebuilding and Transitional Justice in Colombia

Institutionalized and Challenged Meanings of Gender[1]

Anika Oettler

Introduction

In the midst of armed conflict, Colombian feminist and LGBT[2] movements have successfully advocated for Colombia to become a pioneer in the implementation of LGBT rights and women's agency in peacebuilding and transitional justice. The 2011 Victims Law (Ley 1448) was a breakthrough on the road to inclusive peace. It gave voice and entitlement to LGBT victims of the armed conflict and led to the establishment of the National Center for Historical Memory (CNMH), which turned out to be a strong institutional framework for the advancement of a holistic understanding of gender in the Colombian process of dealing with the past. This chapter contextualizes and sheds light on the 2016 landmark peace accord between the Colombian government and the oldest and largest guerrilla group in the Western Hemisphere, the FARC-EP (Revolutionary Armed Forces of Colombia – People's Army). This agreement was hailed as a global milestone in the normative development of a gendered agenda for peace. It contained over 100 gender

1 I am grateful for comments and insights to Juan Betancurth, Pascha Bueno-Hansen, Wilson Castañeda, Lina Céspedes-Báez, Erika Gómez, Brandon Hamber, Juanita Millán, Lisa García Reyes, Marcela Sánchez, Victoria Sandino, Philipp Schulz, José Fernando Serrano Amaya, Heleen Touquet, Hunza Vargas, Maria Daniela Villamil, and Manuel Velandia.

2 The initialism *LGBT* (lesbian, gay, bisexual, transgender) has been widely criticized for not capturing the diversity of sexual orientations and gender identities. While some argue for adding more letters (queer, questioning, intersex, asexual, ally, androgynous, pansexual, two-spirit QQIAAAP2+), others reject the *alphabet soup* or propose alternatives such as *people with diverse sexual orientation and gender identities and expressions* (SOGIE). However, *LGBT* (and, to a lesser extent, *LGBTI* or *LGBTQ*) is the most commonly used acronym in Colombian politics. While the *I* entered the Colombian discursive arena rather unnoticed, via a Supreme Court decision on public LGBTI policy (Castillo Vargas 2018: 29), the *Q* is in use in academically informed activist groups. In this chapter, I use the term *LGBT* in the context of politics, rights, and activism (while referring to other terms when exploring the social construction of masculinities and femininities). LGBT is the globally recognized acronym Colombian activists, academics, and politicians use as a strategic discursive resource. *LGBTI* appears in official Colombian documents, such as the peace agreement.

DOI: 10.4324/9781003519522-9

provisions and drew upon a "territorial, differential and gender approach" (*enfoque territorial, diferencial y de género*). It testifies to the inclusive nature of the agreement that the term *LGBTI* appeared 16 times in its final version. Yet gender sensitivity was highly controversial, and debates on *gender ideology, Castrochavism*, transitional justice, and cash payments to demobilized guerilla fighters were among the main reasons for the narrow failure of the plebiscite for the peace accord in October 2016 (Beltrán and Creely 2018; Céspedes-Baéz 2017; Oettler 2019). The following pages gravitate toward the signing of the peace accord. The contours of this key text and the discursive context to which it relates reveal the difficulties of overcoming dominant gender foci. The peace process is the broader context in which the struggle for considering the roles of masculinities and the experiences of LGBT persons unfolds. In Colombia, peacebuilding and transitional justice evolve in mutual relation. While the transitional justice architecture is a product of the peace process, it also nurtures the agenda for peace. The broad set of recommendations of the truth commission is a case in point.

This chapter develops the notion of conceptual plasticity and argues that gender conceptions underlying Colombian approaches to gender-responsive peacebuilding are fairly consistent yet contested and reversible. Gender conceptions are discourse strands comprising the "finite spectrum of what is said and sayable at a particular point in time and place" (Jäger and Maier 2016: 121). The chapter shows that today's normative agenda for inclusive peace is heterogeneous and informed by diverse gender beliefs. So conceived, the politicization of sexuality and gender becomes central in understanding conflicts over the prospects of peace between and within secular and religious discursive fields. Inclusive agendas for peace are shaped by discursive opportunity structures with a strong transnational or multilevel component (Della Porta and Tarrow 2005), and they span multiple understandings and meanings of gender. These include more conservative binary ideas as well as queer conceptions of gender, rooted in indigenous, Black/afro-Colombian, and Iberian creole cultures, Catholic and secular thinking, and diverse urban and rural socio-economic structural conditions. The inclusive nature of the Colombian peace process led to the incorporation of a great variety of specific immediate needs and strategic goals into the peace accord. These stipulations are not connected with all but relate to diverse gender conceptions. Although the peace accord reflects the decisive imprint that decade-long struggles for gendered peace and shifting norms have left on Colombian peace politics, the failed plebiscite led to a revision of the accord, making it more apt to gender conservatism. For peace negotiators and LGBT activists, this experience demonstrates the difficulty of maintaining both focus and inclusiveness. Too much focus on specific goals weakens legitimacy, while too much inclusiveness implies loss of agenda-setting control. The challenge is to bring forward a gendered agenda for peace that is both inclusive and focused.

In Section 2, my goal is to briefly sketch diverse ideas that function as a framework for those involved in negotiating peace. Therefore, I will set out a heterogeneous field of symbolic and representational subuniverses of *gender*, comprised of academically informed conceptions and those political and religious beliefs that often lie behind everyday opinions. Gender debates evolve around primary concerns. These take three different (although often interconnected) forms – colonialism, faith, and discrimination – and bring different lenses to see the problems of the social world, its causes, and its solutions. While Section 3 introduces the Colombian context, Section 4 offers a synopsis of gendered dimensions of pre-2016 peacebuilding and transitional justice. The purpose of Section 5, then, is to explore the full variety and complexity of gender-related provisions of the 2016 peace agreement between the Colombian government and the FARC-EP. Progress has been mixed in the first years of implementation, and Section 5 briefly assesses successes and obstacles. The concluding section summarizes enabling and constraining forces shaping the gender-sensitive approach to peace and transitional justice in Colombia.

Gender and Symbolic Subuniverses

Gender is a floating signifier that can acquire different meanings. In Colombia, signifying practices take place in diverse discursive arenas that overlap, contradict, and sometimes complement each other. Many actors actively involved in discursive struggles form part of transnational advocacy networks (Finnemore and Sikkink 1998) that produce, promote, and transform the ensemble of policy norms and institutions. The symbolic and representational subuniverses of *gender* have changed in Colombia over the decades, just as social and political relations have evolved. According to Berger and Luckmann (1991: 103), subuniverses are "'carried' by a particular collectivity, that is, by the group that ongoingly produces the meaning in question and within which these meanings have objective reality." There are actors who defend and reinforce institutionalized gender concepts and others who challenge them. What is at stake is the power to define whose interests are included, and whose interests marginalized or excluded. As Berger and Luckmann (1991: 103) note: "Each perspective, with whatever appendages of theories or even *Weltanschauungen* will be related to the concrete interest of the group that holds it."

Struggles over discursive repertoires and the meanings of gender are continuous processes that reflect the power to make one's voice heard. A conceptual framework of gender, though, needs to include a diverse array of *Weltanschauungen*, theories, and symbolic universes that provide settings for meanings and, eventually, for collective action. In Colombia, there are overlapping decolonial, Catholic, and (post)structural frames of reference. Each of them appeals to binary as well as queer notions of gender, both separately and as they interweave in academic debate and collective action.

First, colonial legacies are the primary concern of decolonial debates. In her work on decolonial feminism, Ruth Betty Lozano Lerma describes herself as *mujernegra* (Blackwoman) to highlight the impossibility of separating experiences of racialized and gendered oppression. Referring to Lugones, she adds: "and even more, . . . being *mujernegra* is not even being a woman" (Lozano Lerma 2016: 50). In the same vein, many Black activists do not feel represented by the LGBTIQ+ category. Their claim to visualize and recognize "cuerpxs negrxs, cuerpxs diversxs" (Black bodies, diverse bodies) is a claim for emancipatory action: "[W]e are the negation of negation" (Matamba 2020). In many parts of the world, decolonial feminism has evolved as an emancipatory anti-capitalist movement that brings together local struggles against racism, patriarchy, capitalism, and heteronormativity. In naming and examining intersectional forms of oppression, decolonial feminists add a fourth dimension to decolonial debates on the "central elements that affect the quotidian life of the totality of the global population: the coloniality of power, capitalism, and Eurocentrism" (Quijano 2008: 193). In her now-seminal work, María Lugones (2007) introduced the concept of the "modern-colonial gender system" that proposes that "gender" has a colonial origin and essence. Colonization provided the contextual conditions for the establishment of racialized social relations founded on the category of "gender." Indigenous and Black women were violently suppressed and classified as animals and inferior beings, "sexually marked as female, but without the characteristics of femininity" (Lugones 2007: 203). On the other hand, the modern-colonial gender system fostered the ideas of biological dimorphism, heterosexualism, and patriarchy, establishing White bourgeois women as fragile, submissive, dependent, and sexually passive human beings confined to reproductive functions and charitable activities. Some controversy over the place of gender in precolonial societies (Segato 2014; Paredes 2010; Cabnal 2010) exists, but there is consensus that gender is not an ahistorical concept. The coloniality of gender manifests itself in persistent racialized social relations and provinces of meaning.

Second, faith and God's will are the primary concern of religious debates. The religious field in Latin America has undergone important changes in recent years, and many societies have witnessed "reactive politicization and strategic secularism" (Vaggione 2015: 137), with conservative religious speakers resorting to legal, scientific, and bioethical arguments for justifying their agenda. In Colombia, Catholic moral theology still provides a strong and influential spiritual foundation for political and social life. Although the numbers of Colombians identifying themselves as "religious non-practitioners" are rising (Beltrán 2012), curial and laical religious actors possess significant mobilizing power. Regarding gender roles, in many Catholic discursive arenas, prominent voices begin to argue for what most Catholics would be inclined to accept. What is most visible today is a Catholic morality that deems any gendered behavior acceptable, so long as that behavior does not question the primacy of heterosexual marriage and procreation. Curial voices build discursive bridges between inherited dogma and liberal norms, opening up new conciliatory avenues to those who seek to liberate men and women from the devastating effects of patriarchy. As the Holy Father Francis stated in his post-synodal apostolic exhortation Amoris Laetitia on Love in the Family (2016: §286):

> [It] is true that we cannot separate the masculine and the feminine from God's work of creation, which is prior to all our decisions and experiences, and where biological elements exist which are impossible to ignore. But it is also true that masculinity and femininity are not rigid categories. It is possible, for example, that a husband's way of being masculine can be flexibly adapted to the wife's work schedule.

While conservative Catholics tend to reject "gender ideology" and post-structuralist feminism, they accept the term "gender" to refer to cultural and social characteristics of women and men, with sexual differentiation and the male–female dyad being perceived as fundamentals of God's plan of procreation (Burggraf 2006). However, the term *gender* has come to be used with a wide range of meanings in different Catholic contexts which cover conservative feminisms, pro-life feminism (Derr et al. 2005), feminist liberation theology (Vuola 2001), Catholic LGBT activism (Castillo Vargas 2018), and queer theology (Althaus-Reid 2005). While the fields of Catholic morality are hierarchical, they are by no means homogenous. There is a high degree of contestation, questioning, and resistance, and Catholic feminist as well as more conservative female activists have set in motion discursive dynamics and opened up avenues for political participation.

Third, discrimination is the primary concern of (post)structuralist debates. Feminist thinking involves various approaches within liberal, Marxist, structuralist, and poststructural thinking. One structural strand points to the recursive relationship between structure and agency: *structure* shapes individual performance as well as social interaction, and *agency* makes, creates, and changes the macro-structures of social life (Giddens 1984; Connell 1987). Connell (2009: 11) defined *gender* as "the structure of social relations that centres on the reproductive arena, and the set of practices that bring reproductive distinctions between bodies into social processes." Another strand is interpretative intersectional research that focuses on power structures and the creation of social categories. A key concept is the "matrix of domination" (Collins 2000), in which people experience oppression as well as privilege relative to others. Intersectional approaches argue that race, class, gender, sexuality, age, ability, and other categories interact in specific geographical and historical contexts, producing dynamics of opportunities and oppression. These interconnected categories stand for the unstable and socially constructed foundations of identity, individual performance, social interaction, and the social institutions on which society is built. Anticategorical intersectional research "challenges the very notion of categories as artificial and reductionist" (Misra 2018: 122) and shows that their meaning varies from context to context. Most recent research builds on Connell's basic insight that gender is relational: masculinities are always constructed in relation to other masculinities as well as in relation to femininity (Connell 1987, 1995). Connell coined the terms *hegemonic*, *complicit*, *subordinate*, *marginalized*, and *protest* masculinities, whereas other authors speak of *dominant*, *positive*, and *protective* masculinities (Messerschmidt and Messner 2018), or *hybrid* masculinities, that borrow symbols and lifestyle elements from non-hegemonic masculinities and femininities but fail to undermine gender inequality (Bridges and Pascoe 2018). In gender theory, femininity and masculinity are increasingly framed as non-essentialist concepts transcending the boundaries of male- or female-bodiedness. While there is a strong concern for identity, subjectivity, embodiment, and performance (Butler 1990), feminist and queer scholars constantly point to various modes of oppression, discrimination, and violence. Gender justice, then, is the demystification and dismantling of power structures along the lines of racism, patriarchy, capitalism, and heterosexism. The primary concern is not uniformity and obedience but diversity, liberation, and the negotiation of new and non-violent masculinities and femininities.

Where does this brief conceptual journey take us? It delineates the terrain Colombian academics, activists, politicians, and practitioners not just rely on but expand and deepen. Social theory evolves in a global space, with key insights emerging from the so-called Global South (Connell 2007). Gender theories, though, are not only applied in the Colombian context but rather also co-produced, challenged, and taken further. As Connell (2018: 344) recently claimed, it is important "to see gender and sexual politics in terms of multiple projects, both emancipatory and repressive, that often interweave and often go down separate tracks." In the polarized political climate of Colombian politics, diverse actors pursue conflicting interests inside and outside feminist and anti-feminist, LGBT, religious, and authoritarian movements. What is at stake here is a battle over meaning.

The Dynamics of Violence and Peace in Colombia

The gendered agenda for peace in Colombia was the product of women's activism and, later, LGBT struggles (Oettler 2019). Their cause was boosted in the context of the development of a transitional justice infrastructure, created to overcome the legacies of a decade-long conflict that costed the lives of more than 300,000 people. At the time of writing, the official Colombian Victims Registry (*Registro Único de Víctimas*) has documented 9,218,796 victims of the armed confrontation. The statistics include 8,203,478 victims of forced displacement, 188,008 disappeared, and 1,072,602 killed persons,

37,481 kidnapped persons, and 34,346 victims of sexual and gender-based violence. With regard to gender, the statistics include 4,000 LGBTI victims, 374 victims with non-identified gender, and 434 intersexual victims (Registro Único de Víctimas [RUV] 2021).[3] The statistics on gender-related violence reveal only the tip of the iceberg. Obviously, much of gender-based violence is either undetected, silenced, or considered a minor aspect of the plight of families or communities during or after displacement.

In contrast to other countries of the region, there were only short periods of dictatorial rule in Colombia. The country's political scenario went through different stages of collective violence, with a stable electoral democracy coexisting with organized violence, including excessive use of force and poor respect for the rule of law. Early climaxes of violence were the Thousands Days' War (1899–1902) and the Violence (*La Violencia*, 1948–1953), a civil war between Conservatives and Liberals. Rural poverty, the success of the Cuban revolution, limited possibilities for political participation during the National Front (*Frente Nacional*) – a power-sharing pact between Liberals and Conservatives – and a long history of armed insurrection were the main reasons for the rise and consolidation of different guerrilla groups. The most important guerrilla groups to be founded in the 1960s were the National Liberation Army (ELN – *Ejército de Liberación Nacional*) and the Revolutionary Armed Forces of Colombia (FARC – *Fuerzas Armadas Revolucionarias de Colombia*). From the 1970s on, the violent conflict rapidly passed to increasingly complex scenarios of violence. The expansion and mutation of the drug economy in the 1980s turned Colombia into one of the world's leading coca producers. In response to and in anticipation of leftist insurgency, rural elites and drug cartels formed paramilitary groups that quickly transformed into powerful actors filling political spaces. These groups went far beyond their initial task of countering guerilla activities, labor union organizing, and social movement activities. The strategy of massive internal displacement, used by insurgent, counterinsurgent, and criminal actors alike, led to alarming levels of violence and a continuous humanitarian crisis. Gender-based violence was systematically used by paramilitary groups, guerillas, and state actors as a means to restructure social life (Bouvier 2016; Taussig 2003; CNMH 2015a, 2018a, Serrano Amaya 2018; Esguerra Muelle and Sánchez Buitrago 2006).

Alarming levels of collective violence were paralleled by strong and continuously expanding peace initiatives. Since 1982, several presidents engaged in peace negotiations. Some were successful and some were not (Nasi 2009). In the course of the past few decades, several armed leftist groups, such as the M-19 (*Movimiento 19 de Abril*) and the MAQL (*Movimiento Armado Quintín Lame*), demobilized and ceased to exist as armed groups. These

3 These data exemplify the erroneous use of categories, with the LGBTI and intersexual victims obviously overlapping.

efforts were repeatedly crushed by tides of violent repression. For civil society, political and discursive opportunities opened and closed again, often in unpredictable ways. The creation of the leftist *Unión Patriótica* (UP) in the climate of peace and democratic opening during the Betancour administration (1982–1986) was a traumatic experience. Approximately 3,000 party members, UP presidential candidates, mayors, and members of parliament were killed by paramilitary forces.

Pre-2016 Differential Approaches to Transitional Justice

Already in 2002, during the presidency of Álvaro Uribe (2002–2006; 2006–2010), discussions began on how to apply mechanisms of transitional justice and how to promote reconciliation (Rettberg 2005, 2012; Oettler 2019). Paradoxically, Uribe's *democratic security* policy, designed to extend the military's presence to rural regions, provided the context for "building peace in a time of war" (Bouvier 2009). Over the past 18 years, Colombia has developed an ample state-sponsored and internationally backed transitional justice architecture. Over 50,000 paramilitary and guerilla fighters have been demobilized, and over nine million victims have been registered and promised individual and collective reparation.

In contrast to Law 975/2005, the Law of Victims and Land Restitution (Law 1448/2011, or *Ley de Víctimas y Restitución de Tierras*) was an ambitious, victim-centered legal instrument. It is comprised of individual and collective, material, and symbolic components aiming at restoring the dignity of victims, compensating for loss, and guaranteeing non-repetition. Law 1448 gave rise to the creation of the National System for the Assistance and Comprehensive Reparation of Victims (*Sistema Nacional de Atención y Reparación Integral a las Victimas*, SNARIV), with the Victims' Unit, the Land Restitution Unit, and a number of ministries and public agencies being responsible for implementation (Sánchez and Rudling 2019: 34–37). Law 1448/2011 adopted a transformative and differential approach sensitive to age, gender, sexual orientation, disability, social condition, family or national background, language, religion, and political or philosophical opinion (Congreso de la República 2011: Art. 6 & 13). There is, however, a "large implementation gap between what has been delivered on the ground, what victims' expect, and what they are entitled to in terms of reparations" (Sánchez and Rudling 2019: 7; Weber 2020).

This legal milestone, which responded to the demands voiced by women's, LGBT, and feminist movements, was important in another respect. As part of the reparations envisioned in Law 1448/2011, a National Center for Historical Memory (CNMH) was to be created (Congreso de la República 2011: Art. 144). The CNMH was an institution to follow up on the previous effort made by the Historical Memory Group (GMH), a product of

Law 975/2005. As its predecessor, the CNMH operated under the leadership of the renowned sociologist Gonzalo Sánchez. Its working group on gender provided technical assistance and elaborated a series of cutting-edge reports on sexual and gender-based violence. As we tend to ignore previous achievements, ending up trying to reinvent the wheel, it is crucial to set out the historiographic production of the CNMH in some more detail. Most reports focused on emblematic cases and patterns of violence, highlighting the voices of survivors and witnesses of discrimination and atrocity. Two GMH reports on Wayúu women and the Bahía Portere massacre (CNMH and GMH 2010) and on women in the Caribbean (CNMH and GMH 2011a) were followed by regional reports on the Colombian Caribbean (CNMH and GMH 2011b) and Bajo Putamayo (CNMH 2012), as well as reports on *social cleansing* (CNMH 2015a), the situation of lesbians, gays, bisexuals, and transgender (CNMH 2015b), and the bodily effects of war (CNMH 2017). Moreover, the CNMH published a series of synthesis reports on academic lessons learned and best practices in 2018. That year, 2018, was a turning point in the history of historical clarification, with the truth commission starting its work in November and the second round of the presidential elections won by Iván Duque in May. Duque, backed by former president Álvaro Uribe, had campaigned against the peace accord, and it was clear that this would affect the work of the CNMH. Duque soon announced to replace Gonzalo Sánchez with the far-right Mario Pacheco, and – after harsh reactions from civil society – appointed far-right Dario Acevedo new CNMH director in February 2019. A few months earlier, Sánchez's team reported on lessons learned. The report on the contribution of the CNMH to historical clarification (CNMH 2018a) contained chapters on women (2018a: 47–88), LGBT persons (2018a: 89–118), ethnic groups (2018a: 119–154), peasants and rural communities (2018a: 155–182), and political culture and the media (2018a: 183–208). The CNMH stressed the link between sexual violence and traditional gender arrangements (2018a: 50), the legitimization of paramilitary *corrective* violence aimed at establishing a militarized social order (2018a: 51), and the rationale of militarized masculinity in relation to other males. With regard to LGBT victims, the authors stressed both the continuum of violence and the legitimizing narrative, with violence being perceived as the price people have to pay for being "like this" (CNMH 2018a: 93). An additional report on the CNMH's contribution (CNMH 2018b) contains a chapter on gender and the differential approach (2018b: 15–59), coordinated by Nancy Prada Prada. On the conceptual level, the authors point to the continuum of violence (2018b: 27–28), the difference between masculinity/femininity, sex, and gender (2018b: 25), and delineate the repertoire of violence used by armed actors to impose social and moral orders (2018b: 29). Moreover, they refer to agency and the variety of experiences that include combat experiences of women and LGBT people (2018b: 30). This argument is taken up by Lina Céspedez-Báez, who examines the gender concepts visible in CNMH's historiographic contributions (CNMH and Céspedez-Báez 2018). She concludes that there are liberal feminist as well as radical perspectives in CNMH's work, and she identifies a significant lacuna in research on feminization and masculinization (CNMH and Céspedez-Báez 2018: 103). While the phenomenon of female paramilitary combatants (and perpetrators) remains under-researched, even less attention has been paid to male (non-gay and non-trans) victims of sexual violence.

As shown in the preceding paragraph, Colombia is a global forerunner in bringing public attention to sexual violence, violence against minorities, and the role of militarized masculinities. The CNMH reports form part of a repository of cultural memory that needs actualization and symbolic practice to produce meaning. These reports are fundamental historiographic achievements reflecting diverse primary gender concerns (as described in Section 2). They made subsequent achievements easier.

Contested Gender Sensitivity: The 2016 Peace Agreement and Its Implementation

The signing of the 2016 peace accord between the Colombian government and the FARC-EP significantly accelerated this supply of resources and space. Colombia now accounts for an ambitious and comprehensive effort to deal with past atrocities – and present human rights violations (Oettler 2020). The Integral System of Truth, Justice, Reparation, and Non-Repetition, product of the 2016 peace accord, is considered to be holistic. It comprises three newly established institutions: the Special Jurisdiction for Peace (JEP), a truth commission (CEV), and a Unit for the Search of Disappeared (UBPD). These institutions are connected to other components of the peace accord as well as to formerly created mechanisms for land restitution and reparation.

The victim-centered chapter 5 of the peace accord sets out the institutional framework for transitional justice in Colombia. As a result of decade-long struggles for a gendered agenda for peace (Oettler 2019), the peace agreement incorporated gender into almost all efforts to achieve peace and transitional justice. Therefore, Colombia has been showcased as a case that testifies to "the positive impact of women's participation on the chances of having a peace agreement with gender provisions" (True and Riveros-Morales 2019: 36). And indeed, the terms *gender*, *women*, and *LGBT* appear 280 times in the 310-page peace agreement signed in November 2016. The term *men* appears frequently, always forming part of the dyad *men and women*, and the terms *masculinity* and *femininity* are not used at all. While *ONU Mujeres* identified 100 gender-related measures, the official implementation plan (*Plan Marco de Implementación* 2016) listed 50 gender-related strategies and indicators. As will be described in greater detail later, two aspects deserve particular attention (Oettler 2021): First, the agreement went through a stage of incoherent revision after the failed plebiscite and became more conservative but highly ambiguous. Second, the impressive number of gender provisions turns out to be connected to rather vague and redundant dispositions. Both aspects are crucial for understanding the promises of inclusiveness in the shadow of ongoing contestation.

The failure of the plebiscite was an unanticipated yet brief moment of crisis which reinforced and accentuated existing ideological polarizations. In the run-up to the plebiscite in October 2016, those campaigning for No were against concessions to an armed organization that was responsible for massive acts of violence such as killings, kidnappings, rape, and drug-related crimes. They were against mild penalties, the political representation of FARC, and truth-finding efforts. The No campaign, led by former president Álvaro Uribe and members of Protestant and Catholic churches, had particular resonance in the echo chambers of social media, making viral everything that fed rumors about the devastating effects of a peace deal with FARC. Rumors triggered a variety of fears, with a communist takeover (*Castrochavism*), food shortages, expropriations and the violation of property rights, higher taxes and lower pensions, the destruction of the family, and the homosexualization of society being the main concerns (for details, see Gil Hernández 2020; Posada-Carbó 2017; Beltrán and Creely 2018; Fundación Ideas para la Paz 2016).

The comparison of the two versions of the peace agreement – dated 24 August 2016 and 12 November 2016[4] – reveals inconsistent decisions on the choice of terms. While the terms *gender*, *women*, and *LGBTI* appear 114, 185, and 10 times in the pre-plebiscite version, the revised version contains these terms (in the same order) 55, 209, and 16 times. The discursive strategy of the negotiating parties is revealed in these numbers. The revised version of the peace agreement obviously avoids the term *gender*. The aim was not to substantially change the text but rather to hide a term that provokes *anti-gender* campaigns. Although "the definition of gender was reduced to denote women" (Céspedes-Báez 2019: 58), the overall picture was messy, and the term *gender* was replaced by other signifiers that were at once related to conservative and emancipatory concepts of gender. Just to mention but a few examples, "*equidad de género*" (gender equity, Gobierno Nacional and FARC-EP 2016a: 9) was replaced by "*igualdad de oportunidades entre hombres y mujeres*" (equality of opportunity between men and women, Gobierno Nacional and FARC-EP 2016b: 10), "*personas con orientación sexual e identidad de género diversa*" (persons with diverse sexual orientations and gender identities, Gobierno Nacional and FARC-EP 2016a: 21) became "*grupos en condición de vulnerabilidad*" (vulnerable groups, Gobierno Nacional and FARC-EP 2016b: 25), and the "*enfoque diferencial y de*

4 For a useful tool for comparison see https://draftable.com/compare/JjypTOknafBktqvc (last accessed 14 August 2020). The following quotes refer to the pre-plebiscite (AI) and final (AII) versions of the peace agreements.

género" (differential and gender focus, Gobierno Nacional and FARC-EP 2016a: 27) was reframed as the "*situación particular de las mujeres*" (particular situation of women, Gobierno Nacional and FARC-EP 2016b: 31). These discursive patterns strengthened the rather binary approaches to gender expressed by liberal feminism and gender mainstreaming policies. The revisions, however, did not seem to follow a coherent strategy, as the following example demonstrates: "*identidad de género diversa*" (diverse gender identity, Gobierno Nacional and FARC-EP 2016a: 47) was replaced by *LGBTI* (Gobierno Nacional and FARC-EP 2016b: 53). The primary concern in revising the gender provisions of the peace agreement was avoiding the controversial term *gender*.

Table 7.1 synthesizes two dimensions of the gender provisions: the level of concertedness and their primary focus on resolving root causes of conflict, addressing its consequences, or regulating the conflict between FARC-EP and the government. This table does not contain every mention of gender-related terms but rather 100 gender provisions as identified by ONU Mujeres (2018). What a typifying structuring of the gender provisions in the final version of the peace agreement reveals is a low level of concreteness, with nearly half of all gender-related provisions referring to mission statements, rather vague principles, and fields of action (for more details, see Oettler 2021). The general and abstract nature of these provisions makes operationalization of success or failure of implementation difficult.

On the other hand, it is remarkable that the majority of gender-related provisions refer to efforts addressing the root causes of conflict, especially regarding rural reform, political participation, and drug economy (see Table 7.1). In the gender-related provisions of the agreement, LGBT persons are mostly referenced as one of many social groups to be recognized and attended (Gobierno Nacional and FARC-EP 2016b: 3, 47, 53, 80, 117, 126, 131, 134, 189). One guiding principle of the peace accord is the "promotion of the non-stigmatization of groups in condition of vulnerability

Table 7.1 Gender provisions in the peace agreement between the Colombian government and the FARC-EP (2016)

	Provision's focus			
	Causes of conflict	*Consequences of conflict*	*Conflict regulation*	*Sum*
Principles, fields of action	30	9	7	46
Participation/representation	17	8	2	27
Project	18	3	5	26
Institution	2	4	2	8
Sum	67	24	16	107

Source: Own elaboration, based on ONU Mujeres (2018).

or stigmatization such as women, ethnic communities, LGBTI population, youth, children and elderly people, disabled people, political minorities and religious minorities" (Gobierno Nacional and FARC-EP 2016b: 47). Again, this list of social groups exemplifies the underlying revision strategy of avoiding the term *gender*, with the pre-plebiscite formula referring to the "promotion of the non-stigmatization based on sexual orientation and gender identity" (Gobierno Nacional and FARC-EP 2016a: 41). The revision stage of the peace negotiations led to an ambiguous and far from theoretically grounded picture of the groups to be included in peacebuilding. However, LGBTI persons kept being recognized in the revised version of the peace accords. There were also some mentions of special needs, such as overcoming LGBT stereotyping in public education on drug consumers (Gobierno Nacional and FARC-EP 2016b: 119) and special needs for protection from gender-based violence (Gobierno Nacional and FARC-EP 2016b: 144). Importantly, LGBT organizations and LGBT needs were explicitly included in some provisions on transitional justice and implementation (Gobierno Nacional and FARC-EP 2016b: 137, 234). The peace agreement, however vague it may be in this respect, recognizes *LGBTI* both as lived experience and political category.

In the initial phase of the implementation, the FARC-EP demobilized, laid down 8,900 weapons, started a process of collective reincorporation, and transformed into a political party, the Alternative Revolutionary Force of the People (*Fuerza Armada Revolucionaria del Común*, FARC). The initial phase of the implementation witnessed progress as well as blockades and setbacks (McFee and Rettberg 2019). As it is so often the case, peace optimism faded quickly, and critiques stress that "the half-hearted implementation of the peace agreement and the persistence of violence suggest a grim outlook" (García Pinzón 2020: 1). The COVID-19 pandemic made this perspective even grimmer (Gpaz 2021), especially with regard to gender-based violence and the increasing numbers of human rights defenders and social leaders killed by paramilitary groups and other armed actors. As in other regions of the world (O'Rourke 2020), the pandemic is paralleled by higher levels of sexual harassment, more violent reactions to gender non-conforming behavior, and a redirection of public attention and state resources to other priority areas. Before the outbreak of COVID-19, however, gender-sensitive issues had rather remained at the margins of the implementation process. In its 2018 report on the implementation of the gender-related provisions of the peace agreement, the Kroc Institute stated that gender-sensitive issues were being implemented but lagged behind other provisions within the accord. "As of June 30, 2018, 51% of the commitments had not been initiated; 38% were minimally implemented; 7% had reached an intermediate level of implementation; and 4% of the commitments (five stipulations) had been fully implemented" (Kroc Institute 2018: 6). In its latest report, GPaz raised concern over the slow and declining pace of implementation in 2020 (Gpaz

2021: 16). Yet another aspect of implementation that deserves mention is the gap between policy commitments and actual financing for gender-responsive peace. To date, gender-related budget expenditures and estimates are neither clearly disaggregated nor completely reported (for a detailed overview, see Secretaría Técnica del Componente Internacional de Verificación CINEP/PPP-CERAC 2021: 104–130).

In this rather frustrating atmosphere, the cause of reconstructing masculinities and addressing LGBT rights developed further than activists had imagined precisely because national and international scaffolders of peace opposed the aggressive anti-feminist and homophobic attitudes of the *uribista* No campaign. Notable advances in the field include political representation (e.g., the Special High-Level Forum for monitoring the gender-based approach, created in July 2017; see Kroc Institute 2018: 30) and gender-sensitive approaches to historical clarification, justice, and reparation. The Unit for the Search of the Disappeared applies a gender-sensitive approach addressing the needs of LGBT persons. As transgender and gender-nonconforming people were in an extremely vulnerable position, often violated or killed by acquaintances or strangers, civilians or members of armed groups, their situation requires special attention. In most milieus, LGBT persons live in hostile social environments, experiencing stigma and discrimination, and often fearing retaliation from their families. The UBPD therefore addresses the question of how to search for missing people who eventually have not been missed by their families. This also implies reconsidering rituals of closure and inventing forms of symbolic reparation focusing on non-biological social networks, such as families of choice and communities of experience. The JEP is moving ahead. To date, it has prioritized seven *macro-cases* (*macro casos*) on emblematic violations (case 1: kidnappings by FARC; case 3: falsos positivos – deaths presented as combat casualties by state agents or regional contexts; case 6: repression against the Patriotic Union; case 7: recruitment of children) and regional contexts (case 2: Nariño; case 4: Urabá; case 5: Northern Cauca/Southern Cauca Valley). Although there are high expectations and a number of reports submitted by women's and LGBT organizations (e.g., Colombia Diversa 2011; Díaz Villamil 2020), it is rather unlikely that the JEP will open a macro-case related to gender-based violence. The Truth Commission (CEV) has a highly visible gender working group led by Commissioner Alejandra Miller. Soon after its inauguration, the commission – building on a vast body of knowledge – engaged in ceremonies of public recognition of patterns of violence. Most notably, the first Encounter for Truth (*Encuentro de la Verdad*), realized with victim representatives in Cartagena in June 2019, was about gender-based violence. The symbolic importance of this event cannot be underestimated, and its title, My Body Speaks the Truth (*Mi Cuerpo dice la Verdad*), implicitly recognized the struggle of the LGBT movement, which had entered the debate on peace in the early 2000s, preparing a document titled "Body – First territory of peace" (*Cuerpo – primer territorio de paz*).

In Colombia, insights into the importance of overcoming gender stereotypes and "opening space for alternative masculinities" (Theidon 2009: 32) had some practical consequences. While the reinsertion programs of the 1990s were gender-blind (ibid. 154–155), the 2010 reintegration strategy of the High Council for Reintegration (ACR – *Alta Consejería para la Reintegración*) included aspects such as demilitarization, the promotion of alternative masculinities and shared household responsibilities, the empowerment of women, and the prevention of sexual violence. The transformation of gender relations, however, was not high on the political agenda, being an "add-on" at best. Post-2016 reintegration agenda priorities happen to be the same. The National Reincorporation Strategy (CONPES 3931) includes a gender component, and the gender working group of the National Council for Reincorporation (*Mesa Técnica de Género del Consejo Nacional de Reincorporación CNR*) elaborated guidelines for the inclusion of a gender and masculinity perspective in the process of reincorporation (CNR 2019). In its harsh recent critique of the implementation of the peace accords, a Bogotá think tank condemned "simulation" and a "sophisticated form of non-compliance" (FARC-CSIVI-CEPDIPO 2019: 21). The implementation of the gender perspective is characterized as weak and as being restricted to some internationally funded projects instead of a coherent state-sponsored effort (FARC et al.: 85–89). Indeed, the first phase of implementation has seen some consciousness-raising efforts, but these were far from being a high priority.

Five years after the signing of the peace accord, the implementation record continued to be mixed, and the Kroc Institute (2022: 8) highlighted that only 12% of the gender provisions have been completed. While the Special Jurisdiction for Peace did not open a macro-case to investigate sexual violence and gender-based violence during the armed conflict, the truth commission issued a volume dedicated to gender concerns. It would go beyond the scope of this chapter to discuss the 400-page volume "My Body Is the Truth: Experiences of Women and LGBTIQ+ persons in the Armed Conflict" (CEV 2022, own translation) in detail. But there are two general observations connected to the main argument of this chapter. First, the volume consists of two separate reports – "Women: Voices, which defend and care for life" (pp. 10–221) and "Truth Is Rainbow" (pp. 222–360) – and a glossary and bibliography. These reports differ strikingly in their conceptual frameworks (and potential audiences). While the first report focuses on sexual and gender-based violence against women, the second report gravitates around the argument that the widespread practice of violence against LGBTIQ+ people corresponded to hegemonic cultural norms. While the LGBTIQ+ report takes up decolonial and poststructuralist gender concerns, the report on women's experiences speaks to a broad spectrum of audiences, including discursive communities that do not question binary conceptions of gender (religious communities, liberal feminism). It is revealing that the report and the glossary do not include a definition of "woman." The volume of the CEV shows the difficulty of integrating the diverse symbolic and representational subuniverses of *gender* exposed in Section 2. Second, both sub-volumes contain recommendations. The authors state that they identified 3,400 recommendations given by witnesses or included in the 54 reports the CEV received from civil society organizations (CEV 2022: 203). All of us working in the field of qualitative research know how difficult condensation, categorization, and systematization are. In preparing the final report, the gender working group prioritized some recommendations and subordinated or excluded others. The result was a catalogue of recommendations connected to international norms, the national legal framework, and the 2016 peace accord.

Conclusions

All formulas fall short, yet the commonplace (and overused) metaphor of the glass being half empty, or being half full and getting fuller, captures the Colombian experience quite well (Rettberg 2012). Early engagements with peacebuilding and transitional justice were being further consolidated in recent years, and Colombia has developed an impressive institutional structure for addressing root causes of conflict, ensuring accountability and achieving reconciliation. Nevertheless, illicit economies and armed actors continue to pose an imminent threat to civil society. In times of COVID-19 and increasing killings of *líderes sociales* and non-militarized young people, peace optimism faded. The most pessimist view would suggest that the peace negotiations between the Colombian government and the FARC-EP resulted in a half-empty glass with no refill option – and then the water was tipped into the desert. Still, in defense of moderate optimism, one could argue that there are severe implementation gaps and shifting priorities, but opportunities for some historically marginalized social groups opened up. The 2022 election results and the ambitious "total peace" agenda of newly elected president Gustavo Petro fueled hopes.

The history of the Colombian peace process demonstrates that discursive opportunities are never fully closed or opened. In countercultural political spheres, feelings of hope and resentment, optimism, and anxiety fluctuated over time, and the overall peace process was characterized by multilayered advances and setbacks. In sum, both consensus and dissent within and outside LGBT and women's movements were an essential part of the evolution of the gendered agenda for peace (Céspedez-Báez and Jaramillo Ruiz 2018; Chaparro González and Martínez Osorio 2016; Rojas 2009), which brings together decolonial, Catholic, and (post)structuralist frames of references and *Weltanschauungen*, connected to binary as well as queer notions of gender. Over the past decades, academic thought involved a radical poststructuralist questioning of identities and representation, paving the way for "queering women, peace and security" (Hagen 2016) and for implementing a gendered agenda for peace that takes into account overlapping and mutually reinforcing dimensions of discrimination. In some ways, the advent of a de-essentialist agenda for peace suggested that the patriarchal gender regime had weakened. Not only in Bogotá but also in many regions of Colombia, there is a long history of activists resorting to decolonial, queer, and poststructuralist subuniverses of gender to make sense of the world and develop political agendas (Caro Romero 2020). On the other hand, the Colombian architecture of peace opens up diverse possibilities of discursive and practical alliance building across deep-rooted divides.

Most survivors of violence confronted realities such as displacement, poor housing and living conditions, poverty, and violence in its many manifestations. Therefore, women's organizations from all over the country developed a comprehensive agenda for gendered peace gravitating around "practical gender interests" (Molyneux 1985), often related to public health, rural reforms, or political participation. This agenda, to a large extent, reflected curial and laical calls for an end of gender inequality and violence against women, children, and minorities. For decades, the gendered agenda for peace was expanded or compressed accordion-like, opening up, lubricating, and condensing visions for a just society (Oettler 2019). Countless debates and documents became precursors to the 100 gender provisions in the peace agreement between the Colombian government and the FARC-EP, designed to meet strategic as well as practical gender interests. The entire negotiation process was a veritable exercise of feminist encouragement and consciousness-raising among delegates and civil society organizations (Corporación Humanas and CIASE 2017). It was a process of consultation that was to culminate in the high-level public presentation of the gender subcommission in mid-2016 and the signing of the gendered peace accord in December 2016. The discursive pendulum swung between binary conceptions of gender and decolonial/poststructuralist concerns. In the course of the recent politicization of gender and sexuality, however, a mainstream approach to gender that speaks to religious worldviews became the dominant pole of discourse. The differential approach of the peace agreement appears – to borrow Connell's words – as an "updated categorialism, a static cross-classification of 'race, class, and gender'" (Connell 2018: 341). Yet *gender* is an unstable horizon, unfixed, and open to interpretation of its significance. The 310 pages of the peace agreement imply subtexts of conservative notions of gender, but they may open up their full emancipatory potential in the future.

References

Althaus-Reid, M. (2005). From the Goddess to Queer Theology: The State We Are in Now. *Feminist Theology* 3(2): 265–272.

Beltrán, W. (2012): Descripción cuantitativa de la pluralización religiosa en Colombia. *Universitas Humanística* 73: 201–237.

Beltrán, W. and S. Creely (2018). Pentecostals, Gender Ideology and the Peace Plebiscite: Colombia 2016. *Religions* 8(12): 1–19.

Berger, P. and T. Luckmann (1991). *The Social Construction of Reality. A Treatise in the Sociology of Knowledge*. London: Penguin Books.

Bouvier, V. (ed.) (2009). *Colombia: Building Peace in a Time of War*. Washington, DC: United States Institute of Peace Press.

Bouvier, V. (2016). *Gender and the Role of Women in Colombia's Peace Process*. New York: UN Women.

Bridges, T. and C. Pascoe (2018). On the Elasticity of Gender Hegemony: Why Hybrid Masculinities Fail to Undermine Gender and Social Inequality. In: Messerschmidt, J., Messner, M., Connell, R. and Martin, P. (eds.): *Gender Reckonings. New Social Theory and Research*. New York: New York University Press: 254–274.

Burggraf, J. (2006). Gender. In: Pontifical Council for the Family (ed.): *Lexicon of Ambiguous and Debatable Terms Regarding Family Life and Ethical Questions*. Vatican: Human Life International: 399–408.

Butler, J. (1990). *Gender Trouble: Feminism and the Subversion of Identity*. London and New York: Routledge.

Cabnal, L. (2010). Acercamiento a la construcción del pensamiento epistémico de las mujeres indígenas feministas comunitarias de Abya Yala. In: ACSUR Las Segovias (ed.): *Feminismos diversos: el feminismo comunitario*. Madrid: ACSUR Las Segovias: 10–25.

Caro Romero, F. (2020). Una pequeña historia de las marchas del orgullo en Colombia. In: *Museo Q: Devenir queer: al límite del patrimonio*. Bogotá: MQ: 164–179.

Castillo Vargas, E. (2018). *No somos etcétera. Veinte años de historia del movimiento LGBT en Colombia*. Bogotá: Penguin Random House.

Céspedes-Baéz, L. (2017). En los confines de lo possible: inclusión del enfoque de género en el Acuerdo de la Habana. In: Céspedes-Baéz, L. and Prieto Rios, E. (eds.): *Utopía u oportunidad fallida. Análisis crítico del Acuerdo de Paz*. Bogotá: Editorial Universidad del Rosario: 295–326.

Céspedes-Báez, L. and F. Jaramillo Ruiz (2018). Peace Without Women Does Not Go! Women's Struggle for Inclusion in Colombia's Peace Process with the FARC. *Colombia Internacional* 94: 83–109.

Céspedes-Báez, L. M. (2019). A (Feminist) Farewell to Arms: The Impact of the Peace Process with the FARC-EP on Colombian Feminism. *Cornell International Law Journal* 52(1): 39–63. Available at: https://ww3.lawschool.cornell.edu/research/ILJ/upload/Cespedes-Baez-final-2.pdf

Chaparro González, N. and M. Martínez Osorio (2016). *Negociando desde los márgenes: la participación política de las mujeres en los procesos de paz en Colombia (1982–2016)*. Bogotá: Dejusticia.

CNMH – Centro Nacional de Memoria (2012). *El placer. Mujeres, coca y guerra en Bajo Putamayo*. Bogota: CNMH.

CNMH – Centro Nacional de Memoria (2015a). *Limpieza social: Una violencia mal nombrada*. Bogotá: CNMH.

CNMH – Centro Nacional de Memoria (2015b). *Aniquilar la diferencia. Lesbianas, Gays, Bisexuales y Transgeneristas en el marco del conflicto armado colombiano*. Bogotá: CNMH.

CNMH – Centro Nacional de Memoria (2016). *Mujeres en resistencia*. Bogotá: CNMH.

CNMH – Centro Nacional de Memoria (2017). *La guerra inscrita en el cuerpo*. Bogotá: CNMH.

CNMH – Centro Nacional de Memoria (2018a). *Sujetos victimizados y daños causados. Balance de la contribución del CNMH al esclarecimiento histórico*. Bogotá: CNMH.

CNMH – Centro Nacional de Memoria (2018b). *Memorias Plurales. Balance de la contribución del CNMH al esclarecimiento histórico*. Bogotá: CNMH.

CNMH – Centro Nacional de Memoria and L. Céspedez-Báez (2018). Género y memoria histórica. *Balance de la contribución del CNMH al esclarecimiento histórico*. Bogotá: CNMH.

CNMH and GMH – Centro Nacional de Memoria Histórica & Grupo de Memoria Histórica (2010). *La masacre Bahía Portete: mujeres wayúu en la mira*. Bogotá: CNMH.

CNMH and GMH – Centro Nacional de Memoria Histórica & Grupo de Memoria Histórica (2011a). *Mujeres y Guerra. Víctimas y Resistentes en el Caribe Colombiano*. Bogotá: CNMH.

CNMH and GMH – Centro Nacional de Memoria Histórica/Grupo de Memoria Histórica (2011b). *Mujeres que hacen historia: tierra, cuerpo y política en el Caribe Colombiano*. Bogotá: CNMH.

CNR – Mesa Técnica de Género del Consejo Nacional de Reincorporación (2019). *Herramientas para la inclusión del enfoque de género en procesos de reincorporación económica*. Bogotá: CNR, ONU Muheres. PNUD. Available at: https://www2.unwomen.org/-/media/field%20office%20colombia/documentos/publicaciones/2019/08/herramientas%20para%20la%20inclusin%20%20del%20enfoque%20de%20gnero%20en%20procesos%20de%20reincorporacin%20econmica.pdf?la=es&vs=5733. Accessed on: 12 January 2020.

Collins, P. (2000). *Black Feminst Thought*. New York: Routledge.

Colombia Diversa (2011). *Todos los deberes, pocos los derechos. Situación de derechos humanos de lesbianas, gay, bisexuales y transgeneristas en Colombia 2008–2009*. Bogotá: Colombia Diversa.

Congreso de la República (2011). *Ley 1448, 10 de junio de 2011*. Available at: http://wp.presidencia.gov.co/sitios/normativa/leyes/Documents/Juridica/LEY%201448%20DE%202011.pdf. Accessed on: 12 January 2020.

Comisión para el Esclarecimiento de la Verdad, la Convivencia y la No Repetición (CEV) (2022). *Mi cuerpo es la verdad. Experiencias de mujeres y personas LGBTIQ+ en el conflicto armado*. Bogotá: CEV.

Connell, R. (1987). *Gender and Power: Society, the Person and Sexual Politics*. Cambridge Polity Press.

Connell, R. (1995). *Masculinities*. Cambridge: Polity Press.

Connell, R. (2007). *Southern Theory: The Global Dynamics of Knowledge in Social Science*. Cambridge: Polity Press.

Connell, R. (2009). *Gender. A Short Introduction*. Cambridge: Polity Press.

Connell, R. (2018). Conclusion: Reckoning with Gender. In: Messerschmidt, J., Messner, M., Connell, R. and Martin, P. (eds.): *Gender Reckonings. New Social Theory and Research*. New York: New York University Press: 331–346.

Corporación Humanas and CIASE (Corporación de Investigación y Acción Social y Económica) (2017). *Vivencias, aportes y reconocimiento de las mujeres en el proceso de paz en La Habana*. Bogotá: Corporación Humanas, CIASE.

Della Porta, D. and S. Tarrow (eds.) (2005). *Transnational Protest and Global Activism*. Lanham: Rowman & Littlefield.

Derr, M., R. McNair and L. Naranjo-Huebl (eds.) (2005). *Prolife Feminism: Yesterday and Today*. Kansas City: Feminism and Nonviolence Studies Association.

Díaz Villamil, M. (2020). *Los órdenes del prejuicio: crímenes cometidos sistemáticamente contra personas LGBT en el conflicto armado colombiano*. Bogotá: Colombia Diversa.

Esguerra Muelle, C. and M. Sánchez Buitrago (2006). Atención a la violencia contra personas LGBT en Colombia. In: Serrano Amaya, J. (ed.): *Otros Cuerpos, Otras Sexualidades*. Bogotá: Instituto Pensar: 154–167.

FARC-CSIVI-CEPDIPO (Centro de Pensamiento y Diálogo Político) (2019). *La implementación del Acuerdo de Paz durante el gobierno de Iván Duque. Tendencia a la perfidia y simulación*. Bogotá: Impresol Edicionesl. Available at: https://cepdipo.org/wp-content/uploads/2019/10/La-paz-simulada-CEPDIPO.pdf. Accessed on: 12 January 2022.

Finnemore, M. and K. Sikkink (1998). International Norm Dynamics and Political Change. *International Organization* 52(4): 887–917.

FIP – Fundación Ideas para la Paz (2016). *Radiografía del Plebiscito y el Posplebiscito*. FIP. Available at: http://www.ideaspaz.org/especiales/posplebiscito/. Accessed on: 24 August, 2020.

García Pinzón, V. (2020). Colombia: Between the Dividends of Peace and the Shadow of Violence. *GIGA Focus Latin America* 2. Hamburg: GIGA. Available at: https://nbn-resolving.org/urn:nbn:de:0168-ssoar-66908-5. Accessed on: 10 January 2022.

Giddens, A. (1984). *The Constitution of Society: Outline of the Theory of Structuration*. Berkeley: University of California Press.

Gil Hernández, F. (2020). The Case of Colombia. In: Corrêa, S. (ed.): *Anti-Gender Politics in Latin America. Summaries of Country Case Studies*. Rio de Janeiro: Associação Brasileira Interdisciplinar de AIDS: 79–91.

Gobierno Nacional and las FARC-EP (2016a). *Acuerdo Final para la Terminación del Conflicto y la Construcción de una Paz Estable y Duradera (AI)*, 24 August. Available at: https://www.eltiempo.com/contenido/politica/proceso-de-paz/ARCHIVO/ARCHIVO-16682558-0.pdf. Accessed on: 24 August 2020.

Gobierno Nacional and las FARC-EP (2016b). *Acuerdo Final para la Terminación del Conflicto y la Construccion de una Paz Estable y Duradera (AII)*, 12 November. Available at: https://www.cancilleria.gov.co/sites/default/files/Fotos2016/12.11_1.2016nuevoacuerdofinal.pdf. Accessed on: 24 August 2020.

GPaz – Grupo de Género en la Paz (2021). *La paz avanza con las mujeres. III Informe de observaciones sobre los avances en la implementación del enfoque de género del Acuerdo de Paz*. Bogotá: Edición Cuatro Ojos Editorial.

Hagen, J. (2016). Queering Women, Peace and Security. *International Affairs* 92(2): 313–332.

Holy Father Francis (2016). *Post-Synodal Apostolic Exhortation Amoris Laetitia on Love in the Family*. Vatican: Libreria Editrice Vaticana.

Jäger, S. and F. Maier (2016). Analysing Discourses and Dispositives: A Foucauldian Approach to Theory and Methodology. In: Wodak, R. and Meyer, M. (eds.): *Methods of Critical Discourse Studies*. London: Sage Publications: 109–136.

Kroc Institute (2018). *Special Report of the Kroc Institute and the International Accompaniment Component, UN Women, Women's International Democratic Federation, and Sweden, on the Monitoring of the Gender Perspective in the Implementation of the Colombian Final Peace Accord*. Bogotá: Kroc Institute. Available at: https://kroc.nd.edu/assets/297624/181113_gender_report_final.pdf. Accessed on: 12 January 2022.

Kroc Institute (2022). *Five Years After the Signing of the Colombian Final Agreement. Reflections from Implementation. Executive Summary*. Bogotá: Kroc Institute. Available at: https://curate.nd.edu/show/0z708w35p43. Accessed on: 4 January 2023.

Lozano Lerma, B. (2016). *Tejiendo con retazos de memorias insurgencias epistémicas de mujeres negras/afrocolombianas. Aportes a un feminismo negro decolonial*. PhD Thesis, Quito: Universidad Andina Simón Bolívar.

Lugones, M. (2007). Heterosexualism and the Colonial/Modern Gender System. *Hypatia* 22(1): 186–209.

Matamba (2020). Nota Editorial. *Matamba Revista Afro Juvenil* 10.

McFee, E. and A. Rettberg (2019). Contexto de los deafíos de la implementación temprana en Colombia. In: McFee, E. and Rettberg, A. (eds.): *Excombatientes y acuerdo de paz con las FARC-EP en Colombia: balance de la etapa Temprana*. Bogotá: Ediciones Uniandes: 1–18.

Messerschmidt, J. and M. Messner (2018). Hegemonic, Nonhegemonic, and 'New' Masculinities. In: Messerschmidt, J., Messner, M., Connell, R. and Martin, P. (eds.): *Gender Reckonings. New Social Theory and Research*. New York: New York University Press: 35–56.

Misra, J. (2018). Categories, Structures, and Intersectional Theory. In: Messerschmidt, J., Messner, M., Connell, R. and Martin, P. (eds.): *Gender Reckonings. New Social Theory and Research*. New York: New York University Press: 111–130.

Molyneux, M. (1985). Mobilization Without Emancipation? Women's Interests, the State, and Revolution in Nicaragua. *Feminist Studies* 11(2): 227–254.

Nasi, C. (2009). Colombia's Peace Processes, 1982–2002: Conditions, Strategies, and Outcomes. In: Bouvier, V. (ed.): *Colombia: Building Peace in a Time of War*. Washington, DC: United States Institute of Peace Press: 39–64.

Oettler, A. (2019). The Struggle for Gendered Peace and LGBT Rights in Colombia. *Violence, Security, and Peace Working Papers 2*. London: LSE-GIGA-CCDP. Available at: https://www.lse.ac.uk/lacc/publications/PDFs/VSP2-Oettler-Gendered-Peace-LGBT-Rights-Colombia-web.pdf. Accessed on: 12 January 2022.

Oettler, A. (2020). *Colombia's Ongoing Violence Has Shifted Truth and Reconciliation from the Past into the Present*. LSE Blog. Available at: https://blogs.lse.ac.uk/latamcaribbean/2020/01/13/colombias-ongoing-violence-has-shifted-truth-and-reconciliation-from-the-past-into-the-present/. Accessed on: 12 January 2022.

Oettler, A. (2021). Gender und der überfrachtete kolumbianische Frieden. *Zeitschrift für Friedens-und Konfliktforschung* 10(12): 103–126.

ONU Mujeres (2018). *100 medidas que incorporan la perspectiva de género en el Acuerdo de Paz entre el Gobierno de Colombia y las FARC-EP para terminar el conflicto y construir una paz estable y duradera*. ONU Mujeres. Available at: https://colombia.unwomen.org/es/biblioteca/publicaciones/2017/05/100-medidas-genero-acuerdos. Accessed on: 12 January 2022.

O'Rourke, C. (2020). *COVID-19 and Gender-based Violence in Conflict: New Challenges and Persistent Problems*. Political settlements Research Programme. Available at: http://www.politicalsettlements.org/2020/04/21/covid-19-and-gender-based-violence-in-conflict/. Accessed on: 12 January 2022.

Paredes, J. (2010). *Hilando fino. Desde el feminismo comunitario*. La Paz: El Rebozo/Grietas/Lente Flotante.

Posada-Carbó, E. (2017). The Difficult Road to Peace in Colombia. *Current History* 116: 74–76.

Quijano, A. (2018). Coloniality of Power, Eurocentrism, and Latin America. In: Moraña, M., Dussel, E. and Jàuregui, C. A. (eds.): *Coloniality at Large. Latin America and the Postcolonial Debate*. Durham and London: Duke University Press: 181–224.

Registro Único de Víctimas (RUV) (2021). *Víctimas Conflicto Armado. Gov.co*. Available at: https://www.unidadvictimas.gov.co/es/registro-unico-de-victimas-ruv/37394. Accessed on: 12 January 2022.

Rettberg, A. (2005). *Entre el perdón y el paredón: preguntas y dilemas de la justicia transicional*. Bogotá: International Development Research Centre (IDRC) – Ediciones Uniandes.

Rettberg, A. (2012). Construcción de paz en Colombia: context y balance. In: Rettberg, A. (ed.): *Construcción de paz en Colombia*. Bogotá: Universidad de los Andes: 3–50.

Rojas, C. (2009). Women and Peacebuilding in Colombia: Resistance to War, Creativity for Peace. In: Bouvier, V. (ed.): *Colombia: Building Peace in a Time of War*. Washington, DC: United States Institute of Peace Press: 207–224.

Sánchez, N. and A. Rudling (2019). Reparations in Colombia: Where to? Mapping the Colombian Landscape of Reparations for Victims of the Internal Armed Conflict,

Reparations, Victimhood and Responsibility. *Transitional Societies Policy Paper*. Belfast: Queen's University of Belfast. Available at: https://reparations.qub.ac.uk/assets/uploads/ColombiaReparationsPolicyReportFORAPPROVAL-SP-HR-NoCrops.pdf. Accessed on: 12 January 2022.

Secretaría Técnica del Componente Internacional de Verificación CINEP/PPP-CERAC (2021). *Quinto informe de verificación de la implementación del enfoque de género en el Acuerdo Final de Paz en Colombia*. Bogotá: CINEP/PPP-CERAC.

Segato, R. (2014). Colonialidad y patriarcado moderno: expansión del frente estatal, modernización, y la vida de las mujeres. In: Yuderkys Espinosa, D. and Ochoa, K. (eds.): *Tejiendo de otro modo: Feminismo, epistemología y apuestas descoloniales en Abya Yala*. Popayán: Editorial Universidad del Cauca: 75–90.

Serrano Amaya, J. (2018). *Homophobic Violence in Armed Conflict and Political Transition*. Cham: Palgrave Macmillan.

Taussig, M. (2003). *Law in a Lawless Land*. New York and London: The New Press.

Theidon, K. (2009). Reconstructing Masculinities: The Disarmament, Demobilization, and Reintegration of Former Combatants in Colombia. *Human Rights Quarterly* 31(1): 1–34.

True, J. and Y. Riveros-Morales (2019). Towards Inclusive Peace: Analysing Gender-Sensitive Peace Agreements 2000–2016. *International Political Science Review* 40(1): 23–40.

Vaggione, J. (2015). Sexuality, Religion and Politics in Latin America. In: Corrêa, S., de la Dehesa, R. and Parker, R. (eds.): *Sexuality and Politics: Regional Dialogues from the Global South I*. Rio de Janeiro: Sexuality Policy Watch, Associação Brasileira Interdisciplinar de AIDS: 136–165.

Vuola, E. (2001). *La ética sexual y los límites de la praxis. Conversaciones y críticas entre la teología feminista y la teología de la liberación*. Madrid, Quito: Ediciones Abya-Yala/IEPALA.

Weber, S. (2020). Trapped Between Promise and Reality in Colombia's Victims' Law: Reflections on Reparations, Development and Social Justice. *Bulletin of Latin American Research* 39(1): 5–21.

Section 3

Gendering Justice and Transitions Across Contexts

Chapter 8

Justice and Forced Marriage and Pregnancy in Wartime

A Gender-Inclusive Approach

Camile Oliveira and Erin Baines

Introduction

On 4 February 2021, former rebel commander of the Lord's Resistance Army (LRA), Dominic Ongwen, was convicted of 61 of 70 charges of crimes against humanity and war crimes at the International Criminal Court (ICC). These charges included the practice of forced marriage and pregnancy in the armed group, the latter setting a legal precedent in the Court. While a milestone for the ICC and for the 4,000 victims who testified, Ongwen's conviction was informed by a limited interpretation of how gender shapes the multifaceted and ongoing harms of forced marriage and pregnancy. The Court, for instance, did not consider the coercive setting in which men and boys were sometimes forced into marriage and parenting in the LRA. While it is not our interest to argue whether Ongwen was justly charged, the case of the LRA provides an opportunity to explore how the crimes of forced marriage and pregnancy impinged on and inflicted harm against men and boys (Denov and Drumbl 2020).

For more than two decades, the armed conflict in northern Uganda displaced up to a million people into internal camps that were poorly serviced and protected by the Ugandan military. The LRA, led by spiritual leader Joseph Kony, conducted mass abductions of children and youth to increase the capacity of the rebel group – it is estimated that between 54,000 and 75,000 people were abducted, most of whom came from the Acholi subregion (Pham et al. 2007). Ongwen himself was abducted as a young child and suffered from the physical and mental abuse tactics used by the rebel group to train and indoctrinate young abductees to fight against the government of Uganda. Under highly coercive circumstances, Ongwen became a child soldier and moved up the ranks to become one of LRA's top commanders, staying in the group for a total of 27 years. During this time, Ongwen is reported to have had up to nine so-called wives, resulting in multiple forced pregnancies and the birth of children. Several of his former "wives" provided damning evidence in their testimonies before the Court. However, several others problematized the prosecution's assumption of his perpetrator status. At least

DOI: 10.4324/9781003519522-11

one wife, Florence Ayot, argued that not all relationships were forced, and more so, there is no justice for Ongwen's children, who are now left without a father. In an interview with the *Justice Hub*, Ayot shared her hopes that Ongwen would come back to the community, so that "[they] could join hands and take care of [their] two children." She adds, "I don't know what he did exactly at the frontline, but he has a good character. If he were bad hearted, Kony himself would've killed him" (My Justice 2018).

Transitional justice mechanisms, to date, focus disproportionately on redress for sexual and gender-based violence against women and girls, overlooking gendered experiences of men and boys. The Office of the Prosecutor of the ICC launched its Policy Paper on Sexual and Gender-Based Crimes to counter such criticisms and called for a "deeper and more holistic application of gender analysis to an evaluation of harms in situation of mass atrocity" (Oosterveld 2018: 444). When it came to charges of forced marriage and pregnancy, however, the gender perspective constituted mainly of women's accounts of the crimes. The possibility that Ongwen – or, more generally, any male combatant – may have also been affected by such occurrences is foreclosed, as it does not align with dominant legal or policy discourse. As Bunting (2012: 181) notes, "Nowhere have I seen mention of indictments citing the crime of being forced to marry – men are not seen as 'victims' of forced marriage and this form of sexual violence." Such prosecutorial process also overlooks an affected third party related to this crime – the children born from forced unions – and, in turn, the subject position of men as fathers.

This chapter investigates men's experiences of forced marriage, which elucidate the forceful circumstances under which conjugal unions were formed and their children were born. We draw on research with men demobilized from the LRA now living in northern Uganda which considers how becoming a father shaped their decision-making during the war (Matarazzo and Baines 2019) and their capacity to assume responsibility for their children in the post-war period (Oliveira and Baines 2020; Madhani and Baines 2020). In our analysis, we consider how men were subjected to the institutionalization of forced marriage and pregnancy contingent on gender expectations and roles. The relationship between the former combatant and child brings into conversation forms of justice grounded in lived experiences and judgments issued by the ICC. We take a gender-inclusive approach to unsettle dominant notions of men's and women's role in war and question the static categories of victim and perpetrator. Finally, we conclude by highlighting future directions for consideration in the pursuit of justice after war.

A Note on Methods

This chapter is the result of over ten years of research and collaboration between Baines and two community-based organizations in northern Uganda, the Women's Advocacy Network (WAN) and the Justice and Reconciliation

Project (JRP). Baines worked with JRP from 2011 to 2016 to document the experiences of female survivors of abduction and forced marriage and pregnancy. In 2016, she developed a proposal to examine the impact of becoming a father in the LRA on men's experiences of war and post-war life. The participants were identified with the assistance of WAN, and then through snowball methods of contact. The research team, composed of Benard Okot, Evelyn Amony, and Joyce Abalo, observed that ex-combatants were initially wary of the intentions of the research, due to fears that the stories shared would later be used to prosecute them. Hence, the research context demanded a slow approach to build relationships of trust with participants, most of whom were interviewed over a period of three years from 2016 to 2019. Baines, Amony, Okot, and Abalo developed semi-structured research questions and conducted the interviews, maintaining contact with former combatants over the years. The research was conducted either in English or in Luo-Acholi. Most interviews were digitally recorded and later transcribed and translated into English. In total, 18 demobilized men were interviewed in-depth, and 13 participated in two focus group discussion. Participants determined the time, duration, frequency, and place of all interviews. Most interviews, for example, were held in the commanders' homes, where they felt most comfortable and in charge of the process. Interviews and focus groups were conducted with minimal interruption, allowing the participants to control the narrative pace and response. Each meeting lasted between 20 and 120 minutes, according to the participant's wishes.

Approaches to Justice and Gender Inclusivity

Transitional justice is one part of a larger complex process of reckoning with past abuses to hasten a peaceful coexistence following periods of mass violence such as state repression, conflict, or genocide. However, the field of study and practice has been critiqued for its liberal assumptions regarding the who, what, and when of justice after conflict (Nagy 2008). Retributive, restorative, and reparative approaches within transitional justice seek to address discrete crimes against humanity and war crimes, locating these in the past. Overt forms of violence are documented and prosecuted, but enduring legacies of political violence are often outside of the scope of transitional justice. Categories of victim and perpetrators reproduce gendered binaries of consent and culpability located in autonomous individuals, masking the complexity of violence and diffusion of responsibility (Baines 2015; McEvoy and McConnachie 2012). In contrast, transformative approaches to justice recognize that harms of the so-called past fold into and take the shape of structural, institutional, or symbolic violence in the present (Evans 2016; Gready and Robins 2014). For instance, racialized, gendered, or class inequalities shape social, economic, and political opportunities and so limit the realization of justice (Mani 2008; Miller 2008). Justice is lived in the everyday realities of those who endured violence and continue to face social and economic exclusion or political oppression and marginalization (Anyeko, forthcoming). A transformative approach calls for localized approaches to justice (Shaw et al. 2010), one articulated by and centrally inclusive of the voices of diverse victim groups (Robins 2011).

A transformative gender justice approach considers how mass violence against women and girls are "rooted in existing and surviving gender ideologies and inequalities" that "normalise women's subordinate position in society" (Boesten and Wilding 2015: 75). In order to prevent sexual and gender-based violence against women and girls, the root causes of it must be addressed, "both as 'extraordinary violence' in wartime and their continuation as 'ordinary violence' following the end of armed conflict. For many women, gender-based violence is an ongoing reality that precedes the period of mass violence and continues in the aftermath" (Lambourne and Rodriguez Carreon 2016: 89). Men's and boys' experiences of sexual and gender-based violence similarly intersect with deeply rooted gendered assumptions, beliefs, and institutions that negate the frequency of harm and limit or deny social, political, and judicial recognition, rehabilitation, and recourse (Schulz 2020a). Schulz deftly articulates the transformative possibilities of centering men's and boy's experiences and senses of justice (2020b) and, in collaboration with Touquet and Schulz (2021: 1), argues that men's and boy's agency reveals "a more holistic examination of the dynamics of wartime sexual violence" and what is possible after it.

In other words, examinations of masculinities and men and boys in war must go beyond the study of violent masculinities in conflict studies (Myrttinen et al. 2017), to recognize the vulnerabilities they incur during war which give gender-based violence its form (Carpenter 2006). As Hamber further urges scholars, "an analysis of masculinity and its relationship to transitional justice processes should recognise the complexities of individual and socio-political processes in which masculinity is deeply linked to notions of femininity and the social positioning of men post-conflict" (2007: 390). Expectations to perform masculinities may shape but do not determine behavior, values, beliefs, and desire of men, women, and gender non-binary persons. Nor does one's performance of masculinity come in opposition to, and is asymmetrically performed in relation to, femininities and war, nor even one form of masculinity (such as militarized) excludes the possibility of a person embodying another (such as paternal). A gender analysis is an analysis of power, but power actualized in relation to becoming, rather than being, and informed by both contexts and the relationship in question (Baines 2017). Working toward a gender-inclusive approach to transitional justice, Schulz (2020c) challenges us to "let go of prevailing notions about gendered victimhood" and problematize approaches in transitional justice that focus solely on militarized masculinity as a threat (Theidon 2007). In sum, a gender-inclusive approach, as Schulz (2020c) suggests, transcends a gendered "victim–perpetrator" binary.

A gender-inclusive approach attends to the everyday, situational, and relational ways protagonists work through violent pasts and presents, "while creating the possibilities for new ways of being in the future" (Franke 2006: 823). Or as Schulz (2020c) argues:

> [It is a] means to imaginatively think outside the prevailing standardized TJ toolkit, instead considering autonomously driven processes that can address survivors' needs and facilitate agency, outside the purview of masculine and heteronormative institutions. Such an understanding of TJ can facilitate a more inclusive and holistic engagement with gender and justice in the context of transitions [and further] imply the potential to better address certain gendered conflict experiences in a more fluid and inclusive capacity.
>
> (Schulz 2020c: 702)

In the next section, we situate the crime of forced marriage and pregnancy in wartime within a gender-inclusive, transformative approach to justice.

TJ, Forced Marriage, and Pregnancy

Forced marriage, a widespread practice of the Revolutionary United Front (RUF) during the war in the country, was first recognized as a crime against humanity by the Special Court for Sierra Leone. Forced marriage was later prosecuted in the Extraordinary Chambers in the Courts of Cambodia (ECCC) following the Khmer Rouge's widespread use of the practice and, most recently, the International Criminal Court (ICC) in the trial of LRA leader Dominic Ongwen, who was convicted not only for his active organization of forced marriage but also, for the first time in international law, forced pregnancy. Scholars debate the appropriateness of the term "forced marriage" to capture the intersecting harms of abduction, sexual violence, and forced labor, with some suggesting *conjugal slavery* or *forced conjugal associations* to be more appropriate (Bunting and Quirk 2017). However, the subject of both legal prosecutions and interpretations is, by and large, to consider its relevance to women and girls as victims of the practice (Park 2006). The possibilities of men and boys as anything other than perpetrators are foreclosed in international law and the field of transitional justice, yet more recent studies suggest the practice is more complicated. In their study of men's experiences and perspectives of forced marriage in the LRA, Aijazi and Baines (2017) introduce a relational approach, arguing that relations within the armed group were infused with power as "socially constitutive and diffuse," and agency is exercised within a "wider web of social entanglements through which power circulates and is contested" (2017: 6). Recognizing that most men exercised little choice on when, who, or how to marry in the LRA, Aijazi and Baines (2017) offer a potential to think of power agentively, as the capacity to act from the socially and historically specific relations of domination and subordination.

A relational approach, they posit, helps transcend binary thought and reveals the complexity of relations of harm and care within forced marriage; in effect, it queers assumptions of responsibility and militarized masculinity, the gender binaries attendant within legal or socio-legal studies of forced marriage and pregnancy that assume women and girls as static victims.

Drawing on an ethnography with demobilized men in post-conflict northern Uganda, Denov and Drumbl (2020) seek to understand the ways men and boys are subject to the many harms of forced marriage to redress the current shortcoming in international law and transitional justice practices. Given the coercive circumstances through which men and boys arrived to the position of soldier in the LRA (abduction) and the militarization of intimate relations, they argue that men and boys endured different but no less gendered forms of harm that included

> the evisceration of agency in fundamental associative decisions: the purging of ceremony; destroying community relations and cultural practices; the militarization of private life; the weaponization of the family; and ordering of private relations in accordance with socially engineered strictures of public life including fidelity to the state or organization.
>
> (Denov and Drumbl 2020: 367)

Denov and Drumbl's (2020: 368) intervention is intended to peel "away . . . assumptions and stereotypes" to "further enrich the epistemology of forced marriage," which, in turn, may inform more gender-inclusive approaches to transitional justice scholarship and policy. Indeed, a plethora of studies on how forced marriage and motherhood shape the post-war/genocide moment of women and children born of forced marriage exists (Kiconco and Nthakomwa 2018; Mukasa 2017; Woolner et al. 2019). The harms of the past fold into relations of the present; women and girls are often unable to be "at home" and are rejected by community and family and marginalized and devalued in multiple social, economic, and political institutions (Atim et al. 2018). As Florence Ayot reflects on life after return to Uganda (quoted in The New Humanitarian 2012):

> The relatives of my parents don't want my children. They say the children are of a top LRA commander who killed their people. The relatives of my husband have also abandoned me. They don't give me any assistance yet they know that I am stranded with the children. We are always stigmatized by the community. My children are always reminded that their father is a notorious rebel commander who killed people and that they were born in captivity. . . . Since I am illiterate, I can't do any office work. I am struggling daily doing petty jobs like fetching water for people, washing clothes and digging in gardens in order to get some money. The little I get, I use for buying greens, charcoal and cassava. I can't afford to cook beans and posho [maize meal], which

> consume a lot of charcoal. We don't take tea as I can't afford to buy sugar. For change of diet, children taste meat only once a month.

An unspoken assumption in the study of forced marriage after war is that reunion would only impose a new form of victimization by women; a consideration of children's rights is obfuscated as they are subsumed by their mother's victimization in transitional justice or associated with a father's perpetrator status (Sanchez Parra 2018). This despite initial evidence from northern Uganda that some demobilized fathers seek to assume responsibility for their children born of forced marriage (Oliveira and Baines 2020), and that some marriages resume post-conflict (Dubal 2018). Further, some mothers – who may not wish such a relationship themselves – seek to establish one between her child or children and that of their father or his extended family (Baines and Oliveira 2020). Reflecting on Ongwen, Florence Ayot stated:

> I loved him because of the way he would live with people. He was not quarrelsome, and I felt it was good for me to go to him. There was nothing I disliked about him because I had not seen anything wrong he had done before. . . . We lived happily together.
>
> (BBC 2021)

This stands in contrast with women who testified against Ongwen on the charges of forced marriage and pregnancy, and we do not deny they suffered at his hands. But Ayot and others raise the possibility that some marriages were, or became, "consensual."

The rights of children born of war are seldom understood in relation to their right to know their families, as protected by the Convention on the Rights of the Child (Daniel-Wrabetz 2007). Denov and Cadieux Van Viliet's (2020) research with children born of forced marriage in the LRA and their perspectives of justice revealed that most children hold complex memories toward their fathers: on the one hand, most were aware of, even witnessed, the crimes of war their fathers committed; on the other, they held good memories of their fathers as persons who loved and cared for, raised, and provided for them. The children's experiences provide the kind of grounded, historically contextual understanding of relations of power described by Aijazi and Baines (2017: 21) earlier, opening "possibilities for thinking about culpability and consent as negotiated in webs of relations" and transcending binaries that categorize and obscure the "dynamic ways in which human relations unfold and are imbricated in one another."

Forced Marriage in the LRA

We turn now to men's perceptions and experiences of forced marriage and parenting in the LRA, attending to the historical circumstances surrounding the practice and the ways men sought to act within spaces of coercion before and after the war to assume responsibility for their children. A gender-inclusive approach, we suggest, renders visible such efforts and situates them in the remit of transformative justice approaches. In her study of forced marriage within the LRA, Baines (2014) explores how the practice was part of the group's larger political project to create a new, spiritually pure Acholi society. To support the practice, the LRA abducted thousands of women and girls and forced them into marriage with commanders, forcefully creating familial units within the organization which, in turn, formed the basic military unit. In this context, forced marriage and pregnancy serve as a forced heteronormativity and so violently governed sexuality and sexual and gender identity. LRA commanders strictly regulated forced unions, and any infraction such as flirting or adultery could result in severe punishment or death.

Only top commanders, and often Kony himself, decided which combatants would enter into marriage, when, and with whom, creating a coercive environment for both men and women. AR, who spent close to ten years in the LRA, recalls how he was offered a wife to strengthen his ties to the rebel group and dissipate any previous thoughts of escaping. At first, he refused the woman he was told to "marry," claiming that they were from the same community and, if they returned home, people would accuse AR of abducting her. When another girl was brought to be his wife, he could no longer refuse. He shares: "[W]ith fear, I had no option at that moment because if I had refused to take the second girl again, the commander would become suspicious and that would make them know my intention [to escape]." Other combatants also described the non-consensual nature of unions in the LRA and highlighted their inability to disagree with the decision of who was "assigned" as their partner. Lonyo Pe Kuc elaborates:

> So, [in the case of marriage] there isn't any dating and there is nothing like saying, "I like you". They just call both the boy and the girl and they will tell you that, this is your husband and they will then tell how you are supposed to live [together] and what takes place there and that is all. So, for that I see it as if it wasn't according to the wishes of the two people but it was forceful.

Nevertheless, combatants could and did find ways to navigate the strict rules and regulations of sexual or intimate relations for their own or another person's benefit. RA, who was a spiritual leader in the LRA, recalls an instance when Dominic Ongwen leveraged the practice of forced marriage to secure the safety of another LRA member. He shares:

> Florence [Ayot] had lost her husband and people didn't like her because she was old. Dominic felt pity for the lady because every time she would be begging people to help her with clothes, she never had clothes and she had children. There was no one to take care of her. Dominic felt the pain she was going through and looked at her with a human heart. He picked her and they started living together.

In the preceding case, forcing Ayot to become Ongwen's wife was not seen as a malicious act. Instead, it ensured that Ayot would have a husband to provide for her and her children and protect them during conflict. In a precarious context where resources are scarce and life can easily be taken away, forming a familial unit could be beneficial for some. Additionally, some combatants shared that, over time, a relationship of care could be developed between forced husband and wife. Lonyo Pe Kuc shares his experience but also notes that this was contingent on having a partner of a similar age:

> But if given the same size [age], conflicts may not even arise. . . . They will have a good relationship. But, if given to the size that she doesn't want, conflict will arise. Me and [my wife], we had a good relationship, because our size had matched. . . . And after when we had gotten used to each other, we used to stay as if we had just dated and we weren't just given to each other. We used to stay and live well and also everything was okay.

When a bond was formed between forced husbands and wives, their relationship could continue in a post-conflict context, when both returned to their communities. Male combatants would sometimes release their wives and allow them to return to home, with the promise that they would be reunited in the future. Lucura describes how he supported his wife and arranged her escape:

> I gave her a mattress, bedsheets, clothes and shoes. . . . I also picked some money and gave it to her. That money belonged to the movement but I was the one keeping it. As I handed her all those things, I told her: "Go well and may God bless you." She broke into tears. She told me she would wait for me until I return home.

Studies of forced marriage in the LRA have largely documented the experience from the perspective of women and girls who, in turn, highlight the brutal circumstances surrounding the process: abduction, deprivation, beating, rape. Men in the study recognized that women and girls were married against their will and endured tremendous suffering. However, relationships of care could and did develop between wife and husband over time (Dubal 2018). The strength of these connections, respondents argued, depended on the characters of the two persons involved, their age, and their shared experience, but most importantly, the birth of a child.

Fatherhood in War

The LRA high command forced unions in order to reproduce the Acholi nation (Baines 2014), but also as a mechanism of control, to prevent men from escaping. This might be interpreted in one of two ways. First, that men were "rewarded" for their loyalty and "hard work," a euphemism for adhering to orders, even if these orders contradicted one's sense of morality. Second, it was a strategy to make men "work harder" to provide for and protect their families, drawing on gendered expectations of men as head of family. If a commander disobeyed, he could be stripped of rank, denied access to resources, or imprisoned and beaten – a form of emasculation. Thus, although familial units were meant to consolidate ties between the combatants and the rebel group, for many male combatants, having children changed the dynamics of the armed conflict and switched their focus from defeating enemy forces to ensuring that they can secure better conditions for their descendants. As OL puts it, "instead of thinking so much about the war, you tend to forget about it [and concentrate on your children] because you see their hope in life." Some men relegated their duties as soldiers and prioritized their identity and responsibilities as fathers. OG comments on this shift:

> When I got a child, it became challenging because that was a time the war was intense, and sometimes when we are close to our enemies, children are not even allowed to cry, so looking at the condition my child was going through, that gave me the heart that "why are I am suffering and my child is also suffering. . . ." That is what came into my mind because it became painful seeing my wife and child suffer. That is why I sacrificed my life and decided to send my wife home. . . . I just told her one thing "go back home, this war is unbearable."

Focus groups with male civilians in Uganda described expectations of fathers to

> be a strong provider for [their] immediate and extended family. . . . Fulfilling this role [of father] implies having/owning land to farm . . . sending the children to school for an education, paying the school fees . . . and taking care of the child.
>
> (Madhani and Baines 2020)

In the LRA, however, the nature of armed conflict made it difficult for them to balance their role as soldiers and fathers. As Lucura explains, "during fighting, a man may be in one group and his wife is in another group. . . . There is no one with the responsibility of taking care of your [family]." This situation propelled some male combatants in the study to release their wife and children to return home, in hopes that they will live in better conditions. Others stated that they wanted their children to carry their lineage even if they died in combat. After they became fathers, the future of the children became a major preoccupation, and many also began considering the possibilities of escaping only after having children. As CM puts it: "When I became a father, I started to feel like I should escape home." Others clarified that releasing one's family or escaping was sometimes motivated by other reasons: their families were slowing them down and putting them in danger, they were injured in battle, or the exhaustion of little food, water, and fighting. In any event, expectations of the paternal masculinity could and was often directly in contradiction with the expectations of performing a hyper-militarized masculinity: the former to provide and protect, and the latter to control and decimate.

Establishing paternal identity is intimately linked to realizing a sense of belonging and access to land and resources in northern Uganda (Stewart 2017). In a patrilineal and patrilocal society, children inherit land, maintain a connection to the ancestral world, and learn teachings about their history and living together in a harmonious way all through the paternal clan. However, it was commonplace for abductees to adopt an alias to protect their families who remained home. In some cases, if an abductee attempted to escape, the LRA would punish, torture, or kill the person's family. Hence, fathers were fearful to share their real identities with their children and wives; for others, they feared if their partners were captured, they could reveal their identity to the Ugandan military, and this may lead to pressure or force against their families. OM, a former senior commander who spent 17 years in the LRA, describes this challenge:

> It was difficult to reveal your home to your wife. Not because you don't have love for her but for security reasons. We were doing that to protect our parents. First of all, not all mothers and fathers who lived in captivity had the same heart reason being when you reveal your home this person may report and will use that opportunity to destroy your family.

Some fathers improvised ways to share the identity and location of their clan, fearing they may perish and their children never know their home. Orwat recounts when another soldier, Oruk, entrusted him to take his wife and child to his home before he died from a bullet wound:

> Before Oruk died, he told me that since I know their home, I should ensure that I take his wife and child to his home in Lamogi. . . . We continued our movement until one time we reached the husband's home area and then I released [his wife] to go.

Others secretly showed their wives their homes when passing close to it or named their children after relatives to help them remember who they are and how to locate paternal families should they not survive the war.

Post-Conflict Integration

In the majority of the cases, unification between forced partners was not desired by women (Denov and Lakor 2017). Oweyo-Adola, who spent eight years in the LRA, reflected on how some women were treated as less-than-human:

> Some men when given wives they would want to treat them as slaves. . . . That is why most girls returned and rejected them, most girls did it due to the challenges they faced with their husbands from the bush.
>
> (16 September 2017)

Severing of relationships was also encouraged by numerous rehabilitation centers created to respond to the health and social integration of those who escaped the LRA. Rehabilitation centers such as the Gulu Support the Children Organization (GUSCO) were often the first point of contact for those who escaped the LRA and the families they were stolen from. Yet as demonstrated in this study, there are cases where men and women choose to reunite post-return and where fathers want to continue to care for their children; however, this course of action came with its own set of challenges.

In our study, all fathers returned home after their wives and children had done so. It could be a matter of days, months, or years before a male combatant managed to safely escape from the rebel group. Upon return, some swiftly began to search for their families; others waited until they were settled or had picked up the courage to do so. Stigma and socio-economic challenges were an obstacle to successful reunification with children, resulting in disappointment and frustration for willing fathers. Acholi customary practices – although not fixed but negotiated – hold that conjugal unions be mediated between the man's and women's respective clans. More than an individual decision, marriage is contingent on both clans agreeing on the value of bridewealth and/or *luk* to be paid to the maternal clan, a fine paid to legitimize a child as belonging to the paternal lineage if payment of bridewealth has not been completed before the couple's firstborn (Kiconco and Nthakomwa 2018). For those who wanted to reunite after their escape, maternal clans could demand compensation via payment of bridewealth and/or *luk*. It was the maternal clan, then, who often held decision power over whether unions would be legitimized in a post-conflict context. Michael Atube, who works at the International Committee of the Red Cross, shares the negotiation process that goes into reunifications of wives and husbands:

> I have heard a lot of stories whereby they say the mother coming out first with the children and the father coming out later, then the clan of the father would approach the clan of the mother then agree because what usually come out is that [the marriage was] not the will of the husband or the wife that is why whether it was forceful, they understand the circumstances. . . . So usually they ask for a normalization of the process so that the two can live together.

Not all maternal clans are as willing. Regardless of the woman's wishes, many maternal clans blame the fathers for their daughter's suffering and prevent any connection between the two parties. Those who returned also face stigma from their home communities, with name-calling such as *olum olum* (those from the bush) and suspected of *cen*, or vengeful ghosts of the wronged or neglected dead (Meinert and Reynolds Whyte 2020). OG shares his experience trying to re-establish a connection with his forced wife:

> So, when I returned home I sent the message informing [the maternal clan] that I was back. She also understood but there was resistance from her

> home. They said I am *olum olum* and that I should not stay with their daughter. . . . Everyone seems to see me as a killer. It is true I accept I am "a killer" but it was not my wish.

Other families require payment of fines to ensure that the union continues in accordance with Acholi cultural norms. Furthermore, since bridewealth had never been paid, the children belong to the maternal clan until the father pays *luk*. For OL in Kalongo, this was a source of humiliation. His age-mates whose children had since grown constantly reminded OL that he had returned home from the war with none. Because of his inability to find employment, there was little he could do to meet cultural expectations of paying *luk*. Several other participants described being treated as children on return, which they also attribute to returning as an adult with no family. Still others felt the sting of discrimination when community members would warn off prospective partners to the men, telling them they would never be cared for, and that they carried the demons of the past. The perception of impairment – compounded if the man also returned with a disability – equated those who returned as "useless," even "dangerous" partners and parents. Men could not live up to such an expectation of responsibility as a man, compounding an already-difficult reintegration. Two respondents explicitly explained that these circumstances taken together informed his decision to join the Ugandan military. However, we do not wish to reify the perception men performed a hypermasculinity specifically because they could not realize a paternal one. One the contrary, the majority of men did not join the military and did settle into their communities peacefully, continuing to look for ways to support their children, as we elaborate next.

Given the paternal clan's importance in informing one's sense of belonging, fathers felt that it was imperative to reconnect with their children upon returning. MB reflects:

> [A child] should know who his or her father is, where his or her father and mother comes from and should possess a clan especially in Acholi. The clan is very important to every child especially the boy child who becomes the head of the family.

Nevertheless, in the context of limited economic opportunities and poverty, payment of fines became a major obstacle. One participant shares his frustrations:

> "I released [my wife] to return home. . . . And she gave birth normally and my child is living with her. There was a time I went to their home with the intention of picking my child. Her parents said I should pay 3 million shillings in order to pick up my son. . . . So with my condition, I couldn't afford that money so I left my child with them up to date. . . . If at all there was money, I would have picked my child.

Placing their trust that patriarchal ideals will prevail, some fathers believe their children will one day want to discover their identity, even if their mother does not want a connection with the father: "let the woman fulfill her interests, but time will come when these children will come back to us. Some children will definitely look for their paternal family." Another combatant, CA, also remembers "meeting some children who were born from captivity, and they would ask [him] about their fathers; they want to know whether their father is still alive."

Some participants in the study expressed care and love for their children, and not being able to see them upon returning brought them a keen sense of sadness and frustration. However, for those who were able to reconnect, reuniting with children brought a sense of renewed purpose and opened possibilities for the future. OG, for instance, who first encountered resistance from the head of the maternal clan and was unable to reunify, ends his story on a positive note:

> I started my own life and forgot about my father-in-law. After some weeks, I received a call from my wife. . . . My wife promised that she would come back at the end of the year. I did not believe it because I thought that her father would interfere. Surprisingly one day I saw my wife together with my son came back home. I felt so happy and ran for them because I thought they would never come back and I would not see them again. Life changed for me and it strengthened our relationship. Even her father could now come to visit us and I did the same.

Ex-combatants in the study also expressed a sense of responsibility for their children's well-being and particularly emphasized their wish to secure their children's education. Fathers saw their own future as being compromised by the conflict but wanted to ensure their children did not have to go through similar experiences. Orwat remarks:

> I want to ensure that my children study now that I have missed and failed to study due to staying in captivity. So that in the future, my family that originates from me, who is not educated, can stand a chance to have children who are educated.

Fathers expressed care for their children, and that they look to them for a sense of hope. As AR notes, "My children are everything to me, and if anybody tempers with them, then I would rather die with them." Likewise, OM discusses what children signify to them:

> The future which people normally ask about, it is the children. The future are the young ones because, like us, at least we know the miles we have walked, how old you are, and even the abduction were all lesions which

> made us face sufferings and some of these sufferings are supposed to bring changes in our lives so that we make sure that our children don't go through the same sufferings and we have to take good care of them.

For the fathers in this study, questions of forced marriage and forced parenthood shaped their lives while in captivity and upon returning home. Although unions in the LRA were forceful, the relationships forged within difficult circumstances continued post-return, amidst a myriad of challenges. Fathers navigated a post-conflict setting imbued with resentment, which created challenges when they tried to reunite with their "forced wives" and children, given that was also desired by the latter party. Notwithstanding, for those who are now providing for their children, securing their livelihoods provides hope that they will be able create better conditions for their descendants.

Conclusions

In this chapter, we took a gender-inclusive approach to the study of forced marriage and parenting in wartime, documenting men's experiences and perspectives. We began with consideration of the unprecedented conviction of Dominic Ongwen for forced marriage and pregnancy and suggested that a gender-inclusive approach might broaden how we understand these crimes and attenuate senses of justice in the post-war moment. In doing so, we hope to open new possibilities for thinking about forced marriage and pregnancy in transitional justice beyond legal encapsulations of innocence and guilt (Clarke 2019). A gender-inclusive approach, moreover, may offer important interventions for thinking about justice and its transformative possibilities for redressing past and present violence and reimagining the future. We conclude here by gesturing toward three implications for moving beyond legal approaches and toward a transformative approach.

First, a gender-inclusive approach illuminates how forced marriage and pregnancy in the LRA served as a violent mechanism of control not only of women and girls but also of men and boys. While the LRA sought to build cohesion and unity within the LRA through forced marriage and parenting, the opposite was also true. Some men took decisions to provide for and protect their families that went against the rules of the LRA, often jeopardizing their own security. Some respondents described their decision to release their wives and how they facilitated their escape, as well as the male soldiers' own plan to later escape to join them. Women and children were more than objects or property. They were more than mere markers of status or providers of labor to support the commander, as often referenced in popular media or scholarly literature. To limit their character to such is to problematically assume men were incapable of forming meaningful relationships toward their children (Suarez and Baines 2021).

Indeed, children born of forced marriage feel and hold their father's love, with memories of care, compassion, and a unified family (Denov and Piolanti 2020). Others long to reunite with their father, and their fathers want to reunite with them (Mutsonziwa et al. 2020). Mothers may help facilitate this union, and extended families negotiate it (Baines and Oliveira 2020). Such instances also challenge problematic reductions of men to performances of militarized masculinity and how very complex relations within forced unions are in the post-war moment (Madhani and Baines 2020). We recognized that in certain circumstances, men were compelled to enter marriage and parenting in the LRA, but importantly, they often had little choice in resuming a relationship to a wife or child/ren following their demobilization.

Second, we recognize that our study assumes heteronormative familial relationships as the norm. A gender-inclusive approach should address how sexuality is governed in the context of forced marriage, and how expectations of sexual and gendered identity shape the behavior, opportunities, and decisions of combatant men during and after conflict. Within the LRA, one's sexuality was violently governed, and any deviation was understood as a serious infraction. Past research on the LRA indicates intolerance for non-normative sexual and gender identities within the group (Dolan 2009). How this intersects with gender-based harm might further reveal other forms of harm to be considered under international law, and to address in the process of seeking to rebuild the social fabric and re-write the social contract after war.

Third, bringing children into the conversation of forced marriage and pregnancy begins to fray problematic, gendered, and binary categories. As we previously discussed, children born of war hold no particular victim status in transitional justice. Rather, they are often subsumed under the victim status of their mother. This reinforces a gender exclusion of their fathers as perpetrators, unwilling or incapable of assuming a relationship of care with their children. Considerations of relationships between father and child flesh out the post-war moment more fully than the current exclusive focus on relationships between mother and child, or mother and child in relation to families and communities that reject them. As Drumbl and Denov (2020: 367) argue, if we understand compelled parenthood as a harm affecting men and women differently, then it "ought to be more centrally considered as a key life-altering outcome occasioned by this odious practice." And so understanding forced parenting as such

> would highlight the needs of the children born of these unions and, in this sense, instantiate a broader protection of the "best interests" of these children in line with . . . the United Nations Convention on the Rights of the Child.

Lastly, we find resonance with the emerging conceptualization of justice as transformative, hastened by "local agency and resources, the prioritization of process rather than preconceived outcomes and the challenging of unequal and intersecting power relationships and structures of exclusion" (Gready and Robins 2014: 340). Attention to men's and boy's experiences of forced marriage and parenting over the *long durée* locates agency in the complicated folds of power relations during and following war. It emphasizes the desire to become a father as one possibility of this post-war moment, and justice as a process of working against and in the contestation of legal enclosures. In transitional spaces where the violence of the conflict permeates and shapes post-conflict dynamics, justice for those affected is not attained through a court decision. Communities live in a constant reckoning with the past that impacts daily relationships in ways that transitional justice mechanisms may not be able to remedy. By listening to the life stories of men in this study, we demonstrate the rich potential of inclusion of father's voices and experiences in transitional justice generally and flesh out the discussion on an inclusive gender approach and transitional justice specifically. We seek to contribute to a study of justice that focuses on collective efforts to maximize opportunities for life through the development of accountability mechanisms. Future studies might expand to understand the experiences and the negotiations rendered outside of the judicial system of men, women, and children born of war.

Decisions at the ICC are imperative to name the crime and hold those most responsible accountable. Dominic Ongwen's conviction responded to calls for accountability for the LRA violence against the Acholi peoples and marked a significant moment in Uganda's history. Nevertheless, for those who continue living in the aftermath of war, other forms of justice may focus on securing a future that was disrupted during the conflict. Hence, a gender-inclusive approach opens new historical, legal, and sociocultural possibilities to imagining new futures. In such exploration, justice can be understood as less of "a" transformation and more of a process that continuously reaches toward a future not defined by conflict, a future in which younger generations can thrive.

References

Aijazi, O. and E. Baines (2017). Relationality, Culpability and Consent in Wartime: Men's Experiences of Forced Marriage. *International Journal of Transitional Justice* 11(3): 463–483.

Atim, T., D. Mazurana and A. Marshak (2018). Women Survivors and Their Children Born of Wartime Sexual Violence in Northern Uganda. *Disasters* 42: 61–78.

Baines, E. (2014). Forced Marriage as a Political Project: Sexual Rules and Relations in the Lord's Resistance Army. *Journal of Peace Research* 51(3): 405–417.

Baines, E. (2015). 'Today, I Want to Speak Out the Truth': Victim Agency, Responsibility, and Transitional Justice. *International Political Sociology* 9(4): 316–332.

Baines, E. (2017). *Buried in the Heart: Women, Complex Victimhood and the War in Northern Uganda*. Cambridge: Cambridge University Press.

Baines, E. and C. Oliveira (2020). Securing the Future: Transformative Justice and Children 'Born of War'. *Social & Legal Studies* 30(3): 341–361.

BBC News (2021). Dominic Ongwen – From Child Abductee to LRA Rebel Commander. *BBC News*. Available at: https://www.bbc.co.uk/news/world-africa-30709581. Accessed on: 13 February 2021.

Boesten, J. and P. Wilding (2015). Transformative Gender Justice: Setting an Agenda. *Women's Studies International Forum* 51: 75–80.

Bunting, A. (2012). 'Forced Marriage' in Conflict Situations: Researching and Prosecuting Old Harms and New Crimes. *Canadian Journal of Human Rights* 1(1): 165–185.

Bunting, A. and J. Quirk (eds.) (2017). *Contemporary Slavery: Popular Rhetoric and Political Practice*. Vancouver: UBC Press.

Carpenter, R. (2006). Recognizing Gender-Based Violence Against Civilian Men and Boys in Conflict Situations. *Security Dialogue* 37(1): 83–103.

Clarke, K. (2019). *Affective Justice: The International Criminal Court and the Pan-Africanist Pushback*. Durham: Duke University Press.

Daniel-Wrabetz, J. (2007). Children Born of War Rape in Bosnia-Herzegovina and the Convention on the Rights of the Child. In: *Born of War. Protecting Children of Sexual Violence Survivors in Conflict Zones*. Colorado: Kumarian Press: 21–39.

Denov, M. and A. Cadieux Van Vliet (2020). Children Born of Wartime Rape on Fatherhood: Grappling with Violence, Accountability, and Forgiveness in Postwar Northern Uganda. *Peace and Conflict: Journal of Peace Psychology*: 1–9.

Denov, M. and M. Drumbl (2020). The Many Harms of Forced Marriage: Insights for Law from Ethnography in Northern Uganda. *Journal of International Criminal Justice* 18(2): 349–372.

Denov, M. and A. Lakor (2017). When War Is Better Than Peace: The Post-Conflict Realities of Children Born of Wartime Rape in Northern Uganda. *Child Abuse & Neglect* 65: 255–265.

Denov, M. and A. Piolanti (2020). 'Though My Father was a Killer, I Need to Know Him': Children Born of Genocidal Rape in Rwanda and Their Perspectives on Fatherhood. *Child Abuse & Neglect* 107: 1–8.

Dolan, C. (2009). *Social Torture: The Case of Northern Uganda, 1986–2006*. New York: Berghahn Books.

Dubal, S. (2018). *Against Humanity: Lessons from the Lord's Resistance Army*. Oakland: University of California Press.

Evans, M. (2016). Structural Violence, Socioeconomic Rights, and Transformative Justice. *Journal of Human Rights* 15(1): 1–20.

Franke, K. (2006). Gendered Subject of Transitional Justice. *Columbia Journal of Gender and Law* 15: 813–828.

Gready, P. and S. Robins (2014). From Transitional to Transformative Justice: A New Agenda for Practice. *International Journal of Transitional Justice* 8(3): 339–361.

Hamber, B. (2007). Masculinity and Transitional Justice: An Exploratory Essay. *The International Journal of Transitional Justice* 1(3): 375–390.

Kiconco, A. and M. Nthakomwa (2018). Marriage for the 'New Woman' from the Lord's Resistance Army: Experiences of Female Ex-Abductees in Acholi Region of Uganda. *Women's Studies International Forum* 68: 65–74.

Lambourne, W. and V. Rodriguez Carreon (2016). Engendering Transitional Justice: A Transformative Approach to Building Peace and Attaining Human Rights for Women. *Human Rights Review* 17(1): 71–93.

Madhani, D. and E. Baines (2020). Fatherhood in the Time of War and Peace: The Experiences of Demobilized Male Soldiers in Northern Uganda. *Women's Studies International Forum* 83: 1–8.

Mani, R. (2008). Dilemmas of Expanding Transitional Justice, or Forging the Nexus Between Transitional Justice and Development. *The International Journal of Transitional Justice* 2(3): 253–265.

Matarazzo, A. and E. Baines (2019). Becoming Family: Futurity and the Soldier-Father. *Critical Military Studies:* 1–18.

McEvoy, K. and K. McConnachie (2012). Victimology in Transitional Justice: Victimhood, Innocence and Hierarchy. *European Journal of Criminology* 9(5): 527–538.

Meinert, L. and S. Reynolds Whyte (2020). Legacies of Violence: The Communicability of Spirits and Trauma in Northern Uganda. In: Seeberg, J., Roepstorff, A. and Meinert, L. (eds.): *Biosocial Worlds: Anthropology of Health Environments Beyond Determinism*. London: UCL Press: 168–190.

Miller, Z. (2008). Effects of Invisibility: In Search of the 'Economic' in Transitional Justice. *The International Journal of Transitional Justice* 2(3): 266–291.

Mukasa, N. (2017). War-Child Mothers in Northern Uganda: The Civil War Forgotten Legacy. *Development in Practice* 27(3): 354–367.

Mutsonziwa, T., K. Anyeko and E. Baines (2020). Child Tracing: Locating the Paternal Homes of 'Children Born of War'. *Development in Practice* 30(5): 635–644.

My Justice (2018). Dominic Ongwen's Former Bush Wife: 'Ongwen Will Be Accepted Too'. *Justice Hub*. Available at: https://justicehub.org/article/dominic-ongwens-former-bush-wife-ongwen-will-be-accepted-too/. Accessed on: 13 January 2022.

Myrttinen, H., L. Khattab and J. Naujoks (2017). Re-thinking Hegemonic Masculinities in Conflict-Affected Contexts. *Critical Military Studies* 3(2): 103–119.

Nagy, R. (2008). Transitional Justice as Global Project: Critical Reflections. *Third World Quarterly* 29(2): 275–289.

The New Humanitarian (2012). Florence Ayot, 'My Children Are Always Reminded that Their Father Is a Notorious Rebel Commander'. *The New Humanitarian*. Available at: https://www.thenewhumanitarian.org/report/95645/uganda-florence-ayot-my-children-are-always-reminded-their-father-notorious-rebel-commander. Accessed on: 13 January 2022.

Oliveira, C. and E. Baines (2020). Children 'Born of War': A Role for Fathers? *International Affairs* 96(2): 439–455.

Oosterveld, V. (2018). The ICC Policy Paper on Sexual and Gender-Based Crimes: A Crucial Step for International Criminal Law. *William & Mary Journal of Women and the Law* 24(3): 443–458.

Park, A. (2006). 'Other Inhumane Acts': Forced Marriage, Girl Soldiers and the Special Court for Sierra Leone. *Social & Legal Studies* 15(3): 315–337.

Pham, P., P. Vinck and E. Stover (2007). *Abducted: the Lord's Resistance Army and forced conscription in northern Uganda*. Berkeley: Human Rights Centre.

Robins, S. (2011). Towards Victim-Centred Transitional Justice: Understanding the Needs of Families of the Disappeared in Post-Conflict Nepal. *International Journal of Transitional Justice* 5(1): 75–98.

Sanchez Parra, T. (2018). The Hollow Shell: Children Born of War and the Realities of the Armed Conflict in Colombia. *International Journal of Transitional Justice* 12(1): 45–63.

Schulz, P. (2020a). *Male Survivors of Wartime Sexual Violence*. Oakland: University of California Press.

Schulz, P. (2020b). Examining Male Wartime Rape Survivors' Perspectives on Justice in Northern Uganda. *Social & Legal Studies* 29(1): 19–40.

Schulz, P. (2020c). Towards Inclusive Gender in Transitional Justice: Gaps, Blind-Spots and Opportunities. *Journal of Intervention and Statebuilding* 14(5): 691–710.

Shaw, R., L. Waldorf and P. Hazan (eds.) (2010). *Localizing Transitional Justice: Interventions and Priorities after Mass Violence*. Stanford: Stanford University Press.

Stewart, B. (2017). *'I Feel Out of Place': Children Born into the Lord's Resistance Army and the Politics of Belonging*. PhD Thesis, Vancouver: University of British Columbia.

Suarez, C. and E. Baines (2021). 'Together at the Heart': Familial Relations and the Social Reintegration of Ex Combatants. *International Peacekeeping*: 1–23.

Theidon, K. (2007). Transitional Subjects: The Disarmament, Demobilization and Reintegration of Former Combatants in Colombia. *The International Journal of Transitional Justice* 1(1): 66–90.

Touquet, H. and P. Schulz (2021). Navigating Vulnerabilities and Masculinities: How Gendered Contexts Shape the Agency of Male Sexual Violence Survivors. *Security Dialogue* 52(3): 213–230.

Woolner, L., M. Denov and S. Kahn (2019). 'I Asked Myself If I Would Ever Love My Baby': Mothering Children Born of Genocidal Rape in Rwanda. *Violence Against Women* 25(6): 703–720.

Chapter 9

Delineating Perpetratorhood

On Race, Masculinities, and Fighting Impunity for Sexual Violence in DRC[1]

Chloé Lewis and Susanne Alldén

Introduction

During a side event of the 68th United Nations General Assembly in September 2013, the then UK foreign secretary, William Hague, launched *A Declaration of Commitment to End Sexual Violence in Conflict (the Declaration)*. By the end of the event, two-thirds of member states had endorsed the non-binding "commitment of agreement" between states to end sexual violence in conflict. Copies of the Declaration were distributed to audience members, the opening paragraph of which painted a clear picture of the nature and gravity of sexual violence committed in conflict and emphasized the importance of fighting impunity for conflict-related sexual violence crimes as critical to its prevention:

> The widespread use of rape and other forms of sexual violence in armed conflicts around the world is one of the greatest, most persistent and most neglected injustices. Sexual violence in conflict inflicts unimaginable suffering. It is designed to destroy individuals, families and communities. In so doing it perpetuates conflict and instability, often for generations. But

1 The authors extend their gratitude to the NGO Working Group on Women, Peace, and Security (NGOWG) and to the Human Rights Center Sexual Violence Program at the University of California, Berkeley (HRC), for making this research possible. We are particularly grateful to Sarah Taylor and Kristina Mader at the NGOWG for supporting this research in New York, and to Kim Thuy Seelinger and Julie Freccero at HRC for spearheading the research in DRC. We also extend our gratitude to Milli Lake for supporting the research in DRC and for her generous comments on the manuscript. We thank Rosalie Biaba and Nephtaly Abassa for their invaluable assistance conducting the data collection and are profoundly grateful to everyone who shared their time and insights as part of this research. We are also grateful to Elena Fiddian-Qasmiyeh, Henri Myrttinen, Annette Idler, and Marsha Henry for their comments on earlier versions of this chapter. Finally, we are thankful to the editors for their thoughtful comments on the manuscript and their tenacious patience putting together this important volume during the pandemic. This research was made possible through the generous funding from the Economic and Social Research Council (ESRC) and the MacArthur Foundation. All errors are our own.

DOI: 10.4324/9781003519522-12

> it is not an inevitable consequence of war. . . . As an international community we can – and must – do more to prevent and respond to these acts of barbarism. . . . We must shatter the culture of impunity for those who commit these crimes, by bringing those responsible to justice – as a critical element of our prevention efforts. There should be no safe haven for the perpetrators.
>
> (FCDO 2013: 1)

As part of the UK Prevention of Sexual Violence Initiative (PSVI), this high-level event was chaired by the Rt. Hon. Hague, with statements given by the then special representative to the secretary-general (SRSG) on sexual violence in conflict, Zainab Bangura, and a representative from the London-based organization Survivors Speak Out. A pre-recorded statement was also delivered by Angelina Jolie in her capacity as UNHCR special envoy and co-founder of the PSVI, via video-link. Opening the event, Hague echoed the language of the Declaration, proclaiming that it marked a "historical turning point" in an "awareness and a willingness to act on sexual violence in conflict." In her statement, SRSG Bangura spoke of the "heart-breaking stories" of survivors who have experienced "the most degrading form of treatment by combatants" and whose "bodies are [considered] less worthy than rats." Bangura affirmed that the Declaration represented the international community standing together, saying, "Enough is enough," marking a date on which "we can say that [the] world stood together to challenge this historic injustice" (*fieldnotes*, New York, 24 September 2013). Given the endorsements the Declaration received, this event and the document itself are emblematic of the international community's focus vis-à-vis sexual violence in conflict. They are, in other words, illustrative of the kinds of harms internationally driven efforts to fight impunity are designed to redress and – crucially for the purposes of this chapter – perpetrated by whom.

Throughout the event, participants frequently referred to the experiences of women and girls in eastern provinces of the Democratic Republic of Congo (DRC), with several participants recounting their own visits to the region. In the final minutes of the event, Hague announced a last and unplanned intervention by the representative of DRC to the Francophonie, Isabelle Tshombe. Given the centrality of DRC to the event and in efforts to address sexual violence in conflict more broadly, Hague stated that the country should be represented. Rushing in from a meeting, Tshombe addressed the audience by foregrounding her own identity as a Congolese woman, expressing that "as a Congolese woman," she felt very "moved" that "the cry of the Congolese woman has finally been heard and amplified." She continued, "The Congolese woman has carried her problem across the world and has been heard by the international community. . . . The Congolese woman is no longer alone." She closed by "infinitely" thanking delegates "for having heard the cry of the Congolese woman" (*fieldnotes*, New York, 24 September 2013). Tshombe's repeated references to "*the* cry of *the* Congolese woman" were striking in their singularity. They reified a sense that there exists a shared imaginary of the "Congolese woman," centering on who she is, the nature of the harms she has (inevitably) endured, and the redress she thus (inevitably) seeks. Reflecting on this shared imaginary, a Congolese women's rights activist interviewed in this study aptly posited: "What does this say about our men?" (*interview*, Bukavu, April 2014).

This chapter explores this question by examining delineations of male "perpetratorhood" in efforts to fight impunity for conflict-related sexual violence and considers their implications for the gender dimensions of transitional justice. Through the case study of the Democratic Republic of Congo (DRC), it explores gendered and raced assumptions of male perpetrators underpinning, construed by, and contested within institutions driving efforts to fight impunity for sexual violence in conflict across policy and practice. Doing so, it investigates imaginaries of sexual violence in conflict settings underpinning international policy and advocacy pertaining to efforts to fight impunity and complicates assumptions of conflict-affected masculinities – characterized by brutally violent perpetratorhood – these rely on and reproduce. Fighting impunity for sexual violence is a key focus of debates surrounding and interventions promoting transitional and gender justice in conflict and its aftermath. Through international and increasingly domestic courts (Seelinger and Freccero 2015; Weill et al. 2020), such efforts are largely driven by the interrelated aims of delivering justice to survivors, restoring a sense of faith in the rule of law and deterring potential perpetrators from committing similar crimes (FCDO 2014). Amidst these efforts, the relationship between men, (assumptions of) male perpetratorhood in conflict, and transitional justice processes and their outcomes remains underexplored (Hamber 2007).

Recognizing the significant and important strides made in efforts to hold perpetrators of conflict-related sexual harms to judicial account, policy and advocacy discourses underpinning efforts to fight impunity rest on a carefully curated, but nevertheless restrictive, understanding of sexual violence in conflict. Crudely, this sexual violence is widespread and systematic: it is perpetrated by male combatants against civilian populations; it is used to displace, and at times even destroy, communities. Meeting these criteria, sexual violence is a crime under international humanitarian law and, with the adoption of UN Security Council (UNSC) Resolution 1820 (2008) on women, peace, and security, is recognized as a threat to international peace and security. It is this manifestation of sexual violence that has driven international responses and, for a time, at the exclusion of diverse forms of sexual and gendered harms in conflict (Dolan 2014; Myrttinen and Swaine 2015; Westendorf and Searle 2017). Initially inscribed in the resolutions is, therefore, a carefully delineated – and quint-*essentializing*[2] – understanding of sexual violence in conflict, defining the nature of the harm (brutal, widespread, and systematic), its victims (civilian women and girls),[3] and the redress they seek (justice). In turn, this conception relies on and reproduces a contradistinctive set of assumptions vis-à-vis the perpetrators of such harms (armed men in uniform) and the retribution they warrant (judicial accountability).

This chapter argues that this understanding reifies long-standing, limiting, and troublesome depictions of men and masculinities as characterized by violent, militarized, and brutal (sexual) perpetratorhood and, therefore, as *ipso facto* warranting punitive judicial accountability. The predominance of such imaginaries of masculinities – and attendant presumed perpetratorhood – obscures more complex realities of sexual crimes in conflict-affected contexts and of interactions between victims, perpetrators, and judicial mechanisms in practice. Analyses of judicial data on sexual violence crimes in eastern DRC presented in this chapter reveal a discordance between who efforts to fight impunity are intended to target and who, in practice, is typically held to account for sexual violence crimes in the region. By complicating quint-*essentializing* depictions of male "perpetratorhood," this chapter contributes to evolving literature on masculinities and transitional justice by reviving calls for more nuanced appraisals of *who* is being prosecuted for *what* kinds of crimes in efforts to fight impunity for sexual violence in conflict and its aftermath (Fawcett 2012; Grewal 2012). In this vein, this chapter argues that rather than redressing sexual harms typically associated with the region, in their quotidian application, efforts to fight impunity in DRC may instead be operating to punitively regulate masculinities, sexual relations between young people, and "normative arrangements of intimacy" through the courts (Bedford 2007: 304).

This chapter begins by situating the analysis in literature on gender, peace, and security and transitional justice. Second, it contextualizes the fight against impunity for sexual violence in DRC and outlines the methods behind the studies forming the basis of this discussion. The third section begins by tracing deliberations leading to the adoption of UNSCR 1820, emphasizing

2 This term denotes the idea that the institutional discourses of sexual violence in DRC – centering on its exceptionally brutal and widespread nature – became not only illustrative representations of sexual violence in conflict but also *defining* of understandings of and, in turn, responses to sexual violence in such settings. Speaking to the long-standing feminist concern with and challenge to gendered and raced essentialisms (Fuss 1989; Mohanty 1984), this concept encapsulates the defining and limiting set of assumptions relating to sexual violence in conflict. These are determined, in large part, by the nature of the harm (brutal and widespread), the profile of its victims (civilian women and girls), and its perpetrators (armed men in uniform).

3 More recent UNSC resolutions addressing conflict-related sexual violence, notably UNSCR 2106 (2013), acknowledge that men and boys are also affected by sexual violence.

the deliberate delineation of the male perpetrator figure for institutional and political purposes. The discussion then turns to the prosecution of sexual violence through domestic courts in eastern DRC. Through a granular analysis of the high-profile Minova trial and of the less-exceptional everyday functioning of the justice system, this section demonstrates that the carefully construed male perpetrator figure is less easily discernible in domestic courts. The chapter concludes by emphasizing the importance of granular analysis of masculinities and perpetratorhood interacting with transitional justice mechanisms to discerning the latter's capacity to redressing the conflict-related harms they are intended to redress in a given setting, and thus to securing gender justice for survivors in their pursuit of a gendered peace.

"All the Men Are in the Militias": Masculinities, Conflict, and Transitional Justice

Recent decades have seen a surge in scholarship, policy, and practice on the gender dimensions of armed conflict, which has propelled possibilities for promoting gender justice (Lake 2018; Medie 2017; Pankhurst 2008). Understanding and responding to sexual violence in conflict continue to be a significant focus of this rapidly growing body of work, particularly in eastern DRC (Autesserre 2012; Eriksson Baaz and Stern 2013; Lewis 2021). Feminist approaches to transitional justice in particular have made significant inroads, not least by encouraging us to consider "how transitional justice helps or hinders projects to secure material gains for women" (Bell and O'Rourke in Hamber 2007: 376). While feminist engagement across the arenas of scholarship, policy, and practice often proves mutually reinforcing, some tensions also arise. One area of contestation centers on the tenacity of gendered and raced essentialisms permeating efforts to redraw the boundaries of international security and international law (Mertens and Pardy 2017; Otto 2006; Oyěwùmí 1997). *Essentialism* refers to a belief in "the real, true essence of things, the invariable and fixed properties, which define the 'whatness' of a given entity" (Fuss 1989: xii). Following anti-essentialist traditions, a common thread in critical feminist international legal and international relations scholarship has long been to expose the ways in which women have been "excluded, marginalised, silenced, misrepresented, patronised, or victimised by [international] institutions" (Munro in Edwards 2010: 2).

Such ideas were at the core of critiques of UNSCR 1820 (2008). While significant in the development of the international normative and operational frameworks addressing sexual violence in conflict (Anderson 2010), the resolution was seen by some to undermine a long-standing feminist commitment to challenging pervasive and essentializing depictions of women-as-victims (Otto 2010). Postcolonial feminist scholars and activists in particular call critical attention to monolithic constructions of the "third world woman" produced "under western eyes" (Mohanty 1984). Underscoring the ways in women in the Global South embody the "most authentic victim subject" in international law, policy, and practice, this literature maintains that such depictions are "far from liberating for women" (Kapur 2002: 7). As sexual difference becomes "coterminous with female subordination, and power is automatically defined in binary terms: people who have it (read: men), and people who don't (read: women)" (Mohanty 1984: 344). Such a dualistic model, Mohanty argues, is "ineffectual in designing strategies to combat oppression" and ultimately serves to "reinforce the oppression of the group spoken for" (Mohanty 1984: 344; Alcoff cited in Fiddian-Qasmiyeh 2014: 7).

Discourses of gender and violence in Africa, and arguably in DRC especially, have long been prone to such depictions and are typically laden with especially stark assumptions of (female) sexual victimization and attendant (male) sexual danger (Eriksson Baaz and Stern 2013; Mertens 2016; Tamale 2011). As discussed later, reports of sexual violence in eastern DRC played an important role in positioning the issue on the Security Council agenda and produced a shared imaginary of the (Congolese) survivor premised on the nature of the harms she endures, at whose hands, and the redress she seeks. Whether explicitly stated or not, the shared imaginary of the (Congolese female) survivor of sexual violence relies on and reifies contradistinctive assumptions about the (Congolese male) perpetrator. While there is an extensive body of scholarship challenging pervasive representations of "women-as-victims" in conflict, there is comparatively less scholarship devoted to complicating conventional representations of men in conflict (Myrttinen et al. 2017). This upholds a unidimensional model of gender whereby the dominant position of (all) men relative to (all) women is unquestioned and sustains the idea that – as succinctly stated by Enloe – "all the men are in the militias [or the army], and all the women are victims" (2004: 99).

Scholarship on masculinities in conflict and transitional justice has grown significantly in recent years (Myrttinen et al. 2017). The focus of existing research often centers on militarized masculinities, generating important insights into the motivations, causes, and experiences of violence, including sexual violence, in conflict (Bitenga et al. 2021; Duriesmith 2017; Eriksson Baaz and Stern 2009). Alongside this research is a growing body of work foregrounding and elucidating male victimhood and vulnerability in conflict, in particular to sexual violence (Dolan 2014; Misra 2015; Schulz 2020; Touquet 2022). This literature nuances long-standing and limiting associations of "women-as-victims" and "men-as-perpetrators" paradigm and contributes to ensuring that the diversity of gendered harms perpetrated in conflict is addressed in transitional justice and enables us to understand why they are not (Leiby 2009).

Much of this work on masculinities and sexual violence, implicitly or explicitly, addresses particular – and habitually particularly brutal – kinds of conflict-related sexual harms. By extension, it tends to rest on and reify an imaginary of a male perpetrator figure deemed intrinsically culpable and capable of committing such crimes. This is especially clear in DRC. Indeed, long cast under an "*Afrientalist*" gaze depicting exceptionalized violence perpetrated on Congolese (women's) bodies (Everill and Kaplan 2013: 17; Eriksson Baaz and Verwijen 2018), less rigor and sensitivity are often applied to understanding and representing its gendered subjectivities (Daley 2015). Contemporary depictions of Congolese masculinities typically center on images and accounts of uniformed armed men presented as responsible for widespread, systematic, and "barbaric" acts of sexual violence perpetrated against civilian women and girls (Laurent 2014; Eriksson Baaz and Stern 2009). As scholars have noted, such depictions "reinforc[e] stereotypes of African warriors as primitive and archaic driven by innate violence and tribal hatred" (Eriksson Baaz and Stern 2008: 57; Mertens 2016). As explored further later, these long-standing, pervasive, and racialized depictions of masculinities in Africa are integral to producing and sustaining the figure of the "quint-*essentialist* perpetrator" in international policy and advocacy discourse and limit understandings of the patchwork of masculinities and their relationships to violence in eastern DRC. In this vein, and viewed through the prism of transitional justice, Hamber argues that "[m]asculinity should be seen as central to how we conceptualise the outcomes that transitional justice processes can deliver in terms of gender justice more broadly and women's security in particular," meaning that "[a]ny analysis of masculinity and its relationship to transitional justice needs to recognise multiple masculinities" (2007: 387). Assessing the nature of sexual violence cases – characterized in large part through the profiles of victims and their perpetrators – addressed by domestic courts in eastern DRC in efforts to fight impunity, this chapter heeds this call and delineates a more complex constellation of male "perpetratorhoods" and their interaction with the judicial system in eastern DRC.

A Note on Methods

This chapter draws on data generated as part of two studies addressing in whole or in part judicial responses to sexual violence in eastern DRC. The first study was conducted by one of the authors between 2013 and 2017 with diverse stakeholders at the United Nations Headquarters in New York and in eastern DRC. This study examined how ideas of gender in conflict shape and are shaped by responses to sexual violence. While the broader study was grounded in over 300 interviews with a range of respondents – including policymakers, NGOs, civil society, security forces, service providers – this chapter draws primarily on a subset of 13 interviews conducted with women's rights advocates working with and within the UN Security Council on its women, peace, and security agenda. These interviews took place alongside a year of ethnographic participant observation by the authors with the NGO Working Group on Women, Peace, and Security. The second study was conducted by both authors in North and South Kivu provinces in 2014–2015 as part of a multi-country study on accountability for sexual violence in conflict and post-conflict conducted by Human Rights Center Sexual Violence Program, situated in the University of California, Berkeley, School of Law (Seelinger and Freccero 2015). Both authors were contracted as independent researchers on the DRC case study of the broader accountability study. The authors conducted over 100 interviews with actors working across the military and civilian justice systems across five sites in North and South Kivu, including Goma, Rutshuru, Bukavu, Uvira, and Walungu. In addition, it draws on anonymized case register data and records provided to the authors by judicial and police actors, detailing the nature of sexual violence cases and the demographic profiles of the victims/survivors and their perpetrators.

This multi-sited and multi-institutional approach, therefore, permits an understanding of how and why certain discursive essentialisms are made and remade in a powerful entity, such as the Security Council, *as well as* of their effects as they "travel" through distinct institutional prisms (Said 2001). In line with Buss, this analysis upholds the institutional context as an "important site, in its own right, for the production of knowledge and consensus [and discord] about conflict sexual violence" (2014: 16–17). We add "discord" to Buss's quote here, given this chapter points to discordances in the discursive and material character of the gendered subjects produced by different institutional structures. To bring these nuances and their implications to light, we draw on the sensory metaphor of sight. Elaborating a distinction between the act of "making visible" as a long-standing central motif in feminist scholarship and activism – and "sight" as an analytical tool – Buss emphasizes that the latter enables a "series of intellectual moves through which to explore women and armed conflict" (2014: 5). In other words, it usefully permits one to ask: "[W]ho sees, who is seen, what is seen, and how?" (ibid.). Applying this analytical lens to efforts to fight impunity for sexual violence in DRC, we explore distinct – and often discordant – institutional delineations of male perpetratorhoods.

Fighting Impunity for Sexual Violence in DRC

In the early to mid-2000s, reports emerged of brutal, systematic, and widespread sexual violence perpetrated in the conflicts in eastern DRC. Such reports frequently featured haunting testimonies of survivors and perpetrators alike, rendered only more horrifying by the distressing statistics with which they were presented (e.g., HRW 2002; Réseau des Femmes pour un Développement Associatif, Réseau des Femmes pour la Défense des Droits et la Paix and International Alert 2005). Since then, sexual violence has remained a defining feature of the conflicts in DRC, as well of responses, and remains a significant security threat facing civilians (UNSC 2021: 12). Despite challenges posed by the COVID-19 pandemic, the UN Secretary General details important progress in the fight against impunity for war crimes and crimes against humanity over the last year, including sexual violence. These include the conviction and imprisonment of three former armed group commanders and the ongoing trials of one other in Kinshasa. The report also documents the conviction of an additional 131 members of national security forces and eight members of non-state armed groups in 2020 through mobile military courts (UNSC 2021: 12–13). The report does not give further information on the nature of these crimes, or the legislation under which they were prosecuted.

Fighting impunity for sexual violence in conflict is driven by the dual objectives of delivering justice for survivors and deterring potential future perpetrators from committing similar crimes. Such efforts are, therefore, geared toward "restoring faith in rule of law" on the one hand and preventing conflict-related sexual violence in the longer term on the other (FCDO 2014: 5). Convictions, therefore, carry significant symbolic and pedagogical potential in conveying who is punishable and for what kinds of crimes. As such, whether through international or, increasingly, domestic courts, fighting impunity to date typically prioritizes criminal prosecutions, including for sexual violence crimes, and the promotion of gender justice. This has been a significant and significantly funded component of multi-sectoral responses to sexual violence in eastern DRC over the last decade. A multitude of actors, including (inter)government ministries, donors, and NGOs supporting law enforcement and judicial capacity-building by developing robust sexual violence legislation, has established specialized sexual violence police units – the squadron for the protection of children and the prevention of sexual violence, known by their French appellation *l'escadron de protection de l'enfant et la prevention des violences sexuelles* (PEVS) – and prosecution cells, as well as legal clinics, and continue to conduct trainings and convene mobile courts to improve access to justice for survivors (Lake 2018; Lake et al. 2016; OSF 2012).

These efforts have led to some important successes in recent years, including the typically elusive convictions of high-profile conflict actors, as well as more concerted effort to prioritize sexual violence in the justice system (Lake 2018). These appraisals are perhaps all the more significant, and surprising, given the immensely challenging operational environment of eastern DRC, characterized by vast distances across often-inaccessible terrain, structurally under-resourced judicial and law enforcement entities, and chronic insecurity (UNGA 2008; UNDP 2012). Such constraints contribute to frequently disappointing judicial outcomes, including in the Minova trial detailed later. This chapter takes seriously the importance of securing accountability for survivors of sexual violence, including conflict-related sexual violence. Given the enormity of the challenges facing judicial actors and the important pedagogical value accorded to convictions, this chapter equally takes seriously the importance of carefully assessing the operationality of efforts to fight impunity in practice. To do so, it pays particular attention to who is prosecuted, for which kinds of (sexual) crimes, and what this tells us about masculinities and transitional justice in conflict-affected contexts.

Introducing the Quint-*Essentialist* Perpetrator

Contemporary reporting on sexual violence in conflict, notably in DRC, predominantly centers on acts committed by "armed men in uniform." From the onset, this limited focus was made explicit and was sustained as part of the advocacy strategy adopted to establish conflict-related sexual violence as a self-standing issue on the Security Council agenda (HRW 2002; Goetz 2015). A requisite component of this strategy was to delineate which kinds of rape fall under the ambit of the Council's mandate. This resulted in a definition and discourse of conflict-related sexual violence resting on "a combination of *who* (the profile of victims and perpetrators); *what* (the elements of the offence); *how* (the method) and *why* (the motive)" (UN Action 2011: 2). Crudely, "sexual violence in conflict" was defined as sexual harms perpetrated by conflict parties against civilians with a demonstrable link to a conflict.

While the story behind Resolution 1325 on women, peace, and security (WPS) is well documented, those of subsequent WPS resolutions, including UNSCR 1820, are less well-known (Basu 2016; Goetz 2015). In the aftermath of the landmark adoption of UNSCR 1325, a number of women's rights advocates working with and within the UN sought to push for the adoption of a standalone resolution on sexual violence in conflict. With this advocacy goal set, it was met by a resistant Council. A UN women's rights advocate recounted that they were presented with two challenges: convincing Council members of the relevance of sexual violence to its mandate on the one hand and to delineate *which* specific forms of sexual violence fall within the Council's remit on the other. By developing a clear, coherent, and legally grounded set of arguments, drawing on "*illustrative examples*," they made the case that "not every rape is for the Security Council." Acknowledging that a focus on institutional divisions of labor "sounds very bureaucratic," this was, the UN Women's Rights Advocate affirmed, "where the debate was" (UN women's rights advocate, *interview*, New York, January 2014).

In particular, women's rights advocates at the UN explained that part of this strategy required delineating perpetrators as conflict actors, typically sporting military fatigues. Respondents explained that certain member states would not accept that "a husband raping his wife – unless he's being held at gunpoint by, you know, a military officer – should count on the sexual violence in conflict agenda" (senior women's rights advocate, *interview*, New York, January 2014). Emphasizing that the perpetrator profile represents an evident defining feature of conflict-related sexual violence, the UN women's rights advocate stated that the military uniform *ipso facto* represents a "symbol of being a [sexual] predator" (UN women's rights advocate, *interview*, New York, January 2014). Yet while key, the distinction between "armed men in uniform" and "civilian men" was not the only one made in delineating the perpetrators of sexual violence for the purposes of the Security Council. Not all acts of sexual violence committed by an individual in a military uniform constitute "sexual violence in conflict" under the WPS agenda, nor do they trigger the same institutional response mechanisms. Notably, sexual violence perpetrated by UN peacekeepers falls under the separate policy category of sexual exploitation and abuse (SEA), addressed under the remit of conduct and discipline. This distinction is no coincidence (Westendorf and Searle 2017). According to the UN women's rights advocate, conflation between conflict-related sexual violence and SEA "created a number of closed doors" as troop-contributing countries were concerned that advancing conflict-related sexual violence on the Council agenda would place a spotlight on sexual abuses perpetrated by their troops. This second delineation was therefore a "tactical and strategic decision that [they] made . . . very deliberately." They continued, "And I can tell you honestly that had we not done that, we would be nowhere [with conflict-related sexual violence]" (UN women's rights advocate, *interview*, New York, January 2014).

At this time, increasing reports of mass rapes in conflict were emerging, notably from Darfur and DRC. This, combined with a series of "fortuitous events" and unexpected champions, contributed to galvanizing the requisite political will to lift the notion of a standalone resolution on sexual violence off the ground (Goetz 2015). One such fortuitous and catalytic backstory involves the 2007 award-winning documentary *The Greatest Silence: Rape in the Congo* by American filmmaker Lisa F. Jackson. Interspersed with testimonies from survivors describing their experience with varying degrees of detail and emotional distress, the film incorporates a number of lasting narratives about sexual violence in DRC. The story told is that "rape is used as a method to create continued instability," that it is "the monstrosity of the century," and that "silence kills thousands of women in the forests of the Congo" (Jackson 2007: 01:22 min., 02:36 min., 01:53 min.). It is committed by (Black) men in uniform on a brutal and unimaginable scale, and the solution is fighting impunity.

The Greatest Silence contributed to placing DRC center stage in policy debates pertaining to sexual violence in conflict. In an "Enloesque" turn of events, the women's rights advocate recounted that Cheryl Bernard – who was the wife of the US ambassador to the UN at that time – watched the documentary. Horrified by what she saw, she mobilized senior women in the UN as well as her husband, the ambassador, to respond to this violence (UN women's rights advocate, *interview*, New York, January 2014; Goetz 2015). According to Goetz (2015), the ambassador immediately accepted his invitation to the Wilton Park Conference – at which UNSCR 1820 was drafted – after having watched the film. Due to the catalytic role the documentary played in galvanizing Council action, *The Greatest Silence* was credited as "the inspiration for a 2008 U.N. Resolution classifying rape as a weapon of war" (HRW 2010).

The centrality of sexual violence in eastern DRC to UNSCR 1820 was further evidenced in the Council's open debate during which the resolution was adopted. Of the country situations referred to during the deliberations, DRC was referenced the most frequently, and by a significant margin, pointing not only to its influence on this policy development but also on defining the essence of sexual violence of concern to the Council. Throughout the debate, *sexual violence* was described as "a brutality," "heinous," "horrific," "an outrage," and as "a cruel weapon of war to obliterate the enemy and destroy the family, whole communities and, above all, the dignity of women" (UNSC 2008: 3, 10, 15, 23, 28). These depictions came to define what sexual violence in conflict looks like, considered by some as "the quintessential harm of war" (Heathcote and Otto 2014: 11). Those who endure, and indeed survive, such extraordinary violence might therefore be considered the quintessential survivors of war; those deemed responsible for committing such harms might thus, in turn, be considered its quintessential perpetrators. Taking this further, as experiences of sexual violence documented in DRC came to represent the dominant, defining, and quint-*essentializing* frame through which sexual violence in the region, and in conflict more broadly, is understood, those responsible for perpetrating such violence in DRC may thus represent the dominant, defining, quint-*essentialist* perpetrators of sexual violence in conflict.

That this understanding of sexual violence in conflict is at the forefront of internationally driven policy responses was evidenced by policymakers and shapers at the United Nations Headquarters. When we were asked about who the perpetrators of sexual violence are in conflict, the presumption was almost always that we were talking about individuals "belonging to militia, or uncontrolled government forces" (special advisor, permanent mission to the UN, *interview*, New York, January 2014). Stated more explicitly still, a member of the UN Team of Experts on Sexual Violence and the Rule of Law explained, "What we do is armed groups, like in DRC, going in and raping people, or sexual slavery. . . . [T]hat's what characterises our work" (UN Team of Experts on Sexual Violence and the Rule of Law Member, *interview*, New York, January 2014). The respondent explained that there are some contexts where distinguishing between sexual violence and *conflict-related* sexual violence – the former referring to sexual violence "in the community" or the "usual domestic violence" – is "a little bit more difficult." However, he continued, "when you talk about the DRCs or Somalias, no one usually questions or argues that the distinction [exists] or how you label it [conflict-related sexual violence]" (UN Team of Experts on Sexual Violence and the Rule of Law Member, *interview*, New York, January 2014). From this perspective, in a context like DRC, sexual violence and *conflict-related* sexual violence are presumed to be easily distinguishable, while incidents reported to and addressed by response structures are typically presumed to be perpetrated by armed men in uniform with a direct link to conflict dynamics.

Re-tracing the politics behind the establishment of sexual violence in conflict as a standalone issue on the Security Council agenda illuminates the political necessity of the quint-*essentialist* narrative of sexual violence in conflict toward achieving this end. It formed part of a carefully constructed and legally grounded set of arguments, grounded in realities reported from DRC, crafted to establish sexual violence as a threat to international peace and security. Yet acknowledging the strategic necessity of the quint-*essentialist* perpetrator in spurring international policy on conflict-related sexual violence, the discursive centrality of DRC reproduced long-standing and troubling imaginaries of violently sexualized masculinities in Africa, and in DRC specifically. Indeed, the institutional success of the quint-*essentialist* script in the UN Security Council relied on and reified the idea that (Black) African men, especially those wielding military fatigues, are not only believed to be (always-already) potentially capable of such brutal sexual harms but, equally, that they are also perceived as (always-already) potentially culpable of them.

We use the language of essentialism here with some caution, not least due to its "sheer rhetorical power [as] an expression of disapprobation and disparagement" (Fuss 1989: xi). We certainly do not intend to use the term disparagingly, nor do the authors intend for it to be read as denying the materiality of the experiences of sexual violence in eastern DRC, including by uniformed combatants (Lewis 2021). This analysis recognizes that the radicality or conservatism of an essentialism is contingent on its "deployment," calling for a careful investigation of "*who* is utilising it, *how* it is deployed, and *where* its effects are concentrated" (Fuss 1989: 20). That said, the following sections of this chapter challenge the notion that the effects of a strategically, instrumentally, or functionally deployed essentialism can be situationally concentrated, particularly when dealing with a powerful entity such as the UN Security Council.

The Quint-*Essentialist* Perpetrator in Practice: The Minova Trial

A handful of incidents of mass rape has become particularly notorious in eastern DRC. One such event took place in November 2012 when, following a defeat to the M23, hundreds of soldiers from the national army – the *Forces armées de la République démocratique du Congo* (FARDC) – retreated to the town of Minova, on the shores of Lake Kivu and bordering North and South Kivu. What ensued was "a 10-day frenzy of destruction" which included widespread looting and sexual violence, with some reports estimating that "more than 1,000 women, children, and men were raped in this town alone" (Alhindawi 2014). Most reports estimated the numbers of incidents to be around 130 (Lake 2014). Because of the scale of the attack and the outcry that followed, Congolese authorities came under significant pressure to hold those responsible to account in the immediate aftermath of the attack (Nichols 2013). The events that took place at Minova were viewed by many as representing a clear and incontrovertible incident of conflict-related sexual violence and thus came with high hopes and expectations of the trial.

Portrayals of the Congolese judicial system in DRC often center on its weaknesses and failings in securing justice, particularly for survivors of sexual violence (UNGA 2008). Despite significant pressure and support from the international community, the outcomes of the Minova trials appeared only to affirm such depictions. Initial hearings were held in Goma in December 2013, and the final trials were held over ten days *in situ* in Minova in May 2014. For jurisdictional context, as the crimes were committed during an active military operation against the M23, the case fell under the operational military court, meaning, there could be no appeals process. Seventy-six charges were brought against 39 defendants. These included charges of rape as a war crime (under individual and command responsibility), rape as an "ordinary crime" under the 2009 Child Protection Law, pillage, murder, theft, extortion, and disobeying military orders. Thirty-three of the charges were for rape as a war crime, and one charge for the rape of a minor under domestic legislation. Seventy-six civil parties testified at the trial; this included 50 testimonies for rape and 26 testimonies for crimes of pillage, although most of the parties testifying for rape were also victims of pillaging. Only two convictions were secured for sexual violence, one of which was for rape as a war crime, the other for the rape of the minor as an ordinary crime. All other defendants accused of rape as a war crime were acquitted, although some were charged with lesser crimes (CMO 2014a). The verdict was thus widely viewed as a "disappointment" and a "failure to deliver justice" to survivors (Nichols 2014; UN News Centre 2014).

According to the court ruling, acquittals for rape as a war crime under command responsibility were made largely on the grounds of effective control. The court determined that some defendants were no longer exercising their function at the time the crimes were committed (CMO 2014a: 80). For others, it determined that, given the circumstances in Minova at that time, it was beyond the bounds of "all necessary and reasonable" measures in their power to "prevent or repress the commission" of the crimes (CMO 2014a: 81). Finally, with respect to command responsibility – whereby commanders are expected to report crimes committed by troops under their command to relevant authorities – the court determined that the defendants had met their requirements under this principle (CMO 2014a: 81).

External observers took issue with this reasoning and the overall ruling. In particular, Human Right Watch reported on a number of procedural discrepancies on the part of the military prosecution office in the steps leading up to the trial, which called into question the veracity of their intention to hold those responsible for the attacks to account (HRW 2015). Similar views were shared by the defense counsel, who claimed that "even the population told [them] the ones on trial were not the perpetrators" (defense counsel, *interview,* Goma, October 2014). This points to a tension in the trial between balancing international pressure to convict on the one hand with the fragile politico-military context on the other. As explained by one of the judges at the trial:

> It was a fragile time [as] there wasn't any trust, there was a fear that some [soldiers] might jump to the other camp [M23]. . . . People said we can't investigate now, the situation needs to calm down a bit. You know, with justice, it goes first peace, security, and then justice will follow.
>
> (military judge, *interview*, Goma, December 2014)

These factors impacted on the investigation, including the selection of defendants, and contributed to the strong sense of disappointment vis-à-vis the outcomes of the trial. As such, while "perpetratorhood" appeared clear to many, identifying and prosecuting those responsible were more elusive in practice.

The question thus emerges of who *was* convicted under individual sexual violence charges and on what grounds? As previously noted, two convictions for sexual violence charges were delivered at the Minova trials: one for rape as a war crime, and the second for rape of a minor under the 2009 Child Protection Law. The indictment for rape as a war crime required both evidence of individual criminal responsibility and contextual elements linking the crime to the conflict (CMO 2014a: 68). The preceding analysis made clear some of the challenges of identifying and prosecuting defendants accused of sexual violence under international law. The operational military court shed further light on the challenges of identifying perpetrators accused under individual criminal responsibility, explaining that:

> Generally, with respect to sexual violence, perpetrators take measures to not be identified by their victims. They favour acting when it's dark, blinding their victims with the light of their electric torches, intimidating them with threats to stop them from staring at them, [and] warding off potential witnesses. The victim becomes the only witness to the aggression. Herein lies the importance of her statement so that the judge can appreciate her credibility.
>
> (CMO 2014a: 68)

The officer convicted on the charge of rape as a war crime was recognizable by virtue of an exceptional physical feature: a missing thumb. According to the verdict, the victim "recognised the suspect whom she had previously seen fetching water from the fountain and who had a missing finger on his hand, a feature she easily remembered" (CMO 2014a: 75). So central was this feature to the proceedings that the suspect's defense argued that the victim had only noticed the missing thumb during the preliminary investigations, a claim that was later proven unfounded. In effect, in the aftermath of the attack, the victim had "brought the facts to her cleric giving a distinctive sign on his body: his cut thumb" (CMO 2014a: 57). This particular case underscores the difficulties, first, of identifying individual perpetrators of conflict-related sexual violence and, second, of proving individual criminal responsibility beyond reasonable doubt. Overall, even when the circumstances of the crime align closely with those associated with the quint-*essentialist* perpetrator, this case points to the necessity of an exceptional physical characteristic to prove individual criminal responsibility.

The second case resulting in a conviction for sexual violence was of a different nature and was adjudicated under the 2009 Child Protection Law, thus as an ordinary crime. The defendant was a corporal from the 8th Military Region (North Kivu) who was lodging with a first sergeant and his family, including the latter's daughter, who was 6 at that time (CMO 2014a: 57). While the victim's parents were out, the suspect took the young girl to an isolated area, where he raped her. The accused challenged this account; his version of events was contested by three witnesses. Assessing the evidence, the presiding judge determined "there [was] no shadow of a doubt as to [the defendant's] intent and the Court considers that all the constitutive elements for the rape of a child are brought together" (CMO 2014a: 76). The success of this conviction in this case thus rested on the fact that there were three witnesses, including a superior officer, and because the victim was a child, the notion of consent was legally void (CMO 2014a: 76).

As the next section demonstrates, this case aligns more closely with the types of sexual violence cases adjudicated by domestic courts in eastern DRC. This is perceptible across three axes: the perpetrator profile (lower-ranking and/or lower socio-economic status), the legislation applied (domestic legislation), and the nature of the case presented (girls under the age of 18). As such, while the violence that took place in Minova in November 2012 echoed the familiar stories of sexual violence in eastern DRC, the outcomes of the trial affirmed the challenges associated with fighting impunity for sexual violence at the domestic level and, thus, with holding quint-*essentialist* perpetrators to judicial account.

The "Male Perpetrator" in Everyday Justice

By virtue of its scale, the resources invested, the nature of the cases adjudicated by a domestic court, and the high-level spotlight on its outcomes, the Minova trial was exceptional (Candeias 2015: 32). The military and civilian justice systems operate outside such exceptional cases and outside such a bright spotlight, including in relation to sexual violence cases. Examining the less-exceptional, everyday functioning of the justice system in eastern DRC further reveals a more complex interaction between the law, gender, and masculinities. Indeed, our analysis of case registers kept by judicial actors, combined with interviews with medico-judicial actors, revealed a number of striking trends across penal and judicial institutions relative to the plaintiffs' and accused perpetrators' profiles, which frequently bore little resemblance to the dominant and quint-*essentialized* narrative.

There is no consistent mechanism for recording judicial data in eastern DRC, complicating case monitoring through the penal chain (UNJHRO 2014: 11). Some figures are nonetheless available. In 2014, UNJHRO observed a "slow but steady progress in the prosecutions of sexual violence" (UNJHRO 2014: 11). Its figures show that between July 2011 and June 2012, 269 judgments for sexual violence were recorded, and that from July 2012 to June 2013, 383 judgments were recorded (UNJHRO 2014: 11). Covering a similar period, UNDP counted 6,554 sexual violence cases reported to judicial structures across South Kivu, North Kivu, and Ituri, of which 7% were in the military judicial system. The vast majority, then, were civilian cases. Of these, 652 had received a judgment, 60% of which resulted in a conviction (UNDP 2012: 24). A 2012 evaluation of mobile courts in North and South Kivu found that of 127 dossiers for rape presented to the courts, 74% resulted in convictions (OSISA 2012: 15). These numbers indicate that, unlike the image presented by high-profile and highly mediatized court cases such as Minova, the conviction rate for sexual violence cases is generally high. Reflecting on a three-year sexual violence program she had overseen, a respondent recounted that of the 8,000 (female) beneficiaries of the program, "200 or 250" started a judicial process. Of those, "only 57 got to the end," that is, to trial and sentencing. Of the 57, 47 resulted in a conviction. "Once you get to the trial," she noted, "apparently, it's okay" (European donor representative, *interview*, Bukavu, May 2014). With particular attention to the profiles of accused perpetrators, this raises the question: What kinds of sexual violence cases make it to and *through* the courts in North and South Kivu?

In our analysis of judicial case records, three trends in the case profiles were especially noteworthy. First, police and judicial structures are addressing a higher number of cases of sexual violence involving civilian suspected perpetrators than those involving members of the military or of an armed group. Turning to the specialized sexual violence police units (PEVS) first, case registers in Goma indicated that from January 2013 to July 2014, the unit recorded 477 cases of sexual violence, in which the accused perpetrator was identified as civilian in 99% of incidents. A similar trend was perceptible in the PEVS unit in Bukavu, where 96% of reported perpetrators were identified as civilian. Cases involving uniformed personnel or a member of an armed force may be more likely to be reported to the military justice system directly, if reported at all. Even with this in mind, 857 cases of sexual violence were reported to the civilian magistrates' office in Goma in 2013–2014, a number that is seven times greater than in the military judicial equivalent in Goma – *the auditorat militaire général* – where 122 cases were recorded in 2013–2014.

The second striking trend was that, more often than not, the accused perpetrator was known to or identifiable to the victim to a significant level of detail. In the civilian judicial registers accessed in both Bukavu and Goma, with the exception of three cases, all suspected perpetrators were noted as being known to, or at least identifiable by, the victim (PGI 2014a, 2014b; TGI 2014a, 2014b). In the military magistrates' office in Goma, the suspect was recorded as *inconnu* in only one of the 122 cases reported (AMG 2014; AMS 2014). Respondents explained that it is rare for incidents of sexual violence committed by someone unknown to be reported or investigated, as these are often seen as "a lost cause from the outset" due in large part to weak investigative capacities of judicial actors (international judicial organization representative, *interview*, Bukavu, October 2014).

The third striking pattern relates to the age, education, and socio-economic demographic of the accused perpetrators. In the PEVS, reported perpetrators were primarily identified as students (including school pupils) and as unemployed. A third of perpetrators reported to the PEVS in Goma were minors under the age of 18, while the average age of suspected perpetrators recorded by the unit in Bukavu was 25 years old, with 82% being between 15 to 30. When asked about trends in perpetrator profiles reported, a general prosecutor stated that "very often, very often they are idle young men" (general prosecutor, *interview*, Bukavu, October 2014). In military structures, the socio-economic standing of reported perpetrators was marked by rank, which were typically of low military grades. Describing the kinds of cases typically addressed by his office, the secretary of a military prosecution office remarked, "The 2006 Law [on sexual violence] came with a lot of rigour, we arrest boys who are nineteen or twenty here in the cantonment who rape young girls who are minors" (military court secretary, *interview,* Goma, December 2014).

The 2006 Sexual Violence Law was heralded by many for broadening the legal definition of *sexual violence*, aligning the definition of *rape* with the sex-inclusive definition of the Rome Statute, as well as introducing strong punitive measures, including sentencing for perpetrators and financial reparations for victims (Zongwe 2012). The law also raised the age of consent from 15 to 18. This provision created a new – and relatively easy to prosecute – category of sexual crimes for which consent is legally void. As a military judge explained, "even if [the victim] consented, the law is very clear that the perpetrator will be convicted" (military judge, *interview*, Uvira, October 2014). This category of cases was the most represented in judicial structures analyzed in this study. Our analysis of court registers indicated that between 70 and 95% of sexual violence cases recorded by judicial structures in Goma and Bukavu between 2013 and 2014 were of statutory rape. It is also worth noting here that the average age of the victims recorded in the case registers was 16.

Still, this does not say very much about the nature, dynamics of, or the stories behind these cases. Known as *copinage*, or "boyfriend–girlfriend" cases, respondents across police and judicial structures in North and South Kivu explained that since the advent of the 2006 Sexual Violence Laws, they are seeing growing numbers of cases, often reported by a parent, involving adolescent girls who are in sexual relationships with young, sometimes adolescent, men. Respondents across both the military and civilian judicial systems described "surprising scenarios" wherein victims brought food to the prison for their perpetrators or brought their children to the prison to visit their fathers (international judicial reinforcement organization representative, *interview*, Goma, October 2014; defense counsel, *interview*, Goma, October 2014). In one account, a military judge recounted a scene during a mobile court in Walikale wherein a 16- or 17-year-old girl threatened to kill herself if her (military) boyfriend was sent to prison (military prosecutor, *interview*, Bukavu, October 2014). In another, a legal clinic coordinator recounted that "one girl was so upset" that in the courtroom she said, "Arrest my dad [who reported the relationship], he is the problem here!" (legal clinic representative, *interview*, Bukavu, October 2014). Reflecting on similar scenarios he encountered, a civilian prosecutor observed that "the big problem here [is that] the victims are not always with us [the courts]," noting that "if [the judge] has a sensitive disposition . . . he can give a sentence that is not too heavy and that does not break the young girls' heart" (civilian prosecutor, *interview*, Goma, August 2014).

The experiences described through these vignettes are a far cry from those encoded in the quint-essentialized narrative of sexual violence in eastern DRC. This discordance was aptly captured by a civilian magistrate who emphatically stated:

> [Y]ou [the international community] say sexual violence as a weapon of war here, those are not the cases we [magistrates] see every day. It's young people who are in relationships, who love each other, and they have sexual relations. This is what we see day to day.
>
> (civilian magistrate, *interview*, Goma, December 2014)

The adolescent girls depicted by judicial actors appeared more akin to victims of the law than of their (legally prescribed) perpetrators, let alone of the sexual harms typically associated with the region. Analyses of the discordance between dominant and quint-*essentialized* understandings of sexual violence in DRC and the types of cases addressed by the formal justice system are sparse. Nevertheless, similar observations were made in an unpublished report commissioned by a large-scale judicial reform program in eastern DRC – the *Programme d'Appui à la Justice à l'Est de la RDC* (PARJ-E) – which concluded that "the majority of accused severely condemned and detained for rape are young boys because of relations of *copinage* with young girls of their generation" (Kateta 2014: 22–23, authors' translation; see also Douma et al. 2016; Mansfield 2009). A study conducted on the prosecution of sexual violence as part of the Special Courts in Sierra Leone pointed to similar trends, demonstrating that this is not unique to DRC (Grewal 2012). It is, however, perhaps all the more striking in eastern DRC, given the widespread and quint-essentialized reporting of sexual violence in the region.

What does this mean for understandings of masculinities and race in efforts to fight impunity for sexual violence in conflict-affected DRC? Before addressing this question, it is important to state that our intention is not to suggest that all cases in the civilian and military judicial systems in eastern DRC, including those involving minors, are of *copinages*, or that these are representative of sexual violence perpetrated in eastern DRC more broadly. Of note, during this study, harrowing reports emerged out of Kavumu, just outside Bukavu, which indicated that at least 50 girls between the ages of 6 months and 11 years of age were taken from their homes in the night and later found in urgent need of medical care. In June 2016, the "ringleader" and 67 of his men were convicted following a long and complex judicial process (Wolfe 2016). Cases of this kind, evidently, do not constitute the cases of *copinages* depicted earlier. Moreover, through this analysis, we do not proclaim to make any normative or, indeed, legal claim on how cases of *copinages* and statutory rape should be addressed. Such a discussion is warranted but lies beyond our scope here. Instead, this discussion calls for a more nuanced appraisal of the kind of cases of sexual violence making it to and addressed by the justice system in conflict-affected contexts.

It is pertinent to revisit here the underlying rationale behind the prosecution-led fight against impunity, driven in large part by the importance of justice being (seen to be) done and its presumed deterrent effect. The belief that fighting impunity for sexual violence committed in conflict "offer[s] an irreplaceable lesson for the public about the scourge of sexual violence and the potential to bring perpetrators to account" is pervasive and was echoed by respondents (OSF 2012: 6). Thus, if convictions are important because they communicate what is punishable by law, it is surely important to "pay more attention to what is prosecuted and why" (Fawcett 2012: 76–77). If we consider convictions for *copinages* and those for sexual violence committed as part of a military operation, the messages conveyed are qualitatively – legally and socially – distinct. The latter aligns with the objectives of the fight against impunity as outlined earlier; the former does not. Recalling the words of the civilian prosecutor earlier, through its application to cases of *copinage*, efforts to promote accountability for sexual violence in DRC instead function to "break young girls' hearts" (civilian prosecutor, *interview*, Goma, August 2014) by prosecuting their legally prescribed perpetrator. In less-affective terms, the operation of the law here appears more akin to one of (sexual) regulation than one of redress for sexual harms, let alone of the types of sexual harms typically associated with eastern DRC. Omitting to critically assess the nature of the sexual crimes addressed by domestic courts and law enforcement may contribute to misrepresenting the socio-legal operation of transitional justice in local contexts. In addition, it leaves unchallenged, and sustains, long-standing and intimately sexuo-racialized gaze casting Congolese masculinity as always-already, quintessentially defined by a capacity for exceptionally brutal sexual perpetratorhood.

Conclusion

Recent years have seen more concerted efforts to fight impunity and address the gender dimensions of conflict in transitional justice, notably by prosecuting perpetrators of sexual violence through international and domestic courts. Affirming the important potential of fighting impunity to promoting a sustainable and gendered peace, this chapter critically examined gendered and raced assumptions underpinning such efforts. Re-tracing deliberations leading to the adoption of UNSCR 1820 (2008) revealed the institutional maneuvering behind the carefully curated definition of sexual violence in conflict encoded in the resolution, along with the central role of the documented experiences of women and girls in eastern DRC, to generating requisite political will within a resistant Security Council. Grounded in documented realities, these experiences came to embody a quint-essentialist narrative of sexual violence in conflict, defining the nature of the harm (brutal, widespread, and systematic), its victims (civilian women and girls), its perpetrators (armed men in uniform). While instrumental to establishing sexual violence as a standalone issue on the Security Council agenda, the centrality of DRC relied on and reproduced troubling imaginaries of exceptionally and violently sexualized masculinities in Africa, and in DRC specifically.

Against the backdrop of the institutionally delineated quint-*essentialist* perpetrator, a close analysis of efforts to fight impunity for sexual violence in eastern DRC demonstrated that this figure is less easily discernible in judicial practice. As shown in Minova, the powerful interplay of politico-military factors and weak investigative capacities frustrates the already-difficult task of delivering justice for survivors of grave international crimes. An analysis of the less-exceptional, everyday functioning of the judicial system in North and South Kivu indicated that that the internationally supported fight against impunity for sexual violence is playing a different function than intended. Rather than redressing grave, often brutal, crimes of conflict-related sexual violence, such efforts are instead disproportionately functioning to prosecute cases of *copinages*, or boyfriend–girlfriend cases. In such cases, rather than providing redress, the convictions described earlier were instead a source of distress for the legally prescribed victims.

Returning to the socio-legal and pedagogical potential of campaigns to fight impunity: these are, in large part, intended to deter future crimes from being committed, by demonstrating that sexual violence in conflict contexts will not go unpunished. Yet with the exception of notable recent successes, this chapter suggests that the message conveyed to those who perpetrate, command, or condone sexual violence, as defined by international law, is that impunity prevails. Moreover, the relative ease of prosecuting cases involving a minor since the introduction of renewed sexual violence legislation in DRC indicates that convictions alone may be a misleading metric of success, particularly when insufficient attention is paid to *who* is prosecuted and for *what kinds* of sexual crimes. It is important to restate that our intention is not to make any normative or legal claim as to how statutory rape should be addressed – such a discussion lies beyond the scope of this chapter. Instead, our intention is to demonstrate that omitting to heed attention to the nature of sexual crimes prosecuted not only risks mischaracterizing the socio-legal outcomes of fighting impunity in local contexts but also leaves the presumed ubiquity of the quint-*essentialist* male perpetrator – and attendant assumptions of brutally violent perpetratorhood and conflict-affected masculinities – unchallenged in transitional justice discourse, policy, and practice.

References

Alhindawi, Z. D. (2014). *They Will Be Heard: The Rape Survivors of Minova.* New York: Al Jazeera. Available at: http://america.aljazeera.com/multimedia/2014/3/they-will-be-heard-therapesurvivorsofminova.html. Accessed on: 4 January 2022.

Anderson, L. (2010). Politics by Other Means: When Does Sexual Violence Threaten International Peace and Security?. *International Peacekeeping* 17(2): 244–260.

Autesserre, S. (2012). Dangerous Tales: Dominant Narratives on the Congo and Their Unintended Consequences. *African Affairs* 11(443): 202–222.

Basu, S. (2016). Gender as National Interest at the UN Security Council. *International Affairs* 92(2): 255–273.

Bedford, K. (2007). The Imperative of Male Inclusion: How Institutional Context Influences World Bank Gender Policy. *International Feminist Journal of Politics* 9(3): 289–311.

Bitenga, A., K. Mutondo, J. Balegamire, A. Emile and D. Mukwege (2021). Motivations for Sexual Violence in Armed Conflicts: Voices from Combatants in Eastern Democratic Republic of Congo. *Medicine, Conflict and Survival* 37(1): 15–33.

Buss, D. (2014). Seeing Sexual Violence in Conflict and Post-Conflict Societies: The Limits of Visibility. In: Buss, D., Lebert, J., Rutherford, B., Sharkey, D. & Aginam, O. (eds.): *Sexual Violence in Conflict and Post Conflict Societies: International Agendas and African Contexts*. London and New York: Routledge: 3–27.

Candeias, S., L. Côté, E. Papageorgiou and M. Raymond-Jetté (2015). *The Accountability Landscape in Eastern DRC: Analysis of the National Legislative and Judicial Response to International Crimes (2009–2014)*. New York: International Centre for Transitional Justice.

Daley, O. P. (2015). Researching Sexual Violence in the Eastern Democratic Republic of the Congo: Methodologies, Ethics, and the Production of Knowledge in an African Warscape. In: Gray, C. L., Momsen, A. and Momsen, J. (eds.): *The Routledge Handbook of Gender and Development*. Abingdon: Routledge: 429–440.

Dolan, C. (2014). *Into the Mainstream: Addressing Sexual Violence Against Men and Boys in Conflict*. Briefing Paper Prepared for the Workshop Held at the Overseas Development Institute. Available at: https://reliefweb.int/report/world/mainstream-addressing-sexual-violence-against-men-and-boys-conflict. Accessed on: 10 January 2022.

Douma, N., D. Hilhorst and J. Matabaro (2016). *Getting the Balance Right?: Sexual Violence Response in the Democratic Republic of Congo. A Comparison between 2011–2014*. London: Secure Livelihoods Research Consortium & Justice and Security Research Program, LSE. Available at: https://reliefweb.int/report/democratic-republic-congo/getting-balance-right-sexual-violence-response-drc-comparison. Accessed on: 10 January 2022.

Duriesmith, D. (2017). *Masculinity and New War: The Gendered Dynamics of Contemporary Armed Conflict*. Abingdon and New York: Routledge.

Edwards, A. (2010). *Violence Against Women Under International Human Rights Law*. Cambridge: Cambridge University Press.

Enloe, C. (2004). *The Curious Feminist: Searching for Women in a New Age of Empire*. Berkeley: University of California Press.

Eriksson Baaz, M. and M. Stern (2008). Making Sense of Violence: Voices of Soldiers in the Congo (DRC). *The Journal of Modern African Studies* 46(1): 57–86.

Eriksson Baaz, M. and M. Stern (2009). Why do Soldiers Rape? Masculinity, Violence and Sexuality in the Armed Forces in the Congo. *International Studies Quarterly* 53: 495–518.

Eriksson Baaz, M. and M. Stern (2013). *Rape as a Weapon of War?: Perceptions, Prescriptions, Problems in the Congo and Beyond*. London and New York: Zed Books.

Eriksson Baaz, M. and J. Verweijen (2018). Confronting the Colonial: The (Re)production of 'African' Exceptionalism in Critical Security and Military Studies. *Security Dialogue* 49(1–2): 57–69.

Everill, B. and J. Kaplan (2013). Introduction: Enduring Humanitarianism in Africa. In: Everill, B. and Kaplan, J. (eds.): *The History and Practice of Humanitarian Intervention and Aid in Africa*. Basingstoke and New York: Palgrave Macmillan: 1–22.

Fawcett, A. (2012). Improvements in the Legal Treatment of Systematic Mass Rape in Wartime: Where Do We Go from Here? In: St. Germain, T. and Dewey, S. (eds.): *Conflict-Related Sexual Violence: International Law, Local Responses*. Sterling, VA: Kumarian Press: 53–70.

FCDO (Foreign, Commonwealth and Development Office). (2013). *A Declaration of Commitment to End Sexual Violence in Conflict*. Available at: https://assets.publishing.service.gov.uk/government/uploads/system/uploads/attachment_data/file/274724/A_DECLARATION_OF_COMMITMENT_TO_END_SEXUAL_VIOLENCE_IN_CONFLICT.pdf.

FCDO (Foreign, Commonwealth and Development Office). (2014). *International Protocol on the Documentation and Investigation of Sexual Violence in Conflict*(1st ed.). Available at: http://www.refworld.org/docid/53f2fed34.html. Accessed on: 30 August 2016.

Fiddian-Qasmiyeh, E. (2014). *The Ideal Refugees: Gender, Islam, and the Sahrawi Politics of Survival*. Syracuse, NY: Syracuse University Press.

Fuss, D. (1989). *Essentially Speaking: Feminism, Nature and Difference*. London and New York: Routledge.

Goetz, A. (2015). *Conflict-Related Sexual Violence: The Politics of the UN Security Council's Approach to the Protection of Civilians*. London: Department of International Relations Fred Halliday Memorial Lecture, London School of Economics and Political Science. Available at: http://www.lse.ac.uk/publicEvents/events/2015/11/20151119t1830vOT.aspx. Accessed on: 30 August 2016.

Grewal, K. (2012). International Criminal Justice: Advancing the Cause of Women's Rights?: The Example of the Special Court for Sierra Leone. In: St. Germain, T. and Dewey, S. (eds.): *Conflict-Related Sexual Violence*. Sterling: Kuarian Press: 76–77.

Hamber, B. (2007). Masculinity and Transitional Justice: An Exploratory Essay. *The International Journal of Transitional Justice* 1(1): 375–390.

Heathcote, G. and D. Otto (2014). Rethinking Peacekeeping, Gender Equality and Collective Security: An Introduction. In: Heathcote, G. and Otto, D. (eds.): *Rethinking Peacekeeping, Gender Equality and Collective Security*. Basingstoke and New York: Palgrave McMillan: 1–20.

HRW (Human Rights Watch) (2002). *The War within the War: Sexual Violence Against Women and Girls in Eastern Congo*. New York: HRW.

HRW (Human Rights Watch) (2010). *The Greatest Silence: Rape in the Congo*. Human Rights Watch Film Festival. Available at: https://ff.hrw.org/film/greatest-silence-rape-congo. Accessed on: 4 January 2022.

HRW (Human Rights Watch) (2015). *Justice on Trial: Lessons from the Minova Rape Case in the Democratic Republic of Congo*. Human Rights Watch. Available at: https://www.hrw.org/report/2015/10/01/justice-trial/lessons-minova-rape-case-democratic-republic-congo. Accessed on: 30 August 2016.

Jackson, F. (2007). *The Greatest Silence: Rape in the Congo*. HBO [documentary film]. Trailer. Available at: http://www.hbo.com/documentaries/the-greatest-silence-rape-in-the-congo. Accessed on: 30 August 2016.

Kapur, R. (2002). The Tragedy of Victimization Rhetoric: Resurrecting the Native Subject in International/Postcolonial Legal Politics. *Harvard Human Rights Law Journal* 15(1): 1–37.

Kateta, B. (2014). *Rapport de l'Etude sur le traitement des infractions de violences sexuelles par le système judiciaires et les acteurs concernés dans les Provinces des Nord et Sud Kivu et dans le District de l'Ituri Du 04 mai au 04 Juin 2014*. PARJ-E (unpublished).

Lake, M. (2014). *After Minova: Can War Crimes Trials Overcome Violence in DRC?* African Arguments. Available at: https://africanarguments.org/2014/05/after-minova-can-war-crimes-trials-overcome-violence-in-the-drc-by-millie-lake/. Accessed on: 4 January 2022.

Lake, M. (2018). *Strong NGOs and Weak States: Pursuing Gender Justice in the Democratic Republic of Congo and South Africa*. Cambridge: Cambridge University Press.

Lake, M., I. Muthaka and G. Walker (2016). Gendering Justice in Humanitarian Spaces: Opportunity and (Dis)empowerment Through Gender-Based Legal Development Outreach in the Eastern Democratic Republic of Congo. *Law and Society Review* 30(3): 539–574.

Laurent, O. (2014). Things Fall Apart: Masculinity and Violence in Congo. *Time*. 21 July. Available at: https://time.com/3387309/things-fall-apart-masculinity-and-violence-in-congo/. Accessed on: 30 January 2023.

Leiby, M. (2009). Digging in the Archives: The Promise and Perils of Primary Documents. *Politics and Society* 37(1): 75–99.

Lewis, C. (2021). The Making and Remaking of the 'Rape Capital of the World': On Colonial Durabilities and the Politics of Sexual Violence Statistics in DRC. *Critical African Studies* 12(3).

Mansfield, J. (2009). Prosecuting Sexual Violence in the Eastern Democratic Republic of Congo: Obstacles for Survivors on the Road to Justice. *African Human Rights Law Journal (AHRLJ)* 9(2): 367–408.

Medie, A. P. (2017). Rape Reporting in Post-Conflict Côte d'Ivoire: Accessing Justice and Ending Impunity. *African Affairs* 116(464): 414–434.

Mertens, C. (2016). Sexual Violence in the Congo Free State: Archival Traces and Present Reconfigurations. *The Australian Review of African Studies* 37(1): 6–20.

Mertens, C. and M. Pardy (2017). 'Sexcurity' and Its Effects in Eastern Democratic Republic of Congo. *Third World Quarterly* 38(4): 956–979.

Misra, A. (2015). *The Landscape of Silence: Sexual Violence Against Men in War*. London: Hurst & Company.

Mohanty, T. (1984). Under Western Eyes: Feminist Scholarship and Colonial Discourse. *Boundary 2* 12(3): 333–358.

Myrttinen, H., L. Khattab and J. Naujoks (2017). Re-Thinking Hegemonic Masculinities in Conflict-Affected Contexts. *Critical Military Studies* 3(2): 103–119.

Myrttinen, H. and A. Swaine (2015). Monster Myths, Selfies and Grand Declarations: A Conversation on the Global Summit to End Sexual Violence in Conflict. *International Feminist Journal of Politics* 17(3): 496–502.

Nichols, M. (2013). *U.S., Britain Push Congo to Prosecute Soldiers Over Minova Rapes*. London: Reuters. Available at: https://www.reuters.com/article/us-congo-democratic-rapes-idUSBRE9950J820131006. Accessed on: 4 January 2022.

Nichols, M. (2014). *United Nations Disappointed by Congo Mass Rape Trial Verdict*. London: Reuters. Available at: https://www.reuters.com/article/uk-congodemocratic-rape-un-idUKKBN0DM1H320140506. Accessed on: 4 January 2022.

Open Society Foundations (OSF) (2012). *Justice in DRC: Mobile Courts Combat Rape and Impunity in Eastern Congo*. Available at: https://www.opensocietyfoundations.org/sites/default/files/justice-drc-20130114.pdf. Accessed on: 29 May 2018.

Open Society Initiatives for Southern Africa (OSISA) (2012). Helping to Combat Impunity for Sexual Crimes: An Evaluation of the Mobile Gender Justice Courts. *On Learning* 4. Available at: https://www.yumpu.com/en/document/view/5837349/helping-to-combat-impunity-for-sexual-open-society-initiative-of-. Accessed on: 29 May 2018.

Otto, D. (2006). Lost in Translation: Re-Scripting the Sexed Subjects of International Human Rights Law. In: Orford, A. (ed.): *International Law and Its Others*. Cambridge: Cambridge University Press: 318–356.

Otto, D. (2010). Power and Danger: Feminist Engagement with International Law through the UN Security Council. *Australian Feminist Law Journal* 32(1): 97–121.

Oyěwùmí, O. (1997). *The Invention of Women: Making an African Sense of Western Gender Discourses*. London and Minneapolis: University of Minnesota Press.

Pankhurst, D. (2008). *Gendered Peace: Women's Struggle for Post-War Justice and Reconciliation*. Abingdon: Routledge.

Programmes des Nations Unies pour le Développement (UNDP) (2012). *Monitoring Judicaire: Rapport sur les données relatives aux cas de violences sexuelles à l'Est de la République démocratique du Congo*. PNUD & le Ministère de la Justice et des Droits Humains. Available at: https://www1.undp.org/content/dam/dem_rep_congo/docs/demgov/UNDP-CD-Monitoring-Judiciaire-2011.pdf. Accessed on: 13 January 2022.

Réseau des Femmes pour un Développement Associatif, Réseau des Femmes pour la Défense des Droits et la Paix & International Alert (2005). *Women's Bodies as a Battlefield: Sexual Violence Against Women and Girls During the War in the Democratic Republic of Congo, South Kivu (1996–2003)*. London: International Alert. Available at: https://repositories.lib.utexas.edu/bitstream/handle/2152/4949/4053.pdf. Accessed on: 1 July 2017.

Said, E. (2001). Traveling Theory. In: Bayoumi, M. and Rubin, A. (eds.): *The Edward Said Reader*. London: Granta Books: 195–217.

Schulz, P. (2020). *Male Survivors of Wartime Sexual Violence: Perspectives from Northern Uganda*. Oakland: University of California Press.

Seelinger, T. and J. Freccero (2015). *The Long Road: Accountability for Sexual Violence in Conflict and Post Conflict Settings: Kenya, Liberia, Sierra Leone, Uganda*. Berkeley: Human Rights Center, University of California. Available at: https://www.law.berkeley.edu/wp-content/uploads/2015/04/Accountability_report_2015_final_web2.pdf. Accessed on: 10 January 2022.

Tamale, S. (ed.) (2011). *African Sexualities: A Reader*. Cape Town, Dakar, Nairobi and Oxford: Pambazuka Press.

Touquet, H. (2022). Silent or Inaudible?: Male Survivor Stories in Bosnia-Herzegovina. *Social Politics: International Studies in Gender, State and Society* 29(2): 706–728.
UN Action (2011). *Analytical and Conceptual Framing of Conflict-Related Sexual Violence.* UN Action Against Sexual Violence in Conflict. Available at: http://peacemaker.un.org/sites/peacemaker.un.org/files/AnalyticalConceptualFramingConflictrelatedSexualViolence_UNAction2011.pdf. Accessed on: 30 August 2016.
United Nations General Assembly (2008). *Promotion and Protection of All Human Rights, Civil, Political, Economic, Social and Cultural, Including the Right to Development. Report of the Special Rapporteur on the Independence of Judges and Lawyers, Leandro Despouy Addendum Mission to the Democratic Republic of the Congo*, A/HRC/8/4/Add. Available at: https://digitallibrary.un.org/record/1477246?ln=en. Accessed on: 10 January 2022.
UNJHRO (UN Joint Human Rights Office) (2014). *Avancées et Obstacles dans la Lutte Contre l'Impunité des Violences Sexuelles en République démocratique du Congo.* MONUSCO & Haut-Commissariat des Nations Unies pour les Droits de l'Homme. Available at: https://reliefweb.int/report/democratic-republic-congo/avanc-es-et-obstacles-dans-la-lutte-contre-l-impunit-des-violences. Accessed on: 10 January 2022.
UN News Centre (2014). DR Congo Mass Rape Verdict Fails to Deliver Justice to Victims, Say UN Envoy. *UN News Centre.* Available at: https://news.un.org/en/story/2014/05/467912-dr-congo-mass-rape-verdict-fails-deliver-justice-victims-says-un-envoy. Accessed on: 4 January 2022.
UNSC (UN Security Council) (2008). *Security Council Resolution 1820 on Women, Peace and Security*, Adopted by the Security Council at its 5916th Meeting on 19 June 2008, S/RES/1820.
UNSC (UN Security Council) (2013). *Security Council Resolution 2106 on Women, Peace and Security.* Adopted by the Security Council at its 6984th Meeting on 24 June 2013, S/RES/2106.
UNSC (UN Security Council) (2021). *Report of the Secretary-General: Conflict Related Sexual Violence*, 30 March, S/2021/312. Available at: https://documents.un.org/doc/undoc/gen/n21/069/02/pdf/n2106902.pdf?token=f572eltU6Gk3ealcbE&fe=true. Accessed on: 21 July 2024.
Weill, S., K. Thuy Seelinger and K. Bree Carlson (eds.) (2020). *The President on Trial: Prosecuting Hissène Habré.* Oxford: Oxford University Press.
Westendorf, J. and L. Searle (2017). Sexual Exploitation and Abuse in Peace Operations: Trends, Policy Responses and Future Directions. *International Affairs* 93(2): 365–387.
Wolfe, L. (2016). *What It Takes to Get an Alleged Mass Rapist and 67 Militiamen Arrested in Congo.* Washington: Foreign Policy. Available at: http://foreignpolicy.com/2016/06/23/how-i-got-an-alleged-mass-rapist-and-67-militiamen-arrested-in-congo/. Accessed on: 10 January 2022.
Zongwe, P. (2012). The New Sexual Violence Legislation in the Congo. *African Studies Review* 55(2): 37–57.

Interviews and Field Notes Cited

Civilian Magistrate, *interview*, Goma, December 2014.
Congolese Women's Rights Activist, *interview*, Bukavu, April 2014.
Defence Counsel, *interview*, Goma, October 2014.
European Donor Representative, *interview*, Bukavu, May 2014.
General Prosecutor, *interview*, Bukavu, October 2014.
International Judicial Organisation Representative, *interview*, Bukavu, October 2014.

International Judicial Reinforcement Organisation Representative, *interview*, Goma, October 2014.
Launch of the Declaration to End Sexual Violence in Conflict *Fieldnotes*, New York, 24 September 2013.
Legal Clinic Representative, *interview*, Bukavu, October 2014.
Military Court Secretary, *interview*, Goma, December 2014.
Military Judge, *interview*, Uvira, October 2014.
Military Prosecutor, *interview*, Bukavu, October 2014.
Senior Women's Rights Advocate, *interview*, New York, January 2014.
Special Advisor, Permanent Mission to the UN, *interview*, New York, January 2014.
UN Team of Experts on Sexual Violence and the Rule of Law Member, *interview*, New York, January 2014.
UN Women's Rights Advocate, *interview*, New York, January 2014.

Judicial and Police Data

AMG (2014). *Sexual Violence Cases Recorded by the Auditorat Militaire de Garnison (Military Magistrates) in Goma* 2013–2014 [Copy on file with authors].
AMS (2014). *Sexual Violence Cases Recorded by the Auditorat Militaire Supérieur in Goma 2013–2014*, unpublished [Copy on file with authors].
CMO (2014a). *Pro-Justitia Arret*, RP N°003/2013, RMP N°0372/BBM/013, 5 Mai 2014 [Copy on file with authors].
CMO (2014b). *Sexual Violence Cases Recorded by the Cour Militaire Operationelle (Military Operational Court) in Goma 2008–2014*, unpublished [Copy on file with authors].
PEVS (2014a). *Perpetrator Profiles in Sexual Violence Cases Recorded by PEVS Unit in Goma 2013–2014*, unpublished [Copy on file with authors].
PEVS (2014b). *Sexual Violence Cases Recorded by PEVS Unit in Bukavu 2013–2014* [Copy on file with authors].
PEVS (2014c). *Perpetrator Profiles in Sexual Violence Cases Recorded by PEVS Unit in Bukavu 2014*, unpublished [Copy on file with authors].
PGI (2014a). *Sexual Violence Cases Recorded by the Parquet de Grande Instance (Civilian Magistrates) in Goma 2013–2014* [Copy on file with authors].
PGI (2014b). *Sexual Violence Cases Recorded by the Parquet de Grande Instance (Civilian Magistrates) in Bukavu 2013–2014* [Copy on file with authors].
TGI (2014a). *Sexual Violence Cases Recorded by the Tribunal de Grande Instance (Civilian Tribunal) in Goma 2013–2014*[Copy on file with authors].
TGI (2014b). *Sexual Violence Cases Recorded by the Tribunal de Grande Instance (Civilian Tribunal) in Bukavu 2013-2014* [Copy on file with authors].

Chapter 10

Croatian Veteran Masculinities and Exclusive Narratives

Points of Identification With the "Myth of the Homeland War" in the 2010s[1]

Catherine Baker and Heleen Touquet

Introduction

In July 2018, the Croatian men's national football team returned home from reaching the World Cup final to a public celebration in the capital, Zagreb. The players, who had mostly been boys during Croatia's 1991–1995 War of Independence against the Yugoslav People's Army (JNA) and Serb paramilitaries (the "Homeland War"), were unexpectedly joined by a musician to whom many of them looked up, Marko Perković Thompson. Thompson had famously been a serving volunteer in the Homeland War when his career as a controversial patriotic musician began in 1992. Now the generation of 1990s youth like team captain Luka Modrić had grown to adulthood, and Thompson had aged into a representative of the politicized veterans' movement but was still popular among youth of the late 2010s who agreed with his stances on politics and memory. As time has passed since the 1990s and the mythologized generation of wartime soldiers, or "branitelji" ("defenders"), have become middle-aged veterans, contemporary Croatian popular culture in the 2010s was producing an idealized veteranhood that obscured the material vulnerabilities of ageing veterans and of youth facing prolonged economic disparity. Where transitional justice processes are still salient a generation after conflict, this phenomenon suggests, understanding the relationship between masculinities and transitional justice requires attention to how age and conflict-related masculinities interact. In Croatia, the production of "veteran masculinities" through media is an ongoing process which affirms the dominant narrative of the Homeland War and even makes proximity to veteran masculinities a potential political resource for male civilians and women in politics.

Focusing on Croatia, this chapter thus offers an analysis of the enduring influence of veteran masculinities post-conflict. Veteran masculinities in

1 This chapter was drafted in March 2020 and does not attempt detailed coverage of the July 2020 Croatian general elections, or later developments, including Škoro's break with the Homeland Movement in 2021.

DOI: 10.4324/9781003519522-13

Croatia permeate different spheres of civilian life and youth culture through sports and music, as evidenced in the digital public sphere. This enduring influence is an important tool to gauge the state of transitional justice as veteran masculinities are intimately connected to the societally hegemonic narrative of the Homeland War. This narrative offers an attractive black-and-white picture of the 1990s conflict based on a clear delineation of Croatian victims and heroes and Serb enemies but has constrained space for acknowledgment of injustices against Serbs or behavior by Croats that did not fit the heroic ideal. The institutionalization of this nationalist narrative by political and cultural elites has thus been one of the main causes of the lack of recognition of Serb civilian victims in society, the disavowal of war crimes perpetrated by Croatian soldiers, and the reluctance to contemplate the implications of the chain of command now known to have existed between the wartime Croatian leadership and separatist Croat forces in Bosnia-Herzegovina (BiH), which committed crimes of their own. The cross-generational attractiveness of the pure, sacrificial, and heroic war veteran ensures the enduring impenetrability of the Homeland War narrative.

This chapter's concept of "veteran masculinities" relates to concepts of military or militarized masculinities (for a discussion, see Hamber et al., this volume) as veterans' social identities relate to military ones. Veteran masculinities are those shaped by the "long and contradictory afterlife" (Bulmer and Eichler 2017: 161) of past militarized masculinities once veterans have re-entered civilian life. While veterans are often recognized as important actors for transitional justice processes to engage with (Sokolić 2019) and the social construction and transformation of masculinities are becoming acknowledged as a significant dimension of the gender politics of transitional justice (Hamber 2016), the masculinities *of* veterans are still understudied in transitional justice research. Veteran masculinities are important to consider in the context of transitional justice, however, not only because they influence the ways in which it is socially acceptable for the generation(s) that fought to relate to the wartime past, but also because of their effect on the young, for whom they represent masculinities of their parents', and specifically their fathers', generation. Structurally, in the terms defined by James Messerschmidt and Michael Messner (2018: 41–42), veteran masculinities operate as both "dominant" and "hegemonic" masculinities in contemporary Croatian public culture: that is, they are "the most celebrated . . . form of masculinity in a particular social setting," that of war memory (they are dominant), and they "legitimate an unequal relationship between men and women . . . and among masculinities" which relates differently to the institutionalized narrative of the war (they are hegemonic). The dominant Homeland War narrative has now been enshrined in Croatian public culture for more than 30 years, reaffirmed during the Croatian state's clashes with the International Criminal Tribunal for Former Yugoslavia (ICTY) in the 2000s and, even more so, during the 20th anniversary celebrations of the war's final offensive

("Oluja") in 2015. Both through formal education and through less-formal but highly significant channels of social and cultural activity aimed at youth, young people have thus had a sanitized narrative of the glorious wartime past offered to them as common sense for their entire lives.

Outside self-consciously left-wing or "alternative" circles, the social costs for young people to criticize this narrative can be high, and its heroic treatment of the veteran in lived experience interacts in complex ways with the subjectivities of young people whose own family lives and paternal relationships were seriously affected by the war. As Ivor Sokolić (2019: 2) contends in his own study of post-conflict memory and justice in Croatia, where top-down "judicial narratives" set out by the ICTY and domestic tribunals fail to conform with bottom-up "everyday narratives" grounded in the emotions of how individuals experienced the war, "they struggle to take hold in society." The ways in which veteran masculinities have been mediated to youth help constitute the everyday narratives that young people assemble with influences from family memory, education, traditional and social media, peer groups, and associational culture as a "postmemory" (Jelača 2016: 184) of the war. Moreover, they have sustained a public culture in which proximity to hegemonic veteran masculinities has become a political resource for figures who do not themselves embody them. Through these processes, the dominant Homeland War narrative and its idealized image of the veteran are reinvested with social and political meaning. They constitute, therefore, part of the everyday "gendered negotiations . . . around silence and speech" which, as Johanna Mannergren Selimović (2020: 2) argues, "link to larger processes of social remembering and forgetting" – in this case, the social forgetting of acts committed by Croats that would undermine the heroic memory of the nation at war.

Methodologically, this chapter is informed by past qualitative content analysis of recorded songs, music videos, and newspaper/magazine articles by the first author, including exploratory research for a project which did not proceed after the COVID-19 pandemic began (see Baker 2019). Before developing our argument about the enduring influence of veteran masculinities, we first elaborate on the dominant Homeland War narrative and its gendered underpinnings. We then focus on the links between veteran masculinities and post-conflict youth through music and sports and, in a second part, on local politicians' identifications in proximity to veteran masculinities.

The Dominant Homeland War Narrative

Croatian public culture and its structure of gender relations were defined by the gendered and ethnicized politics of Croatia's War of Independence (the "Homeland War") in the 1990s; a generation later, they still are. Croatian media in the 1990s, "alternative" outlets aside, combined in an effort to ethnically and politically homogenize the public around a consensus that Croatia was an inherently peaceful, Western-oriented, central European nation forced into a war of self-defense against the historic aggression of an Eastern, Balkan, and totalitarian adversary with which it had nothing culturally in common. While Croatia had been attacked and was fighting in self-defense, this frame created a stark ethnopolitical separation. Croatian anthropologists observing wartime media at first hand witnessed the beginning of this process (e.g., Feldman et al. 1993; Senjković 2002), including ethnomusicologists who first demonstrated that popular music was integrally embedded in them as well (e.g., Pettan 1998) – that is, that the cultural politics of ethnonationalism reached into spheres of everyday life beyond news media.

This hegemonic discursive frame, following the narrative of national identity espoused by Croatia's founding president, Franjo Tuđman (see Bellamy 2003), was infused by a hierarchical gender order which located masculine virtue in readiness to defend the nation and feminine virtue in readiness to bear children for it, mourn for it, or – in limited circumstances – fight for it as well (Ceribašić 2000; Žarkov 2007). So tacitly as to go almost completely unspoken, the move also aligned the nation with the Whiteness of a Europe already beginning to fortify its borders against migration from the Global South (and then, until states met conditions for EU accession, south-east Europe itself). Military masculinities were central in this frame, specifically the emblematic masculinity of the Croatian "branitelj," or "defender," a term for Homeland War veterans which enshrines the all-encompassing narrative of defensive war in the very language conventionally used throughout Croatian public life to refer to those who fought in it. The archetype of the branitelj, once a soldier and now a veteran, continues to define gender relations in Croatia even as it has adapted to the war passing out of living memory for the nation's youngest members, who extensively populate (yet are not the whole of) Croatia's digital public sphere.

"Transitional justice" processes and other efforts to bring about public reckoning with more complex and less-savory aspects of Croatian participation in the war confront these contexts (Sokolić 2019). They find the boundaries of acceptable Croatian public discourse about the nation and its recent past still governed by what Dejan Jović (2017: 20) calls "the myth of the Homeland War." This narrative was affirmed under Tuđman and reaffirmed in the early 2000s through several episodes of resistance to indictments issued against Ante Gotovina and certain other wartime Croatian generals by the International Criminal Tribunal for Former Yugoslavia (ICTY): this period cemented the phrase "the truth about the Homeland War" to signify the idea that, since Croatia's war was defensive, no crimes could have been committed on the Croatian side. The abstract figure of the male veteran around which it revolves has tended to silence the wartime participation of Croatia's 23,080 female veterans (see Berdak 2013: 55) but has also been constructed out of the genuine and material social exclusion and disappointment of hundreds of thousands of men – some of whom have found their experiences represented in the organized veterans' movement, and others have not.

Paradoxically, although Croatia operates what sociologists describe as a highly "clientelist" veterans' welfare system (Dolenec 2018: 72), large numbers of veterans in economically marginalized areas who experience material vulnerabilities feel embittered their sacrifice was in vain (see Schäuble 2014). The right wing explains this as a cultural crisis caused by "war profiteers" "ratni profiteri") and sympathizers with the old socialist Yugoslav order. These contentions have existed since war's end but worsened during the crisis brought on by the global financial crash in 2007–2008 and the continued inability of solutions based on neoliberal economic integration to deliver prosperity or adequate psychosocial care in economically marginalized regions, often the very frontline areas of 1990–1995 – exacerbating the material vulnerabilities of veterans and other inhabitants and causing high youth immigration, which has depopulated regions like Dalmatinska zagora (the Dalmatian hinterland). A third layer of crisis since 2015 has become Croatia's imbrication in the global refugee crisis as the EU member state tasked with securing the boundary between the EU's external border and its Schengen border, to which the Croatian state has responded with intimidating pushbacks of refugees by police.

Significant developments in the cultural politics of Croatian war memory have occurred during these years, within the overarching "myth of the Homeland War." One is the transformation of the branitelj archetype to become meaningful to today's Croatian youth, who were not even born during the war and now might not even remember Tuđman firsthand. Another is the rising prominence of resentment against "war profiteers," whose self-serving management of the economy is cited as a major reason that the youth are now immigrating en masse (Jurić 2017: 363).

Veteran Masculinities and Post-Conflict Youth

Veteran masculinities in contemporary Croatia are caught between the symbolic image of the branitelj as national martyr-hero and the material realities of men who have often been left without sufficient care for their service's physical and psychic consequences and certainly feel they have been left without sufficient recompense. This was already the case in the late 1990s when the Association of Croatian Homeland War Military Invalids (HVIDRA) established itself as the leading politicized veterans' association, and in the early 2000s, when HVIDRA and other groups protested against cooperation with the ICTY. What has changed as more time has elapsed is how the social repertoire of veteran masculinities is filtered through the category of age. The iconic youthful volunteer who went to the front in summer 1991 with Walkman and rosary in hand, in an archetype largely crafted by Croatian war journalists (Senjković 1996: 42–43), would now be 50 or above; his older counterparts, always more numerous than the "rocker-soldier" myth implied, are now of retirement age. For late-1990s/early 2000s youth, whose own lived experience of the war informed what they understood veterans had fought for, the masculine archetype of the veteran might well map onto an older brother or cousin marked by the war; for today's Croatian youth, veterans signify the father's generation, and their understandings of veteran politics may well be filtered through how they perceive their own fathers' lives. This influences their postmemory of the war.

The evolving public persona of the controversial patriotic musician Marko Perković Thompson illustrates this temporal shift in archetypical veteran masculinities. Thompson famously served in the Homeland War, as continuously denoted by his stage name, referencing the submachine gun he carried in the volunteer platoon that mobilized to defend his home village of Čavoglave in Dalmatinska zagora; he became a professional musician after a song he wrote honoring the platoon became a nationwide hit on Croatian radio in spring 1992. The song, "Bojna Čavoglave" ("The Čavoglave platoon"), expresses the camaraderie, defiance, and fighting spirit it attributed to the men. It inextricably connotes the ongoing presence in Croatian society of symbols of the fascist Ustaša movement and the 1941–1945 Independent State of Croatia (NDH), since it begins with the Ustaša salute "Za dom spremni"; the Croatian Defence Forces (HOS) paramilitary group adopted this salute, along with black uniforms, on forming at the beginning of the war.[2] After almost three decades in showbusiness, Thompson has aged in the public eye, from a long-haired biker to a gray-haired father of five. His significance to youth has shifted in the meantime from a participant in a conflict they remember to a participant in a conflict they do not.

Narratives of veterans' heroism and sacrifice as the foundation of Croatian freedom, in this context and others, remain embedded across Croatian society today as points of identification for youth. Veterans whose engagement with the recent past transgresses the hegemonic myth, such as Ranko Britvić, who has been trying to reconcile Homeland War and anti-fascist Partisan heritage since 1996 (Ljubičić 2017), have no comparable representation in the celebrity sphere, narrowing the range of veteran masculinities available to mainstream youth consciousness in the digital public sphere. Although appeals to what the veterans fought for no longer index young people's direct lived experiences, which no longer date back far enough, heroic and sacrificial narratives remain live as points of collective identification with an

2 Thompson shouts the first two words, and a group of male voices (or the live crowd) offers the third. In recent public controversies over the slogan, he has justified its continued use by explaining it was the wartime slogan of HOS (Thompson 2017), who have been legally recognized as branitelji. Its supporters also date it to the Croatian general Nikola Šubić Zrinjski's battle cry at Szigetvár in 1566.

ethnically and politically bounded vision of the Croatian nation and its path through the war. This vision is ethnically bounded because it revolves around the Croat ethnic majority, and politically bounded because it delimits loyalty as uncritical support for the veterans' movement and its moral claims. By implication, critical modes of citizenship toward the war (such as questioning how Croatian forces treated Serbs, the oppressive everyday atmosphere that Croatian Serbs behind the lines experienced, and the Croatian state's wartime intentions toward territory in Bosnia-Herzegovina claimed as Croatian) risk being pushed to, or beyond, the margins of what being Croatian today is allowed to mean. While hegemonic veteran masculinities involving consensus with the myth of the Homeland War are lauded, counter-hegemonic veteran masculinities which could champion critical reckoning with the myth are become closed down.

Veteran masculinities and war memory are prominently tied together in the sphere of popular culture for Croatian youth both through Thompson's stardom in general and through the relationship that the Croatian Football Association (HNS) and certain players have forged between his persona and the men's national football team. A symbolic link between men's sport and the Croatian nation in arms dates back to Tuđman and wartime journalists identifying male Croatian sportsmen with fighting for the nation on the sports field (Brentin 2013: 6–7). HNS's alliance with Thompson, and certain players' public affinities with him, made this link material in the 2010s by attaching Thompson's well-known star narrative as a veteran (and thus, by association, his contentious repopularization of "Za dom spremni") to HNS's notion of how the team represents the nation.

Veteran Masculinities at the Nexus of Popular Music and Sport

Since at least 2012, Thompson's "Lijepa li si" has been played before the team's home matches and international tournament games (Holiga 2012), and HNS named it the team anthem after a fan survey in January 2016 (Tportal 2016). This song, which Thompson first recorded in 1998 and re-recorded in 1999 with five other male singers from different regions of Croatia and Bosnia-Herzegovina,[3] praises the constituent regions of what it constructs as the Croatian homeland, in poetic couplets. One of these, "Herceg-Bosno, srce ponosno" ("Herceg-Bosna, proud heart"), contentiously puts "Herceg-Bosna" (the name of the separatist Croat entity that the Croat Defence Council (HVO) attempted to create during the war in BiH by expelling Bosniaks) alongside Dalmatia, Slavonia, Lika, Istria, and Dalmatinska zagora as if they all had

3 Alen Vitasović (from Istria), Mladen Grdović (Zadar), Giuliano (Split), Miroslav Škoro (Slavonia), and Mate Bulić (Herzegovina).

equal status – which, in "integralist" Croat nationalism, they do. The song and video represent the union of regional masculinities into one national homeland united by Thompson, ending with "let us embrace in front of them all, let them see that we are here [neka vide da nas ima]" – a slogan since adopted by veterans (Braniteljski.hr 2015), sports fans (Lipovac 2013), Thompson himself when supporting both groups (Jutarnji.hr 2015; Herceg 2018), and even, satirically, the Croatian LGBTQ movement, especially when they were direct targets of the clericalist right during the 2013 anti-equal-marriage referendum campaign (Index.hr 2014).[4]

In 2012, Thompson was also chosen to record an anthem for HNS's official supporters' club before that year's European Championships. Titled "Uvijek vjerni tebi" ("Always faithful to you"), after the club's name, Uvijek Vjerni ("Always Faithful"), it directly linked sport and war memory by encouraging the team to "fight for the nation [narod] and the colors of your home . . . when you hear the anthem, fight for Vukovar" ("bori se za narod/i za boje doma svog . . . kada čuješ himnu, bori se za Vukovar"). Its video connected them even more tightly by intercutting sequences of Thompson and his band performing to assembling fans first with iconic footage from previous Croatia matches, then also with wartime footage of Croatian artillery firing and soldiers celebrating (Thompson 2012). The emotions of identification toward Thompson and of rewatching the team's historic goals, within this video's affective politics of spectatorship, are thus invited to be transferred on to Croatian military heroism during the Homeland War, and to remembrance of Vukovar as a sacrificial site (see Kardov 2007). Both here and when stadia play "Lijepa li si," Thompson's veteran background means the official presentation of the men's football team fuses the emotions of audience identification with the team with national military masculinities, in the live match atmosphere and also the digital public sphere.

In 2018, Thompson's background and music were even bound into celebrations of Croatia's astonishing successes in the men's World Cup, through individual players' agency and, eventually, collective spectacle, when he joined the team's welcome reception in Zagreb (Dnevno.hr 2018). Thompson's meaning to members of today's national team is filtered through their own experiences as Croats who were boys during the war and who would have begun listening to him (or at least known of him as a celebrity) years before they were celebrities themselves. Modrić, born in a village near Zadar with his ancestors' name, was aged 5 when war broke out and spent

4 The repertoire of the Croatian lesbian choir Le Zbor (see Hofman 2020) includes a version of "Lijepa li si" (renamed "Banana," their vocalization of the song's introductory phrase on gusle and flute, instrumentation that sonically ascribes it to the Dinaric region) which turns the place-names into words denoting each region's women – transforming the sentiments of masculine love for a feminine homeland into expressions of same-gender desire that satirically reconciles queerness and nationhood (Le Zbor 2015).

seven years living in a displaced persons' hotel after RSK police attacked his village and executed his grandfather in December 1991. Dejan Lovren was born in 1989 to a family in the central Bosnian village of Kraljevska Sutjeska who fled the war in BiH to Munich when he was aged 3 (post-war, German authorities expected his family and other Bosnian refugees to return to BiH; the Lovrens moved to Croatia instead). The patriotic music of Thompson and other musicians in the early 2000s was part of their adolescence and now has ritual significance when they celebrate victories.[5] As star footballers, they are themselves now points of identification for youth, where any youthful identifications with Thompson's music they may have had become translated into how they embody the nexus between sporting masculinities and mythologized Homeland War commemoration.

The military masculinity celebrated in Thompson's wartime anthem and commemorated in his later songs expressing war memory is one of bravery, aggression, toughness, skill at directing firepower, and determination to defeat a much stronger adversary (the larger, better-equipped JNA). HNS has readily mapped these qualities onto the self-image of the men's national team, whose official nickname is the "Vatreni" ("The Men of Fire") and who represent the smallest nation to appear in a World Cup final since Uruguay in 1950. The idea of having embodied them in his youth is simultaneously the foundation of Thompson's veteran masculinity and thus of the "authenticity" of his star meta-narrative; Modrić and Lovren, meanwhile, embody a generational post-conflict masculinity grounded in experiencing the conflict as boys. Both these masculinities stem directly from the war and, within the dominant Homeland War narrative's gender order, are interdependent: the veterans' generation fought to defend the children's generation so that boys could grow into men and make a free nation proud (though women and girls of both generations are invisible).

Besides direct connections to the war like these, the "myth of the Homeland War" even permits those with more distant personal connections to the conflict to claim authenticity or authority through proximity to the myth's core masculinities, especially to veterans. The musician Miroslav Škoro, who, like Thompson, was heavily involved in early 2000s anti-ICTY campaigns alongside the veterans' movement, for instance, has been able to project a civilian masculinity expressing brotherhood with veterans including Thompson himself. The evolution of his public persona from patriotic musician to anti-political right-wing presidential candidate exemplifies why understanding masculinity, security, and conflict requires appreciating the construction of civilian masculinities as well as overtly military ones (Millar 2019): in

5 Lovren and teammate Šime Vrsaljko were filmed singing along to an excerpt of "Bojna Čavoglave" in their locker room after their World Cup defeat of Argentina in 2018 (Index.hr 2018a).

Škoro's case, proximity to and fraternity with veterans as embodied in his music and performance have granted him authority to speak on patriotism and politics.

Proximity to Veteran Masculinities

Škoro's third place in the 2019–2020 Croatian presidential elections (where HDZ's Kolinda Grabar-Kitarović came second and the Social Democratic Party (SDP) candidate Zoran Milanović won) was not his first political experience, since he served a year as an HDZ parliamentary deputy in 2007–2008 and had held diplomatic office in 1995–1997 as a consul-general in Hungary. His activity as a patriotic musician had begun during the Homeland War, when "Ne dirajte mi ravnicu" ("Don't touch my plains"), a song he had written as an immigrant in the USA, was taken up by the Croatian music industry as an anthem for Croats displaced from the front lines in Slavonia, his own home region. He returned to Croatia and became a music industry entrepreneur alongside his performance career. During the early 2000s contentions with the ICTY, Škoro asserted his authority to speak through music on the war's significance for Croatian national memory in a duet with Thompson, "Reci, brate moj" ("Tell me, my brother"). This appeared on both their 2002–2003 albums, and Škoro joined Thompson to sing it at Thompson's first large stadium concert in 2002 in Split.

Škoro's proximity to Thompson and the authenticity of veteran masculinity that Thompson lent "Reci, brate moj" – which Škoro had written, then offered to Thompson as a duet because "[Thompson is] a warrior" and should sing it (Ivić 2005) – became part of his own accreting "meta-narrative," aligning with his service to wartime morale to position himself within the circle of patriotic brotherhood even though his own background was civilian. This circle, in both his music and Thompson's during the 2000s, extended back through time. His 2003 song "Sude mi" ("They're judging me") narrates "a knight of my people, chained up in a faraway country" ("vitez roda moga u dalekoj zemjli okovan"), telling his love he is being tried "because [he] defended what was dearest to [him]" ("što sam branio moje najdraže") and because "[his] brothers betrayed [him]" to have him sent there. Its chorus, in folkloric phrasing, expressed faith that time would vindicate him, since "[his] enemies . . . do not know that truth is deep water" ("dušmani . . . ne znaju/ da je istina voda duboka"). This used sometimes also to be performed with Thompson – including in its official video, recorded during Škoro's 2003 album tour (Škoro 2013) – though they no longer cooperate directly.

In the midst of General Ante Gotovina's flight from indictment by the ICTY, "Sude mi" recalled Gotovina and his potential imprisonment very readily, as several YouTube montages setting it over photos of Gotovina confirm. The song's very idea of truth was simultaneously being politicized through the discourse of "the truth about the Homeland War," that is, the insistence that the war was and was only "defensive, legal, legitimate and liberatory" (in Sanader's words when committing his government to supporting Gotovina's defense in 2005 (Lamont 2010: 1698). A "Foundation for the Truth About the Homeland War" was founded in January 2006 to raise funds for defending Gotovina and other generals, with Škoro on its board (Vlašić et al. 2006).

Škoro's production of patriotic music narrating Croatian veterans' plight as a betrayal continuing the treatment of Croatian military heroes in the past continued on his 2005 and 2008 albums. His song "Svetinja" ("Holy thing"), title track of his 2005 album, framed the mid-2000s as a time when "even brother is cheating brother – what are the bad servants of bad masters doing to us?" ("i brat brata vara/što nam rade lose sluge loših gospodara"), and when "the best among us are drinking water at night, hiding their white faces" ("a najbolji među nama noću vodu piju, bijelo lice kriju") – images typically associated with hajduks' hideouts in epic poetry. The chorus established a triad of "holy things": "faith, love and the homeland" ("vjera, ljubav i domovina"). His music in the 2010s, after the global financial crisis, linked the betrayal narrative more specifically to a populist economic program: his 2014 song "Od kud ti pravo" ("Where do you get the right?"), for instance, directed itself at false patriots and liars who had compromised the nation's fraternal community but would still eventually be buried under its flag.

Thematizing the material vulnerabilities of many ageing veterans, this latter song's video (Škoro 2014) directly opposed worthless and worthy masculinities by contrasting two identical men sitting to eat on either side of a park bench. The left-hand man is expensively dressed, with a chauffeur, fine dining, female companionship, media attention, a national medal (awarded by an actor resembling the then president Ivo Josipović), and enough money to shower banknotes at an accordion band (who, in a Croatian context, is likely to be playing Bosnian/Serbian NCFM). The right-hand man, wearing jeans and an old leather jacket, walks up with a cheap bicycle and eats a modest mortadella sandwich from his battered satchel, alone; while the rich man celebrates, the poor man sells his own medal to an ungrateful gangster but still readily gives the money (in a Christian act of charity) to a young beggar who needs it more. Even before the poor man has revealed his medal, the socio-economic clues of his age and dress position him as a typical representative of the disadvantaged veterans' generation in the 2010s. Though this phase of Škoro's music primarily depicts economic betrayal, the prior context of his own and others' music in the 2000s heightens the implication that – as the Croatian right continually argues – economic betrayal also betrays the legacy of the Homeland War. As Sokolic demonstrates, many Croats see the processes of neoliberal transition and transitional justice as inherently connected (Sokolić 2019: 141–164).

Retrospectively, these songs can now be seen as a prelude to Škoro's 2019 presidential campaign. As a candidate, then, after the election, as founder of a new party called the Homeland Movement, Škoro campaigned under the slogan "Let's give Croatia back to the people [vratimo Hrvatsku narodu] – now or never!" and his homepage called it a campaign "from the people, with the people, for the people." His program to expand the presidential mandate with powers to declare binding referendums, preside over parliamentary sessions, temporarily veto laws and reform the Constitutional Court aimed to promise voters the bypassing of a parliamentary political elite which, one infers, his target voters were thought to see as out of touch. His campaign website's biography mentioned his record label directorships (Croatia Records and Orfej in 1997–1999) as evidence of his business experience, and the success of his 2003 and 2005 lead singles (including "Svetinja"), though not "Sude mi" or "Reci, brate moj." His campaign's language nevertheless often indexed his wider repertoire of patriotic songs, potentially activating whatever personal associations and memories voters already attached to his music.[6] The fact that most voters encountered these either as Facebook statements or in posts on sympathetic online portals made these allusions and points of identification inherently part of the digital public sphere. The image of moral worth and veracity Škoro presented to voters rested, one can suggest, on his record of defending Croatian military heroes and proximity to the veterans' movement through popular music: this was not a military masculinity yet was still a militar*ized* one (see Eichler 2014: 84), being structured by the primacy of military concerns.

Appeals to the authenticity of everyday experience in Škoro's music hint at a challenge Croatian campaigners have always faced in advocating for public reckoning with wartime persecution of Serbs and the state's wartime entanglement with Bosnian Croat separatism: the fact that describing the war as defensive, legal, legitimate, or liberatory *is* justified in itself and in the personal everyday truth of how many Croatians experienced the war. It is the mobilization of such descriptions to silence critical investigation and discussion of acts which undercut them that interferes with open public examination of the recent past. This issue, already well-worn for transitional justice scholars in the 2000s (e.g., Lamont 2010; Pavlaković 2010), manifests today as a consequence of its embedding in popular culture during the 2000s. Reasserting "Sude mi" as part of his contemporary public persona in 2017, Škoro told the right-wing talk show *Bujica* he had dedicated the song to "all the Croatian generals," including Tihomir Blaškić, Ivan Čermak, Mladen Markač, and "all the generals from BiH who are in The Hague today," as

6 His very campaign slogan "now or never" dated back to "Mata" and its model narrative of recent Slavonian family history (Mata's father says it to him as the 1990s begin). During the campaign, while he was commenting on the arrest of a mountain rescue worker for an alleged nationally motivated assault on a Serb man, his statement began and ended with "truth is deep water" ("istina je voda duboka"), from the chorus of "Sude mi" (Škoro 2019).

well as Gotovina, and to "every Croat person who has been in the situation of defending his testimony of love for his country"; he also said he had lost a show on the RTL network as a result (Direktno.hr 2017). Early 2000s music is thus still politically significant today.

Remembering and defending Homeland War memory is moreover, in this repertoire, a masculine homosocial experience, even though women (in mixed-gender groups) are within Škoro's and Thompson's audiences as fans. A limited expansion of the gendering of Croatian veteranhood did occur in the mid-2010s with the novel visibility of certain female Homeland War veterans, such as the disabled veterans' protestor Nevenka Topalušić and the former military police officer Tanja Belobrajdić.[7] Both these women's biographies pointed to aspects of the war that were hard to reconcile with prevailing Croatian national memory, and neither was easily contained within the frame of "girlish innocence" (Žarkov 2007: 196) with which Croatian media represented female soldiers during the war. In the 2019–2020 Croatian presidential elections, Škoro's proximity to military and veteran masculinities was placed directly in competition with the persona of another candidate whose public persona had been defined by proximity to the military sphere, the incumbent president Kolinda Grabar-Kitarović – who had made a "militarized femininity" (Sjoberg 2007) part of her public persona, after winning her first term in 2015, by making frequent appearances in Croatian military uniform while visiting bases in Croatia and Afghanistan.

Grabar-Kitarović, as Croatia's first female president, was also Croatian forces' first female commander-in-chief; thus, her presidency was the first time state command over the Croatian military was not being personified by a man. The construction of her presidential persona traded on her proximity to military masculinity, bringing to mind the provocative question of Marysia Zalewski (2017: 201): "What does the concept of military masculinities look like when removed from the male body?" Grabar-Kitarović's Homeland War service had been in a civilian capacity as a foreign ministry official, so she had no firsthand military record of which to remind the public. She could, however, still claim authority through proximity to the military sphere through her time at NATO, when (only two years after Croatia's 2009 admittance) she served as assistant secretary-general for public diplomacy and became "the unofficial figurehead for NATO's engagement with [the] Women, Peace and Security [agenda]" (Wright et al. 2019: 32) as its Afghanistan mission implemented UN Security Council Resolution 1325.

7 Topalušić, a military nurse seriously wounded in Operation Una in September 1995 (an operation taking place *after* Oluja), died in October 2014 at a disabled veterans' protest camp outside the veterans' ministry in Zagreb (Boduszyński and Pavlaković 2019: 810). Belobrajdić, author of a 2015 novel about the war, sued three alternative media outlets in 2018–2019 for reporting on allegations about her wartime conduct (Vragolović 2020).

Her presidential persona's relationship to leadership and Croatian statehood fused this personal background with an implicit claim to be achieving and embodying the fulfilment of Franjo Tuđman's presidential dream, cut short by his death in December 1999. Her January 2015 victory speech, for instance, had revived Tuđman's language of national unity (calling for a dissolution of political divisions into one shared patriotic endeavor) and called on Croats, "[L]et us finish the path we began under the first Croatian president Dr Franjo Tuđman, let us bring Croatia into prosperity" (Grabar-Kitarović 2015) – an emotional peak interrupted by the crowd's chorus of the patriotic song "Zovi, samo zovi" ("Call, just call"), much like fans at a Croatian football match or waiting for a Thompson concert to start.

Grabar-Kitarović's public persona also, however, harnessed proximity to *veteran* masculinity, articulated – just as with HNS – through associating herself with late 1990s/early 2000s patriotic popular music. This included several occasions during her presidency when she was filmed singing along with "Lijepa li si"[8] – despite the implications of a Croatian president joining in lyrics containing a separatist term for part of a neighboring state (Klix.ba 2017; Index.hr 2018b). Even the tight associations Grabar-Kitarović created between herself and the men's national football team in 2018 by attending their World Cup matches can be seen, in this context, to go beyond their briefly sensational impact in world media.[9] The fusion of sport and Homeland War memory in Croatian public culture since the 1990s has created a master narrative for sport in the 2010s in which world-class feats by Croatian athletes reassert the interpretation that they could not have happened if not for victory in the Homeland War – since Croatia would not have its sovereignty and the athletes would not be representing Croatia. Both HNS and Grabar-Kitarović contributed to producing this narrative by aligning themselves with popular culture which mediated the Homeland War narrative through hegemonic and dominant veteran masculinity.

Grabar-Kitarović's performance of acceptance within and leadership of these conventionally masculine spaces represented a symbolic identification with the military masculinities of war commemoration and the militarized masculinity of Croatian team sport which, as of 2018, appeared tightly connected. During the 2019 presidential race, Škoro nevertheless outflanked her on the patriotic right. Even though Grabar-Kitarović beat him into the second round against Milanović, it was Škoro who ended the campaign with

8 For example, a military pilgrimage to Lourdes (Hina 2017), an Armed Forces Day ceremony where the Navy klapa (male voice choir) sang it (Milekić 2017), visiting the National Federation of Croat-Americans (Index.hr 2018), and after a national football match on the 2019 campaign trail (Dalmatinski portal 2019);

9 For example, the World Economic Forum produced a Twitter video with images of Grabar-Kitarović joining the players on the pitch after the final, hailing her "powerful lessons in leadership" (WEF 2018).

more political momentum and an agenda for the 2020 general elections, suggesting that her ability to embody a point of identification with the myth of the Homeland War was ultimately more fragile than his. Her last viral image on social media at the time of revising this chapter was joining other female Croatian public figures in raising a middle finger to Škoro following his contentious comments about abortion in June 2020 (Jutarnji.hr 2020). In July 2020, HDZ won the general elections, the center-left Restart Coalition came second, and Škoro's party came third with 16 seats.

Conclusion

Contemporary Croatian public culture is a milieu in which the civilian sporting masculinities of footballers such as Modrić and Lovren, the poetic and entrepreneurial masculinity of Škoro, and the militarized femininity of Grabar-Kitarović's presidential public persona have all been constructed in proximity to veteran masculinities, in whom the "myth of the Homeland War" has invested the most power to define the "truth" of the conflict. This has made them both dominant and hegemonic. Three months before the 2018 World Cup, when the roles of sport, Thompson, and Grabar-Kitarović in producing the contemporary myth of the Homeland War would be internationally publicized, the historian Ivo Goldstein was already connecting all three, in a critical column written after Grabar-Kitarović had invited Vladimir Putin on a state visit to Croatia without consulting the HDZ prime minister Andrej Plenković:

> KGK by and large reduces her public activities to banal nationalistic symbolism, supporting Croatian teams dressed in the national strip, and singing tribal [plemenskih] Thompson songs. On the military pilgrimage to Lourdes in France, she sang "Lijepa li si", which openly flatters the secessionist longings of Herzegovinan Croats with the line "Herceg-Bosno, srce ponosno". A humane [uluđenoj] and decent Croatia does not need a president who jumps on to the middle of the pitch after the handball team has won a match and who, singing, calls the integrity of a neighbouring state into question. Not to mention her defending the notorious Ustaša-nostalgic [ustašonostalgičara] Thompson in the name of free speech – too much is too much [kaj je preveč, preveč je].
>
> (Goldstein 2018)

Goldstein's linkage between Grabar-Kitarović's public persona, Thompson's music, and the politics of Croatian men's football (from which he distances himself and an imagined Zagreb progressive intelligentsia by making his pronouncement in Zagreb's kajkavian dialect) summarizes the convergence of politics, popular music, and sport that has infused the "myth of the Homeland War" with new affective tissue for members of the nation who were not even alive during the war. Yet the power to manipulate that convergence is unequally distributed, reflecting the hegemonic nature of veteran masculinities in legitimating unequal relationships between genders and among masculinities. Grabar-Kitarović could associate herself with the revisionist patriotism of early 2000s politicized veteran masculinities as late as November 2019, when she captioned a Facebook post of photos from collecting re-election signatures in Zadar "Neka vide da nas ima" (Grabar-Kitarović 2019). But as Škoro became her rival on the right, over-identifying herself with "Lijepa li si" had its risks, since Škoro had been among Thompson's guests on it; the organizer of one Grabar-Kitarović rally in Zagreb where it was played during a patriotic medley heard Škoro's line and appeared to cut the song short (Asipi 2019). The legitimacy Grabar-Kitarović, a female defense diplomat and politician, could gain through proximity to veteran masculinities was ultimately more conditional than what Škoro could gain as a civilian entertainer and businessman, suggesting that gender retains a structuring role in determining who can claim such proximity more credibly.

The sustenance of the "myth of the Homeland War" through celebrities whose public personas have been constructed in proximity to veteran masculinities supports Sokolić's suggestion that public distrust in "all sources of information" about war crimes and transitional justice is high, but "individuals who took part in the conflict" and "television images (e.g. of the shelling of Vukovar or Dubrovnik)" are trusted much more (Sokolić 2019: 19). The biographies and meta-narratives of Modrić, Lovren, Škoro, and Thompson come with a gendered authenticity that invites such trust, and the audiovisual technologies of popular music even enable war experience and war images to be combined in examples such as Thompson's "Uvijek vjerni tebi." Such continued mythologizations of the veteran occur even as the actual veterans' generation in young people's everyday lives is the age of older parents, contemplating their exit from the workforce in a system which, 25 years after "victory," can still not provide most of them a dignified retirement or offer most youth a prosperous future that does not involve working abroad. Within the confines of the "myth of the Homeland War," the only solution offered to young people is to regenerate the sentiments of the betrayal narrative anew.

The example of how new points of identification with veteran masculinities continue to be created in Croatia illustrates the challenges of dislodging militarized masculinities from their hegemonic place in post-conflict societies, as scholars of transitional justice and gender have frequently argued is necessary for societal understandings of the conflict to themselves transform (Theidon 2009). The field's focus on militarized and otherwise violent masculinities has, admittedly, left non-violent, non-militarized, and non-heterosexual masculinities, and even masculine vulnerability in general, deprioritized in much transitional justice scholarship (Myrttinen et al. 2017; Schulz 2020). The production of veteran masculinities in contemporary Croatian popular culture, including through routes aimed at youth, illustrates how the material vulnerabilities of ageing veterans and fathers, and of youth facing conditions of prolonged economic precarity, where milestones of maturity are difficult to realize, are subsumed into an idealized veteranhood. This keeps the dominant narrative of the Homeland War alive while closing down space for former combatants, and non-combatants, to interpret their service in ways that complicate it. Bound by the constraints of resources, space, and time, transitional justice processes in Croatia and other settings where conflict occurred a whole generation ago may find this an even greater task to tackle as postmemory goes on.

References

Asipi, E. (2019). *Pustili Škoru pa ga prekinuli: "ma to su tehničke poteškoće"*.Zagreb: 24 sata. Available at: https://www.24sata.hr/news/pustili-skoru-pa-ga-prekinuli-ma-to-su-tehnicke-poteskoce-666266. Accessed on: 28 January 2023.

Baker, C. (2019). Veteran Masculinities and Audiovisual Popular Music in Post-Conflict Croatia: A Feminist Aesthetic Approach to the Contested Everyday Peace. *Peacebuilding* 7(2): 226–242.

Bellamy, A. J. (2003). *The Formation of Croatian National Identity: A Centuries-Old Dream*? Manchester: Manchester University Press.

Berdak, O. (2013). Reintegrating Veterans in Bosnia and Herzegovina and Croatia: Citizenship and Gender Effects. *Women's Studies International Forum* 49: 48–56.

Boduszyński, M. P. and Vjeran Pavlaković (2019). Cultures of Victory and the Political Consequences of Foundational Legitimacy in Croatia and Kosovo. *Journal of Contemporary History* 54(4): 799–824.

Braniteljski.hr (2015). *Neka vide da nas ima*. Zagreb: Braniteljski.hr. Available at: https://braniteljski.hr/neka-vide-da-nas-ima/. Accessed on: 28 January 2023.

Brentin, D. (2013). 'A Lofty Battle for the Nation': The Social Roles of Sport in Tuđman's Croatia. *Sport in Society* 16(8): 993–1008.

Bulmer, S. and M. Eichler (2017). Unmaking Militarized Masculinity: Veterans and the Project of Military-to-Civilian Transition. *Critical Military Studies* 3(2): 161–181.

Ceribašić, N. (2000). Defining Women and Men in the Context of War: Images in Croatian Popular Music in the 1990s. In: Moisala, P. and Diamond, B. (eds.): *Music and Gender.* Urbana, IL: University of Illinois Press: 219–238.

Dalmatinski Portal (2019). Video: *Kolinda na islasku sa stadiona zapjevala "Lijepa li si"*. Dalmatinski Portal. Available at: https://dalmatinskiportal.hr/sport/video--kolinda-na-izlasku-sa-stadiona-zapjevala--lijepa-li-si-/52553. Accessed on: 28 January 2023.

Direktno.hr (2017). *Zbog potpore Gotovini i pjesme "Sude mi" na RTL-u su mi ukinuli emisiju*. Zagreb: Direktno.hr. Available at: https://direktno.hr/direkt/zbog-potpore-gotovini-i-pjesme-sude-mi-rtl-su-mi-ukinuli-emisiju-81973/. Accessed on: 28 January 2023.

Dnevno.hr (2018). *Zašto je Thompson uopće bio u autobusu s Vatrenima?: konačno smo doznali odgovor*. Zagreb: Dnevno.hr. Available at: https://www.dnevno.hr/sport/sp-rusija/zasto-je-thompson-uopce-bio-u-autobusu-s-vatrenima-konacno-smo-doznali-odgovor-1195124/. Accessed on: 28 January 2023.

Dolenec, D. (2018). A Soldier's State?: Veterans and the Welfare Regime in Croatia. *Anali Hrvatskog politikološkog društva* 14: 55–78.

Eichler, M. (2014). Militarized Masculinities in International Relations. *Brown Journal of World Affairs* 21(1): 81–93.

Feldman, L., I. Prica and R. Senjković (eds.) (1993). *Fear, Death and Resistance: An Ethnography of War: 1991–1992*. Zagreb: IEF.

Goldstein, I. (2018). *Ugrožava li predsjednica stabilnost političkog sustava?*. Zagreb: Globus. Available at: https://www.jutarnji.hr/globus/Globus-komentari/pise-ivo-goldstein-ugrozava-li-predsjednica-stabilnost-politickog-sustava/7191621/. Accessed on: 28 January 2023.

Grabar-Kitarović, K. (2015). Video: *Kolinda Grabar-Kitarović prva hrvatska predsjednica! Pobjednički govor*. YouTube. Available at: https://www.youtube.com/watch?v=ahFdAZl3hNE. Accessed on: 28 January 2023.

Grabar-Kitarovićm, K. (2019). *Neka vide da nas ima*. Facebook. Available at: https://www.facebook.com/KolindaGrabarKitarovic/posts/2542122995854644. Accessed on: 28 January 2023.

Hamber, B. (2016). There Is a Crack in Everything: Problematising Masculinities, Peacebuilding and Transitional Justice. *Human Rights Review* 17(1): 9–34.

Herceg, M. (2018). *Sjajna atmosfera u autobusu – Thompson: "Zagrlimo se pred svima, neka vide da nas ima . . ."*. Zagreb: Narod.hr. Available at: https://narod.hr/sport/foto-sjajna-atmosfera-autobusu-thompson-zagrlimo-se-pred-svima-neka-vide-da-nas. Accessed on: 28 January 2023.

Hina (2017). *Vesela atmosfera na hodočašću u Lourdesu*. Jutarnji list. Available at: https://www.jutarnji.hr/vijesti/hrvatska/video-vesela-atmosfera-na-hodocascu-u-lourdesu-pogledajte-kako-predsjednica-ministri-i-vojnici-pjevaju-lijepa-li-si/6099503/. Accessed on: 28 January 2023.

Hofman, A. (2020). Disobedient: Activist Choirs, Radical Amateurism, and the Politics of the Past after Yugoslavia. *Ethnomusicology* 64(1): 89–109.

Holiga, A. (2012). *Euro 2012: The Problem with Croatia's Nationalistic Fans Starts at the Top*. London: The Guardian. Available at: https://www.theguardian.com/football/blog/2012/jun/26/euro-2012-croatia-racism-uefa. Accessed on: 28 January 2023.

Index.hr (2014). *Prvi Osijek Pride pod sloganom: Osijek – nepokoreni grad; LGBTQ – nepokoreni građani*. Zagreb: Index.hr. Available at: https://www.index.hr/vijesti/clanak/Prvi-Osijek-Pride-pod-sloganom-Osijek---nepokoreni-grad;-LGBTIQ---nepokoreni-gradani/765519.aspx. Accessed on: 28 January 2023.

Index.hr (2018a). *Igrači objavili prve fotografije nakon pobjede: Ćorluka oduševio porukom, Lovren zapjevao Čavoglave*. Zagreb: Index.hr. Available at: https://www.index.hr/sport/clanak/igraci-objavili-prve-fotografije-nakon-pobjede-corluka-odusevio-porukom-lovren-zapjevao-cavoglave/2006206.aspx. Accessed on: 28 January 2023.

Index.hr (2018b). *Kolinda u Americi pjevala Thompsona*. Zagreb: Index.hr. Available at: https://www.index.hr/vijesti/clanak/video-kolinda-u-americi-pjevala-thompsona/2025827.aspx. Accessed on: 28 January 2023.

Ivić, S. (2005). Nikad ne bih prijavio Gotovinu. *Arena*, 2 June.

Jelača, D. (2016). *Dislocated Screen Memory: Narrating Trauma in Post-Yugoslav Cinema*. London: Palgrave Macmillan.

Jović, D. (2017). *Rat i mit: politika identiteta u suvremenoj Hrvatskoj*. Zagreb: Fraktura.

Jurić, T. (2017). Suvremeno iseljavanje Hrvata u Njemačku: karakteristike i motivi. *Migracijske i etničketeme* 33(3): 337–371.

Jutarnji.hr (2015). *Thompson zove na skup potpore braniteljima*. Zagreb: Jutarnji list. Available at: https://www.jutarnji.hr/vijesti/hrvatska/thompson-zove-na-skup-potpore-braniteljima-osokolile-se-vrazje-sile-i-fasistoidni-ljevicari/486031/. Accessed on: 28 January 2023.

Jutarnji.hr (2020). *Bivša predsjednica samo za Jutarnji: "Prošlo je vrijeme kad je žena čekala što će 'baja' reći"*.Zagreb: Jutarnji list. Available at: https://www.jutarnji.hr/vijesti/hrvatska/bivsa-predsjednica-samo-za-jutarnji-proslo-je-vrijeme-kad-je-zena-cekala-sto-ce-baja-reci-15003295. Accessed on: 28 January 2023.

Kardov, K. (2007). Remember Vukovar: Memory, Sense of Place, and the National Tradition in Croatia. In: Ramet, S. P. and Matić, D. (eds.): *Democratic Transition in Croatia: Value Transformation, Education and Media*. College Station, TX: Texas A&M University Press: 63–88.

Klix.ba (2017). *Predsjednica Hrvatske zapjevala Thompsonovu pjesmu u kojoj se veliča Herceg-Bosna*. Sarajevo: Klix.ba. Available at: https://www.klix.ba/vijesti/regija/predsjednica-hrvatske-zapjevala-thompsonovu-pjesmu-u-kojoj-se-velica-herceg-bosna/170521015. Accessed on: 28 January 2023.

Lamont, C. K. (2010). Defiance or Strategic Compliance?: The Post-Tuđman Croatian Democratic Union and the International Criminal Tribunal for the Former Yugoslavia. *Europe–Asia Studies* 62(10): 1683–1705.

Le Zbor (2015). Video: *Le Zbor – Banana LIVE – Lisinski 1.4.2015*. YouTube. Available at: https://youtu.be/wy6hzqxEb_0. Accessed on: 28 January 2023.

Lipovac, N. (2013). Foto: *Reykjavik u kockicama*. Zagreb: Jutarnji list. Available at: https://www.jutarnji.hr/sport/nogomet/foto-reykjavik-u-kockicama-navijaci-stizu-sa-svih-strana-sad-svedska-kanada-norveska. . ./920483/. Accessed on: 28 January 2023.

Ljubičić, S. (2017). *Ovo je Ranko Britvić, čovjek čija udruga okuplja branitelje i partizane*. Split: Slobodna Dalmacija. Available at: https://slobodnadalmacija.hr/vijesti/hrvatska/ovo-je-ranko-britvic-covjek-cija-udruga-okuplja-branitelje-i-partizane-zbog-sacice-galamdzija-ljudi-misle-da-su-braniteljske-udruge-desnicarska-banda-495023. Accessed on: 28 January 2023.

Mannergren Selimović, J. (2020). Gender Silences in Post-Conflict Societies: A Typology. *Peacebuilding* 8(1): 1–15.

Messerschmidt, J. W. and M. A. Messner (2018). Hegemonic, Nonhegemonic, and 'New' Masculinities. In: Messerschmidt, J. W., Yancey Martin, P., Messner, M. A. and Connell, R. (eds.): *Gender Reckonings: New Social Theory and Research*. New York: New York University Press: 35–56.

Milekić, S. (2017). *Croatian leaders sing praises for Herzeg Bosnia*. Belgrade: Balkan Insight, 30 May. Available at: https://balkaninsight.com/2017/05/30/croatian-leaders-sing-praises-for-herzeg-bosnia-05-30-2017/. Accessed on: 28 January 2023.

Millar, K. (2019). What Do We Do Now?: Examining Civilian Masculinity/ies in Contemporary Liberal Civil Military Relations. *Review of International Studies* 45(2): 239–259.

Myrttinen, H., L. Khattab and J. Naujoks (2017). Re-thinking Hegemonic Masculinities in Conflict Affected Contexts. *Critical Military Studies* 3(2): 103–119.

Pavlaković, V. (2010). Croatia, the International Criminal Tribunal for the Former Yugoslavia, and General Gotovina as a Political Symbol. *Europe–Asia Studies* 62(10): 1707–1740.

Pettan, S. (1998). Music, Politics and War in Croatia in the 1990s: An Introduction. In: Pettan, S. (ed.): *Music, Politics and War: Views from Croatia*. Zagreb: IEF: 9–28.

Schäuble, M. (2014). *Narrating Victimhood: Gender, Religion and the Making of Place in Post-War Croatia*. New York: Berghahn.

Schulz, P. (2020). Towards Inclusive Gender in Transitional Justice: Gaps, Blind-Spots and Opportunities. *Journal of Intervention and Statebuilding* 14(5): 691–710.

Senjković, R. (1996). Image of the Warrior. *Narodna umjetnost* 33(1): 41–57.

Senjković, R. (2002). *Lica društva, likovi države*. Zagreb: IEF.

Sjoberg, L. (2007). Agency, Militarized Femininity and Enemy Others: Observations from the War in Iraq. *International Feminist Journal of Politics* 9(1): 82–101.

Škoro, M. (2013). Video: *Miroslav Škoro & Marko Perković Thompson – Sude mi*. YouTube. Available at: https://www.youtube.com/watch?v=nUjsydvnTc8. Accessed on: 28 January 2023.

Škoro, M. (2014). Video: *Miroslav Škoro – Od kud ti pravo*. YouTube. Available at: https://www.youtube.com/watch?v=4pgchEmasRA. Accessed on: 28 January 2023.

Škoro, M. (2019). *Istina je voda duboka*. Facebook. Available at: https://www.facebook.com/MiroslavSkorooofficial/photos/a.1361864807214181/2452092994858018/?type=1&theater. Accessed on: 28 January 2023.

Sokolić, I. (2019). *International Courts and Mass Atrocity: Narratives of War and Justice in Croatia*. London: Palgrave Macmillan.

Theidon, K. (2009). Reconstructing Masculinities: The Disarmament, Demobilization and Reintegration of Former Combatants in Colombia. *Human Rights Quarterly* 31: 1–34.

Thompson (2012). Video: *Thompson – Uvijek vjerni tebi*. YouTube. Available at: https://www.youtube.com/watch?v=nxBY2NQ9QVc. Accessed on: 28 January 2023.

Thompson (2017). *Gospodin Bojan Glavašević nas je preko media zamolio da objasnimo prvi stih Thompsonove pjesme "Bojna Čavoglave"*. Facebook. Available at: https://www.facebook.com/marko.perkovic.thompson/posts/1397690603620755:0. Accessed on: 28 January 2023.

Tportal (2016). *HNS potvrdio: Thompsonov hit himna Hrvatske na Euru*. Zagreb: Tportal.hr. Available at: https://www.tportal.hr/sport/clanak/hns-potvrdio-thompsonov-hit-himna-hrvatske-na-euru-20160127. Accessed on: 28 January 2023.

Vlašić, B., A. Plišić and M. Goreta (2006). *Zaklada za istinu o Gotovini želi prikupiti 20 milijuna dolara*. Zagreb: Jutarnji list. Available at: https://www.jutarnji.hr/arhiva/zaklada-za-istinu-o-gotovini-zeli-prikupiti-20-milijuna-dolara/3377873/. Accessed on: 28 January 2023.

Vragolović, A. (2020). *Tužba: sredstvo ušutkivanja neprofitnih medija (dio II)*. Zagreb: Maz.hr. Available at: http://www.maz.hr/2020/03/29/tuzba-sredstvo-usutkivanja-neprofitnih-medija-dio-ii/. Accessed on: 28 January 2023.

WEF (2018). Different Goals. Read More. *Twitter*, 17 July. Available at: https://twitter.com/wef/status/1019197076444516352. Accessed on: 28 January 2023.

Wright, K. A. M., M. Hurley and J. I. G. Ruiz (2019). *NATO, Gender and the Military: Women Organizing from Within*. London and New York: Routledge.

Zalewski, M. (2017). What's the Problem with the Concept of Military Masculinities? *Critical Military Studies* 3(2): 200–205.

Žarkov, D. (2007). *The Body of War: Media, Ethnicity and Gender in the Break-Up of Yugoslavia*. Durham, NC: Duke University Press.

Chapter 11

Possibilities and Improbabilities

Reflections on "Queering" Transitional Justice in Colombia and Lebanon/Syria

Henri Myrttinen, Laura Camila Barrios Sabogal, and Charbel Maydaa

Introduction

> "I can't explain the amount of fear that I have when it comes to going anywhere and having the visible expression of a woman; there is not a single chance that I will not be harassed or attacked."[1]

The previous quote from a Syrian trans woman, interviewed in Lebanon after she had fled the Syrian Civil War, not only encapsulates the everyday nature of violence and discrimination against persons of diverse sexual orientations, gender identities and expressions, and sex characteristics (SOGIESC) in peacetime as in war; it also points to the challenges of addressing these harms through transitional justice (TJ) processes, not only because of societal and political resistance to diverse SOGIESC inclusion, but also because the continuums of violence and harm transcend the boundaries usually set for these processes.

As discussed in previous chapters of this book (see "Introduction"; Hamber et al.; Fobear, this volume), TJ processes have increasingly taken gender perspectives into account to varying degrees; "gender mainstreaming" has often only meant a narrow focus on women and, in particular, on acts of sexual and gender-based violence (SGBV) against women and girls only, rather than gendered harms against women and girls, as well as others, more broadly (see, for example, Buckley-Zistel and Zolkos 2012; Simic 2016). The experiences and concerns of persons of diverse SOGIESC in times of conflict and under repressive regimes have, to date, only seldom been taken into account, as emphasized by Fobear in this volume (also see Fobear 2014).[2]

1 KII, Beirut, April 2022.

2 We use the term *SOGIESC* rather than *LGBTIQ+* (lesbian, gay, bisexual, trans, intersex, queer, and other gender identities) as in our experience in both Colombia and Lebanon, the latter acronym was not accepted by all interviewees, as they felt that it did not represent their identities and expressions. See also Daigle and Myrttinen (2018: 105–106) and Chapter 1 for a further discussion.

DOI: 10.4324/9781003519522-14

This, however, has started to shift, both in terms of transitional justice (see Fobear, this volume) and the field of gender, peace, and security more generally (Hagen et al. 2021; Verhelst López 2018).

In this chapter, we seek to interrogate what transitional justice processes might mean for persons of diverse SOGIESC, following Fobear's call in this volume (Chapter 3). We focus here on three contextual settings that have arguably been central to the increased interest in broadening research and policy on diverse SOGIESC in relation to peace and security: Colombia and Lebanon/Syria. Although the situations in Lebanon and Syria are interlinked, they will be examined separately, as the social and political processes in the two locations are also quite divergent. While Colombia has an ongoing, comprehensive transitional justice process in which diverse SOGIESC experiences are explicitly taken into account (see Chapters 13, 14), there has been a very limited transitional justice process in Lebanon which has been completely gender-blind, and Syria has had no transitional justice processes. Using these three cases, we summarize what has and has not been possible to date and also zoom out, so to say, from the mechanisms and processes to raise more fundamental questions about what an inclusion of diverse SOGIESC in TJ possibly can and most likely cannot do. We also stress the need for thinking more broadly about what "justice" might mean beyond formal TJ processes, such as through the work of grassroots and informal support networks for survivors.

While the focus of the chapter was initially only on Lebanon and Syria due to two of the authors' ongoing research in these two countries, we decided during the data collection stage to expand this to Colombia as well. The reason for adding a very different context was, in a sense, driven by hope. While the prospects of either any kind of transitional justice or improved SOGIESC rights in Syria at the time of writing are more or less nil, and extremely slim in Lebanon,[3] we wanted to contrast these with a case study that did offer at least a glimmer of hope of what might be possible. While the situation in Colombia and its transitional process have been far from perfect (see Oettler, this volume), it is nonetheless vastly more than what would be currently possible in Lebanon, let alone Syria.

This chapter is based on fieldwork conducted over various intervals by the authors between September 2019 and October 2022 in four locations: Colombia, Lebanon, Syria, and Turkey. In addition to desktop research, it involved 16 interviews and six focus group discussions. In Colombia, these were mainly with representatives of diverse SOGIESC rights organizations engaged with

3 Given the degree to which the parties – and individuals – responsible for abuses and atrocities in the Lebanese Civil War remain entrenched in the political system, diverse SOGIESC rights have, to a very limited degree, been able to advance a tiny bit further than the moribund transitional justice process.

the TJ process. These interviews were conducted prior to the launching of the final report of the Truth Commission in 2022. In Syria, the interviews were with gay men, lesbian, and trans women, and in Lebanon and Turkey with Syrian, Lebanese, and other persons of diverse SOGIESC, including both refugees and members of the "host community." In addition to this, interviews were conducted with representatives of international organizations working with refugees in Lebanon and Turkey. The research in Lebanon, Syria, and Turkey was part of the *Masculinities and Sexualities research stream* of the UKRI GCRF-funded *Gender, Justice and Security Hub* (AH/S004025/1) hosted by the LSE Women, Peace, and Security Centre, as well as further research on the experiences of Iranian, Lebanese, and Syrian lesbian, bisexual and trans women funded by the Sexual Violence Research Initiative.[4]

We first give an overview of the impacts of armed conflicts on persons of diverse SOGIESC, followed by a discussion of integrating diverse SOGIESC perspectives into transitional justice processes. This is followed by an in-depth examination of the cases of Colombia, Lebanon, and Syria and a discussion of what these cases can tell us about the possibilities and challenges of "queering" transitional justice.[5]

Persons of Diverse SOGIESC in Conflict and Transition

While the body of literature on gender and conflict – and, in particular, the experiences of women and girls and impacts of violent conflict on them – has grown enormously over the past two decades, research on diverse SOGIESC is comparatively new and relatively limited (Hagen et al. 2021). The Colombian and Syrian Civil Wars have been an exception to an extent, as different NGOs and academics have highlighted SOCIESC dimensions as well, far more than in other conflicts.

As José Fernando Serrano-Amaya (2018: 41–42) points out, there can be a range of motivating factors that shape armed actors' violent targeting of persons of diverse SOGIESC, such as shaming, humiliation, and dehumanization; reinforcing control of territory; achieving support of the wider community; "re-education"; maximization of resources through extortion; and impeding social mobilization in occupied areas. Some of the violence is, however, also non-strategic and motivated by individual perpetrators' desires and impulses, be they for subjugating others, financial gain, out of bigotry and hatred, or other reasons. However, unlike many civilians affected by armed

4 See Maydaa et al. (2020) and Erdem et al. (2024) for findings.

5 We use "queering" here mostly in a narrow sense of broadening the scope of transitional justice to also examine diverse SOGIESC, rather than in a broader sense of disrupting heteronormativity or of using approaches that disrupt normative frameworks. See also "Introduction" and Moussawi 2020 for a discussion of queering as a concept.

conflict, persons of diverse SOGIESC also often face constant discrimination and threats of violence from other civilians as well, as we explore in the next section on continuums of violence.[6]

The forms of discrimination as well as open or structural violence also often come in layers. For example, a lesbian Syrian refugee woman may face discrimination not only because of her sexual orientation but also for being a woman in a patriarchal society, for being a refugee, for being Syrian (given Lebanon's complicated historical relationship), possibly for being from a lower-income bracket, possibly for her religious background, on top of which comes homophobia. It should, however, also be noted here that these gendered vulnerabilities are not innate to the person and their SOGIESC but constructed, or as Lewis Turner (2016) puts it:

> Ultimately, a person is not vulnerable because they are a man or a woman [or of another gender identity], but because of what being a man or a woman [or of another gender identity] means in particular situations. A person is made vulnerable by the circumstances, challenges and threats they face.

A further particular risk factor is often that of visibility, as also discussed further later: the degree to which others can "read" the person as being "visibly" non-heterosexual, non-gender-conforming, or non-cisgender (even if this does not correspond to their SOGIESC) often acts as a major driver or triggering factor of discrimination, violence, and abuse (Daigle and Myrttinen 2018; Moussawi 2020).

Continuums and Spectrums of Violence

As the wide body of feminist research on gender, conflict, and displacement has shown, the massive social, economic, and political disruptions caused by conflict and displacement both create new opportunities for different gender roles to emerge as well as to exacerbate pre-existing gender power imbalances and vulnerabilities. Feminist researchers have also long argued that dichotomies of public vs. private and peace vs. war are much less distinct for those in positions that are subjugated based on gender, race, or other factors. This is the case for persons of diverse SOGIESC, who can face different spectrums or "continuums of violence,"[7] exploitation, abuse, and discrimination

6 Depending on the context, other civilians may also face discrimination from other civilians based on their gender, ethno-religious background, disability, social class, or other factors (e.g., widowed or divorced women, substance abusers, or commercial sex workers).

7 The term *continuum of violence* has been used by feminist researchers Elizabeth Kelly (1988) and, later, Cynthia Cockburn (2004) to disrupt common dichotomies of war/peace and public/private by highlighting how women face various forms of violence prior, during, and after violent conflict and in both public and private spaces.

in multiple ways, including ones not necessarily affecting other civilians (see Daigle and Myrttinen 2018; Serrano-Amaya 2018). For persons of diverse SOGIESC, we have identified the following continuums or spectrums, which intersect and build on each other:

- A spectrum of **perpetrators** of discrimination, abuse, and violence, including family members, other civilians, security forces, militias, and extremist groups – but also, at times, from other persons of diverse SOGIESC. These perpetrators may come from across the political and ideological spectrum, as from religious extremists of all major religions, various secular right-wing and left-wing groups, as well as apolitical persons and groups.
- **Temporally**, in pre-conflict times, during and throughout the escalation of armed conflict, and in its aftermath.
- **Spatially**, in private spaces, in semi-private spaces, in spaces hidden from public view (such as places of detention), and in public.
- **Geographically**, in rural areas, in urban areas, throughout their flight from conflict zones, in refugee camps, and in areas of re-settlement.
- Over a spectrum of various **forms of abuse**, including everyday, mundane micro-aggressions, looks, and verbal abuse; systemic discrimination (including the criminalization of one's sexuality and/or gender identity); blackmail and extortion; physical and sexual violence, including excessive and spectacular violence staged as a public spectacle.
- Involving a range of **different vectors of discrimination** and hatred, including homophobia, biphobia, transphobia, misogyny, racism, xenophobia, Islamophobia, and class-based discrimination (e.g., for "looking too poor").
- Furthermore, the risk of discrimination, abuse, and violence is **intersectional**, and various forms of oppression can compound each other.

These continuums and spectrums echo in many ways the experiences of other civilians, especially women and girls, who also face potential violences and discrimination across spatio-temporal continuums and from a range of civilian and military actors, as identified in feminist literature on continuums of violence (Cockburn 2004; Kelly 1988). However, based on our findings, the risks and frequency can increase dramatically the more a person is identified by others as being non-heterosexual or non-cisgender.

The degrees to which persons of diverse SOGIESC are exposed to and at risk from these continuums and spectrums of violence are not distributed evenly: those who are also otherwise potentially marginalized due to their socio-economic position, their lack of support networks, or are visible to others as "non-conforming," are most likely to be also the most vulnerable.

The variety of violences and actors further presents a major challenge to "queering" transitional justice, quite apart from having to overcome institutional reluctance to address diverse SOGEISC issues in these processes in the first place. While there are clearly a range of systematic violences occurring, where should a transitional justice process draw a line, spatially, temporally, in terms of forms and assumed severity[8] of violence addressed, in holding not only states and armed actors but also civilians accountable? To what degree can a transitional justice process or instrument really address deep-seated social norms? We explore these questions in the following sections.

What Is Transitional Justice from a Diverse SOGIESC Perspective?

As argued by Fobear's chapter in this volume, to date, only a handful of transitional justice processes have taken diverse SOGIESC experiences and perspectives into account in any way (Bueno-Hansen 2017; Fobear 2014; Verhelst López 2018). These are South Africa (1995–2002), Peru (2001–2003 – see Comisión de la Verdad y Reconciliación 2003), Paraguay (2004–2008), Ecuador (2008–2009), Brazil (2012–2014), and the Colombian *Sistema Integral de Verdad, Justicia, Reparación y no Repetición* (SIVJRNR – Comprehensive System of Truth, Justice, Reparation, and Non-Repetition, 2017–present). Of these, only the Brazilian and Colombian processes have been explicit in taking on diverse SOGIESC perspectives in their work, and the others have only done so cursorily (Bueno-Hansen 2017; Fobear 2014; Muddell 2007; Verhelst López 2018). The Colombian process has thus far gone the furthest, thanks especially to the groundbreaking work by civil society and the *Centro Nacional de Memoria Histórica* (CNMH) (Oettler 2019), discussed further later, which has also included examining the structural, social, and historical roots of anti-LGBTIQ+ violence and discrimination. It is for these reasons that Colombia as a case study is reflected in this chapter and features so prominently throughout this volume at large.

Transitional justice processes usually cover all or some of the following four areas: truth-seeking or truth-telling, criminal justice and/or prosecutions, reparations to victims/survivors,[9] as well as longer-term institutional or governance reform and societal change (e.g., Bueno-Hansen 2017; Buckley-Zistel and Zolkos 2012; Fobear 2014). The aim of these processes is to help both individuals and communities who have been wronged, as well as the transitioning society itself, to *heal* from the wounds of the past and ensure that past wrongs are not repeated. According to Kimberly Theidon, one explicit goal of a transitional justice process is "the writing of new national narratives that are more inclusive of groups that are historically marginalized within the nation-state" (2006: 457). Furthermore, as pointed out by Martha Minow (1998: 60), "the most distinctive element of truth commissions, in

8 This is also difficult to establish, given the cumulative impacts of seemingly "little violences."

9 We use both the terms *victims* and *survivors* here, given differing wishes of those affected by violence in different contexts as to which term they prefer.

comparison with prosecution, is the focus on victims, including forgotten victims in forgotten places."

As Katherine Fobear points out (2014: 53), the integration of diverse SOGIESC experiences in transitional justice processes, and there the recognition and protection of their rights, can thus be

> one step towards dismantling hegemonic norms of patriarchy, racial hierarchy, inequality, sexism, and heterosexism whether brought on by colonization, state insecurity, or civil conflict. . . . Allowing sexual and gender minorities the protection and freedom to speak to past violence and discrimination can also be the next step for breaking down the structural and symbolic barriers that limit access by sexual and gender minorities to living a safe and secure life in the present.

Furthermore, the work of transitional justice processes can show how violence and discrimination against particular groups of people can be systematic and structural rather than random and individualized, allowing for an "understanding of the causes and underlying mechanisms that allow particular patterns of abuse to occur," and for an examination of the "larger social, religious, economic, political, and national ideologies from which these types of violences stem," thus constituting "one step towards dismantling hegemonic norms of patriarchy, racial hierarchy, inequality, sexism, and heterosexism whether brought on by colonization, state insecurity, or civil conflict" (Fobear 2014: 53–54).

As the Colombian CNMH (2015: 438) states, "the recognition of full citizenship of these [diverse SOGIESC] victims requires the elimination of heteronormative representations and imaginaries that legitimate violence against women and people that do not adhere to gender and sexual norms."

Therefore, at least theoretically, transitional justice processes offer the potential for addressing the multiple wrongs faced by persons of diverse SOGIESC in armed conflicts and at the hands of repressive regimes. However, as Pascha Bueno-Hansen (2017) and Katherine Fobear (2014) caution, previous experiences of integrating gender into transitional justice as well as broader experiences of trying to bring in diverse SOGIESC perspectives into mainstream political discourses point to a range of potential risks in this.

In examining the integration of diverse SOIGESC perspectives into Latin American transitional justice processes, Pascha Bueno-Hansen (2017: 3, emphasis added) highlights the following three potential pitfalls:

> The **first pitfall** comes to light through the lessons learned from two decades of headway around women's rights and recognition of gender-based violence, including the homogenization of the victim subject, the 'add-on' approach to gender analysis and the reduction of gender to women. Inclusive conceptions of citizenship and reparations offer pathways to counteract this pitfall.

The **second pitfall** surfaces by placing the study of Latin American gender and sexual minority experiences in a global context. Western notions of sexuality and gender have become the default metric of modernity. Dominant frameworks utilized to comprehend LGBTI struggles globally are riddled with false dichotomies, such as modern LGBTI-friendly countries versus uncivilized homo- and transphobic countries. A call for attention to local versions of gender and sexual diversity guards against this pitfall.

The **third pitfall** presents itself in relation to the limited conception of temporality within transitional justice. Given the temporally bounded nature of transitional justice and the short-term mandate of transitional justice mechanisms, scholars and practitioners struggle with the vexing problem of accounting for structural and historic violence and ongoing impunity.

A further drawback of transitional justice processes, as highlighted by Hamber et al. in this volume (Chapter 2), is the limited focus on direct violence and, in terms of "integrating gender in transitional justice," almost exclusively on men's sexualized violence against women. This narrow focus invisibilizes both the structural factors which exacerbate violent masculinities as well as the systematic discrimination and non-physical forms of violence and abuse faced by those who are not part of the dominant group, be it ethnic minorities, women, persons of diverse SOGIESC, and others. Transitional justice processes' focus on exceptional and egregious acts of direct violence also leaves little space for the less-spectacular, everyday, constant, and systematic discrimination and violence. The requirements of some transitional justice processes of establishing that patterns of violence were widespread and systematic can also act as a hurdle to prosecutions if there are not enough documented violations, as has happened in Colombia.

Furthermore, in their current set-up, transitional justice processes are often ill-equipped to deal with multiple and/or fluid identity categories. Would, for example, violence against a secular, left-wing Kurdish lesbian woman in Syria be classified as violence against her based on her gender, her sexual orientation, her political orientation, her ethnic background, her perceived lack of religiosity, and/or as part of a geographical pattern of abuse? And how much agency would she, as a victim/survivor, have as to how the transitional justice process decides to frame her story? Persons of diverse SOGIESC may not want that to be the primary identity, be it because of the risks entailed of coming out or because they see other aspects of their identities as more important and/or regard SOGIESC more as a practice than an identity (see also Moussawi 2020 on contestations of the centrality of sexual/gender identity in the Lebanese context).

What Is Possible (If Difficult): "Queering" Transitional Justice in Colombia

As discussed in Oettler's (Chapter 7) and Serrano-Amya's (Chapter 11) contributions, the Colombian conflict is perhaps the best-documented case study in terms of impacts of armed violence on persons of diverse SOGIESC.

As discussed in greater detail in Chapter 14 in this volume, the integration of diverse SOGIESC perspectives into debates about transitional justice in Colombia dates back to the early 2000s. The 2011 Victims' and Land Restitution Law was an important step in securing the inclusion of SOGIESC perspectives as being relevant to transitional justice processes. The law provided for the establishment of the CNMH and the Victims' Unit (*Unidad de Atención y Reparación de Víctimas*, UARIV), with the latter being the first Colombian state institution to include an LGBTI category in its victim registry (Bueno-Hansen 2017). Under the law's reparations programs, 1,321 individuals of diverse SOGIESC were awarded monetary reparations (Colombia Diversa 2020). In 2016 and 2018, two LGBT groups – *Mesa LGBT de la Comuna 8 de Medellín* and *Colectivo Crisálida* – were recognized respectively as collective reparation subjects. This was a noteworthy achievement, as Colombia became the first country to acknowledge SOGIESC-based collective harms (Colombia Diversa 2020). However, it was the signing of a peace agreement between the Colombian government and the FARC–EP in 2016 that was arguably a more significant landmark. It included, as a historical first, provisions on SOGIESC rights (see Chapter 14). However, the successful mobilization of homo-, lesbo-, trans-, and biphobia by conservative opponents of the deal, ultimately seeing it defeated by national plebiscite that same year, also shows the political power of anti-LGBTIQ attitudes and the limits of societal openness on these issues (Krystalli and Theidon 2016).

According to the Colombian SOGIESC rights activists interviewed, the revised final agreement did significantly not weaken the provisions regarding gender (see Chapter 13); rather, the revised peace agreement helped activists to pressure for the inclusion of these perspectives into the SIVJRNR institutions and to promote their accountability.[10] This legal recognition has protected the work of these institutions from anti-gender groups opposed to the inclusion of SOGIESC perspectives in the transitional justice mechanisms. All three institutions of the SIVJRNR process have created working groups in charge of ensuring diverse SOGIESC participation,[11] and all three institutions have also hired gender-sensitive officials (see Chapter 12).

Nonetheless, the process of integrating diverse SOGIESC perspectives into the transitional justice process has been hard and complex, both due to external and internal dynamics. Externally, conservative groups have continued their opposition to diverse SOGIESC inclusion in the implementation of the Peace Agreement. Targeted violence by armed actors and social stigma against persons

10 Interviews, Colombian SOGIESC rights groups, October 2020.

11 These are the Truth Commission (Comisión para el Esclarecimiento de la Verdad, la Convivencia y la No repetición – CEV), the Special Jurisdiction for Peace (Jurisdicción Especial para la Paz – JEP), and the Missing Persons Unit (Unidad de Búsqueda de Personas dadas por Desaparecidas – UBPD).

of diverse SOGIESC have kept survivors from coming forward. Lastly, the coronavirus pandemic and attendant restrictions have hampered involvement of survivors in the SIVJRNR process as well as the work of diverse SOGIESC rights organizations in documenting past violence (Colombia Diversa 2020).

There are also internal challenges within the SIVJRNR institutions. The need to establish that patterns of violence are widespread and systematic has been an obstacle in at least one case in which not enough LGBTIQ+ victims have come forward and been verified as victims. Other obstacles identified by SOGIESC rights organizations included the limited expertise on SOGIESC concerns, internal disconnections, and information gaps on homo-, lesbo-, bi-, and transphobic violence during the conflict.[12]

The various institutions also face particular challenges: the CEV has a mandate that ends 2022, but at the time of writing (mid 2022), there is still no clarity on the inclusion of diverse SOGIESC perspective into its final report, be it as either a stand-alone chapter or as a cross-cutting topic.[13] The temporal, budgetary, and technical barriers also limit its work, in particular achieving its ambitious internal target for diverse SOGIESC victim testimonials. Furthermore, the CEV has adopted a restrictive definition of conflict-related sexual violence (CRSV), which risks leaving out victims/survivors of opportunistic sexual violence, leaving these cases to the ordinary justice system, where levels of impunity are very high.[14]

JEP has sought to prioritize diverse SOGIESC cases and has brought in two cases, but there are still many challenges to this tribunal. Like the CEV, JEP has adopted a restrictive definition of CRSV, in contradiction of its own Gender Commission's guidelines and Constitutional Court jurisdiction. JEP has organized events across the country to encourage diverse SOGIESC victims/survivors to come forward, but according to rights groups, these calls often fail to consider the political, security, and judicial risks faced by survivors. Furthermore, in order to access JEP's jurisdiction, individuals often require the assistance of a SOGIESC rights organizations, as there are many legal barriers to the direct participation of survivors. These events can also create unrealistic expectations of victims'/survivors' prospects for justice.[15] The UBPD chose to leave reporting presumed disappeared persons up to their families (consanguineous or chosen), which runs the risk of missing or disappeared persons of diverse SOGIESC not being reported if they had been forced to run away from their families due to discrimination, had not been in contact with their families due to their rejection, or families are ashamed of reporting them.[16]

12 Interviews, Colombian SOGIESC rights groups, October 2020.
13 Interviews, Colombian SOGIESC rights groups, October 2020.
14 Interviews, Colombian SOGIESC rights groups, October 2020.
15 Interviews, Colombian SOGIESC rights groups, October 2020.
16 Interviews, Colombian SOGIESC rights groups, October 2020.

The Colombian case thus highlights the multiple ways in which transitional justice processes can, in practice, if there is a political will, start integrating diverse SOGIESC perspectives across the wide spectrum of its activities. However, it also highlights the multiple challenges and barriers that this integration faces, and this is merely at the very first stages of the justice processes, where information is being collected and analyzed. Justice for crimes past, let alone more fundamental transformations of gendered societal power dynamics, thus still remains a long way off.

What Is Improbable: Queer (Or Any Kind Of) Transitional Justice in Lebanon/Syria

While the Colombian transitional justice process is by no means perfect, it presents a far more comprehensive and multifaceted TJ machinery and process, and one where much more is possible in terms of an examination of gender than what is in existence or on the horizon in Lebanon, let alone in Syria. In Lebanon, there have been very limited but wholly gender-blind steps toward transitional justice, while in Syria the decades of repression and over a decade of war continue, with little hope of peace. In both countries, persons of diverse SOGIESC face legal discrimination, abuse, and physical violence.[17] Unlike in Colombia, where both civil society and state actors have embraced, at least to a degree, both diverse SOGIESC rights and transitional justice processes, this is not the case for state actors in Lebanon and Syria, and only partially the case for civil society actors.

Lebanon's Unaccounted-For Past

Since its independence, Lebanon has been engulfed in numerous armed conflicts, either directly or indirectly affected by them, and political violence has been a constant. The main armed conflict was the 1975–1990 Lebanese Civil War, in which over 100,000 civilians were killed and approximately 17,000 disappeared. Yet as stated by the International Center for Transitional Justice, "[n]o serious measures have ever been implemented to address the violations committed during the war. No one has ever been prosecuted for these abuses, in large part due to a comprehensive amnesty law passed in 1991" (ICTJ 2020). There has also been no judicial follow-up to the 2006 Lebanon War with Israel or crimes committed during the decades-long occupation of parts of Lebanon by Israel and Syria. The degree of violence against persons of diverse SOGIESC in any of the political and armed violence in Lebanon

17 This includes French mandate–era legislation in both countries outlawing "unnatural sexual acts," though the laws have been interpreted more liberally in Lebanon in recent years and the degree of its use in Syria is unclear (Maydaa et al. 2020; Human Rights Watch 2020).

has not been researched or documented, and even CRSV has not been systematically researched or documented. Lebanon is also one of the main host countries for Syrian refugees, including persons of diverse SOGIESC, and is, in many ways, directly and indirectly affected by the Civil War, which is why we cover the two cases partially together here.

The only act of political violence in Lebanon which has had judicial consequences was the 14 February 2005 assassination of then prime minister Rafiq Hariri, which led to the establishment of the Special Tribunal for Lebanon (STL) in 2007. Its mandate is, however, limited only to the assassination and directly related political violence, and no gender perspectives have been taken into account in its work. The only other major development in Lebanon was the passage of Law 105 on the Missing and Forcibly Disappeared Persons in November 2018, which, in June 2020, led to the government appointing the members of National Commission for the Missing and Forcibly Disappeared (ICTJ 2020). Neither the law nor the commission has any mandate to integrate diverse SOGIESC perspectives.

While Lebanon, and in particular Beirut, has regionally often been seen as one of the more diverse SOGIESC-friendly societies in the region, discrimination and abuse are nonetheless still common and widespread (Helem 2017). Although court rulings have established that the colonial-era Article 534 criminalizing "unnatural" sexual acts cannot be used against persons of diverse SOGIESC and that the Internal Security Forces (ISF) can no longer conduct anal examinations on suspected homosexual men, the article itself remains in place, and homo-, lesbo-, bi-, and transphobic discrimination, abuse, and harassment by the ISF and other officials are widespread. Acceptance of diverse SOGIESC varies, and while there are diverse SOGIESC-friendly spaces, families, and communities, social ostracization as well as verbal and physical abuse are also common. The degree of freedom in terms of sexual orientation and gender expression also varies with wealth, social connections, and other forms of social capital (e.g., in terms of style, fashion, and speech) and visibility and also differs for lesbian and bi women, for gay and bi men, and for trans men and women (Moussawi 2020). Lebanon has, for years, been a destination not only for diverse SOGIESC refugees from conflict-affected countries and repressive regimes in the region but also for other LGBTIQ+ migrants. Diverse SOGIESC refugees often face multiple forms of gender-based and xenophobic stigmatization and discrimination, as well as abuse, extortion, and violence, even from within the Lebanese LGBTIQ+ community (Heartland Alliance 2014; Helem 2017; Maydaa et al. 2020; Saleh and Qubaia 2015).

The Syrian Civil War

The outbreak of the Syrian uprising and subsequent civil war impacted persons of diverse SOGIESC differently in different parts of the country, though on the whole restricting what little freedoms of gender expression and diverse SOGIESC-friendly spaces existed prior to the war. Fadi Saleh (2020) highlights that in the initial stages of the uprising, homophobic verbal assaults and taunts by the government against opposition demonstrators did not lead to homophobic violence. However, upon taking up arms and controlling territory, various armed opposition groups – including the Free Syrian Army, Jabhat al-Nusra, and Daesh/Islamic State – started using violence against persons of diverse SOGIESC (HRC 2018; Human Rights Watch 2020; Kıvılcım 2017; Maydaa et al. 2020; Myrttinen et al. 2017). The policing of gender norms and violence committed by the Islamic State in Syria and Iraq has been best documented and allegedly included, making public spectacles (including internet distributions) of its executions of suspected homosexuals (Human Rights Watch 2015, 2020). The one opposition group which has taken a more progressive stance toward diverse SOGIESC is the Kurdish *Partiya Yekîtiya Demokrat* (PYD), where its forces have allegedly included an openly pro-LGBTIQ+ unit of foreigner volunteer fighters (Ghazzawi 2017).

As documented by human rights organizations and UN agencies (Human Rights Watch 2020; UNHCR 2017) and the UN Commission of Inquiry on Syria (HRC 2018), CRSV has been used against Syrians of all gender identities in house raids, checkpoints, and detention centers as a widespread and systematic abuse by state and non-state armed groups, including by pro-government militias. According to our interviews and Human Rights Watch, "although men and boys are stopped at checkpoints regardless of their sexual orientation and gender identity, gay and bisexual men and transgender individuals were often sexually and verbally harassed and sexually abused on the basis that they were 'soft looking'" (2020: 38). In our interviews with diverse SOGIESC Syrians, a further recurring theme was the risk of violence and death either directly at the hands of (extended) family members or indirectly by being reported to militias by community and family members, as well as forced heterosexual marriage, especially for women of diverse SOGIESC (Erdem et al. 2024; Maydaa et al. 2020). Sexual assault and abuse of suspected gay men have also been documented as occurring within the Syrian armed forces (Human Rights Watch 2020), and possibly in other armed groups as well.

There is currently no transitional justice mechanism in place in Syria, although first cases have been filed against Syria with the International Criminal Court (Killingsworth 2019) as well as in human rights cases before regional courts in Germany, such as the *al-Khatib* trial. The first cases before the ICC focus on forced displacement, however, and political opposition to diverse SOGIESC has meant that the Rome Statute of the ICC is ambivalent on issues of non-binary gender identity and silent on sexual orientation. While international and state-level transitional justice processes for Syria and Lebanon have either advanced at a glacial speed or not at all, some civil society groups and NGOs have been pushing for community-level reconciliation processes, including a Syrian Charter for Truth and Justice.[18] As far as we can tell, these efforts have not integrated a diverse SOGIESC perspective, at least not openly, though issues such as sexual violence are raised (Woods et al. 2017).

The prospects for achieving justice for diverse SOGIESC persons in Lebanon and Syria thus remain very slim, indeed, both in terms of having any kind of transitional justice process and on SOGIESC rights, even if there have been small advances in Lebanon in terms of societal acceptance over the past years. Our interviewees had few illusions about the prospects of success, and especially, Syrian refugees were emphatic about even a post-war society likely not being safe for them:

> I hate Syria. I hate to go back there. I can't imagine Syria to be just and fair.[19]
>
> I do not think that a day will come where Syria is going to be just.[20]
>
> There is no respect [for diverse SOGIESC persons] at all. It is impossible to achieve justice in Syria. Justice in Syria is merely talk; nothing will happen.[21]

A majority of our respondents, including more well-off and secure Lebanese, expressed a wish to leave the Arab region as a whole, as they saw little hope for societal change on SOGIESC issues (see also Heartland Alliance 2014; Maydaa et al. 2020). Those respondents with the requisite economic means, social cachet, and informal support networks were able to create temporary safe spaces or "bubbles" for themselves, but these are also often marked by precarity and their temporary nature (see also Moussawi 2020).

A striking feature in our interviews and focus group discussions was the impact of the constant, everyday fear, discrimination, micro-aggressions, and abuse faced by our respondents. The negative cumulative effect of this was an all-pervasive sense of physical, emotional, personal, economic, and social insecurity and distrust. It was these abuses, and the fear of them, which respondents focused on, more than larger narratives of the Syrian civil war. Respondents highlighted repeatedly how, even if there was no war, they would not be safe in Syria, and how, even in their comparative safety of Lebanon and Turkey, they faced continued risks and abuses. With some respondents, there was even a degree of frustration of us asking about justice, war, and displacement, given how much more salient other abuses, forms of discrimination, and socio-economic vulnerabilities were in their everyday lives.

18 https://syriaaccountability.org/new-justice-charter-gives-voice-to-victims-demands/.
19 KII, Syrian cisgender gay man, Beirut, April 2022.
20 KII, Syrian trans woman, Beirut, April 2022.
21 KII, Syrian trans man, Beirut, April 2022.

Discussion – Alternative, Complementary Ways of Seeking Justice?

While Colombia, Lebanon, and Syria, like so many other societies, share patterns of violence and discrimination against persons of diverse SOGIESC by civilians and armed groups, the three cases also differ in important ways. While the patterns of anti-LGBTIQ+ violence by armed actors have been documented to at least some degree in Colombia and Syria, there is little to no information about the impacts of past conflicts on persons of diverse SOGIESC in Lebanon. Colombia and, to a lesser degree, Lebanon also have a civil society that is open to and able to advocate on SOGIESC issues, whereas in Syria this is practically non-existent. In Colombia, unlike Syria and Lebanon, there is also importantly an openness and the political will in state structures to take seriously both diverse SOGIESC perspectives and addressing the wrongs of the past (see Chapter 14) – both of which are not present in Lebanon, and even less so in Syria.

The Colombian case has highlighted a number of practical and institutional challenges of SOGIESC inclusion in transitional justice, but there are broader questions that our research raises. The narrow mandates that focus on direct physical violence committed only by particular actors during a limited period of time (or even narrower understandings, as in Colombia and the Lebanese STL) fail to address the continuums of gendered violence we outlined, let alone other gendered wrongs of conflict and oppression. Furthermore, the critique of an excessive insistence on placing victims'/survivors' experiences in one fixed identity category rather than examining how multiple intersecting identities create different axes and dynamics of oppression and vulnerability in conflict and under repressive regimes also needs to be taken seriously, not only for persons of diverse SOGIESC.

The findings from Lebanon and Syria also raise troubling questions. If the likelihood of any kind of transitional justice is extremely low; if an eradication of patriarchal, heterosexist, and militarized structures and mindsets is so far off; and if persons of diverse SOGIESC have so many other pressing, essential needs[22] to attend to, how much energy should be or can be spent on a seemingly quixotic quest for transitional justice? This question is made all the more vexing as many of our research participants – and thus potential intended beneficiaries of transitional justice – saw little point in returning to Syria or even remaining in the broader Arab region to build a more just and equal society.

Nevertheless, the seeming futility of the quest for SOGIESC-inclusive transitional justice in Lebanon and Syria does not necessarily mean that the quest for justice should be abandoned. As much as they are currently improbable

22 This includes basic survival needs, such as physical security, shelter, or health care, but also economic survival, psychosocial support, and fostering support networks.

for Lebanon and Syria, there is at least a potential pathway now for criminal justice prosecutions, for state reparations to victims/survivors, as well as for longer-term institutional or governance reform and societal change in Colombia, even if these are, in no way, guaranteed. However, as much as these tend to be some of the main goals of national and international transitional justice processes, there are also other, less-institutional, and more personal impacts that these processes can have, such as truth-seeking or truth-telling, as well as contributing to fundamental changes in social norms. The most direct, potential benefits are those for the victims/survivors who, so it is hoped, can find a sense of justice being done, of a recognition of the wrongs committed against them, of restitution and rectification, and help with the process of healing. Transitional justice processes, as stated by one of our Colombian interviewees, offer an opportunity to include marginalized diverse SOGIESC voices, to understand the origins of different prejudices, and to contribute to the transformation of social imaginaries and undoing of historical and recurring wrongs. As another Colombian respondent underscored, these processes should, however, not only focus on victimization but also remember the agency, the dignity, the resistances, and the contributions to peacebuilding of persons of diverse SOGIESC.

In the absence of a prospect of any, let alone diverse, SOGIESC-responsive national transitional justice process in Lebanon or Syria, and the challenges of the one in Colombia, perhaps it makes sense to focus more support to localized, community- and civil society–based efforts to provide these truth-seeking and social norm change opportunities – an argument also proposed by Oettler in this volume (Chapter 7). As in the case of Colombia, these community and civil society efforts can help achieve more tangible benefits for survivors and may contribute to institutional uptake and prosecutions in the future.[23] As Schulz (2019) argues:

> [A] shift from the macro- to the micro-level implies opportunities to circumvent some of the hetero-patriarchal blind-spots of top-down TJ measures, and to open up space for more creative and inclusive engagements with gender in post-conflict processes, including the incorporation of masculinities and/or queer perspectives.[24]

Localized, alternative approaches that focus less on formal criminal justice and more on social justice can also be more survivor- rather than

23 In no way should, however, a pivot to supporting local, informal efforts mean opening the door to impunity. Rather, these processes should ideally be complementary.

24 As Schulz (2019), however, cautions, the often heteropatriarchal nature of the contexts in which such work is pursued needs to be taken into account, though, on the other hand, it is precisely these social norms which the work would seek to transform.

prosecution-centric, that is, taking the survivors' needs, concerns, and wishes of how they want to frame their own stories as a starting point, rather than prioritizing the prosecution's wish to build a winnable case at all costs. For such localized, complementary transitional justice processes to have a direct, tangible, and positively transformative impact for victims/survivors, more localized community-based alternative approaches can be more important – and these can also directly focus on the kinds of needs and vulnerabilities raised by many of our respondents, be it psychosocial support, improving their socio-economic security, or addressing everyday abuse and discrimination. When asked about what justice would look like for them, while in no way suggesting impunity for past wrongs, many of our interviewees longed to have a basic, everyday sense of security, of being able to be themselves and enjoy the same rights as other citizens:

> I wish to be able to get married and form my own family with someone from another religion. I dream to be able to walk on the streets the way that I am, as myself, without having others harass me or subject me to any form of abuse.[25]

Conclusion

The comparison of Colombia, Lebanon, and Syria has shown the multiple continuums and spectra of gendered violence and discrimination which persons of diverse SOGIESC face, both in conflict and ostensibly peaceful settings. From a theoretical perspective, "queering" of transitional justice processes offers openings to not only address individual and collective wrongs but also tackle root drivers of violence and oppression against persons of diverse SOGIESC and transform heteronormative gendered power relations in society more broadly. However, in practice, transitional justice processes have remained limited in scope and all too often gender-blind. The Colombia case, however, does offer a glimpse of what can be possible, while also highlighting many of the challenges. The Colombia case, with its persistent work by civil society activists both on SOGIESC rights and transitional justice, also underscores the importance of localized, grassroots work, as illuminated by Serrano-Amya's exploration of "queering transitional justice from below" in this context (see Chapter 12). Nonetheless, even in this most positive of our three cases, these hard-won victories have been in the face of resistance and setbacks. Given the broad continuums and spectrums of harm experienced by persons of diverse SOGIESC, TJ processes, with their limited mandates and often arcane proceedings, cannot realistically be expected on their own to transform societal norms. They can only be one aspect, albeit a

25 KII, Syrian trans woman, Beirut, April 2022.

potentially powerful one, of recognizing past wrongs and reformulating gendered norms and dynamics in the aftermath of violent conflict or repressive governments. While recognition of past harms is important, for those directly affected, the practical, quotidian support that grassroots efforts and informal support networks can provide may be more impactful, and these require more external support. In Colombia, the space for doing so is greater, and it is conceivable that both state actors at the national and local level as well as civil society can build upon the outcomes of the TJ process. In Lebanon and Syria, state engagement in a positive sense is highly unlikely, and in the absence of TJ processes, grassroots efforts remain the only avenue of support available to survivors. The degree to which TJ processes at various levels can indeed affect or contribute to broader societal change and shift heteronormative beliefs, practice, and systems of governance will need to be established by future research.

Both the history of SOGIESC rights movements and of transitional justice processes show how much perseverance is needed to achieve change – but also how quickly major shifts can happen. In Lebanon, for example, it has taken 30 years of persistent lobbying for a commission on missing persons to be set up. On the other hand, in spite of resistance and setbacks, both Colombian and Lebanese societies have come very far in a comparatively short time over the past decade in taking diverse SOGIESC issues more seriously – including in transitional justice in the former case. While we wish we could be more hopeful about gendered justice in the case studies we have covered here, it is perhaps at this localized level where most can be achieved at the moment to help survivors (re)gain a sense of justice, integrity, security, and dignity.

References

Buckley-Zistel, S. and M. Zolkos (2012). Introduction: Gender in Transitional Justice. In: Buckley-Zistel, S. and Stanley, R. (eds.): *Gender in Transitional Justice*. London: Palgrave Macmillan: 1–36.

Bueno-Hansen, P. (2017). The Emerging LGBTI Rights Challenge to Transitional Justice in Latin America. *International Journal of Transitional Justice* 12: 1–20.

CNMH (2015). *Aniquilar la diferencia: lesbianas, gays, bisexuales y transgeneristas en el marco del conflicto armado colombiano*. Bogotá: CNMH.

Cockburn, C. (2004). The Continuum of Violence: A Gender Perspective on War and Peace. In: Giles, W. and Hyndman, J. (eds.): *Sites of Violence: Gender and Conflict Zones*. Oakland: University of California Press: 24–44.

Colombia Diversa (2020). *Responses to Questionnaire for the Report on Gender Perspective in Transitional Justice Processes for the 75th Session of the General Assembly* [unpublished internal document].

Comisión de la Verdad y Reconciliación (2003). *Informe Final*. Lima: Comisión de la Verdad y Reconciliación.

Daigle, M. and H. Myrttinen (2018). Bringing Diverse Sexual Orientation and Gender Identity (SOGI) into Peacebuilding Policy and Practice. *Gender & Development* 26(1): 103–120.

Erdem, Z. P., C. Maydaa, H. Berchtold, C. Wilmot and H. Myrttinen (2024). *Violence Against Refugee Women of Diverse SOGIESC in Lebanon and Türkiye*. Beirut: MOSAIC MENA.

Fobear, K. (2014). Queering Truth Commissions. *Journal of Human Rights Practice* 6(1): 51–68.

Ghazzawi, R. (2017). Decolonising Syria's So-Called 'Queer Liberation', *Al Jazeera*, 5 August.

Hagen, J., M. Daigle and H. Myrttinen (2021). Sexual Orientation and Gender Identity or Expression (SOGIE) in Violent Conflict and Peacebuilding. In: Confortini, C., Feron, E., Parashar, S. and Väyrynen, T. (eds.): *Routledge Handbook of Feminist Peace Research*. London: Routledge.

Heartland Alliance International (2014). *No Place for People Like You: An Analysis of the Needs, Vulnerabilities, and Experiences of LGBT Syrian Refugees in Lebanon*. Chicago: Heartland Alliance. Accessed at: www.heartlandalliance.org/wp-content/uploads/sites/13/2016/02/no-place-for-peoplelike-you_hai_2014.pdf.

Helem (2017). *Human Rights Violations Against Lesbian, Gay, Bisexual, Transgender, and Queer (LGBTQ) Individuals in Lebanon*. A Shadow Report submitted to the Human Rights Committee. Available at: https://www.ecoi.net/file_upload/1930_1493282102_int-ccpr-ico-lbn-27152-e.pdf.

HRC (2018). 'I Lost My Dignity': Sexual and Gender Based Violence in the Syrian Arab Republic. *Conference Room Paper of the Independent International Commission of Inquiry on the Syrian Arab Republic*, United Nations Human Rights Council, Thirty-Seventh Session 26 February – 23 March 2018. Geneva: Office of the United Nations High Commissioner for Human Rights. Available at: https://www.ohchr.org/sites/default/files/Documents/HRBodies/HRCouncil/CoISyria/A-HRC-37-CRP-3.pdf

Human Rights Watch (2015). Islamic State's War on Gays. *Los Angeles Times*, 8 June. Accessed at: www.hrw.org/news/2015/06/08/"slamic-states-war-gays.

Human Rights Watch (2020). *"They Treated Us in Monstrous Ways" – Sexual Violence Against Men, Boys, and Transgender Women in the Syrian Conflict*. New York: Human Rights Watch.

ICTJ (2020). *Our Work – Lebanon*. ICTJ. Available at: https://www.ictj.org/our-work/regions-and-countries/lebanon. Accessed on: 2 December 2020.

Kelly, E. (1988). *Surviving Sexual Violence*. Cambridge: Polity.

Killingsworth, M. (2019). Justice, Syria and the International Criminal Court. *Australian Outlook Blog*, 24 December. Available at: https://www.internationalaffairs.org.au/australianoutlook/justice-syria-international-criminal-court/. Accessed on: 6 December 2020.

Kıvılcım, Z. (2017). Lesbian, Gay, Bisexual and Transsexual (LGBT) Syrian Refugees in Turkey. In: Freedman, J., Kıvılcım, Z. and Özgür Baklacıoğlu, N. (eds.): *A Gendered Approach to the Syrian Refugee Crisis*. London: Routledge: 26–41.

Krystalli, R. and K. Theidon (2016). Here's How Attention Gender Affected Colombia's Peace Process. *Washington Post*, 9 October. Available at: https://www.washingtonpost.com/news/monkey-cage/wp/2016/10/09/heres-how-attention-to-gender-affected-colombias-peace-process/.

Maydaa, C., C. Chayya and H. Myrttinen (2020). *Impacts of the Syrian Civil War and Displacement on Diverse SOGIESC Populations*. Beirut: MOSAIC MENA.

Minow, M. (1998). *Between Vengeance and Forgiveness: Facing History after Genocide and Mass Violence*. Boston: Beacon Press.

Moussawi, G. (2020). *Disruptive Situations – Fractal Orientalism and Queer Strategies in Beirut*. Chicago: Temple University Press.

Muddell, K. (2007). *Sexual Minorities Study: LGBT Issues and Transitional Justice*. Paper presented at the Open Society Institute Forum: Gender and Transitional Justice. New York City, 7 February.

Myrttinen, H., L. Khattab and C. Maydaa (2017). 'Trust No One, Beware of Everyone': Vulnerabilities of LGBTI Refugees in Lebanon. In: Freedman, J., Kıvılcım, Z. and Baklacıoğlu, N. (eds.): *A Gendered Approach to the Syrian Refugee Crisis*. London: Routledge: 61–76.

Oettler, A. (2019). *The Struggle for Gendered Peace and LGBT Rights in Colombia.* Violence, Security and Peace Working Papers (2). London: London School of Economics and Political Science.

Saleh, A. and A. Qubaia (2015). *Transwomen's Navigation of Arrest and Detention in Beirut: A Case Study*. Civil Society Knowledge Centre, Lebanon Support.

Saleh, F. (2020). Queer/Humanitarian Visibility: The Emergence of the Figure of the Suffering Syrian Gay Refugee. *Middle East Critique* 29(1): 47–67.

Schulz, P. (2019). Towards Inclusive Gender in Transitional Justice: Gaps, Blind-Spots and Opportunities. *Journal of Intervention and Statebuilding* 14(5): 691–710.

Serrano-Amaya, J. F. (2018). *Homophobic Violence in Armed Conflict and Political Transition*. London: Palgrave Macmillan.

Simic, O. (2016). Engendering Transitional Justice: Silence, Absence and Repair. *Human Rights Review* 17: 1–8.

Theidon, K. (2006). Justice in Transition: The Micropolitics of Reconciliation in Post-war Peru. *The Journal of Conflict Resolution* 50(3): 433–457.

Verhelst López, J. J. (2018). *Voices from the Margins: An Analysis of the Emerging LGBTIQ-subject of Truth Commissions*.MA Thesis, University of Lund, Lund, Sweden.

Woods, A., T. Murphy and M. Christina Vibe (2017). *Transformation Through Justice for Syria: Lessons from South Africa, Indonesia and Colombia*. Istanbul: Istanbul Policy Center.

Section 4

Beyond Violation-Centric Views

Chapter 12

Queering Transitional Justice From Below

Some Inputs From Queer Masculinities[1]

José Fernando Serrano-Amaya

Introduction

Calls for a perspective "from below" and for a people-centered approach have gained increasing prominence in scholarship and practice of peacebuilding in the past three decades. The concept of "peacebuilding from below" was coined in the 1990s as a response to a focus on militaristic approaches to conflict resolution, challenging top-down approaches, emphasizing civil society experiences and bottom-up practices. The call for consideration to the micro-level has also been extended to transitional justice, seeking to challenge, contrast, and complement the more common top-down, institutionalized, and legalistic approaches that dominate the field (McEvoy and McGregor 2008). Further developments of the call have explored the collective action of human rights networks and victims' organizations in claims for justice (Kreft 2019; Paredes 2020; Rudling 2019) or power asymmetries among demobilized paramilitaries and civil society victims as subjects of transitional justice laws and policies (Krystalli 2019).

Throughout this emerging literature, however, little remains known about the meanings and practices of transitional justice from below from the perspectives of diverse and heterogeneous queer subjectivities– which remain marginalized and largely ignored in debates about transitional justice and peacebuilding at large (Bueno-Hansen 2015; Schulz 2020). This contribution addresses that gap by connecting debates about transitional justice from below with discussions of queer men and masculinities. It also dialogues with relational gender analysis that problematizes masculinities, considering power differences between women and men and among men (Connell 2009).

The chapter argues that as much as it is important to include more diverse voices and experiences of men into TJ processes (Hamber 2016; Schulz

1 I appreciate the comments made on previous versions of this chapter by the editors of this contribution, by Raewyn Connell, Pascha Bueno-Hansen, and Anika Oettler, and by the participants on the writers' workshop in September 2021.

DOI: 10.4324/9781003519522-16

2020) – and in particular those in subordinated positions – it is also important to queer transitional justice and to queer the below in transitional justice. This queering is an attempt to unsettle the illusion of transition from chaos to order and the return to "normality" that still underlines conflict resolution, peacebuilding, and transitional justice. It is also a discussion on the homogenizing use of "below" that renders power disparities among those in subordinated positions invisible. If there is not a movement from inclusion to queering, I suggest, the result will continue to be the already-criticized "add and stir" approach to gender perspectives (Duriesmith 2019; Wright 2019) that simply expands the list of subjects to be added: from women to men to queers.

The queering suggested here does not operate in a negative way of disruption or disordering. It is an invitation to focus attention on the struggles for dignity of those in subordinated positions of power. If civil society is one of the sites of the "below" in transitional justice, queer men are situated even below "the below." Still, as I will illustrate in the chapter, they are progressing change in their communities throughout a variety of social, political, and cultural practices.

The chapter starts with a theoretical discussion on the conception of the "local" and "below" in transitional justice, and on "subaltern" perspectives in masculinities studies, to establish connections and differences with queerness as a position and perspective. Then, it offers three aspects of what the process of queering of transitional justice can look like, particularly from the perspective of those below and of queer masculinities. A common thread in the sections is how violence affects a sense of collectiveness and the different ways in which queer men struggle for collective action and exercise agency. A discussion on trans masculinities is introduced later in the chapter, to call attention to the limits of queerness and studies on masculinities, and to suggest the need of more concentrated analyses of the notion of "transition" in transitional justice. This chapter offers some ideas of how this process of queering TJ can be understood – thereby offering concrete empirical and analytical contributions to what remains an under-developed and largely conceptually driven discussion.

On Methodology, Ethics, and Positionality

This chapter is based partially on data collected in four cities in the Colombian Caribbean region – Cartagena, Barranquilla, Santa Marta, and Monteria – in 2013 for my PhD research (Serrano-Amaya 2014). It also uses information produced some years after, when the peace agreement between the Colombian State and the former FARC guerrilla was signed. Both sets of information are of relevance nowadays with the increasing academic interest on LGBT topics in peacebuilding and the implementation of transitional justice instruments such as the Truth Commission or the Special Jurisdiction for Peace in Colombia.[2] In revisiting data from two different points in time, the aim is to show that, from the perspective of queer men, there are experiences of violence that occur before conflicts arise, develop with them as they are mutually constituted, and are reshaped after peace negotiations. This personal and academic trajectory acts also as the leading thread of the piece.

For the first set of data, I interviewed a selected sample of activists, human rights advocates, and public employees using networks from previous collaborations I have had with Caribe Afirmativo, a national organization working on LGBT rights. Interviews were realized according to the ethics protocol authorized by the University of Sydney. Participants in the research were involved in the creation of memories and in the collective histories of the groups they work for or to which they are related. Several of them were working for the recognition of lesbian, gay, bisexual, and transgender people as victims of the socio-political conflict or were involved in rights-lobbying activities.

Interviews were based on an oral history perspective based on the work of feminist scholars (Haug 1987) and queer researchers (Epprecht 2004). In their perspective, oral history is a process of engagement, expression, empowerment, reflexivity, and collective organization. I approached participants as expert producers of knowledge. The oral histories they shared were considered narratives that involve complex interactions between reflection on their lived experience of violence and their practices to transform social injustices. The knowledge they have acquired can be seen in terms of "practical knowledge," a knowledge drawn from experience (Maddison and Scalmer 2006) that they use and transform in their work and activism.

Participants were not requested to narrate personal experiences of violence, but they did so several times, challenging ethics protocols that intended to avoid such descriptions of events. The possible traumatic effect of the interview was ameliorated by the participation, in some of the interviews, of a peer from the local organization. For some participants, the international context of the research – a PhD dissertation at an Australian university and with a comparative perspective with other countries – became a space to denounce, exchange ideas, and ask the researcher about the situation in other places. As a result, interviews were also conversations and opportunities for mutual learning, discussion, and drafting ideas for activism, troubling constantly our positionalities.

This chapter and its primary research are based on a permanent discussion on the politics of not-knowing, those politics of knowledge that intentionally

2 This chapter was written before the presentation of the final report of the Colombian Truth Commission in June 2022. The report has a volume dedicated to gender, with a focus on women and "LGBTIQ+" communities. The volume has raised several debates on the notion of gender used and on how it addresses issues of masculinities. I will not cover those debates here, but mentioning them is important to show ongoing discussions on the topic.

make invisible some issues for public or academic interest even if there is data about them (Nordstrom 1999). Politics of not-knowing affect the ways in which issues of gender and sexuality, in particular queer topics, are managed in peacebuilding and transitional justice policies and politics. The information I revisit here was produced as part of a longer commitment with the production of knowledge for activist and academic purposes. I have participated in activist and advocacy initiatives for the protection of the rights of gays, lesbian, bisexual, and transgender people and for the recognition of their role in peacebuilding not just as victims but as collective actors. Denouncing the invisibility and sometimes intentional denial of the victimization of LGBT[3] individuals and collectives has been part of the political context in which I have produced my academic contributions.

My positionality affected the information used in this contribution in several ways. I have had a long-term commitment with struggles for LGBT rights that facilitated dialogue with some activists and advocates at the regional level but also raised questions among others about the uses of the information collected or my alignment in activist politics. The fact that I collected some information as a Colombian studying abroad facilitated me access to some spaces as it was perceived as neutral or external to the local context. It was also restrictive because of these same factors and the suspicion by participants of co-optation of their life stories. The Colombian racial and regional orders were also present, since, as someone born in the Andean inner lands, a *cachaco*, I was often perceived as alien in the *costeño* – coastal culture. Since I was working in LGBT issues, I was sometimes read as a gay man, but my gender and sexuality were often under question due to a permanent representation of my own subjectivity as foreigner. All these contradictions created a relationship of partial acceptance and rejection that affected the spaces in which I could participate and the expectations of those I collaborated with. The tension insider/outsider (Naples 1997) happens not only in the division activist/academic work but also in the geopolitics of knowledge production and in the multiplicity of elements that, in my case, create a researcher position.

This chapter is also a struggle with politics of translation and of academic scholarship. It is tempting to find equivalents of *queer* and *queering*

3 The acronym *LGBT* is a matter of intense debates for homogenizing and creating a parallelism among disparate political agendas and forms of victimization. It has become part of the language to discuss some issues of gender, sexualities, identities, and collective organization. It has even more entered in the language of public polices sometimes associated with other descriptive terms. I tend not to use the "I" for *intersex*, unless it is explicitly referred that way, since, in the case of Colombia, intersex activism has taken a different path from LGBT activism. In a similar way, I do not add the "Q" from *queer*, because the queer activism I have witnessed tends to stress a difference with LGBT activism. In my use, *LGBT* is a particular political and identity subjectivity that is not just the summary of individual identities but a kind of new and emerging subject of governability.

in Spanish and Latin American cultures. In Mexican jargon, an equivalent could be *joto*, as a noun, and *jotear*, as the verb. In Colombia, it would be *marica* and *mariquear. Mariquear* has interesting associations. As a verb, it suggests the action of disturbing, annoying, or losing time. It can also be associated with changing the gender of a person, an action, or a word. As a noun, *marica* is gaining a new use in activism that retakes its previous negative or pejorative meaning and makes it affirmative and a matter of pride, in a similar way that happened with *queer* in the United States gender and sexual politics in the 1980s. *Marica* has also been adopted in research on the memories of armed conflict by LGBT individuals and collectives (CNMH 2019), or in literary and cultural studies on Latin American gender and sexual politics of dissidence (Falconí 2018; Sutherland 2021). However, I am reluctant to make a direct or mechanic translation of *queer* to *marica* since it would erase the particular meanings and stories behind the uses of each term, in special its combination of gender, sexual, class, and generational politics.

The possibilities and limitations of translating *queer* and *queering* to languages such as Spanish and its use in activism have been a matter of intensive discussions. The discussion has moved from a matter of translation of the word (Viteri et al. 2011) to an analysis of political practices that defy hegemonic or dualist definitions of citizenship and social change (Vidal et al. 2014) to a recognition of the multiplicity and incommensurability of the term in Spanish- and non-Spanish-speaking contexts (Pierce et al. 2021). In this perspective, I see *queer* less than a nomination, identity, or typology of subjects and more as an analytical perspective and a political position.

In 2005, I had the chance to lecture on gender, sexuality, and conflict to political science students at the university I am working at currently. When teaching the results of my master dissertation, I translated *queering* conflict to *mariquiar el conflicto*. The reactions of students ranged from disgust, for the still-pejorative meaning of the term, to unsettling and attraction. Somehow, this contradictory reaction is similar to the intention of queering transitional justice that will be suggested here in terms of challenging politics of knowledge. Still, I am reluctant to make immediate associations between *queering* and *mariquiar*, and I use *queer* in Spanish always in reference to its uses and contestations in English contexts. If I were writing this chapter in Spanish, I would use other terms and locate the discussions in other political and theoretical contexts. From this view, positionality is also the possibility of taking distance.

On "Below" and "Subaltern" in Transitional Justice: Same, but Different

In their introduction to a pivotal text on transitional justice from below, Kiran McEvoy and Lorna McGregor (2008) offer three understandings of the perspective "from below." The first understanding looks at the intense groundwork of grassroots organizations and communities to achieve justice.

The second understanding considers mobilizations at the community level and at less-recognized sites where transitional justice is enacted. The third understanding intends to bring to the center the agency of the dominated and oppressed. For McEvoy and McGregor (2008: 2), transitional justice from below is a critique to dominant perspectives "from above" and an attempt for an "actor-oriented" perspective that emphasizes grassroots actors and community mobilizations, in particular those less represented in mainstream accounts of conflict transitions. It is also an invitation to explore the diverse and many times creative ways in which local actors have taken a protagonist role in facilitating political transitions and their required changes.

Transitional justice from below can be seen as an explanatory concept and a political project. Several authors and perspectives have contributed to both goals, with direct or indirect involvement with the concept. The result is a wide range of understandings and applications of the interest on localized actors' perspectives and on the enactment of transitional justice that challenges any attempt of contention in one unified concept. "From below" can be seen as emphasis on localized practices to challenge legalistic and lineal assumptions in transitional justice mechanisms, as documented in the compilation by Rosalind et al. (2010) or a focus on social actors such as human rights networks as studied by Gómez Sánchez (2012) or Tapia (2019). However, "the local" is not necessarily a subordinated position, since at local levels there could be many power positions and important differences in terms of access to resources and legitimacy among civil society organizations. The call to recognize local voices in transitional justice could lead to more integrative frames in which they are involved in all the steps of the process, as suggested by Lundy and McGovern (2008). It can also question the desirability of institutional mechanisms for transitional justice when other practices are seen as more desired delivers of justice, such as religious engagement or agricultural activities, as deduced by the work of Martin (2016). These examples illustrate the disparities and nuances in the purpose of transitional justice from below among practitioners, academics, and activists, reflecting its complexity as concept and as political project.

These problems require further discussion when connecting with issues of queer masculinities. The three understandings of TJFB mentioned earlier are relevant to offer a different angle on a discussion of masculinities in relation to transitional justice and will be illustrated in the next sections. The first two understandings are a request for looking at everyday practices of collective organizing and mobilization for justice in communities and organizations. From a relational perspective of gender, the two definitions would be useful to explore the participation of men in transitional justice practices on the ground and to discuss issues of masculinities in activism, for example. The third understanding connects with the interests of subaltern studies (Guha 1997) and other related areas, such as feminist methodologies (Harding 1987) or decolonial studies (Castro-Gómez and Grosfoguel

2007), in challenging dichotomist explanations of power and in departing analyses from the perspective of the subordinated and excluded. It also offers a theoretical and political challenge when discussing issues of men and masculinities. However, how can masculinities, in relation to grounded practices of transitional justice, be discussed as subaltern experiences?

A first possible answer can be found going back to a core idea in the studies of masculinities: their diversity and dissimilar location in relations of power. In Raewyn Connell's conceptualization of masculinities (Connell 2005), they are distributed alongside different dimensions of power, from hegemonic to subordinated positions, from marginalized to complicit positions. While hegemonic masculinity became the focus of attention in most discussions on masculinities, what remain less frequently discussed are configurations of masculinities in subordinated or marginalized power positions. A call for considering masculinities in transitional justice from below can thus be associated with a focus on understanding subordinated, marginalized, or complicit masculinities. This is useful, for example, to understand the situation of young men and antimilitaristic masculinities, as studied by Daniel Conway in the anti-conscription movement during South African apartheid (2004). The case of men who resist, escape, or evade incorporation in armed groups in context of conflict would offer also a relevant example of struggles for justice at the ground level. Yet another example points to the cases of those men who decide not to displace from disputed areas while women, children, and other men are forced to flee.

It is important not to make an immediate equivalence between "the below" in transitional justice and the "subordinated" in masculinities. While the first is a perspective to approach the infrastructures for building peace from a topography of actors and levels, the second is an analysis of the relational dimension of power. The "below" in TJFB refers more to a location and calls for a focus on local experiences when the tendency is to consider mostly the perspective of those in top or elite positions. The "subordinated" in the study of masculinities is part of the analysis of power relations to exercise hegemony and is required to define others in dominated positions. The example provided by Connell at first to explain subordination was the situation of homosexual men in relation to heterosexual men. However, the direct association between homosexuality and subordination was discussed in further developments of the concept of hegemonic masculinities (Connell and Messerschmidt 2005) that emphasized the dynamics and internal complexity of masculinities and called attention on the problems of an automatic location of homosexual men or queer masculinities in subordinated positions.

When connecting transitional justice from below with a relational model of masculinities, it is not enough to consider subordinated masculinities to look from below. A connection between the interest on the "below" from TJFB and the relational analysis of power relations in masculinities (1) helps problematize the focus on local experiences without assuming the "local" as homogeneous or as self-evident expression of the opposite of elites and (2) recalls the importance of power relations in the analysis of what is seen as "the below" as a simplistic descriptive location, and (3) a relational model of power relations in the study of "the below" invites to explore all actors involved in the production of such position, such as the role of men in local experiences on TJFB and, among them, those in subordinated position as queer men.

Acknowledging these problems and possibilities, in this chapter I will look at TJFB as a concept relevant to criticize and explore power relations in transitional justice and as a project to emphasize the agency and protagonist role of those in subordinated positions in its enactment. However, the call for a people-centered approach and the uses of "below" need also to be challenged for their limited discussion of queer subjectivities, their cis-heteronormativity, and their limited understanding of power relations among those in subordinated positions, such as queer men. Queering transitional justice and queering the below in transitional justice are analytical and political strategies to question both issues. They are also useful for exploring issues of gender and sexuality in transitional justice and for engendering the field. In the next section, I will expand these topics.

Queering Transitional Justice

There have been several attempts for queering mainstream issues in relation to peacebuilding, such as conflict analyses (Duggan 2012), truth commissions (Fobear 2014), security and peacebuilding (Hagen 2016; Maier 2020), or transitional justice (Bueno-Hansen 2015). In these cases, *queering* implies both the inclusion of women and sexually diverse subjectivities in the recount of political conflict and the challenging of dualistic or heteronormative assumptions in core concepts and practices in the field of peacebuilding (also see Fobear in this volume). However, the meanings of what is included in this queering, how this is to be done, and the scope of the theoretical challenge expected by a queering perspective vary.

In some cases, queering as inclusion means taking the perspectives of some queer subjectivities into account in the reports of violence during conflicts or in peace activities (Maier 2020). This inclusion is done by the translation of experiences of violence by expert voices, such as academics and professional activists, and through mechanisms for testimony, such as human rights reports, and findings of emblematic cases. Which voices are being included and which voices do not obtain acknowledgment, or what makes some experiences "emblematic," are a matter that deserves further discussion in the broader realm of debates around queering peacebuilding or transitional justice.

In other cases, queering as a challenge to normative systems implies a discussion of the implicit pursue for normalization embedded in conflict resolution strategies (Serrano-Amaya 2004), the limits of core notions of peacebuilding to consider the needs of women and queer subjects (Hagen 2016), or the disruption of binaries and dichotomist divisions of sex/gender that support heteronormative frameworks (Schulz and Touquet 2020). It may also be a request to consider the intersection between systems of oppression, such as heteronormativity, cisnormativity, and coloniality, in the analysis (Bueno-Hansen 2018). In these cases, queering goes further toward an interpellation of peacebuilding and transitional justice as produced and producers of normative systems. However, there are differences on what those normative systems are. While for some (Hagen 2016; Serrano-Amaya 2004) the focus is normative systems of peacebuilding industries, for others (Schulz and Touquet 2020) the focus is on heteronormativity and other gender systems of oppression (Bueno-Hansen 2018).[4]

Still, such inclusion and discussion do not imply or directly require a perspective "from below." Challenging heteronormative and dualistic notions of gender and sexuality in policy documents about peace (Langlois 2018) can typically be seen as a process of "queering from above." Such queering from above is of importance to discuss normative considerations of gender and sexuality in legal documents and in the legalist approaches to deal with transitions. As stated in the compilation by McEvoy and McGregor (2008), a focus on "from below" does not imply excluding the relevance of the "from above," and their combination can be considered a more successful strategy for change. Still, it is affected by the over-emphasis in norms, codes, and rules that are embedded in queer theory.

The process of queering transitional justice from below and the below in transitional justice as suggested here follows the queer intersectional analysis proposed by Bueno-Hansen (2018) but further expands on systems of domination such as politics of knowledge and expert knowledge production and representation. This queering of TJFB serves as a call for a radical emphasis on the lived and embodied experience of violence, transitions, and peace for those social actors in subordinated and oppressed positions. Queering TJFB and the below directs the attention not only to policing and regulation or to

4 Defining *queering* mostly in terms of heteronormativity may be problematic, especially for the diverse set of meanings associated with the later concept. *Heteronormativity* is a concept that uses a language of codes and social orders based on gender divisions and (hetero)sexuality as norm in order to explain the functioning of regulatory systems. "Heteronormativity," as a concept, has gained space in Anglophone literature in recent decades and has been defined in different ways (Chambers 2007; Jackson 2006; Schneider and Ward 2009), with no single definition of the norms, institutions, or regulations that constitute it. Despite that the wording of the concept is associated with Warner (1993), Jackson (2006) considers that the idea was already present in the work of early lesbian feminists, such as Gayle Rubin or Adrienne Reich, who conceptualized "compulsory heterosexuality" not only in terms of regulation of sexuality but also of gender relations. For the discussion here is relevant the role of heteronormativity as core concept in US-based queer theory and the differences with other queer theories and politics.

practices of resistance, as often considered in queer analyses, but also to the diverse, contradictory, and creative ways in which individuals, grassroots organizations, and collective actors navigate systems of oppression and their fractures. This call has been already introduced in perspectives that call for radical participatory approaches (Lundy and McGovern 2008) in order to critique standardized top-down analyses and strategies for change. Still, I suggest moving the approach a step further. In a prospective sense, queering TJFB allows for opening the space for emancipatory peacebuilding practices, as suggested in critical peacebuilding theory (Richmond 2007). It also connects with developments on "transformative justice" that challenge the main focus on temporal institutional legal changes in transitional justice and instead emphasizes the processual and long-term protagonist role of communities on socio-political dimensions of justice (Gready and Robins 2014). It is a request for knowledge production and theory building based on the situated experiences and practices of those most marginalized in societies in transition in their struggles for dignity and social justice.

On the Lived Experience of Violence

Victor[5] is a gay man and an HIV activist. He was born in 1967 in Santa Marta, one of the three biggest cities on the Colombian Caribbean coast, important for tourism and exportation economy. Since the late 1990s, Victor has been the owner of gay bars, a hairdresser, a makeup artist, a *transformista*, and an HIV activist. By the time of the interview, he was running a charity organization that provided HIV education and organized beauty pageants with five other friends. These events are an important space for socialization and collective organization for a diverse range of gender and sexually diverse marginalized people. There, they not only resist gender and sexual orders but also create a variety of innovative cultural and political practices that allow them to negotiate their position within communities and produce a sense of collectivity and belonging. For this work, they were also the target of armed actors who have been active in the inner lands of the Caribbean coast and in other areas of the country (CNMH 2018b; González 2021). Few months after I interviewed him, Victor was threatened for his activism and was requested to reveal the names of those who tested positive for HIV by a member of a local armed group. For denying doing it, he was forced to displace to two other cities in the area, closing his organization and reducing his activism.

The day that I met Victor and his colleagues, I walked with them in Cienaga, a town in the Caribbean with a long history of social resistance and unionism in banana plantations that started in the early twentieth century. In the last decades, Cienaga and the surrounding areas in the Caribbean were

5 Names were changed to protect identities.

badly affected by the violence committed by *paramilitares* (CNMH 2018a). LGBT communities were a particular target of those violences. They faced permanent threats, forced displacement, torture, and killings that were fundamental for the social, economic, and political orders imposed by paramilitary armies (CNMH 2015; Serrano-Amaya 2018). Social cleansing was the common category used to explain violence against those considered contrary to social orders, queers included (CNMH 2016). It was not just a concept but a lived experience in the conversations. By the early 2010s, new forms of criminal bands that emerged after the demobilization of *paramilitares* were fighting to control the zone, creating a complex landscape of overlapping violences that give a unique character to my fieldwork in the region.

Victor and his friends showed me the areas where they do outreach work with sex workers, "gay men," and other populations for their sexual education work. I noticed that some members of the community recognized them and talked to them in a friendly way. I also noticed others looking at us with caution. On two occasions, I heard jokes and mocking whistles aimed at us as we passed. My companions did not react to any of these comments. The constant surveillance of gender behaviors was evident, and I could notice how our non-verbal interactions changed. There may also have been surveillance by legal or illegal armed actors.

During one of my visits, I met Guillermo, Ignacio, and Oscar – Victor's peers in a local organization offering sexual health counselling and promoting LGBT rights. Guillermo was born in Bogota in 1963, Oscar in 1993, and Ignacio in 1995 in Cienaga. Guillermo was in a heterosexual relationship and recently became a father. Ignacio AND Oscar defined themselves as *gay and transformistas*.[6] In our conversation, they often interchanged masculine and feminine pronouns to describe themselves and other men. Oscar sometimes described himself as a transgender person. The three share an abject position in their community. Guillermo, as a recovered drug addict, was perceived as a source of pollution and a threat to others. His activism with sex workers and the fact that his house was also the place where he conducted workshops about sexual education have caused several conflicts with neighbors. Ignacio's and Oscar's sexuality and femininity troubled their families since they were kids and kept them under the permanent gaze of other members of their community. At the same time, they described a rich and complex sexual culture in which they engaged with heterosexual men in many ways, even those in legal or illegal militarized positions.

6 *Transformista* is a term associated with the representation of female characters, often well-known singers and actresses for cultural and entertaining activities. It has a local meaning that emphasizes popular culture and makes a difference with drag queen cultures, which are seen more as foreigner, urban, and modern. In the context of my fieldwork, I could see an overlapping between *transformista* and ways to refer to transgender experiences.

Early in our conversation, they described different types of violence they have been exposed to. A gay soccer referee was killed last year while training in a park. A guy driving a motorbike appeared out of nowhere and shot him dead. A transgender woman was decorating the house of her sibling for Christmas, and suddenly two men appeared, chased, and killed her. She had been warned before about not coming back to that area. Two years earlier, a lesbian girl was raped and killed. Her body was found in a deserted place. The weekend before the interview, a *chica trans* – a trans girl – who is also doing sex work was sitting in a bar when, suddenly, a guy arrived and shot her in front of everybody. She was badly injured but survived. The descriptions of Guillermo, Ignacio, and Oscar were rich in detail and covered a wide spectrum of temporalities and localities. In their life course, violence was not just an event they witnessed but a permanent factor that has given shape to their experiences as members of a community and, specifically, as queer men. When exploring with them what these different descriptions and incidences of violence had in common, one recurring explanation referred to the fact that all these cases were close to them and that they could have happened to them as well, even if they did not know the victims personally.

Research on the gender and sexual dimensions of conflict in Colombia has documented extensively how armed actors use and reshape gender and sexual orders to support their strategies to gain political and territorial control (Caribe-Afirmativo 2019; CNMH 2015). The concept of a "continuum of violence" (Moser 2001) has been useful for feminist scholarship to call attention to the extension of structures of gendered violence across different contexts, including from non-war context to conflict situations and reverse. The previous examples of violence can well be explained with that concept.

However, explaining these instances only through the lens of continuity and a continuum of violence may not allow us to consider what emerges as new as well as the specificities of this type of violence. There are also methodological and theoretical issues in explaining what was said before with such concept, since it is based on understandings of gendered violence against women. If there is a continuum on violence against queer men, its reasons, expressions, and effects are not necessarily the same. In this case of violence exercised by some men in positions of power against other men in subordinated positions, the use of the concept can render invisible the agency of the perpetrator and the specific contexts, situations, and purposes leading to the use of violence.[7] What Victor and his friends were describing can better be characterized as a spiral of violence, moving at uneven speed with some moments of intensification, densification, and apparent relaxation. A relaxation, however, that did not imply for queer men to loosen the feeling of being a possible victim.

7 This was an issue raised by Raewyn Connell in one of her comments to this chapter.

In the case of Victor, his situation as a person living with HIV and his activism on this topic have exposed him to particular forms of violence. He remembered that when he was working in a bar, he received an intimidating phone call; someone called him *sidoso*, a pejorative term that not just describes living with HIV but implies a disease carrier, and threatened to burn his working place. Something similar has happened to people he knew. Once, he met a couple at the beach that had to leave their hometown in the inlands because people learned about their positive HIV status. They left when a funeral crown was delivered to their house. Victor gave them accommodation for several months and helped them find a job. Another friend was beaten on the street close to his home because his neighbors were informed that he was HIV positive.

The emergence of particular forms of violence with a focus on gender, sexuality, and queerness is also materialized in the distribution of threatening leaflets, common in areas affected by socio-political violence in Colombia. The use of threatening leaflets has been documented and denounced by human rights and LGBT organizations due to its intense impact in the regulation of everyday life in areas under dispute by armed actors (Caribe-Afirmativo 2017; Colombia-Diversa 2013). Leaflets are used by illegal armed actors from all political landscape, including criminal gangs, revealing a hybrid space of fear and surveillance in which politically motivated violence mixes with other forms of social and collective violence. Leaflets represent well an assemblage of stigmatized identities from the perspective of armed actors. Guillermo was the one who offered most information on that topic. He received one of those leaflets days before we met. The pamphlet was left under his front door. Guillermo linked this leaflet to the fact that people knew that they offer services in the house for trans women and sex workers. The leaflet included a death threat to *maricas, putas y drogadictos* – "faggots, whores, and drug users." Guillermo emphasized that it did not affect them much, since it was not the first time that this has happened. At the time, there was a new wave of those leaflets, and the practice had acquired a certain kind of everydayness – indicating the extent to which violence and threat of violence were inherently normalized in queer people's lived realities.

This interconnection between marginalized collectives deserves attention in a discussion on queerness since it reflects the porosity, instability, and fluidity of hierarchies of exclusion. For the research that supports this chapter, I analyzed 39 of these threats.[8] In most of the analyzed threats, the victims were gendered and sexualized individuals associated with other marginalized groups. The most common association was between queers and *prostitutas* (sex workers), which appeared in 23 of the cases. The second association was with drug users, who were mentioned in 16 cases,

8 For an extended description of the results, see Serrano Amaya (2018).

and with drug dealers, mentioned in 11 cases. The third association was with petty crime and youth cultures. These associations create abject subjects that serve to mark limits between populations, defining explicitly some as sources of pollution and rendering others implicitly as standards of good citizenship. In this segregation of populations, non-normative gender identities or sexualities are an assemblage with other social hierarchies of exclusion. This assemblage challenges explanations of homophobic and transphobic violence in armed conflict that isolate some violence from others. This isolation can be seen, for example, in reports written by *Centro Nacional de Memoria Histórica* (CNMH 2015, 2019) that tend to explain trans and homophobic violence mostly as result of heteronormativity, erasing other forms of exclusion. Instead of the enacting of heteronormativity, what the associations mentioned before suggest is the permanence and actualization of racialized divisions around order.

Recent research has found that armed actors in the Caribbean and Pacific coastal areas of Colombia have acted with particular attention on racialized LGBT communities and individuals through forms of violence that combine hyper-sexualization with attempts to "correct" their sexualities and gender experiences and with direct elimination (VV.AA. 2021). In a country that has denied its structural racism and homo/transphobia, armed actors have enacted forms of violence that were gendered, sexualized, and racialized. Those violences were rooted in a history of *mestizaje* – miscegenation as core element of nation-building project that imposed not only a racial whitening order but also a social order based on ideas of cleanness and purity. I suggest that such order is continued in social cleansing operations and expressed in the impact of threatening leaflets.

Asked about the impact of the leaflets, Guillermo explained that by now they are used to them. Since they have become so common, it is better to ignore them, he stated. However, he also explained that it does not mean that the leaflets are harmless. Leaflets announce who are those marked as dangerous others. Once leaflets are distributed, people stop going out, "trans girls" do not dress up and prefer to stay at home, and public spaces are emptied. This situation runs parallel with the presence of criminal gangs struggling for power. *Bandas Criminales Emergentes* – Criminal Emerging Gangs – emerged after the demobilization of *paramilitares* (2003–2006), and it is commonly assumed that they are just a new phase of paramilitary armies. These forms of everyday violence are targeting not just queer men but also other marginalized individuals and groups. This permanent surveillance is of relevance to understand the mutual constitution of masculinities and nationalism in which, as Slootmaeckers (2019) argues, forms of violence such as homophobia act as technology of othering. I would add that it is not just homophobia but also violence against transgender people and subordinated masculinities, such as those outside expected models of productivity and citizenship.

Being a Queer Man in Context of Conflict: Struggling with Abjection

The descriptions that Guillermo, Oscar, and Ignacio offered about the current situation of violence in their region contrasted with the references they offered on changes in gender and sexual orders. Those changes were seen as creating tension between the permanence of traditional gender and sexual orders, mostly explained as *machismo*, and the *avances* ("advancements") and *reconocimiento* ("recognition") due to collective actions. The interviewees' narratives challenge oversimplifying approaches to gender and sexuality as mostly places of oppression and instead call attention to their agency for change. The *avances* are the result of their collective action and materialize their struggles for dignity; struggles often reduced to the last pages of human rights reports mostly constructed around denouncing victimization. The tension between *machismo* as oppressive social and cultural structure and the acknowledgment of the changes produced by collective action can be seen to make sense of their experiences amid protracted violence. It is an attempt to express agency.

In the previous section, I focused on how queer men lived in several overlapping regimes of violence. Those regimes can be seen as a result of the heteronormative patriarchal system that produces social order through the naming of what is legitimate and what is abject, as Butler (1990, 1993) discussed extensively. The *abject*, in Butler´s perspective, are those zones of uninhabitability, unintelligibility, or lifelessness in which marginalized others are cast to exist. The violences discussed earlier have a destructive power not only in terms of annihilation but also in terms of producing certain social orders by the marginalization of some life projects. In this section, I expand on how queer men navigate in those zones of abjection. I argue that such navigation is done by finding ways to acquire some elements of acceptance, such as the respect and responsibility associated with hegemonic masculinities, and at the same time creating strategies to survive as queer men in a context in which legal and illegal armed actors are active agents in producing gender and sexual orders for their socio-political purposes. It is a combination of agency, collective mobilization, and action at grassroots level.

Early in the interview, Guillermo, Oscar, and Ignacio agreed on *machismo* as a common element of the local culture. "Machismo" was offered as an all-encompassing explanation that would speak for itself to describe not only male power but also lack of caring for others and for oneself, risk-taking, and the making of violence as intrinsic and definitional elements of one's identity. Guillermo mentioned how his work on sexual rights often faces the problem that responsibility on sexual behavior and reproductive consequences – including sexual care – is seen as the obligation of women. Because of machismo, men do not participate in those caring activities and decision-making duties. For example, introducing the use of condoms is often seen as difficult for men or even opposed to masculinity. Even more, Guillermo mentioned with concern how the city may be facing a high level of vulnerability to HIV because of the "myths and ignorance" around topics of sexuality and the virus. As such, *machismo* was stated by these queer men as an explanatory trope to locate themselves in gender and sexual orders in which they are part and to take a step aside at the same time.

Victor has a 12-year-old son who is the biological son of a friend involved in sex work. Victor used to be his godfather. One day, however, Victor's friend asked him to take care of the kid for a few days. She left and only returned three years after, telling Victor that she could not continue raising the kid. Victor registered him under his family name. They live together, in a house that Victor inherited from his mother. Being a caring father for his kid and even supporting the education of a niece and a cousin have given Victor a role in his family that challenges the rejection he faced due to his homosexuality. Still, now that his son is becoming a teenager, Victor has reduced his work as *transformista*.

In the case of Ignacio, his family did not accept his homosexuality, and his father refuses to talk to him. He had to leave his family when they discovered his sexual orientation. After that, he worked as a *transformista* in gay discos for a while. Nowadays, his relationship with his family is improving. As far as he acts *serio* – "straight acting" – his family would accept him, he explained. Nevertheless, he still feels rejection in his family and community.

Rejection seems to work also in connection with creation. For 11 years, Victor has been an active member of the board of the *Reinado Gay Nacional del Mar* – the National Gay Maritime Beauty Contest. Contestants from all around the country come to the city for a week of activities, such as parades in the beach, visits to organizations, and community work. Victor remembered that, at the beginning of the contest, there was a lot of discrimination and jokes about it. Now, the *Reinado* is an event of the city and has partial support by local authorities. Three years before the interview, for example, there was the first *Desfile de la Diversidad Sexual* – a sexual diversity parade that Oscar and Ignacio remembered with pride. They were just a few participants and walked with fear. Despite some negative reactions, people "behaved properly," they commented. In the second year, there were more participants; nobody used masks to cover their faces, and they even had the accompaniment of the police. The community was expecting the parade; people wanted to see them from the best places on the street, and even the wife of the mayor was present, they said enthusiastically. Commenting on that event, Guillermo said that he sees more respect in a place like Cienaga than in the interior of the country. There is now even space for a trans beauty pageant during *Fiestas del Caiman*, Alligator Festivities, the most important local festivities in Cienaga and highly recognized as cultural heritage in the country.

Ignacio, Oscar, and Victor described a dense network of parties and beauty pageants that happen all year through and in different places in the region.

They even mentioned a little town close to the extended banana plantations policed by *paramilitares* where sometimes *transformistas* organize events. Part of the conversation was about what happened in the last pageant when the best candidate was someone coming from the other side of the country. They were proud that they have people from so far coming here for these events. Asked about how this could happen in an area where *paramilitares* had a significant territorial, political, and economic control, they associated this effect with the logic underlying some male-to-male sexual interactions. For them, it happens for the same reason that straight men, while enhancing expressions of hegemonic masculinity, look for *maricas* to have sex with. They may also be the first ones "throwing stones at them" when they are in company of other men.

What they were describing was a regulated integration of diverse sexual practices, sexual subjectivities, and gendered interactions. The navigation in these contradictory gender and sexual orders also requires a constant control of their embodiment of gender and sexuality and a permanent renegotiation of their belonging to family, community, and social networks. Oscar started the interview by explaining how important the support of his family has been to overcome bullying because of his sexual orientation and gender expression. He does not fear to react to bullying on the streets by turning back and facing the situation, because he is sure his family will support him. He also emphasized that what makes a difference in his case is that he leads his life as a gay man in a "responsible" way, meaning, that he is not being promiscuous or causing problems.

It is important to explore in detail these references to the acceptance of prescribed responsibilities in relation to masculinities and embodiment. A first reaction might be to explain this as proof of the power of hegemonic masculinity and heteronormativity over queer masculinities. It is not possible to locate queer masculinities totally outside of the regulation of gender and sexuality imposed by those regimes. The fact that it occurs in contexts of socio-political violence where armed actors regulate several aspects of everyday life, including gender expression and sexual interactions, needs to be taken into account. I could see less of a desire of looking straight and more a search for demonstrating belonging, solidarity, and interconnection with social networks. Even more, to protect or reduce risk of exposure to relatives and those in close interactions. The search for some grade of acceptance through responsibility associated with traditional gender roles and the embodiment of markers of gendered respect could be seen more as strategies to survive in oppressive gender, sexual, and socio-political regimes.

Micro-activism and Reasons for Change

If there is a common element among the diverse approaches to the meanings of peacebuilding and transitional justice from below, it is the recognition of activism as a key element in the challenge of war, violence, and power systems (McDonald 1997). The increasing acknowledgment of issues of women and gender (O'Rourke 2013), and of gender and sexual diversity in conflict analyses and transitional justice mentioned earlier, is the result of lobbying and activism by a diverse range of organizations (El-Bushra 2007; Lambourne and Rodriguez Carreon 2016). This is certainly the case in Colombia, where much of the knowledge on gender and sexual diversity has been gathered and occurred outside of academia. There is, indeed, extensive evidence to argue that it is thanks to activists' knowledge and advocacy that gender and sexual diversity, LGBT topics, or queer analyses have entered the field of peacebuilding and transitional justice in this context (see Oettler, this volume).

Activism is indeed a key element in a perspective from below. Activism often involves a call for change. There is a reason that those in powerful and hegemonic positions often oppose and fight back activism for change: because they resist to give up power that is sought to be changed and redistributed as a result. These processes also have direct implications for discussions around masculinities. As Raewyn Connell stated in an analysis of research on masculinities and the promotion of peace (2000: 24) "the most powerful groups of men usually have few personal incentives for gender change." Even though many men and boys may have a tense or oppositional relationship with hegemonic masculinity, their claims may be shamed or despised in favor of violence and militarism. Literature on youth masculinities in contexts of socio-political violence has described extensively the interconnection between violence and the achievement of masculinity (Riaño 2006). The legitimation and normalization of violence depend on the dismissal of alternative gender and life projects.

The analysis of activism, collective struggles, and reasons for change is a key element in the queering of below in transitional justice. Change, in terms of changing collective patterns of being men, has been extensively discussed in the social studies of masculinities and in activism for changing masculinities (Aguayo and Sadler 2011; Careaga and Cruz Sierra 2006; Connell 2015; Gonzalez 2012; Valdés and Olavarría 1998). Here, I suggest moving that interest and these discussions a step further. Queering the below in transitional justice implies a discussion on the strategies to promote change, on activism, and in particular an understanding of struggles for change led by those in oppressed and marginalized positions. It is within the practices and discourses of those acting in social mobilizations, civil society organizations, and diverse landscapes of collective action that the "below" is enacted.

Activism can reproduce hierarchies of power. Therefore, a queer perspective is also a discussion of the resources that some may or may not have to make their voices recognized and to advance an exploration of the mechanisms that make their experiences intelligible for the peacebuilding and transitional justice industries. TJFB requires close attention to micro-activisms and to those with fewer resources to be heard in official mechanisms of transitional justice. This certainly applies to the experiences and subject positioning of queer-identifying men in Colombia, as discussed thus far in this chapter. In contexts of socio-political violence and intense regulation of both state institutions and social infrastructure, the limits and possibilities of activism, and therefore their scope of change, are intensively regulated and limited. The overlapping violences described earlier are an evident expression of how destructive power can limit and impede social mobilization. Other power relations, such as cultural and political capital, can also affect the possibilities for activism.

Victor remembered how a well-known *paramilitar* gave him food and let him use a house where he could offer care for people at the latest stage of the syndrome. The *paramilitar* was infamous for his cruel actions and for helping people in need. It was through a woman's humanitarian assistance organization that Victor was introduced to him. That was the time in which *paramilitares* infiltrated community organizations to get some support for their actions and to control what was happening in social mobilizations. They even controlled some of the provision of health services. Accepting such offer of help was not an easy decision for Victor. There was a general lack of resources, and in this context, *paramilitares* managed several aspects of institutional and everyday life. Rejecting such an offer would have ended up acting against himself and his work. It was hard work, and there was a lack of state-sponsored support.

Victor's history as an activist resembles those stories of people who struggle to transform injustices using all resources available, including their own income. It also remembers a common situation in countries like Colombia where, because of the lack of services provided by the state, people organize themselves to solve basic needs, such as access to medicines or health care. In the case of Guillermo, his house was his office, workshop saloon, and community meeting room. Their micro-activism reminds how queering is a constant blurring of the public–private divisions.

However, their micro-activism does not follow the pattern of building structured organizations as illustrated by other interviewees and was kept on a more personal level, raising questions on different patterns for building a sense of collective action. None of them had the literacy required to participate in human rights lobbying that required sophisticated legal language, or in the alliance-building strategies required to escalate their influence from the bottom up. They also lack the class and political capital that could connect them with local political and economic elites. Despite having a long career in activism, they did not reference belonging to recognized national or regional networks of social movements. Still, their work was significant enough to catch attention of those in favor and against their leadership in social transformation.

Queering TJFB implies also discussing the strategies used by collective actors to produce change. The examples mentioned earlier have in common a distance with legal activism as core strategy for mobilization. Legal activism is somehow equivalent to top-down perspectives in peacebuilding that focus on action at institutional level to produce transformations. It is in a privileged power position due to its proximity to the language of the state that locates micro-activisms in subordinated relationships. Micro-activism expands the idea of the "local" to the dimension of the intimate.

I had the chance to get in contact with Victor in early 2020 for a research on the impact of political violence on people living with HIV (Serrano-Amaya et al. 2021). After I first met him, he was unable to return to his natal city due to continuing threats to him and his family. As a father, he did not want to expose his son. Despite the enactment of new legal frames for transitional justice, such as compensations for victims of armed conflict, he could not even present his case as victim of conflict in his town, fearing that his testimony could be known by illegal armed actors. He was registered in the legal system recognizing victims with the help of a local NGO working in his new residence. The changes promised with transitional justice have had little impact on him.

Which Transition? Transition and Trans Masculinities in Transitional Justice

By early 2010s, the time of previous narratives, possibilities of a political transition in Colombia were still a blur. By the late 2010s, the political landscape has changed dramatically. The signing of the 2016 Peace Agreement between former FARC guerrilla and the Colombian government was simultaneously a time of hope, deception, and suspicions about the possibilities for change. The failing of the 2 October 2016 plebiscite to ratify the peace agreement among discussions against and in favor of gender perspective made evident the fragility of a gendered peace perspective. I was among those who lobbied and contributed to give meaning to the inclusion of LGBT topics in the peace agreement and in peacebuilding and witnessed how difficult it was still to bring gender and sexuality to the center of transitional justice initiatives.

For the argument I am weaving here, it is important to discuss the notion of "transition" in TJFB from perspectives less considered in the more legalist approaches to the topic. "Transition" in transitional justice tends to be a less-discussed category from gendered or sexualized perspectives. However, for the perspective of queer subjects, the meaning of *transition* needs to be put at the center, especially when such transition from some forms of violence may imply its reconfiguration in post-conflict or post-political agreements. As the stories I have described before, the change delivered for queer subjects after political negotiations may be little or relative.

In the increasing development of the field of transgender studies, issues of transitional justice, peacebuilding, and transgender lives in general and trans masculinities are gaining interest. Key studies have shown how individuals who identify as transgender participated actively in struggles for social change (Morgan et al. 2009) and how the narrative of change and sex transition operated also as a device to explain political transitions (Carvajal 2018; Swarr 2012). Still, including the experiences of trans women or men under notions of queerness or in the frameworks of social studies of masculinities is problematic, as it is adding the experiences of trans men in descriptions of masculinities and transitional justice without considering theoretical implications, such as conceptual appropriation or homogenization of life experiences. My attempt here is not to equate trans masculinities to queer masculinities but to contribute to a discussion on the possibilities of trans masculinities to transforms the field of transitional justice and masculinities.

In order to open a discussion on transgender lives and transitional justice, we arranged a panel on political and social transition at Universidad de los Andes, Bogotá, on 6 September 2019. The panel was held in an international conference on critical studies of political transitions and was intended to connect fields of discussion often presented separately. By the 2010s, there was in Colombia an increasing interest in connecting gender identity, sexual orientation, and peace and conflict issues, but mostly in terms of inclusion and recognition and less in terms of challenging core concepts of justice or political change. Queering those fields of knowledge and expertise was still a limited discussion.

The panel invited Colombian transgender scholars and activists Simón Uribe, Laura Weinstein, and Nikita Dupuis to discuss issues of gender, sexual, and political transitions. We have had the chance to collaborate before in activism and public policies for LGBT rights, and the event was the chance to reconnect our work and personal trajectories in a different political moment. A common element raised by them was that gender transitions and political transitions are interconnected. Peace, social justice, and transgender rights activist Nikita Dupuis made it explicit when introducing himself in the opening of the event:

> I believe in peace. I believe in dissidence. Without dissidence there will not be the utopia of peace. I have learnt from my experience of transitioning that everything can change. Peace is possible because I have lived utopia in my body and my life experience.

In his intervention, Nikita discussed the overlapping and embodiment of several forms of violence and several transitions without a neat or clear separation among each other. Male privilege, a key concept in discussions on masculinities, as something to be obtained, exercised, or excluded from, was not the key issue of his description of facing and living violence. Passing as a cisgender man in the working-class neighborhood where he grew up was not the desire of assimilation to male privilege pictured in some discussions on transgender masculinities. It was a strategy to survive gender-based, sexual, and socio-political violence. A strategy combined with a constant learning to read contexts to be aware of threats and the ability to create alliances and networks of support to move when needed. Transition has been embodied not only through the technologies of gender, as he described, but also through a constant negotiation of subjective identities and socio-political positioning. It is transition in terms of movement and not in terms of resolution.

Here I identify a connection with the previous discussion with the queering of TJFB: the blurring of the division public/private and the enactment of the intimate as space for micro- and macro-activisms different than the reification of the local as a space for change by itself. However, there are also differences. The local, in Nikita's analysis, can be, in fact, as violent as the structural, and privilege is not an intrinsic or taken-for-granted departing point. Even more, if in TJFB there is a displacement from the more legalist to more social-political perspective to transitional justice, here is an experience that runs outside to the top/down or bottom/up call.

Conclusion

This contribution offered a frame for connecting fields that have developed in separation, such as the studies of queer men and of transitional justice, in order to show the possibilities of queering transitional justice not just as the addition of another subject of study but to discuss some of the core ideas in the topic. The importance of the epistemological perspective "from below" is to emphasize the protagonist role of civil society and social movements in peacebuilding and transitional justice. Their agency and their creativity. It offers a significant paradigm change useful to consider the perspectives of those who are not often considered in the accounts of peacebuilding and queer men. As many other changes, such a perspective is the result not just of theoretical shifts but of the collective efforts of social actors to produce change. However, such paradigmatic change requires a constant discussion of the risks of instrumentalization, homogenization, exoticization, or coaptation.

Challenging homogenization has been a key element in the recent interest on masculinities in peacebuilding and transitional justice. In the extended literature on women and gender in peace and transitional justice, studies of masculinities or of gender and sexual diversity are just recently starting to develop as a particular field of attention. In that literature, militarized and violent dimensions of masculinities have had more attention due to the disproportionate suffering imposed on women and feminized bodies. Other dimensions of masculinities, such as non-militarized masculinities, the experiences of older men, trans or queer men, are less explored.

That risk happens also in the explanatory models of peacebuilding. The common representation of the peacebuilding enterprise as a pyramid locates the "below" at the bottom of the structure. "From below" suggests approaching from a certain topography that pictures elites and decision-making actors at the top and civil society at the bottom. in this representation, there is not a differentiation of the power relations among those social actors located at the top or at the bottom. The discussion on what is the "below" in those explanatory frames is limited and tends to create polarized and homogenized representation of who are the producers of change, particularly the ones in subordinated positions.

Nevertheless, as I intended to illustrate before, change is delivered not just through resistance but also with creativity and invention. These efforts are often produced with limited resources, and even against state institutions and armed actors. In the previous discussion, I called attention on the pivotal role of collective action in the queering of transitional justice but also warned about the problems of using a homogenized or standardized idea of how it acts. There is agency and collectiveness in the cases of the queer men described, but it is also limited and restricted by the destructive power of multiple forms of violence they are facing. Here is a space for comparisons with the ways in which women exercise agency and collective action in their dealing with socio-political violence. Describing what I mentioned before as a "mobilization" of queer men as used for describing women's mobilizations in contexts of armed violence and political transitions would be problematic and misleading. Still, there is a sense of collectiveness and belonging, even if atomized and micro-localized.

There are also other relevant differences. The call to acknowledge "the below" is a call to recognize local ownership and participation in the return to a state disrupted by conflict. The return to the "normal" or to certain everydayness is part of the promises of transitional justice and sometimes celebrated as proof of the success of communities and organizational movements. However, there is again a relevant difference here when considering the disparate subjects in "the below." For queer subjects and those in subordinated gender and sexual positions, the "before" was already a violent order that must not be restored or recovered but radically transformed. The "return to the normal" is, in fact, the announcement of continuing violence. Not by surprise, there were no key movements of rupture in the narratives of the queer men I encountered. Which normal, if there is any, for whom, and for which reasons, seems to be one of the biggest critiques from a queer perspective of transitional justice.

The interest on masculinities in general, and in queer masculinities in particular, in relation to transitional justice is to open and expand the field of conflict transformation and peacebuilding. Social studies of masculinities had a strong connection with feminism and with gender as a category for social analysis and for changing power relationships. The queering of TJFB (1) is useful to interrogate who becomes, and for which reasons, the subject of attraction on the accounts of transitional justice and under which regimes of existence, particularly nowadays, when we are facing more public policy interest in issues of gender, men, masculinities, and peacebuilding; (2) helps explore why there is certain attention on some men on dealing with forms of gendered, sexualized, and socio-political violence while silence on others; (3) expands the gendered dimensions of conflicts to issues not often considered relevant, such as in the examples I provided earlier, giving space to voices not often heard in these debates; (4) challenges, with the focus on the below and the subaltern, the risk of imposing a new order of authority and expertise in the making of masculinities and transitional justice as a new field of academic and political concern; (5) reminds us that in masculinities there are several structures of power in interaction, including those of the global order of knowledge; and (6) finally, strengthens the gendered and sexualized dimension of justice in TJ with the acknowledgment of how gender hierarchies still have disproportionated impact in women and those feminized subjects and the inclusion of gender-related inequalities and part of agendas for justice in a dimension broader than a political transition.

References

Aguayo, F. and M. Sadler (eds.) (2011). *Masculinidades y politicas publicas: involucrando hombres en la equidad de genero*. Santiago: Universidad de Chile.

Bueno-Hansen, P. (2015). *Feminist and Human Rights Struggles in Peru: Decolonizing Transitional Justice*. Champaign, Illinois: University of Illinois Press.

Bueno-Hansen, P. (2018). The Emerging LGBTI Rights Challenge to Transitional Justice in Latin America. *International Journal of Transtional Justice* 12(1): 126–145.

Butler, J. (1990). *Gender Trouble: Feminism and the Subversion of Identity*. New York: Routledge.

Butler, J. (1993). *Bodies That Matter: On the Discoursive Limits of "Sex"*. London: Routledge.

Careaga, G. and S. Cruz Sierra (2006). Introducción. In: Careaga, G. and Cruz Sierra, S. (eds.): *Debates sobre Masculinidades. Poder, Desarrollo, Políticas Públicas y Ciudadanía*. México: Universidad Nacional Autónoma de México: 9–28.

Caribe-Afirmativo (2017). *"Arco iris en blanco y negro" Reflexiones en torno a derechos, condiciones de vida y construcción de Paz de personas LGBTI en los municipios de Maicao (La Guajira), Ciénaga (Magdalena), Soledad (Atlántico) y El Carmen de Bolívar (Bolívar) en el caribe colombiano en el año 2017*. Barranquilla: Caribe Afirmativo.

Caribe-Afirmativo (2019). *Nosotras resistimos. Informe sobre violencias contra personas LGBT en el marco del conflicto armado en Colombia*. Barranquilla: Caribe Afirmativo.

Carvajal, F. (2018). Image Politics and Disturbing Temporalities: On 'Sex Change' Operations in the Early Chilean Dictatorship. *Transgender Studies Quarterly* 5(4): 621–937.

Castro-Gómez, S. and R. Grosfoguel (2007). Giro decolonial, teoría crítica y pensamiento heterárquico. In: Castro-Gómez, S. and Grosfoguel, R. (eds.): *El giro decolonial: reflexiones para una diversidad epistémica más allá del capitalismo global*. Bogotá: Siglo del Hombre Editores; Universidad Central; Pontificia Universidad Javeriana: 9–46.

Chambers, S. A. (2007). An Incalculable Effect': Subversions of Heteronormativity. *Political Studies* 55(3): 656–679.

CNMH (2015). *Aniquilar la diferencia. Lesbianas, gays, bisexuales y transgeneristas en el marco del conflicto armado colombiano*. Bogotá: Centro de Memoria Histórica.

CNMH (2016). *Limpieza social: una violencia mal nombrada*. Bogotá: CNMH.

CNMH (2018a). *Paramilitarismo. Balance de la contribución del CNMH al esclarecimiento histórico*. Bogotá: CNMH.

CNMH (2018b). *Un carnaval de resistencia: Memorias del reinado trans del río Tuluní*. Bogotá: CNMH.

CNMH (2019). *Ser marica en medio del conflicto armado. Memorias de sectores lgbt en el Magdalena Medio*. Bogotá: Centro Nacional de Memoria Histórica.

Colombia-Diversa (2013). *Impunidad sin fin. Derechos humanos de lesbianas, gays, bisexuales y personas trans en Colombia 2010–2011*. Bogotá: Colombia Diversa.

Connell, R. (2000). Arms and the Man: Using the New Research on Masculinity to Understand Violence and Promote Peace in the Contemporary World. In: Breines, I., Connell, R. and Eide, I. (eds.): *Male Roles, Masculinities and Violence: A Culture of Peace Perspective*. Paris: UNESCO Publishing: 21–33.

Connell, R. (2005). *Masculinities* (2nd ed.). Berkeley: University of California Press.

Connell, R. (2009). *Gender*. Cambridge, Oxford and Malden: Polity.

Connell, R. (2015). *El género en serio. Cambio global, vida personal, luchas sociales*. México: Universidad Nacional Autónoma de México.

Connell, R. and J. Messerschmidt (2005). Hegemonic Masculinity: Rethinking the Concept. *Gender & Society* 19(6): 829–859.

Conway, D. (2004). 'Every Coward's Choice'? Political Objection to Military Service in Apartheid South Africa as Sexual Citizenship. *Citizenship Studies* 8(1): 25–45. http://doi.org/10.1080/1362102042000178418.

Duggan, M. (2012). *Queering Conflict: Examining Lesbian and Gay Experiences of Homophobia in Northern Ireland*. Farnham, Surrey: Routledge.

Duriesmith, D. (2019). Engaging or Changing Men? Understandings of Masculinity and Change in the New "Men, Peace and Security" Agenda. *Peacebuilding*: 1–14.

El-Bushra, J. (2007). Feminism, Gender, and Women's Peace Activism. *Development and Change* 38(1): 131–147.

Epprecht, M. (2004). *Hungochani: The History of a Dissident Sexuality in Southern Africa*. Montreal and Ithaca: McGill-Queen's University Press.

Falconí, D. (ed.) (2018). *Inflexión marica. Escrituras del descalabro gay en América Latina*. Barcelona: Egales.

Fobear, K. (2014). Queering Truth Commissions. *Journal of Human Rights Practice* 6(1): 51.

Gómez Sánchez, G. I. (2012). Asimetrías del poder, resistencias y derechos de las víctimas frente a los procesos de justicia y paz. *Estudios de Derecho* 153: 90–112.

González, D. A. (2021). 'Teatro, lo tuyo es puro teatro': memoria visual travesti en el trópico (1984–2020). (Spanish). *"Theater, Yours Is Pure Theater":Visual Transvestite Memory in the Tropics (1984–2020) (English)* 16(1): 140.

Gonzalez, J. (2012). *Red Iberoamericana y Africana de Masculinidades*. Available at: http://www.redmasculinidades.com/content/qui%C3%A9nes-somos.

Gready, P. and S. Robins (2014). From Transitional to Transformative Justice: A New Agenda for Practice. *The International Journal of Transitional Justice* 8(3): 339–361. http://doi.org/10.1093/ijtj/iju013.

Guha, R. (1997). *A Subaltern Studies Reader, 1986–1995*. Minneapolis: University of Minnesota Press.

Hagen, J. J. (2016). Queering Women, Peace and Security. *International Affairs* 92(2): 313–332. http://doi.org/10.1111/1468-2346.12551.

Hamber, B. (2016). There Is a Crack in Everything: Problematising Masculinities, Peacebuilding and Transitional Justice. *Human Rights Review* 17(1): 9–34.

Harding, S. (1987). Is There a Feminist Method? In Harding, S. (ed.): *Feminism and Methodology*. Bloomington and Indianapolis: Indiana University Press.

Haug, F. (1987). *Female Sexualization: A Collective Work of Memory*. London: Verso.
Jackson, S. (2006). Gender, Sexuality and Heterosexuality: The Complexity (and Limits) of Heteronormativity. *Feminist Theory* 7(1): 105–121.
Kreft, A.-K. (2019). Responding to Sexual Violence: Women's Mobilization in War. *Journal of Peace Research* 56(2): 220–233. http://doi.org/10.1177/0022343318800361.
Krystalli, R. C. (2019). *'We Are Not Good Victims': Hierarchies of Suffering and the Politics of Victimhood in Colombia*. PhD, The Fletcher School of Law and Diplomacy. Medford: Tufts University.
Lambourne, W. and V. Rodriguez Carreon (2016). Engendering Transitional Justice: A Transformative Approach to Building Peace and Attaining Human Rights for Women. *Human Rights Review* 17(1): 71–93. http://doi.org/10.1007/s12142-015-0376-0.
Langlois, L. L. (2018). Gender Perspective in UN Framework for Peace Processes and Transitional Justice: The Need for a Clearer and More Inclusive Notion of Gender. *International Journal of Transitional Justice* 12(1): 146–167.
Lundy, P. and M. McGovern (2008). Whose Justice: Rethinking Transitional Justice from Bottom up. *Journal of Law and Society* 35(2): 265–292.
Maddison, S. and S. Scalmer (2006). *Activist Wisdom: Practical Knowledge and Creative Tension in Social Movements*. Sydney: UNSW Press.
Maier, N. (2020). Queering Colombia's Peace Process: A Case Study of LGBTI Inclusion. *International Journal of Human Rights* 24(4): 377.
Martin, L. S. (2016). Practicing Normality: An Examination of Unrecognizable Transitional Justice Mechanisms in Post-Conflict Sierra Leone. *Journal of Intervention & Statebuilding* 10(3): 400–418.
McDonald, G. (1997). *Peacebuilding from Below: Alternative Perspectives on Colombia's Peace Process*. London: Catholic Institute for International Relations.
McEvoy, K. and L. McGregor (2008). *Transitional Justice from Below: Grassroots Activism and the Struggle for Change*. Oxford and Portland: Hart Publishing.
Morgan, R., C. Marais and J. Wellbeloved (2009). *Trans. Transgender Life Stories from South Africa*. Johanesburgh: Gala.
Moser, C. (2001). The Gendered Continuum of Violence and Conflict. An Operational Framework. In: Moser, C. and Clark, F. (eds.): *Victims, Perpetrators or Actors? Gender, Armed Conflict and Political Violence*. London: Zed Books: 30–51.
Naples, N. (1997). A Feminist Revisiting of the Insider/Outsider Debate: The 'Outsider Phenomenon' in Rural Iowa. In: Hertz, R. (ed.): *Reflexivity and Voice*. Thousand Oaks: Sage: 70–94.
Nordstrom, C. (1999). Wars and Invisible Girls, Shadow Industries, and the Politics of Not-Knowing. *International Feminist Journal of Politics* 1(1): 14–33.
O'Rourke, C. (2013). *Gender Politics in Transitional Justice*. London: Routledge.
Paredes, V. (2020). Una experiencia de justicia transicional transformadora desde abajo. Las contribuciones de OIM a la participación de las víctimas de Pasto. *A Bottom-Up Transformative Transitional Justice Experience. IOM's Contributions to the Victim's Participation of Pasto* 22(44): 98–109. http://doi.org/10.29375/01240781.3825.
Pierce, J., M. A. Viteri, D. Falconí, S. Vidal-Ortiz and L. Martínez-Echázabal (2021). Queer/cuir de las américas: Traducción, decolonialidad y lo inconmensurable. *El lugar sin límites. Revista de estudios y políticas de género* 5: 1–20.
Riaño, P. (2006). *Jóvenes, memoria y violencia en Medellín*. Bogotá: Editorial Universidad de Antioquia, Instituto Colombiano de Antropología.
Richmond, O. (2007). Emancipatory Forms of Human Security and Liberal Peacebuilding. *International Journal* 62(3): 458.
Rosalind, S., W. Lars and P. Hazan (eds.) (2010). *Localizing Transitional Justice: Interventions and Priorities After Mass Violence*. Stanford, CA: Stanford University Press.

Rudling, A. (2019). What's Inside the Box? Mapping Agency and Conflict within Victims' Organizations. *International Journal of Transitional Justice* 13(3): 458–477. http://doi.org/10.1093/ijtj/ijz025.
Schneider, B. and J. Ward (2009). The Reaches of Heteronormativity: An Introduction. *Gender & Society* 23(4): 433–439.
Schulz, P. (2020). Towards Inclusive Gender in Transitional Justice: Gaps, Blind-Spots and Opportunities. *Journal of Intervention & Statebuilding* 14(5): 691.
Schulz, P. and H. Touquet (2020). Queering Explanatory Frameworks for Wartime Sexual Violence Against Men. *International Affairs* 96(5): 1169–1187. http://doi.org/10.1093/ia/iiaa062.
Serrano-Amaya, J. F. (2004). *Queering Conflict: The Invisibility of Gender and Sexual Diversity in Peace Building* (Master in Conflict Resolution). Bradford: University of Bradford.
Serrano-Amaya, J. F. (2014). *Chiaroscuro: The Uses of 'Homophobia'and Homophobic Violence in Armed Conflicts and Political Transitions.* PhD, The University of Sydney, Sydney.
Serrano-Amaya, J. F. (2018). *Homophobic Violence in Armed Conflict and Political Violence.* Cham: Palgrave Macmillan.
Serrano-Amaya, J. F., H. Mejía, C. Martínez, S. Pachón and S. Luna (2021). *VIHdas Truncadas: Informe sobre violencias contra personas viviendo con VIH en relación con el conflicto armado en Colombia.* Bogotá: Caribe Afirmativo.
Slootmaeckers, K. (2019). Nationalism as Competing Masculinities: Homophobia as a Technology of Othering for Hetero- and Homonationalism. *Theory and Society* 48(2): 239–265. http://doi.org/10.1007/s11186-019-09346-4.
Sutherland, J. P. (2021). *Nación marica. Prácticas culturales y crítica activista latinoamericana.* Santiago: Los Perros Románticos.
Swarr, A. L. (2012). *Sex in Transition: Remaking Gender and Race in South Africa.* Albany: State University of New York Press.
Tapia, N. (2019). The Category of Victim 'From Below': The Case of the Movement of Victims of State Crimes (MOVICE) in Colombia. *Human Rights Review* 20(3): 289–312.
Valdés, T. and J. Olavarría (eds.) (1998). *Masculinidades y equidad de género en América Latina.* Santiago: Flacso, UNFPA.
Vidal, S., M. A. Viteri and J. F. Serrano Amaya (2014). Resignificaciones, prácticas y políticas queer en américa latina: Otra agenda de cambio social. *Nómadas* 41: 185–201.
Viteri, M. A., J. F. Serrano-Amaya and S. Vidal-Ortiz (2011). Como se piensa lo 'queer' en America Latina? *Iconos* 35(1): 47–60.
VV.AA. (2021). *Nos decían: "tras de negras, maricas" Experiencias e impactos del conflicto armado en personas Afro-LGBT del Sur de Bolívar y el Pacífico Sur Colombiano: Instituto sobre Raza.* Igualdad y Derechos Humanos, Caribe Afirmativo, Fundación Afrodescendiente por las Diversidades Sociales y Sexuales, Arco Iris de Tumaco.
Warner, M. (1993). Introduction. In: Warner, M. (ed.): *Fear of a Queer Planet. Queer Politics and Social Theory.* Minneapolis and London: University of Minnesota Press: vii–xxi.
Wright, H. (2019). "Masculinities Perspectives": Advancing a Radical Women, Peace and Security Agenda? *International Feminist Journal of Politics*: 1–23.

Chapter 13

Reclaiming the Post-War Self

Masculinities, Political Prisoners, and Transitional Justice in El Salvador

Ursula Mosqueira

Introduction

Responding to TJ scholars who advocate for "thick description" and exploration of how survivors' lived experience and gender representations matter for TJ, this chapter investigates what masculinities "do" in three key moments of war survivors' lives. Based on ethnographic data and survivor narratives, I explore the lived experience of former political prisoners who endured torture during El Salvador's Cold War–era armed conflict (1980–1992) as they continue to make sense of their experience and seek justice. I argue that post-conflict and violence settings – such as post-war El Salvador – require that we avoid identifying survivors as either "agents" or "victims," which often tends to be the case (Schulz 2019). In this research, masculinities reveal an inevitable double character: vulnerability and agency appear as two sides of the same coin, suggesting that these "states of being" closely coexist and mutually condition one another.

Results shed light on how survivorhood and gender intersect. Survivor narratives show individuals who are able to exert agency by critically and creatively giving meaning to their present, reclaiming power over their lives. At the same time, these stories reveal deep forms of vulnerability, reflecting the effect of systems of power on individual lives: elements of class inequality, state repression, the moral duty to engage in armed revolutionary combat in their youth, and the gendered mandates to disguise vulnerability all reveal the burdensome sequelae of the past on them. This interplay of agency/victimhood reflects the gendered possibilities they find to elaborate and express who they are in ways that feel honest and dignifying. While displays of hegemonic masculinity emerge, demanding the masking of emotion and assuming the duty to protect others, "cracks" in this war hero identity also arise; as TJ scholars and practitioners, we must learn from the complexity of these expressions and accommodate for their multiplicity.

These findings are important, considering the modest amount of research we have yet produced on masculinities in TJ contexts and the little we know about Cold War Latin America's torture survivors (Park

DOI: 10.4324/9781003519522-17

2014). Also, they help enrich our comprehension of victims' needs, which is essential not merely in the interest of theoretical precision but, most importantly, to help identify how gendered scripts mediate individuals' access to reparations and justice. The case of former political prisoners in El Salvador provides insight into how post-conflict societies can implement transitional justice measures and practices that complement or go beyond the standard legalist approach in TJ[1] – such as reconciliation or reparation measures – especially in the absence of a strong state. Survivors' views are key vis-à-vis the legal impunity they face and the mixed evidence we have about whether and how conventional TJ mechanisms (trials and truth commissions) actually deliver the reparation that victims require (Akhavan 2001; Mallinder 2007; McEvoy 2007; Mendeloff 2009; Minow 1998, 2019; O'Connell 2005). While these mechanisms undoubtedly represent crucial advancements, the few and far between TJ measures implemented in El Salvador (including civil society–led restorative justice tribunals) follow the "legalist" model of testimony-giving (Frisso 2016), emphasizing survivors' role as witnesses of grave human rights violations. While these legal-type processes have been crucial to democratic transitions in post–Cold War Latin America by fomenting the rule of law and seeking a more efficient delivery of formal justice (Brooks 2003), reparations necessitate a fuller rendering of human experience.[2]

As Giorgio Agamben has argued, justice and restitution are a matter of subjects (Agamben 1999; Chare 2006). The subject "becomes witness to its own disorder" and "its own oblivion as a subject" (Agamben 1999: 106) when social relationships are torn by violence. Reconstituting a subjective order and escaping from oblivion therefore require transitional justice theory and practice to concern itself with subjectivity. Redistributing responsibility and shame (for the harms inflicted) and achieving a sense of restitution and recovery are necessarily a symbolic and narrative endeavor that is also conditioned by gender. Hence, Salvadoran former political prisoners can be important actors in transitional justice that push the boundaries on restitution and

1 *Legalism* generally refers to how the law tends to shape and regulate our behavior, our political relations, our language, and the way we think (Ewick and Silbey 1998). Not only in El Salvador but also in the rest of Latin America, official discourse has typically rendered torture survivors through a legal perspective, considering them important witnesses to the facts of repression, especially in truth commissions and judicial trial–type instances (Boesten and Wilding 2015; Franke 2006; Hayner 2011; Theidon 2007a).

2 In the best-case scenarios, legalism in transitional justice translated into truth commissions and human rights trials. They helped breed important advancements by culturally sanctioning impunity across countries, create legal tools to punish crimes against humanity, and produce vital research on violent histories to avoid their future repetition (Hayner 2011; Mani 2005; Neier 1998; Thakur and Malcontent 2005). In less-optimal scenarios, these mechanisms became standard-setting references.

reparations, contributing important knowledge on the post-authoritarian healing process of individuals, groups, and societies.[3]

Authoritarianism and Political Prisoners in El Salvador: A Brief Overview

El Salvador is a small country in Central America whose recent experience speaks eloquently of Latin America's Cold War transit. In 1980, an armed conflict of nationwide dimension broke out as a leftist revolutionary guerrilla movement attempted to overthrow a right-wing authoritarian government backed by the US government. As done previously during the twentieth century, state terror was implemented to destroy the voice of political dissent challenging an oligarchic status quo cemented during colonization (Ching 2016; Corradi et al. 1992; Leslie 2001; Montgomery 2018; Sluka 2000). A powerful authoritarian state apparatus focused on quelling the revolutionary effort. As the country's 1993 UN-led Truth Commission concluded, at least 85,000 people would be killed, 95% of them by government forces (Betancur et al. 1993), and widespread torture would be applied throughout the country (Hammond 1996; Leiby 2015).[4]

In the post-war period, absence of accountability for these crimes continues to be the norm, while the road to truth, justice, and reparations for victims of systematic human rights violations remains long and challenging. To date, a nearly unshakeable context of impunity prevails, supported by a broad-sweeping amnesty law (in place until late 2016), a weak judiciary, corruption, and lack of political will. The Salvadoran state has implemented minimal reparation programs, and there have been very few convictions for forced disappearances, extrajudicial executions, and torture committed on a

3 For example, in the Argentinian case (which takes the lead in state-implemented TJ efforts within the Latin American region), Rebekah Park identifies former political prisoners' juridical role in pushing for trials and truth commissions, and their political role in pushing for memorialization. In Northern Ireland, quantitatively based research suggests that victims can, in fact, "act as a positive and inclusive force in terms of the rehabilitation and re-integration of former combatants in societies emerging from conflict" (Brewer and Hayes 2015, 741; Joyce and Lynch 2017).

4 According to the Truth Commission, over 4,400 of the human rights violations documented during the armed conflict correspond to torture and mistreatment. Out of 22,000 complaints of serious acts of violence that occurred in the country between January 1980 and July 1991, over 20% concern torture (Betancur et al. 1993). This is an approximation, given the Truth Commission did not capture every act of violence and only received a significant sample of human rights violations during its three months of testimony-gathering (Betancur et al. 1993). However, the estimates also convey the widespread character of these violations and reveal the context in which my interviewees experienced torture. Many abuses were inextricably linked to other abuses documented by the truth commission and other human rights organizations: forced disappearances, arbitrary detention, denial of due process, extralegal assassinations, and massacres.

broad scale (Binford and Alarcón Medina 2014; Silber 2011). This state of impunity makes the country stand out among its Latin American neighbors, as it notably lags behind in securing victims' access to rights (Martínez Barahona et al. 2012; Skaar et al. 2016).

Regardless, persisting organizations in El Salvador made up by civil war survivors continue the uphill battle of seeking truth, justice, and reparations vis-à-vis the country's authoritarian past. COPPES, the Committee of Former Political Prisoners of El Salvador, or *Comité de Ex-Presos Políticos de El Salvador*, is one such organization. It brings together individuals who were detained without due process and tortured for their participation in political activities associated with leftist ideals during the country's armed conflict (1980–1992).

Gender in Transitional Justice: Expanding Current Boundaries

My research speaks to gender and transitional justice scholars who emphasize the need to explore alternative masculinities and thick description of the complex diversity of masculinities in peacebuilding and transitional justice processes in the everyday (Hamber 2016; Theidon 2009; see Campbell, this volume; see Serrano-Amaya, this volume). Creating a "thicker"[5] understanding of TJ can help us consider how power relations mediate access to rights – an aspect typically neglected by conventional approaches – and therefore interrogate how intersectional dimensions like gender, race, class, sexuality, and involvement in the political conflict at hand may condition the attainment of justice (McCann 2014; Ní Aoláin 2012; Scheingold 1974).

We have learned that gender is something we "do" (Butler 1988; Jurik and Siemsen 2009; West and Zimmerman 1987, 2009) in relation to the norms, expectations, and social environment created around one's concept of self (Hamber 2016; Human Rights Campaign 2020; West and Zimmerman 2009; Widmer 2006). As many contributors of this volume highlight, masculinities and other gender identities remain underexplored in the TJ field, which, in turn, engages the risk of appropriating survivors' discourses in ways that perpetuate limiting stereotypical notions, such as that of victims (especially women) as passive actors (Boesten and Wilding 2015; Campbell 2007; Franke 2006; Hamber 2016; Hayner 2011; Nesiah 2006; Ross 2003; Theidon 2007b, 2018; O'Rourke 2011; Sjoberg 2011).

5 Distinguishing between "thick" and "thin" theories in the social sciences implies juxtaposing multilayered, complex explanations of social reality focused on the meaning and context surrounding human behavior, with more unidimensional, narrowly descriptive, or positivistic analysis (Coppedge 1999; Geertz 1973; McEvoy 2007).

Moreover, we should also be aware of the ways that eliciting testimony can harmfully perpetuate the unequal distribution of shame in society (Theidon 2018). To serve justice and truth-telling more faithfully, TJ theory and practice can, for example, further consider the silences that surround men's sexual victimization (Touquet and Schulz 2021) and the implications for women to bear the "narrative burden" (Theidon 2018: 147) of sexual violence (Dolan 2018). This investigation aims to be cognizant and critical of the ways that public testimony sometimes shapes survivors' ability to give meaning to their experiences of pain, their needs, and their realities – both for themselves and for collective memory (Franke 2006; Hamber 2016; Hayner 2011; Nesiah 2006) – by more wholly exploring survivors' subjectivity than legal-type testimonies often allow.

To study political prisoners' masculinities, this chapter finds inspiration in two avenues proposed by critical TJ scholars. One of them involves shifting the focus of our analyses from the prevention of violent masculinities to, instead, considering "how hidden masculine cultures operate within a variety of hierarchies and social spaces" (Hamber 2016: 30) – a claim that is made centrally in Chapter 2 of this volume. The other avenue involves exploring the factors that structure survivors' vulnerability (Carpenter 2005; Dolan 2018; Theidon 2007b). My research follows these scholars' lead while also suggesting that we focus on factors that structure survivors' agency (Mosqueira 2020; Touquet and Schulz 2021). As many other populations involved in political violence, the individuals whose lives I explore are not only victims but also individuals who enact agency and reclaim power over their lives through social and political participation. By helping to "push the envelope" on understanding what gender does, we can shed light on how men's narratives – elicited in their various dimensions – could potentially begin to disarm existing gendered messaging around shame (Brown 2006, 2008).

Methodological Remarks

The empirical results discussed in this chapter come from my sociological doctoral dissertation analyzing Salvadoran former political prisoners' lived experience and how they reclaim power over their lives (Mosqueira 2020). I employed qualitative research methods to gather data: ethnographic interviews, participant observation (of informal conversations, group therapy sessions, meetings, group meals, and gatherings), and focus groups that were co-led with a male psychologist (and integrated other participatory methodologies). For the portion of results described in this chapter, I specifically explored how victimization affected individuals' sense of self and how this process is gendered.

I developed a relationship with the organization of former political prisoners in El Salvador named COPPES (Committee of Former Political Prisoners of El Salvador) through my work at the University of Washington Center for

Human Rights (UWCHR, in Seattle, USA) as a graduate student for multiple years. I deepened my relationship with COPPES through collaboration on TJ projects and multiple visits. Due to my pre-existing relationship with them and IDHUCA (the Human Rights Institute at UCA, a Jesuit university) through the Center for Human Rights, I was in an advantageous position to conduct this research. COPPES supported my research endeavors, and colleagues at IDHUCA provided crucial support and feedback throughout. I carried out my fieldwork between August and November 2015. In total, I carried out 38 in-depth interviews with Salvadoran former political prisoners (14 women and 28 men). I also carried out three additional interviews with key informants, including mental health professionals and NGO leaders, and held extensive informal conversations with human rights experts at IDHUCA. During my research, I used snowball sampling based on initial contacts provided by COPPES' leadership.

In terms of data analysis, I transcribed interviews and used iterative identification of codes to analyze them, finding inspiration in grounded theory to let analysis categories emerge (Katz 2001). Like any research endeavor, this study is hardly exempt of limitations. Any ethnographic work involves the possibility of doing symbolic violence to participants. I attempted to avoid this as much as possible by building rapport with each interviewee and securing a temporal and physical space in which we were not bothered. Interviews took place in locations that were viewed as neutral and safe to both interviewees and myself. I carried out the majority of interviews at UCA (the Jesuit University of El Salvador) and REDES (a non-profit organization where one of COPPES's leaders works and often offers up its offices for COPPES meetings). The rest took place in other third-party locations (people's homes, offices, or cafés).

Because of the sensitive content of this research endeavor, and in order to avoid the pitfalls of re-victimizing interviewees, I continuously received support from mental health professionals who know this population well. As part of doing respectful and ethical research, I obtained informed oral consent from each person prior to beginning interviews. I also made it clear that they could refrain from discussing any topic they were not comfortable with and that I would not inquire directly about their experience of victimization. I have protected their privacy by leaving out identifying information and substituting interviewees' real names with pseudonyms.

Some of the ethical implications of this work involve the level of trauma that many of the interviewees bring to the table. To minimize the risk of triggering traumatic reactions, I was as respectful and empathetic as possible and also availed myself with tools to handle unforeseen crisis situations. Mental health professionals who have worked with this specific population trained and advised me in this respect. While mental health professionals accompanied me in the first six interviews, I later decided to continue doing interviews by myself. I felt capable of handling challenging situations and considered that a more intimate dialogue became possible when only two of us were involved in the conversation. Time and resource constraints also made it difficult for a mental health practitioner to accompany me in all interview sessions. However, I also made it clear to interviewees that an additional conversation with me or a mental health professional after the interview could be arranged when needed.

While I recognize that adopting roles such as "researcher" and "research subject" engages power differences, I bear in mind self-reflective methodologies that consider both the researcher and the researched as subjects with agency, even if with differing power statuses (Ackerly et al. 2006; Björkdahl and Selimovic 2015; Jakoby 2006; Thapar-Björkert and Henry 2004). In all instances, I was open about my identity as a Chilean and native Spanish speaker, and I believe that having a shared cultural and linguistic background as a Latin American helped foster trust. Because of my previous work in El Salvador, I felt welcomed into a community as a colleague, collaborator, and friend. For men, it is possible that having a young woman (age 32 at that time) interviewing them on some of the most challenging episodes in their life may have caused difficulty. However, the two men-only focus groups I co-led with a male psychologist created a different space where aspects of vulnerability could be shared more safely.

The Double Character of Political Prisoners' Masculinities

In this section, I primarily focus on analyzing and describing masculinities. Yet because masculinities and femininities in this context emerge in inter-relational ways, at specific junctions, I also refer to observations and interviews that involve women. The section argues that the lived experiences of Salvadoran former political prisoners reveal masculinities shaped by a double character: aspects of vulnerability and agency alike structure them. These masculinities emerge in three key moments of interviewees' lives: when they became involved in a national revolutionary struggle, during torture and imprisonment, and in the post-war period, when trying to reclaim power over their lives.

By highlighting these specific moments, results shed light on how survivorhood and gender intersect. In this case, survivor experiences elucidate subjects who are able to engage in productive elaborations of the self by shaping their reality and creating resistance, as opposed to being completely determined by social power (Foucault 1985, 1986). They are able to exert agency, meaning, the ability to engage critically and creatively with their present (Taylor and Vintges 2004: 3), by reflecting, deliberating, and making "informed decisions about matters that affect [them] and reveal the sorts of persons [they] are" (Porter 2016: 39). Survivors' agency here translates into the ability to give meaning to their experiences of pain and survival, and to their needs and realities, not only for themselves, but also for collective memory. In turn, this agency is also conditioned by social structures such as gender, race, class, ethnicity, and culture, as positionality within these structures conditions possibilities of access to opportunities and resources or to multiplying layers of discrimination and violence (Ní Aoláin 2012). In this particular case, survivor narratives reveal deep forms of vulnerability reflecting the effect of systems of power on their individual lives: elements of class inequality, state repression, the moral duty to engage in armed revolutionary combat in their youth years, and the gendered mandates to disguise vulnerability all reveal the burdensome sequelae of the past on them.

In this particular case, agency/victimhood is mediated by gender scripts that shape individuals' possibilities of expressing vulnerability, pain, emotionality, and self-determination. Empirical results highlight the interplay between hegemonic masculinity displays, expression of vulnerability, and efforts to resist gendered messaging around shame.

Participation in the Revolutionary Struggle: Tensions Between Traditional and Modern Gender Roles

When individuals decided to participate in the armed revolutionary movement, they chose identities that challenged and redefined traditional gender roles (Lagarde 2005; Sharim 2005). This produced tensions that unveil conflict between roles linked to the family and roles linked to political life. These strains speak of broader social changes affecting gender roles in Latin America (and the Global North) during the second half of the twentieth century (Giddens 1992; Jelin 2005; Lagarde 2005; Olavarría 2017; Sharim 2005). Transformations in the traditional sex/gender/sexuality system that predominated in the region accelerated during the 1970s, owing to factors such as women's increasing participation in the labor force, the precarization of men's employment, structural adjustment policies, the redefinition of the state's role in society, increasing globalization, and demographic changes (Olavarría 2003).

In the Salvadoran context, masculinities convey tension between traditional and newer forms (Olavarría 2017). When asked about their revolutionary participation, men speak about the challenge of combining political activism with their immediate family ties. On one hand, they define masculinities in terms of a more traditional duty to protect a national family, leaving their personal home to engage in armed combat. On the other hand, they define masculinities around the vulnerabilities (pain, guilt, shame) that arose as they neglected a more modern masculine role in the home, which would have involved being present fathers and husbands (Olavarría 2017).

When interviewees describe their desire to protect others through armed combat, they express a more traditionally defined masculine role. They construct masculinities around what scholars have called "hegemonic" or "militarized masculinity" (Hamber 2016; Theidon 2007a; Wetherell and Edley 1999), structured around men's responsibility to protect and provide, which is also consistent with memoirs published by Salvadoran former combatants (Ching 2019). In fact, interviewees spent numerous hours describing civil war events and feats that align with this type of masculinity, which has been defined as a performance enacted through a narrow set of behaviors that are viewed as acceptable: for example, masking emotion, disguising fear, and prioritizing aggression and obedience (Eriksson and Stern 2012; Hamber 2016; Theidon 2007a; Trenholm et al. 2013). A growing body of literature has discussed how violent masculinities help perpetuate cycles of violence in society, and how they link to various forms of sexual violence, including during times of war (Kent 2014; Kirby 2013; Miranda 2007; Skjelsbaek 2001; Wood 2009). My interviewees' narratives cannot completely be reduced to the "dark" side of hegemonic masculinity, however, as their descriptions of war situations also reflect worthy qualities like courage and the desire to serve others through considerable risk-taking. Interviewees in my sample find a sense of agency in having participated in a crucial historical moment for their country.

Alternatively, empirical results expose different forms of masculinities that reflect "cracks" in the war hero identity. Interviewees' experiences unmask a more nuanced practice of masculinities during and after the revolutionary effort involving the expression of vulnerabilities. These mainly associate with the pain of severed family relationships and the loss of home. Talk of vulnerability does not arise automatically in men's narratives, however, as they tend to speak indirectly about their feelings. They express emotionality in other ways and during instances when a specific kind of rapport was built: during informal one-on-one conversations, weekly group therapy sessions, and men-only focus groups.

While the duty of having to fight "for a greater cause" has provided them with a sense of ownership and agency over their lives, this coexists with a sense of vulnerability and loss. Family is a key issue here. Tensions between conflicting notions of the family (immediate family versus a "national family") needing their time, protection, and engagement characterize the gendered worries experienced by men. An interviewee describes a concept of the family that prevails in men's depictions:

> My family was relegated to a secondary position, so to speak. From that time on, I understood the family to be – well, it's all of us. In fact . . . family involves our entire community, the people, the entire country, all of Latin America, the entire planet. So I can basically say that when I left [home], my [immediate] family was relegated to second place. Actually, I just couldn't be with them anymore. It wasn't ever the same.

Many men in my sample still struggle to resolve these tensions. Their choice to prioritize broader definitions of the family (a Salvadoran or Latin American "family") through their political engagement created notable pressure on their relationships with spouses and children. Interviewees repeatedly mention the disappointment that their political activism generated in their immediate family environment. When speaking of truncated family relationships, they mention neglected children who were hurt by their political involvement in multiple ways and who have not yet forgiven them for it. They also mention children who have not entirely "succeeded in life" as a result of their decision to leave home or their being forced to leave at some point. Neglecting ties to their immediate family often resulted in losing an important social space of belonging. It has led them to a feeling of "failing" as a father or spouse.

Damián describes his sense of loss around home and family, which crystallized on the night he was kidnapped by security forces:

> The past screwed me over. The moment I was taken out of my home in the middle of the night truncated my life. It made a crack in my personal structure, and now I'm feeling that crack. I had mentioned I have a family. I have kids, but I'm not with them anymore because they're already adults and now they fend for themselves. We used to have a house that we built for our family. Later on, I came to be homeless. . . . I went from living in my own home with my family to living in a rental place by myself. Off to start a new life.

A third example articulately reflects the felt sense of duty to protect the nation while leaving the comfort of the home behind and separating from loved ones (especially romantic partners). It is a piece of prose poetry that an interviewee wrote in the 1980s and generously shared with me:

> We renounced you. Without ever ceasing to love you, we made you believe, and we made ourselves believe, that the war or the organization was what we loved. Without waiting for there to be a reward, without imagining the possibility of finding you again, without announcing our departure, without anything . . . but with you all, always in our memory: mother, sister, woman, dream. . . .
>
> How can I tell someone I love that I love her? If the answer will be . . . "if you love me stay, don't go, come back"? How can I return to combat if I'm sad? And the years went by, the battles, the nights and their dead and you were alive, like every breath on my back, like every morning facing my future. . . .
>
> And what if none of this were true? For sure I would still have mom to cry with for the woman I no longer have, for the children who left, for the siblings who'd rather believe I'm dead, for the compañeros [comrades] who know I'm still alive . . .

Out of all the richness held in this passage, I would like to underline how it reflects men's discourses throughout. The author highlights his sense of loss around intimate/family relationships while describing his duty to leave for combat and not being able to stay, as the women in his life might desire (or even as he himself might). This elaboration of masculinity hits on a key element of this political duty – the emotional duty of "making himself believe" that this is what he loved. Needing to cover his emotions with a sense of responsibility (as sadness did not find a place when it was time for combat) underscores the kinds of vulnerability masked by the role of active combatant.

The Contours of Interrogation and Torture

While men in this study do not readily discuss their emotional vulnerability in regards to interrogation, they more openly describe vulnerability in relation to physical abuse done to their bodies. Scholars indicate that shame in society is distributed along gendered lines (Brown 2006, 2008) and have described war contexts in which shame resists verbalization (Diken and Laustsen 2005; Theidon 2016). So by prioritizing descriptions of the physical sequelae of torture on their bodies and acknowledging that they endured severe beatings (as opposed to recognizing other kinds of vulnerability), they are likely exerting agency in order to resist shame.

In addition, men tend to discuss the facts of interrogation and the beatings they experienced under torture in more detail than women, although they do not mention any sexualized elements of abuse. Such elements of shame and intimidation did emerge in women's narratives and referred to sexual aspects as well. However, men did not describe this kind of intimidation, sexualized or not. While silences are of course unspoken, men's silence about this is noteworthy, given the prevalence of sexual forms of torture applied in El Salvador: 66% of victims of sexual violence in Salvadoran detention facilities were men, a finding that was confirmed by the non-governmental human rights commission of El Salvador, the CDHES (Leiby 2015: 134).[6]

Men's refusal to discuss any element of sexual victimization during my research likely speaks to the extreme position of vulnerability that discussing this topic would put them in vis-à-vis a female interviewer, the weight of shame around these issues in Salvadoran/Latin American society (Neumann and Anderson 2014; Mantilla Falcón 2005; Porter 2016; Theidon 2012), and the little practice men in this context seem to have in speaking with others about situations that made them susceptible to harm.

6 "The most frequent forms of sexual violence used against detainees were sexual humiliation (42 percent), rape and gang rape (23 percent), sexual torture (21 percent), and attempted or threatened acts of sexual violence (11 percent)" (Leiby 2015: 133).

Descriptions of beatings and precarious detention conditions are commonplace. For example, an interviewee describes physical ailments he currently experiences as a result of torture:

> I have lumbago now. They've just diagnosed me. Right now, I have back pain. They found I have two joined vertebrae and they are exerting pressure on the nerve. So that gives me a tingling sensation. . . . I attribute that part to torture. And the rib, the rib, I felt they hit me in this area. Not with their fist, though . . . this right here, with the edge of something.

Beyond only the physical concerns and consequences of violence on their bodies, however, men also express more complex elaborations around the intricacies of vulnerability, trauma, and agency. During a focus group session with only a few men guided by a male mental health professional, participants chose one place in their body that they viewed as a wound or injury from the time of imprisonment. This participatory therapy space created a different environment to the one we experienced during individual interviews or other (mixed-gender) group settings. It took a few hours and generated some of the richest exchanges I had with men regarding their experiences of pain and vulnerability.

A participant, while describing himself as "not very expressive but analytical" as a person, explains his major wounding around the loss of his family:

> The reason for locating my spot here [in my heart] has to do with history, and basically with the fact that I lost my family when I was imprisoned. That also created conflict with my children, in the sense that they basically became orphans. . . . [They had] no father, I was in prison, and no mother [because she disappeared]. That's a very long story . . . about the persecution of my three children. It didn't only happen at the first place [safety home] they went to. It also happened later when they were hiding with family. They had to leave that place too and go live with my sister. After that, they all went to the United States as mojados.[7] My family supported me with this but then my children were captured in the United States and they spent about ten days in detention at the border.

When the participant made this statement, his pain could be felt in the air. Male research participants tended to describe their feelings through factual descriptions of events rather than by explaining the feelings themselves. However, they reached this depth of expression only when prompted by a mental health professional in the context of an intimately defined focus group, in

7 An expression used in Central America to refer to individuals who migrate to the United States without documents.

which he and I participated on equal terms, by doing the same exercises as participants and speaking of our own vulnerabilities. This suggests that it takes a very specific kind of rapport to make way for the full spectrum of survivors' experiences to emerge. The findings in this section also point to the way in which vulnerabilities and agency are intricately linked: understanding how hegemonic masculinities occlude displays of emotion, fear, and "weakness" makes it all the more necessary to explore social spaces in which "cracks" to the war hero identity can let in some light.

After the War: Gendered Tensions in Seeking Justice and Healing

In this section, I explore masculinities as they emerged in the collective spaces that former political prisoners have constructed to seek justice and healing. On one hand, these mixed-gender spaces emphasize the sense of agency that survivors draw from their past and current political participation. In post-war El Salvador, collective truth- and justice-seeking efforts have been key to resist a staunch socio-political context of impunity; most research participants actively seek some measure of healing and justice through work with COPPES or involvement in labor unions, church organizations, and other community organizations. On the other hand, these spaces reveal important tensions between femininities and masculinities which relate to individuals' sense of vulnerability. While achieving a degree of collective involvement seems crucial in this context, when it comes to collaborating with others as victims in therapy and justice-seeking spaces organized by COPPES, gendered differences appear to get in the way. As shown by interview data, femininities constructed around victimization seem to place greater emphasis on experiences of vulnerability, while masculinities prefer to emphasize strengths. This difference creates gaps that still mediate individuals' ability to work through victimization experiences together.

A paradigmatic kind of tension I witnessed during COPPES's weekly mixed-gender therapy sessions (ten weeks in total) sheds light on these gendered difficulties. This space bore important emotional weight for all participants because it evoked how they elaborate their most personal, ethical, and political struggles. Initially, there were about 15 individuals who committed to participating in the ten weekly sessions. However, by the third week, a few of the women who have been active participants in COPPES (and founded the feminist organization DIGNAS) decided to stop participating. During one of the sessions, a woman brought up the issue of not feeling emotionally safe in the group therapy space. She had noticed in the previous session that her male counterparts were not displaying the emotional vulnerability she would have expected when discussing experiences of torture and imprisonment. The men responded, not agreeing with what the woman and her peers were expressing. They tried to assure them: if that was the way they felt, they understood and would support them in their own healing. But they could not be forced to say they were traumatized. The tension escalated, with both parties trying to find some resolution, but the effort only caused more frustration.

The following excerpt summarizes men's perspective on the issue and hints at why the women's position may have been too much for them to concede to. At least according to this group of men, identifying their war experience as being mostly traumatic would feel dishonest. The following quote comes from the men-only focus group that I co-led with a male psychologist, in which a different kind of rapport was built in comparison to individual interviews and the mixed-gender therapy sessions:

> I really don't want to feel like the war is a trauma. I don't drag that along with me as trauma. On the contrary, I think if that hadn't happened . . . maybe I'd have who knows how many children, and I'd continue being the tenant farmer at the Girona estate. Who knows! So, I feel that, speaking for myself . . . I'm completely satisfied. I view all this [justice-seeking work that I'm involved in] as a demand [we're making] to avoid further abuse. But not as trauma. I feel like it's our payment for – just like when you're in love with someone . . . all the suffering that comes afterwards is part of your payment for the happiness you enjoyed during a period of time [with that person].
>
> Whenever I'm having a shitty time, I think to myself, "damn, I've had such a great time [in the past], and the last thing I have to do is pay for it." I feel that torture and the other stuff was just the bill for everything I got out of this. Look, my knees are all screwed up and my feet are ruined [where torture was applied]. Sure! . . . But if I could, I would gladly give someone the chance to be a guerrilla if they got to experience the badass stuff we lived through, because I think it's all fascinating. I don't think there's a more badass profession than being a guerrilla. Definitely, you get to have the time of your life. . . . Despite all the darkness it creates, it also gives you incredible moments.

The sincerity and enthusiasm with which this participant shares his interpretation of the past highlight the rich narratives that healing spaces can accommodate when participants feel at ease with openly sharing their experiences. A sense of gratitude and awe infuses the narrative of this survivor, who prefers to emphasize the strengths he derives from his past experience rather than focus on the vulnerabilities it created. This is a trend that appears throughout masculine discourses. By doing so, he asserts his agency in refusing to dwell on pain or speak about his experiences publicly in the fashion that his *compañeras* (female comrades) may have liked during the group therapy sessions. Just as researchers have spoken of the danger of appropriating women's discourses by eliciting testimony in pre-scripted ways, men in this case are resisting a similar kind of appropriation.

In the Salvadoran context, and as a result of prominent social-cultural ideologies on gendered behavior, the masculinities–vulnerability link may be doing very different work for survivors than the femininities–vulnerability link. Social work and psychology scholarship, specifically relational-cultural theory, suggests that displays of self-conscious emotions like shame and social messaging around them are organized around gender (Brown 2006, 2008; Else-Quest et al. 2012; Hartling and Lindner 2016; Hartling et al. 2000; Tangney and Dearing 2002). Research on the effects of shame in victims of sexual violence also point to significant gender differences (Weiss 2010a, 2010b). For men, showing weakness is typically a source of shame (Touquet 2021).

Therefore, in this case, engaging in displays of vulnerability may seem especially risky for men. On the other hand, while femininity is also surrounded by negative messaging around social displays of vulnerability, research shows that building a safe community around sharing this emotion has been key for women's achievement of well-being (Brown 2006, 2008). While these conclusions stem from a US context, the comparable definitions of traditional/modern gender roles in Latin America and the Global North suggest the plausibility of these interpretations. As far as I could observe, this insight on femininities and vulnerability reflects the Salvadoran context well, as women in my sample have found safe spaces with other women to discuss their painful experiences. Men, to my knowledge, have not yet to the degree that women have.

Women and men may have to continue working separately in order to achieve a productive level of comfort in the presence of others, because all survivors carry with them considerable sequelae. Mental health experts I worked with claimed that a fruitful path forward involves holding healing spaces separated by gender identity; in this way, it would be easier to generate rapport, feel included, and exert voice in equal measure. Once individuals reflect on the gender representations that shape their lives, they may be able to listen to their peers across gender divides without demanding that they express themselves in any given way. This would be an important task for COPPES to consider and should be a crucial element of any reparation program or policy targeting political violence survivors.

Conclusions

This chapter analyzes how masculinities shape the lived experience of torture survivors in El Salvador, revealing the "work" of gender in three key moments. These data indicate that post-conflict and violence settings such as post-war El Salvador require that we avoid identifying survivors as either "agents" or "victims," which often tends to be the case (Schulz 2019). Masculinities here reveal an inevitable double character: vulnerability and agency appear as two sides of the same coin, suggesting that these "states of being" closely coexist and mutually condition one another.

The ethnographic data collected in this study reveal masculinities that are shaped by tensions between traditional and newer forms. Tensions also appear in narratives of interrogation and torture between expressing vulnerability and asserting agency; men prefer to describe painful experiences through factual descriptions of beatings but tend to sidestep emotional or sexualized aspects of victimization. Finally, in the post-war process of seeking reparations and justice through collective efforts, tensions surface between masculinities and femininities when negotiating identities as victims of torture. Particularly in mixed-gender therapy spaces, clashing expectations on how individuals discuss elements of agency and vulnerability reflect critical gendered troubles. Gendered social messaging around shame is probably key in creating these divides.

A central element of agency for masculinities (and also femininities) in this context is taking political action. At various points in time, this has involved breaking with the status quo, standing up for rights before and after the war, and participating in collective efforts. A subtler element of survivors' agency underlined in my results involves reclaiming and portraying the self in empowering ways or, as TJ scholars have called it, resisting the appropriation of their discourses. Masculinities here seem to be engaging in what anthropologist Audra Simpson calls "ethnographic refusal"[8] (McAllister 2013; Simpson 2007, 2014). Men resist describing their experiences in a predetermined way (for example, through the lens of victimization and vulnerability) that does not feel honest to them. On their part, women refuse to bear the burden of victimhood and vulnerability alone in their collective mixed-gender spaces.

By prioritizing masculinities in this study, I have spoken to key challenges that persist in TJ theory and practice in regards to gender, such as the risk of appropriating survivors' discourses in detriment of more dignifying public truth-sharing and framing gender as a limited dimension that leaves masculinities and other identities out of the gender question. Responding to critical TJ scholars, I have attempted to expand our understanding of the intricacies of masculinities in various social spaces and explore the factors that structure survivors' vulnerability. I have also proposed the need to investigate factors that structure survivors' agency, which allows us to transcend stereotypical notions of victims as passive actors (see Touquet and Schulz 2021). Additionally, this case study underlines the importance of studying masculinities in relation to other gender identities, as they condition and co-construct one another. Ultimately, this research emphasizes masculinities not merely for the sake of theoretical precision but, most importantly, to illustrate how gender

8 Audra Simpson defines "ethnographic refusal" as a rejection to a settler colonial structure of research that manifests itself in the right to speak and not to speak (Simpson 2007, 2014). It involves the refusal to be ordered, ranked, governed, or possessed.

performance conditions survivors' ability to maintain meaningful relationships with their own community and thus participate more unreservedly in reparation and justice-seeking spaces.

Results confirm the importance of exploring how survivors' sense of justice and restitution is a "subjective" matter in which gendered scripts play a role. Masculinities here sway between hegemonic masculinity displays, expressions of vulnerability, and efforts to resist gendered messaging around shame. The interrelatedness of these dimensions suggests several lessons for TJ mechanisms and practices. First, methodological considerations related to securing confidentiality, emotional safety, and diminishing power differences between research "subjects" and researchers are crucial to visibilizing narratives that convey the manifold facets of survival. While eliciting witness-style testimony in legal-type instances may result to productivity in certain contexts, reparation spaces become all the more necessary in the absence of state-implemented TJ mechanisms.

Furthermore, nuanced depictions of vulnerability and agency indicate that disclosure of victimization requires allowing stories to emerge in survivors' own terms. This means not imposing specific scripts for how vulnerability or agency need to be discussed and not pushing any specific agenda. Finally, these results not only indicate the power of prevalent gender norms to hinder the construction of justice-seeking and healing spaces based on respectful and honest relationships; by the same token, they also reveal the potential contained within collective survivor-led spaces to disarm shame and (unwanted) silence by empowering individuals to define their vulnerabilities and their agentic qualities in empowering ways. One stepping stone toward this could be expanding dialogue among survivors on the effects of gendered pressures and expectations on them. Another would be for survivors and relevant TJ stakeholders (academics, human rights organizations, international contributors, etc.) to take on some of the same questions addressed by this edited volume regarding the specific challenges faced by various gender identities. These discussions can, in turn, lead to cementing reparation programs that create new meeting points and participatory therapy spaces cemented on survivors' sense of voice. In Agamben's terms, these could become particular and local spaces focused on building subjects' sense of restitution and recovery – social spaces for men to explore "cracks" in the all-too-familiar war hero mandates in order to build renewed communities.

References

Ackerly, B., M. Stern and J. True (eds.) (2006). *Feminist Methodologies for International Relations*. Cambridge: Cambridge University Press.

Agamben, G. (1999). *Remnants of Auschwitz: The Witness and the Archive*. New York: Zone Books.

Akhavan, P. (2001). Beyond Impunity: Can International Criminal Justice Prevent Future Atrocities? (Symposium: State Reconstruction After Civil Conflict). *American Journal of International Law* 95(1): 7–31.

Betancur, B., R. Planchart and T. Buergenthal (1993). From Madness to Hope: The 12 Year War in El Salvador: Report of the Commission on the Truth for El Salvador. *Commission on the Truth for El Salvador*. Truth Commission Digital Collection, United States Institute of Peace. Available at: www.usip.org/sites/default/files/file/ElSalvador-Report.pdf. Accessed on: 14 December 2021.

Binford, L. and R. Medina Alarcón (2014). Revisiting the El Mozote Massacre: Memory and Politics in Postwar El Salvador. *Journal of Genocide Research* 16(4): 513–533.

Björkdahl, A. and J. Mannergren Selimovic (2015). Gendering Agency in Transitional Justice. *Security Dialogue* 46(2): 165–182.

Boesten, J. and P. Wilding (2015). Transformative Gender Justice: Setting an Agenda. *Women's Studies International Forum* 51: 75–80.

Brewer, J. and B. Haye (2015). Victimisation and Attitudes Towards Former Political Prisoners in Northern Ireland. *Terrorism and Political Violence* 27(4): 741–761.

Brooks, R. (2003). The New Imperialism: Violence, Norms, and the 'Rule of Law'. *Michigan Law Review* 101: 2275–2340.

Brown, B. (2006). Shame Resilience Theory: A Grounded Theory Study on Women and Shame. *Families in Society: The Journal of Contemporary Social Services* 87(1): 43–52.

Brown, B. (2008). *I Thought It Was Just Me (But It Isn't): Telling the Truth About Perfectionism, Inadequacy, and Power*. New York: Gotham Books.

Butler, J. (1988). Performative Acts and Gender Constitution: An Essay in Phenomenology and Feminist Theory. *Theatre Journal* 40(4): 519–531.

Campbell, K. (2007). The Gender of Transitional Justice: Law, Sexual Violence and the International Criminal Tribunal for the Former Yugoslavia. *The International Journal of Transitional Justice* 1: 411–432.

Carpenter, R. C. (2005). Women, Children and Other Vulnerable Groups: Gender, Strategic Frames and the Protection of Civilians as a Transnational Issue. *International Studies Quarterly* 49(2): 295–334.

Chare, N. (2006). The Gap in Context: Giorgio Agamben's Remnants of Auschwitz. *Cultural Critique* 64: 40–68.

Ching, E. (2016). *Stories of Civil War in El Salvador: A Battle Over Memory*. Chapel Hill: University of North Carolina Press.

Ching, E. (2019). Relatos de la Guerra Civil en El Salvador: Una Batalla Narrativa [Stories of the Civil War in El Salvador: A Narrative Battle]. *Realidad: Revista de Ciencias Sociales y Humanidades* 153: 23–47.

Coppedge, M. (1999). Thickening Thin Concepts and Theories: Combining Large-N and Small-N in Comparative Politics. *Comparative Politics* 31(4): 465–476.

Corradi, J., P. Weiss Fagen and M. A. Garretón (eds.) (1992). *Fear at the Edge: State Terror and Resistance in Latin America*. Berkeley: University of California Press.

Diken, B. and C. Bagge Laustsen (2005). Becoming Abject: Rape as a Weapon of War. *Body and Society* 11(1): 111–128.

Dolan, C. (2018). Victims Who Are Men. In: Ní Aoláin, F., Cahn, N. and Haynes, D. F. (eds.): *The Oxford Handbook of Gender and Conflict*. New York: Oxford University Press: Chapter 19.

Else-Quest, N. M., A. Higgins, C. Allison and L. Morton (2012). Gender Differences in Self-Conscious Emotional Experience: A Meta-Analysis. *Psychological Bulletin* 138(5): 947–981.

Eriksson Baaz, M. and M. Stern (2012). Beyond Militarized Masculinity: The Case of the DRC. In: Eriksson Baaz, M. and Utas, M. (eds.): *Gender and Stir: Reflections on Gender and SSR in the Aftermath of African Conflicts*. Uppsala: The Nordic Africa Institut: 331–334.

Ewick, P. and S. Silbey (1998). *The Common Place of Law: Stories from Everyday Life*. Chicago: University of Chicago Press.

Foucault, M. (1985). *The History of Sexuality. Volume 2: The Use of Pleasure*. Trans. Robert Hurley. New York: Vintage.
Foucault, M. (1986). *The History of Sexuality. Volume 3: The Care of the Self*. Trans. Robert Hurley. New York: Vintage.
Franke, K. (2006). Gendered Subjects of Transitional Justice. *Columbia Journal of Gender and Law* 15: 813–828.
Frisso, G. (2016). *El Derecho Internacional Penal como Instrumento de Resistencia en los Tribunales Populares: el Tribunal Internacional para la Aplicación de la Justicia Restaurativa en El Salvador*. Universidad del Rosario, Editorial Tirant Io Blanch, Instituto Iberoamericano de La Haya.
Geertz, C. (1973). *The Interpretation of Cultures: Selected Essays*. New York: Basic Books.
Giddens, A. (1992). *The Transformation of Intimacy: Sexuality, Love, and Eroticism in Modern Societies*. Stanford, CA: Stanford University Press.
Hamber, B. (2016). There Is a Crack in Everything: Problematising Masculinities, Peacebuilding and Transitional Justice. *Human Rights Review* 17(1): 9–34.
Hammond, J. (1996). Organization and Education Among Salvadoran Political Prisoners. *Crime, Law and Social Change* 25(1): 17–41.
Hartling, L. and E. Lindner (2016). Healing Humiliation: From Reaction to Creative Action. *Journal of Counseling and Development* 94(4): 383–390.
Hartling, L., W. Rosen, M. Walker and J. Jordan (2000). *Shame and Humiliation: From Isolation to Relational Transformation* (Work in Progress No. 88). Wellesley, MA: The Stone Center, Wellesley College.
Hayner, P. (2011). *Unspeakable Truths: Transitional Justice and the Challenge of Truth Commissions*(2nd ed.). New York: Routledge.
Human Rights Campaign (2020). *Sexual Orientation and Gender Identity Definitions*. Human Rights Campaign. Available at: https://www.hrc.org/resources/sexual-orientation-and-gender-identity-terminology-and-definitions. Accessed on: 15 December 2021.
Jakoby, T. (2006). From the Trenches: Dilemmas of Feminists in Fieldwork. In: Ackerly, B., Stern, M. and True, J. (eds.): *Feminist Methodologies for International Relations*. Cambridge: Cambridge University Press: 153–173.
Jelin, E. (2005). Las Familias Latinoamericanas en el Marco de las Transformaciones Globales: Hacia una Nueva Agenda de Políticas Públicas. In: Arriagada, I. (ed.): *Políticas Hacia las Familias, Protección e Inclusión Sociales*. Serie Seminarios y Conferencias N. 46. Santiago de Chile: CEPAL: 69–88.
Joyce, C. and O. Lynch (2017). 'Doing Peace': The Role of Ex-Political Prisoners in Violence Prevention Initiatives in Northern Ireland. *Studies in Conflict and Terrorism* 40(12): 1072–1090.
Jurik, N. and C. Siemsen (2009). 'Doing Gender' as Canon or Agenda: A Symposium on West and Zimmerman. *Gender and Society* 23(1): 72–75.
Katz, J. (2001). Analytic Induction Revisited. In: Emerson, R. (ed.): *Contemporary Field Research: Perspectives and Formulations*. Prospect Heights, IL: Waveland Press: 331–334.
Kent, L. (2014). Narratives of Suffering and Endurance: Coercive Sexual Relationships, Truth Commissions and Possibilities for Gender Justice in Timor-Leste. *International Journal of Transitional Justice* 8(2): 289–313.
Kirby, P. (2013). Refusing to be a Man? Men's Responsibility for War Rape and the Problem of Social Structures in Feminist and Gender Theory. *Men And Masculinities* 16(1): 93–114.
Lagarde, T. (2005). *Para mis Socias de la Vida: Claves Feministas para el Poderío y la Autonomía de las Mujeres, los Liderazgos Entrañables y las Negociaciones en el Amor*. Nicaragua: Puntos de Encuentro.

Leiby, M. (2015). Sexual Violence Against Political Prisoners: An Examination of Empirical Evidence in El Salvador and Peru. In: Ackerman, A. and Furman, R. (eds.): *Sex Crimes: Transnational Problems and Global Perspectives*. New York: Columbia University Press: 129–142.

Leslie, H. (2001). Healing the Psychological Wounds of Gender-Related Violence in Latin America: A Model for Gender-Sensitive Work in Post-Conflict Contexts. *Gender and Development* 9(3): 50–59.

Mallinder, L. (2007). Can Amnesties and International Justice be Reconciled? *The International Journal of Transitional Justice* 1(2): 208–230.

Mani, R. (2005). Rebuilding an Inclusive Political Community After War. *Security Dialogue* 36(4): 511–526.

Mantilla Falcón, J. (2005). The Peruvian Truth and Reconciliation Commission's Treatment of Sexual Violence Against Women. *Human Rights Brief* 12(2): 1–5.

Martínez Barahona, E., M. L. Gutiérrez Salazar and L. Rincón Fonseca (2012). Impunidad en El Salvador y Guatemala: 'De la Locura a la Esperanza': ¿Nunca Más. *América Latina Hoy: Revista de Ciencias Sociales* 61: 101–136.

McAllister, C. (2013). Testimonial Truths and Revolutionary Mysteries. In: McAllister, C. and Nelson, D. (eds.): *War by Other Means: Aftermath in Post-Genocide Guatemala*. Durham and London: Duke University Press Books: 92–115.

McCann, M. (2014). The Unbearable Lightness of Rights: On Sociolegal Inquiry in the Global Era. *Law and Society Review* 48(2): 245–273.

McEvoy, K. (2007). Towards a Thicker Understanding of Transitional Justice. *Journal of Law and Society* 34(4): 411–440.

Mendeloff, D. (2009). Trauma and Vengeance: Assessing the Psychological and Emotional Effects of Post-Conflict Justice. *Human Rights Quarterly* 31(3): 592–623.

Minow, M. (1998). *Between Vengeance and Forgiveness*. Boston: Beacon Press.

Minow, M. (2019). Do Alternative Justice Mechanisms Deserve Recognition in International Criminal Law?: Truth Commissions, Amnesties, and Complementarity at the International Criminal Court. *Harvard International Law Journal* 60(1): 1–46.

Miranda, A. (2007). Wartime Sexual Violence: Women's Human Rights and Questions of Masculinity. *Review of International Studies* 33(1): 75–90.

Montgomery, T. S. (2018). *Revolution in El Salvador: From Civil Strife to Civil Peace* (2nd ed.). New York: Routledge.

Mosqueira, U. (2020). *Reclaiming the Self: Political Prisoners, Gender, and Subjectivity in Post-War El Salvador*. PhD Thesis, University of Washington Libraries. Available at: http://hdl.handle.net/1773/46193.

Neier, A. (1998). *War Crimes: Brutality, Genocide, Terror, and the Struggle for Justice*. New York: Times Books.

Nesiah, V. (2006). Discussion Lines on Gender and Transitional Justice: An Introductory Essay Reflecting on the ICTJ Bellagio Workshop on Gender and Transitional Justice. *Columbia Journal of Gender and Law* 15: 799–885.

Neumann, K. and D. Anderson (2014). Introduction: Violence, Justice and the Work of Memory. *International Journal of Conflict and Violence* 8(1): 4–15.

Ní Aoláin, F. (2012). Advancing Feminist Positioning in the Field of Transitional Justice. *International Journal of Transitional Justice* 6(2): 205–228.

O'Connell, J. (2005). Gambling with the Psyche: Does Prosecuting Human Rights Violators Console Their Victims? *Harvard International Law Journal* 46(2): 295–345.

Olavarría, J. (2003). Los Estudios Sobre Masculinidades en América Latina. Un Punto de Vista. *Anuario Social y Político de América Latina y el Caribe* 6: 91–98.

Olavarría, J. (2017). *Sobre Hombres y Masculinidades: "Ponerse los Pantalones"*. Santiago: Ediciones Universidad Academia de Humanismo Cristiano.

O'Rourke, C. (2011). Transitioning to What? Transitional Justice and Gendered Citizenship in Chile and Colombia. In: Buckley-Zistel, S. and Stanley, R. (eds.): *Gender in Transitional Justice*. New York: Palgrave Macmillan: 136–162.

Park, R. (2014). *The Reappeared: Argentine Former Political Prisoners*. New Brunswick, NJ: Rutgers University Press.

Porter, E. (2016). Gendered Narratives: Stories and Silences in Transitional Justice. *Human Rights Review* 17(1): 35–50.

Ross, F. (2003). *Bearing Witness: Women and the Truth and Reconciliation Commission in South Africa*. London: Pluto Press.

Scheingold, S. (1974). *The Politics of Rights: Lawyers, Public Policy, and Political Change*. New Haven: Yale University Press.

Schulz, P. (2019). Towards Inclusive Gender in Transitional Justice: Gaps, Blind-Spots and Opportunities. *Journal of Intervention and Statebuilding* 14(5): 691–710.

Sharim, D. (2005). La Identidad de Género en Tiempos de Cambio: Una Aproximación Desde los Relatos de Vida. *Psykhe* 14(2): 19–32.

Silber, I. C. (2011). *Everyday Revolutionaries: Gender, Violence, and Disillusionment in Postwar El Salvador*. New Brunswick, NJ: Rutgers University Press.

Simpson, A. (2007). On Ethnographic Refusal: Indigeneity, 'Voice' and Colonial Citizenship. *Junctures: The Journal for Thematic Dialogue* 9: 67–80.

Simpson, A. (2014). *Mohawk Interruptus: Political Life Across the Borders of Settler States*. Durham: Duke University Press.

Sjoberg, L. (2011). Gender, the State, and War Redux: Feminist International Relations Across the 'Levels of Analysis'. *International Relations* 25(1): 108–134.

Skaar, E., J. Garcia-Godos and C. Collins (eds.) (2016). *Transitional Justice in Latin America: The Uneven Road from Impunity Towards Accountability*. New York: Routledge.

Skjelsbaek, I. (2001). Sexual Violence and War: Mapping Out a Complex Relationship. *European Journal of International Relations* 7(2): 211–237.

Sluka, J. (2000). *Death Squad: The Anthropology of State Terror*. Philadelphia: University of Pennsylvania Press.

Tangney, J. P. and R. Dearing (2002). *Shame and Guilt*. New York: Guildford Press.

Taylor, D. and K. Vintges (eds.) (2004). *Feminism and the Final Foucault*. Urbana and Chicago: University of Illinois Press.

Thapar-Björkert, S. and M. Henry (2004). Reassessing the Research Relationship: Location, Position and Power in Field Accounts. *International Journal of Social Research Methodology* 7(5): 363–381.

Thakur, R. and P. Malcontent (eds.) (2005). *From Sovereign Impunity to International Accountability*. Tokyo: United Nations University Press.

Theidon, K. (2007a). Transitional Subjects: The Disarmament, Demobilization and Reintegration of Former Combatants in Colombia. *The International Journal of Transitional Justice* 1(1): 66–90.

Theidon, K. (2007b). Gender in Transition: Common Sense, Women, and War. *Journal of Human Rights* 6(4): 453–478.

Theidon, K. (2009). Reconstructing Masculinities: The Disarmament, Demobilization, and Reintegration of Former Combatants in Colombia. *Human Rights Quarterly* 31(1): 1–34.

Theidon, K. (2012). *Intimate Enemies: Violence and Reconciliation in Peru*. Philadelphia: University of Pennsylvania Press.

Theidon, K. (2016). A Greater Measure of Justice: Gender, Violence, and Reparations. In: Lewin, E., Silverstein, L., Bolles, L., Boellstorff, T., Dudgeon, M. and Khandelwal, M. R. (eds.): *Mapping Feminist Anthropology in the Twenty-First Century*. New Brunswick: Rutgers University Press: 191–210.

Theidon, K. (2018). 1325 + 17 =?: Filling in the Blanks of the Women, Peace, and Security Agenda. In: Ní Aoláin, F., Cahn, N., Haynes, D. F., Valji, N. and Theidon, K. (eds.):

The Oxford Handbook of Gender and Conflict. Oxford: Oxford University Press: Chapter 12.
Touquet, H. (2021). Silent or Inaudible? Male Survivor Stories in Bosnia–Herzegovina. *Social Politics*: 1–23.
Touquet, H. and P. Schulz (2021). Navigating Vulnerabilities and Masculinities: How Gendered Contexts Shape the Agency of Male Sexual Violence Survivors. *Security Dialogue* 52(3): 213–230.
Trenholm, J., P. Olsson, M. Blomqvist and B. M. Ahlberg (2013). Constructing Soldiers from Boys in Eastern Democratic Republic of Congo. *Men And Masculinities* 16(2): 203–227.
Weiss, K. (2010a). Too Ashamed to Report: Deconstructing the Shame of Sexual Victimization. *Feminist Criminology* 5(3): 286–310.
Weiss, K. (2010b). Male Sexual Victimization: Examining Men's Experiences of Rape and Sexual Assault. *Men and Masculinities* 12(3): 275–298.
West, C. and D. Zimmerman (1987). Doing Gender. *Gender and Society* 1(2): 125–151.
West, C. and D. Zimmerman (2009). Accounting for Doing Gender. *Gender and Society* 23(1): 112–122.
Wetherell, M. and N. Edley (1999). Negotiating Hegemonic Masculinity: Imaginary Positions and Psycho Discursive Practices. *Feminism and Psychology* 9(3): 335–356.
Widmer, M. (2006). 'Real Men' Without Guns. *New Routes: A Journal of Peace Research and Action* 11(4): 12–14.
Wood, E. J. (2009). Armed Groups and Sexual Violence: When Is Wartime Rape Rare? *Politics and Society* 37(1): 131–161.

Chapter 14

Mind and Body

Civilian Enactment of Masculinity in the North of Ireland and the Occupied Palestinian Territories

Seamus Campbell

Introduction

There has been much theorizing about masculinities and their enduring associations with warfare and collective violence (Ni Aoláin et al. 2011; Hutchings 2008; Myrttinen et al. 2016). As scholars of conflict and violence have rightly noted, it is primarily men who participate in war and dominate the discourses and value systems which lead to war, while in many parts of the world, manhood remains characterized by a readiness to engage in battle (Skjelsbaek 2001; Cockburn 2001). However, in undertaking the important work of highlighting the linkages between masculinities and conflict violence, scholars have largely overlooked the experiences and identities of men who do not take up arms but instead retain their civilian identities (Foster 2011; MacKenzie and Foster 2017). This chapter, therefore, seeks to address this gap by examining the experience and identities of civilian men within transitional and conflict-affected contexts.

Specifically, this chapter will examine the experiences and identities of civilian men within the North of Ireland and the Occupied Palestinian Territories.[1] Utilizing empirical evidence, I explore how, in the North of Ireland, the pursuit of a popular sport, namely, boxing, enabled young men to construct masculine identities which, although civilian in character, were nevertheless highly respected and contributed to informal peacebuilding processes. With regard to the Occupied Territories, I show how, despite the oppressiveness of the occupation and the checkpoint regime, those who participated in this study remained civilian and affirmed their masculinities primarily through the utilization of various forms of situated knowledge, knowledge which may hasten the process of any potential transition. In doing so, I reveal how the participants of the North of Ireland affirmed their masculinities and mitigated the effects of conflict primarily through the cultural capital associated

1 Although the island's six most northeasterly counties which remain part of the United Kingdom are officially known as Northern Ireland, herein I prefer to use the term *North of Ireland* in recognition of the contested and colonial nature of its creation and preservation.

DOI: 10.4324/9781003519522-18

with their bodies, while the participants of the Occupied Territories did so principally by utilizing the cultural capital associated with their minds.

For the former group of participants, the pursuit of boxing proved to be a form of "salvation." Not only did it enable them to attain high-status forms of civilian masculinity in the midst of violent conflict, but it also provided spaces of safety and sanctuary, mentorship and camaraderie, and opportunities to encounter the often previously feared "other." In this context, therefore, I argue that the sport functioned as a culturally appropriate peacebuilding intervention, one which addressed young men's culturally sanctioned gendered interests and identities whilst steering them away from a path of political violence or social deviance. Whilst lacking the formality of other forms of intervention, it nevertheless remains the case that the sport's impact on both individuals and communities in the North of Ireland has been considerable.

In the absence of a formal transitional process and spaces of relative safety, the latter participants, the majority of whom were students at Palestinian universities, drew upon situated forms of knowledge to affirm their masculinities and more successfully navigate the conflict environment. At checkpoints and other sites of interaction with Israeli military forces, participants drew upon knowledge of the conflict environment, knowledge of Hebrew, and knowledge accrued through academic endeavors to more skillfully exercise caution and vigilance and thus demonstrate their capacity for agency and masculine self-reliance. Whilst such forms of knowledge may not be considered transformative per se, their utilization as gendered coping mechanisms highlights forms of civilian masculinity present within Palestinians which are based on courage pragmatism and persistence, forms which are likely to prove invaluable in any future transitional process. This chapter, therefore, seeks to provide a textured analysis of civilian masculinities and the continuum of men's experiences within conflict-affected and transitional settings – echoing calls made by Brandon Hamber et al. in Chapter 2 of this volume. Moreover, it draws attention to the ways in which relatively mundane and everyday experiences, such as engaging in a popular sport or utilizing one's knowledge whilst crossing a security checkpoint, may enable individuals to cope with experiences of violence and insecurity in a manner compatible with their gender identities. Although such micro-level dynamics may be outside the purview of formal peacebuilding or transitional justice processes, they can nevertheless provide further nuance and insight on how masculinities operate within conflicted societies and, indeed, about transitional and peacebuilding processes more broadly.

Overview of the Conflicts

The conflict in North of Ireland, often referred to as "The Troubles," claimed the lives of over 3,500 people between 1969 and 1998 (Sutton 2001). Although its causes and workings are complex, it has broadly been defined as a conflict between the Protestant/unionist/loyalist community, which aims to maintain links with the rest of the United Kingdom (UK), and the Catholic/nationalist/republican community, which seeks unification with the Republic of Ireland (Brown and Ni Aoláin 2015). While the 1998 Good Friday or Belfast Agreement succeeded in considerably reducing levels of political violence, significant peacebuilding challenges remain (Wilson 2016), and transition remains ongoing and uncertain. Examining the North of Ireland thus permits an exploration of how protracted (internal) conflict and subsequent transition have impacted upon civilian men and their masculinities within a Western and democratic setting.

By contrast, while the North of Ireland now enjoys a relative, if precarious, semblance of peace, the conflict in the Occupied Palestinian Territories and Israel remains active and ongoing. Described as ethnonational in nature (Milton-Edwards and Hinchcliffe 2008), with its roots within settler colonialism (Sharoni 2001; Shalhoub-Kevorkian 2015), the conflict has cost more than 8,000 lives in the past three decades and is considered one of the most entrenched in the modern world (Handelman 2011; Uppsala Conflict Data Program 2021). While the 1993 Oslo Agreement sought to reset relations between Palestinians and Israelis, the years which followed saw progress falter, and at present, the prospect of any meaningful transition appears remote. Investigating the Occupied Territories thus allows for an examination of how protracted conflict and military occupation have impacted upon civilian men and their masculinities within a Middle Eastern context much exposed to international intervention.

A Note on Methodology

Within the North of Ireland, interviews were conducted with 23 individuals who had been involved in boxing either during or after the conflict. Of these, 22 were male, and all were at least 40 years old at the time of interview. Almost all the participants had been amateur or professional boxers in their youth and had grown up in nationalist and unionist communities in the midst of ongoing violence. Many remained active within the sport in a coaching, referring, or organizational capacity. By contrast, and as highlighted earlier, the research conducted within the Occupied Territories was focused not on boxing but on the ongoing effects of conflict and military occupation, including the gendered impacts of the Israeli checkpoint regime. Within this context, therefore, interviews were conducted with 27 individuals, 20 of whom were undertaking or had recently completed their studies at Palestinian universities.[2] Of these, 13 were male and 7 were female, and all were in their late teens or early twenties at the time of interview. Two focus groups, comprising

2 The remaining participants were comprised of two male members of staff employed at Palestinian universities, a male lawyer/community activist, a male secondary school teacher, and four females active within Israeli human rights organizations (also see Campbell 2020).

primarily of male students, were also conducted on campus, and a research journal was maintained throughout.

These sites clearly differ in terms of geographical location as well as the character and status of their respective conflicts. What is more, the interests, as well as demographics, of the research participants also vary significantly in terms of age, class, educational attainment, and gender representation, with more women represented among the younger, better-educated, and more upwardly mobile Palestinian cohort. Despite this, however, civilian masculinities within both contexts remain greatly influenced by experiences of conflict, insecurity, and precarity. Moreover, the aim of this research was not to conduct a rigid comparison but to enable an exploration of the complexity of civilian masculinity in varied cultural settings. It was thus felt that examining these sites in tandem could provide insights which would surpass those gained as a result of examining either site individually and facilitate a more varied and nuanced understanding of male identity and conflict.

Civilian Men, Masculinities, and Conflict

While scholarship on masculinity and conflict has focused overwhelmingly on violent and militarized masculinities (Steans 2006; Merry 2009; Ni Aoláin et al. 2011), significantly less attention has been devoted to exploring the masculinities of civilian men (Foster 2011; MacKenzie and Foster 2017). Although it has been acknowledged that many men do not take up arms during periods of violent conflict (Wright 2014), it remains the case that civilian men remain largely overlooked within scholarship, the media, and humanitarian policy and practice (Foster 2011; Hutchings 2011; Allsopp 2015). The tendency to think of "women and children" as civilians at the expense of unarmed adult men (Carpenter 2006; Enloe 2000) has, it seems, served to locate civilian men on the wrong side of the gendered peace and violence dichotomy (Moran 2010), thus perpetuating their status as "the big forgotten ones, the ones nobody talks about" (Carpenter 2006: 9).

Considering this, this chapter seeks to render visible something which has been largely invisible, namely, the gendered experiences and identities of civilian men within conflict-affected and transitional settings (see Hamber et al., Agarwal, this volume). To date, when the experiences and identities of such men have been examined, it has usually been in relation to their vulnerabilities and victimization, for example, in relation to sexual violence (Schulz 2020).[3] It has also been noted that men (including civilian men) are often those most likely to lose their lives during periods of armed conflict (Vess

3 A body of literature outside of conflict studies also exists which has examined themes within masculinity such as fatherhood and coming of age within conflict-affected societies (see, for example, Strier 2014; Gokani et al. 2015: Otman 2020).

et al. 2013; Wright 2014). In the North of Ireland, 91% of all those who died as a result of the conflict were male, 47% of whom were civilians (Sutton 2001),[4] while within Israel and the Occupied Palestinian Territories, 85% of Palestinians who lost their lives to the conflict since 2008 have been male, 54% of whom were civilians (United Nations Office for the Coordination of Humanitarian Affairs 2021).[5] Whilst recognizing their vulnerabilities, however, this chapter seeks to move beyond transitional justice narratives which tend to locate men as either victims or perpetrators of violence (see Hamber et al., this volume) and instead aims to provide critical insights in relation to their lived realities as both civilians and gendered beings.

Judicially, distinguishing between the civilian and the combatant is formally known as the principle of distinction (Kinsella 2011).[6] The principle attempts to differentiate between armed forces conducting hostilities and those presumed not to be participating (Melzer 2009) and holds that persons clearly not responsible for the prosecution of war should not be intentionally attacked or killed (Hartigan 2010). While profoundly shaped by the Christian tradition of just war (Slim 2008), the civilian ethic is essentially a product of international law and international relations and represents an evolving concept in both legal and cultural terms (Kinsella 2011; De Búrca 2014). Within international law, however, civilians remain characterized by what they are not, that is, combatants or members of military forces (Slim 2008; Rothbart et al. 2012).

While civilian immunity is not a gendered norm per se, it has been, as suggested earlier, more often associated with "women and children" than with adult men (Carpenter 2003; Enloe 2000). Within both the Geneva Conventions of 1949 and their Additional Protocols, for example, reproductive capacity and sexual vulnerability are used to distinguish between the combatant and the civilian (Kinsella 2011). Similarly, the website of the International Committee of the Red Cross (ICRC) lists women and children, as well as the sick and the old, as those considered "highly vulnerable" to the effects of armed conflict (ICRC 2010), while the phrase "vulnerable women" is given special consideration in several UN declarations (Hirsch 2012: 255). By contrast, it seems that civilian men have often struggled to credibly assert their

4 Herein, statistics attributed to Sutton (2001) have been sourced from the *Sutton Index of Death* and have been created using the tabulations functions on the Conflict Archive on the Internet (CAIN) website. They include deaths which resulted from the conflict in Ireland between 14 July 1969 and 31 December 2001.

5 These figures have been created using the cross-tabulations function on the *Data on Casualties* page of the United Nations Office for the Coordination of Humanitarian Affairs website. They include deaths resulting from the context of occupation and conflict between 1 January 2008 and 14 October 2021.

6 See Articles 48, 51(2), and 52(2) of Protocol Additional to the Geneva Conventions of 12 August 1949 and relating to the Protection of Victims of International Armed Conflict (Protocol I) of June 1977.

civilian identities to either enemy forces or international protectors (Hirsch 2012; Turner 2019), and that international legal norms continue to judge men of battle age as less worthy of protection than those commonly associated with civilian status (Myrttinen et al. 2017; Carpenter 2006).[7] Male vulnerability during conflict, it seems, remains "essentially unimaginable" (Myrttinen et al. 2016: 8), the consequences of which may be far reaching, as has been highlighted by scholars such as Charli Carpenter (2003) and Adam Jones (2004).[8] As noted earlier, while the purpose of this chapter is to examine men as civilians rather than as victims of armed conflict, there is a need to recognize the centrality of vulnerability to civilian experiences and identities within conflict-affected contexts. The sections which follow, therefore, seeks to shed light on civilian men's lived realities of conflict and vulnerability within the North of Ireland and the Occupied Palestinian Territories; this cross-cultural analysis permits a more extensive level of theorization which may resonate in numerous conflict-affected and transitional contexts.

Boxing and Civilian Masculinities in the North of Ireland

As the research underpinning this chapter progressed, it was decided that civilian masculinities and experiences of conflict within the North of Ireland would be explored through the prism of boxing. The reasons for this were fourfold. Firstly, boxing has, historically at least, been a highly masculinized sport within which the male body is central to the construction of identity (Woodward 2007). Secondly, boxing has existed in Belfast in one form or another for at least 200 years (Sugden 1996), and the city once had a rich tradition of "hard" men – working-class men who engaged in bare-knuckled street fights and gained notoriety for doing do (Feldman 1991: 52).

Thirdly, boxing in the North of Ireland is a predominantly working-class sport (Sugden 1996), which thus enabled the recruitment of those from communities which had suffered disproportionally from the effects of conflict-related violence (Coulter 1999). And lastly, and perhaps most significantly, there appeared to be a consensus that boxing had facilitated respectful contact between those from differing sides of the community/religious divide even during the most violent periods of the conflict (Sugden and Harvie 1995). Boxing thus provided an opportunity to explore how the civilian masculinities forged

7 Under the Obama administration, for example, it has been claimed that men of battle age killed as a result of drone strikes were presumed to be "terrorists" (Friedersdorf 2012).

8 Jones (2004), for example, has argued that men are often the primary victims of armed conflict and, thus, that they may, in fact, be more in need of civilian protection than other groups. Similarly, Carpenter (2003) has highlighted the gendered dynamics of the mass killing of men and boys within the context of the former Yugoslavia and has contended that, of the civilians present, men were those most likely to lose their lives at the hands of enemy forces.

within the sport contributed to the building of peace among those considered specialists in the (controlled) infliction of bodily violence.

Whilst boxing may perhaps be regarded as a relatively apolitical pursuit, its centrality in shaping the lives and identities of research participants soon became apparent. As alluded to earlier, many of the participants felt that the sport had been their "salvation," providing spaces of safety and sanctuary within which unlikely friendships were formed and high-status forms of civilian masculinity were attained. In this respect, therefore, boxing functioned as an everyday form of engaging with the lasting effects of conflict, one which offered a degree of protection from the effects of political violence and social deprivation, whilst also facilitating the imagining of communities characterized by respect, inclusion, and solidarity, rather than scarcity, fear, or division

Boxing as Salvation

In analyzing the narratives of the participants from the North of Ireland, one of the most significant and surprising findings was the frequency with which they spoke about having found "salvation," or having been "saved," as a result of their pursuit of boxing. The sport, it seemed, had saved many of them from the dangers associated with coming of age within their respective working-class communities, including the perils of either perpetrating or falling victim to political violence. From a gendered perspective, boxing had seemingly saved the participants from forms of masculinity which were either more violent or more vulnerable than forms commonly associated with boxing. Of such forms, however, it appears that it was the role which boxing played in deterring the adoption of militarized masculinities which was at the forefront of the minds of participants when they spoke of salvation, as revealed in the following extracts:

> When I think about it like (boxing) it was the savior for me in many ways. Like if I hadn't of had the boxing . . . what other . . . ? I would probably have ended up in Long Kesh (prison). And I have no doubts about it whatsoever.
>
> (Harry)[9]

> You know I was in the boxing gym . . . punching the bags, sparring; boxing became my life.[10] If I hadn't have had boxing, I might otherwise have been out joining paramilitaries or joyriding or whatever so boxing was my salvation.
>
> (Matthew)

9 In order to protect their identities, all those who participated in the study have been attributed pseudonyms.

10 The names of clubs and specific areas have been omitted in order to protect the anonymity of participants.

The preceding extracts are typical of the ways in which participants described the critical intervention which boxing had made in their lives. Maurice, for example, similarly spoke of how boxing had been his "savior," deterring him from getting "mixed up in the Troubles," while Jason was convinced that the sport had "saved hundreds of people's lives" by keeping them "away" from the conflict and providing an alternative "path." Others, whilst perhaps avoiding overtly discussing the terms previously cited, told of how getting involved in the sport had been the "best thing" that had ever happened to them (James), or of how boxing had been a "big help" whilst growing up in the midst of the conflict (Andrew). It was clear, therefore, that regardless of the specificity of their language, many of the participants felt very grateful, or even "blessed" (Conor), that the sport had intervened in their lives in such a positive manner.

Theidon (2009: 32) has argued that in situations of conflict, "carving out space to be a civilian and act like one is crucial." I argue that within this context, boxing, as a powerful expression of masculinity, carved out space for young men to remain civilian in a way that did not feminize them or call their "hard-won" masculinities into question (Ducat 2004: 12). It seems that the securing of this authentically masculine yet civilian form of identity was made possible in part as a result of the enduring connections between masculinity and sport (Delgado 2005), and indeed between masculinity and violence (Dekeseredy and Schwartz 2005), which found expression within boxing.

Moreover, it was also facilitated by the similarities which exist between forms of masculinity associated with militarism and those associated with boxing. Like war, boxing has long been characterized by danger, courage, and indeed, violence (Woodward 2007), and like the soldier, the boxer is viewed as fearless, strong, and someone with heart – in short, the definitive alpha male (Paradis 2012). It is within these gendered parameters, then, that boxing offered salvation to those who pursued it. It did so by facilitating the attainment of secure masculine identities which, although civilian in character, were viable alternatives to the militarized forms of masculinity which were highly visible within working-class communities during the period.

The salvation which many participants found within boxing also appears to have been at least partly due to the time and dedication devoted by boxing coaches to those under their tutelage. We know from cross-cultural research that models or mentors can have a significant influence on "lifelong outcomes" for teenage boys (Wilson et al. 2014: 2). It has also been argued that emotionally connected relationships between men and boys may provide for the modelling of positive forms of masculinity, forms which allow for emotional vulnerability and the transcendence of stereotypical norms (Spencer 2007).

Within this context, it seems that boxing coaches modelled forms of masculinity which transcended traditional stereotypes and were based not on wanton violence but on the controlled use of aggression within highly regulated environments. Participants appear to have been largely receptive to the forms of masculinity modelled by their coaches, referring to such figures in brotherly, fatherly, or even messianic terms, as outlined in the extracts which follow:

> So the coach . . . was like a father figure to us. When we turned up to go to trips, he would have washed your face and cut your hair.
>
> (Matthew)

> I'm basically doing what (my former coach) did for me . . . passing on the same wee bit of knowledge and encouragement. No, he was a savior, a savior to a lot of people.
>
> (Jason)

As alluded to in Jason's quotation, several participants felt a debt of gratitude to their former coaches, as well as duty to give back what their coaches had given to them. In doing so, some were aware of the many roles which they were now expected to play, and perhaps of the positive forms of masculinity they were now expected to model. Harry, for example, told of how he attempted to offer those he now trained "a different range of things," including encouragement and "direction in life," while Peter spoke of how a boxing coach is expected to be a "teacher," "educator," and "father" and, as such, occupied a position of significant responsibility. Such responsibilities are thus in stark contrast to common perceptions of the sport as one within which hypermasculine identities predominate (Woodward 2007).

With this context, therefore, there is ample evidence to support Wilson et al.'s (2014) argument that models or mentors can have a significant influence on lifelong outcomes, as well as to support Spencer's (2007) observation that emotionally connected relationships may provide for the modelling of positive forms of masculinity. Boxing coaches provided examples of ways to perform civilian masculinities which, although predicated upon a rejection of political/social violence, were not based upon suggestions of cowardice or weakness. Coaches also displayed many of the qualities that one might associate with positive fatherhood, such as care, compassion, patience, and respect, modelling what Gokani et al. (2015: 215) have referred to as "appropriate and fruitful ways of 'being a man.'"[11]

In examining the saving or protective role that the sport played in the lives of participants from the North of Ireland, it is also necessary to examine the sanctuary provided by both boxing clubs and the environment surrounding the

11 I am conscious here that what might constitute "positive" fatherhood or masculinity is always likely to be contested and context-specific. Hence, while conscious to highlight the forms of masculinity modelled by boxing coaches within this context, I am also cognizant of the need to avoid reinforcing normative judgments attached to such forms.

sport itself. As argued by Sorek (2009), a physically unsafe social environment often increases the attractiveness of fighting sports, such as boxing. Within this context, the conflict certainly created an unsafe social environment. The majority of participants grew up in Catholic communities which had to contend with violence from both British military forces and loyalist paramilitaries, the latter groups responsible for killing upwards of ten times more civilians than paramilitary members between 1969 and 1993 (Coulter 1999). Hence, given the relatively limited protection conferred by civilian identity, boxing clubs, as spaces of comparative safety, were both attractive and accessible to youths from working-class communities during the period. Moreover, as quintessentially masculine spaces, they provided a form of sanctuary which was highly compatible with the gendered aspirations of young men from such communities who were disproportionally vulnerable to the effects of conflict violence.

Indeed, participants referred to their boxing clubs as spaces of safety and "sanctuary" (Robert; Gavin), where one could hope to find "refuge" and "solace" (Matthew). At many clubs, it appeared that such feelings of safety emanated from the fact that those from both sides of the community could train without fear of having their community/religious identity questioned, with politics said to be "left at the door" (Ryan). Moreover, such clubs were said to be safe emotional spaces, spaces within which patrons could hope to find something of themselves, a sense of self-worth, identity, and acceptance "for who they are" (John). They were thus spaces which engendered a sense of belonging, with "belonging to oneself" said to be a metaphor for the establishment of a secure masculinity (Woodward 2007: 11).

While boxing was almost exclusively a male sport during the period, several participants spoke of how their mothers would be reassured by knowing they were attending their respective boxing clubs. Harry, for example, recalled how his mother would tell others she had "no worries" about her son as she knew he was "safe" whilst attending his club. It perhaps says something about the dangers inherent within such communities that mothers were reassured that their sons were protected whilst participating in a relatively violent sport. It seems, however, that they calculated that the relative safety which boxing clubs provided more than compensated for whatever physical harm their sons might come to as a result of their pursuit of the sport. In seeking to protect their sons therefore, some mothers were at least tacitly supportive of the aggressive masculinity inherent within the sport, and thus its cultural status was not solely upheld by men.[12]

12 Indeed, it would seem that in many conflict-affected societies, women, for a variety of reasons, have an interest in maintaining aggressive and/or violent masculinities. Theidon (2009), for example, has noted that in situations of violence and poverty, the desire to be protected and provided for means that women often play an active role in affirming forms of masculinity that are aggressive well beyond the confines of competitive sport.

While it must be noted that boxing clubs were only as safe as both paramilitary and state forces permitted them to be, it seems that the perception that those training were under the protection of hypermasculine actors negated the threat posed by hypermasculine actors of a more militarized kind. The outward similarities, therefore, between the masculine regimes ruling (or thought to rule) within boxing clubs and those ruling within paramilitary organizations appear to have provided the basis of the protective capabilities of such sites. The masculine nature of such spaces ensured that those who frequented them could feel sufficiently safe to express vulnerability, receive emotional support, and perhaps start to come to terms with the pain and emotional distress associated with the reality of ongoing conflict and socio-economic deprivation. As such, these spaces enabled patrons to engage in what transitional justice scholars might consider to be processes of transition, by creating conditions for acceptance, healing, and the imaginings of futures free from fear and brutality.

As Cahn and Ni Aoláin (2010) note, in many contexts, men often engage in violence to gain social status, value, and security. Within the North of Ireland, it seems that young men joined boxing clubs for similar reasons, with the pursuit of boxing affording participants a defense against the expectation to the joint paramilitary groups, as well as a degree of protection against the violence perpetrated by such groups.[13] In relation to the former, Maurice, for example, described how the "respect" he gained as a boxer helped counteract the "guilt" he felt for failing to join a paramilitary group, while for Harry, boxing acted as a "safety valve," affording him "a bit of status" which he "didn't have to go chasing through any paramilitary organization." With regard to protection against paramilitary violence, Conor opined that this was because "paramilitaries on both sides of the divide respect(ed) amateur boxers," while Peter noted that there was "an understanding" that if you were involved in boxing, "there wouldn't be any bad will against you."

The forms of masculinity embodied by boxers during the period, based upon the inflicting and suffering of violence (albeit within highly controlled environments), were also valued within working-class communities more broadly on both sides of the divide. Harry, for example, argued that such communities "understood what it was to be a man," which thus enabled boxers to gain status and respect beyond the confines of their own community. Their ability to at least partially transcend community divisions, therefore, was possible because of, rather than despite, their rootedness within working-class communities.

13 Paramilitaries in the North of Ireland were responsible for over 85% of all conflict-related deaths (Sutton 2001).

Boxing, Community Relations, and Peacebuilding

As suggested earlier, boxing's power to save was due in part to its ability to bring together those from both sides of the community divide, with cooperation and mutual respect seemingly pervading relations during the period. Participants recalled, for example, how international boxing teams would come to Belfast during the 1970s and 1980s and how the subsequent boxing show alternated between Catholic and Protestant areas, drawing crowds from both sides of the community and uniting those who had previously been kept apart. They also described how "sectarianism never came into boxing" (Maurice), how the sport "brought communities together" and engendered "mutual respect" (Matthew), and of its ability to build "bridges" and "transcend politics" (Peter; Matthew). Such evidence points to what might be considered an "inclusive" masculine culture existing within the North's boxing community, one predicated on the social inclusion of identities normally marginalized by prevailing masculine norms (Anderson 2011). It also underlines the extent to which those involved in the sport embraced a wide range of masculine behaviors beyond those narrowly associated with traditional or hyper forms of masculine identity.

It was evident that the inclusive nature of boxing had made a lasting impression on many of those who pursued it. Numerous participants spoke of how the sport had broadened their outlook, enabled them to form friendships beyond the confines of their own community, and ultimately to humanize those from the other community. Matthew, for example, spoke of how boxing helped him see that those from the Protestant/unionist community were "just like" him, while John described how his involvement within the sport "completely changed" his "recognition" of those from the Catholic/nationalist community. Perhaps their endeavors within a physically tough sport gave those from both sides something they could identify with and enabled them to see the other both in terms of their masculinity and their humanity.

Indeed, on two separate occasions, the term "friends for life" was used when describing the nature of relationships which had crossed community divides (Peter; George), while participants also referred to the boxing community in the North as a "family" (Matthew; Jason; Maurice). As Messner (1992) notes, men who have worked, fought, or played together often form deep and lasting friendships. Male friendship, therefore, as part of the performance of masculinity (Migliaccio 2009), was not derailed or made impossible by community background, masculine bonds proving stronger than community division.

Notwithstanding the friendships, shared values, and solidarity which undoubtedly existed within the sport even amid conflict, a note of caution is warranted. As Sugden and Bairner (1993: 107) argue, "sport is not and never can be a panacea for social cleavages." While those involved in boxing within this context may have been bridging divides and breaking down barriers, they were doing so in a way that affirmed their own masculinities and shared masculine values. They were not, however, championing wider social change, and the extent to which they influenced political beliefs or social values outside of boxing is questionable. Moreover, boxing did not claim to have a formal community relations agenda, something which a number of participants, as well as sporting bodies of the day, believed would have proven counterproductive (Sugden and Harvie 1995). Nevertheless, in a context within which most other sports were deeply implicated in perpetuating division, boxing largely succeeded in ensuring the separation of sport and politics. As suggested earlier, having examined the role which boxing played in the lives of participants, I argue that boxing within this conflict-affected and transitional context functioned as an informal and culturally appropriate peacebuilding intervention. By this I mean that boxing created safe spaces for men for the collective enhancement of masculinities whilst also facilitating respectful contact with those on the other side of the community divide. Moreover, in reducing the expectations upon young men to prove their masculinities through paramilitary membership, it seems that the sport managed to address young men's culturally sanctioned gendered interests and identities whilst steering them away from a path of political violence or criminality.

Within this context, therefore, boxing was primarily harnessed for peace rather than war. Boxers could be both alpha males and civilian men and, indeed, could be celebrated for being so. While few may advocate for utilizing the sport to address male violence or advance gender equality,[14] it did provide viable civilian alternatives to the militarized forms of masculinity which were highly visible within working-class communities during the period. It also contributed to the building of peace amongst those considered specialists in the art of the controlled infliction of bodily violence. Hence, whilst the pursuit of boxing may be considered a relatively mundane pursuit far removed from transitional processes, within this context it nevertheless played a critical role in assisting young men from working-class communities to cope with experiences of violence and insecurity, and to imagine futures beyond fear and division. It is illustrative, therefore, of processes of peacebuilding which occur in the below and which, while lacking formality and fanfare, may have a significant impact upon those involved.

Civilian Masculinities in the Occupied Palestinian Territories

I now turn to the exploration of the conflict-related experiences and identities of civilian men living within the Occupied Palestinian Territories, with

14 It should be noted, however, that in recent years, boxing in the North of Ireland has become much more inclusive of women and girls, as highlighted by the significant success of figures such as Katie Taylor.

a focus on the Israeli checkpoint regime. While the North of Ireland has made the transition to relative (if precarious) peace, no such transition has occurred within the Occupied Territories, and the lives of those who live there continue to be blighted by insecurity and violence. The first nine months of 2021, for example, saw the deaths of 337 Palestinians, 72 of which occurred in the Occupied West Bank (United Nations Office for the Coordination of Humanitarian Affairs 2021), that is, the area of the Territories within which many of the participants lived, worked, and studied. While in theory the security needs of the occupying power should be balanced against the maintenance of the civil life of those occupied (Ben-Naftali et al. 2005), in practice it seems that the Israeli state struggles to view those occupied as civilians,[15] thus severely limiting the utility of civilian identity within this context. At the level of everyday experience, the violence and insecurity experienced by Palestinians within the Occupied Territories are perhaps most visible and exemplified by the Israeli checkpoint regime. Military checkpoints have been ever present since the early 1990s, when Israel began implementing a policy of closure and siege within the Territories (Mansbach 2009). Various types of obstructions, including manned checkpoints, roadblocks, metal gates, and earth mounds, now pave the Territories, and together with the separation barrier, they have become one of the most prominent technologies of the occupation (Kotef and Amir 2014). Not only do they serve to separate Palestinians from Israelis, but as they are often located within the Territories, they also frequently separate Palestinians from each other (Korsten 2011) and have thus resulted in a myriad of physically unconnected communities (Hammami 2006). While Israel maintains that the checkpoint regime is necessary for national security (Korsten 2011), for Palestinians, the extensive security screening to which they are routinely subjected represents a continual undermining of their civilian identities and the perceived irrelevance of international law to their experiences of conflict.[16] As Amir (2014) notes, checkpoints are overwhelmingly masculine spaces. The majority of soldiers/security personnel are men, as are most of those crossing the more formalized checkpoints (which control entry into Israel) at least. They are thus sites

15 Israel's apparent reluctance to confer civilian status upon those living within the Occupied Territories was recently highlighted when Israeli defense minister, Avigdor Lieberman, declared that those who had lost their lives whilst protesting behind the security fence in the Gaza Strip were not "innocent civilians" but "Hamas members." This is despite the fact that among those who lost their lives was Yaser Murtaja, a Palestinian journalist who, at the time of his shooting, was wearing a blue jacket which was clearly marked "press" (Middle East Monitor 2018).

16 While Palestinians in the Occupied Territories are regarded as "protected persons" under Article 4 of the Fourth Geneva Convention (Imseis 2003: 100), Israel regards its presence not as an occupation but an "administration" (Imseis 2003: 93) and thus has violated almost every provision of the Convention since the occupation's inception (Imseis 2003).

at which masculinities confront each other in particularly acute ways, albeit from very different positions of power (Hochberg 2010). As well as emphasizing the violence of such sites, scholarship has also drawn attention to their ability to subjugate, humiliate, and even emasculate those who must cross them (Foster 2011; Naaman 2006; Korsten 2011). As MacKenzie and Foster (2017) note, experiences of being stripped, verbally demeaned, and having to ask for permission to move from place to place seem designed to humiliate and intimidate the Palestinian populace.

Indeed, a significant number of my research participants also spoke of experiencing humiliation at these sites. Many lamented that young soldiers, whom they frequently referred to as "kids," could "boss" them around at will even though the participants were often their seniors in terms of age (Focus Group 2). While the insults which the soldiers directed at younger men seemed to be somewhat expected or even accepted, those directed at older men were considered beyond the pale. The potential of body/strip searches to embarrass and humiliate was similarly highlighted (Ahmed; Focus Group 1), with such searches functioning to produce the Palestinian body as both a symbol of danger and an object of complete subjugation (Hochberg 2010).

It seems, therefore, that while the checkpoint regime is maintained, the masculinities of Palestinians will continue to be undermined. Foster (2011: 80), for example, argues that if children at such sites witness those who they view as "almost holy" stripped of their power and defenseless, it can call into question their very status as masculine guardians and thus can be experienced as deeply emasculating. Despite this, however, many of the participants appeared to suggest that the masculinized power that the (particularly young) soldiers possessed by virtue of their military positions was ultimately illegitimate, an aberration of the normal process of proving one's masculinity through, for example, weathering life's many storms over several decades. By contrast, it seems the participants regarded the masculinities of older Palestinian men as much superior, including morally superior (see Korsten 2011), to their young and armed Israeli counterparts, even if this was not reflected within the power dynamics present at checkpoints. The perceived illegitimacy of such militarized masculinities may thus have provided something of a bulwark against the worst effects of humiliation and masculine subjugation suffered by Palestinians. Thus far, I have largely examined how ongoing conflict and military occupation have exposed Palestinian men to insecurity and vulnerability, undermining their roles as (masculine) providers and protectors (Gokani et al. 2015; MacKenzie and Foster 2017). As Nordstrom (1997) notes, however, war is not something that happens to people as static, passive, or generic victims. Instead, those affected by conflict typically respond in dynamic ways and negotiate their daily survival based on what is possible (also see Mosqueira, this volume). My research also found this to be the case, and as I will show, participants responded to their circumstances with agency and creativity and continued to find ways to express their masculinities based on the resources at their disposal.

One way in which the participants expressed or affirmed their masculinities within this context was by exercising a significant degree of caution and vigilance. While risk-taking has often been associated with masculinity, and with militarized and hegemonic forms in particular (Higate and Hopton 2005), it seems that many of the participants had become risk-averse rather than risk-takers. Indeed, all the participants who spoke of the need to exercise caution and vigilance were male,[17] a number of whom emphasized the particular precarity of military checkpoints. Sari, for instance, spoke of how he was reluctant to stand near soldiers at such sites, lest he be accused of carrying out a stabbing attack. Similarly, Hasheem explained how, when passing through such sites by car, one could not even afford to allow one's foot to slip off the brake, as even "a small accident" could prove fatal (Focus Group 1). More broadly, participants emphasized that in order to live within the Occupied Territories, it was necessary to keep "on the safe zone" and to avoid doing anything which could be considered suspicious (Mustafa). One was required to be "cautious" and to "adjust and tune" oneself depending on the situation at hand (Bashir). Being "really careful," avoiding active involvement in politics, and using social media with caution were also advised (Ahmed). Ultimately, the participants expended considerable energy doing what they could to simply "live and stay alive" (Omar).

Within this context, therefore, caution and vigilance appear to have been (at least partially) redefined as markers of masculinity. While such attributes may be in stark contrast to ideals often associated with hegemonic masculinity, they nevertheless functioned as gendered coping mechanisms which enabled participants to maximize their safety and affirm their masculinities within this conflict-affected context. What is more, while acting with caution and vigilance may have involved participants accepting a degree of subjugation, it also enabled them to utilize their agency and knowledge in order to navigate the conflict environment more effectively, as is further discussed in the section which follows.

The Role of Knowledge

As Schulz (2020) contends, the gathering, keeping, and passing on of knowledge can be regarded as a marker of masculinity in numerous cultural contexts. In the context of the Occupied Territories, analysis of the data revealed the extent to which situated knowledge, in various forms, was utilized by participants to both negotiate the complexities of the occupation and affirm their masculinities. A broad understanding of the political context and its practical implications was one such form of knowledge. Participants suggested that

17 This, I believe, shows the extent to which civilian men in the Occupied Territories experience relative powerlessness and vulnerability, and perhaps how cautions are already set for women by virtue of their gender.

the more knowledgeable one was in this respect, the more effectively one could read a given situation and exercise caution and vigilance accordingly, thereby enabling one to avoid or navigate some of the challenges associated with the conflict environment. This acquisition of this form of knowledge was thus held as both a masculine responsibility and a marker of masculinity.

The value which participants placed on knowledge of the conflict environment is evident in the extracts which follow. Abdul, for instance, contended that men should be "street-smart" and know how to "interact" with Israeli soldiers (Focus Group 2). Similarly, his colleague Salman argued that men should "know what they are doing when it comes to the occupation" and "should maybe have a background about what is going on" (Focus Group 2). Others spoke of how men in the Occupied Territories needed to be "clever a little bit" (interview with Ahmed) or just simply "aware" of "things" (interview with Fatima; interview with Ghada). Utilizing this form of knowledge to maximum effect thus enabled participants to utilize their agency and maximize their safety within an environment which provided little of either.

Another form of knowledge utilized by participants to both negotiate the complexities of the occupation and affirm their masculinities was an understanding of the Hebrew language. As highlighted by postcolonial studies, colonial language has often been appropriated by those subjected to colonial rule in order to confront their oppressors (Said 1994; Katrak 1989). Within this context, it has been noted that the ability to speak Hebrew provides significant symbolic capital for Palestinian men, providing proof that they have been able to "figure out" the language and also that they have worked (or can work) within Israel (Rothenberg 2006: 97).

In their interactions with Israeli soldiers, participants suggested that their ability to understand or respond in Hebrew reduced their vulnerability to mistreatment or abuse. As Ghada stated: "[T]he soldiers, they are talking Hebrew, so if you don't understand you may be yelled at, treated badly." By contrast, Anis explained that "speaking Hebrew gives you a plus, because it shows them (the soldiers) that you understand what they're saying." By understanding their language, therefore, Palestinians could hope to gain a measure of "safety" during these interactions (Rashida).

In addition, a number of participants suggested that the ability to speak Hebrew made it easier for soldiers to humanize them, thereby reducing the tensions associated with such interactions. Ghada, for instance, explained how speaking in Hebrew could enable one to gain the "respect" of soldiers, while Hasan expressed the view that using the language helped create a sense of "familiarity" and ensured that such interactions were "a little less unfriendly."

Beyond its utility during checkpoint interactions, various participants expressed the view that the ability to speak Hebrew was a marker of Palestinian masculinity in a broader sense. Rashisa, for instance, contended that "to be a successful man in Palestine you have to know the Hebrew language," such knowledge potentially enabling one to access more lucrative employment within Israel. For Sahar, learning Hebrew was also a way for men to "deal" with the occupation and was, therefore, something of a masculine expectation alongside "working" and "trying not to get killed," while for Raed learning Hebrew was a (masculine) necessity as Palestinians were "living right next door" to those who spoke this language. In short, therefore, while this form of knowledge, like knowledge of the conflict environment, could, in theory at least, proves as advantageous to women as to men, in practice it seems that it had largely been appropriated by men to validate or affirm their masculinities within public space.[18]

A third form of knowledge which the participants both valued and used to their advantage was scholarly or academic knowledge. As De Sondy (2015) states, there is great emphasis on the pursuit of learning within Islamic traditions. Within this context, participants suggested that academic knowledge was something that men should possess or strive to acquire. It was also said to be something which not even the machinery of occupation could take away (field notes, 25 October 2016).

In expressing her belief in the value of a good education, Sahar, for instance, highlighted its potential to increase one's employment opportunities and income and the enhanced role that one could subsequently play in one's community. Others highlighted the extent to which the knowledge gained as a result of educational endeavors, such as English language skills or knowledge of the law of occupation, reduced vulnerability during interactions with Israeli soldiers (Raed; Rashida). Moreover, a good education was said to provide one with enhanced opportunities to gain employment in an occupation that did not require crossing checkpoints as part of one's daily commute or could afford one increased social status and thus ease of crossing when one was required to pass through such sites (Hasan).

Participants also opined that academic achievement could enable one to persist in Palestine and even push back against the occupation. Sayed argued that having a good education meant that one could hope to remain in Palestine "like the olive tree," while Sami was of the belief that education was their "greatest weapon" in their battle against oppression. And again, while men and women could both hope to benefit from the knowledge gained as a result of higher education, in practice it seems that the more public nature of men's responsibilities (MacKenzie and Foster 2017), including that of providing and protecting, meant that they could hope to accrue more benefits from it. Academic knowledge, therefore, like the other forms of knowledge

18 Male participants expressed the view that men were the ones "expected" to do the talking at checkpoints (Focus Group 2) and, indeed, to "deal" with the occupation more generally (Habib). However, as Shalhoub-Kevorkian (2009) notes, women are often asked to cross checkpoints when their male kinfolk are too afraid of suffering violence or humiliation to do so.

discussed earlier, was thus primarily a masculinized form of knowledge which the participants could draw upon to affirm their masculinities and gain at least a measure of protection against the effects of conflict and occupation. Indeed, it appears that the participants drew upon these forms of knowledge, much more so than any recourse to their civilian identities, in order to reduce their vulnerability to conflict violence. These findings thus reveal that within the Occupied Territories, there appeared to be paucity of spaces which the participants considered safe, with not even family homes or university campuses considered places of refuge (Emad; Sayed). In response, therefore, participants attempted to ensure that their behavior rendered the space around them to be as safe as possible, by behaving in ways not perceived to be threatening in the eyes of the Israeli security forces (or indeed the Israeli state). Their actions, then, were guided by the premise that hyper-vigilance, rather than hypermasculinity, would best serve them in their efforts to avoid falling victim to conflict-related violence. Hence, in the absence of a meaningful transition, such actions functioned as gendered coping mechanisms, enabling participants to cope with the insecurity and (masculine) subjugation associated with ongoing conflict and military occupation in a practical and peaceful manner. As suggested earlier, forms of civilian masculinity based on quiet persistence and the negotiation of complex practicalities are likely to prove invaluable to any future transitional or formal peacebuilding processes.

Negotiating Civilian Masculinities: Bodies and Minds

While violent conflict has often been thought of as a theater within which men may enhance their masculinities through the use of violence (Friðriksdóttir 2018), the findings herein add to the body of literature which suggests that conflict may undermine men's roles and identities and limit the resources and strategies available for attainment of normative forms of masculinity (Dolan 2002; Wright 2014). However, the findings also reveal how civilian men continue to utilize the resources and strategies available to them to meet the challenges associated with conflict-affected and transitional settings. Specifically, I argue that the participants from the North of Ireland affirmed their masculinities and gained a measure of protection from the effects of conflict-related violence primarily by utilizing the cultural capital associated with their bodies, while their counterparts in the Occupied Territories did so principally by utilizing the cultural capital associated with their minds.[19]

As suggested earlier, the "masculinization opportunities" available to the participants from the North of Ireland were profoundly shaped by their

19 Whilst recognizing the respective strategies and resources utilized by the participants, it is important to note that I am not attempting to uphold or reinforce the mind–body dualism found within some strands of scholarship (Gill et al. 2005).

position within the region's class hierarchy (Baird 2012: 183). As noted earlier, such participants hailed from areas characterized not only by high levels of conflict violence but also relative deprivation (see Coulter 1999; Mesev et al. 2009). Within such communities, the relative lack of employment or educational opportunities would have meant there were comparatively few resources and strategies available for the attainment of normative forms of masculinity. However, given the esteem within which pugilists were held within working-class communities on both sides of the divide, the pursuit of boxing enabled participants to acquire highly protective and valued forms of civilian masculinity. With boxing being a sport within which the body is central and highly visible, the masculine capital associated with their bodies afforded participants both masculine affirmation and (bodily) protection from the effects of conflict-related violence.[20]

By contrast, participants from the Occupied Territories primarily drew upon resources and strategies associated with situated knowledge, that is, their minds. Participants utilized knowledge of the conflict environment, knowledge of Hebrew, and the knowledge which they had accrued through further education. Utilizing these forms of knowledge, which appeared to remain primarily the preserve of men, enabled participants to more skillfully exercise caution and vigilance, and hence to navigate conflict spaces more successfully. It also permitted them to demonstrate agency and self-reliance, their vulnerability within such spaces permitting the affirmation of their masculinities.

The sites thus reveal that even in situations of conflict and transition, when masculinization opportunities may be restricted and masculine subjugation may be patently apparent, resources and strategies for the affirmation of civilian masculinities are likely to remain. Within such contexts, therefore, it may be within relatively mundane and everyday spaces, such as the boxing club or the security checkpoint, where gendered coping mechanisms are enacted, and where processes of peacebuilding and transition, or at least the recognition of the necessity of such processes, may begin to take root.

Conclusion

This chapter has examined the experiences, identities, and vulnerabilities of civilian men within two conflicted societies, namely, the North of Ireland and the Occupied Palestinian Territories. It has explored how civilian men within these contexts respond to conflict and its effects on their gender identities in context- and culturally specific ways. In relation to the North of Ireland, it has shown how the participants found salvation within boxing, primarily by utilizing their bodies to affirm masculine identities which were both highly

20 Numerous scholars, including Whitehead (2002) and Connell (2005), have discussed the centrality of the body to the construction of masculinity.

protective and civilian in character. With regard to the Occupied Territories, the chapter has revealed how the participants responded to the effects of conflict by drawing upon various forms of knowledge, principally by utilizing their minds, in the hope of affirming their masculinities and safely navigating the conflict as civilians.

The chapter has thus sought to deliver a more holistic understanding of the continuum of men's experiences within conflict-affected and transitional societies. Through the examination of two seemingly quite disparate settings, it has provided for a nuanced examination of masculinity and conflict beyond soldiering and violence, the findings from which may have resonance in numerous conflict-affected contexts. Moreover, by making explicit reference to their civilian identities, it has endeavored to make non-combatant men visible as gendered beings, and thus to contribute to an area of scholarship which has long been neglected. As Myrttinen et al. (2014) note, a truly gendered approach to understanding both conflict and peace is not possible without bringing men, as gendered beings, into the analysis. There is a need, therefore, to look beyond those whom we often consider to be "ideal" (Hirsch 2012: 254) or "paradigmatic" (Kinsella 2011: 16) civilians and recognize the identities, vulnerabilities, and protection requirements of non-combatant men. The chapter has also shown how gendered coping mechanisms, such as the pursuit of a popular sport or the utilization of various forms of knowledge, are enacted in context and culturally specific ways. While such mechanisms may be beyond the confines of formal transitional justice processes, they may nevertheless function to diminish barriers to peacebuilding, hasten processes of transition, or foster agency and masculine self-reliance within environments of danger and subjugation. Within conflict-affected settings, therefore, let us not overlook how men often seek not to fuel violence but to avoid it, navigate it, adapt to it, and pursue micro-processes of peacebuilding and transition in pragmatic and courageous ways.

References

Allsopp, J. (2015). *The Refugee Crisis: Demilitarising Masculinities*. openDemocracy. Available at: https://www.opendemocracy.net/en/5050/refugee-crisis-demilitarising-masculinities/. Accessed on: 18 November 2021.

Amir, M. (2014). Women Speaking of National Security: The Case of Checkpoint Watch. *International Political Sociology* 8(4): 363–378.

Anderson, E. (2011). *Inclusive Masculinity: The Changing Nature of Masculinities*. Oxon: Routledge.

Baird, A. (2012). The Violent Gang and the Construction of Masculinity Amongst Socially Excluded Young Men. *Safer Communities* 11(4): 179–190.

Ben-Naftali, O., A. M. Gross and K. Michaeli (2005). Illegal Occupation: Framing the Occupied Palestinia Territory. *Berkeley Journal of International Law* 23(3): 551–614.

Brown, K. and F. Ni Aoláin (2015). Through the Looking Glass: Transitional Justice Futures Through the Lens of Nationalism, Feminism and Transformative Change. *International Journal of Transitional Justice* 9(1): 127–149.

Cahn, N. and F. Ni Aoláin (2010). Gender, Masculinities and Transition in Conflicted Societies. *New England Law Review* 44(1): 101–188.

Campbell, S. (2020). *Civilian Masculinities and Conflict: An Examination of Northern Ireland and the Occupied Palestinian Territories*. PhD Thesis. Belfast: Ulster University.

Carpenter, R. C. (2003). 'Women and Children First': Gender, Norms, and Humanitarian Evacuation in the Balkans 1991–95. *International Organization* 57(4): 661–694.

Carpenter, R. C. (2006). *'Innocent Women and Children': Gender, Norms and the Protection of Civilians*. Aldershot: Ashgate Publishing.

Cockburn, C. (2001). The Gendered Dynamics of Armed Conflict and Political Violence. In: Moser, C. O. and Clark, F. C. (eds.): *Victims, Perpetrators or Actors? Gender, Armed Conflict and Political Violence*. London: Zed Books: 13–29.

Connell, R. (2005). *Masculinities*(2nd ed.). Cambridge: Polity Press.

Coulter, C. (1999). *Contemporary Northern Irish Society: An Introduction*. London: Pluto Press.

de Búrca, A. (2014). *Preventing Political Violence Against Civilians: Nationalist Militant Conflict in Northern Ireland, Israel and Palestine*. Basingstoke: Palgrave Macmillan.

Dekeseredy, W. and M. D. Schwartz (2005). Masculinities and Interpersonal Violence. In: Kimmel, M. S., Hearn, J. and Connell, R. (eds.): *Handbook of Studies on Men and Masculinities*. Thousand Oaks: Sage Publications: 353–366.

Delgado, F. (2005). Golden But Not Brown: Oscar De La Hoya and the Complications of Culture, Manhood, and Boxing. *The International Journal of the History of Sport* 22(2): 196–211.

De Sondy, A. (2015). *The Crisis of Islamic Masculinities*. London: Bloomsbury.

Dolan, C. (2002). Collapsing Masculinities and Weak States – A Case Study of Northern Uganda. In: Cleaver, F. (ed.): *Masculinities Matter! Men, Gender and Development*. London: Zed Books: 57–83.

Ducat, S. (2004). *The Wimp Factor: Gender Gaps, Holy Wars, and the Politics of Anxious Masculinity*. Boston: Beacon Press.

Enloe, C. (2000). *Maneuvers: The International Politics of Militarizing Women's Lives*. Berkeley and London: University of California Press.

Feldman, A. (1991). *Formations of Violence: The Narrative of the Body and Political Terrorism in Northern Ireland*. Chicago: University of Chicago Press.

Foster, A. (2011). *"Pulling the Tail of the Cat": An Exploration of Palestinian Peacebuilders' Conceptualisations of Men and Masculinities in the Israeli-Palestinian Conflict*. Master Thesis. Wellington: Victoria University of Wellington.

Friedersdorf, C. (2012). Under Obama, Men Killed by Drones Are Presumed to be Terrorists. *The Atlantic*, 29 May. Available at: https://www.theatlantic.com/politics/archive/2012/05/under-obama-men-killed-by-drones-are-presumed-to-be-terrorists/257749/. Accessed on: 27 February 2019.

Friðriksdóttir, G. S. (2018). Soldiering as an Obstacle to Manhood? Masculinities and Ex-Combatants in Burundi. *Critical Military Studies*: 1–18.

Gill, R., K. Henwood and C. McLean (2005). Body Projects and the Regulation of Normative Masculinity. *Body & Society* 11(1): 37–62.

Gokani, R., A. Bogossian and B. Akesson (2015). Occupying Masculinities: Fathering in the Palestinian Territories. *NORMA: International Journal for Masculinity Studies* 10(3–4): 203–218.

Hammami, R. (2006). *Human Agency at the Frontiers of Global Inequality: An Ethnography of Hope in Extreme Places*. Inaugural Address as 2005/2006 holder of the Prince Claus Chair. Utrecht: Utrecht University, 20 April.

Handelman, S. (2011). *Conflict and Peacemaking in Israel-Palestine*. Oxon: Routledge.

Hartigan, R. S. (2010). *Civilian Victims in War: A Political History*. New Brunswick: Transaction Publishers.

Higate, P. and J. Hopton (2005). War, Militarism and Masculinities. In: Kimmel, M. S., Hearn, J. and Connell, R. (eds.): *Handbook of Studies on Men & Masculinities*. Thousand Oaks: Sage Publications: 432–447.

Hirsch, S. (2012). Civilians Under the Law: Inequality, Universalisms and Intersectionality as Intervention. In: Rothbart, D., Korostelina, K. and Cherkaoiu, M. (eds.): *Civilians and Modern War: Armed Conflict and the Ideology of Violence*. Oxon: Routledge: 251–271.

Hochberg, G. Z. (2010). 'Check Me Out' Queer Encounters in Sharif Waked's Chic Point: Fashion for Israeli Checkpoints. *GLQ: A Journal of Lesbian and Gay Studies* 16(4): 577–597.

Hutchings, K. (2008). Making Sense of Masculinity and War. *Men and Masculinities* 10(4): 389–404.

Hutchings, K. (2011). Gendered Humanitarianism: Reconsidering the Ethics of War. In: Sylvester, C. (ed.): *Experiencing War*. London: Routledge: 28–41.

Imseis, A. (2003). On the Fourth Geneva Convention and the Occupied Palestinian Territory. *Harvard International Law Journal* 44(1): 65–138.

International Committee of the Red Cross (2010). *Civilians Protected Under International Humanitarian Law*. ICRC. Available at: https://www.icrc.org/en/document/protected-persons/civilians-protected-international-humanitarian-law. Accessed on: 18 November 2021.

Jones, A. (2004). Gendercide and Genocide. In: Jones, A. (ed.): *Gendercide and Genocide*. Nashville: Vanderbilt University Press: 1–38.

Katrak, K. H. (1989). Decolonizing Culture: Toward a Theory for Postcolonial Women's Texts. *Modern Fiction Studies* 35(1): 157–179.

Kinsella, H. M. (2011). *The Image Before the Weapon*. Ithaca: Cornell University Press.

Korsten, V. (2011). *Soldiers and Students: Macro-Politics Played Out in the Micro-Setting of Checkpoints*.Master Thesis. Amsterdam: University of Amsterdam.

Kotef, H. and A. Merav (2014). (En)Gendering Checkpoints: CheckpointWatch and the Repercussions of Intervention. *Signs: Journal of Women in Culture and Society* 32(4): 973–996.

MacKenzie, M. and A. Foster (2017). Masculinity Nostalgia: How War and Occupation Inspire a Yearning for Gender Order. *Security Dialogue* 48(3): 206–223.

Mansbach, D. (2009). Normalizing Violence: From Military Checkpoints to 'Terminals' in the Occupied Territories. *Journal of Power* 2(2): 255–273.

Melzer, N. (2009). *Interpretive Guidance on the Notion of Direct Participation in Hostilities Under International Humanitarian Law*. Geneva: International Committee of the Red Cross. Available at: https://www.icrc.org/eng/assets/files/other/icrc-002-0990.pdf. Accessed on: 10 February 2016.

Merry, S. E. (2009). *Gender Violence: A Cultural Perspective*. Oxford: Wiley Blackwell.

Mesev, V., P. Shirlow and J. Downs (2009). The Geography of Conflict and Death in Belfast, Northern Ireland. *Annals of the Association of American Geographers* 99(5): 893–903.

Messner, M. A. (1992). Male Athletes' Friendships. In: Kimmel, M. and Messner, M. (eds.): *Men's Lives*. New York: Macmillan: 215–231.

Middle East Monitor (2018). *Israel's Lieberman: No Innocent Civilians in Gaza*. Available at: https://www.middleeastmonitor.com/20180409-israels-lieberman-no-innocent-civiliansingaza/ Accessed on: 10 April 2018.

Migliaccio, T. (2009). Men's Friendships: Performances of Masculinity. *The Journal of Men's Studies* 17(3): 226–241.

Milton-Edwards, B. and P. Hinchcliffe (2008). *Conflicts in the Middle East Since 1945* (3rd ed.). Oxon: Routledge.

Moran, M. H. (2010). Gender, Militarism, and Peace-Building: Projects of the Post-conflict Moment. *The Annual Review of Anthropology* 39: 261–274.

Myrttinen, H., L. Khattab and J. Naujoks (2017). Re-thinking Hegemonic Masculinities in Conflict-Affected Contexts. *Critical Military Studies* 3(2): 103–119.

Naaman, D. (2006). The Silenced Outcry: A Feminist Perspective from the Israeli Checkpoints in Palestine. *NWSA: National Women's Studies Association Journal* 18(3): 168–180.

Ni Aoláin, F., D. F. Haynes and N. Cahn (2011). *On the Frontlines: Gender, War, and the Post Conflict Process*. Oxford: Oxford University Press.

Nordstrom, C. (1997). *A Different Kind of War Story*. Philadelphia: University of Pennsylvania Press.

Otman, A. (2020). Handcuffed Protectors? Palestinian Fatherhood-Protection Unlocking Its Chains. *International Journal of Applied Psychoanalytic Studies* 17(2): 146–164.

Paradis, E. (2012). Boxers, Briefs or Bras? Bodies, Gender and Change in the Boxing Gym. *Body & Society* 18(2): 82–109.

Protocol Additional to the Geneva Conventions of 12 August 1949, and Relating to the Protection of Victims of International Armed Conflicts (Protocol I), 8 June 1977. Available at: https://www.icrc.org/en/doc/assets/files/other/icrc_002_0321.pdf. Accessed on: 8 December 2021.

Rothbart, D., K. Korostelina and M. Cherkaoiu (2012). The Place and Plight of Civilians in Modern War. In: Rothbart, D., Korostelina, K. and Cherkaoiu, M. (eds.): *Civilians and Modern War: Armed Conflict and the Ideology of Violence*. Oxon: Routledge: 1–17.

Rothenberg, C. E. (2006). 'My Wife Is from the Jinn': Palestinian Men, Diaspora and Love. In: Ouzgane, L. (ed.): *Islamic Masculinities*. London: Zed Books: 89–104.

Said, E. W. (1994). *Culture and Imperialism*. New York: Vintage Books.

Schulz, P. (2020). *Male Survivors of Wartime Sexual Violence: Perspectives from Northern Uganda*. Berkeley: University of California Press.

Shalhoub-Kevorkian, N. (2009). *Militarization and Violence Against Women in Conflict Zones in the Middle East: A Palestinian Case-Study*. Cambridge: Cambridge University Press.

Shalhoub-Kevorkian, N. (2015). *Security Theology, Surveillance and the Politics of Fear*. Cambridge: Cambridge University Press.

Sharoni, S. (2001). Re-thinking Women's Struggles in Israel-Palestine and in the North of Ireland. In: Moser, C. O. N. and Clarke, F. (eds.): *Victims, Perpetrators or Actors? Gender, Armed Conflict and Political Violence*. London: Zed Books: 85–98.

Skjelsbaek, I. (2001). Is Femininity Inherently Peaceful? The Construction of Femininity in the War. In: Skjelsbaek, I. and Smith, D. (eds.): *Gender, Peace and Conflict*. London: Sage Publications: 47–67.

Slim, H. (2008). *Killing Civilians: Method, Madness, and Morality in War*. London: Cinco Puntos Press.

Sorek, T. (2009). 'The Only Place Where an Arab Can Hit a Jew and Get a Medal For It': Boxing and Masculine Pride Among Arab Citizens of Israel. *Sport in Society* 12(8): 1065–1074.

Spencer, R. (2007). 'I Just Feel Safe with Him': Emotional Closeness in Male Youth Mentoring Relationships. *Psychology of Men & Masculinity* 8(3): 185–198.

Steans, J. (2006). *Gender and International Relations*. Cambridge: Polity Press.

Strier, R. (2014). Fatherhood in the Context of Political Violence: Los Padres de la Plaza. *Men and Masculinities* 17(4): 359–375.

Sugden, J. (1996). *Boxing and Society: An International Analysis*. Manchester: Manchester University Press.

Sugden, J. and A. Bairner (1993). *Sport, Sectarianism and Society in a Divided Ireland*. Leicester: Leicester University Press.

Sugden, J. and S. Harvie (1995). *Sport and Community Relations in Northern Ireland*. Coleraine: Centre for the Study of Conflict, University of Ulster.

Sutton, M. (2001). *An Index of Death from Conflict in Northern Ireland*. CAIN Web Service. Available at: https://cain.ulster.ac.uk/sutton/. Accessed on: 1 May 2018.

Theidon, K. (2009). Reconstructing Masculinities: The Disarmament, Demobilization, and Reintegration of Former Combatants in Colombia. *Human Rights Quarterly* 31(1): 1–34.

Turner, L. (2019). Syrian Refugee Men as Objects of Humanitarian Care. *International Feminist Journal of Politics* 21(4): 595–616.

United Nations Office for the Coordination of Humanitarian Affairs (2021). *Data on Casualties*. Available at: https://www.ochaopt.org/data/casualties. Accessed on: 20 May 2021.

Uppsala Conflict Data Program (2021). *Israel*. Department of Peace and Conflict Research, Uppsala University: Available at: https://ucdp.uu.se/?id=1&id=1#country/666. Accessed on: 12 May 2021.

Vess, J., G. Barker, S. Naraghi-Anderlini and A. Hassink (2013). *The Other Side of Gender: Men as Critical Agents of Change*. Special Report 340. Washington, DC: The United States Institute of Peace. Available at: https://www.usip.org/sites/default/files/SR340.pdf. Accessed on: 26 February 2018.

Whitehead, S. (2002). *Men and Masculinities: Key Themes and New Directions*. Cambridge: Polity Press.

Wilson, N. J., R. Cordier and S. Wilkes-Gillan (2014). Men's Sheds and Mentoring Programs: Supporting Teenage Boys' Connection with School. *International Journal of Men's Health* 13(2): 92–100.

Wilson, R. (2016). *Northern Ireland Peace Monitoring Report: Number 4*. Community Relations Council. Available at: https://www.community-relations.org.uk/sites/crc/files/media-files/NIPMR-Final-2016.pdf. Accessed on: 9 May 2018.

Woodward, K. (2007). *Boxing, Masculinity and Identity: The 'I' of the Tiger*. Oxon: Routledge.

Wright, H. (2014). *Masculinities, Conflict and Peacebuilding: Perspectives on Men Through a Gender Lens*. Saferworld. Available at: https://www.saferworld.org.uk/resources/publications/862-masculinities-conflict-and-peacebuilding-perspectives-on-men-through-a-gender-lens. Accessed on: 22 November 2021.

Chapter 15

Civilian and Caring Masculinities and the Questions of Justice in Kashmir

Amya Agarwal

Introduction

Throughout scholarship on masculinities in times of war and conflict, the persistent association of men with violence continues to be a predominant, if not *the* hegemonic, theme of inquiry. Military masculinity, for instance, is used as a significant concept to examine male gender roles, performances, and embodiments in military and military-like institutions and organizations (Duncanson 2009). In the South Asian context, too, efforts to examine war and armed conflict as a masculine activity have contributed toward highlighting the gendered nature of institutions and matters linked to national security, where feminist voices are excluded (Parashar and D'Costa 2017). These significant efforts are, without a doubt, crucial in the study of gender, peace, and conflict. However, other forms of masculinities also coexist in conflict settings – sometimes paradoxical and overlapping – that often get overlooked. These include non-militarized notions of masculinity, civilian masculinities (Carpenter 2006; Campbell, this volume), or non-heterosexual masculine identities (Serrano-Amaya, this volume). Going beyond a primary focus on militarized masculinities in critical scholarship on men and masculinities (CSMM) (Bjarnegård and Murray 2018), through qualitative research in different contexts, has specifically highlighted the significant role of civilian agency (Hollander 2014; Krause 2019; Kunz et al. 2018).

Drawing inspiration from critical masculinities scholarship in different contexts around the world, in this chapter I specifically explore the role of civilian masculinities around questions of justice, care, and processes of social repair in the ongoing Kashmir conflict in India. Like other conflicts, Kashmir also entails a web, or a mosaic, of entangled masculinities. These include, among others, competitive militarized masculinities of the state armed forces and militant groups, masculinities associated with religion, conflict-affected civilian masculinities, demobilized masculinities, and other non-militarized forms of masculinity. In this context, the agency of both men and women affected by the conflict can be better understood by foregrounding their engagement with masculinities. This is because the context and surroundings in which both

DOI: 10.4324/9781003519522-19

men and women exercise their choices and perform practices are shaped and informed by the interplay of gender in general (Ahäll 2012), including masculinities (Touquet and Schulz 2021). In this context, studying the roles and identities of civilian men may be significant to arrive at a more meaningful understanding of informal mechanisms of social repair, justice, and agency. As an illustrative example of civilian masculinity in Kashmir, I study the role of Imran (name changed), who is a prominent lawyer and human rights activist in Kashmir. His efforts to question the human rights violations in Kashmir are recognized widely across the region. Despite threats and attacks on his life, Imran's long struggle to render injustices visible illuminates the significant and crucial roles that civilian and unarmed men can play in conflicts but which nevertheless remain unrecognized by dominant discourses around gender, conflict, and transitional justice (see Hamber et al. and Mosqueira, this volume).

Through the discussion of one particular expression of civilian masculinity represented by Imran, the chapter will specifically highlight, in line with this volume, the inadequacy of studying transitional justice only from a top-down perspective and through the lens of state actors and institutionalized processes, as well as exclusively in so-called *post-conflict* contexts. To engage with Kashmir from a transitional justice perspective is in itself a unique exercise – for it being an ongoing conflict and without institutional mechanisms in place for peace and justice – the chapter shows how informal processes of transitional justice are an integral part of an active conflict setting as well. In doing so, the chapter challenges the limited scope and dimensions of "transitional justice" perspective that is usually not applied to an ongoing conflict.

Civilian masculinity is usually understood as an opposite of, in contradiction to, military and violent forms of masculinities – typically viewed through men portrayed as soft, living their lives without being impacted by the conflict. Through the case of Kashmir, the chapter shows that there is not one homogeneous notion of civilian masculinity but a multiplicity of civilian masculinities. These are neither static nor necessarily exclusive. Men can embody (or may have embodied) military masculinity in the battlefield but also represent civilian masculinities at home. Similarly, civilian men's lives are not unaffected by militarization – militarism, state, and the conflict itself have a strong influence on the civilian masculinities. The examples of demobilized former militants and young male participants of the stone pelting movement in Kashmir (as discussed at greater length later) simultaneously represent both militarized and non-militarized forms of masculinities. At the same time, some human rights activists and NGO workers represent more caring and non-violent forms of civilian masculinities. There are, of course, men who are neither former militants nor resisters or activists – who are *only* living their lives in the context of a conflict, which in itself is troublesome enough, with often severe implications for their masculinities (Dolan 2002; Hollander 2014). As such, it is not an exaggeration to say that conflict impacts the lives of all inhabitants in some way or another, even if they are *ordinary* civilians just living their lives. Together, the different (sometimes contradicting) identities of men in the civilian sphere show that there is no singular form of civilian masculinity embodied in Kashmir. These insights carry important implications for further nuancing conceptual and theoretical takes on civilian masculinities and alert us to avoid over-romanticizing or essentializing civilian masculinities as a complex and heterogeneous conceptual category.

Through the case of Imran, the chapter highlights the significant role that male activists of human rights and NGO workers play in conflict-affected societies. To avoid romanticizing or equating the category of civilian masculinity with inherently peaceful and non-violent men, it is important to reiterate that Imran's case is only one of the many ways in which civilian men identify themselves in Kashmir. The chapter will further look into the ways Imran tells us the story of some civilian men making sense of their everyday lived realities, constantly rebuilding themselves and their community – or how, in other words, they are remaking a world (Das et al. 2001) in the midst and wake of violence. Through Imran's case, the chapter presents an example of a civilian man's masculinity as positioned against militarism, and yet his agency is shaped by the experiences of militarism and violence. This focus evidences the need to move beyond dominant scripts of transitional justice associated with post-conflict contexts, as this limits the view of social repair and justice within ongoing conflict scenarios and in the midst of violence.

Secondly, it highlights men's involvement in the informal mechanisms for social repair that are equally significant in understanding the role of non-state actors in conflicts. In a way, this also validates the existence of multiple stakeholders in conflict situations as compared to state-centric approaches to understanding conflict and enacting transition – speaking to the normative concern across many of the chapters to move beyond an emphasis on state and institutions as the primary, if not exclusive, custodians of transitional justice processes (see, for example, Serrano-Amaya, Mosqueira, Thiyagaraja, Campbell, this volume). Thirdly, the practices undertaken by men to make sense of their positions, question injustices, and provide support to victims and survivors of violence are important to understand the agency of civilian men as shaped by masculinities (Touquet and Schulz 2021). Additionally, the chapter does not just look at the multiplicity of masculinities, but that these are always being contested by other men. In an attempt to address the aforementioned issues, the chapter is divided in four sections. In the first section, I give an overview of the research context and methods, after which I explore what civilian masculinities mean in the Kashmir conflict and who represents this form of masculinity. In the third section, I locate Imran's unique role and his agency, following which I analyze the significance, relevance, and contribution that Imran's case makes in expanding our understanding of the role of caring masculinities in relation to questions of justice and social repair in the civilian life of Kashmir.

Research Context: Kashmir in Transition

The conflict in Kashmir is traced back to the partition of the Indian subcontinent into two countries, India and Pakistan, in accordance with the Mountbatten Plan in 1947. The princely states of British India were given the choice to accede to either India or Pakistan, under the Indian Independence Act of 18 July 1947. The ruler of the princely state of Kashmir, during the partition, decided to accede to India despite the contestation and resistance from within Kashmir (Akbar 2002; Habibullah 2008; Whitehead 2007; Dasgupta 2002).

Throughout the period after partition, Kashmir's existence has been marked with discontent, resistance, and stringent counter-resistance measures by the Indian state. Continuity of failed promises of the Indian state, internal resistance politics, and rigged elections resulted in the growth and fostering of the militancy movement in Kashmir. The movement reached its peak in the late 1980s and early 1990s, with many young men joining the militancy. The militant resistance initially received widespread support from the local inhabitants (Puri 1993). Women not only encouraged men to join the militancy – illustrating how women can often be involved, or complicit, in the social co-production of specific forms of masculinity, including militarized masculinities – but also themselves performed supporting activities in the form of providing shelter, food, and aid to the militants (Parashar 2011), thereby demonstrating the manifold roles and forms of agency of women in armed struggles (Sjoberg and Gentry 2007).

The Indian state implemented strong counter-insurgency practices as a response to the rising militancy. The Armed Forces Special Powers' Act (AFSPA) gave impunity to the Indian army that further led to, and accelerated, a number of human rights violations against the civilian population. A few human rights organizations and civil society bodies, both in Kashmir and internationally, have been actively involved in documenting and protesting against these human rights abuses. The resistance movement in Kashmir once again gained momentum in 2008, when the Indian government reached an agreement with the state of Jammu and Kashmir to transfer 99 acres of forestland to the Amarnath Shrine Board (which facilitates the religious pilgrimage from mainland India to the Amarnath cave). People in Kashmir considered this decision as a grave violation of the autonomy of the state of Kashmir. A large number of people gathered for a rally and protested against this decision (New York Times 2008).

Furthermore, in 2010, the killing of a young boy from Kashmir who was caught in a clash between the resisters and the Jammu and Kashmir (J&K) state police forces ignited more anger and gave rise to a fierce rebellion in the Kashmir valley. Many young boys and girls protested on the streets, confronted and pelted stones at the Indian state armed forces. The Indian state, in response, used repressive measures to quell dissent and protests. Several young boys suffered pellet injuries and, shaped by these experiences, decided to join the militancy. Kashmir thus saw the rise of a new form of militancy from within Kashmir, composed of young educated boys. They posted pictures on social media platforms and became popular heroes in the valley. Many women approved of and provided wholehearted support to the aspiring militants. In 2016, the leader of this new militancy movement, Burhan Wani, was killed by the Indian armed forces, which led to huge protests. Men and women gathered in large numbers at his funeral procession. Once again, the valley experienced widespread resistance on the streets, which in turn was met by strict counter-resistance measures by the state. Kashmir politics took a turn in 2019 when the Indian government, ruled by the Bhartiya Janata Party (BJP), abrogated Article 370 that granted a special status to the J&K state. A curfew was imposed, Kashmiri political leaders were placed under house arrest, and internet services were cut off for months after the decision was announced. Up until today, the situation in Kashmir after the removal of Article 370 has not significantly improved, at least not in the manner as promised by the government.

The research underpinning this chapter can be located in the past context of the rise of human rights organizations and activism of several key actors and people who opposed the human rights violations inflicted by the Indian state armed forces. As a result of their efforts, cases of enforced disappearances, rape, unmarked graves, and other forms of human rights violations started coming to the forefront. The Association of Parents of Disappeared Persons (APDP) and the Jammu and Kashmir Coalition of Civil Society (JKCCS), founded in 1994 and 2000, respectively, are two prominent examples of organizations operating in this particular context. They contributed significantly to documenting cases of enforced disappearances, sexual violence, torture, and other human rights violations, examined the specific problems faced by wives of the disappeared, commonly referred as *half widows* in Kashmir. Over time, several other NGOs – both Kashmiri and international – were formed to provide support and relief for (half) widows and other survivors of violence.

Research Methods and Positionality

This chapter draws from my PhD field research conducted in the Kashmir valley between 2013 and 2016. Most of the empirical data collected is now included in a monograph, but the case of civilian masculinities could not be included, due to its specific exploration of militarized masculinities of the state and non-state actors. Keeping in my mind the sensitivity of doing research in Kashmir, it is important to write a few sentences about the context of my field research. These reflections are also included in my book (Agarwal 2022: 13), but for methodological transparency, it may be important to reiterate a few points here. In 2013, I was recruited as one of the field researchers for a project on conflict governance headed by my PhD supervisor at that time. As part of this project, field researchers from Delhi were teamed up with Kashmiri researchers. My partner was a Kashmiri student, Abid (name changed), who became a close friend, advisor, and guide. After our project-related field trip was over, we remained in touch along with a few other Kashmiri researchers. After many discussions on my PhD topic, they offered to help me with my PhD field research.

I made several trips between 2013 and 2016, and Abid (with the help of his friends and teachers) meticulously arranged my interviews with various stakeholders for each trip. We hired a driver, who drove us to several districts tirelessly without charging much and also became a good friend later. I am so grateful for his kindness and friendship. Abid accompanied me for each interview and even translated the interviews in Kashmiri. My PhD field research was funded partly by the university teaching assistantship scholarship that I received from 2010 to 2014, and money borrowed from my mother.

The study was ethnographic in form, and qualitative interviews were held with activists, NGO workers, separatist leaders, widows, wives of the disappeared, mothers of sons killed in the conflict, women representatives of the village Panchayat Halqas, ex-militants, surrendered militants, army personnel, and young men who participated in the stone pelting movement. All these interviews were arranged with the help of my Kashmiri interlocutors, and there was no involvement of the Indian government, my university, or my PhD supervisor in arranging these interviews. The purpose of my research was clearly explained to all the participants, and I am very grateful to them for their time, effort, and trust in me. Their consent was central in the pursuit of the research. The ethical dimensions of this research are in line with certain parameters as previously developed by scholars conducting field research in conflict and other politically sensitive contexts (Cronin-Furman and Lake 2018; Mwambari 2019). The study adopts a *do no harm* ethical imperative, which is in accordance with Wood's (2006) understanding of informed consent of the respondents toward the research project, to protect the politically sensitive data and to decide what material to publish.

A word on my positionality is also important. The researcher's positionalities play a huge role in influencing the ways in which interlocutors participate and the research is affected (Mwambari 2019). Henry et al. (2009) suggest important questions to consider while conducting research: "Does it matter whether a researcher is white and female? Is she, he or they academic? Who is the research for – UN, the University or an NGO?" (Henry et al. 2009: 469). Critical reflection on these questions definitely opens up spaces to "consider the boundaries interfaces of power relations and knowledge systems between the researcher and the researched" (Henry et al. 2009: 470). My field research experience involved constant reflection of my political situatedness and multiple positionalities, such as being a female, Indian, outsider, non-Muslim, as well as the influence each of these identity vectors had on the research process. For a more detailed background and my positioning,

I provide my book reference (Agarwal 2022). But in short, I belong to an upper-caste Hindu family. I was raised by a single mother with the support of my maternal grandparents in Bhopal, the capital city of Madhya Pradesh state in India. I have not known my biological or stepfather's family, so I only speak of my maternal family. After completing school, I moved to Delhi in 2003 for higher studies. I was married at the time of my PhD research. Neither my family nor my ex-husband's family had any direct association with politics in Kashmir. My interest in the gender dimension of the Kashmir conflict was an extension of my MPhil research on women's peacebuilding efforts in the Northeast India, and I wanted to initially pursue a comparative study.

As a woman coming from Delhi, I was mostly considered an outsider in Kashmir – but the families of my interviewees generally welcomed me; and being accompanied by my Kashmiri (male) friend greatly helped in receiving some acceptance. There were one or two cases where I was asked to leave or even threatened, but overall, the interlocutors not only gave interviews but also invited me for nun chai (famous Kashmiri pink tea) or lunch. When I mentioned my daughter, the women, and especially mothers of sons killed, opened their hearts, and often we cried together. Some male survivors of violence were reluctant to share their stories with me and instead spoke to my collaborator, while showing him the wounds on their bodies.

My interview with Imran, the main character in this chapter, was arranged with the help of my friend in 2014 at Imran's organization's office. It was a long interview, and Imran shared both his professional and personal life story. I learned a lot from his story – and above all, the valuable insights, and his courage and determination in adversity, were inspiring. This was the only one time I met Imran, and I have not been in touch after that, but his story has stayed with me forever. I asked Abid if we could seek his permission for publishing his real name in my book/chapter, but the circumstances have changed in Kashmir after the abrogation of Article 370, and it has not been possible to get in touch with most of my interviewees. In order to protect their identities, I have changed all the names in this chapter.

Through Imran's story, the chapter aims to discuss how a civilian lawyer and human rights activist can broaden our understanding of masculinities in conflict situations. There are, of course, other human rights activists and NGO workers who embody a similar role. However, Imran's case is unique because he is one of the first activists to reopen cases of severe forms of human rights abuses committed by the Indian state. He used his legal profession to legally demand recourse. Without much physical or financial support, he started a struggle that involved huge risks to his life. His actions have successfully contributed to organizing the struggle for human rights in Kashmir. Other organizations were also influenced by his work, and that resulted in the acceleration of the documentation of human rights abuses. Over a period of time, the international community also recognized his contributions, and he has been awarded by multiple international human rights bodies. This chapter's aim is not to applaud or glorify Imran's role and work, but his role as a civilian in greatly influencing human rights activism in a conflict-affected society, and what this means for the study of civilian masculinities, is certainly worth exploring.

Entangled Civilian and Militarized Masculinities in Kashmir

The Kashmir conflict offers a suitable example to show the simultaneous existence and dynamic interplays of several conceptions of masculinities. The competitive and militarized masculinities of the state armed forces and the militant groups, masculinities associated with religion, conflict-affected civilian masculinities, and other non-militarized forms of masculinity represented by the human rights activists all form a web, or a mosaic, of masculinities in Kashmir. However, mirroring the persistent emphasis on violent and militarized masculinities in conflict studies more broadly – as attested to by Hamber et al. and Baker and Touquet in this volume – throughout existing scholarship is predominantly understood through the lens of militarized actors. In this process, and as a result, the significant roles played by civilian men in relation to the conflict get overlooked, as is the case throughout research on gender, masculinities, and conflict more broadly, such as in Northern Ireland or Israel/Palestine (see Campbell, this volume). As mentioned before, civilian masculinity is not a unified concept, neither in Kashmir nor in other conflicts, and there are different ways in which civilian men embody masculinities.

It is important to note that the civilian population in Kashmir is as deeply impacted by the conflict as the militarized actors. In such a context, it is difficult to categorize civilian men as ordinary men living their lives unimpacted by the conflict. The category of *civilian* in itself is problematic in a conflict-affected context. Prolonged curfews, violence, threats to life, human rights abuses, and enforced disappearances are only some examples to show that the simplified dichotomies of civilian versus militarized are misleading. Due to such a binarized view, mostly found in conflict studies, militaries masculinities are sometimes associated with violence and aggression, while civilians are treated as non-violent and inherently peaceful. To avoid such essentialized perspectives, it is important to recognize the fluidity between militarized and civilian masculinities. This section shows the different ways in which civilian men embody militarized masculinities – sometimes embodying both militarized and civilian masculinities simultaneously. There are also ordinary civilian men living their lives while simultaneously being impacted by the conflict. They may not have a militarized past, or participate in the resistance movement, or work in NGOs and human rights organizations, but they navigate the challenges of living in conflict in ordinary and mundane ways. So what does the category of "civilian men" really mean in the Kashmir conflict? Before exploring the answer to this question through the solitary case of Imran, I begin by demonstrating the fuzziness of the categories of civilian and militarized men in Kashmir. In doing so, I look into two groups of men who inhabit the civilian sphere but also embody a militarized past or (an imagined) future. The first are young men who participated in the stone pelting movement and aspired to join the new militancy (at the time of the interviews), and the second are ex-militants/surrendered militants who reintegrate in the society after their return.

Young Male Participants of the Stone Pelting Movement

With reference to the research context discussed earlier, some boys and young men had participated in the resistance of 2008 and 2010. They pelted stones and participated in the street resistance as a way to show their dissent toward the Indian state. During 2014 and 2015, I conducted interviews with nine young men who had participated in these protests. These men live ordinary civilian lives as students or employees and simultaneously participated in violent protests. The fluidity of their civilian and militarized identities is significant. When asked about the motivation behind participating in these protests, they responded that it was the inability of the earlier generation to achieve freedom by joining the militancy (in the late 1980s and early 1990s) and that the loss of lives, along with innumerable cases of human rights violations, had so far discouraged these young men from joining the militancy. However, after participating in the stone pelting movement, they faced periodical detentions and interrogations. They felt resentful about the lack of spaces to address their grievances. Most of them felt that joining the new wave of militancy (led by the then popular leader Burhan Wani) would be a better solution than facing regular harassment. Some of them also had (during the interviews) physical injuries due to the pellet guns used by the state armed forces as a way to quell the protests.

The predominant narrative around men joining the militancy in the late 1980s and early 1990s was that they were unemployed and uneducated. The interviewed young men emphasized that being uneducated and unemployed has nothing to do with joining the militancy. Many men who joined the wave of militancy in 2014–2015 were highly educated and came from economically well-off backgrounds. The start of the new militancy, according to them, was a result of the continued oppression inflicted upon the local inhabitants. All the nine interviewees mentioned that, if given a chance, they would not hesitate to give their lives for the cause of freedom and join the militancy movement. Their unwillingness to join the militancy at first was turned into an inclination, not only due to their resentment, but mainly also because of the harassment they faced after their participation in the stone pelting protests – both physical and psychological.

The narratives of these young men provide an understanding of the different ways in which conflict-affected semi-civilian, semi-militarized masculinities respond to the challenges, shape and reshape their perceptions of masculinity, and navigate their realities. Also, the overlapping of victimhood and agency in their responses highlights the need to incorporate a more fluid approach toward studying the experiences of people living in conflict-affected contexts. Krystalli (2020) succinctly articulates the need to look at victimhood and agency as coexisting: "Taking victimhood seriously requires moving away from a view of it as always synonymous with vulnerability or lack of agency or as entirely reduced to the experience of victimization." Kreft and Schulz (forthcoming), drawing on research in Colombia and Uganda, similarly argue for the need to move beyond a dichotomization of vulnerability and agency in the lives of the conflict-affected, instead demonstrating that both agency and victimhood often coexist and can, at times, also be co-constitutive and mutually enforcing each other.

The masculine imaginaries of these young male participants of the stone pelting movement are shaped by past experiences of militancy in Kashmir, the present experiences of harassment, and inspiration derived from the new militant heroes. They were not keen to leave their families to pick up the gun and remained disillusioned by the militant past of the previous generations. However, they also believed that they had no formal or informal space to voice their anger or protest against the injustices. In response to a repressive situation, this newer form of militancy started being perceived as a model for them to express and imagine manhood.

Reintegrated Former Militants

Another example to highlight the problematic constitution of the *civilian* category is the case of former militants who returned to civilian life. There generally is a sociological distinction between ex-militants and surrendered militants with regard to the ways in which they are referred to as honorable and disgraceful categories, respectively. But for this analysis, which mainly focuses on their reintegration, I use the term *former militants* for both groups. As opposed to the overwhelming support the militants received during the peak of the militancy movement, these men were not as respected once they sought to return and transition back to civilian life. Such an observation is not limited to Kashmir, and scholars discuss similar instances of former militants experiencing the loss of respect, honor, and masculinity as a result of the transition. Theidon, for instance, in her study on Colombian ex-combatants, discusses the many obstacles of reintegration, such as bodily capital and difficulties in joining the civilian labor market. Similarly, the struggle masculinities (or *frustration aggression* (Porter 2013)) of ex-combatants, as Xaba (2010) describes in his study of Black South African youth who were associated with the anti-apartheid struggle, were endowed with respect and status as *young lions*, *liberators* within their communities, and their violence was revered. However, the struggle version of masculinity is no longer acceptable in the post-apartheid order, and hence, they faced what can be perceived as a crisis of masculinity.

The withdrawal of public support from the militancy in the 1990s and an increased violence of the Indian state armed forces, along with the disunity among the armed groups, changed the social position of the militancy in Kashmir. The return of militants to civilian life during this period of distrust toward the militancy made their reintegration more challenging. Some interviewed surrendered militants felt unwelcomed and unaccepted by society. For many of the interviewed surrendered militants, the monetary benefits offered by the surrender and rehabilitation policy had attracted them to return. However, the compensation did not cover their return journey and was inadequate to sustain their lives. Many also said that it came at a high cost, including detentions, social rejection, and subordination. Experience of physical violence and *torture* alongside difficulties of settling into civilian life heightened the feelings of inadequacy among these former militants (Agarwal 2022).

With very little formal support from the state or non-state organizations, the former militants had to find their own coping mechanisms. Being discreet about sharing their experiences, sometimes remaining silent, selectively engaging with NGOs, sometimes performing traditionally women-centric roles at home, finding solace in the company of fellow former militants who went through similar experiences – all these acts are representative of their agency. Illuminating the hybridity of civilian and militarized worlds, the case of former militants is significant to question the exclusiveness of *civilian* in the embodiment of masculinities in the Kashmir conflict.

Caring Masculinities in Kashmir: The Case of Imran

The militarization in Kashmir (of both the state and non-state actors) has hugely influenced the civilian lives of inhabitants. Thus, a more fluid understanding of civilian is significant to view how men embody masculinities in this sphere. In this section, I explore a more caring expression of masculinity that certain men embody in the civilian sphere. Imran's agency can be located within such an embodiment. The agency deployed by male human rights activists and NGO workers in conflict-affected societies is often not recognized as gendered in the study of conflicts. Men are viewed as significant actors of human rights activism, but not necessarily as gendered subjects. Outside the victim or perpetrator category, the gender influence on this group of men is understudied. This category includes men who work as agents of change in society – including activists, lawyers, journalist, or staff in NGOs who actively oppose injustices and human rights violations resulting from the conflict. They dedicatedly work on a range of issues, such as enforced disappearances, rape and sexual violence, welfare of widows and half-widows, support for orphans and some organizations broadly on human rights violations. Some of them document human rights abuses, and some are involved in providing relief to survivors.

The struggle of these male activists is challenging, as they are seen as threats to both sides of the conflict (state and non-state) that inflict human rights violations. There have been instances of them receiving life threats and even being physically attacked several times. In the past, journalists from leading local news houses writing about the killings and covering stories about the conflict have been attacked and even killed (Ashiq 2019). As one journalist remarked:

> [W]e are prepared for death. The nature of our jobs is such that we are always on target. That cannot stop us from writing about the truth. My very close colleague and senior lost his life and I am prepared for the worst.[1]

Despite the volatile and stressful environment, these male activists, journalists, and lawyers have continued their fight against human rights abuses. Some provide care to the victims and survivors way beyond their contracted working hours. I refer to these men as embodying caring masculinities in Kashmir, a term used by Karla Elliott (2016). As Elliott (2016) rightly points out:

> Caring masculinities can be seen as masculine identities that exclude domination and embrace the affective, relational, emotional and interdependent qualities of care defined by the feminist theorists of care.

The avoidance of care has traditionally been seen as a feature of "being a man," and this can be redefined as normal for boys and men (Hearn 2001). Furthermore, Hanlon (2012) outlines several reasons for the absence of care from the traditional construction of masculinities, which include care being defined as feminine, doing care viewed as a feminized activity, the notion that men are ill-equipped to take care, and lastly, care as giving up power associated with traditional masculinity. As a response to traditional constructs of masculinity, a new wave of CSMM focused on men's caring and nurturing practices has emerged, particularly in European literature and largely positioned in the European Union (EU). The applicability of the notion of caring masculinities, however, is widespread and also speaks well to Imran's example from Kashmir. Imran's choice of practicing everyday acts of care toward his community (discussed in the next section) and enacting and performing that caring masculinity as a particular manifestation/branch of civilian masculinity (in contrast to (semi-)militarized forms of masculinity), he facilitates and influences micro-level processes of social repair. The intention is not to present a romanticized account or to make this an idealized category but

1 As told in a telephonic conversation on 11/10/2019.

instead to show that masculinities in conflict might also embody identities of care rather than aggression. Aspects of care, in general, receive only insufficient attention in research on violence, conflict, and transitions (Krystalli and Schulz 2022), and even more so, it is seldom linked to masculinities. The story of Imran describes how a few men also embrace more positively connotated emotions (such as compassion and empathy), practices, and interdependence. These stories are not often heard, but that does not mean they do not exist. They coexist within and amid the dominant narratives of violence, aggression, and dominance and need to be acknowledged, heard, and included in the study of conflicts.

Imran: Contributions and Agency

Imran is a lawyer and human rights activist who has worked extensively on documenting cases of human rights violations and questioning injustices. He actively opposed injustices and human rights violations. From providing legal assistance to several victims of conflict in Kashmir to reopening important cases of human rights violations and documenting the injustice, Imran, in his capacity as a lawyer, has been able to bring some hope in the lives of the families who had nowhere else to turn. His struggle became visible in the 2000s, when he started a human rights organization. His struggle is widely recognized by both the international community and local inhabitants of the valley. As a recognition of his efforts and contributions, he has received awards by international human rights bodies. Both militarized camps (the state armed forces and the militant groups), however, perceive his work as a potential threat, as he follows the violations of human rights closely and because the research conducted by his organization tends to reveal and bring awareness of excessive crimes committed by both sides to the conflict. His life was attacked a few times and he has received death threats but still remains dedicated to the cause. As he explains:

> There have been unprecedented human rights violations in this part of the world. I have myself been attacked a number of times (not sure by whom) but nothing can stop me from my work. I don't want to feel guilty on my deathbed that I didn't do anything for people who have been subjected to so much injustice in front of my eyes. This is the least that I can do. My profession of being a lawyer can help be a medium for the injustice to come in front of people's eyes. Also, a credible documentation is missing in Kashmir. Our organization aims to do that. Someone needs to do it. I have devoted my life for this cause.[2]

2 Interview on 03/09/2014.

Imran's most significant contributions include the reopening of a mass rape case in Kashmir. Inhabitants of the village where the mass rape happened had alleged that personnel of the Indian state armed forces had repeatedly raped women. A public interest litigation (PIL) in the J&K High Court was filed by Imran on behalf of the survivors of the mass rape in demanding the reopening of and reinvestigation into this case. As a response to his PIL, the closure report by the J&K state police was revisited, and the judicial magistrate directed further investigation to unravel the identity of those who happened to be the perpetrators of the alleged crime. Later, a division bench of State Human Rights Commission (SHRC) had also asked the government to constitute a Special Investigation Team (SIT) for reopening the case and had also recommended to prosecute the then director prosecution for "deliberately scuttling" the investigation into the matter and seeking closure on the grounds that the perpetrators were "untraced." Criminal accountability and justice also relate to the transitional justice (TJ) aspects of legal redress, and Imran's ability to influence the state mechanisms inspires us to explore the potential of caring masculine identities in conflict situations. Along with reopening the mass rape case, Imran also diligently explored the case of the unmarked graves in Kashmir.

While surveying disappearance cases in villages across two districts of Kashmir valley, from where the three men vanished in 2010, villagers showed Imran a hitherto unknown network of unmarked and mass graves: muddy pits and mossy mounds pockmarking pine forests and orchards. According to eyewitnesses, all had been dug under the watch of the Indian security forces and all contained the bodies of local men. Some were fresh; others had decayed. Imran widened his search, mapping almost 1,000 locations. Imran's team alerted the government's SHRC. "We suspected the missing of Kashmir were buried at these secret sites," he said. The SHRC agreed to an inquiry.

Yet another significant contribution toward human rights activism made by Imran was that he provided legal assistance to several families whose relatives had disappeared while in the custody of the Indian security forces. He filed numerous petitions on behalf of these families and often spent time listening to the agony and frustration of the families. As I was waiting for my interview with Imran, I the saw the father of a disappeared person walk to his office and Imran discuss his case with care and compassion. He wrote all the details about the incident, provided updates and assurance. Many such families and survivors of violence find solace in the presence of Imran, who answers their questions and provides legal assistance as and when required. The space of support that Imran has created for the parents and families in distress gives them the courage to navigate the challenges. His knowledge of the steps to be taken through law gives strength to these families. The agency deployed by Imran shows how important his role has been in serving as an agent of visibilization of human rights abuse in the Kashmiri society. His fight has served crucial in revealing human rights violations, and he has brought awareness about the different injustices in the conflict. His petitions have compelled not only state apparatus, like the SHRC, but also international organizations like the UN to take action because of his findings. From a masculinities perspective, where and how do we locate Imran's identity, and what can this embodiment contribute toward the study of masculinities in Kashmir?

Embodiment of Care Rather Than Domination

When asked about his motivation toward his tireless struggle to document human rights abuses, Imran responded by saying: "It is difficult to see the helplessness of people resulting from the human rights abuses. Anyone should feel prompted to question such injustices." As a man of few words, Imran lets his actions and practices speak volume of his motivation and dedication to provide care and solace to the people who come to him. Men like Imran have brought about positive change in the lives of survivors through peaceful and compassionate practices – representing engagement of masculine identities with care. However, by rendering Imran as embodying care, I do not just mean his compassion and empathy toward the families of the disappeared or survivors of violence but more radical forms of care that also involve larger social repair. Elliott shows how hook's idea of non-domination forms the core of caring masculinities – "hook's ideal of a connected, peaceful culture that rejects domination also captures the core of caring masculinities: the rejection of domination and the adoption of values of care" (Elliott 2016: 252; hooks 2004: 117). The traits of caring masculinities represent what are often perceived as *softer* forms of masculinity, such as compassion, sacrifice, and peace, that form a very important part in the discourse on conflict but which remain invisible due to the dominance of the hegemonic masculine norms of violence and aggression (Allsopp 2015). The struggle and practices of Imran suggest that while he (like other Kashmiri inhabitants) was impacted by militarization, he chose to identify himself with attributes of care, peace, and compassion. As highlighted earlier, some men in the civilian sphere identify themselves with militarized action, whereas some, like Imran, choose care over domination. Why is there a need to highlight Imran as the embodiment of a caring and nurturing masculinity?

Imran's case, from a non-Western vantage point, builds on the significance of highlighting care-related approaches among conflict situations. Such experiences are not new in men's everyday lives in conflict but are mostly overlooked to circulate dominant narratives of masculine attributes. It becomes even more important to highlight men's care as usual occurrences that coexist with the violence and suffering in conflicts. Hanlon (2012) demonstrates that masculinities and care are not anti-thetical to each other. They are intertwined, but in need of reconstruction. "We cannot appreciate masculinities without understanding relations of power and dominance, but we cannot understand power and dominance without also appreciating men's emotional lives" (Hanlon 2012: 66). Through the case of Imran, this chapter only reinforces the analysis made by scholars like Elliott (2016), that masculine identities can be reconceptualized as caring ones and show potentials of caring masculinities for change. It is, however, imperative to ask the question of how care is defined in such theoretical reworkings of masculine attributes. Here, the feminist ethics of care is a useful parameter to define men's engagement with care.

In non-conflict scenarios, the engagement of men with care is mainly understood through care work at home, such as childcare, care for the elderly, and other significantly nurturing acts. In conflict-affected contexts, along with the nourishing and enriching acts of care at home, care-related approaches also take the form of social repair and the idea of what Veena Das calls *remaking a world*. The everyday lived experiences of the civilians and how they make sense of and respond to violence provide us with invaluable insights on nurturing processes and approaches of social repair. As Baines and Rosenoff-Gauvin (2014: 282) rightly argue, the everyday can be seen as a "space of negotiation and re-negotiation of social relationships that make life meaningful." Similarly, Kent (2016), through her research in Timor-Leste, also highlights the importance of paying close attention to the everyday strategies and practices of social repair through which people seek to rebuild their lives. Krystalli and Schulz (2022: 1) further remind us through their respective research in Colombia and Uganda that "centring practices of love and care open up different sites and spaces and highlights a different set of actions through which to understand the work of remaking a world in the wake of violence."

Viewing such everyday acts of care, social repair, and remaking of a world is particularly significant in exploring caring masculinities, especially in societies and communities that survive violence and social harms. This is because the stories of care, especially those practiced by men, are often erased while primarily focusing on experiences and shaping of violence and harms. In an attempt to change the storyline of how masculinities are usually constructed in conflicts, this chapter centers Imran's care-related approach for his community and his quest for justice amidst the violence and domination of both the state and non-state militarized actors. His choice, his practices, and the positive implications of his actions signify the potential of caring masculinities to bring positive change in conflict and violence-affected situations.

Conclusion

In the violent context of Kashmir, there are a few stories that carry the potential of altering the predominant view of conflict and masculinities. The chapter started with the exploration of *civilian* as a framework to illuminate these overlooked stories. However, the fluidity of the *militarized* and *civilian* categories makes it difficult to contextualize an exclusive form of civilian masculinity. Examples of reintegrated former militants and young men who pelted stones show that men in Kashmir can simultaneously embody militarized and civilian masculinities. It may be useful to add here that the marker of civilian is still important to include several actors who may not actively participate in the conflict, and this chapter is in no way dismissing the civilian category. However, the chapter has attempted to show the fluidity between binaries of militarized and civilian in conflict settings. Additionally, the chapter also acknowledges the complexities and multiplicities of civilian masculinities that are intersectionally conditioned and defined. They intersect with class, religion, and care, and the chapter also refrains from creating any new essentialisms that may equate civilian with caring. Not all civilian men choose to practice care or work for social repair; some are pre-occupied with making ends meet or to survive. Some men in the civilian sphere use care-oriented approaches to navigate and make sense of their everyday lived realities, Imran being one of them. However, Imran, being a well-educated lawyer, does not represent the average Kashmiri man. Not all men might have the conditions for practicing care in a recognized way that Imran did, and caring masculinities can also exist in more everyday, mundane forms, such as caring fathers. Imran's story, however, tells us that it is possible to rework the theorization of masculinities in conflict and that caring masculinities have strong prospects of positively influencing both state-centric justice processes and bringing positive change in people's lives, in terms of social repair and remaking lives in the wake of violence.

Imran's long struggle to oppose human rights violations like mass rape, enforced disappearances, and unmarked graves, among others, is acknowledged by the Kashmiri locals and recognized by the international human rights bodies. His extensive documentation of human rights abuses has given hope to many Kashmiris who often go to his small office for solace. Imran's use of his profession as a high court lawyer to question injustice, meet families affected by the conflict, and file cases on behalf of the victims of conflict is an everyday act of social repair, an act of care, and an act of remaking and rebuilding a world. He provides a significant validation for research on caring masculinities and their potential of social change for men and gender relations (Elliott 2016). Imran's story also tells us that the everyday lives of *ordinary men* in conflicts can have a strong impact on the processes of transitional justice and also disrupt violence and harms, to some extent. Paying closer attention to caring masculinities in conflict and transitional settings broadens an engagement with masculinities in relation to justice and shows how performing a caring notion of masculinity provides new insights for how processes of social repair unfold.

Through Imran's story, there is also a possibility to revisit transitional justice as a concept. Imran's everyday acts of investigation – spending time with family members of the disappeared, meeting survivors of violence, documenting human rights violations, outside his contracted hours and then influencing governmental bodies to take action – all show the significance of, firstly, integrating the informal mechanisms and processes of justice within the study of transitional justice and, second, questioning the limited scope of transitional justice that usually involves post-conflict contexts and state-centric discourses. There is a continuum of transitional justice in both conflict and post-conflict contexts. In addition, the mundane acts of care, social repair, and rebuilding selves, in the midst of violence and in the absence of institutional mechanisms, are also empowering forms of transitions, and they may further open more pathways to justice.

References

Agarwal, A. (2022). *Contesting Masculinities and Women's Agency in Kashmir*. London: Rowman and Littlefield.

Ahäll, L. (2012). The Writing of Heroines: Motherhood and Female Agency in Political Violence. *Security Dialogue* 43(4): 287–303.

Akbar, M. J. (2002). *Behind the Vale*. New Delhi: Roli Books.

Allsopp, A. (2015). *The Refugee Crisis: Demilitarising Masculinities*. Accessed at: https://www.opendemocracy.net/en/5050/refugee-crisis-demilitarising-masculinities/. Accessed on: 14 April 2022.

Ashiq, P. (2019). Rising Kashmir Editor Shujaat Bukhari Murder Probe Reveals Grave Security Lapses. *The Hindu*. Available at: https://www.thehindu.com/news/national/other-states/rising-kashmir-editor-shujaat-bukhari-killed-in-second-attempt-within-24-hours/article61996391.ece. Accessed on: 26 March 2022.

Baines, E. and L. Rosenoff-Gauvin (2014). Motherhood and Social Repair after War and Displacement in Northern Uganda. *Journal of Refugee Studies* 27(2): 282–300.

Bjarnegård, E. and R. Murray (2018). Critical Perspectives on Men and Masculinities in Politics: Introduction. *Politics & Gender* 14(2): 264–265.

Carpenter, R. (2006). Recognizing Gender-Based Violence Against Civilian Men and Boys in Conflict Situations. *Security Dialogue* 37(1): 83–103.

Cronin-Furman, K. and M. Lake (2018). Ethics Abroad: Fieldwork in Fragile and Violent Contexts. *PS: Political Science & Politics* 51(3): 607–614.

Das, V. Arthur Kleinman, M. Lock, M. Ramphele and P. Reynolds (2001). *Remaking a World: Violence, Social Suffering, and Recovery*. Berkeley, CA: University of California Press.

Dasgupta, C. (2002). *War and Diplomacy in Kashmir: 1947–48*. Delhi: Sage.

Dolan, C. (2002). Collapsing Masculinities and Weak States – A Case Study of Northern Uganda. In: F. Cleaver (ed.): *Masculinities Matter!: Men, Gender, and Development*. New York: Zed Books: 57–84.

Duncanson, C. (2009). Forces for Good? Narratives of Military Masculinity in Peacekeeping Operations. *International Feminist Journal of Politics* 11(1): 63–80.

Elliott, K. (2016). Caring Masculinities: Theorizing an Emerging Concept. *Men and Masculinities* 19(3): 240–259.

Habibullah, W. (2008). *My Kashmir: Conflict and the Prospects for Enduring Peace*. Washington, DC: United States Institute for Peace Press.

Hanlon, N. (2012). *Masculinities, Care and Equality: Identity and Nurture in Men's Lives*. Basingstoke, UK: Palgrave Macmilan.

Hearn, J. (2001). Men and Gender Equality: Resistance, Responsibilities and Reaching Out. *Keynote at the Conference Men and Gender Equality*, Örebro, Sweden, 15–16 March.

Henry, M., P. Higate and G. Sanghera (2009). Positionality and Power: The Politics of Peacekeeping Research. *International Peacekeeping* 16(4): 467–482.

Hollander, T. (2014). Men, Masculinities and the Demise of a State: Examining Masculinities in the Context of Economic, Political and Social Crisis in a Small Town in the Democratic Republic of the Congo. *Men and Masculinities* 17(4): 417–439.

hooks, b. (2004). *The Will to Change: Men, Masculinity and Love*. New York: Atria Books.

Kent, L. (2016). Sounds of Silence: Everyday Strategies of Social Repair in Timor-Leste. *Australian Feminist Law Journal* 42(1): 31–50.

Krause, J. (2019). Gender Dimensions of (Non) Violence in Communal Conflict: The Case of Jos, Nigeria. *Comparative Political Studies* 52(10): 1466–1499.

Kreft, A. K. and P. Schulz (2022). Political Agency, Victimhood and Gender in Contexts of Armed Conflict: Moving Beyond Dichotomies. *International Studies Quarterly* 66(2): sqac022.

Krystalli, R. (2020). Women, Peace, and Victimhood. *IPI Global Observatory*. Available at: https://theglobalobservatory.org/2020/10/women-peace-and-victimhood/. Accessed on: 18 January 2021.

Krystalli, R. and P. Schulz (2022). Taking Love and Care Seriously: An Emergent Research Agenda for Remaking Worlds in the Wake of Violence. *International Studies Review* 24(1): 1–25.

Kunz, R., W. Udasmoro and H. Myrttinen (2018). Preachers, Pirates and Peacebuilding: Examining Non Violent Hegemonic Masculinities in Aceh. *Asian Journal of Women's Studies* 24(3): 299–320.

Mwambari, D. (2019). Local Positionality in the Production of Knowledge in Northern Uganda. *International Journal of Qualitative Methods* 18: 1–12.

New York Times (2008). *Land Transfer to Hindu Site Inflames Kashmir's Muslims*. Available at: https://www.nytimes.com/2008/06/28/world/asia/28kashmir.html. Accessed on: 25 November 2021.

Parashar, S. (2011). Gender, Jihad and Jingoism: Women as Perpetrators, Planners and Patrons of Militancy in Kashmir. *Studies in Conflict and Terrorism* 34(4): 295–317.

Parashar, S. and B. D'Costa (2017). Feminist Foreign Policy: The South Asia Conundrum. *Disrupted* 1: 27–30.

Porter, A (2013). What Is Constructed Can Be Transformed: Masculinities in Post-Conflict Societies in Africa. *International Peacekeeping* 20(4): 486–506.

Puri, B. (1993). *Kashmir: Towards Insurgency*. New Delhi: Orient Longman.

Sjoberg, L. and C. Gentry (2007). *Mothers, Monsters, Whores: Women's Violence in Global Politics*. London and New York: Zed Books.

Touquet, H. and P. Schulz (2021). Navigating Vulnerabilities and Masculinities: How Gendered Contexts Shape the Agency of Male Sexual Violence Survivors. *Security Dialogue* 52(3): 213–230.

Whitehead, A. (2007). *A Mission in Kashmir*. New Delhi: Penguin.

Wood, E. (2006). The Ethical Challenges of Field Research in Conflict Zones. *Qualitative Sociology* 29: 373–386.

Xaba, T. (2010). Masculinity and Its Malcontents: The Confrontation Between 'Struggle Masculinity' and 'Post-Struggle Masculinity' (1990–1997). In: Morell, R. (ed.): *Changing Men in Southern Africa*. London: Zed Books.

Chapter 16

Queering Post-War Transitions

Exploring Queer Potentials of the "Butterfly for Democracy" Movement in Sri Lanka

Thiyagaraja Waradas

Introduction

At around 8:00 p.m. on 26 October 2018, I was waiting at a train station in a suburb of the Sri Lankan capital, Colombo, expecting a train, when I was struck by the sudden noise of firecrackers from all directions. My first thought was that this was an auspicious time for a wedding ceremony that must have been happening nearby. Soon, however, I realized that this was something rather unusual, as the firecrackers went on for a while. In the meantime, the television screen in the train station was turned on, as breaking news revealed that President Sirisena has unconstitutionally removed the prime minister of the Unity Government and appointed Mahinda Rajapaksha, the wartime president who was defeated by Sirisena during the 2014 elections. This political act in the democratic history of Sri Lanka marked what some observers referred to as a *constitutional coup*, which lasted 52 days, until the 16th of December, when the prime minister of the Unity Government was reinstated after the Supreme Court ruling against President Sirisena's decision. During these 51 days, Sri Lanka has witnessed an unprecedented level of public protest both in the streets and in public offices, demanding the president to respect the Constitution and restore democracy in the country. Civil society activists and different pressure groups took the protests to the streets and courts, including Sinhalese queer community groups in Colombo – thereby marking a historical turn in the politics of gender and sexual justice rights in Sri Lanka.

As has been well established in the literature, democratization processes are key ingredients, intended outcomes, and immediate goals of transitional justice processes (Leebaw 2008). And by no means are post-war democratization and transitional justice processes meant to be queer-blind. Yet what role queer activism and emancipation can play in these democratization processes, and how these processes affect and involve sexual and gender minorities, has not yet been explored – mirroring the persistent lack of queer curiosities and understandings in the field of transitional justice more broadly (Bueno-Hansen 2018; Fobear and Baines 2020; Schulz 2020). As

DOI: 10.4324/9781003519522-20

Katherine Fobear notes elsewhere in this volume, research and engagement with sexual and gender minorities in the field of transitional justice remain slow and limited. This is largely due to the adherence of TJ processes to narrow constructions of heterosexualized normative male–female gender binaries (Bueno-Hansen 2018). What is more, even if there is engagement with queer communities, experiences, and concerns and with the lived realities of people with diverse sexual orientations, gender identities and expressions, and sex characteristics (SOGIESC) in post-war transitional justice and reconciliation processes (see Fobear, this volume), this is often confined to a victimization logic (also see Hamber et al., this volume), whereby SOGIESC communities are considered as mere victims of violence that need to be redressed during transitional justice processes (see Akı, this volume). Such approaches typically take on forms of technocratic interventions, focused on institutionalized processes or mechanisms (see Bueno-Hansen, this volume). Taking this limitation seriously, a few scholars who began investigating the agency of SOGIESC communities during transitional justice processes have also failed to move beyond macro-institutional and policy interventions in the form of top-down approaches to TJ processes. Against this background, some, such as Katharina Hoffmann and Thokozani Mbwana in this volume, have stressed the potential of moving from the macro- to the micro-level in order to achieve an inclusive framework for TJ (also see Schulz 2020).

In light of this, here I will pick up Fobear's question of "what it would mean to better incorporate and engage with queer bodies and theory in transitional justice" (Fobear, this volume) and apply this specifically to the post–civil war transitional justice context of Sri Lanka. In this chapter, I will move beyond normative, technocratic, and institutionalized processes rooted in top-down vs. bottom-up debates. By focusing specifically on the Sri Lankan Butterflies for Democracy (B4D) movement as an exemplary case of micro-level queer engagements during transitional period, the chapter unpacks the intersections between queer emancipation and democratization in a post-war and transitional context and on the grassroots level. I will reflectively explore the nature and dynamics of the responses of queer activists in the context of the ongoing post-war transition period in Sri Lanka. Centered on queer agency in transitions from conflict outside official processes of transitional justice efforts, this research transcends gender dichotomy and binaries of top-down vs. bottom-up approaches.

I will demonstrate how interventions of SOGIESC communities during the constitutional coup, through the B4D movement, have enabled queer people in Sri Lanka to respond to transitional contexts with their own experiences and somehow enact a sense of justice informed by their own experiences of reclaiming their collective identities. By devising an intersectional political space called *Butterflies for Democracy* that connects sexual and gender justice and democratic rights, SOGIESC communities produced two key outcomes that contributed to the process of queering the post-war transitions in Sri Lanka. First, it has foregrounded the potential of queer agency to effectively reclaim and redefine the term "butterfly" in this particular context and thereby constitute their own notion of justice against state-sponsored queerphobic violence occurring in transitional context. The B4D movement specifically emerged in response to the so-called "butterfly speech" by President Sirisena, a state-sponsored queerphobic hate speech, as described in greater detail in what follows. *Butterfly* is a derogatory slur for *queer*, symbolizing queerphobia, but thanks to advocacy by the B4D movement, the term has now been turned into a symbol of unity, courage, and solidarity. As such, SOGIESC communities who feared self-censorship at the beginning of the constitutional coup have become an energized, proactive force for queering the post-war transition toward democracy in the country. An initially invisibilized group of oppressed communities has become visible through its proactive political role during the struggles for democracy. This reclaiming process represented a sense of justice for queer communities in Sri Lanka who navigate sponsored queerphobia emanating from the forces that define the terms of TJ landscape of the country. Reclaiming collective identity in TJ context is in line with the idea of justice through being in a group (Schulz 2019), where they enact a sense of justice informed by the praxis of the queer movement.

Second, queer organizing in Sri Lanka has unearthed a *new* way of politics that offers a critique of and alternative to conventional TJ and reconciliation mechanisms and processes that are heavily focused on formal technocratic TJ and reconciliation mechanisms (Sharp 2013). This focus has presented the hybridity of engagements on many levels, the messiness of contexts, and the complexities of entire TJ processes. It also demonstrates the need to move beyond the liberal democratic normative framework to conceptualize the potential of queer curiosities and praxis in the context of TJ processes in heavily ethnically polarized contexts. As such, this attention presents queering TJ as not only about the inclusion of SOGIESC grievances into the transitional justice processes but, rather, also as redefining the TJ and reconciliation landscape from the perspectives of queer subjectivities that transcend dualities and polarized identities (also see Fobear, this volume). The research underpinning this chapter thus shows that queer curiosities and praxis may offer fresh avenues of imagination and conceptions of post-war transitions that are not necessarily confined to the parameters of the liberal democratic paradigm. In the next section, I will first contextualize Sri Lanka's civil war and transitional justice processes. Then, I will analyze the events leading to the B4D movement, which will be followed by an assessment of the queer potential of B4D in Sri Lanka's democratic transition process.

Sri Lanka's Civil War, Transitional Justice Processes, and SOGIESC Communities

Sri Lanka's three-decade-long civil war between the Liberation Tigers of Tamil Eelam (LTTE), also known as Tamil Tigers, fighting for a separate Tamil homeland, and the government of Sri Lanka (GoSL) ended in 2009 with the military defeat of the LTTE by government forces led by President Mahinda Rajapaksha.

The first five years since the end of the war were marked by a declining democratic nature of the state and an unprecedented level of centralization of power by President Mahinda Rajapaksha, with severe violations of human rights laws. The level of corruption and nepotism within the family and relatives of the president also constituted a major concern. The government of Sri Lanka and the LTTE were accused of war crimes and human rights violations by the international community and UN Human Rights Council in 2014 (UNHCR 2014). In terms of reconciliation, apart from a few concessions, such as the government-appointed Lessons Learnt and Reconciliation Commission (LLRC), very little progress was made (Walton and Thiyagaraja 2020). To that effect, achieving sustainable peace constituted a challenge due to the reinforced ethnic divisions and a lack of credible efforts in addressing the root causes of the conflict (Höglund et al. 2016). Sri Lanka has eventually become a prime example of *Victors Peace*, contributing to theorizing of illiberal peacebuilding (Smith et al. 2020; Walton and Thiyagaraja 2020).

The electoral victory of President Sirisena in 2015 came at a time when the country was being led toward an autocratic-turn regime under his predecessor. One might therefore consider that the electoral victory of President Sirisena was a clear mandate from the public, not only to reverse the autocratic turn of rule, but also to take the country forward in an inclusive path informed by ideas and principles of post-war peacebuilding. Although Sri Lanka is known as one of the oldest and uninterrupted majoritarian democracies in Asia, the country's democratic governance has been affected by the tensions caused by the legacies of war – tensions between its political elites and parties, ongoing militarization, and issues related to wartime accountability and justice. As democracy is a key intended outcome of the transitional justice process (Leebaw 2008), the new government has to implement reforms that would restore the democratic nature of the governance and facilitate the transitional justice and reconciliation process.

The government took a few key steps to ensure to stop an autocratic turn. The most immediate outcome of the regime change was to bring a sense of relief to the masses, whose dissenting voices have been oppressed by the wartime Rajapaksha regime. The government passed the 19th amendment to the Constitution to restore the democratic nature of the government by reimposing the two-term limit to the president, removing the executive president's power to dissolve the parliament and certain immunities of it. It has also granted more powers to the prime minister and the cabinet and empowered independent commissions on police, judiciary, and human rights (Keenan 2015). The government also relaxed the censorship and suppression of media and reduced the military presence in civilian affairs, including in the northern and eastern parts of the country. In a conciliation step to the long-standing call from the international community for reconciliation and accountability, the government, in September 2015, co-sponsored the UN Human Rights Council Resolution, culminating in the so-called "Geneva Process." This process called for four transitional justice mechanisms: a truth commission, an office for reparations, an office for missing persons (OMP), and an independent special court for war crimes, with the participation of foreign judges. In addition, the government also agreed to conduct public consultations with victims and all stakeholders and to a political settlement to the conflict through constitutional reforms. Out of these measures, the *Unity Government* was only able to implement the office for missing persons, a public consultation on reconciliation mechanisms, and some constitutional reforms. The government also enacted the Right to Information Act (RTI) and subsequently established the RTI Commission. These efforts returned the hope for democratic governance in the central organs of the state.

Sri Lanka's post-war transition has also been largely defined by heterosexualized terms and confined to the groups whose ethnic identities were the major contestation of the conflict – Tamil and Sinhalese. This exclusive focus is despite the fact that Sri Lanka inherits one of the earliest SOGIESC rights movements in the South Asian region. Starting in 1995 with the first SOGIESC organization, called Companions on a Journey (COJ), Sri Lanka's SOGIESC communities have been fighting to eliminate historical oppression imposed on them since the introduction of anti-sodomy laws into Sri Lanka's penal code by the British colonial rule, which made homosexuality a crime. This has been further extended in 1995 to include sex between women, which was not a crime earlier. Sri Lanka remains one of the 63 countries in the world that continue to criminalize homosexuality and actively prosecute them. Today, Sri Lanka's SOGIESC movement consists of more than ten SOGIESC organizations, including entities located in the former war-torn areas of Jaffna and Batticaloa and economically marginalized NuwarEliya – the central highlands, navigating a queer landscape consisting of homo-ethnonationalists, queer left, and homo-liberals (Thiyagaraja 2022).

Unlike Nepal – a country that decriminalized homosexuality and has accommodated SOGIESC rights within its transition process produced through a negotiated settlement – Sri Lanka's transition process has been a challenging political landscape for queer curiosities and inclusion of SOGIESC rights. Sri Lanka's SOGIESC communities, in part, also emerged during the conflict and lived through it. However, SOGIESC persons' experiences and their victimization during this period have not been documented. There are hardly any testimonials of SOGIESC experiences represented to the LLRC commission. The plight of SOGIESC persons in the war-affected areas remains unexplored. The movement started during the intense war in 1995, faced the short-lived Norwegian-facilitated peace process during 2001–2006 with steady but slow growth and expansion, which was later subject to degeneration under the first five years' period after the war (2009–2014). Both post-war governments not just refused to show signs of any serious accommodation of the grievances of the SOGIESC communities but also proactively promoted the hate campaign against queer subjectivities and suppressed the SOGIESC NGOs. SOGIESC NGOs were not only considered as traitors but also actively othered and jettisoned from the national imaginary of citizenhood. Again in 2017, President Sirisena refused to include decriminalization as an action point of the National Plan of Action of Human Rights 2017–2022 and defended his decision publicly by claiming that homosexuality shall not be legalized as it is "against" the moral ethics and culture of the country.

In this context, the constitutional coup in October 2018 shocked the SOGIESC groups and reminded them of the fears and oppression faced under Rajapaksha's post-war period. Making those fears worse, President Sirisena employed state-sponsored queerphobic hate speech against SOGIESC communities for the first time directly to justify his unconstitutional move, claiming the ousted prime minister and his decision-making circles are full of queer subjectivities that need to be jettisoned from the power to save the country. He called them *butterflies* at a public rally, invoking a queerphobic slur used to demonize SOGIESC identities. This so-called *butterfly speech* marked a key juncture where a unique political process comprising the queer agency eventually led to a political outcome, what I would name as queering transitional justice in Sri Lanka. What follows is a careful presentation of this political juncture, its dynamics, and its outcomes.

Before I step into examining the role of SOGIESC agency during the transition process with the emergence of Butterfly momentum, a note on the method and my positionalities is warranted. As a gay activist from the ethnic minority Tamil community, I witnessed and narrated my experiences during the coup and its consequences. My work with the SOGIESC communities since 2015 has been nationally visible, which positions me as an insider on the one hand. However, on the other hand, I am also positioned as an outsider, as I am also based in the UK for studies and research. Most of my articulations here are informed by my experiences as part of the movement and as one of the key architects of the B4D movement. This may, on one hand, offer an in-depth subjective exposition of the events that occurred during this time. At the same time, it also warrants readers to understand the limitations I had as being part of this movement. The inability to distance myself from the volatile events and the object of the study can also serve as a limitation of the analysis. This research emerged as part of my PhD fieldwork in Sri Lanka, where I was affiliated with an organization co-founded by me called Community Welfare and Development Fund. Interviews, archival research, participants observations, and reflective journals are key data collection methods that have been employed to gather data for the study. The research has benefited from several individuals and fellow activists whom I am unable to disclose here due to sensitivities of the identities.

Initial Responses to the Constitutional Coup

This failed constitutional coup of 51 days that started with the dismissal of Prime Minister Ranil Wickremasinghe by President Sirisena sparked mixed reactions within Sri Lanka. Rajapaksha supporters were reassured and celebrated his unconstitutional return. His supporters were lighting firecrackers and celebrating the change with much less regard to the undemocratic and unconstitutional nature of the appointment. Rajapaksha allies and trade unions have already started obstructing the ministers and members of the ousted prime minister's government in fulfilling their duties a day after President Sirisena declared that the cabinet is dissolved and after appointing the new prime minister (Reuters 2018). On the other hand, the United National Front (UNF) alliance, led by ousted prime minister Ranil Wickremasinghe, started protesting the unconstitutional move by the president, as Wickremasinghe refused to step down and continued to be the legitimate prime minister of the country. Soon, protests sparked in the capital city of Colombo, and the battle was taken also in the courtrooms of the highest judiciary of the country, while President Sirisena and the new prime minister, Mahinda Rajapaksha, were trying to consolidate power both within and outside the parliament. Opposition political parties such as JVP and Tamil National Alliance (TNA) have condemned the move and requested to uphold the democracy and Constitution of the country.

Civil society groups and human rights defenders, including SOGIESC activists, were undecided and shocked to witness the abrupt move by the president. Liberal circles of the SOGIESC activists and groups were worried that the broken relationship between the two leaders of the unity government was apparent for some time. Civil society groups who had witnessed the oppression under the wartime Rajapaksha regime were concerned about their freedom to work and the protection of human rights. Even a proposal made by me to have a political stocktaking among SOGIESC activists was seen as too contentious. Some felt this coup could lead to the resurgence of an era of sabotage and oppression. As such, many did not want to resort to proactive meetings and gatherings.

The fear was also evident in conducting regular activities by SOGIESC groups. One of the groups I co-founded was tasked to create a queer social space in the country's second-largest city of Kandy, a sacred city hosting the holy temple of Buddhists and known for its religious and conservative political landscape. Members of the organizing team were extra-vigilant, and the event was discreetly organized with the support of a public university in Kandy. A movie screening was held and attended by a good crowd with much caution. This was the first event held outside of Colombo during the coup, and with much reluctance. Another manifestation of fear is the renewal of discussions among SOGIESC groups on reducing to be visible in conducting their activities, which is an indication of caution.

However, this is not the case with other civil society groups working on human rights issues – such as women's rights groups, human rights defenders, liberal NGOs, or artists – to discuss the changing political situation and to explore ways of navigating the situation. These dynamics are thereby rather different from the position adopted by many within the circles of SOGIESC activism. As a way of avoiding visibility, certain SOGIESC activists joined the other NGOs and civil society initiatives to raise their voice for democracy without necessarily invoking SOGIESC identities. One such example was a statement issued by a group of Sri Lankan students studying abroad titled "A Coup in Asia's Oldest Democracy" (Daily FT 2018). This statement was also endorsed by SOGIESC students, including myself. Similarly, certain queer artists joined the initiatives and dialogues in responding to the crisis.

Butterfly Speech: State-Sponsored Political Queerphobia

On 5 November 2018, at a mass political rally in Colombo organized to garner public support for his move and to the new prime minister, President Sirisena made a derogatory statement accusing sacked prime minister Ranil Wickremasinghe to live as a "*butterfly*" (Ada Derana 2018). As reported by a journalist, Sirisena accused him by saying that "he forgot to solve peoples' problems and entered into a butterfly life." He further accused that all the decisions of the government were made by the circle of butterflies and the prime minister. His accusations were targeted at Ranil Wickremasinghe and his inner circle of decision-makers in the government.

Butterfly – *samanalaya* – stands as a homophobic slur against non-heterosexual conduct in the Sinhalese language, spoken by the majority of Sri Lankans, which denotes a carefree, socially non-conforming lifestyle of non-heterosexual men. It is also used as a derogatory term for effeminate men or queer men in most parts of the country. The term is considered to be a hate expression toward men who are considered not "manly" or "masculine" enough. It is a term widely known to demonize queer individuals by a society embedded in heteropatriarchal values. Being queer in the context of Sri Lanka, where sodomy is a crime and socially stigmatized, is a legitimate ground for discrimination. Sri Lanka criminalizes same-sex conduct through the laws of Sections 365 and 365(a) housed in the country's penal code introduced by British colonizers. Since then, society continues to discriminate and stigmatize SOGIESC persons. Queer is considered as abnormal, weak, less human, and unpreferred citizenry for a society led by nationhood shaped by masculine, strong, and fatherhood figures. Hence, it is much easier to reinforce the idea that being queer translates to being unfit to rule the expectations of heterosexual society.

Sirisena's use of the term and accusing Wickremasinghe and his rule, in which all the decisions were made by his *butterfly gang*, is a clear attempt to delegitimize his rule by invoking homophobia and thereby justifying the unconstitutional removal. The president's political utilization of derogatory terms to delegitimize forces that do not conform with heteropatriarchal values can thus be identified as state-sponsored queerphobia. Queerphobia is instrumentalized by the state to reinforce the heteropatriarchal nature of the state and nationhood by naming queerness as a condition to be excluded from access to the state (Rao 2020). Sirisena's act of hate speech constitutes a clear endorsement that not being heterosexual serves as a disqualification to hold power to rule the country. This has effectively heterosexualized the state by proclaiming heterosexual citizens as the only legitimate actors to access (or, for that matter, to rule) the state. Further, queer has been labeled as the cause of economic and political instability in the country. Queerness is blamed for the failures of governance and security of the state. Therefore, these dynamics and assumptions can be seen as creating a binary logic, whereby *queer* is placed as disloyalty while *heterosexuality* is a synonym of loyalty to the nation (Wanniarachchi 2019). It also draws a parallel with ongoing Islamophobia and xenophobia that is actively propagated by the ethnonationalist lobby in the country. Hence, the state and nation should be defended from the queer constituency, and its "intrusion" into heterosexualized spheres has become the political intention of his speech. Therefore, one could argue that Sirisena's butterfly speech is not merely directed against one person but rather against the entire SOGIESC community and is politically instrumentalized to appeal to the queerphobic lobby emboldened by ethnonationalist ideas deployed for electoral gains.

Immediate responses to the speech came from the audience gathered at the rally. The crowd chuckled, and the fellow political leaders on the stage laughed. Soon, Sirisena's explanation is followed by a roaring approval from the crowd. A crowd not only consisting of heterosexuals but also *butterflies* rumbled President Sirisena's statement. This conduct of "fitting in" with the trend as a survival mechanism for those queer individuals was also noticeable. The heterosexualized audience – including both heterosexuals and butterflies trying to fit in – became actively engaged with the state-sponsored queerphobic act (Jayasinghe 2018). Sirisena's speech popularized queerphobia as an acceptable political logic of exclusion in just a few minutes which was not publicly articulated before. Sirisena's butterfly speech thus had a wider reach compared to those at present. Every corner of the Sinhalese community became aware of the speech, and within minutes, evoking the language of *butterflies* has become a generalized logic of delegitimizing queerness. Individuals from rural areas also started to use butterfly slurs to demonize and identify dissenting voices of the ethnonationalist sentiments.

In responding to Sirisena's queerphobic speech, the late foreign minister of the Wickremasinghe government, Mangala Samaraweera, who is also open about his sexual identity of being a gay man, responded immediately on Twitter, stating, "I would rather be a butterfly than a leech, Mr. President"

(Ameen 2018). The initial public criticism of the butterfly speech was mainly recorded on Twitter by a minuscule community of English-speaking urban-based individuals. Samaraweera's mild opposition did not radically question the effort of state-sponsored queerphobia but instead continues to put queer and corruption on the same spectrum. It did place queer in a relatively better position, rather than advancing radical emancipation. Hence, this response statement did not produce the much-needed opening to respond to the state-sponsored queerphobia as evoked in the initial butterfly speech (Thiyagaraja 2017).

Butterflies Waking Up

The butterfly speech presented a challenge to the defensive and self-censored approach of SOGIESC groups adopted to respond to the constitutional coup. Unlike the position-invisibility and self-censorship as adopted by the SOGIESC groups in the first few days of the constitutional coup (see earlier text), the speech has brought the queer community and activism into the center of political debates, making it a visible target of state-sponsored hate speech. The first organized response came from a group of activists led by me and a Sri Lankan transgender woman residing abroad to initiate a public online petition against the butterfly speech. After the initial decision to refrain from proactive measures to the coup, the like-minded SOGIESC group which I was part of was convinced that there is nothing more to lose and that silence would risk the political credibility of the movement. The response from the "openly" queer politician mentioned earlier also encouraged the like-minded group to initiate an online petition. The petition was signed by more than 200 persons online, with their names visible, and disseminated through news sites for visibility (Sri Lanka Brief 2018). The statement condemned the queerphobia used by the head of state and called for the president to be held accountable for the consequences of his act:

> We condemn his use of homophobia to amuse his political gallery. By trivializing homophobia in this fashion, President Sirisena should be held responsible for any homophobic incidents that Sri Lankan citizens may experience in the coming days.
>
> (Sri Lanka Brief 2018)

It carried a strong word of protest against the president's actions, which asked further actions against any possible repercussions of the speech. This petition has marked one of the strongest protests from the SOGIESC communities in the recent period.

The petition was followed by a media briefing and a group of SOGIESC persons joining a protest organized by civil society groups in Colombo. The media briefing, held on 6 November 2018, was attended by four SOGIESC activists, including myself. The briefing was aimed at showing our support for democracy and protesting the president's hate speech. It was a success, with very few criticisms and hate responses. It has strengthened the demand articulated in the collective public petition and demanded an apology from the president (*Daily Mirror* 2018b): "Sirisena should apologize to the LGBTQI+ community over his remark made at Government's rally on Monday in Colombo" (*Daily Mirror* 2018b). This brave tone of the press conference highlighted that those worst affected by the hate speech would be the rural SOGIESC communities across the country. "It is the minority LGBTIQ+ community in rural areas who will have to undergo the repercussions of this statement" (*Daily Mirror* 2018b). This important element of highlighting the fate of poorer segments of the SOGIESC communities is part of the media tactic to counter the hate speech of the government which had the support of SOGIESC persons from rural areas. The demands were also not related to decriminalizing homosexuality – a demand considered as Western by the nationalist lobby – but rather holding the president accountable for hate speech, which may not necessarily invoke the Western label that is used to delegitimize SOGIESC demands.

At the end of the press conference, SOGIESC groups have also organized themselves and joined an ongoing continuous evening protest organized by a group of civil society activists demanding to restore the democracy of the government in a place near to the prime minister's official residence in Colombo every day since the coup from 6:00 p.m. The SOGIESC groups carried slogans saying, "Butterflies vote too," or "Butterfly Power" (Duffy 2018). The protest was acknowledged in the international media and did not result in any major backlash. Individuals working in SOGIESC NGOs and "independent" SOGIESC activists also joined the evening protest to the butterfly speech.

In addition to these collective initiatives, two queer individuals have written strongly but appealing letters addressing the president. A gay (Gamage 2018) and a lesbian person (Wijesinghe 2018) wrote letters highlighting their suffering due to the prevalent stigma and criminalization of homosexuality in Sri Lanka: "I'm young. Yes. But I've gone through the bullying. The teasing. The endless nights crying and cutting myself because I hated myself, because of statements and ridicule that the society in general directed at me" (Gamage 2018). Similarly, Aloka Wijesinghe (2018), in her letter, also highlighted the continuous oppression against queer women: "Our queer lives were always hanging on a ceiling. Some queer Sri Lankan citizens have been beaten to death or banned from their native towns and villages." The letters were well received and created an appealing conversation on social media which offered crucial support for the online petition.

These responses present a clear change from the sentiments and positions adopted by the SOGIESC groups during the early weeks of the coup, which was to maintain self-censorship and to keep a low profile. Sirisena's hate speech provided a reality check for the defensive approach of the SOGIESC communities adopted for the constitutional coup. It has recentered sexual and gender justice politics, putting sexual and gender identities as the center of contestations. The realization that being restrained and withdrawn was no longer a viable option became evident, as indicatively reflected in this statement by a lesbian activist:

> When I browsed through a couple of articles, I just said to myself, "Wait, I'm just an 18 years old and I never had a thing for politics unless it affected my right to live."
>
> (Wijesinghe 2018)

This sentiment of distancing from politics becomes redundant as it created a situation and strategic invisibility is no longer politically prudent. Hence, many SOGIESC groups have decided to respond to the "new" circumstances in more active ways, which can be termed as an act of waking up.

Mainstreaming of Butterflies for Democracy

The responses of butterflies took a different shape when a proactive collective political mobilization was launched by the SOGIESC communities. On 7 December 2018, SOGIESC groups staged a protest in Colombo at the Lipton Circus roundabout under the theme of "Butterflies for Democracy," demanding democracy and dignity. A press statement released to the media before the protest stated as follows:

> "Butterflies for Democracy" will stand in solidarity along with allies, family, and friends of the LGBTQIA community to protest the blatant disregard for democracy currently prevailing in the country.
>
> (135 Campaign 2018)

This is a clear demand that aligns with the politically pressing issue at that time: democracy. The statement further stated that:

> We demand that democracy prevails and insist that democracy is nothing without equality, respect, and dignity for all citizens of this country. We stand in solidarity with the many groups who have been speaking out for the same at this moment in time, and warmly invite them to join us.
>
> (135 Campaign 2018)

The latter part of the statement demanding democracy articulates the connection between democracy and equality, respect and dignity, with key demands that SOGIESC communities have been fighting for a long time. It perfectly blends the sexual and gender justice demands along with democracy to widen the meaning of democracy as a political ideology where many forces can come under one umbrella. Protestors carried slogans saying, "Butterflies are voters too," "We stand for equality and Democracy" (Aththa Withthi 2018), and the protestor's key slogans were "defend democracy," as well as demand for complete democracy and a better political culture. Compared to the previous protest joined by the SOGIESC NGOs and groups on 7 November 2018, this protest had clear slogans and demands centered on democracy, rather than just a resistance to hate speech. As listed in the following table, the focus of the protest was explicitly on democracy demanded by SOGIESC communities.

However, an inclusive and collective equality agenda for sexual and gender justice was manifested by the leadership of SOGIESC communities proactively in organizing the protest and taking ownership of the initiative as compared to the previous one in November 2018. The inspiration to organize an inclusive and collective protest of all SOGIESC communities came from the women's march, organized by a group of women activists who demanded democracy during the coup. A group of SOGIESC leaders from different segments of the SOGIESC communities, including the author, has organized this protest and named it the *Butterflies for Democracy* protest. The rest of the civil society groups had no hand in organizing this, but the majority of them supported the initiative by joining the protest. This has become the landmark protest where SOGIESC communities have come forward for an issue that affects each citizen of the country. The protest also communicated to the public that the SOGIESC community – a community often criticized for not voicing common issues – too, stand together with the general public in demanding democracy. This is a clear difference from the protest held in November, where the SOGIESC community engaged in a defensive approach of joining an ongoing protest with limited ownership. Hence, it can be argued that the December protest constitutes a successful mainstreaming of the *Butterflies for Democracy* agenda. An invisible group of oppressed communities has become visible through its proactive political role during the struggles for democracy.

Devising an Intersectional Agenda

The series of interventions by SOGIESC communities characterizes the ability of queer agency in formulating an intersectional agenda. It is an agenda where gender and sexual identities have intersected with the collective need of other groups from different classes, social statuses, political affiliations, different ethnic and religious identities – to promote democracy and demand justice. To do so, SOGIESC groups radically articulated the political contexts in which the hate speech was conducted and the ideas that would inform the response to the speech. As described earlier, state-sponsored queerphobia has been employed as a technique of legitimizing undemocratic political actions of

Table 16.1 Compositions of two protests

Themes	*7 November 2018* *Liberty Roundabout Protest*	*7 December 2018* *Lipton Circus Protest*
Major cause	Protest against president's hate speech calling SOGIESC communities as "butterflies."	Protest for demanding democracy and better political culture while marking the agency of SOGIESC groups.
Participants	Majority of SOGIESC organizations and groups and civil society groups.	Almost all the SOGIESC organizations and groups, civil society groups, and left groups–aligned political parties, artists, professionals, and women's rights groups.
Organizers	SOGIESC community got together and joined the ongoing protest organized by the civil society groups at the Liberty Circus in Colombo.	SOGEISC communities and individuals got together and organized the entire protest and took the lead. The protest was held at Lipton Circus as a separate SOGIESC protest under the theme Butterflies for Democracy.

Source: Created by the author using data collected during a field visit in Sri Lanka.

the ethnonationalist regime that has emboldened the queerphobic lobby in the country. This has revitalized anti-SOGIESC voices and effectively imposed a sense of fear and self-censorship within SOGIESC groups. Hence, any attempt to respond to the speech with existing ideas and campaigns was not considered prudent. This has forced SOGIES groups to devise a different strategy.

In strategizing the focus of the responses, decriminalization as a strategic demand was not utilized, but instead, democracy and non-discrimination were foregrounded as mechanisms of reclaiming the term *butterflies*. The legal approach to decriminalize non-conforming sexualities has been labeled as Western and anti-cultural to the local values and traditions by the queerphobic ethnonationalist lobby. Decriminalization has become a contentious demand to bring many constituencies together, particularly homo-ethnonationalists who also felt threatened by the "butterfly speech" but who were unable to raise their protest. Therefore, "less contentious" but much-needed positions and demands of democracy and non-discrimination were used to frame the reclaiming process. The petition (Sri Lanka Brief 2018), a media briefing (135 Campaign 2018), the November protest (Duffy 2018), and the collective protest in December 2018 (Aththa Withthi 2018) all carried slogans demanding democracy. These slogans and demands highlighted the importance of equality, demanded to hold the president accountable for hate speech, reminded that SOGIESC persons, too, are citizens and have the right to political participation, and demanded to convene the parliament as well as equal respect to SOGIESC communities. All this was also clear from the interviews given by the activists to the media during the December protest, which stated, "[W]e all have a common problem [manifest threat to the democracy] in the country today and we are here for that" (Aththa Withthi 2018).

Such an intersectional approach founded on non-discrimination and democracy played an instrumental role in multiple ways in facilitating the collective agency of the queer community to reclaim their collective identity. First, it functioned as a tactic shield from queerphobic criticisms leveled against the decriminalization approach. By using non-discrimination as the ideological platform to stand for democracy and equality, the movement's approach mitigated the space for usual anti-Western, anti-cultural, foreign-funded, dollar-driven NGO conspiracies, foreign projects criticisms of homophobic ethnonationalist lobbies. Despite a few media responses critiquing the movement (Gossiplanka 2018), most of the media coverage was either sympathetic or curious about these actions. The online petition was well-received on social media, with more than 200 signatures and publicity across websites and other human rights NGOs (Groundviews 2018). The two articles written by the young gay man and a lesbian woman were also widely shared and were able to cultivate a sympathetic and localized discourse, by openly sharing the suffering and the discrimination they endure as Sri Lankan citizens (Gamage 2018; Wijesinghe 2018). The press conference was covered in mainstream media, including audiovisual news channels in Sinhala, Tamil, and English which telecast it without criticism. Even the questions asked from the protestors and activists during these demonstrations were conducive and well exploited by the activists to highlight and elaborate non-discrimination and democracy as key demands of every Sri Lankan citizen, including the SOGIESC communities (Vikalpa 2018; Daily Mirror 2018a; Aththa Withthi 2018; Newsfirst 2018).

Secondly, the intersectional agenda has brought together diverse groups of interests onto a common platform and catalyzed the mobilization. Civil society groups, including human rights groups, women's rights groups, youth groups, and artists, have come forward to support the B4D protest. Political groups aligned with "left" politics also joined the protest, along with liberal civil society groups. The agenda emerged as a spectrum of interests, whose precise interests may not necessarily fully overlap. Those who are not necessarily pro-decriminalization also joined the march, along with SOGIESC groups, as the agenda was not about decriminalization but democracy and non-discrimination. This certainly benefitted their mobilization, as SOGIESC groups are a small number of individuals whose presence might not have been a significant factor in a protest without the power of allies and other interest groups, providing the necessary numbers, ideas, and slogans.

Thirdly, it was also a platform to bring together highly divisive SOGIESC groups and NGOs onto a single platform. Pro-coup elements – mostly the homo-ethnonationalists within SOGIESC communities, who did maintain silence to Sirisena's move – also joined the protest, as their identity has been threatened with the "butterfly speech." Sinhalese homo-ethnonationalists are often identified with ideas related to the majoritarian democracy, in which Sinhalese dominance is legitimized and any accommodation to minority rights – and particularly any contention to the rights of Sinhalese to the dominance of the Sri Lankan state – will not be tolerated. This movement of Sinhalese ethnonationalists believes any efforts to change the nature of the majoritarian state as a threat to the Sinhalese nation and paints international facilitated liberal democratic peacebuilding agenda as a threat to the Sri Lankan nation. This contention creates a gap between homo-ethnonationalists and other segments of the SOGIESC group, including particularly those actors navigating the liberal civil society space. In this context, bringing homo-ethnonationalists to the street in support of the B4D movement is a significant outcome. Devising an intersectional agenda thereby contributed toward bridging the gap between different homo-ethnonationalists, homo-liberals, and the queer left.

Devising an intersectional agenda, and putting that into practice, was not a risk-free exercise, especially in a context where the tide is not necessarily in favor of sexual and gender justice demands and developments. The SOGIESC groups initially had to endure a strategy of invisibility and low profiles to navigate the space produced by the constitutional coup. However, the "butterfly speech" triggered a response from the SOGIESC communities which was a radical U-turn from the previous defensive policy of being invisible. The series of discussions held within SOGIESC groups is indicative of some of the concerns and risks that are embraced and avoided. The idea of an online petition was a result of concerns by many within the SOGIESC movement that did not want to resort to a visible measure without having a sense of potential responses of the government and to avoid major public attraction to the action. This fear became real when the press conference was called. Key SOGIESC activists did raise concerns about attending a public media conference where they will be seen out opposing the government. As a leading organizer of the press conference, two of the three activists whom the author approached did clearly state that they did not want to take a risk at this juncture, largely due to unpredictable repercussions of opposing the government in mass media. Another activist who has agreed to attend the press conference did not show up, possibly for the same reason of not wanting to endure the risk. As such, the press conference was down to four activists, who finally decided to shield behind the non-discrimination agenda and decided to hold the press conference, which turned out to be a success.

Queer Potentials

What has B4D, as a queer-led movement, offered for comprehending queer potentials in TJ contexts and transitions in general? On the one hand, the movement itself demonstrated its ability to embrace both an internal and external transformation of the sexual and gender justice movement shaped by challenging moments. Internally, B4D symbolized a radical break from the defensive approach adopted by SOGIESC groups in the early stages of the coup. First, invisibility and self-censorship were followed at the beginning of the coup. And then it was changed into a defensive approach when SOGIESC communities joined other civil society groups to protest. Eventually, SOGIESC groups initiated their interventions to the protests, which mainstreamed the B4D movement, marking a proactive collective response to the crisis. It has given much hope within the SOGIESC communities that queerphobic hate speech can be transformed into an opportunity for the queer agency if deployed through a strategically calculated intersectional agenda during transitions. A community that was scared and down to self-censorship at the beginning of the coup has become an energized, proactive force for transforming the post-war transitions toward democracy and enacting a sense of justice in the country. It has gone from being invisible to major news headlines in national media and has become a driving force in the streets, where most of the struggles for democracy and justice took place.

Externally, the movement has gained wider publicity and legitimacy by voicing for a common agenda – democracy – during a national political crisis. The proactive protest of B4D was timely, and some forces from the left political movement have welcomed it as a new political development in the country, when certain radical left groups remained silent during the constitutional coup. Some even praised SOGIESC communities as an example of how to mainstream a specific struggle through the common issue in a creative and nuanced way, by bringing together democracy and queer emancipation struggles into a single platform to the mainstream in a polarized, conflict-affected society, where SOGIESC identities are criminalized and stigmatized (Fonseka 2018). The following presents a section of the English translation of a Facebook post from a radical youth group called *Aluth Parapura* (New Generation) commenting on the role of B4D during the democratization struggle:

> What Butterflies have taught us about politics?
>
> The interventions of the SOGIESC communities into the struggle for democracy are of the greatest importance. Their intervention seems to be politically creative and nuanced. They have gained unprecedented visibility in the public political space by bringing their struggle against "Butterfly" hate speech into the mainstream democratic struggle. . . . [T]he importance is that the SOGIESC communities did not restrain themselves into their struggle in a time of national emergency. Rather, they

> mainstreamed their specific issues while contributing to the struggle for resolving the larger political problems of the country. They are different from the student movement of the country that kept silent throughout the crucial period and confined into their specific struggle only.
>
> (Fonseka 2018)

This statement stands as evidence for the role played by the SOGIESC community during the struggle for democracy. It also shows that the intersectional agenda earned much-needed legitimacy by overcoming the long-standing criticism of dormancy in common issues.

Further, the collective queer agency had effectively reclaimed and redefined the term *butterfly*, demonstrating its ability to contend with queerphobic rhetoric in transitional politics. *Butterfly* as a derogatory slur for *queer*, symbolizing queerphobia, has now been turned into a symbol of unity, courage, and solidarity. Examples such as *butterfly power*, *butterflies vote too*, and coming out as *butterflies* whilst using symbols of butterflies in the protest marked the signs of reclaiming *butterfly* as a term synonymous with queer courage and thereby enacting a sense of justice. The reclaiming process would not have been a reality if it was not combined with the common struggle for democracy. The intersectional agenda provided the necessary machinery for the "new" way of politics of queer emancipation. It is a political process that mainstreams gender and sexual justice issues through a political approach that resonates with other political constituencies.

For transitional politics, the interventions of B4D have widened the transitional space for democratization in post-war Sri Lanka by advancing the struggle for sexual and gender justice. The wider acceptance gained for the queer agency, through the visibilization caused by the intersectional agenda, was instrumental in queering democratic forces. This was done by attracting the support of democratic forces for queer agency. More and more support for the historical grievance of SOGIESC communities came from democratic forces, including traditional parties and human rights groups who had been silent on the rights of SOGIESC communities and who have started publicly supporting the cause. Immediate support came from an organization called the National Intellectual Organization (NIO), consisting of renowned academics and professionals aligned with the center-left party called Janatha Vimukthi Peramuna (JVP – Peoples' Liberation Front). The invitation was to attend their public meeting held in Colombo in demanding democracy on the 12th of November 2018. Surprisingly, it was at this meeting that the leader of the political party, for the first time, declared his party would endorse the rights of SOGIESC communities (Thiyagaraja 2018). This is the first time a political party representing the parliament has publicly endorsed the SOGIESC agenda. In addition to endorsement by the New Left Front and Socialist Equality Party – whose influence in political representation is minuscule – this is considered as a major development, considering the threat posed by the constitutional coup. Another politician and a former member of parliament, Lal Kantha, publicly came out and supported SOGIESC rights weeks later, on 23 November 2018. The late foreign minister of the Unity Government, Mangala Samaraweera, who is also an openly gay politician, previously declared his support for the B4D (Daily Mirror 2018c). Several civil society groups also extended their invitations to the B4D movement to join them in their later initiatives. A left youth group invited the SOGIESC activists to form a youth wing called *New Wings* to join them to fight for a better political culture meeting and to join the subsequent press conference representing the movement (අලුත් පියාපත් 2018). Such invitations provided a good platform for SOGIESC groups to continue the struggle beyond their B4D protest. On 12 December 2018, a united protest organized by the collective of civil society groups was also joined by the B4D, and activists were invited to address the protest. Further, SOGIESC activists did conduct a workshop for the youth wing of the JVP in February 2019, which was a rare engagement that has not previously been done by any political party in the country. In the same month, NIO, in its inaugural convention, declared an LGBT policy in its manifesto, which was endorsed by the JVP leader publicly (Bakamoono 2019).

Further, the SOGIESC community's engagement with the formal transitional justice and reconciliation processes in Sri Lanka exposed the limits of the technocratic formal interventions of TJ processes informed by the liberal peacebuilding paradigm. As explained in the introduction of this chapter, often the engagement of SOGIESC communities with post-war transitional justice and reconciliation processes is confined to technocratic, formal institutionalized interventions (Bueno-Hansen 2018; also see Fobear, this volume). This is partly due to the male–female gender binaries and the victimization logic of SOGIESC communities embedded within the heterosexualized normative framework of transitional justice processes (Bueno-Hansen 2015 and this volume). Sri Lanka's experience in this domain, particularly with the formal process, has been one that has failed to move beyond a mere record of noting the existing demand for SOGIESC rights. It was also met with strong resistance whenever queer agenda was pushed through the track one political space. Unlike processes in Colombia and Nepal (see, for instance, Myrttinen et al., Oettler, this volume), Sri Lanka's transitional justice process informed by the Geneva Consensus continued to be predominantly heterosexualized and left little room for queering the technocratic institutionalized interventions. Exploiting this marginal space that existed within public consultations on reconciliation and constitutional amendment efforts, the SOGIESC groups made their representations to the public consultations on Constitutional Reforms and Public Consultation Taskforce on Reconciliation Mechanisms (CTF 2016; PRC 2016). In addition, the independent legal reform committee established under the leadership of Justice Aluwihare to compile possible reforms to the country's Penal Code was another space where SOGIESC groups submitted their demands in 2018. These recommendations demanded decriminalization of homosexuality and the inclusion of SOGIESC rights into the legal framework of the country when new constitutional and reconciliation measures are implemented. However, none of these demands have been converted into actions and remain as mere records supported by the technocratic entities tasked to consult the public on formulating the parameters of the post-war transitional process of Sri Lanka. In other instances, the advancing of queer rights as part of the government's commitment to the international community was met with the severe backlash that reconfirmed the resistance to queering post-war transition and has emboldened the political queerphobia embedded within the government's approach to the post-war politics of the country. These efforts not only met with resistance but also ended up reaffirming the queerphobic ethnonationalist critique that SOGIESC rights have been part of foreign-funded, dollar-driven NGO conspiracy against the Sinhala-Buddhist nation and culture. This was evident in the attempts made in 2016, as explained in the earlier section of this chapter.

Differently, B4D paved a "new way" of politics outside the formal processes of conflict transition where a sense of justice for queer community was enacted. It offered a pathway for queer communities and allies to come together under one umbrella in responding to a state-sponsored queerphobic hate speech. It operated through a language that was difficult to be demonized by the queerphobic ethnonationalist forces. By transcending the limits of the formal process, it has effectively escaped the usual critique of a foreign conspiracy against the Sinhala-Buddhist nation. It has brought the queer agenda onto the forefront of transitional politics, by foregrounding queer agency in the larger struggle for democracy in Sri Lanka. By doing so, the visible presence of queer agency in transitional politics was normalized through reclaiming collective queer identity, without much resistance that SOGIESC communities otherwise encounter in formalized institutional avenues of the transitional justice process. Indeed, it did not demand decriminalization but certainly enhanced the legitimacy for SOGIESC rights, a vital element that earlier efforts with the formal process have failed to generate. Its agenda expanded beyond sexual and gender justice issues and has effectively contributed to queering the transitional justice and reconciliation processes through enacting a sense of justice served to remedy the state-sponsored queerphobia, as explained earlier. It showed the queer agency's potential beyond victimhood, in the transitional justice and reconciliation process. Its ability to foreground the queer agency also highlights the potential of queer agency outside the formal processes. In other words, it shows the transformation occurring on the street in advancing a common struggle for democracy that is complex, messy, non-linear, and not necessarily following the taxonomy of liberal paradigmatic transitional justice and reconciliation processes. And finally, it shows the merits of not being confined to set categories and pathways of transitional politics.

Reflections and Conclusions

This chapter contemplated the question of what role queer activism can play in the struggle for democratization in broader transitional justice and reconciliation processes. Using the B4D movement in Sri Lanka as a case study, the chapter remedies the persistent lack of queer curiosities and understandings in the field of transitional justice and reconciliation processes (Fobear, this volume). Moving beyond normative, technocratic, and institutionalized processes rooted in top-down approaches, Sri Lanka's B4D movement's intervention during the constitutional coup in October 2018 has been examined as a micro-level queer engagement that unpacks the intersections between queer emancipation and democratization in a post-war and transitional context.

The developments outlined in this chapter indicate the impact of queer potentials in the struggle for democratization in post-war Sri Lanka. The B4D movement demonstrated how queer activism not only continues to work in parallel to the democratization process but also actively supports and advances democratization processes and justice in post-war contexts, beyond the institutionalization of reconciliation and transitional justice processes. By effectively exploiting an injurious, queer-phobic political statement, the B4D movement mainstreamed SOGIESC rights, amplified its space for queer activism, gained visibility for collective queer agency, and eventually reclaimed the term *butterfly* as a symbol of unity, courage, and solidarity. The reclaiming process represented a sense of justice in their own terms by engaging outside of the formal technocratic channels of transitional justice. Collectively, this contributed to queering post-war transitional justice and democratization efforts through an intersectional agenda, indicating a "new way" of politics.

As such, B4D presents a unique queer potential in comprehending the role of queer activism in post-war transitional spaces. By foregrounding the collective agency of queer subjects, it necessitates equal scholarly attention on queer agency as much as queer victimization during post-war transitional justice and reconciliation processes. It also reminds us of the danger of containing queer engagement only to the formal technocratic processes and shows the existence and the capacity of informal, spontaneous, and organic emergence of queer mobilizations. In other words, the intellectual thirst on queer curiosities during transitional spaces must be reminded that the technocratic formalized approach is not the only place where queering transitions occur. Such micro-level spontaneous queer engagement can yield the benefits that formal processes often fail to deliver in their attempts to queer post-war transitions and thereby necessitating the need for moving beyond the dichotomous categorizations of transitional justice approaches. It also reminds policymakers on reconciliation and transitional justice processes to look beyond formal avenues of queer engagements. Allocating resources and strengthening informal micro-level queer interventions might enable post-war queer agenda a feasible project.

References

135 Campaign (2018). *Butterflies for Democracy Press Statement*. Available at: https://www.facebook.com/135campaign/photos/a.1365061660219386/2048056981919847/. Accessed on: 26 February 2022.

Ada Derana (2018). *What I Changed Was a Policy That Didn't Suit the Country*. Colombo: Ada Derana. Available at: https://www.youtube.com/watch?v=JW84UmxGO5o. Accessed on: 25 February 2022.

Ameen, A. (2018). *I Would Rather Be a Butterfly Than a Leech*. Available at: https://www.facebook.com/photo?fbid=1913995528907097&set=a.1549879965318657. Accessed on: 26 February 2022.

Aththa Withthi (2018). *Butterflies for Democracy*. Available at: https://www.youtube.com/watch?v=iDKIth-N7xM. Accessed on: 26 February 2022.

Bakamoono (2019). JVP Includes Decriminalization of LGBTIQ Persons in Election Manifesto. *Bakamoono*. Available at: http://www.bakamoono.lk/en/article/4204/jvp-includes-decriminalization-of-lgbtiq-persons-in-election-manifesto?fbclid=IwAR1vpIEsWrYw3wQZUvF6QDxrkg5AsZXjgEsacKpViKcoOuLUUYPYDSqkHbc. Accessed on: 26 February 2022.

Bueno-Hansen, P. (2015). *Feminism and Human Rights Struggles in Peru: Decolonizing Transitional Justice*. Urbana: University of Illinois Press.

Bueno-Hansen, P. (2018). Decolonial Feminism, Gender, and Transitional Justice in Latin America. In: Ní Aoláin, F., Cahn, N., Haynes, D. and Valji, N. (eds.): *The Oxford Handbook of Gender and Conflict*. Oxford: Oxford University Press.

CTF (2016). *Final Report of the Consultation Task Force on Reconciliation Mechanisms: Executive Summary and Recommendations*. Consultation Report. Colombo: CFT. Available at: https://womenandmedia.org/si/ctf-on-reconciliation-mechanisms-final-report-all-volumes/?msclkid=6bb9bd84ade811ec9fcc23c5a28c7a76. Accessed on: 27 March 2022.

Daily FT (2018). *A Coup in Asia's Oldest Democracy*. Colombo: Daily FT. Available at: https://www.ft.lk/opinion/A-coup-in-Asia-s-oldest-democracy/14-665691. Accessed on: 25 February 2022.

Daily Mirror (2018a). *"Butterflies" Continue Their Fight for Democracy*. Colombo: Daily Mirror. Available at: https://www.dailymirror.lk/news-features/Butterflies-continue-their-fight-for-democracy/131-159649. Accessed on: 26 February 2022.

Daily Mirror (2018b). *Prez Should Apologize, Says LGBTQ+ Community*. Colombo: Daily Mirror. Available at: https://www.dailymirror.lk/breaking_news/Prez-should-apologize-says-LGBTQ-community/108-158026 Accessed on: 26 February 2022.

Daily Mirror (2018c). *I Would Rather Be a Butterfly Than a Leech – Mangala*. Colombo: Daily Mirror. Available at: https://www.dailymirror.lk/article/I-would-rather-be-a-butterfly-than-a-leech-Mangala-157952.html?msclkid=59a599f3ade411ec93aa61c42044fa69. Accessed on: 27 March 2022.

Duffy, N. (2018). *Sri Lanka President Slammed for "Insidious Homophobic Comments"*. London: PinkNews | Latest lesbian, gay, bi and trans news | LGBT+ news. Available at: https://www.pinknews.co.uk/2018/11/08/sri-lanka-president-maithripala-sirisena-insidious-homophobic-comments/. Accessed on: 26 February 2022.

Fobear, K. and E. Baines (2020). Pushing the Conversation Forward: The Intersections of Sexuality and Gender Identity in Transitional Justice. *The International Journal of Human Rights* 24(4): 307–312.

Fonseka, S. (2018). දේශපාලනය ගැන සමනලුන් කියා දුන්නේ කුමක්ද??. දේශාපාලනය ගැන සමනලුන් කියා දුන්නේ කුමක්ද?. Available at: https://m.facebook.com/story.php?story_fbid=470154023510306&id=100015471375191. Accessed on: 26 February 2022.

Gamage, M. (2018). *An Open Letter to President Sirisena by a Young "Samanala" Sri Lankan*. Colombo: Colombo Telegraph. Available at: https://www.colombotelegraph.com/index.php/an-open-letter-to-president-sirisena-by-a-young-samanala-sri-lankan/. Accessed on: 26 February 2022.

Gossiplanka (2018). ඔයාලා 'සමනල රැන' කිව්වම අපගේ හිත් රිදුණා – සමරිසි ක්‍රියාකාරිකයන්. *Gossip Lanka News*. Available at: https://www.gossiplankanews.com/2018/11/samariri-statement.html. Accessed on: 26 February 2022.

Groundviews (2018). *Statement by the Sri Lankan LGBTQI+ Community and allies on President Sirisena's Homophobic comments at ' Jana Mahima'rally'*. Available at: https://www.facebook.com/notes/377997760277736/. Accessed on: 26 February 2022.

Höglund, K., M. Kovacs and W. Thiyagaraja (2016). The Peace Triangle: Capturing Peace After Military Victory in Sri Lanka. In: Firchow, P. and Anastasiou, H. (eds.): *Practical Approaches to Peacebuilding: Putting Theory to Work*. London: Lynner Rienner: 9–33.

Jayasinghe, P. (2018). *Samanalun, Godayas and Our Words*. Colombo: Groundviews. Available at: https://groundviews.org/2018/12/01/samanalun-godayas-and-our-words/. Accessed on: 27 March 2022.

Keenan, A. (2015). *A New Sri Lanka?* Brussels, New York, Washington, DC and London: International Crisis Group. Available at: https://www.crisisgroup.org/asia/south-asia/sri-lanka/new-sri-lanka. Accessed on: 23 February 2022.

Leebaw, B. (2008). The Irreconcilable Goals of Transitional Justice. *Human Rights Quarterly* 30(1): 95–118.

Newsfirst (2018). *Butterflies for Democracy*. Colombo: Newsfirst. Available at: https://www.newsfirst.lk/2018/12/07/butterflies-for-democracy/. Accessed on: 26 February 2022.

PRC (2016). *Report on Public Representations on Constitutional Reform*. Consultation Report. Colombo. Available at: https://www.colombotelegraph.com/wp-content/uploads/2016/05/PRC-Report-English-Final.pdf. Accessed on: 20 September 2019.

Rao, R. (2020). *Out of Time: The Queer Politics of Postcoloniality*. New York: Oxford University Press.

Reuters (2018). *Sri Lanka Police Arrest Sacked Minister Over Shooting*. London: Reuters. Available at: https://www.reuters.com/article/uk-sri-lanka-politics-shooting-idUKKCN1N31EA. Accessed on: 25 February 2022.

Schulz, P. (2019). "To Me, Justice Means to Be in a Group": Survivors' Groups as a Pathway to Justice in Northern Uganda. *Journal of Human Rights Practice* 11: 1–19.

Schulz, P. (2020). Towards Inclusive Gender in Transitional Justice: Gaps, Blind-Spots and Opportunities. *Journal of Intervention and Statebuilding* 14(5): 691–710.

Sharp, D. (2013). Interrogating the Peripheries: The Preoccupations of Fourth Generation Transitional Justice. *Harvard Human Rights Journal* 26: 149–168.

Smith, C., L. Waldorf, R. Venugopal and G. McCarthy (2020). Illiberal Peace-Building in Asia: A Comparative Overview. *Conflict, Security & Development* 20(1): 1–14.

Sri Lanka Brief (2014). *UNHCR March 2014 – Revised Draft Resolution on Sri Lanka (14 March)*. Colombo: Sri Lanka Brief. Available at: https://srilankabrief.org/unhrc-march-2014-revised-draft-resolution-on-sri-lanka-14-march/. Accessed on: 22 February 2022.

Sri Lanka Brief (2018). *Sri Lankan LGBTQI+ Community and Allies Condemn President Sirisena's Homophobic Comments*. Colombo: Sri Lanka Brief. Available at: https://srilankabrief.org/sri-lankan-lgbtqi-community-and-allies-condemn-president-sirisenas-homophobic-comments/. Accessed on: 26 February 2022.

Thiyagaraja, W. (2017). ආඩම්බර පොන්නයකු වීම. *Vikalpa*. Available at: https://www.vikalpa.org/article/30275. Accessed on: 26 February 2022.

Thiyagaraja, W. (2018). *JVP Stands for Non-Discrimination of LGBTIQ+ Persons*. Colombo: Colombo Telegraph. Available at: https://www.colombotelegraph.com/index.php/jvp-stands-for-non-discrimination-of-lgbtiq-persons/. Accessed on: 26 February 2022.

Thiyagaraja, W. (2022). Paradox of "Radical' and 'Non-Radical": Exploring the Origin and Evolution of LGBT NGOs in Sri Lanka. In: Ranawana, A. (eds.): *Discourses on Youth Radicalisation. Colombo: Centre for Poverty Analysis*. Available at: https://www.researchgate.net/publication/361189996_Paradox_of_'Radical'_and_'Non-Radical'_Exploring_the_Origin_and_Evolution_of_LGBT_NGOs_in_Sri_Lanka#fullTextFileContent. Accessed on: 26 February 2023.

Vikalpa (2018). සමනලුන්ට බය ජනපති. Available at: https://www.vikalpa.org/article/33902. Accessed on: 26 February 2022.

Walton, O. and W. Thiyagaraja (2020). Liberal and Illiberal Peacebuilding in Sri Lanka. In: Richmond, O. and Visoka, G. (eds.): *Palgrave Encyclopedia of Peace and Conflict Studies*. Cham: Palgrave Macmillan.

Wanniarachchi, S. (2019). *Of Butterfly Assemblages and Constitutional Coups: Invention and Intersection of Heteromasculinity and Class in Post-Colonial Sri Lanka*. London: LSE Engenderings. Available at: https://blogs.lse.ac.uk/gender/2019/08/26/of-butterfly-assemblages-and-constitutional-coups-invention-and-intersection-of-heteromasculinity-and-class-in-post-colonial-sri-lanka/. Accessed on: 25 February 2022.

Wijesinghe, A. (2018). *Dear Mr. President: Letter from a Sri Lankan Queer Woman*. Colombo: Colombo Telegraph. Available at: https://www.colombotelegraph.com/index.php/dear-mr-president-letter-from-a-sri-lankan-queer-woman/?fbclid=IwAR3-1n8P_C0I-dsyXZf7nu9rUVCer7wbGMTGP5Ud-7jvslOKFgbUOhIxk9M. Accessed on: 26 February 2022.

අලුත් පියාපත් (2018). ප්‍රජාතන්ත්‍රවාදය සහ යහපත් දේශපාලන සංස්කෘතියක් වෙනුවෙන් අලුත් පියාපත් මාධ්‍ය හමුව. Available at: https://www.facebook.com/watch/?v=344092352807372. Accessed on: 26 February 2022.

Chapter 17

Concluding Thoughts and Calls to Action

Heleen Touquet, Philipp Schulz, Pascha Bueno-Hansen, José Fernando Serrano-Amaya, Brandon Hamber, and Katherine Fobear

Introduction: Calls to Action

Let us now turn to the question of what we intended to achieve with this volume. Following the previous sections' thick and detailed case study explorations at the micro-level – honing in on specific questions, phenomena, and cases – with this concluding chapter, we change gears and focus on the macro-level aspects of this book's explorations. To this end, we want to draw out several implications and contributions of this volume, in the conceptual, analytical, empirical, methodological, and practical sense, offering concluding thoughts. In addition, we also aim to orient our gaze forward, in terms of identifying gaps that still remain unaddressed, mapping out directions for further research, and articulating calls for action in terms of facilitating and advancing more inclusive approaches to gender in dealing with the past. As such, this chapter includes broader observations by way of considering the individual chapters as a whole, coupled with ensuing reflections from both the editors as well as particular contributing authors, thereby offering a range of different perspectives.

Implications for Scholarship and Policymaking

This book has sought to move toward creating a more holistic framework for studying masculinities and queer perspectives in transitional justice, creating conversations between a variety of perspectives and different bodies of literature that engaged with some of the key themes covered in this volume – masculinities, queering, gender, and transitional justice – but that for the most part have remained siloed. We specifically aimed to move away from violation-centric views and the ensuing victim/perpetrator binaries that have dominated a lot of the scholarly work on masculinities and queer perspectives, as well as on transitional justice (see Hamber et al., this volume). Instead, the book moves to center the experiences and positionalities of those men and persons with diverse SOGIESC who are neither active combatants nor victims of violence. Guided by a feminist and queer curiosity, we

DOI: 10.4324/9781003519522-21

aimed – rather than merely making men and people with diverse SOGIESC visible – to critically interrogate patriarchal and heteronormative frames that govern transitional justice processes and their implementation. All the chapters in this volume therefore recognize the relationalities and intersections between gender identities and sexual orientations, as well as the enduring influence of patriarchal gendered hierarchies and power structures, rooted in feminist traditions of thought. Taken as a whole, the collection of chapters presents a framework that exposes and critiques the deeply gendered structures that inform liberal peacebuilding and its main tenets of liberal democracy, human rights (civil and political rights), and a market economy. The chapters all suggest alternative ways to work toward inclusive TJ, based on masculinities and queer perspectives of dealing with the past, respectively.

In so doing, the chapters in this book carry important implications and offer numerous empirical, conceptual, and analytical contributions for scholarship and policymaking on transitional justice. Taken together, the volume advances an understanding of the gender dynamics of processes of dealing with the past, beyond an equation of "gender" with "women and girls." This leads the discussion toward more inclusive conceptions of and approaches to gender in post-conflict and transitional settings and, in so doing, demonstrates and unearths the heterogeneities and complexities of how a whole variety of intersecting gender constructions, identities, and sexual orientations shape how TJ processes are implemented, felt, and experienced by different groups of conflict-affected communities. In particular, this combination of masculinities and queer perspectives – as hereto under-utilized frames to make sense of gender and dealing with the past – aptly illustrates, critiques, and seeks to undo the heteronormative, patriarchal, neoliberal, and Western-centric lenses that dominate TJ processes in general, but also an engagement with gender and TJ specifically.

Through various methodological and epistemological approaches, from conceptual and theoretical approaches to thick description and case studies based on rich empirical work, the authors included in this volume have considered in-depth how masculine cultures and queer perspectives operate within a variety of hierarchies and social spaces. The first set of theoretical chapters sets the stage for the micro-level studies that follow in the subsequent sections, by showing the inherent limitations of liberal rights approaches to TJ, and instead calls for queering legal theory and TJ more broadly. Specifically, this process of queering is to be understood as a radical rethinking of the heteronormative and patriarchal structures and theoretical concepts that support TJ practice and theory (Bueno-Hansen 2018). It is a critique of how TJ has been conceptualized in liberal peacebuilding and a plea to not merely add legal categories and emphasize political rights but rather think through alternative and intersectional ways of how gender identities and sexual orientations can be included in TJ processes. İrem Akı's chapter proves that we do not necessarily need to invent anything new to achieve that goal; rather, as she suggests, the Yogyakarta Principles could, for example, be used as a basis to start a process of queering legal theory. Another downside of the liberal human rights way of adding categories, rather than addressing the underlying structures, is highlighted by Katherine Fobear. Fobear demonstrates that this dominant approach creates and supports narratives of Western exceptionalism and superiority and an othering of queer lives outside of the West. Queering TJ, therefore, cannot be done without a decolonial approach that is cognizant of epistemic violence and is inclusive of queer voices and non–North American and European epistemes. As Katharina Hoffmann and Thokozani Mbwana argue, it is precisely outside of the liberal traditions and bodies of knowledge that solutions can be found.

In the micro-level studies that follow, we saw how the considerations as laid out in the theoretical chapters play out in the nuances and complexities of lived realities and practical situations of transitional justice across a variety of settings. Among other things, the empirical material from various locations shows the fluidity and malleability of the categories that are sometimes employed rather rigidly in transitional justice discourses. The analyses presented in the book show that many of the categories that are so central to TJ processes are in fact fluid. Individuals navigate in and out of these rigid categories throughout their lives. In Amya Agarwal's chapter, Kashmiri men embody military and civilian masculinities at the same time. In Croatia, Catherine Baker shows how the masculinities promoted by older veterans in Croatia are adopted by younger civilian men in football and music cultures. The categories of perpetrator and victim are blurred and often influenced by colonial and racist imagery. This is shown in Chloe Lewis and Susanne Allden's discussion of the Congolese young men who are being accused of rape. Erin Baines and Camille Oliveira similarly discuss the complexity of the victim/perpetrator paradigm in the case of fathers of children born of war rape in the LRA. In addition, Ursula Mosqueira shows how prevalent gender norms and binary understandings of masculinities, femininities, and gender can hinder the construction of justice-seeking and healing spaces among survivors of torture in El Salvador's political prisons. Thiyagaraja Waradas's chapter on the Butterflies for Democracy (B4D) movement in Sri Lanka points out that creating space for queer voices and experiences is not a sideshow but is central to democratic principles. The interests of the queer movements and the democracy movement for liberation are deeply interlinked. The chapter by Thiyagaraja convincingly demonstrates how queer subjectivities and experiences lead queer men to come out in support of a pro-democracy movement.

The volume also touches upon important issues related to knowledge production: Whose voices are heard and centered within TJ, and how does it impact its outcomes? Who are the actors whose knowledge and whose knowledge production contributions are taken seriously and whose voices and perspectives continue to be omitted from discussions about TJ, within the academy, in policymaking, and locally within the spaces and sites where

TJ is enacted? Both Fernando Serrano-Amaya's and Pascha Bueno-Hansen's chapters illustrate how lesbian and gay activists' and queer individuals' work can steer transitional justice processes in specific directions, in what Fernando Serrano Amaya calls "queering transitional justice from below." Pascha Bueno Hansen shows how the presence of one lesbian activist changed and queered the remit of the truth commission in Ecuador. Like Serrano-Amaya and Bueno Hansen, in their chapter, Henri Myrtinnen, Laura Barios, and Charbel Maydaa call for more support for local agency and grassroots and civil society–led efforts at achieving justice and how these actors, at the micro-level, influence not only how these processes are navigated but also how they ought to be studied and understood.

Many of the chapters in this volume specifically reflect the centrality of Latin American activists in establishing examples and good practices with regards to processes of specifically queering TJ. The Latin American examples and, more specifically, the Colombian peace agreement show the importance of carefully listening to queer and activist voices to move forward. As Oettler points out, though, the inclusion of queer voices in the Colombian peace agreement and the discourse on peace in general has not come without the tireless activism of queer and Indigenous peoples. The peace agreement is also not exclusively progressive, as it is often made to appear, as it contains sections and ideas that are more conservative in nature and that can be mobilized by those who do not support LGBTQ and/or indigenous rights, as the recent past in Colombia has already demonstrated. A queer TJ process thus requires steadfast and continuous support and engagement with queer activists and voices globally. This will be all the more important in a world where the anti-gender movement, "traditional values," and transphobic movements have gained more power in recent years, supported as they are by powerful states as well as a global network of influential political and religious leaders.

Ways Forward and Calls to Action

Integrating a variety of voices and being inclusive require accountability, which must also be attentive to Global South–North power asymmetries and dominant extractivist practices in academia (Bunting et al. 2023). This was also on our editorial agenda for this volume, as the editors issued calls for papers and solicited a diverse range of authors and activists to contribute to the volume. We also designed a collaborative process to work on the book, inviting the authors to comment and reflect upon each other's chapters – thinking and working relationally to the extent possible. Many of the authors involved have long track records of working closely with activists or being activists themselves, primarily in the Global South. In compiling this volume, we have thus also been mindful of not reproducing but instead trying to counter the imbalance of author representation and positionalities and include more strongly the voices and perspectives of activists and authors from the Global South and/or from non-academic spaces. Nevertheless, we must ask ourselves critical questions to what extent we have been able to achieve this in a way that is satisfactory, and there is, indeed, much more potential to continue centering these diverse and more representative voices and perspectives in this book, but even more so in scholarship and policymaking on these topics writ large. We believe that it is paramount to center movement-based knowledge production and hold the expert production of knowledge accountable to those that live through the given armed conflicts, political repression, and/or political violence. The struggles around the recognition of genders and sexualities are lived by activists and advocates before, during, and after peace processes in real time and have been subject to critical debates and scrutiny within these circles and by these actors for a long time already, often much longer than within the academy.

The volume also touches upon and involves crucial debates outside an academic and activist context, but with regards to political processes and developments, with real-time implications for the topics we write about and for the communities whose stories, experiences, and lived realities are discussed, portrayed, and written about across these pages. In particular, our volume shall appear in a period of time which has been governed by a conservative religious and political backlash in many states across the world, which brings with it specific risks. One of these risks for the specific subject area of this book is that SOGIESC perspectives could be added to the TJ toolbox without thinking through broader underlying power differentials and hierarchical structures that cause discrimination. Adding queer perspectives in such a way can also draw unwanted attention to queer bodies, causing them to be seen as a curiosity. Another risk is, the calls for attending to and integrating masculinities perspectives fall flat, as there is no substantial critical masculinities movement that exists in our world. Women's, LGTBQ, and Indigenous rights have been advanced thanks to the existence of strong and broad social movements, but there is no equivalent for critical masculinities. The voices that we hear most in debates about masculinities currently are limited to a conservative masculinist countermovement that supports "traditional values" and individualist and neoliberal discourses, calls, and campaigns for men to refrain from "toxic masculinities" and be "good men." The development of a broader and more critical movement seems a critical step if we are to advance to a more inclusive approach.

Linked to this, and again specifically applied to the overall aims and objectives of this volume, advancing a more inclusive approach to gender in transitional justice and processes of dealing with violent pasts also requires an even greater and more coherent *combination* of feminist, masculinities, and queer perspectives. In this volume, we have sought to build and take that conversation further, rooting it in feminist approaches to conflict, political violence, and peace; the chapters in this volume have brought attention to masculinities and queer perspectives to the study and practice of transitional justice and have placed these alongside as well as in conversation with one another. Yet more work needs to be done to not only place these diverse – sometimes complementary, sometimes contradictory – perspectives and approaches into conversation but to also conceptually and analytically combine them in more coherent ways. One concrete and fruitful example for this intellectual exercise of intertwining masculinities and queer perspectives in a transitional and post-conflict context is the chapter by Jose Fernando Serrano Amaya, interrogating transitional justice from below through queer masculinities, and thereby demonstrating how processes of queering transitional justice can be undertaken through attention to, and an engagement with, masculine bodies, actors, and processes. This chapter, in particular, sets the agenda and illustrates ways forward for effectively facilitating a relational and inclusive engagement with gender in the context of transitional justice, drawing on and taking inspiration from feminist, queer, and masculinities perspectives alike and in combination. Scholarship on gender in the context of armed conflict and peacebuilding more broadly, and in relation to transitional justice in particular, would benefit tremendously from building on this work to achieve a more comprehensive gender examination of these processes. Future research in these areas thus requires a more holistic, radical (and anti-liberal), and relational framework of integrating and combining masculinities, feminist, and queer perspectives – something which this volume sets the path and groundwork for. Most importantly, we believe the book has illustrated the possibilities of the collective creation of knowledge that goes beyond collected individual pieces of work, in that it is also a knowledge and action project that expands some fields and approaches and creates a space that did not exist before.

References

Bueno-Hansen, P. (2018). The Emerging LGBTI Rights Challenge to Transitional Justice in Latin America. *International Journal of Transitional Justice* 12(1): 126–145.

Bunting, A., A. Kiconco and J. Quirk (2023). *Research as More Than Extraction: Knowledge Production and Gender-Based Violence in African Societies*. Athens, OH: Ohio University Press.

Index

abductees 161, 171
abduction 165–166, 169, 174; female survivors of 163; mass 161
abject, abjected 70, 80, 261, 264–265
abortion 128–129, 222
Acevedo, Dario 144
Acholi Nation, LRA attempt to create 168–169
Acholi peoples: bridewealth among 173; cultural norms among 173; customary practices of 172; LRA violence against 177
Acholi region 83, 161
ACHPR *see* African Commission on Human and Peoples' Rights
Acuerdo Final para la Terminación del Conflicto y la Construccion de una Paz Estable y Duradera, 24 August 2016 (Final Agreement to End the Armed Conflict and Build a Stable and Lasting Peace): AI 146n4; AII 146n4
affirmative sabotage 71
Africa and African contexts: de- and anti-colonial 16; decolonial perspectives on queering transitional justice 18, 69–86; homophobia in 78; homosexuality in 77; LGBT/Q/I/A+ as acronym in 72; *queer* in activism in 72; queerness from/within 74; same-sex marriages decriminalized in 78; sexuality and gender in 74–77; violence and discrimination against queers in 72; *see also* [countries by name]
African Centre for Refugees, Ontario, Canada 62
African Charter 69
African Commission on Human and Peoples' Rights (ACHPR) 69; adoption of *Principles and Guidelines on the Implementation of Economic, Social and Cultural Rights in the African Charter* by 69
African homophobia 77–79
"African LGBTI Manifesto" 80
African Union (AU) 69
Afrientalist gaze 187
Afro-feminism 75
AFSPA *see* Armed Forces Special Powers Act
Agamben, Giorgio 279, 294
Ahmed, Sara 128
AI *see* Acuerdo Final para la Terminación del Conflicto y la Construccion de una Paz Estable y Duradera, 24 August 2016 (Final Agreement to End the Armed Conflict and Build a Stable and Lasting Peace)
AII *see* Acuerdo Final para la Terminación del Conflicto y la Construccion de una Paz Estable y Duradera, 24 November 2016 (Final Agreement to End the Armed Conflict and Build a Stable and Lasting Peace)
Aijazi, O. 165, 167
al-Khatib trial 240
Alldén, Susanne 370
Almeida, Ana 131
Aluwihare (Justice) 362
Alvarez, Sandra 129, 131
Alvaro Vive ¡Carajo! 119

Amir, M. 313
Amnesty International: "Crimes of Hate Conspiracies of Silence Torture and Ill-Treatment Based on Sexual Identity" 120–121, 123, 125
amnesty law: El Salvador 280; Lebanon 238
anger 328, 334
APDP *see* Association of Parents of Disappeared Persons
Armed Forces Special Powers Act (AFSPA) 328
Asociación Gay Transgénero Coccinelle 130
Association of Croatian Homeland War Military Invalids (HVIDRA) 212
Association of Parents of Disappeared Persons (APDP) 329
AU *see* African Union
AVC *see* Alvaro Vive ¡Carajo!
Ayot, Florence 162, 166–169

B4D *see* Butterflies for Democracy
Bahamond, Christian 119, 122–123
Bahía Portere massacre 144
Baines, Erin 8, 165, 167
Bairner, A. 311
Bajo Putamayo 144
Bangura, Zainab 182
Barnett, H. 101
Bell, C. 10
Belobrajdić, Tanja 220
Beristain, Carlos 120
Bernard, Cheryl 191
Betancour administration 143
Bhartiya Janata Party (BJP) 329
BiH *see* Bosnia-Herzegovina
bi-phobia or biphobia 11, 232, 236
bisexual *see* LGBT; LGBTQI+
BJP *see* Bhartiya Janata Party
Blaškić, Tihomir 219
Bohlander, Michael 105–106
Boise, S. de 29
Bosnia-Herzegovina (BiH) 209, 214, 216, 219; Dayton Agreement 59; hate crime legislation in 59
boxing (sport of) 23, 300–302; civilian masculinities in North of Ireland and 305–312, 319; community relations and peacebuilding through 311–312; as salvation 306–310
Brussels Tribunal on Crimes against Women 128
Bucaram, Abdalá 130
Bueno-Hansen, Pascha 56–57, 234, 371
Buss, D. 188
Butler, Judith 73, 96, 265
Butterflies for Democracy (B4D) 16, 23, 344–364; mainstreaming of 355–356; as term or homophobic slur 346, 351–352, 361
butterfly gang 351
Butterfly Power 354, 361
"butterfly speech" (Sirisena) 346, 349, 351–353, 359

Cadieux Van Vliet, A. 167
CAIN *see* Conflict Archive on the Internet
care 20, 23, 325; avoidance of 336; embodying 339–342; everyday acts of 340; feminist ethics of 340; feminist theorists of 336; feminization of 336; harm and 166; health 242n22, 269; masculine identity and 336–337; medical 200; positive fatherhood and 308; psychosocial 212; sexual 265
Caribe Afirmativo 253
caring masculinities 23, 326, 335–342; traits of 339; *see also* Imran
Carpenter, Charli 305
Castrochavism 137, 146
Catholic Church 146
Catholic(s): community (Ireland and North of Ireland) 302, 309, 311; conservative 140; frames of reference 138, 151; moral theology 139; thinking 137
CDHES *see* Comision de Derechos Humanos de El Salvador (Human Rights Commission of El Salvador)
Centro National de Memoria Histórica (National Center for Historical Memory) (CNMH)(Colombia) 136, 143–145, 234, 236
Čermak, Ivan 219
Céspedez-Báez, Lina 144–145
CEV *see* truth commission
Chechnya, anti-gay purges in 55
checkpoint regime, Israeli 300, 302, 313–314

checkpoints 240, 316; crossing 317; military 315; power dynamics at 314; security 23, 301, 319
cis-heteronormativity 258
cis-hetero-sexism 116
cisnormativity 259
class *see* working class
class-based discrimination 232
class divide 131
class hierarchy 319
classification in law and legal texts 102, 108–109
class inequality 163, 278
class, race, ethnicity 6, 12, 44, 101 285; categorialism applied to 152; gender intersecting with 101; intersectional approaches to 140
CLS *see* critical legal studies
CMO *see* Cour Militaire Opérationelle
CNMH *see* Centro National de Memoria Histórica (National Center for Historical Memory)
CNR *see* Consejo Nacional de Reincorporación
Coccinelle 130
Cockburn, Cynthia 231n7
COJ *see* Companions on a Journey
Cold War 7, 118, 278–280
Colectivo Crisálida 236
Colombia: gender and peacebuilding in 17–19, 21; LGBTQ activists in 58; National Center for Historical Memory 98; peace agreement 19; peacebuilding in 22; queer masculinities in 38; Thousand Days' War 142; truth commission 115; Violence, the (Civil War) 142; *see also* CEV; CNMH; FARC; FARC-EP
Colombian Victims' Unit 58
colonialism 54, 138; aftermath of 70n1; legacies in Africa of 77, 82, 84; South African 76
coloniality 84, 259
coloniality of gender 76, 79, 86, 139
coloniality of power 77, 80, 86
Comision de Derechos Humanos de El Salvador (Human Rights Commission of El Salvador) (CDHES) 288
Comisión para el Esclarecimiento de la Verdad, la Convivencia y la No repetición – CEV) *see* Truth Commission (Colombia) (CEV)
compañeras (female comrades) 291
Companions on a Journey (COJ) (Sri Lanka) 348
compulsory heterosexuality 96, 128, 259n4
Conflict Archive on the Internet (CAIN) 304
conflict-related deaths 310n13
conflict-related experiences of civilian men: in North of Ireland 318; in Palestine 312, 318
conflict-related masculinities 208
conflict-related sexual harms 186; transitional justice mechanisms to reddress 185
conflict-related sexual violence (CRSV) 39–40, 53, 239–240; boxing in North of Ireland's recruitment from communities affected by 305; CEV's definition of 237; definition and discourse of 190; difficulty of defining 99n5; holding perpetrators to account 183; identifying individual perpetrators of 196; importance of fighting impunity for 181; international policy on 193; lack of systematic research on 239; legal systems' failure to address 201; SEA conflated with 191; securing accountability for 189; sexual violence distinguished from 191–193; UNSC agenda regarding 190–191; UNSC resolutions regarding 184n3; UN Women's Rights advocate on 191; used against Syrians 240; against women and girls 39–40; *see also* Minova trial
Congo *see* DRC
conjugal slavery 165
conjugal unions 162, 172
Connell, Raewyn 31–32, 140–141, 152, 257, 262n7, 268, 319n20
CONPES 3931 *see* Política Nacional para la Reincorporación Social y Económica D Exintegrantes De Las FARC-EP (The National Policy for the Social and Economical Reintegration of Former Members of the FARC-EP)

Consejo Nacional de Reincorporación (CNR) 150
continuums of violence 21, 144, 228, 231–233, 244, 262
copinage 198–201
coping mechanisms 335; gendered 301, 315, 318–319
COPPES *see* Committee of Former Political Prisoners of El Salvador
Cordero, León Febres *see* Febres Cordero, León
Cordero, Tatiana 118, 121–124, 127–131
Correa, Rafael 114, 119, 129
Cour Militaire Opérationelle (CMO) 195–196
Crenshaw, Kimberlé 12, 98n4; *see also* intersectionality
critical scholarship on men and masculinities (CSMM) 325, 336
crime: armed 35; definitions of 93, 100; drug-related 146; feminine 30, 40; gender-based 20; international 201; masculine 30; against men 40; sexual or sexual violence 40, 99, 184, 189–190, 196, 198, 200, 202; *see also* forced marriage; hate crime; war crime
crime of forced marriage and pregnancy 161, 165, 175
crimes against humanity 103, 119–120, 161, 163, 189; legal tools to punish 279n2
crimes of pillage 194
crimes against women 128
critical legal studies (CLS) 100
Croatia 210; Association of Croatian Homeland War Military Invalids (HVIDRA) 212; clientelist veterans welfare system in 212; global refugee crisis and 212; LGTBQ movements in 215; men's national football team 208; post-conflict memory of 210; post-war 13; Restart Coalition 222; veteran masculinities in 13, 21, 208–224; war crimes by soldiers of 209; War of Independence 21, 208–211; war memory of 212; war narratives in 211; Zagreb 208; *see also* Homeland War; Lovren; Modrić; NDH; Škoro; Thompson
Croat Defence Council (HVO) 214
Croatian Defence Forces (HOS) 213
Croatian Democratic Union (HDZ) 217
Croatian Football Association (HNS) 214–216, 221
CRSV *see* conflict-related sexual violence
CSMM *see* critical scholarship on men and masculinities

Daigle, M. 15
Dalmantinska zagora (Dalmatian hinterland) 212, 214
Dankwa, Serena Owusua 75
Darfur 191
Das, Veena 340
Dayton Agreement 59
Democratic Republic of Congo (DRC) 13, 17, 20; 2006 Sexual Violence Laws 198–199; 2009 Child Protection Law 194–196, 198; *copinage* in 198–201; *Greatest Silence: Rape in the Congo* (film) 191; Forces armées de la République démocratique du Congo (FARDC) 193; international crimes in 201; male homoerotic practices in 76; male perpetratorhood in 181–183, 186, 196–202; masculinities in 42; Minova trial 193–196; Programme d'Appui à la Justice à l'Est de la RDC (PARJ-E) 199; sexual crimes in 20, 194, 202; sexual violence in 181–202; violence against women and girls in 182–183, 186–187, 191
Denov, M. 166, 176
deprivation 169, 306, 319; socio-economic 310
DIGNAS *see* Mujeres por la Dignidad y la Vida (Women for Dignity and Life)
disappeared, the: Colombian Victims' Registry numbers 141; Febres Cordero administration and 119; in Kashmir 338, 339; Law 105 on the Missing and Forcibly Disappeared Persons 239; National Commission for the

Missing and Forcibly Disappeared 239; wives of 329; *see also* UBPD
discord 188
discordance 184, 199
DRC *see* Democratic Republic of Congo
Drumbl, M. 166, 176
Dupuis, Nikita 271
Duque, Iván 144

ECCC *see* Extraordinary Chambers in the Courts of Cambodia
ECHR *see* European Court of Human Rights
Ecuador 17; Asociación Gay Transgénero Coccinelle 130; decriminalization of homosexuality in 130; Organization of Lesbian Women/ Organización de Mujeres Lesbianas de Ecuador (OML) 129
Ecuadorian Truth Commission 113–133; final report 57, 113, 115, 117, 132; feminist movement's impact on 117; gender and gender-approach of 19, 114, 116, 124; inner workings of 118; legal cases prepared by 120; *see also* Cordero, Tatiana; Correa, Rafael
Ejército de Liberasión Nacional (ELN) 142
El Instituto de Derechos Humanos de la Universidad Centroamericana (IDHUCA) 283
Elliott, Karla 336, 339–340
ELN *see* Ejército de Liberasión Nacional
El Salvador 17; Comision de Derechos Humanos de El Salvador (Human Rights Commission of El Salvador)(CDHES) 288; overview of authoritarianism in 280–281; political prisoners and transitional justice in 278–294; post-conflict 279; post-war 278; REDES nonprofit 283; torture in 278, 280–281, 284, 288, 290, 370; *see also* COPPES
Enloe, Cynthia 34–35, 45, 186
"Enloesque" turn 191
essentialism(s) 74, 341; deployment of 193; discursive 188; gender 74; language of 193; raced 184–185
ethnocentrisms, Euro-American 74
ethnographic: data 278, 293; interviews 282; participant observation 187; refusal 293; study 330; work 283
ethnography 166
ethnomusicology 211
ethnonational conflict 55
ethnonationalism 352; cultural politics of 211; homo-ethnonationalists 348, 357–359; Northern Irish 59; settler colonialism and 302; Sri Lanka 348, 352, 357–359, 363
EU *see* European Union
European Championships (football, i.e. soccer) 215
European: colonial laws 54; epistemes 370
European Union (EU) 82, 336
executions of suspected homosexuals 240; *see also* extrajudicial executions; murder
exploitation 43, 55, 61, 231; sexual 191
extrajudicial executions 118–119, 130, 280
Extraordinary Chambers in the Courts of Cambodia (ECCC) 165

false dichotomies 235
false distinctions 7
false patriots and liars 218
FARC *see* Fuerzas Armadas Revolucionarias de Colombia – Ejército del Pueblo (Revolutionary Armed Forces of Colombia – People's Army)
FARC-EP *see* Revolutionary Armed Forces of Colombia – People's Army)
FARDC *see* Forces Armées de la République Démocratique du Congo (The Armed Forces of the Democratic Republic of the Congo)
fathers: ageing 224; caring 341; civilian 43; present 285; Ugandan expectations of 170
fathers of children born in war 13, 20, 162, 167, 169–176; of war rape 370
Febres Cordero, León 114, 118–121, 124–125; uprising against 125
female bodies 35, 141

female characters *see* transformista
female experiences in conflict settings 4
female homosexuality 129
female-identifying 78
female military veterans 211, 220
female paramilitary combatants 145
female same-sex intimate relationship 76n2
female subordination 186
female survivors of abduction 163; *see also* forced marriage
female victims or victimhood 7, 10, 97, 126, 186
feminism: Afro-feminism 75; conservative 140; decolonial 139; lesbian 128; liberal 147, 150; pro-life 140; queer theory and 101n8; structuralist 140
feminist activism and activists 115, 132
feminist-informed approach 19
feminist legal scholarship and scholars 101
feminist legal theory 100
feminist liberation theology 140
feminist methodology 256
feminist movements 122, 128, 130, 143; Colombian 136
feminist-movement-informed gendered approach to transitional justice 113–114, 116, 127, 132
feminist organizations and organizing 118, 121, 129; DIGNAS 290
feminist research 231
feminist resistance 117, 124
feminist scholarship and scholars 53, 56, 185, 188, 253; African 74
feminist theory and theorists 73; African 78; Uganda 81
feminist transitional justice scholarship and scholars 97, 99n6
Fiereck, Kirk 74, 83
Finley, L. 102
Fobear, Katherine 93, 228–229, 233–234, 345
Forces Armées de la République Démocratique du Congo (The Armed Forces of the Democratic Republic of the Congo) (FARDC) 193
former militants, as term 334
Foster, Alana 41, 314
frustration aggression 334
Fuerzas Armadas Revolucionarias de Colombia – Ejército del Pueblo (Revolutionary Armed Forces of Colombia – People's Army) 142, 149, 252, 270
Fundación Regional de Asesoría de Derechos Humanos (INREDH) 130–131

gender: Catholic acceptance of term 140; institutionalized and challenged meanings of 136–152; non-normative 131; as term 104; Rome Statute's definition of 104; in transitional justice 281–282
gender-based: abuses 3; crimes 20, 162; experiences 10; harms 116, 176; oppression 55; stigmatization 239
gender-based violence: CNMH reports on 144; Colombian paramilitary groups' use of 142; Colombia Special Jurisdiction for Peace and truth commission's report on 150; COVID-19 and 148; Ecuador Truth Commission's examination of 19, 114–115, 117, 121, 124, 126–127, 132; ICC policy paper on 162; male victims of 4; masculinities associated with 36; men and boys' experiences of 164; ongoing reality of 164; preventing 164; sexual violence as 38n5; systemic nature of 56; transitional justice and 39, 52–53, 60–61, 234; undetected 142; wartime rape as 53; *see also* SGBV
gender-blind 150, 229, 238
gender essentialism 74; *see also* essentialism
gender ideology 140
gender-inclusive approach to forced pregnancy and marriage in wartime 161
gendering of men's experiences 3
gender justice 79–81; defining 79; hybrid forms of 82
Gender, Justice and Security Hub 230
gender-nonconforming people 54–55, 149
Gender Perspective in Transitional Justice Processes (United Nations) 132

gender roles: modern 285–288, 292; traditional 267, 285–288, 292
gender-sensitive truth commissions *see* truth commissions
Geneva Conventions 304, 313n16
Geneva Process 348
Global North 31, 78
Global South 77–78, 141, 371–372; women victims in 186
GMH *see* Historical Memory Group
Goldstein, Ivo 222
Goma 188, 194–195, 197–200
Gómez Sánchez, G. 256
Good Friday Agreement 1998, 59, 302
GoSL *see* Government of Sri Lanka
Gotovina, Ante (General) 211, 217–218, 220
Government of Sri Lanka (GoSL) 346; *see also* Sri Lanka
Grabar-Kitarović, Kolinda (KGK) 217, 220–223
grassroots events and efforts 245, 371; feminist internationalist 128
grassroots organizations 260
grassroots people and actors 16, 23, 70, 72, 84, 86, 256
Guillermo 261–266, 269
Gulu Support the Children Organization (GUSCO) 172
Gunkle, Henriette 76
GUSCO *see* Gulu Support the Children Organization

Hagopian, Andrew Sumner 104–106
Hague, The 219
Hague, William 181–182
Hamber, Brandon 7, 30, 38, 42, 187, 235, 332
Hanlon, N. 336, 339
Hariri, Rafiq 239
hate 45
hate crime legislation 59
hate speech 23; state-sponsored (Sri Lanka) 346, 349, 352–354, 356, **357**, 358, 360, 363
hatred 55, 187, 230, 232
HDZ *see* Croatian Democratic Union
Hebrew language 301, 316–317, 319
hegemonic: as term 141, 285
hegemonic cultural norms 150
hegemonic gender construct 21, 127
hegemonic masculinity 17, 31–34, 44–45, 209–210, 285; concept of 257; dark side of 286; displays of 285, 294; emotion and "weakness" occluded by 290; misogyny and homophobia central to 32; power of 267; respect and responsibility associated with 265; risk-taking associated with 315; straight men and 267; transforming 37; veteran masculinity 214, 221, 223; violence and aggression associated with 339
hegemonic norms of patriarchy 99, 234
hegemonic sexual and gender norms 63, 79
Herceg-Bosna 214
"Herceg-Bosno, srce ponoso" 214, 222
Herzegovina *see* Bosnia-Herzegovina
Herzegovinian Croats 222
heteronormative familial relationships 176
heteronormative frames/frameworks 5–6, 14, 19; masculinity within 38, 41; sexual violence within 98
heteronormative gender regimes and power relations 83, 244, 265
heteronormativity 52; challenging 95, 259; cis-heteronormativity 258; concept of 11; critical engagement with 19; disrupting 230n5, 259; exposing and deconstructing discourses based on 96; forced 168; homophobia and patriarchy and 52, 54–56; law as tool of 102; law as tool to change 103; monolithic 14; non-heteronormative masculinities 18, 44; non-heteronormative people 71, 83; non-heteronormative sexualities 72–74; patriarchy and 16; power of 267; social control enacted through 116; as social organizing principle 97; struggles against 139; as term 76
heterosexual gender regimes 76–77; Western 74
heterosexual hegemony 96
heterosexual/homosexual binary 94–96

heterosexuality: heteronormativity and 11, 16; masculinity(ies) and 5; *queer* as being outside of 52n2, 72; social norms and ideologies of and around 55
heterosexual matrix 96, 102–103, 109
heterosexual male agency 41
heterosexual system: conservative political and religious commitment to 132; Ecuadorian Truth Commission and 113–133; men benefitting from 128; nation-state and 126; violence and 127
Historical Memory Group (GMH) 143–144
HIV *see* human immunodeficiency virus
HNS *see* Croatian Football Association
Hoad, Neville 74
Hollander, T. 42
Holocaust 55
homocapitalism 78, 81
Homeland Movement party 219
Homeland War 208, 208–224; Association of Croatian Homeland War Military Invalids (HVIDRA) 212; "Foundation for the Truth About the Homeland War" 218; myth of 211, 214, 216, 222; narrative of 21, 209–210, 221
homoeroticism 76
homo-ethnonationalists 348, 357–359
homo-liberals 348, 359
homonationalism 78
homonormativity: as term 76
homophobia 11, 16, 52, 231–232; ambivalences in Africa of 71; armed conflict and 264, 266; colonization of Africa and 77; hegemonic masculinity and 32; heteronormativity and patriarchy and 52, 54–56; as historical construction 54; public outcry against 78; Sirisena's political use of 351–354, 357; systems of power and control and 55; *see also* queerphobia
homophobic hate and violence 23, 37, 59, 237, 239–240; *see also* B4D
homophobic countries 235
homosexual: anal exams performed on 239; any penetrated or raped man defined as 125, 127; executions of 240; as term 107–108
homosexuality 35n1; "aggravated" 51; Anti-Homosexuality Act 2014 (Uganda) 51; anti-homosexual laws in Africa 77, 83; criminalization in Sri Lanka of 348, 363; criminalization (and subsequent decriminalization) in Ecuador of 128–131; criminalization in Uganda of 81; Nepal's decriminalization of 348; public discourses in Africa of 77; regulation in Ecuador of 132; Sinhalese slur against 351; subordination and 257
homosexualization of society, fear of 146
homosexual marriage 96
homosociality 220
HOS *see* Croatian Defence Forces
hooks, bell 339
HRW *see* Human Rights Watch
human immunodeficiency virus (HIV) 78; political violence and people living with 270; Victor's case 260, 263, 266, 270
human rights activism 338
human rights organizations 240
Human Rights Watch (HRW) 240
Hurtado, Osvaldo 120
HVIDRA *see* Association of Croatian Homeland War Military Invalids
HVO *see* Croat Defence Council
hypermasculinity 35n1, 35–36, 38, 45; male performance of 173; militarized 171; safety in Palestine and 318; in sports such as boxing 308, 310
hyper sexualization 126, 264
hyper-vigilance 318
hyper-visibility 38n5
hyper-visuality 55, 61

ICC *see* International Criminal Court
ICRC *see* International Committee of the Red Cross
ICTR *see* International Criminal Tribunal for Rwanda
ICTY *see* International Criminal Tribunal for the former Yugoslavia

IDHUCA *see* El Instituto de Derechos Humanos de la Universidad Centroamericana
Ignacio 261–262, 265–266
impunity: accounting for 235; in Colombia 237; in El Salvador 280–281; fighting, in DRC 181–202; justice vs. 7; legal 279; national legacy of (Ecuador) 118, 127; persistent 40; roots of 57
Imran 326–327, 331–333, 335–341
Independent State of Croatia (NDH) 213
Indigenous: actors 53; children in Residential schools 98; communities 98; concepts 72; conceptualization of same-sex erotics 76; cultures 137; gender minorities 58; ideologies around justice 84; languages 73; LGBTQ persons 56; rights 371–372; sexualities 73; voices 63; women 139
informed consent 330
informed decisions 284
INREDH *see* Fundación Regional de Asesoría de Derechos Humanos
International Center for Transitional Justice 51
International Criminal Court (ICC) 40, 103, 161; cases on forced displacement 240; on gender 106; Office of the Prosecutor 106, 162; Policy Paper on Sexual and Gender-Based Crimes 106, 162; Ongwen trial and conviction 165, 177; *see also* Ongwen, Dominic; Rome Statute
International Committee of the Red Cross (ICRC) 304
International Criminal Tribunal for the former Yugoslavia (ICTY) 40, 99, 209–212, 216–217; anti-ICTY campaigns 216
International Criminal Tribunal for Rwanda (ICTR) 99
International Gay and Lesbian Human Rights Commission 117
intersectionality 3, 96, 98n4, 101; anti-queer violence and 56; concept of 11–12, 31; criterion of 115; issue of 37n4
intersex people 69, 95n3, 124, 136n2; as term 107–108; violence against 142; see also LGBTIQ+; SOGIESC
Israel 31, 313n16; Lebanon War with 238; conflict in Occupied Palestinian Territories 302, 304, 313; military forces of 301, 314; Palestinian interaction with 313–314, 316, 318
Istria 214

J&K *see* Jammu and Kashmir
Jackson, Lisa 191
Jackson, S. 259n4
Jammu and Kashmir (J&K) 328–329; High Court 338; state police 338; *see also* Kashmir
Jammu and Kashmir Coalition of Civil Society (JKCCS) 329
JEP *see* Special Jurisdiction for Peace
JKCCS *see* Jammu and Kashmir Coalition of Civil Society
JNA *see* Yugoslav People's Army
Jolie, Angelina 182
Josipović, Ivo 218
joto, *jotear* 255
Jović, Dejan 211
JRP *see* Justice and Reconciliation Project
Justice Hub 162
Justice and Reconciliation Project (JRP) 163
just war 304
JVP *see* Peoples' Liberation Front

Kashmir 17; caring masculinities in 335–340; civilian and caring masculinities in 325–342; conflict in India 23, 325; former militants in 334–335; historical roots of conflict in 328–329; human rights violations in 329; Imran as case study 326–327, 331–333, 335–341; masculinities in 43; Stone Pelting Movement in 333–334
KGK *see* Grabar-Kitarović, Kolinda
Khmer Rouge 165
Kivu *see* Lake Kivu; North Kivu; South Kivu
knowledge: decolonial 70; passing of 315–318; politics of 259

knowledge production 71, 188, 260, 370; activist 118; collective 116, 133; decolonizing 118; expert 259, 372; geopolitics of 254; hidden genealogy of activist knowledge production 121, 127–131; movement-based 372; neoliberal frames of 77; politics of 19, 116–118; privileged 86; transitional justice and 113
Kony, Joseph 161–162, 168
Kreft, A. 334
Krystalli, R. 334, 340
Kuc, Lonyo Pe *see* Lonyo Pe Kuc

Lake Kivu 193
Lauretis, Teresa de 73
law; amnesty (Lebanon) 238; anti-homosexual 77, 83; anti-LGBTIQ+ 85; Child Protection Law 2009 (DRC) 194–196, 198; customary 82; descriptive, normative, and critical perspectives to 100–101; equality 129; European colonial 54; family 103; human rights 107, 122; international 71, 94, 99, 106, 165–166, 176, 185–186, 304, 313; international criminal 99, 103–104; national security 118; politics and 100; power of 93, 108; queer legal theory and 99–103; Sexual Violence Law 2006 (DRC) 198–199; as social discourse 95, 100–101, 103; as tool of heteronormative society 102; Victims Law 2011 (Colombia) 136, 143, 236; see also rule of law
Law 105 on Missing and Forcibly Disappeared Persons (Lebanon) 239
Law 975/2005 (Colombia) 143, 144
Law 1448/20011 (Colombia) *see* Law of Victims and Land Restitution (Law 1448/2011, or Ley de Víctimas y Restitución de Tierras) (Colombia)
Law for Reparation of Victims and Prosecution 2013 (Ecuador) 120
Law of Victims and Land Restitution (Law 1448/2011, or Ley de Víctimas y Restitución de Tierras) (Colombia)136, 143
Lebanese Civil War 229n3, 238
Lebanon 17, 229–230; armed conflict in 238; article 534 criminalizing "unnatural" sexual acts in 239; assassination of prime minister of 239; LGBTIQ+ community in 239; occupation of parts of 238; passage of Law 105 on the Missing and Forcibly Disappeared Persons 239; National Commission for the Missing and Forcibly Disappeared 239; queer TJ in 21, 228–245; SOGIESC in 239–241, 245; Special Tribunal for Lebanon (STL) 239, 242; state actors in 238; unaccounted-for past of 238–241
legal clinics 189
legalism 279n1
legal recognition, of same-sex marriage 59, 96
legal rights approaches 81
legal rights, for sexual and gender minorities 54
legal rules, general 93
legal studies *see* critical legal studies (CLS)
legal theory *see* queer legal theory
Lehr-Lehnardt, Rana 105
lesbian activism and activists 115, 127, 131, 355; *see also* Alvarez, Sandra; Cordero, Tatiana
lesbian choir 215n4
lesbian feminists 259n4; early 259n4
lesbian, gay, bisexual, and transgender (LGBT) 95n3, 144; activism and public policy for 271; criticism of acronym 136n2; rights of 253–254
lesbian, gay, bisexual, transgender, and intersex (LGBTI) 136n2; "African LGBTI Manifesto" 80; anti-LGBTI laws 85; category(ies) of 95, 109; human rights violations against 123, 129; Indigenous sexualities and 73; in legal studies 101n9, 109; living publicly as 104; queer theory and 95; sexual violence against 124, 126–127; studies 101n9; as synonym of queer 95, 101n9; as

term 93n1, 136n2; violation of rights of 125; violence against 114–115, 121
lesbian, gay, bisexual, trans, intersex, queer (LGBTQ): Croatian 215; displaced 18, 53; refugees and displaced populations 60–62; rights of 52, 54, 79; as term 136n2; violence against 56, 61; voices of, in transitional justice 56–60
lesbian, gay, bisexual, trans, intersex, queer, and other gender identities (LGBTIQ+) 228n2, 355; anti-LGBTIQ+ attitudes 236; anti-LGBTIQ+ laws 85; anti-LGBTIQ+ violence 233, 242; Black activists not represented by 139; Kurdish 240; Lebanese 239; "My Body Is the Truth: Experiences of Women and LGBTIQ+ persons in the Armed Conflict" (Truth Commission) 150, 253n2; as term 93n1, 228n2
lesbian identities 75; public 76
lesbian organizations 118
lesbian(s): discrimination against 128; as gender 104; human rights violations against 117; International Gay and Lesbian Human Rights Commission 117; in legal texts 101; Organization of Lesbian Women/ Organización de Mujeres Lesbianas de Ecuador (OML) 129; persecution of 128; rape and murder of 262; sexual violence against 98–99, 124; as term 107–108
lesbian Syrian refugee women 231; left-wing Kurdish lesbian woman in Syria 235
lesbophobia 19, 236–237, 239
Lesotho 78
Lessons Learnt and Reconciliation Commission (LLRC) 347–348
Le Zbor 215n4
Lewis, Chloe 370
Lewis, Desiree 73, 75, 79–80
LGBT *see* lesbian, gay, bisexual, and transgender
LGBTI *see* lesbian, gay, bisexual, transgender, and intersex
LGBTQ *see* lesbian, gay, bisexual, trans, queer
LGBTQI+ *see* lesbian, gay, bisexual, trans, queer, intersex, and other gender identities
Liberation Tigers of Tamil Eelam (LTTE) 346–347
liberators, as term 334
LLRC *see* Lessons Learnt and Reconciliation Commission
Lonyo Pe Kuc 168–169
Lord's Resistance Army (LRA) 20, 51; children born of forced marriage in 167, 169; criminal conviction of leader of 161, 165; escapees from 171–172; fatherhood in 169–172; forced marriage in 167–169, 175–177; GUSCO as support for former members of 172; men demobilized from 162; men and boys abducted into 166; treatment of women in 172; *see also* Acholi Nation
Lovrens, Dejan 216, 222–223
LRA *see* Lord's Resistance Army
LTTE *see* Liberation Tigers of Tamil Eelam
Lugones, María 75, 139
Lundy, P. 256

M-19 *see* Movimiento 19 de Abril
M23 193–195
MacKenzie, Meghan 41, 314
male/female binary 94–98, 102, 104–105, 113
male/female dyad 140
Mannergren Selimović, Johanna 210
MAQL *see* Movimiento Armado Quintín Lame
Marcos, Natalia 118, 120–125, 128, 131
marica 255, 263, 267
mariquear 255
mariquiar el conflicto 255
Markač, Mladen 219
Masculinities and Sexualities research stream (UKRI GCRF) 230
masculinity(ies): alternative 150, 281; civilian enactment in North of Ireland and Palestine of 300–320; conceptualizing 31–36; conflict-affected 183, 186, 202;

conflict violence and 300, 320; Congolese 187; critical mapping of TJ and 29–45; critical 372; Croatian veteran 21, 208–224; as "doing male" 12; dominant 141; DRC sexual violence and 20, 181–202; El Salvadoran 22, 278–294; femininity(ies) and 113, 140–141, 290, 293; gendered 10; hegemonic 257, 268, 285, 290, 293–294; hybrid 141; in Kashmir 23, 325–342; militarism and 36; non-hegemonic 141; non-heteronormative 18; paternal 170; peacekeeping 35; performing 164; passing of knowledge as marker of 315–318; political prisoners' 282, 284–292; positive 141; protective 141; queer 251–274, 373; queer perspectives in TJ and 3–24; risk-taking and 315; scholarship on 4–5; secure 309; sexual crime and 20; SOCIESC and 11; sporting or sports-related 22, 310; structural aspects of 13; subordinated 257, 264; subordinate expressions of 18; trans 270–272; transitional justice and 36–41, 270–272; veteran 209, 221–223; violence and 29, 36–38; violent 164, 235, 286; violently sexualized 193, 201; youth 268; *see also* caring masculinities; Connell, Raewyn; hegemonic masculinity; hypermasculinity; militarized masculinity
masculinization: de-masculinization 55; feminization and 145
masculinization opportunities 318–319
Matebeni, Zethu 73
McEvoy, Kiran 255–256, 259
McGovern, M. 256
McGregor, Lorna 255–256, 259
McQuaid, Katie 14, 61
McWilliams, M. 36, 38
Mellström, U. 29
men: as breadwinners 30; "big man" 44; forgotten status of 4; gendering of the experiences of 4; "hard" 305; violations against 38–41; violations and violence perpetrated by 36–38, 43, 97; violence against 17; *see also* masculinity(ies); perpetrator; SVAM
Mesa LGBT de la Comuna 8 de Medellín 236
Messerschmidt, James 33, 209, 257
Messner, Michael 209, 311
Milanović, Zoran 217, 221
militarized masculinity 17, 21, 34–36, 44–45; violence and 41
Miller, Alejandra 140
Minova trial 185, 189, 193–197, 201
misogyny 19, 32, 63, 116, 125, 232
Missing and Forcibly Disappeared Persons 2018 (Law 105, Lebanon) 239
Modrić, Luka 208, 215–216, 222
Monro, Surya 73
Montoneras Patria Libre 118
Movimiento 19 de Abril (M-19) 142
Movimiento Armado Quintín Lame (MAQL) 142
Moyo, Khanyisela 71
Mozambique 78, 128
Mupotsa, Danai S. 74
murder 194; of LGBTQ people 57–58
Myrtinnen, Henri 41

Naber, Nadine 53
Nagel, Joanne 55
National Commission for the Missing and Forcibly Disappeared (Lebanon) 239
National Intellectual Organization (NIO) (Sri Lanka) 361
nationalism 55; Croat 215; masculinities and 264; *see also* ethnonationalism; homonationalism
National Liberal Army (ELN) 142
NATO *see* North Atlantic Treaty Organization
Nazis *see* neo-Nazis
NDH *see* Independent State of Croatia
Nebot, Jaime 121, 125
neo-Nazis 130
NGO *see* non-governmental organization
Ní Aoláin, F. 36, 38
NIO *see* National Intellectual Organization (Sri Lanka)
Nkambwe, Christopher 62

non-governmental organization (NGO) 75, 187, 189, 332, 335; half-widows in Kashmir supported by 329; human rights 358; SOCIESC 230, 349, 351, 354, 356, 359; Syrian Charter for Truth and Justice pushed by 240–241; TJ and 84, 86; in Uganda 82–83
non-binary: gender identities 30, 32; genders 109; subjectivities 54
non-combatant men 13, 42–43
non-conforming genders 114
non-gender-conforming 231
non-heteronormative: masculinity 18, 44; people 83; sexuality 72
non-heterosexual: individuals 14; masculinity 41; visible to others as 231–232
non-judicial mechanisms 96–97, 108
non-militarized masculinity 23
non-normative: genders 114, 128, 131; sexual identities 101n9
non-stigmatization 145, 147
North Atlantic Treaty Organization (NATO) 220
Northern Ireland 17, 38; Belfast Agreement 302; boxing in Belfast 305, 311; Equality Commission 59; former combatants in 280n3; Good Friday Agreement 1998, 59, 302; nomenclature/naming conventions as 300n1; *see also* North of Ireland
Northern Ireland Act 58
Northern Ireland Human Rights Commission 59
northern Uganda 40, 161–162, 166–167, 171; *see also* Uganda
North of Ireland: boxing in 23, 300–302; civilian masculinities and boxing 300, 305–312, 319; "The Troubles" in 301
North Kivu 187–188, 193, 196–197, 199, 201

Occupied Palestinian Territories 22, 300–302, 304–305, 308, 313n16; civilian masculinities in 312–315; negotiating civilian masculinities in 318–319; role of knowledge in 315–318
Occupied West Bank 313
Office for Missing Persons (OMP) (Sri Lanka) 348
Okesch, A. 80
OML *see* Organización de Mujeres Lesbianas de Ecuador (Ecuadorian Organization of Lesbian Women)
OMP *see* Office on Missing Persons
Ongwen, Dominic 161–162, 167–169, 175, 177; *see also* Ayot, Florence
ONU (Organización de las Naciones Unidas) *see* United Nations)
ONU Mujeres 145, 147
Oosterveld, V.104–106
Organización de Mujeres Lesbianas de Ecuador (Ecuadorian Organization of Lesbian Women) (OML) 129
Organization of Lesbian Women *see* Organización de Mujeres Lesbianas de Ecuador (OML) 129
Oscar 261–262, 265–267
Oslo Agreement 1993 302

Pacheco 144
Palestine *see* Occupied Palestinian Territories; Oslo Agreement
Palestinians 301–302, 304, 313n16, 313–314, 317
Paraguay 57; Truth and Justice Commission 57
parameters: epistemic 114, 116, 133; feminist ethics of care as 340; gendered 307; investigative 131; liberal democratic paradigm as 346; research 330; structural 120
paramilitares 261, 264, 267, 269
paramilitaries and paramilitary groups 35, 58, 98, 142–143; boxing in North of Ireland and 309–310, 312; British 309; Croatian Defence Forces 213; demobilized 251, 264; female combatants in 145; human rights defenders and activists killed by 148; joining 306
paramilitary corrective violence 144
PARJ-E *see* Programme d'Appui à la Justice à l'Est de la RDC (DRC) 199
Park, Rebekah 280n3
peacebuilding 3, 7–8; in Colombia 136–138, 151; conflict transformation and 273; gender

and 10, 14, 18; formal 23; gender sensitivity in 20; illiberal 347; informal 300; liberal democratic 359; masculinity(ies) and 12; micro-level 13; post-war 13, 347; queer bodies and theories in 16; queering 22, 258–259; state 61; TJ and 7–8, 16–17, 251–252, 254, 260, 267–268, 272; undoing violent masculinities as quandary for 37–38, 42; women's 331; women's agency in 136
peacebuilding from below 251, 267
peacebuilding intervention 301, 312
peacebuilding practitioners 13
peacebuilding theory 260
peacekeeper masculinity model 35
peacekeepers: soldiers as 35; UN 191
Peoples' Liberation Front/Janatha Vimukthi Peramuna (JVP) 350, 361–362
perpetrator: male 7; male, in everyday justice 196–201; men as 36–39; quint-*essentialist* 187–197, 201; women as 97
perpetrator and victim binaries 20, 97, 162
perpetratorhood: delineating 181–202; male 183, 188; masculine 13; sexual 184, 201
Peru 117–118
pink tea (*nun chai*) 331
pink triangle 55
Plenković, Andrej 222
Política Nacional para la Reincorporación Social y Económica D Exintegrantes De Las FARC-EP (The National Policy for the Social and Economical Reintegration of Former Members of the FARC-EP) (CONPES 3931) 150
Prada Prada, Nancy 144
Prevention of Sexual Violence Initiative (PSVI) (UK) 182
Programme d'Appui à la Justice à l'Est de la RDC (PARJ-E) (DRC) 199
prostitutas (sex workers) 263
PSVI *see* Prevention of Sexual Violence Initiative (UK)
Puar, Jasbir 78
Putin, Vladmir 222
QQIAAAP2+ *see* queer, questioning, intersex, asexual, ally, androgynous, pansexual, two-spirit
queer agency 363
queer-blind 344
queer-identifying men 269
queer-informed legal theory or legal texts 103, 105–106, 108
queering 14; defining 74; as phenomenological and analytical process 56
queering peacebuilding 22
queering post-war democratization processes 23
queering-to-come 74
queering transitional justice 18, 21, 22, 51–63; African colonialist perspectives on 69–86; connecting homophobia and heteronormativity and patriarchy to 54–56; possibilities of 62–63; *see also* queer transitional justice
queer-led movement *see* B4D
queer legal theoretical perspectives: transitional justice and 93–109
queer legal theory 99–103; defining 101
queer masculinities 251–274
queerness 54, 81; as being against norms and categories 102; from/within Africa 74; hierarchies of exclusion and 263; nationhood and 215, 352; studies on masculinities and 252, 271
queer perspectives in judicial mechanism of transitional justice 103–108
queerphobia 352, 361; political 363
queerphobic: criticism 358; ethnonationalist lobby 357, 363
queerphobic hate speech 349, 360; political 351–353, 356
queerphobic violence 78, 346
queer, questioning, intersex, asexual, ally, androgynous, pansexual, two-spirit (QQIAAAP2+) 136
queer(s): in African activism 72–74; as analytical position 255; as being against norms and categories 102; coded in Sri Lanka as disloyalty 352; *prostitutas* and 263; pursuing justice for 83; translating into other languages such as Spanish

255; as umbrella term 72–74; in US 1980s politics 255; violence and discrimination against 82, 261; as vulnerable victims 86; *see also* LGBTQ
queer theory 71; silent ethnocentrism of 74
queer transitional justice: in Syria/Lebanon 238–241
quint-*essentialized*: narrative 197, 199, 201; reporting 200
quint-*essentialist* perpetrator 187–197, 201
quint-*essentializing* 184
Quito 118, 122

Rainbow Refugee (Canada) 62
Rajapaksha, Mahinda 344, 347, 349–350
Rao, Rahul 72, 78
Reddy, Vasu 73
REDES nonprofit 283
Reich, Adrienne 127–128, 259n4
Refugee Law Project (Uganda) 62
reparation programs 107, 236
reparation(s) 3, 7, 40, 114–115, 124, 234; in El Salvador 279–281, 292–293; Integral System of Truth, Justice, Reparation, and Non-Repetition (Colombia) 145; Law for Reparation of Victims 120; monetary 236; National System for the Assistance and Comprehensive Reparation of Victims (Sistema Nacional de Atención y Reparación Integral a las Victimas (SNARIV) 143; transitional justice 30, 279; state 243; symbolic 149; *see also* Special Rapporteur
reparation subjects 236
Residential schools 98
Restart Coalition (Croatia) 222
restitution 143, 145, 236, 243, 279, 294
Revolutionary Armed Forces of Colombia (People's Army) (FARC-EP) 136, 138, 145–148, 151–152
Revolutionary United Front (RUF) 165
Riaño-Alcalá, Pilar 8
Rich, Adrienne 127–128
Right to Information Act (RTI) (Sri Lanka) 348
Right to Information Commission (Sri Lanka) 348
right-wing: authoritarian government 280; groups 232; talk show 219
Rome Statute 95, 103–106, 108, 198
Rosalind, S. 256
Rosenbloom, Rachel 117
Rosenoff-Gauvin, L. 340
RTI *see* Right to Information Act
Rubin, Gayle 259n4
RUF *see* Revolutionary United Front
rule of law 79, 81, 100–101, 279; as principle of governance 69; restoring faith in 183, 189; UN Team of Experts on Sexual Violence and the Rule of Law 192
Rutshuru 188

Saavedra, Luis Ángel 130–131
Saleh, Fadi 240
Salvioli, Fabián 3, 9, 115, 132
Samaraweera, Mangala 352–353
same-sex erotics and intimacy 76
same-sex relationships 11, 72; decriminalization in African countries of 78; persecution of 77; among working women in Ghana 75; Sri Lankan criminalization of 351
same-sex sexualities and sex 51, 54–55
same-sex unions (i.e. marriage) 59
Sánchez, Gonzalo 144
Scheinert, J. 105–106
Schulz, Philipp 4, 41, 83, 98, 125n8, 164–165, 243, 315, 334, 340
SDP *see* Social Democratic Party
SEA *see* sexual exploitation and abuse 191
Selimović, Johanna Mannergren *see* Mannergren Selimović, Johanna
Serrano-Amaya, José Fernando 230, 244
sexual exploitation and abuse (SEA) 191
sexual and gender-based violence (SGBV) 30, 39–40; against men 39; against women and girls 43, 228
Sexual Minorities Uganda (SMUG) 62
sexual orientation and gender identities and expressions (SOGIE) 136n2

sexual orientation, gender identity, gender expression, and sex characteristics (SOGIESC) 3–7, 13–19; armed actors' violent targeting of 230; armed conflict and 230–231; B4D movement and 23; civilian male violence against 43; in Colombia 17, 229–230, 235–238, 242–245; continuums of violence faced by persons with diverse 231–233; demands for justice by persons with diverse 93–95; everyday violence against persons with 228; experience of armed conflict by people with diverse 98; gendered violence against 21; law and legal system in relationship to 93–95, 102–103; in Lebanon 229–230, 238–239; legal recognition in TJ context of people with diverse 97–99; lived experiences of 22, 245; queer legal perspective on 102, 108; queer legal theory and 19; queer people with diverse 6, 10; rights of and protections for people with diverse 95; research and policy implications of research of 11, 368–369, 372; Rome Statute and 103–106; as sexual minorities 96; in Sri Lanka 345–346, 348–364; in Syria 229–230, 238, 239–241; as term 15, 72; transnational justice and 233–235, 345; victimhood of people with diverse 19, 99; violence against 4, 16, 18, 37–38, 43, 98; Yogyakarta Principles and 106–109

sexual violence *see* conflict-related sexual violence (CRSV)

sexual violence against men (SVAM) 39–40

sexual violence crime *see* crime

Sexual Violence Research Initiative 230

sex workers 35, 122–123, 261, 263; commercial 231n6; transgender 125

Seychelles 78

SGBV *see* sexual and gender-based violence

SHRC *see* State Human Rights Commission

Sika, V. 80

Sirisena (President of Sri Lanka) 23, 344, 346–347, 349–354, 359; *see also* "butterfly speech"

SIT *see* Special Investigation Team (J&K)

Sierra Leone *see* Special Court for Sierra Leone

Škoro, Miroslav 214n3, 216–223

Slootmaeckers, K. 264

SMUG *see* Sexual Minorities Uganda

social actors 118, 256, 249, 273

social cachet 241

Social Christian party 119, 121, 124–125

social cleansing 130, 144

social contract 176

Social Democratic Party (SDP) (Croatia) 217, 222

social discourse 100–101; law 103

social extermination 130

social hierarchies 264

social justice 260

social identity 209

social imaginaries 243

social media 45, 222

social mobilization 269

social morality 57

social order 265; heterosexual 77; threats to 115, 126

social power 284

social relations, gender and 139

social repair 13, 53, 60, 325–327, 342; care and 339; everyday acts of 341; everyday strategies of 340; Imran's work to enact 23; micro-level processes of 336; remaking a world via 340

social status 56

social suffering 6

social theory 141

social unrest 60

SOGIE *see* sexual orientation and gender identities and expressions

SOGIESC *see* sexual orientation, gender identity, gender expression, and sex characteristics

Sokolić, Ivor 210, 218, 223

South Africa 38, 42; anti-conscription movement in 257; apartheid 257; Black South African youth 334; decriminalization of same-sex

relationships in 78; gender justice in 79; hybrid gender justice in 82; LGBTQ in 57; post-apartheid 76; rule of law in 79; SOGIESC perspectives in 233; Ubuntu in 81; women in 79
South Asia 325
South Kivu 187–188, 193, 197, 199, 201
Special Court for Sierra Leone 165, 200
Special High-Level Forum for monitoring the gender-based approach 149
Special Investigation Team (SIT) (J&K) 338
Special Jurisdiction for Peace (JEP) 145, 150, 236n11; Colombia 252–253
special needs for protection 148
Special Rapporteur on truth, reparation and guarantees on non-recurrence (UN) 9, 132; "*Gender perspective in transitional justice processes*" report 123
special representative to the secretary-general (SRSG) 182
Special Tribunal for Lebanon (STL) 239, 242
Spivak, G. C. 71
Sri Lanka: B4D movement in 16–17, 23, 344–; COJ in 348; Colombo 344, 350; constitutional coup in 345–346, 349, 350–351, 353–354, 359, 362, 364; National Intellectual Organization (NIO) 361; protests in **357**; SOGIESCs and SOGIESC rights in 345–346, 348–364; United National Front (UNF) 350; Victors Peace in 347; *see also* B4D; JVP; Rajapaksha; Sirisena; TNA; Wickremasinghe
SRSG *see* special representative to the secretary-general
State Human Rights Commission (SHRC) 338–339
STL *see* Special Tribunal for Lebanon
Stone Pelting Movement in 333–334
Stroessner, Alfredo 57
subaltern perspectives 252; transitional justice from 255–258
subaltern(s) 70, 84, 272
Sugden, A. 311
Survivors Speak Out (UK) 182
SVAM *see* sexual violence against men
Syria 17, 230; Free Syrian Army of 240; Islamic State in 240
Syria/Lebanon 17, 21, 229; queer transitional justice in 238–241; SOCIESC rights and concerns in 21, 228–231, 235, 238–245
Syrian Charter for Truth and Justice 241
Syrian Civil War 228, 230, 239–241
Syrian refugees 231, 235, 239, 241

Taller Comunicación Mujer 129
Tamale, Sylvia 75–77, 80–82
Tamil community 348–349
Tamil homeland 346
Tamil language 358
Tamil National Alliance (TNA) 350
Tamil Tigers 346
Tapia, N. 256
Taylor, Katie 312n14
Theidon, Kimberly 4, 42, 233, 307, 334
Thompson, Marko Perković 208, 213–217, 220–223
Thousand Days' War 142
Timor Leste 115
TJ *see* transitional justice
TJFB *see* transitional justice from below
TNA *see* Tamil National Alliance
Topalušić, Nevenka 220
torture: in Ecuador 127; El Salvador 278, 280–281, 284, 288, 290–291, 293, 370; by Febres Cordero administration 118–119, 122, 124; gendered as masculine crime 30, 40, 99; gendering of victims of 37, 57; in Guayaquil 125–126, 131; as human rights violation 8, 329; in Kashmir 335; by LRA 171; sexual violence as tool of 124
Touquet, Helen 40, 98, 125n8, 164
traditional: femininity 43; gender arrangements 144; gender roles 267, 285–288, 292; justice 7, 83; justice instruments 82; leadership 83; masculinities 293, 336; reconciliation processes in Africa 83; sexual norms 58, 113; sexual order 265; understandings of sex 101; "values" (political conservative) 371–372
traditionalisms 74

transformative gender justice 79
transformista 260–261, 261n6, 266–267
transgendered women 117, 125, 262
transgender experiences 261n6
transgender individuals 3–4; activism by 270; advocacy for 254; Caribe Afirmativo's work for 253; cisgender-homosexual individuals versus 79; discrimination against 130; gender as term and 104; GMH report on 144; queer theory and category of 96; sexual and verbal harassment of 240; violence against 57, 99, 105, 149, 264
transgender studies 270–271
transitional justice (TJ): from "below" 255–258; critical mapping of masculinity and 29–45; defining 7; gender and 7–9; gender in 281–282; gendering 9–10; inclusive gender in 18–20; introducing LGBTQ voices in 56–60; masculinities and 36–41; masculinities perspectives in 12–13; moving beyond a violence-centric lens on 41–43; NGOs and 84, 86; peacebuilding and 7–8, 16–17, 251–252, 254, 260, 267–268, 272; queer, in Lebanon 21, 228–245; queering 258–260; queer legal theoretical perspectives and 93–109; queer perspectives in 14–17; queer perspectives on masculinities and 3–24; subaltern perspectives on 255–258; *see also* queering transitional justice; queer transitional justice
transitional justice from below (TJFB) 22, 244, 255–258; as concept 258; concept of "below" in 252, 257; micro-activisms and 268; practices of 251; producing change via 269; queering 251–274; "transition" in 270
Transitional Justice Policy (AU) 69
transphobia 11, 16, 55, 63, 117, 232, 235–237, 239, 264, 371
travesti and travesty movement 117, 124, 126, 130
truth 3
Truth Commission *see* Ecuador 113
Truth Commission (CEV) (Colombia) 145, 149, 151, 236n11, 237
truth commissions 8, 18–19, 45; gender-sensitive 4; gender and sexuality addressed by 115; Latin American 57; Paraguay 57; men's experiences prioritized by 3; use of mandates to establish 93–94; 114 victims' right to speak in 97
"Truth is a Rainbow" 150
truth-seeking 21, 233, 243, 290
truth-seeking processes 4, 7, 115; *see also* Special Rapporteur on truth, reparation, and guarantees of non-recurrence (UN)
truth-telling 233, 243, 282
Tshombe, Isabelle 182–183
Tuđman, Franjo 211–212, 214, 221
Turkey 229–230, 241
Turner, Lewis 231

UBPD *see* Unit to Search for the Disappeared
Ubuntu 81
Uganda 17; Anti-Homosexuality Act 2014 51; armed conflict in 83; "Kill the Gays" bill 51; forced marriage and wartime pregnancy in 161–177; homophobia in 81; *kuchus* in 73; lived experiences of the conflict-affected in 334, 340; male LRA combatants in 20; male survivors' gender-specific justice needs and conceptions in 40; NGOs in 82; refugee camps in 61; Sexual Minorities Uganda (SMUG) 62; Women's Coalition for Peace 83; *see also* LRA
UK *see* United Kingdom
UKRI GCRF 230
UN *see* United Nations
undesirable 55, 125
UNDP *see* United Nations Development Programme
UNF *see* United National Front (Sri Lanka)
UNGA *see* United Nations General Assembly
UNHCR *see* United Nations High Commissioner for Refugees
Unidad de Búsqueda de Personas dadas por Desaparecidas – UBPD) *see*

Unit to Search for the Disappeared (UBPD) (Colombia)
Unión Patriótica (UP) 132
United Kingdom (UK) 300n1, 302; Prevention of Sexual Violence Initiative (PSVI) 182; Survivors Speak Out 182
United National Front (UNF) (Sri Lanka) 350
United Nations: Convention on the Rights of the Child 176; Headquarters, NYC 187, 192; *Joint Statement on Ending Violence and Discrimination against LGBTI People* 54; Team of Experts on Sexual Violence and the Rule of Law 192
United Nations Development Programme (UNDP) 197
United Nations General Assembly (UNGA) 181
United Nations High Commissioner for Refugees (UNHCR) 182
United Nations Human Rights Commission 51
United Nations Joint Human Rights Office (UNJHRO) 197
United Nations peacekeepers, sexual violence by 191
United Nations Security Council (UNSC) 9; Resolution 1820 on women and peace and security (WPS) 183, 191
United Nations Security Council Resolution (UNSCR) 1325 190, 220; 1820 183–185, 190–192, 201
United Nations Special Rapporteur *see* Special Rapporteur (UN)
United States: 1980s gender and sexual politics of 255; undocumented immigrants to 289
Unit to Search for the Disappeared (UBPD) (Colombia) 145, 149, 236n11, 237
Universidad de los Andes 271
UNJHRO *see* United Nations Joint Human Rights Office
UNSC *see* United Nations Security Council
UNSCR *see* United Nations Security Council Resolution
UP *see* Unión Patriótica
Uribe, Álvaro 143–144; the No campaign by 146
Uribe, Simón 271
Uvira 188, 198

Vásquez, Elizabeth 131
victim/perpetrator binaries 368, 370
victim/survivor 235
violation-centric: foci 22, 31, 42, 44; lens 17, 23, 41–43; logic 4; views 11, 21, 43, 368
Violence, the (Civil War, Colombia) 142
Vukovar 215, 223

Walungu 188
WAN *see* Women's Advocacy Network
war: children born of 167–168; fatherhood in 169–171; femininities and 164; financiers of 45; glorification of 45; hypermasculinity in times of 38; masculinities in 12, 36–37, 44; men's experiences of 163; peace vs. war 231; rape as war crime 194; rape as weapon of 192; sexual violence during 192; survivors of 192; violence in 8, 10, 12; *see* Cold War; Colombia; Homeland War; Lebanon; LRA; Syria; Thousand Days' War; Ukraine
war crimes 9, 161, 189, 194–196, 209; rape as 194
warfare: gendered nature of 29; political economy of 44
War of Independence *see* Croatia
warmongering 45
Warner, M. 259n4
war rape 36, 192, 194–196
warrior: African 187; militarized 35; soldier/warrior, as type 35
wartime: forced marriage and pregnancy in 20, 161–176; sexual violence in 164
Wayúu women 144
Weinstein, Laura 271
Weltanschauung 138, 151
Whitehead, S. 319n20
White middle-class 101; men 31
Whiteness, European 211
whitening, racial 264

White people, rights of 100
White saviorism 84
White women 139
Wickremasinghe, Ranil 350–352
Wilton Park Conference 191
Wojnicka, K. 29
Women's Advocacy Network (WAN) 162–163
Wood, E. 330
working-class men: North of Ireland 305–307, 309–310, 312, 319
working-class women: Ghana 75
Wright, H. 31

Xaba, T. 334
xenophobia 232, 239, 352

Yerovi Proaño, Sebastian 122
Yogyakarta, Indonesia 107
Yogyakarta Principles 15n1, 94, 106–109, 123n7; queering legal theory on the basis of 370
Yogyakarta Principles plus 10 (YP +10) 107
young lions 334
YP +10 *see* Yogyakarta Principles plus 10
Yugoslav People's Army (JNA) 208, 216
Yugoslavia 17; mass killing of men and boys in 305n8; socialist order of 212; *see also* ICTY

Zaatari, Ziena 53
Zadar 214n3, 215, 223
Zagreb 208, 215, 223; dialect 222; intelligentsia 222; veteran's ministry in 220
Zalewski, Marysia 220

www.ingramcontent.com/pod-product-compliance
Lightning Source LLC
LaVergne TN
LVHW021246011026
849160LV00010BA/753
9781032857213